Fiji

Korina Miller
Robyn Jones
Leonardo Pinheiro

LONELY PLANET PUBLICATIONS
Melbourne • Oakland • London • Paris

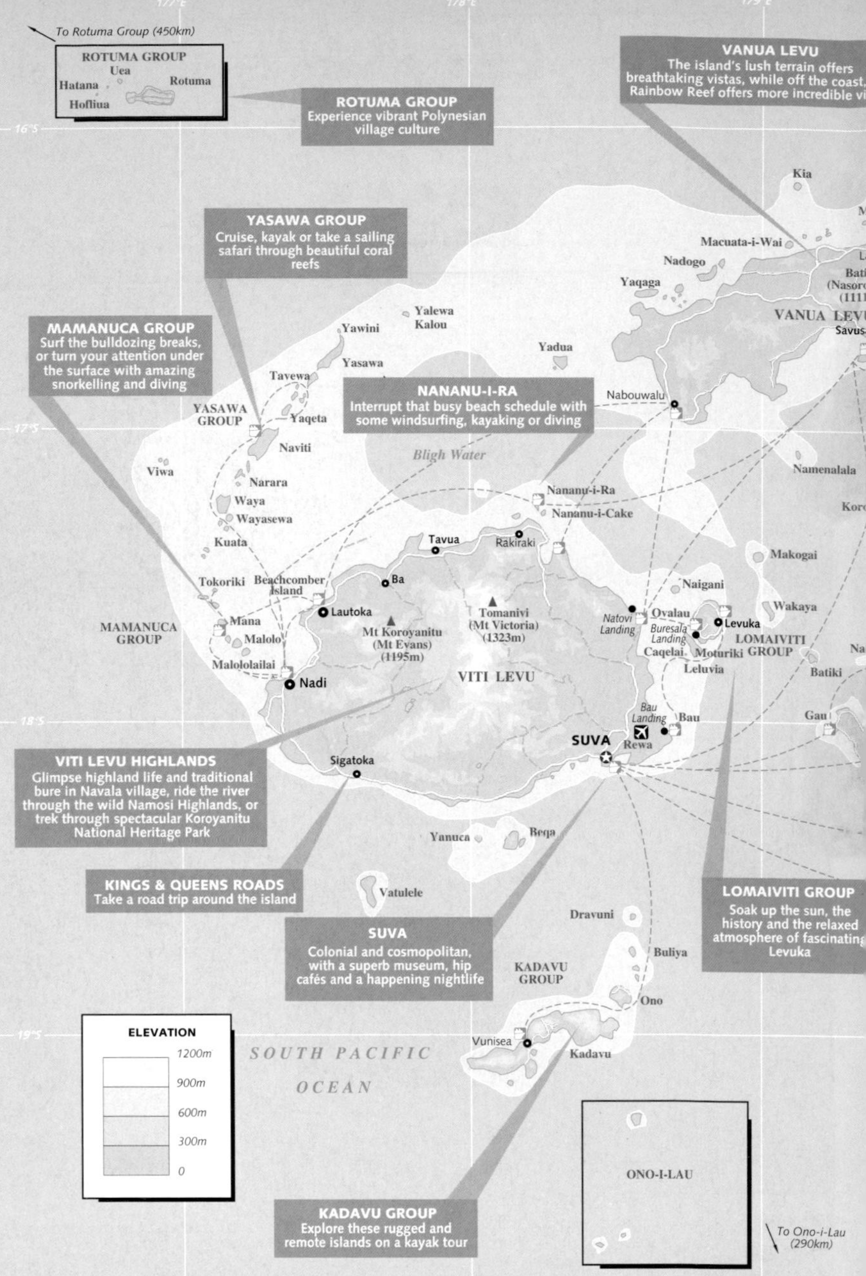

177°E
178°E
179°E
16°S
17°S
18°S
19°S
To Rotuma Group (450km)
ROTUMA GROUP
Uea
Hatana
Rotuma
Hofliua
ROTUMA GROUP
Experience vibrant Polynesian village culture
VANUA LEVU
The island's lush terrain offers breathtaking vistas, while off the coast, Rainbow Reef offers more incredible vie
YASAWA GROUP
Cruise, kayak or take a sailing safari through beautiful coral reefs
MAMANUCA GROUP
Surf the bulldozing breaks, or turn your attention under the surface with amazing snorkelling and diving
NANANU-I-RA
Interrupt that busy beach schedule with some windsurfing, kayaking or diving
Kia
Macuata-i-Wai
Nadogo
Yaqaga
VANUA LEVU
Savusa
Yalewa Kalou
Yawini
Yasawa
Yadua
Tavewa
YASAWA GROUP
Yaqeta
Naviti
Nabouwalu
Bligh Water
Viwa
Narara
Waya
Wayasewa
Kuata
Nananu-i-Ra
Nananu-i-Cake
Namenalala
Tavua
Rakiraki
Makogai
Tokoriki
Beachcomber Island
Ba
Naigani
Lautoka
Tomanivi (Mt Victoria) (1323m)
Wakaya
Mana
Malolo
MAMANUCA GROUP
Mt Koroyanitu (Mt Evans) (1195m)
Natovi Landing
Ovalau
Buresala Landing
Levuka
LOMAIVITI GROUP
Caqelai
Moturiki
Leluvia
Batiki
Malololailai
Nadi
VITI LEVU
Bau Landing
Bau
Gau
SUVA
Rewa
Sigatoka
VITI LEVU HIGHLANDS
Glimpse highland life and traditional bure in Navala village, ride the river through the wild Namosi Highlands, or trek through spectacular Koroyanitu National Heritage Park
Yanuca
Beqa
KINGS & QUEENS ROADS
Take a road trip around the island
Vatulele
LOMAIVITI GROUP
Soak up the sun, the history and the relaxed atmosphere of fascinating Levuka
Dravuni
SUVA
Colonial and cosmopolitan, with a superb museum, hip cafés and a happening nightlife
Buliya
KADAVU GROUP
Ono
ELEVATION
1200m
900m
600m
300m
0
Vunisea
Kadavu
SOUTH PACIFIC OCEAN
ONO-I-LAU
KADAVU GROUP
Explore these rugged and remote islands on a kayak tour
To Ono-i-Lau (290km)

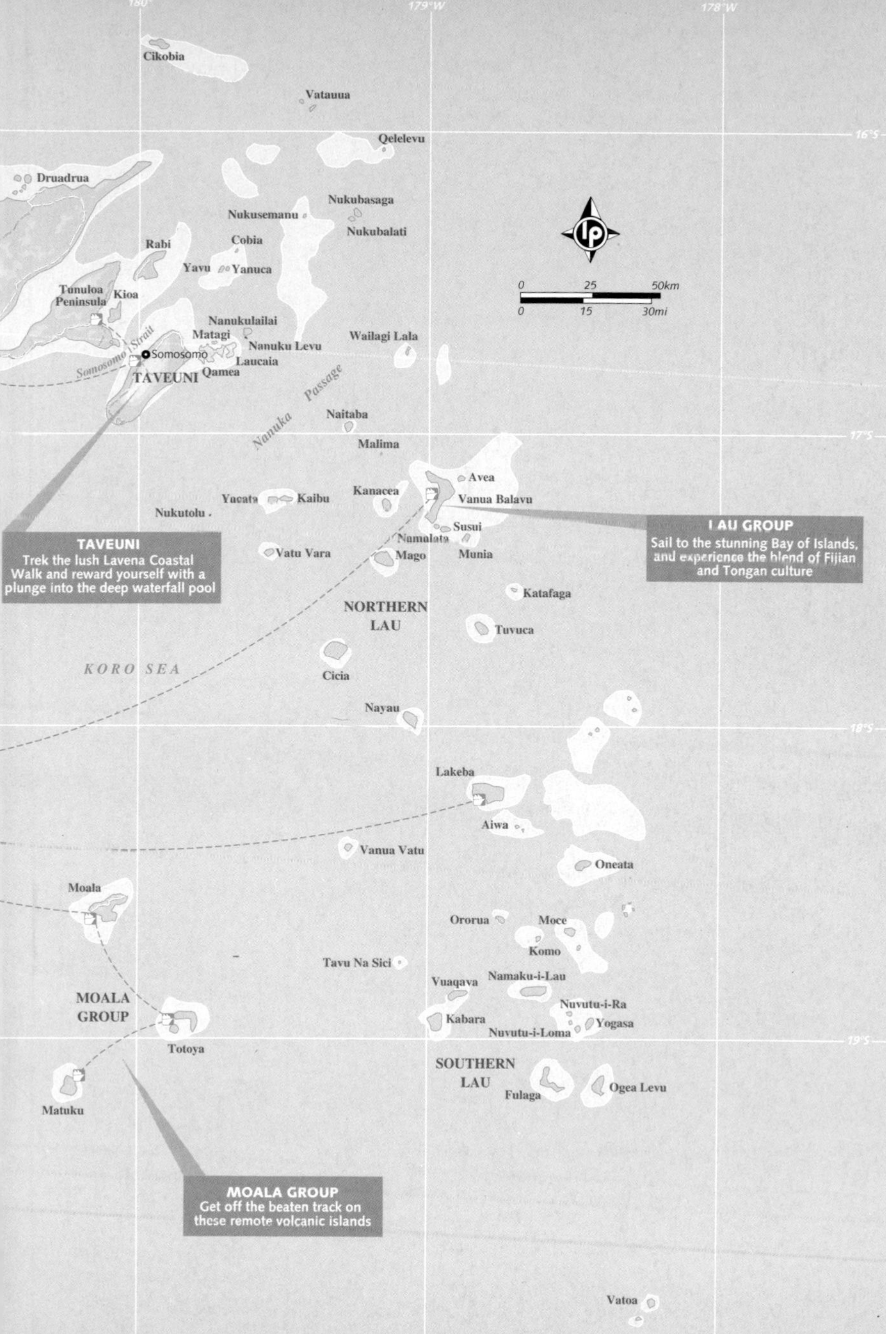
180°
179°W
178°W
16°S
17°S
18°S
19°S
0
25
50km
0
15
30mi
Cikobia
Vatauua
Qelelevu
Druadrua
Nukubasaga
Nukusemanu
Nukubalati
Cobia
Rabi
Yavu
Yanuca
Tunuloa Peninsula
Kioa
Nanukulailai
Matagi
Nanuku Levu
Wailagi Lala
Somosomo Strait
Somosomo
Laucaia
Qamea
TAVEUNI
Nanuka Passage
Naitaba
Malima
Avea
Kanacea
Vanua Balavu
Yacata
Kaibu
Nukutolu
Susui
Namalata
Mago
Munia
Vatu Vara
TAVEUNI
Trek the lush Lavena Coastal Walk and reward yourself with a plunge into the deep waterfall pool
LAU GROUP
Sail to the stunning Bay of Islands, and experience the blend of Fijian and Tongan culture
Katafaga
NORTHERN LAU
Tuvuca
KORO SEA
Cicia
Nayau
Lakeba
Aiwa
Vanua Vatu
Oneata
Moala
Ororua
Moce
Komo
Tavu Na Sici
Namaku-i-Lau
Vuaqava
MOALA GROUP
Nuvutu-i-Ra
Kabara
Yogasa
Nuvutu-i-Loma
Totoya
SOUTHERN LAU
Fulaga
Ogea Levu
Matuku
MOALA GROUP
Get off the beaten track on these remote volcanic islands
Vatoa

Fiji
6th edition – June 2003
First published – March 1986

Published by
Lonely Planet Publications Pty Ltd ABN 36 005 607 983
90 Maribyrnong St, Footscray, Victoria 3011, Australia

Lonely Planet Offices
Australia Locked Bag 1, Footscray, Victoria 3011
USA 150 Linden St, Oakland, CA 94607
UK 10a Spring Place, London NW5 3BH
France 1 rue du Dahomey, 75011 Paris

Photographs
Many of the images in this guide are available for licensing from Lonely Planet Images.
w www.lonelyplanetimages.com

Front cover photograph
Man watching breaking wave, Fiji (Warren Bolster/Getty Images)

ISBN 1 74059 134 8

Printed by The Bookmaker International Ltd
Printed in China

Contents – Text

Contents – Maps

INTRODUCTION

GETTING AROUND

VITI LEVU

MAMANUCA GROUP

YASAWA GROUP

LOMAIVITI GROUP

VANUA LEVU

TAVEUNI

KADAVU GROUP

LAU & MOALA GROUPS

ROTUMA GROUP

The Authors

Korina Miller

Korina spent the first 17 years of her life on Vancouver Island and has been on the move ever since. Her travels have taken her to many corners of the world, from Alaska to Sicily and Colombia to Scotland. She studied in Japan and Denmark; lived and worked with remote tribal peoples in India and Southwest China; ran a hotel in the mountains of Ecuador and arts organisations in Vancouver and London. En route, she picked up a degree in Communications, an MA in Migration Studies and a limey husband. She's now roaming New Zealand in search of a home. Korina is the co-author of LP's *China* and *South-West China* and the author of *Beijing Condensed*.

Robyn Jones

Robyn, a farm girl from rural Victoria, Australia, spent a formative year as an exchange student in the Brazilian megalopolis of São Paulo. While at university she explored a bit of Australia and Europe and eventually returned to Brazil to get to know her future in-laws. With Leonardo, she has worked on Lonely Planet's *Brazil* and *South America*, co-wrote the 4th and 5th editions of *Fiji* and the Fiji and Tuvalu chapters of the 1st edition of *South Pacific*, and contributed to *Travel with Children*. In between travels Robyn works as an architect in Melbourne, where she lives with Leonardo and their sons Alex and Nicholas (who both helped research this book).

Leonardo Pinheiro

Leonardo was born and raised in Rio de Janeiro, Brazil. At 15, curious to roam further than Rio city, he jumped on a bus to the northeast coast. From then on he travelled around the country as much as his pocket money and time would allow. After tertiary studies in agricultural science, Leonardo headed for Sydney to do post-grad studies and to check out the Australian surf. He met Robyn, and moved to Melbourne where they now live with their two sons Alex and Nicholas. He has recently finished his PhD in biochemistry.

Contributing Author
Clement Paligaru

Clement is an Indo-Fijian who came to Australia in 1984. He has reported extensively on the Pacific region for the Australian Broadcasting Corporation and is currently the Senior Producer of *Pacific Beat*, a daily current affairs programme on Radio Australia's international service.

FROM THE AUTHORS

Korina Thank you to John and Marilyn in Levuka for the many tips and banana pancakes; to Andrea of Levuka for getting us on a boat to Leluvia; to Tom and his staff in Colo-i-Suva for the birthday cake; to Vasemaca in Suva for her help with statistics; to Bob and Lui on Vanua Levu for their hospitality and the sea views; to Jackie of Tunuloa Peninsula for babysitting my book; to Bibi and his family on Taveuni for the herbal medicine from their garden; and to Morica, Tige, Chet and their crew for a very memorable tour. Many thanks to editor Errol for never being more than an email away, to Jane and Simone at LP and to co-authors Robyn and Leo. Thanks and love to Paul, my favourite travel crony. A special Vinaka to the many beautiful Fijians we met on the road – your friendliness was the highlight of my trip.

Robyn & Leonardo A warm *vinaka vakalevu* (thank you very much) to all the great people we met along the way for helping make this trip to Fiji our most enjoyable so far. Special thanks to the following: Tups and others at the FVB; Vili, Eddie and Co in Nadi; Paul; Nancy on Nananu-i-Ra; Julie, Annalise and Ledua in Kadavu; Kevin and the friendly staff aboard the *Yasawa Flyer* and the *Tiger IV* in the Yasawas and Mamanucas, as well as Peter, Bruce, John, Tony and Lance; and Tom for sharing his bottle of rum. At home, thanks to Casey and Ian for their understanding and flexibility, Maryanne for the last-minute computer, and Mum for again looking after our bills while we were away. Thanks especially to Alex and Nicholas who coped brilliantly with being carted all over the place.

Clement A big thank you to Hilary Ericksen, Tamani Nair, Samisoni Pareti, Matthew Oakley and the Paligaru clan for all the invaluable suggestions, feedback and encouragement.

This Book

This latest edition of *Fiji* is thanks to a collaboration of authors: Korina Miller, Robyn Jones, Leonardo Pinheiro and Clement Paligaru. Robyn and Leonardo wrote the previous two editions. Robert Kay wrote the first three editions.

FROM THE PUBLISHER

This edition was produced by a chorus of production staff at Lonely Planet's Melbourne office. Chris Tsismetzis was responsible for the 40 maps. Cris Gibcus orchestrated design and layout and Chris Love was Project Manager. Simone Egger edited the book in unison with: Craig Kilburn, Darren O'Connell, Barbara Delisson, Jocelyn Harewood and Suzannah Shwer. Errol Hunt commissioned the book (with help from Corie Waddell, Kusnandar, Susie Ashworth and Ann Seward); he also updated the Health section and kept everything harmonious. Adriana Mammarella and Kate McDonald carried out design and layout checks, and Carol Chandler handled print production.

Vinaka to Quentin Frayne for the Language chapter, Maria Vallianos who designed the front cover, and Annie Horner & Kerrie Williams at Lonely Planet Images. Thanks to Te Puna Maturanga o Aotearoa, National Library of New Zealand and the National Library of Australia for permission to re-use historical images.

Thanks

Many thanks to the travellers who used the last edition and wrote to us with helpful hints, useful advice and interesting anecdotes:

Jenny Amery, Elissa Arkinstall, Lauren Baldoni, Robert Barash, Brad Beecroft, Peter Beer, Garet Benavides, Liz Benge, Ingrid Bengtsson, William Berg, Loris Biaggio, Derek Bissell, Helle Bjerre, Ramie Blatt, Steve Booth, Leon Bowles, Anne Bowyer, Alan Bradley, Michael Bridge, Chris Briggs, Richard Brunt, Stuart Bulloch, Lawrence Burness, Shayne Burnet, Jacqueline Calder, Do Cammick, Yvette Carman, Jackie Carver, Brian Cassey, Jeff Catherwood, Eva Cermak, Stuart Chambers, Ingrid Champion, Neelam Charan, Brooke Charles, Alanna Clifton, Stephanie Cone, Paul Corwin, Malcolm Craig, Rachael Cramer, Christine & Rosemary Crouch, Hollis Dana, Ellen Daniell, Sandra Davidson, Russel Deamer, Ernst Deitrich, Liz DeLoughrey, Luis Di Criscio, Julia Ditrich, Felette Dittmer, John Donkin, Andrew Dorkins, Michael & Pia Dowling, Mark Duvall, Phillip East, Frances Edwards, Nivine Emeran, Gordon Evans, Caroline Ewing, Mike Fee, Lorraine Folder, Russell Fong, Kathy Forsyth, Carolyn & Tevita Fotofili, Dan Fowler, David Frid, Danielle Friedli, Bob Fry, Diego M Gabathuler, Charo Garcia, Aki Ghani, Scott Gilmore, Duncan Gilroy, Chris Godfrey, Bill Grable, Scott Graham, Lynne Greenwood, Lucky Grewal, Paul Griffiths, Nathan Gutsell, Paul Harris, Kirsten Hartshorne, Sara Hatton, James Henderson, Ingela Hermansson, Terri Higashi, Richard Hindes, Mark Holland, Natalie Holland, Djamila Holmlund, Nikola Hopkins, Lillian Houston, Lee Hubbard, Rob Hulls, Lisa Humphrey, William Hurrey, Suein Hwang, Scott Hyams, Per Hylle, Robin Irwin, Prue Jackson, Sara Jelley, Nicola Jellyman, James Jordin, Tim Joslin, Noga Kadman, Matthew Kandiah, Ingrid Karlsson, Louise Kawakami, Jennie King, Pat Kirikiti, Tim Kniep, Barbara Krantz, Martin Kyllo, Jay Kyne, Harriet Lamb, Gerhard Lammel, Andrea Lanyon, Klaus Latta, Lory Leacock, Leslie Leung, Travis Lopez, Julie Louttit, Rachel Lynch, Barbara Mackney, Philip K Maini, Tomas Maltby, Susie Markham, Janette Mather, Scott Mather, Stuart Matthews, Kelly McCarthy, Tracey McGregor, Angie McGuire, Collin McKenny, Kat Mclean, George McLelland, Hilary McNamara, Jim McNamara, Nathalie Meunier, Andrew Mitchell, Sara Molan, Gregory Mooney, Kirsty Morris, Daniel Munday, Monique Nagelkerke, N & M Nakamura, Margery & Ken Nash, Victoria Nason, Jenny Natusch, Linda Nawava, Rahni Newsome, Victoria Nickerson, Trine Nielsen, Lisa Nowacki, Sheryl Onuma, Jodie Page, Cherie Palmer, David Palmer, Matt Papaphotis, James Parry, Wim Peeters, Doreen Pfaeltzer, Wolfgang Pfaeltzer, Sara Pines, Elizabeth Pollard, David Powell, Rae & Terry Powell, Thomas Proft, Freda Prouty, John Radford, Riju Ramrakha, Michael Rausch, Alaisdair Raynham, Anna Reiss, Lindsay Rieger, Donna Roemling, Catherine Ross, Joseph Ross, Kevin Russell, Denise Ruygrok, Sara Sande, Robert Saunders, Paul Schmidt, Peter Selwyn, Gemma Seville, William Sharp, Mark Sigman, Joanne Sims, Marinus JJ Sinke, David Sinn, Ron Skates, , Guybe Slangen, Chris Souilivaert, N Southern, GE Spence, Becky St John, Siegfried Stapf, Eric Steinert, Geoff & Nerolie Stodart, Neil Stollznow, Georgia Stone, Kate & Nick Stonier, Astrid Striedl, Helen Sykes, Jochen Tekotte, Sue Thewlis, Geoffrey Tickell, Deborah Todd, Helene & Joe Tuwai, Andy Ulery, Leon D Urbain, Caroline & Herman van den Wall Bake, Frank van Kampen, Peter Paul van Reenen, Frederique van Tijen, Marion Vanson, Paul D Varady, Jenny Visser, Eldad Vizel, Jennifer Wade, Richard Walker, Andy Walters, Gabrielle Watson, Jenni Weir, Kristina Wendhorst, Sally Weston, Graham Whitehead, Donna Widdison, Noelene Williams, John Winter, Dorothy Wirth, Jim Wirth, Eleanore & John Woollard, Lincoln Young, Gene Yuson, Monika Zilch, Simone & Amir Zimmermann

Foreword

ABOUT LONELY PLANET GUIDEBOOKS

The story begins with a classic travel adventure: Tony and Maureen Wheeler's 1972 journey across Europe and Asia to Australia. There was no useful information about the overland trail then, so Tony and Maureen published the first Lonely Planet guidebook to meet a growing need.

From a kitchen table, Lonely Planet has grown to become the largest independent travel publisher in the world, with offices in Melbourne (Australia), Oakland (USA), London (UK) and Paris (France).

Today Lonely Planet guidebooks cover the globe. There is an ever-growing list of books and information in a variety of media. Some things haven't changed. The main aim is still to make it possible for adventurous travellers to get out there – to explore and better understand the world.

At Lonely Planet we believe travellers can make a positive contribution to the countries they visit – if they respect their host communities and spend their money wisely. Since 1986 a percentage of the income from each book has been donated to aid projects and human rights campaigns, and, more recently, to wildlife conservation.

Although inclusion in a guidebook usually implies a recommendation we cannot list every good place. Exclusion does not necessarily imply criticism. In fact there are a number of reasons why we might exclude a place – sometimes it is simply inappropriate to encourage an influx of travellers.

UPDATES & READER FEEDBACK

Things change – prices go up, schedules change, good places go bad and bad places go bankrupt. Nothing stays the same. So, if you find things better or worse, recently opened or long-since closed, please tell us and help make the next edition even more accurate and useful.

Lonely Planet thoroughly updates each guidebook as often as possible – usually every two years, although for some destinations the gap can be longer. Between editions, up-to-date information is available in our free, monthly email bulletin *Comet* (w www.lonelyplanet.com/newsletters). You can also check out the *Thorn Tree* bulletin board and *Postcards* section of our website, which carry unverified, but fascinating, reports from travellers.

Tell us about it! We genuinely value your feedback. A well-travelled team at Lonely Planet reads and acknowledges every email and letter we receive and ensures that every morsel of information finds its way to the relevant authors, editors and cartographers.

Everyone who writes to us will find their name listed in the next edition of the appropriate guidebook. The very best contributions will be rewarded with a free guidebook.

We may edit, reproduce and incorporate your comments in Lonely Planet products such as guidebooks, websites and digital products, so let us know if you don't want your comments reproduced or your name acknowledged.

How to contact Lonely Planet:
Online: e talk2us@lonelyplanet.com.au, w www.lonelyplanet.com
Australia: Locked Bag 1, Footscray, Victoria 3011
UK: 10a Spring Place, London NW5 3BH
USA: 150 Linden St, Oakland, CA 94607

Introduction

Lapped by warm azure waters, fringed with vibrant coral reefs and cloaked in the emerald green of the tropics, Fiji is a paradise-seeker's dream come true. Its sun-soaked, white-sand beaches and resorts are bliss, but only a slice of the country's allure. The abundant sea life and clear waters make Fiji a diving and snorkelling mecca. Rugged highland interiors offer stunning landscapes, remote villages and treks through extinct volcanic craters. Giant waterfalls plunge through areas of rainforest in well-maintained reserves while archaeological sites dotted throughout the country allude to Fiji's mysterious past.

Amid this wealth of natural beauty, Fiji's true magic lies in its people and their fascinating blend of cultures. The majority of the population is made up of indigenous Fijians and Indo-Fijians. Most indigenous Fijians continue to live a village lifestyle under the authority of a local chief and maintain traditional values and culture. While their ancestors once gained Fiji the fearsome reputation of the 'Cannibal Isles', indigenous Fijians of today are some of the friendliest people on the globe and your contact with them will undoubtedly be a highlight of your trip. A visit to a village will give you the chance to experience a *lovo* feast, *meke* dancing and the traditional kava welcoming ceremony.

Indo-Fijians have called Fiji home for over four generations; their ancestors were brought as indentured labourers from India to work on British sugar plantations. Sari shops, temples and curry houses are now Fijian fixtures as is the Indo-Fijian warm humour and hospitality. You'll also see Fijians of European decent; Fiji was once the centre for trade in the South Pacific and a British colony for nearly 100 years (gaining independence in 1970). Added to this diverse population are people from neighbouring South Pacific countries, as well as a growing number of Chinese immigrants. The result is an eclectic blend: as you travel around Fiji, you can feed on curries and chop suey, visit temples, churches and mosques, hear Urdu and Mandarin, and sip spiced *chai* or kava. While the common language is English, the universal greeting is a warm *bula!*

Unlike many countries, the indigenous people of Fiji have not lost their traditional land rights, and retain ownership of 83% of the country. Land access and political equality for Fiji's many ethnic groups remain controversial topics, with governmental coups in the country's not-so-distant past. However,

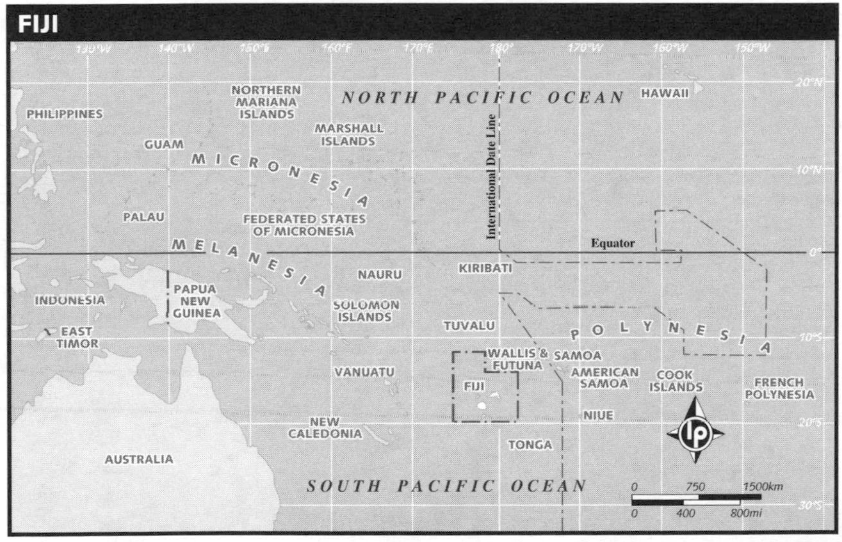

other than getting an earful about it from your taxi driver or a local village guide, it's extremely unlikely to affect you as a tourist. Instead, you might notice that, despite ethnic tensions, Indo-Fijians and indigenous Fijians are crossing cultural boundaries more and more. In urban centres, you'll spot a few mixed couples, in Fijian villages you might be served up roti and curry, and behind the hotel reception desk you'll probably find both Indo-Fijian and indigenous Fijian staff.

Fiji is a relatively easy country in which to travel: it has a pleasant tropical climate, no malaria is present, it has an amazing range of activities and accommodation for all tastes and ages, and the extensive transportation network is efficient and generally trouble-free. It's also got some easy options for those travelling on a package tour who are looking to embellish their trip with a bit of independent travel. Take an adventure cruise, go trekking, rent a car or hop on a local bus, spend a day or spend two months. With over 300 islands in its archipelago and a fascinating history and culture, Fiji is yours to explore.

Facts about Fiji

HISTORY

Vitian Culture

The name Fiji comes from the Tongan name for the islands and was given to the archipelago after the arrival of the Europeans. Before this the inhabitants called their home Viti. Vitian culture was a complex blend of influences shaped by Polynesian, Melanesian and, to a lesser extent, Micronesian peoples who came and went over 35 centuries.

The Lapita people first settled the Fiji islands about 1500 BC. Linguistic studies suggest that they came from Vanuatu or the eastern Solomon Islands. These people – coastal dwellers who relied on fishing – are thought to have lived in relative peace. However, from about 2500 years ago, a shift towards agriculture occurred along with an expansion of population which led to an increase in intertribal feuding. Cannibalism became common and in times of war, villages moved to fortified sites.

About 1000 years ago Tongans and Samoans invaded from the east, prompting larger scale, more-organised wars. More Tongans invaded in the 18th century and villagers again sought refuge in fortified sites. While there were also extended periods of peace, Viti was undergoing intense social upheaval at the time of the first European settlement in the early 19th century. Local skirmishes between tribes verged on civil wars, leading the Europeans to believe that Viti was in a constant state of war.

No Vitian community was completely self-sufficient and networks for trade operated throughout the islands and even extended to Tonga and Samoa. Viti was, however, never politically unified and there were local variations in culture. Vitian society centred on *mataqali* (extended family groups), which were headed by a *turaga-ni-koro* (hereditary village chief) who was usually male. The chief's everyday role was to chat and solve problems while the men of the village worked in the fields and the women fished, cooked and made crafts. Ownership was collective but the chiefs controlled the allocation of land and labour. Villages were further grouped under a high chief. A chief's immense power over the community was reinforced by the belief that he or she was tabu

Portrait of a Fijian Man – engraving by JD MacDonald, 19th century

(sacred), and their *mana* (spiritual power) was derived from a special relationship with an ancestral god. Many of these beliefs and associated practices continue to exist in indigenous Fijian villages today.

Chiefs were polygamous and intermarriage led to complex interrelationships between *mataqali*. Normally, the position of chief passed through a generation of half-brothers before passing to their sons, but the appointment was often hotly debated by village elders. Rivalry and power struggles were common, resulting in fighting and occasionally all-out war between close neighbours who were invariably related. To further complicate matters, a chiefly woman's sons could claim ownership over property owned by her brothers in other villages. This was known as the *vasu* system.

A startling array of vicious weapons, including barbed spears, javelins, bows and arrows, slinging stones, throwing clubs and skull-piercing battle hammers and clubs, can be seen at the Fiji Museum in Suva.

European Explorers

During the 17th and 18th centuries, Europeans crossed the southwest Pacific searching for *terra australis incognita*, or the 'unknown southern land'.

The first-known European to visit Fijian waters was Abel Tasman, who sailed past the group in 1643, en route to the East Indies. His descriptions of negotiating the treacherous reef system northwest of Vanua Levu and Taveuni kept mariners out of Fijian waters for the next 130 years.

After claiming Australia for Britain, the English navigator James Cook visited Tonga (which was then known as the Friendly Islands) where he learnt of the Fijians' reputation as formidable warriors and ferocious cannibals. Cook visited Fiji uneventfully, stopping on Vatoa in the southern Lau Group in 1774. However the tales of the 'Cannibal Isles' accompanied him back to Europe and further deterred sailors from visiting the islands.

After the famous mutiny on the *Bounty* in 1789, Captain William Bligh and 18 others were cast adrift near Tonga. In their small open boat, with only a few provisions and navigation instruments, they sailed for Timor in the Dutch East Indies – a 6000km trip that lasted 41 days. They passed through southern Lau, across the Koro Sea and between Vanua Levu and Viti Levu (through a channel now known as Bligh Water). Almost clearing the Cannibal Isles without incident, they were chased by two Fijian war canoes near the Yasawas. Bligh managed to make rudimentary charts along the way, which he added to during another voyage in 1792 when he sailed through the Lau Group, the Koro Sea and past Kadavu.

Traders & Beachcombers

Tongans had long been trading with the Lau Group and other more-distant Fiji islands. Colourful *kula* feathers, which were highly valued for their use in ceremonial dress, *masi* (printed bark cloth) and weapons were all traded. From the early 19th century, European traders tackled their fears of the reefs and the cannibals and also began to visit Fijian waters. Whalers and traders of sandalwood and bêche-de-mer (sea cucumber) had a significant and disruptive impact on the local population, introducing firearms and foreign capitalist values.

Sandalwood Trade Fragrant sandalwood timber was highly valued in Asia. Tongans initially controlled the trade, obtaining the sandalwood from the Fijian chiefs of Bua Bay on Vanua Levu, and then selling it to the Europeans. However, when Oliver Slater – who was a survivor of the shipwrecked *Argo* – discovered the location of the supply, he spread the news of its whereabouts and Europeans began to trade directly with Fijians in 1805. See 'The Goods, the Bad & the Ugly' boxed text in the Vanua Levu chapter.

The sandalwood trade was a high-profit business for the Europeans. Initially bartering for metal tools, tobacco, cloth, muskets and powder, the chiefs eventually began to drive harder bargains and often demanded assistance in wars against other chiefs.

While the timber trade provided wealth and advantage for the chiefs of Bua (Vanua Levu) and Bau (southeast Viti Levu), this led to jealousy and conflict with other villages. The introduction of firearms through the trade and the resulting increase in violent tribal warfare were a lasting consequence of the trade. By 1813 the accessible supply of sandalwood was exhausted.

Bêche-de-Mer Trade Considered a tasty delicacy in Asia, bêche-de-mer was another lucrative commodity that Fijians traded with the Europeans. As with sandalwood, this trade was short-lived due to overexploitation, only lasting from 1830 to 1835 and 1844 to 1850.

The intensive harvesting process required hundreds of workers for a single bêche-demer station. Some chiefs sent their villagers to work on the trade to boost their own wealth and power, and this affected the lifestyle and economies of the wider communities. The chief of Bau, for example, received 5000 muskets and 600 kegs of powder in return for helping suppress objections to the trade.

Beachcombers During the 17th and 18th centuries, beachcombers lived with Fijian villagers. They were mainly deserting and shipwrecked sailors or escaped convicts from the British penal settlements in Australia. Some didn't survive long before being eaten, while others were recruited into Fijian society and given special treatment for helping the chiefs in warfare. The wise beachcombers made themselves useful in order to increase their chances of survival, serving as interpreters and go-betweens, carpenters, arms-owners and marksmen.

Charles Savage was an especially influential beachcomber. After being shipwrecked on the *Eliza* in 1808, the Swede retrieved muskets and ammunition from the wreck. Savage helped Bau to become one of the most powerful chiefdoms in Fiji. In return for war service he received a privileged position and many wives, and survived for about five years before being killed in battle. His skull was preserved as a kava bowl. Paddy Connel played a similar role in neighbouring Rewa.

Expanding Chiefdoms

By 1829 the chiefdom of Bau controlled Lomaiviti and the coastal areas of northern and eastern Viti Levu, where trade with Europeans had been most intense. Through intermarriage Bau's chiefly family exerted influence over the regions of Rewa on Viti Levu and Cakaudrove on Vanua Levu, as well as over much of Northern Lau, Ovalau and Moturiki. The chiefdom had accumulated wealth, tools, weapons and influence from dealings with traders and beachcombers. From Bau's strategic location, enormous canoes were used to carry out raids, intervene in disputes and otherwise assert the chief's power.

The competing chiefs of the regions of Bau, Rewa and Verata (north of present-day Suva) in the southeast involved their people in vicious power struggles, and war was the norm from the late 1840s to the early 1850s. Bauan chief Ratu Seru Cakobau, who succeeded his father Chief Tanoa, was at the height of his influence by 1850. He was known to foreigners as Tui Viti (King of Fiji), despite having no real claim over most of Fiji. Cakobau abused the power he commanded through traditional systems of hierarchy and through customs such as *sevusevu* (a gift presented as a token of esteem or atonement) to get exactly what he wanted. This was often to the demise of entire villages and, eventually, his former allies turned against him.

Tongan Influence

In the early and mid-19th century, Tonga began to have more of an influence on Fijian affairs. The chiefdoms of Bau, Rewa and Cakaudrove became dependent on Tongan canoe building and seafaring skills, and Bau received Tongan military support.

In 1848 Tongan noble Enele Ma'afu led an armada of war canoes to capture the island of Vanua Balavu in Northern Lau. His ultimate goal was to conquer all of Fiji, annex it to Tonga, and convert the people to Christianity along the way. In 1853 his cousin, the king of Tonga, made him governor of all Tongans in Lau. By 1854 Ma'afu had become a serious threat to Cakobau's power. By the late 1850s, the Tongans were the controlling force in eastern Fiji.

Missionaries

Missionaries were drawn to Fiji to find converts for Christianity and to preach against cannibalism. In the 1830s the London Missionary Society (LMS) sent a number of Tahitian pastors to Oneata, while Wesleyan Methodist missionaries David Cargill and William Cross set up in Lakeba, both islands in Southern Lau. Cross and Cargill developed and taught a language system using a single letter to represent each Fijian sound (b for 'mb', c for 'th', d for 'nd', g for 'ng' and q for 'ngg'). This system is still in use today.

Fijians were not interested in giving up their own gods and progress for the missionaries was slow. They soon realised that if they were ever to convert the Fijian people they had to convert the chiefs first – especially the powerful chiefs of eastern Viti Levu. Bau and Rewa were warring intensely at the time and it was not until 1839 that the missionaries' first real victory was achieved. The high chief of Viwa (3km from Bau) converted to the new religion, setting a precedent for his villagers and for other chiefs who were under his influence.

Chief Cakobau reluctantly adopted Christianity in 1854, on the threat of withdrawal of Tongan military support. Nevertheless, the Methodist Church saw his conversion as a triumph and Reverend Baker set out to spread the Gospel in the western highlands; in 1867, he was killed and eaten by locals who resented the imposition of ideas associated with Bau. See the 'Headstrong Reverend Baker' boxed text in the Viti Levu chapter.

Some chiefs endured the presence of missionaries in their village for the trade

Tabua

Tabua (carefully polished and shaped whales' teeth) were believed to be shrines for the ancestor spirits. *Tabua* were, and still are, highly valued items and essential to diplomacy. Used as a powerful *sevusevu* – a gift presented as a token of esteem or atonement – the acceptance of *tabua* binds a chief morally and spiritually to the gift-giver and the desired outcome of that person.

Traditionally, a man's body was accompanied to the grave by a *tabua* – along with a war club or a musket and his strangled wives – to help defend his spirit on its hazardous journey to the after-world. Without the company of a *tabua*, his spirit would be left in 'lonely limbo'.

Originally *tabua* were rare, obtained only from washed-up sperm whales or through trade with Tonga. However, European traders introduced thousands of whale teeth and replicas of teeth in whalebone, elephant tusk and walrus tusk. These negotiation tools became concentrated in the hands of a few dominant chiefdoms, consequently increasing their power.

opportunities this brought. Others converted because they were impressed by what they saw as the new god's power, as demonstrated by the machines, guns and warships of its followers. Missionaries and Fijian ministers gradually displaced the priests of the old religion (see Religion later in this chapter) and assumed their privileged positions. The concept of holiness was accepted for its similarity to the existing beliefs of tabu and mana. The influence of missionaries and Europeans on traditional culture and everyday life was all pervasive: dress and once-elaborate body decoration and hairdressing became conservative; rituals such as initiation tattooing were discouraged; tribal warfare was suppressed; and Bauan was promoted over other dialects as the written language. Most Fijians adopted Christianity alongside their traditional spirituality. Today you will find the two religions hand in hand, with Methodist villagers continuing to worship their ancestral gods through such practices as kava ceremony, tabu areas and codes of conduct, and the symbolic *tabua* (whales' teeth).

European Settlement

By the 1830s a small whaling and beachcomber settlement was established at Levuka, on Ovalau. Foreigners married local women and Levuka became one of the main ports of call in the South Pacific for traders and warships. In 1840 Commandant Charles Wilkes led a US expedition to Fiji. His team, consisting of scientists, artists and language experts succeeded in producing the first reasonably complete chart of the Fijian islands. While surveying the islands, Wilkes negotiated with the powerful Chief Tanoa of Bau and created a port-regulation treaty: the chiefdom was paid in return for protection of foreign ships and the supply of provisions.

The mutually beneficial relationship was short-lived. In 1841, relations began to seriously deteriorate when the foreign settlement was razed by fires which foreigners suspected Cakobau of instigating. Whether Cakobau was in fact guilty of trying to assert his power through arson or if the foreigners only attributed the blame to increase their own control remains a secret of history. During the 1849 US Independence Day celebrations – the home of Williams – The US commercial agent was accidentally destroyed by fire and locals helped themselves to his possessions. Williams held Cakobau (as king of Fiji) responsible for the actions of his people and sent him a substantial damages bill. This set a precedent and compensation claims against Cakobau for the loss of American property rose to an inflated US$45,000.

Cakobau came under increasing pressure from all sides. In 1862, claiming to have power over the whole of Fiji, he proposed to England's consul that he would cede the islands to Britain in return for the payment of his debts. The offer was not seriously considered at the time, but representatives were sent to investigate the attractiveness of the proposition. Rumours and speculation caused a large influx of British settlers via Australia and New Zealand. Settlers bickered between themselves and disputes erupted with Fijians over land ownership. Levuka town became a lawless and greedy outpost, which bordered on anarchy and racial war. Cakobau's huge debt was not cleared until 1868 when the Australian Polynesia Company agreed to pay it in exchange for land (see the Suva section in the Viti Levu chapter).

Various attempts to form a local Fijian government met with limited success. In 1865 a council of chiefs was established but it only lasted a couple of years, after which regional governments were formed in Bau (headed by Cakobau), in Lau (headed by Ma'afu), and also in Bua. Finally, in 1871 Cakobau formed a Fiji-wide government based at Levuka but it too collapsed after two years with Cakobau's opponents accusing his government of extravagance, ineptness and corruption.

Blackbirding

Europeans brought other Pacific Islanders to labour on cotton, copra and sugar plantations in Fiji. The American Civil War indirectly stimulated the trade in labourers by prompting a worldwide cotton shortage that resulted in a cotton boom in Fiji.

Most labourers were islanders from the southwest Pacific, especially the Solomons and New Hebrides (now Vanuatu), but Fijians were also coerced. Initially, people were coaxed into agreeing to work for three years in return for minimal wages, food, clothing and return passage. Later, chiefs were bribed and men and women traded for ammunition. By the 1860s and 1870s the practice had developed into an organised system of kidnapping. Stories of atrocities and abuses by recruiters resulted in pressure on Britain to stop the trade. In 1872 the Imperial Kidnapping Act was passed, but this had limited success in regulating the traffic as Britain had no power to enforce it.

Cession to Britain

With Cakobau's government unable to maintain peace, in 1873 the British consul again considered annexing Fiji. This time Britain was interested, citing the need to abolish blackbirding as its principal justification. With Cakobau's support, Fiji was pronounced a British crown colony on 10 October 1874 at Levuka. Signatories to the Deed of Cession were Cakobau ('King of Fiji and warlord'), Ma'afu (then chief of Lau, Taveuni and much of Vanua Levu) and 11 other chiefs. It is significant that all but one of the high chiefs who signed the deed were from eastern Fiji: cession was not universally accepted by Fiji's chiefs.

The Colonial Period

Colonial Government Along with the end of the American Civil War came a slump in the world cotton market and the Fijian economy began to slide into depression. Epidemics spread throughout the country with an outbreak of measles wiping out about a third of the indigenous Fijian population. Social unrest was on the rise.

The fact that Europeans were greatly outnumbered prompted fears that racial war might break out in Fiji. Like the missionaries before it, the colonial government appreciated the influence of the chiefs. If the chiefs could be persuaded to collaborate with the colonialists, then Fiji would be more easily, cheaply and peacefully governed. This was nearly successful, give or take a dissenting chief or two. (See the 'Kai Colo Uprising' boxed text in the Southern Viti Levu section of the Viti Levu chapter.)

Levuka's geography hindered expansion, so the administrative capital was officially moved to Suva in 1882. The early 1880s saw an increase in investment and settlers from New Zealand and Australia; however, it was the policy of the colonial government to protect Fijian land rights by forbidding sales to foreigners. The system was successful in retaining land rights for the indigenous owners, and 83% of the land is still owned by indigenous Fijian communities.

Fijian Labour In an attempt to maintain good relations with its subjects, the new colonial government prohibited the employment of indigenous Fijians as labourers on plantations. Fijian labour had already been exploited in the sandalwood, bêche-de-mer, cotton and copra trade, and this had proved disruptive to village life. Fijians were increasingly reluctant to take full-time wage work, preferring traditional subsistence work that satisfied their village obligations and was less regimented.

The colonial government was under pressure from Britain to make the Fijian economy self-sufficient. Plantation crops, such as cotton, copra and sugar cane, were a potential solution, but these demanded large pools of cheap labour. Slavery had been abolished, blackbirding was under control, and Fijians were unwilling to leave their communal lands to work on the plantations. Indentured labour seemed the perfect solution.

Indentured Labour In 1878, negotiations were made with the Indian government for labourers to come to Fiji on five-year contracts, after which time the labourers, or *girmitiyas*, were free to return to India at their own expense. If they worked for another five years, their return passage home would be paid. While some Indians saw the system as a way to escape poverty, others were recruited through deception and the promise of fine prospects. Indentured labourers began arriving in Fiji at a rate of about 2000 per year.

The *girmitiyas* soon discovered the reality of life on the plantations. Heavy work allocations were given and food was strictly rationed; if the *girmitiyas* failed to complete the daily tasks, wages were withheld and they could be prosecuted. Corporal punishment and human rights abuses by the overseers were rife, checks were rare and there was little or no recourse to legal aid. In this high-pressure situation, crime, suicide, sickness and disease were not uncommon.

About 80% of the labourers were Hindu, 14% Muslim, and the remainder mostly Sikhs and Christians. Overcrowded accommodation gave little privacy, and people of different caste and religion were forced to mix. Social and religious structures crumbled; there was a lack of traditional leadership, little knowledge of correct religious rituals and no education for children other than in Christian missionary schools.

Even though the *girmitiyas'* experience as labourers was of great hardship and even *narak* (hell), the vast majority of Indians decided to stay in Fiji once they had served their contract and many brought their families across from India. Some people of lower caste had much greater prospects if they stayed in Fiji, as those who returned were usually given the social standing of outcastes or untouchables – the lowest status in India.

By the early 1900s the Indian government was being pressured to abolish the indenture system. Mahatma Gandhi denounced the civil and human rights abuses that were occurring on the plantations as did high-profile missionaries. Indians began to strike against low wages and working conditions. In 1916, recruitment stopped and indenture ended officially in January 1919. By this time, a total of 60,537 indentured labourers were in Fiji.

Power Play The colonial government discouraged interaction between Indians and Fijians. Indians, restricted from buying land from indigenous Fijians by the colonial administration, moved instead into small business, trade and bureaucracy, or took out long-term leases as independent farmers.

In 1904, the constitution was amended to include two Fijians in the Legislative Council. However, it was not until 1916 that the governor nominated one Indian member, and 1929 that the first Indian members were actually elected to government.

The 1920s saw the first major struggle for better conditions for Indians. In an effort to quell labour troubles in the Indian-dominated workforce (and protect their own capital), members of the local European community began stirring and manipulating racial strife between the Fijians and Indians. By taking sides with the Fijians, the Europeans diverted attention from their own monopoly on freehold land and their power and influence in the civil service. It was convenient to blame all problems on the Indian community and to exacerbate fears that the Indian population would surpass that of indigenous Fijians.

World Wars Fiji had only a minor involvement in WWI: about 700 of Fiji's European residents and about 100 Fijians were sent to serve in Europe. The conflict in the Pacific during WWII was much closer to home. Around 8000 Fijians were recruited into the Fiji Military Force (FMF) and trained by American and New Zealand forces. From 1942 to 1943 Fijians fought against the Japanese in the Solomon Islands. While there was no armed combat in Fiji, air-raid shelters and batteries were built in Suva and cannons placed at the strategic spots of Vuda Point near Nadi and Momi Bay.

Understandably, after the racism and exploitation experienced in the cane fields during and since the indenture period, Indians did not rush to enlist. Indians considered the low prices they received for their cane as part of this exploitation and, in 1943, held a strike against the Australian-owned Colonial Sugar Refining Company (which monopolised the industry). Many farmers went so far as to burn their crops to the ground. The Fijian and European leaders chose to see the strike and the Indians' lack of support for the war as cowardly and unpatriotic.

Independence

After WWII, Fijians became more conscious of the need for democratically elected government and the importance of forming organisations such as trade unions. The 1960s saw the formation of ministerial government, voting rights for women, the establishment of political parties, constitutional changes and a movement towards self-government. Increasingly, members of the government were elected by the people rather than nominated by the governor.

Fiji became independent on 10 October 1970, after 96 years of colonial administration. In the rush towards independence, important problems such as land ownership and leases, how to protect the interests of a racially divided country, the voting system, and appropriate development, were not resolved. The long history of segregation in Fiji was continued in the division of political seats and with new parties being separated along racial lines.

Post-Independence Fiji

In the immediate post-independence years, Fiji experienced a bit of an economic boom. Hydroelectricity was introduced, the transport infrastructure was improved and building, commerce, tourism and agriculture were all on the rise. This lasted until the early 1980s when there was a decline in the price of sugar (which was the country's main source of wealth) and the reality of the country's accumulating foreign debt began to hit home.

Fiji's first post-independence election was won by the indigenous Fijian Alliance Party. Although the Alliance promoted itself as being pro-multiculturalism, the results in the polls showed a clear racial division in voting. The following year Ratu George Cakobau, the high chief of indigenous Fijians, became the new governor general. Ironically, he was a descendant of the great chief Cakobau, who had ceded Fiji to Britain almost one hundred years before!

Ethnic Tensions

Following independence, Fijians, especially town and urban dwellers, were optimistic and people of different races generally got along well. There were, however, underlying tensions that became more apparent as the economy worsened. In 1975 there was a rise in nationalism among indigenous Fijians. It was led by Sakesai Butadroka who called a parliamentary motion to repatriate the entire Indo-Fijian community, despite the fact that most were fourth-generation Fijians. Although the motion was rejected by both the Indo-Fijian National Federation Party (NFP) and the Alliance Party, many indigenous Fijians agreed with the idea. The following elections in 1977 saw Butadroka's Fijian Nationalist Party (FNP) divide Alliance voters, allowing the Indo-Fijian NFP to win. Its victory was short-lived, however, as the governor general called for a new election and the Alliance regained its majority.

In both urban and rural areas, most retail outlets and transport services were (and still are) run by Indo-Fijian families. A racial stereotype developed portraying Indo-Fijians as obsessed with making money. However, like most indigenous Fijians, the vast majority of Indo-Fijians belonged to poorer working classes; the main difference was that Indo-Fijians did not have the land resources of the indigenous Fijian population.

Meanwhile the economic aspirations of indigenous Fijians were changing: while some wanted to preserve their traditional ways, others sought to modernise their practices and values. Efforts were made by the government to encourage indigenous Fijians to enter business through a 'soft loan scheme' developed by the Fiji Development Bank. Many of these new businesses failed because they attempted to move into already competitive areas. The failure of their own businesses and the competition of the already established businesses tended to be seen in purely racial terms.

The Alliance Party was perceived to be failing indigenous Fijians in their hopes for economic advancement, and Indo-Fijians were tired of the fighting between the Hindu and Muslim factions within the NFP. Greater unity among the working classes led to a shifting of loyalties and the formation of the Fiji Labour Party (FLP) in 1985. In the April 1987 elections an FLP-NFP coalition defeated the Alliance Party by a small percentage. Despite having an indigenous Fijian prime minister and a cabinet comprised of an indigenous-Fijian majority, the new government was labelled 'Indian dominated'.

Military Coups of the 1980s

The victory of the coalition immediately raised racial tensions in the country. The extremist Taukei movement, supported by the eastern chiefs and the indigenous Fijian elite, launched a deliberate destabilisation campaign. In a demonstration in Suva, 5000 Fijians marched in protest against the new government.

Taukei leaders played on Fijian fears of losing their land rights and of Indo-Fijian political and economic domination. They suggested that development would result in the loss of Fijian culture, and pointed to the suppression of Maori and Australian Aboriginal cultures as examples.

In the following weeks there were violent incidents against Indo-Fijian businesses around the country and petrol bombs were thrown into the government offices in Suva. On 14 May 1987, only a month after the elections, Lieutenant Colonel Sitiveni Rabuka took over the elected government in a bloodless coup and formed a civil interim government. His 'government' was comprised mostly of members of the previous Alliance government and it was supported by the Great Council of Chiefs (see Government & Politics later in this chapter). In the face of international condemnation, Rabuka attempted to legitimise his government by negotiating a deal with Ratu Ganilau, the governor general, to head the council of ministers. Rabuka was to retain control over the security forces and home affairs.

In September 1987, when the government was about to announce that elections would be held, Rabuka intervened with military force. The 1970 constitution was invalidated and Fiji declared a republic. Rabuka proclaimed himself head of state and appointed a new council of ministers, which included leaders of the Taukei movement and army officers. Arrests of community leaders and academics followed, a curfew was imposed in urban centres, newspapers closed and all political activities were restricted.

In October 1987, Ratu Ganilau resigned as governor general and Fiji was dismissed from the Commonwealth. By December, Rabuka had nominated Ratu Mara as the prime minister, and Ratu Ganilau returned as the president of the new republic.

Motivation There are different theories as to what motivated indigenous support for the coups. As the majority of indigenous Fijians are Methodist, many believe it was the nationalist movement within the church that greatly supported the deposed Alliance Party. Church leaders took part in the racist Taukei movement and encouraged the military government to impose nationwide post-coup Sunday observances, including a ban on Sunday trading.

There were underlying tensions and some jealousy on the part of indigenous Fijians against the Indo-Fijians, but these racial differences were deliberately exaggerated by the indigenous Fijian elite who stood to lose by the Alliance Party's defeat. The FLP-NFP coalition, with its western Fijian and Indo-Fijian members, threatened the political power of the traditional hierarchy of the Great Council of Chiefs.

The coups, which were supposed to benefit all indigenous Fijians, in fact caused immense hardship and benefited only an elite minority. When the Indo-Fijian element was effectively removed, tensions within the indigenous Fijian community itself were exposed. Clear examples of this are the conflicts and contradictions between chiefs from eastern and western Fiji; between high chiefs and village chiefs; between urban and rural dwellers; and within the church and trade-union movement.

Interim Government

The economic consequences of the coups were drastic. By the end of 1987, Fiji experienced negative growth in GDP, a devalued dollar, inflation, price increases and wage cuts. The economy's two main sources of income were seriously affected: Indo-Fijian sugar farmers refused to harvest their crops, and tourism declined significantly. Aid from Australia and New Zealand was temporarily suspended leading to large numbers of people, including thousands of Indo-Fijians, skilled trades people and professionals emigrating.

While the government largely recovered from the economic effects, racial tensions continued to run high. In 1989 the government relaxed the Sunday observance rules. In protest, the Methodist Church fundamentalist leader, Manasa Lasaro, organised demonstrations and roadblocks in Labasa, resulting in his arrest and that of 57 others. Methodist Church groups also firebombed and destroyed three Hindu temples.

Ratu Mara, the interim government's prime minister, became antagonistic towards Rabuka for his incompatibility with the old cabinet's traditions and political interests. In late 1989, Rabuka resigned from his position in the cabinet and took command of the army as major-general.

Tipping the Scales

On 25 July 1990 a new constitution was proclaimed by President Ratu Ganilau. The constitution greatly increased the political power of the Great Council of Chiefs and of the military while diminishing the position of Indo-Fijians in government. The majority of seats in the House of Representatives were reserved for indigenous Fijians and the Council of Chiefs would effectively have control over the appointment of the president, majority of senators and prime minister, as well as over legislation relating to land ownership and common rights. Compulsory Sunday observance was legislated, imposing Christian religious values on the population.

Indo-Fijian political leaders immediately opposed the constitution, claiming it was racist and undemocratic. A group of Indo-Fijian academics ceremonially burnt a copy of the constitution in a show of protest, prompting soldiers to kidnap and torture Dr Sigh, a lecturer at the University of the South Pacific. The soldiers involved in the kidnapping were merely fined and then set free under suspended jail sentences.

As the 1992 elections approached, the Great Council of Chiefs disbanded the multicultural Alliance Party in March 1991 and in its place formed the Soqosoqo-ni-Vakavulewa-ni Taukei (SVT; Party of Policy Makers for Indigenous Fijians). The General Voters Party (GVP) was formed to represent Europeans, part-Fijians and Chinese while Indo-Fijians were represented by the NFP and the FLP. Rabuka returned to the scene as interim president and party leader of the SVT.

To suit his political ambitions, Rabuka changed his hardline approach and became increasingly populist. Prior to the 1992 elections he promised to repeal labour laws affecting trade unions, to review the constitution and to extend Indo-Fijian farmers' land leases. The SVT won the first post-coup general election held in May 1992, but failed to obtain a clear majority and had to seek coalition partners. Touting his election promises, Rabuka secured the support of the Indo-Fijian members of the House of Representatives.

The new government faced a faltering economy, growing unemployment and crime, and increasing urbanisation of the population. Instead of promised labour reform, companies with more than 50% indigenous-Fijian ownership were offered a 20-year tax exemption. FLP members eventually walked out of parliament in protest against Rabuka's failure to keep promises and the delay in revising the constitution.

Things went from bad to worse. Hurricane Kina hit Fiji at the start of 1993, causing widespread damage. Later in the year, the government presented a budget with a large deficit. When members of the ruling coalition voted against it and quit their parties to form the Fijian Association Party (FAP), Parliament dissolved and a new general election was called. During the election campaign the president, Ratu Penaia Ganilau, died and the Great Council of Chiefs elected Ratu Mara in his place.

The 1994 election saw the SVT re-elected. Rabuka was reappointed as prime minister and continued as leader of the SVT-GVP coalition. The previously defeated budget remained unchanged and was approved by parliament. By 1995, the National Bank of Fiji was bankrupt with debts mounting to F$150 million. Perhaps in a futile attempt to boost trade, 1995 also saw the lifting of the Sunday observance decree and the ban on Sunday trading.

The 1997 Constitution

Rabuka came under increasing pressure to review the 1990 constitution and, finally, in 1995, a Constitutional Review Commission (CRC) was established. In a submission to the CRC, the SVT called to retain the 1990 constitution and to continue political dominance by indigenous Fijians stating: 'Fijians don't trust Indians politically'. In response, a multiracial, multi-interest group called the Citizens' Constitutional Forum (CCF) submitted a report to the CRC. It proposed a move beyond ethnic issues to a national perspective, in non-racial, secular terms.

In 1996 the CRC presented its findings. The 800-page report called for a return to a multiethnic democracy and a move towards open non-communal seats where all Fijian citizens could vote and stand for election. While accepting that the position of president be reserved for an indigenous Fijian, it proposed no provision of ethnicity for the prime minister.

While Nationalists publicly spat on, burnt and destroyed copies of the report, public expectations of reform and a fairer electoral system ran high. The government acted on most of the CRC's recommendations and a new constitution was declared in 1997. Seats were still reserved for ethnic groups, with an indigenous Fijian majority and, contrary to CRC recommendations, the Great Council of Chiefs retained the power to appoint the president. The new constitution also included a Bill of Rights to outlaw racial discrimination, guarantee freedom of speech and association, the independence of the judiciary and the right of equality before the law.

In the same year, Rabuka apologised to Queen Elizabeth for the 1987 military coups, presented her with a *tabua* as a gesture of atonement and the following month Fiji was readmitted to the Commonwealth.

May 19 Coup

In 1998 the Fiji dollar was devalued. Fiji had been badly affected by the Asian economic crisis as it meant a dive in tourist numbers from South Korea and Japan. The country was suffering its worst drought in recorded history and the exodus of professional and skilled workers continued as the 99-year land leases given to Indo-Fijian farmers by the British began to expire.

Under the new constitution voting became compulsory and a record number of political parties joined the competition for seats, dividing voters' traditional preferences. In the May 1999 elections, Fijian voters rejected Rabuka and the SVT. The FLP, led by Mahendra Chaudhry, won the majority of seats and formed a coalition with the FAP. Chaudhry became Fiji's first Indo-Fijian prime minister.

Indigenous Fijians were far from pleased. Convinced that their traditional land rights were at stake, protests increased and many refused to renew leases to Indo-Fijian farmers. On 19 May 2000, armed men, mostly defectors of the Fijian army's Counter Revolutionary Warfare (CRW) unit, entered the Parliamentary Compound in Suva and took 30 hostages, including Prime Minister Chaudhry. Failed businessman George Speight quickly became the face of the coup, claiming to represent indigenous Fijians. He demanded the resignation of both Chaudhry and President Ratu Sir Kamisese Mara and that the 1997 multiethnic constitution be abandoned.

Minor looting and razing took place in Suva as people took the opportunity to swipe some corned beef and stereos. Indigenous Fijians dug *lovo* pits in the parliamentary lawns and police patrolled downtown armed with golf clubs. While the atmosphere was not particularly violent, support for Speight's group was widespread and Indo-Fijians suffered such harassment that many fled. As the land issue was still in debate, many indigenous Fijians reasserted their traditional rights and evicted tenants from property that had been in Indo-Fijian families for nearly a century.

Chaudhry, despite having suffered broken ribs during a beating by his captors, steadfastly refused to resign. Finally, in an attempt to bring the situation to an end, President Mara announced that he was removing Chaudhry from power. Mara acknowledged the seriousness of his actions and the negative reaction that Fiji would face from the international community with the words: 'We are going to face not only purgatory, but hell'. Speight's group demanded Mara's resignation as well and, with lawlessness increasing and the country divided over his role, Mara relinquished power. The head of Fiji's military, Commander Frank Bainimarama, announced martial law.

After long negotiations between Speight's rebels and Bainimarama's military, it was agreed that the rebels would approve a president who would appoint an interim government to rule until elections could be held under a new constitution. Speight's group would release the hostages, return all weapons in return for an amnesty for all coup participants. Many weapons (although, importantly, not all) were returned to the military and, after eight weeks in captivity, the hostages were released. The 1997 constitution was revoked and Ratu Josefa Iloilo was named president. Iloilo appointed Laisenia Qarase as prime minister.

Speight's group had its own preferred prime minister, and when Iloilo, under strict instructions from Bainimarama, refused the candidate, Speight rang the president and allegedly threatened his life. This was exactly what Bainimarama was waiting for – the army moved quickly, and arrested a bamboozled Speight and over 300 sympathisers. Speight and his gang were formally charged with treason, their amnesty erased by the fact that they hadn't returned *all* the weapons and had threatened the president. The rebels' arrest sparked a round of protest across Fiji, much of it involving further violence towards Indo-Fijians.

The coup drew international disapproval meted out as trade sanctions and sporting boycotts. Travellers were given warnings, sometimes severe, to steer clear of Fiji. The economy, particularly the tourism sector, was hit extremely hard. Many businesses folded and economic desperation fell over much of the population.

To Be Continued...

In November 2000, the High Court ruled that the May 19 Coup had no legal standing, and therefore that Ratu Sir Kaimisese Mara was still president of Fiji, the 1997 multiethnic constitution was still in place, and Qarase's interim government had no standing in law. Qarase, with the support of the military and the Great Council of Chiefs, appealed. In March 2001, the Appeal Court decided to uphold the 1997 constitution and ruled that Fiji be taken to the polls in order to restore democracy.

During the election, the police and military were put on high alert and election observers included a 40-strong team from the United Nations. There were reports of vote buying, intimidation and high numbers of invalid votes. An anonymous flyer that was distributed read: 'A vote for FLP is a vote for Bloodshed.' Nevertheless, ousted prime minister Chaudhry ran, as did George Speight from his island prison. Both won seats, however, Speight was unable to take his up due to his inconvenient incarceration.

Qarase, heading his Fijian People's Party (SLD), won 32 of the 71 parliamentary seats in the August 2001 elections. Claiming that a multiparty cabinet in the current circumstances would be unworkable, Qarase proceeded to defy the spirit of the constitution by including no Indo-Fijians in his 18-strong cabinet. The constitution states that any party with eight parliamentary seats is entitled to cabinet positions; Chaudhry's FLP had won 27 seats.

In the meantime, Speight pleaded guilty to treason. He was given a death sentence, which, within a day, was quickly commuted to life imprisonment – likely out of fear of further protests and rioting. Ironically, Speight is serving out this sentence on Nukulau, once a quarantine station where thousands of indentured Indian labourers first set foot in Fiji.

As was the case in the 1980s, the coup has benefited only those indigenous Fijians at the top and not the majority; in fact, trade sanctions, farm closures, the tourism slump and government cuts have cost about 20,000 jobs and more of the population has sunk into poverty. A lot of Indo-Fijians, many of them professionally trained, continue to leave the country and hospitals and schools in particular have suffered massive staff shortages.

Racial tensions have long been upheld and nurtured by those in power as the cause of indigenous Fijians' poverty. By putting Indo-Fijians out of the political (and to a large extent, economical) picture, the indigenous Fijian leaders have effectively lost their scapegoat; it will be interesting to see what the future holds. As the economy slowly struggles to its feet and tourists return to Fiji, racial issues continue to simmer behind the scenes with no resolution in sight.

GEOGRAPHY

The Fiji islands are in the South West Pacific Ocean, south of the equator and north of the tropic of Capricorn. Australia lies 3160km to the southwest, and New Zealand 2120km to the south. Nearby Pacific Islands include Tonga, 770km to the east, and Vanuatu, 1100km to the west.

Fiji's territorial limits cover an area of over 1.3 million sq km, but less than 1.5% of this is dry land. The total land area is about 18,300 sq km. The islands lie between latitudes 12° and 21° south of the equator, and between longitudes 177° east and 175° west. The 180° meridian cuts across the group at Taveuni, but the International Date Line doglegs eastward so that all islands fall within the same time zone – 12 hours ahead of GMT.

Fiji's Islands & Reefs

Wondering what's beneath your feet? The majority of Fijian islands are volcanic in origin. However, you'll also encounter both coral and limestone islands in the archipelago. Fiji's reefs also take three different forms: fringing, barrier and atolls.

Volcanic Islands

Volcanic islands are generally of high relief with a series of conical hills rising to a central summit. Sharp pinnacles indicate the sites of old volcanoes, and crystallised lava flows often reach the coast as ridges, forming cliffs or bluffs. Between these ridges are green valleys, with the only flat land found along the river basins of larger islands. The coasts are lined with beaches and mangrove communities, and the wetter sides of the islands – facing the prevailing winds – support thriving perennial forest vegetation. The leeward hills are home to grasslands with only a sparse covering of trees.

While there are no active volcanoes in Fiji, live volcanic vents have recently been discovered on Taveuni. There is plenty of geothermal activity on Vanua Levu, and in Savusavu some locals use the burbling hot springs to do their cooking! Viti Levu and Kadavu are also volcanic islands.

Limestone Islands

These are characteristically rocky land masses that have risen from the sea. They have cliffs undercut by the sea and are topped with shrubs and trees. Generally, there is a central depression forming a basin, with fertile undulating hills. Volcanic materials also thrust up through the limestone mass. Vanua Balavu in the Lau Group is an example of a limestone island.

Coral Islands

If you're looking for somewhere to swim, you'll likely end up on one of Fiji's coral islands. Small and low, they are generally found in areas protected by barrier reefs, and surface levels raise only to the height at which waves and winds can deposit sand and coral fragments. These islands support simple yet luxuriant vegetation, mostly overhanging palms, broad-leafed trees, shrubs, vines and grasses. The coasts have bright, white-sand beaches and mangroves in the shallows of lagoons. Examples of coral islands are Beachcomber Island and Treasure Island (Elevuka) in the Mamanuca Group, and Leleuvia and Caqelai in the Lomaiviti Group.

Fringing Reefs

Narrow fringing reefs are linked to the shore of an island and stretch seaward, sometimes up to 5km. During low tide the reefs are exposed. Often the bigger fringing reefs have higher sections at the open-sea edge and drainage channels on the inside, which remain filled with water and are navigable by canoes and small boats. Where rivers and streams break the reefs, the fresh water prevents coral growth. The Coral Coast on southern Viti Levu, is an example of an extensive fringing reef. Most islands in Fiji have sections of fringing reefs somewhere along their coast.

Barrier Reefs

As large strips of continuous reef, barrier reefs are broken only by occasional channels some distance from the coastline. They sometimes encircle islands and often occur in combination with fringing reefs. The biggest barrier reef in Fiji is the Great Sea Reef, which extends about 500km from the coast of southwestern Viti Levu to the northernmost point of Vanua Levu. A section of this barrier is unbroken for more than 150km, and lies between 15km and 30km off the coast of Vanua Levu. Other smaller well-known barrier reefs include the one encircling Beqa, and the Astrolabe Reef of Kadavu.

Atolls

Atolls are small rings of coral reef with land and vegetation on top, rising just above sea level. The ring of coral encloses a lagoon, however, an atoll where the land forms a complete circle is rare, and is invariably small when it does occur.

Despite the idyllic representation of atolls in tales of the South Pacific, most have inhospitable environments. The porous soil derived from dead coral, sand and driftwood retains little water, and unless the atoll is situated within a rain belt, it is subject to droughts. The vegetation is usually small and hardy, with species such as pandanus and coconut palms, shrubs and coarse grasses. Fiji has only a few islands that can be classified as atolls. The best-known is Wailagi Lala, east of Nanuku Passage in the Lau Group. There are, however, a number of 'looping' barrier reefs that encircle islands.

The archipelago comprises 300 islands, or many more, depending on how you apply the definition of island. Island sizes vary from tiny patches of land a few metres in diameter, to Viti Levu, which is 10,390 sq km. The second-largest island is Vanua Levu (big land), with an area of 5538 sq km. Only about one-third of the islands are inhabited, mainly due to isolation or lack of fresh water.

Viti Levu has Fiji's highest peak, Mt Tomanivi (also called Mt Victoria) standing 1323m high, near the northern end of a range that separates eastern Viti Levu from western. Suva, the country's capital, is in southeastern Viti Levu. Both Nadi, home to the country's main international airport, and Lautoka, the second most important port after Suva, are on the western side of the island. Viti Levu has the country's largest rivers and most extensive transport and communication systems. The Kings Road and Queens Road join to form a main road around the island's perimeter.

Vanua Levu, 60km northeast of Viti Levu, is of irregular shape with many bays of various shapes and sizes. The huge Natewa Bay between the Natewa Peninsula and the remainder of the island is about 70km long by 15km wide. Like Viti Levu, the main part of the island is divided by a mountain range. Nasorolevu (1111m) is the island's highest peak.

Taveuni, the third-largest island, is separated from Vanua Levu by the Somosomo Strait. Rugged, with rich volcanic soil and luxuriant vegetation, it's known as the 'Garden Island of Fiji'. Its mountainous backbone of volcanic cones includes Uluigalau (1241m), the second-highest summit in Fiji.

The Kadavu Group is south of Viti Levu. It includes Kadavu, of similar size to Taveuni, Ono and a number of small islands, all within the Astrolabe Reef. The main island is three irregularly shaped, rugged land masses linked by isthmuses. Like Taveuni, Kadavu is very scenic, with beautiful reef lagoons, mountains, waterfalls and dense vegetation.

The remainder of Fiji's islands are relatively small and are classified in groups: Lomaiviti, Lau, Moala, Yasawa, Mamanuca and Rotuma. Beqa, Yanuca and Vatulele are small islands off southern Viti Levu. Individual destination chapters contain information on the geography of specific islands.

GEOLOGY

Apart from Kadavu and the islands of the Koro Sea, all of the Fijian islands belong to one massive horseshoe-shaped submarine platform. The largest land masses, Viti Levu and Vanua Levu, are situated on the broader and higher northwestern end of the platform. The eastern arm of the platform extends almost 500km to the southern end of the Lau Group. The whole platform is tilted to the southeast, resulting in deeper waters at the narrower southeastern end. The waters of the Koro Sea almost cut the platform in two at Nanuku Passage – the northeast shipping gateway to the Fijian islands.

About 300 million years ago, Fiji was part of a large Melanesian continent that included eastern Australia, New Zealand and Southeast Asia; it extended as far north as the Philippines and as far east as Fiji. A complex series of geological events built and shaped the archipelago over a long time, with volcanic material and sediments being deposited on the ancient platform. Viti Levu is believed to be the oldest of the Fijian islands, formed as a result of volcanic activity that began to occur 150 million years ago. Erosion over about 35 million years formed river deltas such as the Rewa near Suva, and the sand hills of Kulukulu, near Sigatoka.

CLIMATE

Fiji has a mild tropical maritime climate throughout the year. It's relatively stable due to the large expanse of ocean surrounding the islands. Unlike landmasses that can change temperature in just a few hours, causing local atmospheric disturbances, the sea surface heats and cools slowly.

There are, however, local variations, from hot and dry to warm and wet. All the large islands have mountain ranges lying across the path of the prevailing easterly and southeasterly trade winds, resulting in frequent cloud and greater rainfall on the windward eastern sides. The leeward sides are drier, with clear sky for most of the year and more variable temperatures and wind direction. Smaller islands tend to have dry and sunny microclimates.

Suva is notorious for its cloudy, wet weather. Fiji's resorts, however, are concentrated in areas of abundant sunshine, especially on the southwestern side of Viti Levu and in the Mamanuca Group.

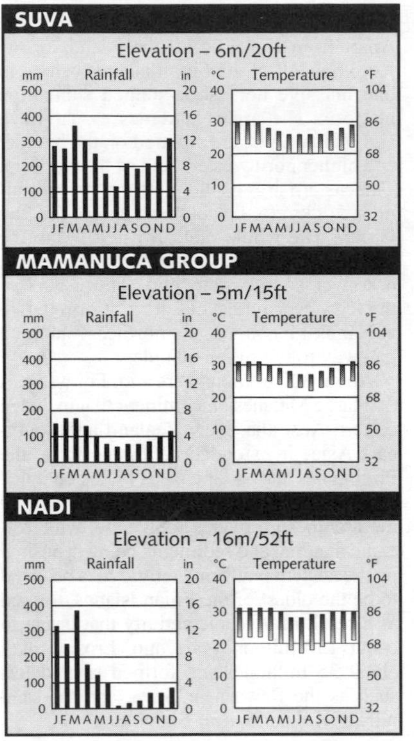

Fiji's 'wet season' is from November to April, and the 'dry season' from May to October, but rainfall occurs all year. Suva, which is in a typical windward locality, has an average rainfall of around 3100mm per year. In comparison, Nadi, on the leeward side of Viti Levu, receives just under 2000mm. The heaviest rains fall from December to mid-April, and during this period the leeward side can get wetter than the windward sides. Strong thunderstorms can occur at any time during the year, but are more frequent around March and are rare in July and August.

Fiji has mild average temperatures of around 25°C, however, summer days can reach 30°C. During the coolest months, July and August, temperatures can drop to 18°C. It can be much cooler in the mountainous interiors of the main islands, especially at night, while temperatures on the smaller islands tend to be more stable. Fiji's warm tropical waters are great for snorkelling and diving, with temperatures averaging 25°C to 28°C year round.

Humidity is high, with averages ranging from 60% to 80% in Suva and 60% to 70% in Lautoka. Hot, windless, summer days with humidity levels of up to 90% can become oppressive. Most of the year, however, the humidity is offset by pleasant sea breezes.

Tropical Cyclones

Tropical cyclones, or hurricanes, are most likely to occur between November and April. Cyclones originate from low-pressure centres near the equator and travel to higher latitudes, accelerating along a curving path. They often reach their full power at latitudes such as Fiji's.

Strong, destructive cyclones are, however, a fairly rare phenomenon in Fiji. The country has been hit by an average of 10 to 12 cyclones per decade, with two or three of these being very severe. On the other hand, in 1985, four cyclones hit Fiji within four months, which caused deaths and millions of dollars worth of damage. Cyclone Kina hit in early 1993 causing severe flooding in northwest Viti Levu, while Hurricane Gavin devastated areas of the Yasawas and Mamanucas in 1997. In 2003, Cyclone Ami hit northeast Fiji leaving Labasa on Vanua Levu under 1.2 metres of water and utterly flattening the surrounding sugarcane fields. People on Kioa and many on Taveuni and in the Lau Group were left homeless and cut off from help for days.

ECOLOGY & ENVIRONMENT

About 2500 years ago the population began to increase and move inland. The burning of forests and clearing of land for agriculture resulted in widespread erosion. The arrival of Europeans, Fiji's entrance into the international market, and the population's growing need for monetary income began to influence traditional communal and subsistence land use, leading to more intensive practices and environmental damage.

Since the 1960s more than 1000 sq km (between 11% and 16%) of Fiji's forests have been cleared. Most of the deforestation is in drier lowland areas while forests in the interiors of the large islands have been cut more sparingly. In recent years some villages have turned to ecotourism as an alternative income source to logging their land. As you travel around Fiji, you may also see the replanting of degraded mangroves.

Tepid Waters

Since the Industrial Revolution in the 18th century, the concentration of greenhouse gases in the earth's atmosphere has risen dramatically – particularly carbon dioxide from burning fossil fuels. These gases block heat from escaping into space, increasing the earth's natural greenhouse effect and raising the earth's temperature. The predicted increase in average temperature may seem small – about 4°C (6°F) in the next 100 years – but this rate of increase is vastly faster than any change in the last 10,000 years.

One of the most obvious effects of global warming will be the melting of polar icecaps and the consequential rise in sea level – estimated at 0.5m to 1m in the next 100 years. Rising sea levels will eventually cause devastating sea flooding and coastal erosion in many Pacific countries, most disastrously on low-lying coral atolls. Even on higher islands, most agriculture, population centres and infrastructure are located in dangerously low-lying coastal areas. As well as the loss of land, the rising seawater table will poison crops and reduce the available fresh groundwater. Fijian islands most likely to be at risk in the future include Beachcomber and Treasure Islands in the Mamanuca Group, and within the next 30 years, Leleuvia and Caqelai in the Lomaiviti Group. Some islands have already been affected by sea-level rise, including the island of Gau in the Lomaiviti Group, which has lost 200m of coast.

Global warming is also bringing an increase in the severity of storms in some regions and an increase in the frequency of droughts in other areas. In recent years, the number of cyclones has increased drastically, from three in the 1940s to 15 in the 1990s. In 2003 Fiji was hit by two cyclones within two weeks. This may well be due to warming, as tropical cyclones only develop where ocean temperatures exceed 27°C.

Over the last few years, Fiji has received its largest wake-up call to global warming – coral bleaching. This occurs when coral is physiologically stressed by raised water temperatures and loses the symbiotic algae that provide its colour and nutrition. If water temperatures return to normal, coral can recover; however, with repetitive bleaching entire reefs can be degraded and die. Following El Nino in 2001, and again in 2002, Fiji's reefs experienced huge amounts of bleaching, effecting 65% of reefs and killing 15%. Environmentalists distinguish between low-level bleaching that has probably always occurred and this massive, recurrent bleaching of entire reefs that is more than likely the result of global warming. As one of the most productive ecosystems on Earth, reefs provide habitat for 25% of marine species; they also protect Fiji's smaller islands and provide a major source of income through tourism. As the bleaching occurs in shallow waters, it has so far had no effect on Fiji's dive-tourism industry; however, continued degradation could quickly spell disaster.

It is extremely difficult to accurately predict the effects of global warming but, while scientists continue their hot debates, Fiji's water temperatures are nonetheless rising, coral is bleaching, cyclones are whipping round the nation and the tide is increasingly nigh.

Unsustainable agricultural practices, such as steep-land sugar-cane and ginger farming, have increased erosion. This has increasingly led to large areas of land becoming unproductive as fertile topsoil is washed away. In an attempt to restore the soil quality, a pine-plantation reforestation programme has been introduced on degraded lands. In the vicinity of indigenous villages, traditional eco-farming practices are generally still in use.

Fiji's plentiful freshwater resources are not well managed, even in areas where water shortages can be a problem. In urban centres water quality is generally good, but supply and quality in many rural areas is poor; the water supply in Rakiraki, for example, has been deemed unfit for human consumption.

The waters around Suva are quite severely polluted, and in certain areas fish consumption is a health hazard. Despite previous 'boom and bust' exploitation of bêche-de-mer and clams, over-fishing continues around the most populated areas. Destructive fishing techniques, such as the use of poisons and explosives, are commonly employed in Fiji without much control, however, the use of drift nets for fishing is officially opposed. Coral harvesting for the aquarium industry continues to occur.

As in many countries, waste management is a national problem. Many villages dispose of their garbage as they always did, as if it were still biodegradable. Being so small, Fiji does not have the luxury of a faraway landfill in which to hide its rubbish. In urban areas, such as Suva, only 60% of sewage goes into a sewerage system and it isn't always processed before being discharged into the sea. There are a number of industries using a variety of toxic materials, with little or no data on the pollution generated. Oil spills are a problem in Suva's Walu Bay.

The World Wide Fund for Nature (WWF) has community-based projects in Fiji that aim to protect biodiversity and encourage the conservation of medicinal and culturally significant plants. One such project aims to conserve *kuta*, the plant used for traditional weaving, by helping local women to restore its habitat, re-learn its cultural significance and hopefully derive an income from the products. South Pacific Action Committee for Human Ecology and Environment (Spachee) has an Ecowoman project that promotes sustainable use of resources and links village women with women in science and technology through community-based projects.

Landowners are increasingly encouraged to become involved in ecotourism. However, while remote villages can benefit from the cash infusion brought by low-impact tourism, they are also faced with additional pollution and rapid cultural change. When visiting remote areas, including the ocean, take your rubbish away with you, try to avoid bumping against or walking on coral reefs and consider whether you really need that shell as a souvenir. You can find ecotourism projects on Taveuni at Bouma and Lavena, and in Koroyanitu National Heritage Park in the Viti Levu Highlands. In areas of intense tourism, such as the Mamanucas, the resorts are being pressured to clean up their acts and implement environmentally sustainable waste practices. While it appears to have become trendy for resorts and tours to tack an 'eco' onto their name, some are more environmentally aware than others.

The following conservation groups are based in Fiji:

Greenpeace (Pacific region office ☎ 331 2861, fax 331 2784) Upstairs, Old Town Hall, Suva.
Spachee (☎ 331 2371, fax 330 3053) On the corner of Ratu Cakobau and Domain Rds, Suva.
Pacific Island Forum (☎ 331 2600, e info@forumsec.org.fj) Forum Secretariat, Private Mail Bag, Suva.
WWF (Pacific region office ☎ 331 5533, 331 5410, e wwfspp@connect.com.fj)

FLORA & FAUNA

Much of Fiji's indigenous flora and fauna is related to those of Indonesia and Malaysia. Many plant and animal species are thought to have migrated to the islands on the prevailing winds and sea currents.

Flora

Most of Fiji is absolutely lush with bright fragrant flowers and giant, leafy plants and trees. Fiji has over 3000 identified plant species, with one-third of these endemic. Much of the native flora is used for food, medicine, implements and building materials.

Rainforest Plants There are hundreds of different fern species in Fiji, a number of which are edible and known as *ota*. *Balabala* (tree ferns) are similar to those in Australia and New Zealand, and are culturally significant. Tree-fern trunks were once used on the gable ends of *bure* (thatched dwelling) but are now commonly seen as carved garden warriors – the counterpart to the Western gnome. Some *wakalou* (climbing fern) species were used to secure roofing and to demarcate the chief's house and temples.

Forest giants include valuable timbers such as *dakua* (Fijian kauri) and *yaka*. These very hard, durable timbers have a beautiful grain and are used for furniture making. However, due to unrestricted logging and the absence of an efficient planting programme, these trees are becoming less common in Fiji.

Degeneria vitienses is a primitive flowering plant found only in Fiji. It is related to the ornamental magnolia. The leaves, known as *masiratu*, were used in the past as sandpaper for wood carving.

Fiji has various species of pandanus and at least two of these are endemic. They are cultivated around villages and the leaves provide the raw material for roof thatching and weaving baskets and mats.

Fiji's national flower is the *tagimaucia* or *Medinilla waterhousei*. This flower only grows at high altitudes on the island of Taveuni and on one mountain of Vanua Levu. Its petals are white and its branches bright red. See 'The Legend of the Tagimaucia' boxed text in the Taveuni chapter.

Orchids are abundant in Fiji's rainforests. Vanilla is a common orchid and there's a renewed commercial interest in its cultivation for use as a natural food flavouring.

Breadfruit – still an important staple in many villages

Edible Plants The Fijian root crops *tavioka* (tapioka; also known as cassava) and *dalo* (taro) are the country's food staples. Cassava is a shrub with starchy tuberous roots that grows up to 3m high. *Dalo*, also known as taro, is high in protein content; its leaves are often used in traditional Fijian dishes and are similar to spinach. Fijians distinguish 80 different varieties of *dalo*.

Breadfruit is still an important staple in many villages. Up to 25cm in diameter, the fruit can be eaten boiled, roasted, fried or fermented underground to produce a type of edible sourdough. In the past, the wood of the breadfruit tree was used to make canoes. The jackfruit is another large tree providing sustenance: Indo-Fijians use its seeds in curries and the ripe flesh of the fruit can be eaten – if you can cope with the unpleasant smell. Bananas are common, as are pawpaw (papaya) and mangoes.

Piper methysticum, or kava, a plant belonging to the pepper family, is widely cultivated in Fiji. The roots are dried, ground and then mixed with water to make *yaqona,* a beverage with relaxing properties, drunk socially and in *yaqona* ceremonies.

Garden Plants Many of Fiji's common garden plants were introduced by JB Thurston in the 19th century. The hibiscus, introduced from Africa, is Fiji's most common and well-known garden plant and is used for decoration, food, dye and medicine. The bougainvillea and the allemanda are also common plants, both introduced from Brazil. The latter produces large yellow flowers all year round. *Bua*, or frangipani, with its strongly scented white flowers, is also an introduced species and often used in soaps and perfumes.

Coastal & River Plants The most distinctive plant communities found along coastlines are mangrove forests. They cover large areas around river deltas and are important for the protection of seashores

Teas & Tonics

It's hard to find a native tree or plant in Fiji that's *not* used by indigenous Fijians for its curative or preventative properties. Pounded into juices, strained into tonics, administered as teas or plasters, herbal medicine is not the alternative here, but the norm. Villagers possess an immense knowledge of the plants around them and their uses, accumulated over thousands of years and passed from generation to generation. If you fall or suffer a bit of indigestion on a village tour, you'll soon be offered a remedy. It might not be tasty but, chances are, it'll work.

One of Fiji's most intriguing herbal remedies is the *noni* tree. A Pacific evergreen growing up to 20ft tall, it produces a warty, foul smelling, bitter tasting fruit. While decidedly disgusting to many of our senses, *noni* juice is gaining growing applause from consumers around the world for its ability to help relieve arthritis, chronic fatigue, high blood pressure, rheumatism, digestive disorders, sinus problems, diabetes and even the effects of ageing (just to name a few). Introduced into Western markets in 1996, *noni* has also been credited with converting cancerous cells back into normal cells and is being studied for its possibilities in fighting HIV.

It sounds too good to be true, and many Western doctors will tell you that's because it's not and that wildly exaggerated claims have not been supported by enough scientific studies. However, many more doctors profess to have seen hundreds of patients use *noni* with fantastic results. Ask a Fijian and they'll likely whip you up some *noni* tea or tonic and let you judge for yourself.

against damage by sea and wind. The aerial roots, sulphurous mud and saline water of mangrove forests also provide breeding grounds for various fish species. Mangrove hardwood is used for firewood and for building houses, and this has led to the destruction of many mangrove areas.

Casuarina, also known as ironwood or *nokonoko*, grows on sandy beaches and atolls. As its name suggests, the timber is heavy and strong and was used to make war clubs and parts of canoes.

The coconut palm has played an important role in human's history in the Pacific. The nuts provide food and drink, the shells are used for making cups and charcoal, the leaves for baskets and mats, the oil for cooking, lighting and as body and hair lotion.

Other common coastal plants include the beach morning glory, with its purple or lavender flowers that only bloom at dawn, wild passionfruit and the *vau*, or beach hibiscus with its large yellow flowers and light wood once used for canoe building. The *vutu* tree flowers only at night; its blooms are white and pink with a distinctive fringe and were traditionally used as poison in fishing.

Aquatic Plants Plants are integral to the structure and energy balance of reefs. The most common is the variety of algae that grows as a film over dead coral. *Nama*, or grape weed, is an algae that looks like miniature green grapes and is often found in lagoons; Fijians consider it a delicacy. Large submerged meadows of sea grass grow in lagoons.

Fauna

Over 3500 years ago, the first settlers introduced poultry and probably also dogs and pigs to Fiji. This coincided with the extinction of at least three bird species (two megapodes, or mound-building birds, and a giant fruit pigeon).

Mammals Due to its distance from other land masses, Fiji has relatively few native mammals. Six species of bat are the only native terrestrial mammals. The most common are the large fruit bats, also known as *beka* or flying foxes, which roost in large numbers in tall forest trees. Two species of insectivorous bats (the free-tailed and the *bekabeka*) are cave dwellers and therefore seldom seen.

All other land-dwelling mammals have been introduced. Perhaps the most common wild animal on Viti Levu and Vanua Levu is the small Indian mongoose, often seen scurrying across the roads. It was introduced in 1883 to control rats in the sugarcane plantations. It succeeded, but it also ate native snakes, toads, frogs, birds and birds' eggs. As they seemed to have eaten everything else, mongooses are also often blamed for the depletion of banded iguanas; it's more likely, however, that feral cats and habitat destruction are the cause. Other domestic animals that have turned feral include the pig, introduced by the Polynesians, and the goat, brought by missionaries. Both damage the native vegetation.

Three species of rat have been introduced. In the 19th century, Europeans inadvertently brought with them the brown-and-black rat and the house mouse. The Polynesian rat came to Fiji much earlier, probably as a food source.

Dolphins, pilot whales and the occasional sperm whale visit Fijian waters, while baleen whales and humpback whales pass by on their annual migration. *Tabua*, the teeth of sperm whales, have a special ceremonial value for indigenous Fijians and are still used as negotiating tokens to symbolise esteem or atonement. See the 'Tabua' boxed text in the History section of this chapter.

Reptiles Fiji has 20 species of land-dwelling reptiles, four species of turtle and four species of sea snake.

Fiji's crested iguana, which was only identified in 1979, is found on the Yasawas and on Yadua Taba (a small island off Bua, Vanua Levu). It can reach one metre in length. Since there are no other species of crested iguana found in Southeast Asia, its ancestors are thought to have floated to Fiji on vegetation from South America. The banded iguana is found here as well as on other Pacific islands, including Wallis, Futuna and Tonga.

Fiji is home to about seven types of gecko, the smallest growing to a mere 8cm in length while the giant forest gecko, which yaps like a dog and changes colour, can reach 30cm. Various types of skink (slim, quick lizards) are also common, some reaching 25cm long.

Two types of terrestrial snakes are found in Fiji. The Pacific boa constrictor were once considered sacred under old religion. Reaching 2m in length, they were raised in rubble-filled pits or around the stone plinth of a spirithouse. Chiefs and priests would eat them during religious rituals, and their vertebrae were threaded for necklaces. Also in Fiji, the venomous burrowing snake *Ogmodon vitianus* is recognisable by a cream chevron on the top of its head but is seldom seen.

There are four sea snakes in Fiji, two of which are semiterrestrial. You are likely to see Fiji's most common snake, the *dadakulaci* or banded sea krait, while snorkelling or diving. Occasionally they enter freshwater inlets to mate and lay eggs on land. They are placid, and locals may tell you that they cannot open their jaws wide enough to bite humans, but don't risk it: the sea krait's venom is three times more potent than the venom of the Indian cobra. Also in Pacific waters, the yellow-bellied sea snake can remain submerged for up to two hours and can be aggressive. Another aquatic snake is *Hydrophis melanocephalus*.

Four turtle species are found in Fijian waters: the hawksbill, the loggerhead (which visits but does not breed in Fiji), the green turtle (named after the colour of its fat) and the leatherback. The leatherback is the largest, growing up to 2m, and is under strict protection to prevent its extinction. As in many other parts of the world, its meat and its eggs are considered a delicacy in Fiji. Taking eggs is banned in Fiji, as is the capture of adults with a shell length under 46cm – a law which doesn't do a lot of good as the turtles only reach breeding age at sizes considerably larger than this. Unfortunately, turtle meat is still sold at the Suva market and the shells, especially of the endangered hawksbill turtle, can still be found in shops and markets even though most countries prohibit their importation.

Leatherback Turtle – endangered and therefore protected

Amphibians The cane toad was introduced from Hawaii in 1936 to control insects in the cane plantations. It has now become a pest itself, competing with the native ground frog in coastal and lowland regions. The tree frog and ground frog have retreated deep into the forests and are rarely seen.

Birds In 2001, in a cave in the Sigatoka Valley of Viti Levu, the bones of a flightless pigeon, several times bigger than a very big turkey, were discovered. It is believed that this bird lived in Fiji 3500 years ago along with giant megapode. Today, there are 25 species of birds in Fiji that are found nowhere else in the world, and it's believed that more may exist in the country's more remote rainforests. Despite the relatively short distance between islands, some birds, such as the Kadavu parrot or the Taveuni dove, are found on one island only. Fiji has around 100 bird species, and Fijian names imitate the birds' sounds; *kaka* for parrots, *ga* for ducks, *kikau* for honeyeaters.

A number of Fiji's bird species are extremely rare and heading towards extinction. In 1983, the Fiji petrel was 'rediscovered', having been sighted only once before in 1854. The long legged warbler hasn't been seen since the 70s and the search for the red throated lorakeet and pink billed parrot finch is still on.

Birds you're more likely to spot include the orange dove and silktail of Taveuni and the barking pigeon which yaps like a dog. The Fiji warbler, the whistling dove, the Kadavu shining parrot, the giant forest honeyeater and the wandering whistling duck also reside in Fiji's forests. Tropical sea birds include the kingfisher, the frigate bird and the booby. Introduced species are common around densely populated areas like Suva. Aggressive species, such as Indian mynahs and bulbuls, have taken over and forced native birds into the forest. Taveuni and Cicia have both imported the Australian magpie.

Birds of the Fiji Bush, by Fergus Clunie, is a good reference for bird-watchers. Also worth checking out is Pacific Bird website **w** www.pacificbirds.com. Taveuni, eastern Vanua Levu, Kadavu, and Colo-i-Suva Park are all good areas for bird-watching.

Insects Fiji, like other islands in the Pacific, is a paradise for insects, and there are many thousands of species here, some of which have evolved into new species unique to Fiji. Most of Fiji's insects have yet to be catalogued but you'll get to know them pretty well anyway. There are plenty of mosquitoes, but fortunately no malaria. There are, however, occasional outbreaks of dengue fever. (See Health in the Facts for the Visitor chapter for more information.)

Marine Life Fiji's richest diversity of fauna is underwater, especially within the reefs and protected lagoons. There are hundreds of species of hard coral, soft coral, sea fan and sea sponge, which are often intensely colourful and fantastically shaped.

Coral needs sunlight and oxygen to survive, so is restricted to depths of less than 50m. Wave-breaks on shallow reefs are a major source of oxygen and corals on a reef-break are generally densely packed and able to resist the force of the surf. Fewer corals grow in lagoons, where the water is quieter, but more fragile corals such as staghorn can be found in these places. Reefs near populated areas can be damaged by alluvial run off, sewage, chemicals, reef-walking, and the use of dynamite to kill fish. Infestations of the crown-of-thorns starfish also kill reefs. Fiji's coral reefs are increasingly being affected by coral bleaching; see the 'Tepid Waters' boxed text in the Climate section of this chapter.

There is a seemingly infinite variety of exquisite tropical fish. Many varieties have descriptive names, such as the soldier fish, surgeon fish, trumpet fish, red lizard fish, goat fish, bat fish, butterfly fish and parrot fish. The ribbon or leaf-nose eel has an interesting life cycle: from a young black male it develops into a brilliant-blue male or bright-yellow female. The territorial anemone fish, or clown fish, lives in a symbiotic relationship with the sea anemone, having developed immunity to its poisonous sting. Some of the most beautiful fish and marine creatures, such as the scorpion fish and lionfish, are also highly venomous. If in doubt, don't touch!

Species such as the barracuda, jackfish, sting ray, small reef shark and large parrot fish can be seen cruising along channels and the edges of reefs. In open sea and deeper waters, larger fish are common, including tuna, bonito, sword fish, rays and sharks. Large sharks, however, normally stay away from the coast. The grey reef shark is most often seen on steeper outer-reef drops. It has a reputation for being aggressive, but it feeds primarily on small fish. Large manta and devil rays feed on zooplankton and small fish. Sting rays are most often found in shallow water near swamp areas and among mangroves.

For an insight into the lives of molluscs, crustaceans, sea slugs, feather stars, starfish, Christmas-tree worms and other marine life, pick up a copy of Paddy Ryan's *The Snorkeller's Guide to the Coral Reef*.

National Parks & Protected Areas

Fiji's outstanding natural beauty, interesting landscapes and vegetation, and rare or unique animals and birds give it immense potential for land reserves.

Since 1971, the Fijian government has proposed environmental policies and plans; implementation, however, has been slow and Fiji still has few legally protected conservation areas. The existing legislation is adequate, but due to a lack of resources, preservation of sites is not being enforced. The recent slump in tourism has also made it economically unviable for some sites to be maintained.

The increased popularity of ecotourism has led to the development of a few forest parks and reserves. The Bouma National Heritage Park now protects over 80% of Taveuni's land area and contains the well-maintained Lavena Coastal Walk, Vidawa Forest Walk and Tavoro Falls Walk. The Koroyanitu National Heritage Park in the Mount Evans Range, near Lautoka in Viti Levu's Highlands, is also well established. Other sites of significance include the Sigatoka Sand Dunes on Viti Levu's Coral Coast; the Sovi Basin and Colo-i-Suva Park in Naitasiri province near Suva; and Tunuloa Silktail Reserve in the Cakaudrove district on Vanua Levu. Refer to the respective chapters for more information.

Indigenous Fijians' traditional land use is very environmentally responsible. Ecotourism is increasing the viability of villagers to unofficially protect their own land by maintaining these traditions.

GOVERNMENT & POLITICS

The SVT-GVP coalition led by Sitiveni Rabuka, leader of the two military coups d'etat of 1987, was ousted in the 1999 elections when Fiji's first Indo-Fijian prime minister, Mahendra Chaudhry, came to power. Before reaching the first anniversary of his election, Chaudhry was also ousted by a coup, this time by failed businessman George Speight and his defected military rebels. The interim leader put in place, Laisenia Qarase, was later elected as prime minister in 2001 as leader of the Fijian People's Party (SDL). His largest opposition, the Fiji Labour Party led by Indo-Fijian Chaudhry, has been granted no seats in the government's cabinet, an act which is against the constitution. For more details, see History earlier in this chapter.

The government is divided into 16 ministries and, for administrative purposes, the country has four political divisions. The Western division includes western and northern Viti Levu, the Rotuma Group, Yasawa Group, Mamanuca Group and Vatulele. The Northern division is comprised of Vanua Levu, Taveuni and their offshore islands. The Eastern division stretches across the Lomaiviti Group, Lau Group, Kadavu group, and Moala Group and the smaller Central division consists of Suva and the southeast side of Viti Levu. Local government includes city, town and municipal councils.

Parliament & the Judiciary

The 1990 constitution was seen by many as racist and detrimental to the country. In 1997 it was replaced by a fairer constitution that would encourage multiethnic governments and has been the cause of further racial tension. Despite being ousted by the May 19 Coup of 2000, the 1997 constitution was reinstated by Fiji's High Court in the same year. Nevertheless, the present indigenous Fijian government refuses to honour the stipulation of ensuring multiethnic cabinet members.

The constitution provides for a parliament consisting of a president, a House of Representatives and a Senate.

The president has executive authority and serves for a period of five years. The position is reserved for an indigenous Fijian appointed by the Great Council of Chiefs and requires support from a majority in the House of Representatives.

The Senate (upper house) consists of 32 members appointed by the president. Of these, the majority are appointed on the advice of the Great Council of Chiefs, one on the advice of the Rotuman Island Council and the remainder on the advice of other communities. The role of the Senate is to revise bills and debate issues.

The House of Representatives (lower house) consists of 71 members. Of these seats 23 are reserved for indigenous Fijians, 19 for Indians, one for a Rotuman, three for members of other races and 25 are open seats.

The position of prime minister is no longer reserved for an indigenous Fijian.

The judiciary is comprised of three courts: a high court, court of appeal and supreme court.

Political Parties

After a history of segregation, Fiji's parties remain largely separated along racial lines. Nearly 30 parties are presently registered in Fiji, however, not all ran in the last elections.

Soqosoqo Duavatani Lewenivanua Party (SDL) Also known as the United Fiji Party and the Fijian People's Party, this hard-line conservative group is led by Qarase and was in power at the time we went to print. It's strongly Christian and believes in paramount rule by indigenous Fijians.

Soqosoqo-ni-Vakavulewa-ni Taukei (SVT) Dubbed the chief's party, the SVT is a Fijian nationalist group sponsored by the Great Council of Chiefs and supported by the Taukei movement

National Federation Party (NFP) Comprised mostly of Indo-Fijians, it was part of the NFP-FLP coalition which won the 1987 election and was then deposed in the first coup

Fiji Labour Party (FLP) Comprised of indigenous Fijian and Indo-Fijian trade-union members

Fijian Association Party (FAP) An ultranationalist party intent on preserving traditional chiefly power

General Voters Party (GVP) Comprised of European, part-Fijian, Chinese and other Pacific Islanders

Christian Democratic Party (Veitokani ni Lewenivanua Lotu Vakarisito) Backed by the Methodist Church – the country's largest Christian denomination

Great Council of Chiefs

Parallel to and intertwined with government administration is the traditional chiefly system. Chiefs make decisions at a local level as well as being extremely influential at a national level through the Bose Levu Vakaturaga or Great Council of Chiefs. When we went to print, the chairman of the council was Ratu Epeli Ganilau.

The basic unit of Fijian administration is the *koro* (village) headed by the *turaga-ni-koro* (a hereditary chief), who is appointed by the village elders. Several *koro* are linked as a *tikina*, and several *tikina* form a *yasana* or province. Fiji is divided into 14 provinces, and each has a high chief.

The Great Council of Chiefs includes members of the lower house as well as nominated chiefs from the provincial councils. The council was originally created by British colonisers to strengthen the position of the cooperating, ruling Fijian elite, and gained great power after the military coups of the '80s and the introduction of the 1990 constitution. The council appoints the president, who in turn is responsible for appointing judges, in consultation with the Judicial & Legal Services Commission. It also has authority over any legislation related to land ownership and common rights.

ECONOMY

Traditional Fijian economic systems are self-sustaining. They rely heavily on kinship and village structure, including the hierarchy of chiefs and villagers. The country's modern economic system has different and often contradictory requirements from the traditional system, introducing individualism into the community and making it difficult for workers to fulfil their village obligations.

Fiji faces grave economic problems. The population is increasing and people's expectations are rising. Poverty and inequality are growing, along with unemployment and increasing urbanisation. Unemployment is especially high among youth as the semi-subsistent village economy is no longer able to absorb large numbers of young people. Cash is required for clothing, school fees, church levies, imported goods and community projects.

With the global push for internationalisation of production and trade, Fiji is becoming more export orientated and open to increased competition. Tourism and sugar are Fiji's main earners and together employ about 80,000 people. Fiji also exports molasses, gold, timber, fish, copra and coconut oil, and clothing. Recent years have seen diversification, with the exportation of forest wood chips and sawn timber, and an expansion in manufacturing to include products such as leather and furniture.

Fiji has long been reliant on overseas aid from Australia and New Zealand, and, more recently, Japan. Economic growth is needed to service Fiji's massive loans. Growth has been hindered by the public's reluctance to invest and make long-term commitments; apprehension that was increased with the coup of 2000 and the further tumbling of the economy. The uncertainty over the renewal of Indo-Fijian farmers' land leases remains a problem; many have been evicted and once productive fields lay idle. Many skilled and educated workers, particularly Indo-Fijians, are leaving Fiji in search of greater security.

The present government's budget proposal for 2003 has brought further protest from the population, with its intention of increasing the Value Added Tax from 10% to 12.5%.

Tourism

Fiji receives about 360,000 visitors every year. Since 1989, earnings from tourism have amounted to about 17% of GDP, surpassing sugar as the primary source of foreign-exchange earnings. Most visitors are from Australia and New Zealand, followed by the USA, the UK and Japan. The industry is promoted by the Fiji Visitors Bureau (FVB) and the South Pacific Tourism Organisation (SPTO).

The May 2000 coup devastated the tourism industry. While backpackers continued visiting, the more lucrative top-end market all but disappeared and many businesses folded or fell into disrepair. Tourists who did arrive directly after the coup were often harassed by desperate vendors, tour operators and hotel owners. These days, tourists are beginning to return to Fiji and the market is once again picking up. It remains a very competitive industry.

Agriculture

Agriculture is the largest sector of the economy. Only about 16% of Fiji's land is suitable for agriculture, and this is mainly along the coastal plains and river valleys and deltas of the two main islands. The principal cane-growing areas are western Viti Levu and northern Vanua Levu, with mills at Lautoka, Ba, Rakiraki and Labasa. Dairy farming is concentrated in the Rewa Delta, near Suva. Other produce includes molasses, copra, cocoa, ginger, rice, vanilla, fruit and vegetables.

The sugar industry was the mainstay of the economy for most of the 20th century, and it currently provides employment for almost a third of the population. The prosperity of the industry is therefore extremely important to the economy, providing taxes to the government and rent from leased land to landowners. In 1998 the economy was badly affected by the sharp fall in sugar production (reduced by 50%), a result of the extended drought.

Due to historical and constitutional reasons, the industry is compartmentalised along racial lines. Most cane is grown by Indo-Fijian farmers on land leased from indigenous landowners. Indigenous Fijians own 83% of the total land area, and, due to rules of ownership, Indo-Fijians cannot buy this land. Long-term land leases began expiring in 1997 and, with evictions looming, many farmers are hesitant to invest in crops and soil when they may not be given the chance to reap the benefits. Much land that has been reclaimed by indigenous Fijians stands empty as the owners prefer to allow it to return to its natural state.

Other Industries

The fisheries industry produces canned tuna, bêche-de-mer, shark fin, trochus shell and trochus-shell buttons.

Pine plantations are common on the western sides of Viti Levu and Vanua Levu. Most forest is on communally owned native land, and has been planted by Fiji Pine Limited.

Gold is being mined at Vatukoula, near Tavua in northern Viti Levu, and until recently at Mt Kasi, in Vanua Levu.

Fiji's manufacturing sector produces clothing, some footwear, cigarettes, food and beverages. Aluminium and plastic products, agricultural equipment, boats, cement, furniture, and handicrafts are also manufactured here.

Standard of Living

Life expectancy is 61.4 years for men and 65.2 for women. Food is relatively plentiful and easy to grow and many rural people live a semisubsistence village lifestyle. About 70% of the population has access to a piped water supply but many rural villages and settlements in the interior and outer islands rely on diesel generators or have no electricity. About 21% of women have jobs outside the home.

About 8% of households have an annual income of less than $3000. The urban poor are less well off, with support networks and extended families less intact. The government provides some housing assistance for low-income earners; however, with poverty and homelessness on the rise, more and more Fijians are ending up in squatter settlements. See the 'Home Away From Home' boxed text in the Suva chapter for more details.

POPULATION & PEOPLE

Fiji has a total population of 840,000 according to the UN's guestimate for 2002 (Fiji last took a census in 1996). About half of the population is under the age of 20 and about two-thirds under 30.

The most populated island is Viti Levu, with 75% of the overall population, followed by Vanua Levu, with 18%. The remaining 7% is spread over 100-odd islands. About 39% of the population are urban dwellers. The highest densities occur in the

Gunusede

A *gunusede,* literally 'drink money', is a village fundraising activity. You may be invited to attend one, and it is considered offensive to refuse. You will need to take some money, and if you are on a tight budget, don't take more than you can afford to give away! You should spend every cent you take to a *gunusede*. If you participate, even to a small extent, it will be appreciated. At a *gunusede*, people buy drinks, usually *yaqona*, for themselves and others. The price is usually a token 10 cents. If someone buys a drink for you and you can't stand another drop (this happens with *yaqona*) you can get out of it by bidding a higher price for someone else to drink it. Otherwise you must drink what is bought for you. These fundraising parties are used to pay for things such as school fees for the village children. It is an example of how the community works together, and it is usually a fun get-together.

Emma Hegarty

major urban centres of Suva, Nadi, Lautoka and in the sugar-cane growing areas of Rewa and Ba.

Fiji's population is the most multiracial of the South Pacific countries. Due to historical factors, such as indenture, many areas have a higher proportion of particular races. The Fijian administration categorises people according to their racial origins and this promotes a lack of national identity. The term 'Fijian' is reserved for indigenous Fijians only. Despite many Indo-Fijian families having lived in Fiji for four or five generations, they are still referred to as 'Indian', just as Chinese-Fijians are referred to as 'Chinese' and Fijians from other Pacific Island decent are referred to by the nationality of their ancestors. People of Australian, New Zealand, American or European descent are all labelled 'Europeans' and those people of mixed Western and indigenous Fijian descent are known as 'part-Europeans'. There is relatively little marriage between other racial groups.

Fijians also use the following terms: *kaiviti* for indigenous Fijian, *kaihidi* for Indo-Fijians, and *kaivelagi*, or literally 'people from far away', for Europeans. The term 'pre-mix' is occasionally used informally to describe people of mixed race.

From the late 1940s until the military coups of 1987, indigenous Fijians were outnumbered by Indo-Fijians. Indigenous Fijians presently account for about 50% of the population and Indo-Fijians for about 45%. A large number of Indo-Fijians emigrated after the 1980s coups and the trend picked up again after the coup of 2000. Some other Pacific countries, including Tonga, refused to let Indo-Fijians into their country.

Indigenous Fijians

Indigenous Fijians are predominantly of Melanesian origin, but with strong Polynesian influences. The result is varied physical features: Melanesian features (such as darker skin and frizzy hair) mix with Polynesian features (lighter skin tone and wavy hair). Strong Melanesian influences, both physical and cultural, are especially evident in the Lau Group due to its proximity to Tonga.

Fijian boys from the Wai-na-Buka (River) – Photograph taken in 1189 by huppeldepup JD MacDonald, 19th century

Melodious Measures

Replaced with guitars and keyboards, traditional indigenous instruments are a rare find in Fiji these days. Yet once upon a time, nose flutes were all the rage. Made from a single piece of bamboo, some 70cm long, the flute would be intricately carved and played by your typical laid-back Fijian, reclined on a pandanus mat and resting his or her head on a bamboo pillow. Whether it was the music or the pose, flutes were believed to have the power to attract the opposite sex and were a favourite for serenading.

Other instruments had more practical purposes, such as shell trumpets and whistles which were used for communication. Portable war drums were used as warnings and for communicating tactics on the battlefield. One instrument you are still likely to see (and hear) is the *lali*, a large slit drum made of resonant timbers. Audible over large distances, its deep call continues to beckon people to the chief's *bure* or to church.

Indo-Fijians

Most Indo-Fijians are descendants of indentured labourers. Initially, most of the Indians came from the states of Bengal (Bangladesh), Bihar and Uttar Pradesh in northeastern India. Later, large groups of southern Indians arrived. The great diversity of languages, religions, customs and subcultures has merged to a certain extent over the years.

Other Indians, mostly Punjabis and Gujeratis, voluntarily came to Fiji soon after the end of the indenture system. These groups are prominent in Fiji's business elite (see the 'Indo-Fijian History & Culture' special section).

Other Groups

There are about 4500 so-called 'Europeans' (see the introduction in this section) who were born in Fiji, and over 10,000 'part-Europeans' living in Fiji. Some of these families established themselves in Levuka during the early 19th century as traders and shipbuilders or on the copra plantations of Vanua Levu, Lomaiviti and Lau. Europeans tend to work in agriculture, business, tourism and in the public sector.

The 8600 Fijians from Rotuma are of Polynesian origin. Most of them live and work in Suva, far away from their remote island. Among the other 9000 Pacific Islanders in Fiji are Tongans and Samoans and 3000 Banabans – Micronesians whose own island was stripped by phosphate mining and who were resettled on Rabi after WWII. Polynesians from Vaitupu atoll in Tuvalu live on the island of Kiao, which they purchased in 1947 to reduce the pressure of overpopulation on their own tiny island. There are also more than 8000 descendants of blackbirder labourers from the Solomon Islands, most living in communities near Suva and on Ovalau.

Officially, about 0.7% of the population (5000 people) is of Chinese or part-Chinese origin. The majority of their ancestors arrived early in the 20th century to open general stores and other small businesses and some of these settlers married indigenous Fijian women. The past decade has brought a new wave of Chinese immigrants to Fiji, many of whom reside on the islands illegally. Some estimates place the Chinese population in Suva alone at 20,000.

EDUCATION

Fiji has a relatively good education system, and is considered the educational centre of the South Pacific. While education is not compulsory, primary and lower secondary education are accessible almost country wide, and the country's literacy rate is high (around 87%).

About 25% of the population is school-aged. Almost all children attend primary school and most complete lower secondary education. There are incentives for poor rural children in the form of free tuition for primary and secondary students, and per capita grants. The government has also been trying to reduce the disparity between rural and urban schools by upgrading teacher quality and student assessments. At some stage during their education, nearly all rural Fijian children move away from their home villages to attend boarding school or to live with relatives in towns.

Education is not officially segregated, but schools are run by the major religions. Normally, Indo-Fijian children attend Hindu or Muslim schools while indigenous Fijians attend Christian schools. There is also a well-established Chinese-Fijian school in Suva. English is the official language taught in all Fijian schools; however, in recent years students have been encouraged to learn either Fijian or Hindi to increase the interaction between different communities. Under the new constitution, students of all races are to be given equal opportunity for government scholarships.

The University of the South Pacific (USP) was established in 1968 as a regional university for 12 Pacific island countries. Its main campus is in Suva, but it has another campus in Western Samoa and centres in the other member countries. The Fiji School of Medicine opened in 1985 to provide medical training in the region. The Fiji College of Agriculture, in conjunction with USP, offers training in tropical agriculture and receives students from other South Pacific countries. The main centre for technical education is Suva's Fiji Institute of Technology (FIT), which runs some programmes in association with local industry and also has campuses in Labasa and Lautoka.

ARTS

Fijian villagers still practice traditional arts, crafts, dance and music. While the majority of these arts remain an integral part of the culture, others are sometimes practiced solely to satisfy tourist demand. *Traditional Handicrafts of Fiji* (1997) by Tabulevu, Uluinaceva and Raimua, is a step-by-step manual of indigenous Fijian crafts and includes their social context. Indo-Fijians, Chinese-Fijians and other cultural groups also retain many of their traditional arts.

Contemporary art includes fashion design, pottery and, though not common, painting and photography. The most likely place to see contemporary work displayed is in Suva. (Check out the University of the South Pacific's Oceania Centre.) There's also a theatre group in Suva that showcases local playwrights, and drama is taught at the university. *Beyond Ceremony: An Anthology of Drama from Fiji*, edited by Ian Gaskel, is a collection of work by Fiji's foremost contemporary playwrights.

Dance

Visitors are often welcomed at resorts and hotels with a *meke*, a dance performance that enacts local stories and legends. While performances for tourists may seem staged, the *meke* is an ongoing tradition. The arrangement of the group and every subtle movement has significance. Important guests and onlookers are honoured with the best seating positions.

In the past, Fijian *meke* were accompanied by chanting either by a chorus or by 'spiritually possessed seers', as well as by rhythmic clapping, the thumping and stamping of bamboo clacking sticks, the beating of slit drums, and dancing. They were held purely for entertainment, for welcoming visitors, or on important religious and social occasions like births, deaths, marriages and property exchanges between villages. Chants included laments at funerals, war incitement dirges and animal impersonations. *Meke* were handed down through generations and new routines were composed for special events.

Men, women and children participated in *meke*. Men performed club and spear dances and the women performed fan dances. In times of war, men performed the *cibi,* or death dance, and women the *dele* or *wate*, a dance in which they sexually humiliated enemy corpses and captives. Dancing often took place by moonlight or torch light, with the performers in costume, and with bodies oiled, faces painted and combs and flowers decorating their hair.

Traditional Chinese dancing is also still practised in Fiji, and Indian classical dance, including Bharat Natyam and *kathak,* is taught at Indian cultural centres.

Music

While in Fiji, try to attend at least one *meke* and a church service to witness fantastic choir singing. Guitar is now the most commonly used instrument and popular local musicians include Seru Serevi, the Black Roses, Danny Costello, Michelle Rounds, the Freelancers, Karuna Gopalan, Laisa Vulakoro, Soumini Vuatalevu, and the more mellow Serau Kei Mataniselala. Reggae has been influential and is very popular, and there are a couple of jazz bands in Suva.

Music from melodramatic Bollywood films is popular among Indo-Fijians, as is Indian dance and pop music. Vocal/harmonium, tabla (percussion) and sitar lessons are given at Indian cultural centres.

A Brush with Culture

If you entered an indigenous Fijian village in the mid-19th century, there was enough make-up flying around to make you think you'd landed backstage of a Broadway show. Before the practice was stamped out by the missionaries, Fijians decked themselves out in face and body paint on a daily basis. They worked from a palette of yellow from ginger root or turmeric; black from burnt candlenut, charcoal or fungus spores; and blue and vermilion introduced by the traders. Vermilion became worth its weight in gold and was traded with the Europeans for baskets of bêche-de-mer.

A typical day saw Fijians made-up in stripes, zigzags and spots. Ceremonies and war called for more specialised designs, often used to carry specific meanings.

Men mostly used red and black, associated with war and death, on their faces and sometimes chests. Young men were covered in turmeric for *buli yaca* (puberty) ceremonies, or renaming ceremonies celebrating their first enemy kill.

Women favoured yellow, saffron, pink and red body paint, with fine black circles drawn around their eyes for beauty. In the first three months of pregnancy, women were painted with turmeric as, during pregnancy, a woman was under sexual tabu. Males found smudged with turmeric paint were ridiculed. After the birth, both mother and baby would be made-up again until the baby was weaned. The bodies of dead or dying women were adorned with turmeric or vermilion paint.

These days, there's not a stripe or a zigzag to be found among indigenous Fijians; however, in the Indo-Fijian society, body painting still remains an important and commonly practiced art. In a tradition brought from India, intricate henna (or *mehndi*) designs are most commonly painted on women's hands and feet for marriage ceremonies. Painting the bride is a ceremony in itself, seen as both therapeutic and spiritual, and most designs are linked to religious beliefs and practices. Hidden in the design will often be the initials of the husband. If the husband can find them, he will be the dominant partner; if he fails, his wife will rule the roost. The henna lasts anywhere from a few days to three weeks; as long as it does, the new bride is exempt from all housework.

As in the rest of the world, henna tattoos are becoming trendy and you may spot young Indo-Fijian women painting them onto customers in the markets.

Pottery

Fiji's best-known potters are Diana Tugea of Nakabuta, in the Sigatoka Valley, and Taraivini Wati of Nasilai, on the Rewa River near Nausori. The pottery-making tradition in these villages has been handed down through the centuries. Different areas had, and still have, different techniques and styles. Both villages receive visitors.

Tugea's clay pots are smooth with a wide belly, open neck and outward curving lip. Used for cooking, the pots are filled with food wrapped in banana leaves or *rourou* (taro leaves).

Wati's pots are highly decorated. This style was traditionally used for water storage and was once reserved for use by high chiefs only. Most of her pots have a smooth outer belly with a raised pattern of triangular spikes and a narrow neck and lip with patterned incisions. The raised spikes are a traditional motif and are thought to represent a type of war fence that was used to defend ring-ditch villages (see the 'Ring-Ditch Fortification' boxed text in the Viti Levu chapter) in the Rewa Delta. She also makes replicas of elaborately designed 19th-century drinking vessels.

Wooden paddles of various shapes and sizes are used to beat the pots into shape, while the form is held from within using a pebble anvil. Coil and slab-building techniques are also used. Once dried, they are then fired outdoors in an open blaze on coconut husks. Pots are often sealed with resin varnish from the *dakua* tree.

Wati displays her work at the Fiji Museum in Suva where she gives demonstrations when she's in town. See the Suva chapter for more information.

Wood Carving

Traditional wood-carving skills are largely kept alive by the tourist trade, which provides a ready market for war clubs, spears and chiefs' and priests' cannibal forks. *Tanoa*, or *yaqona* drinking bowls, are still part of everyday life.

Religious objects, such as *yaqona* vessels, were traditionally made of *vesi*, considered a sacred timber. Carvings in human and animal forms were generally restricted to ceremonial objects. *Yaqona* bowls shaped like turtles are thought to have derived from turtle-shaped *ibuburau* (vessels used in indigenous Vitian *yaqona* rites).

In areas of Tongan influence, wooden articles were traditionally inlaid with ivory, shell and bone; you may still find these materials used today. Traditional designs are still made by the Lemaki people of Kabara, Southern Lau, the descendants of Tongan and Samoan wood carvers and canoe builders who settled in Viti in the 18th and 19th centuries.

The Fiji Museum is the best place to see authentic traditional woodcarvings. You can often see carvings in process at the University of the South Pacific's Oceania Centre, on the campus grounds outside of Suva. Beware that many artefacts for sale at handicraft centres are less than genuine and may have been mass-produced by a machine.

Bark Cloth & Traditional Textiles

Masi, also known as *malo* or *tapa*, is bark cloth with black and rust-coloured printed designs made by indigenous Fijians. In Vitian culture, the status and symbolic worth of *masi* was similar to *yaqona* and *tabua*. *Masi* is associated with celebrations and rituals; it was worn as a loincloth by men during initiation rituals, during renaming ceremonies following killings, and as an adornment in dance, festivity and war. The finest sheet tissue was worn as sashes, waistbands, trains and turbans by priests and chiefs. It was also used to wrap the cord with which a man's widows were strangled for burial with him, so that they would accompany him into the afterlife.

Masi was an important exchange item and was used in bonding ceremonies between related tribes. Chiefs would dance swathed in a huge puffball of *masi* cloth, which was later given to members of the other tribe. Local motifs and patterns were sometimes used to signify allegiance to a particular tribe.

While men wore the *masi*, production has traditionally been a woman's role. The cloth is made from the inner white bark of the paper mulberry bush. The bark is soaked in water, scraped clean and stored in rolls. It's then beaten and felted together for hours, until it has a fine even texture. Large sheets of 2m by 2.2m are not uncommon. Rich, oily, brown cloth is made by soaking the material in coconut oil and smoking it over burning leaves. Intricately painted designs are done by hand or stencil and often carry symbolic meaning. In areas of Tongan influence, patterns are obtained by rubbing the cloth over a tablet made of raised leaf strips. Rusty-coloured paints are traditionally made from an infusion of candlenut and mangrove bark; pinker browns are made from red clays; and blacks are made from the soot of burnt *dakua* resin and charred candlenuts. Modern paints and glues are now often used as shortcuts.

It is difficult for visitors to see *masi* being made. Most Fijian *masi* is made on the island of Vatulele, which has one exclusive resort, on Namuk and Moce in Southern Lau, and on Taveuni. *Masi* is now most commonly made for tourists and is used for postcards, wall hangings and other decorative items. Textile designers have also begun incorporating traditional *masi* motifs in their fabrics.

Mat & Basket Weaving

Most indigenous Fijian homes use woven *voivoi* or pandanus-leaf mats for floor coverings, dining mats and as finer sleeping mats. They are much in demand as wedding presents and for baptisms, funerals and presentations to chiefs.

Traditionally the hereditary role of the women of certain tribes, most girls living in villages learn to weave. The pandanus leaves are cut and laid outdoors to cure, then stripped of the spiny edges and boiled and dried. The traditional method for blackening the leaves for contrasting patterns is to bury them in mud for days and then boil them with special leaves. The dried pandanus leaves, made flexible by scraping with shells, are split into strips of about 1cm to 2cm. Mat borders are now decorated in brightly coloured wools instead of parrot feathers.

Urbanisation and mass-produced goods have inevitably led to a decline in the production of mats. This has, in turn led to a decline in the quality of materials, as *voivoi* bushes need to be harvested regularly.

Literature

The indigenous Fijian oral tradition of telling myths and legends around the kava bowl is still going strong, both as entertainment and as a traditional means for passing on history.

Histories often begin with stories of settlement rather than origin and these stories often validate a village's land rights. As you move from village to village, you will hear stories that contradict one another; the ability of the history to uphold the present seems to be more important than its ability to accurately portray the past. English is the principal written means of expression and many of these traditional stories have been collected in *Myths & Legends of Fiji & Rotuma* by AW Reed & Inez Hames.

Fiji has a small but strong community of poets and writers. Contemporary literature includes works by Joseph Veramu, the author of the short-story collection *The Black Messiah* and the novel *Moving Through the Streets*, which is about urban teenagers in Suva. Jo Nacola's work includes the play *I Native No More*. Other notable authors are short-story writer Marjorie Crocombe and Rotuman playwright Vilsoni Hereniko. The poet Teresia Kieuea Teaiwa, who grew up in Fiji, explores her black American and Pacific Islander identity in *Searching for Nei Nim'anoa* (1995). *Niu Waves* (2001) is a contemporary collection of South Pacific stories and poetry with contributions by Fijians. The Fiji Writers Association has published *Trapped: A Collection of Writings From Fiji*.

Many Indo-Fijian poets write principally in Hindi, but since the 1970s write increasingly in English. Writers of note include Subramani, Satendra Nandan, Raymond Pillai, Prem Banfal and poet Mohit Prasad (*The Eyes of the Mask*, 1998). The theme of the injustice of the indenture experience rates highly in Indo-Fijian literature and the natural environment is often portrayed as harsh and alien. As a body of work it often dwells on a sense of hopelessness and is not necessarily representative of the contemporary or historical Indo-Fijian identity. Prem Banfal's work offers a female perspective.

A Hairy Situation

For indigenous Fijians, the head is tabu or sacred and, in reverence to its sanctity, Vitians spent entire days with the hairdresser.

Until initiation, boys were bald except for one or two upstanding tufts. A man's hair, however, was a symbol of his masculinity and social standing. Men sported flamboyant, extravagant, fantastic and often massive hair-dos, ranging from the relatively conventional giant puffball (up to 30cm tall) to more original shaggy or geometric shapes. Styles were stiffened into place with burnt limejuice. Hair was dyed grey, sky blue, rust, orange, yellow and white, often striped or multicoloured. Before the introduction of the razor and mirror by traders, beards and moustaches were also grown long.

Before initiation, girls wore a lavish cascade of bleached or reddened corkscrew ringlets which hung down to their hips. These ringlets, known as *tobe*, represented the prawns they were destined to fish in later life. Women, on the other hand, wore far more conservative hair-dos – close-cropped with random tufts died rusty brown or yellow. A wife's hair could never outdo her husband's and a husband's could not outdo the chief's.

People slept on raised wooden pillows to keep their coiffure from being spoilt. The head was especially dressed for festive occasions with accessories like scalp scratchers (practical for lice), ornamental combs, scarlet feathers, wreaths of flowers and vines, and perfumed with grated sandalwood.

Shaving one's head was a profound sacrifice for a man and was often done as a symbol of mourning or to appease a wrathful ancestral spirit. Introduced by Europeans, there were special horsehair wigs for balding men or for those who had sacrificed their hair. *Tobe* ringlets (the long ones could take 10 years to grow) were popular war trophies.

Early Europeans were astonished by the variety of elaborate styles. Not long after a missionary measured one indigenous hair-do at 5m in circumference, the custom was deliberately suppressed by the Christians, who regarded it as a 'flagrant symbol of paganism', not suitable for the 'neat and industrious Christian convert'.

These days, you're unlikely to see any hair-dos as fantastical as those that were around before the missionaries took their clippers to them. Nonetheless, it's interesting to notice the increasing amount of long, dyed and relatively big styles worn by the younger indigenous Fijians, compared with the conservative crops sported by the older generations.

Architecture

Traditional The most beautiful example of a traditional village is Navala, nestled in the Viti Levu highlands. It is the only village remaining where every home is a *bure*. *Bure* are cheap, relatively quick to build using local materials of leaves, reeds and bamboo, and withstand the elements incredibly well. *Bure* building is a skilled trade passed from father to son, although the whole community helps when a *bure* is under construction and most village people would know how to maintain the woven walls and thatched roof of a *bure* suffering damage or decay. *Bure*-building skills are also kept alive for the tourist industry with its demand for authentic-looking buildings. These days, however, most villagers live in simple rectangular, pitched-roof houses made from industrialised materials requiring less maintenance. While a *bure*'s structure is generally able to withstand cyclones, the government offers incentives to build concrete cyclone-proof houses.

Most traditional *bure* are rectangular in plan, with a hipped or gabled roof. However, in areas of Tongan and Samoan influence such as Lau, round-ended plans are common. *Bure* have one large room, usually with a sleeping compartment behind a curtain at one end and pandanus mats cover the packed-earth floor. With few windows, the interior space is normally quite dark. Cooking is now normally done in a separate *bure*.

Colonial Levuka, the old European trader settlement and former capital of Fiji, has been declared a historic town and has been nominated for World Heritage Listing. A number of buildings date from its boom period of the late 19th century, and the main streetscape is surprisingly intact, giving the impression that the town has stopped in time.

The British influence on Suva is reflected in its many colonial buildings, including Government House, Suva City Library, Grand Pacific Hotel and other government buildings.

Modern Some modern architecture combines traditional Fijian aesthetics, knowledge and materials with modern technology. Some notable buildings include the new parliament complex, the USP campus in Suva, and the *bure bose* (meeting house) at Somosomo on Taveuni.

Many of the resorts have fairly predictable tropical designs with open, thatched restaurants and bars and beachside bungalows. Resorts with somewhat more distinctive architecture include the upmarket Vatulele Island Resort; Koro Sun Resort near Savusavu, Vanua Levu; and the Raintree Lodge outside of Suva. Young architects with new ideas for tropical architecture are also making an impact on the commercial and resort scene.

SOCIETY

Traditional Culture

Indigenous Fijians Many features of Viti's rich culture were suppressed along with the old religion in the mid to late 19th century. Pre-Christian costume, hairdressing and body decoration were far removed from today's conservative dress style. However, despite the changing influences and pressures, many aspects of the communal way of life are still strong. Throughout the colonial era the chiefly system and village structure remained intact, partly due to laws protecting Fijian land rights and prohibiting Fijian labour on the plantations.

Most indigenous Fijians live in villages in *mataqali* (extended family groups) and acknowledge a hereditary chief who is usually male. Each *mataqali* owns land, and wider groups have a high (or paramount) chief. Each family is allocated land for farming by the chief.

Clans gather for births, deaths, marriages, *meke*, *lovo* feasts and to exchange gifts. *Yaqona* drinking is still an important social ceremony. Communal obligations also have to be met, including farming for the chief, preparing for special ceremonies and feasts, fishing, building and village maintenance. Village life is now only semi-subsistent; cash is needed for school fees, community projects and imported goods.

Village life, based on interdependence, is supportive and provides a strong group identity. It is also conservative; independent thinking is not encouraged and being different or too ambitious is seen to threaten the stability of a village. Conflict arises between those who want change and those who resist it. Profits from any additional business are normally expected to be shared with the whole village. Concepts such as *kerekere* and *sevusevu* are still strong, especially in remote areas. *Kerekere* is unconditional giving

Growing Pains

In traditional Vitian society, growing up may well have been dreaded by young girls. Up until the 20th century, a girl's initiation into adulthood was marked by the *veiqia* rite, the elaborate tattooing of the pubic area. Considered beautiful, girls were also told it would enhance their sex drive. Each village had a female *duabati* (hereditary tattoo specialist) who used a spiked pick, light mallet, bamboo slivers, sharp shells and soot to create the blue-black designs. Often a few girls were tattooed at once, taking turns to hold each other down. The ritual would stretch out over weeks, months, or even a year and was carried out during the day when men were out, to conceal the screaming.

It was believed that untattooed women would be persecuted by the ancestor spirits in the afterlife – slashed about the pubic region or pounded to a pulp and fed to the gods. This was a dreaded fate and girls were loath to defy the custom. Even in the 20th century, after missionaries had suppressed what they saw as a pagan ritual, fake tattoos were sometimes painted on dead girls in an attempt to bluff the gods. These days, you'll often see cosmetic tattoos on the hands and arms of indigenous Fijian men and women, often lucky numbers or initials.

based on the concept that all property is communal; it is especially strong among relatives and friends. This can prove very difficult for anyone attempting to start up commercial ventures in a village, such as a shop. *Sevusevu* is the presentation of a gift such as *yaqona* or, more powerfully, a *tabua* in exchange for certain favours. Again, the receiver is obligated to honour the giver's request. In remote areas the role of men and women is clearly demarcated and many villages still adhere to a strong hierarchy and customs. For example, a man is not supposed to speak directly to his sister-in-law.

Fiji is becoming increasingly urbanised and traditional values and the wisdom of elders are often less respected in towns and cities. Regional cultural, linguistic and social differences that were noticeable in the past are quickly disappearing as Fijians travel more. Villages are increasingly less self-sufficient and many young people travel to the cities for education, employment or to escape the restrictions of village life. For those who have grown up in the relative security and disciplined structure of a village, adapting to urban life is not easy. Together with increased freedom comes competition for jobs and a less supportive social structure. Television, only introduced in the last decade, presents opposing values and contradictory messages.

Indigenous Fijians own about 83% of the land, some of which is leased to others for farming and tourism. In addition to agriculture, mining and the public service, many indigenous Fijians are employed in the tourism industry, so there is some pressure placed on them to retain the more exotic aspects of their culture. While most of the larger resorts are foreign-owned, there are some smaller-scale projects that directly benefit villagers.

See Social Graces in the Facts for the Visitor chapter for a few on-the-road etiquette pointers.

Indo-Fijians Many Indo-Fijian families have been living in Fiji for four or five generations. The majority of the labourers that came to Fiji were young, illiterate farmers from communal villages. The communal living of Indians from diverse backgrounds, the experiences they endured together as labourers and the adaptations they were forced to make, created a more unrestricted, enterprising society distinct from the Indian cultures they left behind. This has been the basis for the Indo-Fijian culture of today (see the Indo-Fijian History & Culture special section).

RELIGION

Religion is extremely influential in all aspects of Fijian society, affecting its politics, government, education as well as interaction within and between different races. Only 0.4% of the population is nonreligious. Together, the different Christian denominations command the largest following (with 52.9% of the population), followed next by Hindus (38.1%), Muslims (7.8%), Sikhs (0.7%) and other religions (0.1%).

Traditional Fijian Religion

The old Fijian religion was based on ancestor worship. The souls of outstanding ancestors were made into local deities so there were many gods and spirits. A hero in battle could become a war god, or an outstanding farmer could become a god of plenty. Appeasing and thanking the gods shaped all aspects of life in Viti, including medicine and mythology. Spirithouses were built for each significant god.

Hereditary chiefs and priests were the representatives of the gods, and the priest served as a medium through which a god spoke to its descendants. Relics and idols kept in the temple were also mediums. Images were carved from sacred *vesi* wood or whales' teeth and sometimes took human form. Food, *yaqona* roots or *tabua* were given as offerings.

The gods demanded that the people carry out mutilative rituals, mourning sacrifices and initiation ceremonies. Mourning sacrifices included amputation of the little finger at the joint and self-induced burns. Shaving one's head was the ultimate religious or mourning sacrifice for a man. For a woman, the equivalent was being strangled to accompany her dead husband to the afterlife. In initiation rituals women were tattooed and men circumcised. It was believed that the demon guardians of the spirit path would ambush and inspect each ghost to see if it had been properly initiated and that its ear lobes had been plugged and little fingers lopped. Concerned friends and family would often try to trick priests and spirits by painting on designs or chopping off a person's fingers after they had died. Belief in the afterlife was a strong incentive for all actions in life.

The early missionaries abhorred the worship of idols and 'heathen' deities and translated *tevoro*, the Fijian word for gods, as devil. The *tevoro* were not necessarily evil, but the label stuck. Most Vitian practices were wiped out and beliefs were suppressed, however, today some of these beliefs and practices remain interwoven with Christianity.

Christianity

Most indigenous Fijians adhere to one of the Christian churches and invariably each village and settlement has at least one church. Church attendance is high and spiritual leaders are very influential. In small villages that

Tread Lightly

Missionaries may have stamped all over traditional Fijian beliefs in the 18th and 19th centuries, but they didn't manage to sweep them out entirely. Despite rigorously following Christian practices, singing hymn after hymn in Sunday mass, and even being lectured on evolution in school, many indigenous Fijians continue to hold parallel beliefs in their traditional ancestral gods.

This is most easily encountered in visits to smaller and more-remote villages. In these areas, *sevusevu* is not simply something done to keep the tourists happy, it's done in the belief that without being granted the permission of the ancestral spirits through this ritual, outsiders treading through the village's tabu areas will bring down the wrath of the gods.

A leaf through a Fijian newspaper will raise more intriguing tales of what the cosmopolitan journalists call 'superstition'. In September 2002, a church-going fisherman from the Lau Group visited the uninhabited island of Yaroua. This island is believed to be the burial ground of an ancient chief from Vanua Levu and the fisherman believes that his rambunctious nephews stirred and angered the chief's spirit. In attempting to leave the island, the group was thrown from the boat and nearly drowned in swells the fisherman had never seen the likes of. Stranded on the island for a week, the fisherman is convinced that his brush with death was the work of the furious ancestral god.

In July of the same year, five babies mysteriously died in the newly built Levuka hospital on Ovalau. The state hospital is built on land traditionally owned by Levuka Village and locals soon linked the deaths to the improper transfer of the land from the village to the state. In fear of the punishment meted out by the ancestral gods, women from Ovalau delivered their babies in hospitals in Suva or Nausori (or in the boat en route). In hopes of clearing the hospital of its ill-fate, health authorities attended a *bolubolu* ceremony with the chief of Levuka Village. This traditional ceremony for apology and reconciliation was a means of gaining acceptance of the land transfer from the ancestors; the hospital has reported no infant deaths since.

The moral of these tales? Watch where you tread.

retain their hierarchical society, people generally follow the religion of the chief. Some villages have a number of religions, occasionally leading to jealousy and conflict. Only about 2% of Indo-Fijians are Christians.

Of all the Christian denominations, the Methodist Church is the most powerful. Extremist factions of the church were supporters of the nationalist movement and the many military coups, and played a role in the Sunday ban on business activities. Other denominations include Catholic, Seventh-Day Adventist, Anglican and Presbyterian. More recently, there has been an increase in the followers of Assembly of God, Mormons and Jehovah's Witnesses.

Even if you are not at all religious, try to attend a church service in a Fijian village. The singing is amazing and visitors are welcome. Leave a small donation to help with community projects.

Indo-Fijian Religions

There are many tiny, beautiful temples and green-and-white mosques scattered around Fiji's countryside, especially in the cane-growing areas of Viti Levu and Vanua Levu. Indentured labourers established temples to pursue their own faith and boost their sense of security in the new alien country. There were, however, a lack of spiritual leaders, and knowledge of the philosophy behind the religions was partly lost. After generations of separation from India, Indo-Fijians are generally less orthodox in terms of caste and religion, and tolerance of religious differences is greater than in India. Most Indo-Fijians are Hindus or Muslims, and Sikhism (combining Hindu and Islamic beliefs) is practiced by some descendants of northwest Indians. Hare Krishnas also have a small following with a temple in Lautoka.

Islam Muslims believe in peace and submission to Allah (God), following the teachings of the prophet Mohammed and the holy book the Koran. Religious festivals include *Ramadan* (30-day, dawn-to-dusk fasting), the *Eid* festival to celebrate the end of fasting, and Mohammed's birthday.

Hinduism Hindus believe in reincarnation when the consequence of all past deeds will be faced – thus the importance of leading a moral life. Most Hindu homes in Fiji have small shrines for worship. High-caste Hindus who are more secure economically tend to be less devoted to religious activities.

Hindus worship one supreme power, *Brahman*, who assumes many forms and names in order to be better understood. The Divine Mother is the personification of nature, which gives life, meaning and purpose to all things. Devotees see every woman as the personified essence of the Divine Mother. The greatest goddess is *Maya Devi* who is all powerful, all knowing, all pervading. All energy is believed to come from her and she is symbolised by water (life giver) and fire (purifier or destroyer). She shows compassion to those who surrender to her, and punishes those who disobey. The green goddess *Parvati* symbolises nature, the dark blue *Kali* represents time, and the red *Lakshmi*, wealth. Other goddess forms include *Durga*, *Maari* and *Shakti*.

Descendants of southern Indians perform a fire-walking ritual in July or August at many temples, including the Mariamma temple in Suva. A group of orthodox Hindus, of north-Indian origin, perform *Durga Gram Puja* each August at Wailekutu, near Suva. This is the worship of the goddess *Durga* – through whipping, piercing the tongue and body, immersing their hands in boiling ghee (clarified butter), and dancing on upturned knife blades. Other important Hindu festivals include *Holi* (Festival of Colours), *Diwali* (Festival of Lights) and the Birth of Lord Krishna. Refer to Public Holidays & Special Events in the Facts for the Visitor chapter for festival dates and more information.

LANGUAGE

English is the official language of Fiji. Only young children in remote areas may not speak it. Most Fijians are multilingual, and speak their vernacular Fijian or Fiji-Hindi. See the Language chapter later in this book for more information, and for more tips, refer to Lonely Planet's *Fijian phrasebook* or *South Pacific phrasebook*.

Facts for the Visitor

Highlights

- Experience the warmth and hospitality of Fiji's multiethnic inhabitants
- Snorkel or dive Fiji's extraordinary coral reefs
- Hike through the lush rainforest and swim in the waterfall pools of Taveuni's Bouma National Heritage Park
- Windsurf or kayak over Fiji's crystal blue waters
- Visit Suva's Fiji Museum for a fascinating look at the migration, cannibalism and culture of Fiji's past
- Go rafting through the gorges and wilderness of the Namosi Highlands
- Enjoy spectacular views from the mountains of Koroyanitu National Heritage Park
- Admire the traditional architecture of the picturesque highland village of Navala
- Visit Levuka, the Wild-West capital of the 19th century
- Hire a 4WD and get lost in the forests and sugarcane fields of Vanua Levu
- Wander along the windswept Sigatoka Sand Dunes
- Encounter the rugged and remote Kadavu Group

SUGGESTED ITINERARIES

Whether you're after an adventure holiday or a laze on the beach, Fiji has lots of options. Package tours are a popular way to visit, but if you're doing this consider tacking on a few days at the end of the tour to visit some of Fiji's more hidden paradises. Ovalau and its offshore islands, Viti Levu's Highlands, Taveuni's national parks, and Savusavu for an adventure cruise are all easily accessible adventures and will give you a chance to experience Fiji's somewhat less beaten track.

Even with only a few days, it's possible to visit any of the islands that have regular flights. Flights in Fiji are responsibly priced, readily available and offer some of the best views. By plane, you can reach most destinations within an hour or so. See the Getting Around chapter for more details.

If you're looking for a beach to swim at, head for one of the smaller coral islands rather than the larger, volcanic islands like Viti Levu, Vanua Levu and Taveuni. Fiji is so well endowed with coral and sealife, you can snorkel off almost every shore. Nature lovers should head for the lush, rugged islands of Kadavu and Taveuni; divers looking to explore the Rainbow Reef and Somosomo Strait should also head for Taveuni, as well as Savusavu on Vanua Levu. Levuka, on Ovalau, is also an excellent place to dive as it's only one of many sights and activities on offer. Note that the eastern sides of the larger islands have wetter climates.

Depending on the time available, your pace and preferences, consider the following itineraries.

One Week

If you're looking for a beach holiday, head to the Yasawas or the Mamanucas to lap up the sun for three or four days. Finish by hopping on a bus or hiring a 4WD and heading up to the picturesque village of Navala and the Nausori Highlands on Viti Levu.

Prefer the less-trodden tourist track? On arrival in Fiji, hop directly on a flight for historic Levuka in the Lomaiviti Group, where you can spend a few days trekking, diving and visiting villages before relaxing for a couple of days on the sandy, offshore island of Caqelai. En route back to Nadi, stop off in Suva for a day to visit the museum.

A good way to pack a lot into a few days is to join an adventure cruise from Savusavu or in the Yasawas.

Two Weeks

Do the above (Yasawas or Mamanucas, the Highlands and the Lomaiviti Group) or spend the second week either exploring Viti Levu's Queens Road and Kings Road or visiting Taveuni with its fantastic nature walks, waterfalls and diving.

One Month or More

Combine some of the above, trying out the ferries as well as flights. Head to Vanua Levu where you can rent a 4WD and get off the beaten track or head to the Kadavu Group for more rainforests and diving.

PLANNING

When to Go

The best time to visit is during the so-called 'Fijian winter' or 'dry season', from May to October. This time of year is more pleasant with lower rainfall and humidity, milder temperatures, and less risk of those pesky tropical cyclones. Fiji can be enjoyed year round, however, and is a great place to escape either southern or northern hemisphere winters.

The end of the year is often busy, coinciding with school holidays in both Australia and New Zealand, and people visiting relatives. In February and March, however, Fiji sees fewer tourists and you're more likely to get bargains on your accommodation. See also Climate in the Facts about Fiji chapter and Public Holidays & Special Events later in this chapter.

What Kind of Trip

There is potential for pretty much any kind of trip you're looking for. You can go for a luxurious beach vacation at a classy resort, a party holiday filled with water sports and Fiji beer, or an adventure trip trekking through villages and kayaking through gobsmacking gorges.

Fiji is one of the South Pacific's major transit hubs. Even if you're just stopping over for a day or two, it's worth getting out and seeing something. Better yet, extend your stay (most airlines will allow you up to three months for a stopover) and really experience Fiji.

Fiji is popular with honeymooners, divers, backpackers, families, bird-watchers, independent travellers and tour groups. There are accommodation options and resorts for every budget as well as many tours on offer.

Maps

The best place to buy maps of the Fiji islands is the **Map Shop** in Suva (see the Suva chapter for more details). It sells big (1:50,000), detailed topographic maps of each island or island group, as well as maps of Suva.

Bookshops sometimes stock town maps, and some tourist brochures also have simple town maps. At the Fiji Visitors Bureau (FVB), or specialist book and map shops overseas, you can usually purchase the latest Hema map of Fiji. Specialist marine charts are usually available at Fijian ports but are expensive; try to buy them overseas.

What to Bring

Pack as little as possible – less to lug around, less to lose. Backpacks should ideally be compact, comfortable, waterproof and have double zips that can be padlocked. Before you leave, walk around with your pack on for awhile; what may seem light at first can feel like a hulking monster 10 minutes later.

Carry money, important documents and some travellers cheques out of sight in a moneybelt. A chain is handy for locking gear to a fixture in shared rooms, or in a hotel's safe-deposit room, and daypacks are good for carrying your valuables onto the bus with you when your bag is out of sight in the storage below. Waterproof bags are handy for carrying stationery, photocopies (see Copies under Visas & Documents later in this chapter) and camera gear on boat trips.

Lightweight, cotton casual clothes are best for Fiji's tropical climate. Bathers, shorts and singlet tops are OK for the resorts; however, when you're not in a resort, respect local customs by covering up. (See Dress under Social Graces in this chapter.) It's wise to take a light jumper as it can get cool in the highlands and elsewhere in the winter months, especially between May and August. Include a light raincoat or compact umbrella, sunglasses, a malleable hat and a lightweight towel or chamois.

Make sure that shoes are worn-in before travelling; the last thing you want are blisters that can lead to infections. You can pretty much live in a good pair of walking sandals and will only need walking boots if you are going hiking in muddy conditions. If you're heading for the nightclubs in Suva or Nadi, you won't be let in wearing flip-flops or tank tops.

Pack toiletries in small containers to reduce bulk. Take resealable plastic bags to avoid those disastrous leaks. Pharmacies and large supermarkets in the main towns stock condoms, tampons and baby items, such as (expensive) disposable nappies, formula and sterilising solution. Most resorts have a shop with basic toiletries but it's usually best to bring your personal needs from home. Include a good insect repellent; vitamins if you will be on the road for an extended period; prescription medicines (with a copy of scripts); and spare glasses or contact lenses (disposables are handy). And you'll never regret carrying some emergency loo roll.

Divers should remember their scuba certification card. While equipment can be hired at most resorts and dive shops, divers and keen snorkellers may prefer to take their own gear. For divers, a lycra suit for summer or a 3mm wetsuit for winter is recommended.

Consider how you will be travelling when packing camera equipment (do you really want to haul that tripod up Koroyanitu?) and bring plenty of film (see Photography & Video later in this chapter). Photos make great thank-you gifts.

Other useful things to consider include an army knife, torch, compass, travel alarm, a mini travel radio and spare batteries. A needle and thread, laundry soap and traveller's clothesline are all handy. Most accommodation places provide mosquito nets or screened windows. You can also buy repellent coils in most shops. Campers and self-caterers will want to bring a lightweight waterproof tent, some plastic dishes and utensils, matches and possibly a camping stove (kerosene is readily available in Fiji).

RESPONSIBLE TOURISM

Tourism is one of the country's main money-spinners and employs a large percentage of the population. Many of the upmarket resorts have foreign owners, however, some money also flows on to local communities. Ecotourism projects are also beginning to take off, some run directly by villagers.

Travellers can minimise their impact by choosing resorts, tours and activities that support local services and people, and that are environmentally and culturally aware. Some tour operators are simply sticking an 'eco' in their name, in hopes of attracting a new market. Don't assume that a resort or tour is ecologically sound just because of its name. See Ecology & Environment in the Facts about Fiji chapter and 'The Responsible Diver' boxed text later in this chapter.

There are a number of cultural issues that travellers should be aware of and respect. An important one is that you can't just head out into the wilderness to camp and hike where you like. Almost all land is owned and protected by villages and you must ask the permission of the local chief as well as his ancestors through offering a *sevusevu* (gift). Even then, you'll likely be accompanied by a local villager to keep you from tramping through sacred and tabu areas. When visiting remote areas, be conscious of your contribution to waste problems. See also Hiking in the Activities section and Camping in the Accommodation section later in this chapter.

The responsible traveller should discourage the trade of shells, coral or turtle products by not purchasing them or bringing them in or out of the country, even if legal.

TOURIST OFFICES

The Fiji Visitors Bureau (FVB) is the primary tourist information body in Fiji. It has many overseas representatives (see Tourist Offices Abroad later). The head office is in Suva, but your first encounter is likely to be at Nadi International Airport. The FVB has a 24-hour, toll-free helpline for complaints or emergencies – ring from anywhere in Fiji (☎ 0800 721 721).

The **South Pacific Tourism Organisation** *(SPTO; ☎ 330 4177, fax 330 1995; e info@spto.org; w www.spto.org; 3rd fl, Dolphin Plaza, cnr Loftus St & Victoria Parade, Suva)* promotes cooperation between the South Pacific island nations for the development of tourism in the region. Check out its website for a Pacific Islands travel directory.

Other useful sources of information include the following publications.

Fiji Magic (☎ 331 3944, fax 330 2852) Free and published monthly, this brochure carries details and prices of accommodation, restaurants, activities and tours. It's widely available (try the FVB, hotels and airline offices) but the information is not always so up-to-date.

Fiji Calling Similar to Fiji Magic, you can pick this one up at FVBs overseas.

Spotlight on Nadi & Spotlight on Suva Both regularly published, these are more freebies from FVB with details of activities and entertainment in the cities

Yacht Help, Fiji's Marine Guide This free booklet is published annually and has loads of useful information like tide tables, resort VHF channels and clearance formalities, as well as tours and maps of port towns. Pick it up at marinas.

Local Tourist Offices

The FVB has offices in Suva and Nadi:

Nadi (☎ 672 2433, fax 672 0141, e fvbnadi@connect.com.fj)
Airport Concourse, Nadi International Airport

Suva (☎ 330 2433, fax 330 0970, e infodesk@fijifvb.gov.fj, w www.bulafiji.com)
Thomas St

Tourist Offices Abroad

For a full list of FVB offices abroad, have a look at **w** www.fiji.nu/fvb-overseas.shtml.

Australia (☎ 1800-251 715, fax (02) 9264 3060, **e** infosyd@bulafiji.au.com, **w** www.bulafiji-au.com) Level 12, St Martins Tower, 31 Market St, Sydney 2000
Canada (☎ 800 932 3454, fax 670 2318) 1275 West 6th Ave, Vancouver, BC V6H 1A6
France (☎ 47-670 0967, fax 670 0918) 13 rue d'Alembery, Grenoble F-38000
Germany (☎ 304-225 6026, **e** fveurope@t-online.de, **w** www.bulafiji.de) Petersburger Str 94, 10247 Berlin
Japan (☎ 03-3587 2038, fax 3587 2563, **e** info@bulafiji-jp.com, **w** www.bulafiji-jp.com) 14th floor, Noa Bldg, 3-5, 2 Chome Azabudai, Minato-Ku, Tokyo 106
New Zealand (☎ 09-373 2133, fax 309 4720, **e** info@bulafiji.co.nz, **w** www.bulafiji.co.nz) 5th floor, 48 High St, Auckland, PO Box 1179
UK (☎ 020 8741 6144, fax 020 8741 6107, **e** allisterbruce@aol.com) 48 Glentham Rd, Barnes, London SW13 9JJ
USA (☎ 800-932-3454, fax 310-670-2318) 5777 West Century Blvd, Suite 220, Los Angeles, CA 90045

VISAS & DOCUMENTS

Passport & Visas

A free tourist visa for four months is granted on arrival to citizens of more than 100 countries, including: most countries belonging to the British Commonwealth, North America, much of South America, Austria, Belgium, Denmark, France, Germany, Finland, Ireland, Italy, the Netherlands, Norway, Spain, Sweden, Switzerland, the UK, Iceland, India, Indonesia, Israel, Japan, Marshall Islands, Mexico, Philippines, Russia, Samoa, Solomon Islands, South Korea, Tanzania, Tonga, Tuvalu, Tunisia, Turkey, Uruguay, Vanuatu and Venezuela. (Check **w** www.bulafiji.com/about/visitor/visitor.shtml for the full list.) You'll need to have an onward ticket and a passport valid for at least three months longer than your intended stay.

Nationalities from countries excluded from the custom's list will have to apply for visas through a Fijian embassy prior to arrival.

Those entering Fiji by boat are subject to the same visa requirements as those arriving by plane. Yachts can only enter through the designated ports of Suva, Lautoka, Savusavu and Levuka. Yachts have to be cleared by immigration and customs, and are prohibited from visiting any outer islands before doing so. Yachties need to apply for special written authorisation to visit the Lau Group (see Travel Permits later in this section).

Visitors cannot partake in political activity or study, and work permits are needed if you intend to live and work in Fiji for more than six months. Foreign journalists will require a work visa if they spend more than 14 days in Fiji (see the Work section later in this chapter).

Visa Extensions Tourist visas can be extended for an extra two months by applying through the Department of Immigration in Nadi, Suva or Lautoka. You'll need to show an onward ticket, proof of sufficient funds and your passport must be valid for three months after your proposed departure. Apply at the **Immigration Department** (☎ *772 2263, fax 772 1720; Nadi International Airport* • ☎ *347 8785; Nausori International Airport* • ☎ *666 1706, fax 666 8120; Namoli Ave; Lautoka* • ☎ *331 2672, fax 330 1653; Gohil Bldg, Toorak; Suva)* You can also apply through police stations in Ba, Tavua, Taveuni, Savusavu, Labasa and Levuka, but allow at least two weeks for the paperwork. If you wish to stay longer than six months you'll have to leave and then re-enter the country.

Yachties can have their stay extended for up to 12 months; apply to authorities at designated ports.

Travel Permits

Yachties intending to sail to the outer islands, such as the Lau Group, will require a customs permit and a permit to cruise the islands, obtained from the **Ministry of Foreign Affairs** *(☎ 321 1458; 61 Carnarvon St, Suva)*, or from the commissioner's office in Lautoka, Savusavu or Levuka. They will ask to see customs papers and details of all crew members. Seek advice from a yachting agent or yacht club in Fiji before applying for the permit.

Travel Insurance

A travel insurance policy to cover theft, loss and medical problems is a good idea. There are many policies available and your travel agent will be able to recommend one. The policies handled by STA Travel and other student travel organisations are usually good value. Some policies offer lower and higher medical-expense options but the higher ones are mainly for countries such as the USA, which have extremely high medical costs. Check the small print. Some policies specifically exclude so-called 'dangerous activities', which can include diving, motorcycling and even hiking. A locally acquired motorcycle licence may not be valid under some policies.

You may prefer a policy that pays doctors or hospitals direct rather than you having to pay on the spot and claim later. If you have to claim later make sure you keep all the documentation.

Check that the policy covers ambulances and an emergency flight home. The Department of Foreign Affairs & Trade now warns travellers that some insurance companies will not pay claims that arise when travellers have disregarded the government's travel advice.

Driving Licence & Permits

If you hold a current driving licence from an English-speaking country you are entitled to drive in Fiji. Otherwise you will need an international driving permit, which should be obtained in your home country before travelling.

Student & Youth Cards

STA Travel and other student travel agencies give discounts on international airfares to full-time students who have an International Student Identity Card (ISIC). Application forms are available at these travel agencies. Student discounts are occasionally given for entry fees, restaurants and accommodation in Fiji. You can also use the student health service at the University of the South Pacific (USP) in Suva.

Copies

Keep copies of vital documents and an emergency stash of about $50 hidden in your luggage. Include a copy of the following: your passport's data pages, your birth certificate, credit cards, airline tickets, travel insurance, driving licence, and, if you are going to work in Fiji, your employment documents and education qualifications. Also include the serial numbers of your travellers cheques, your vaccination details and prescriptions. Remember to leave a copy of all these things with someone at home.

It's also a good idea to store details of your vital travel documents in Lonely Planet's free online **Travel Vault** (w *www.ekno.lonelyplanet.com*). Your password-protected Travel Vault is accessible online anywhere in the world – you can create it at the given website.

EMBASSIES

Fijian Embassies Abroad

Fiji has diplomatic representation in the following countries.

Australia (☎ 06-260 5115, fax 260 5105, e fhc@cyberone.com.au) 19 Beale Crescent, Canberra, ACT 2600

Belgium (☎ 02-736 9050, fax 736 1458, e info@fijiembassy.be) 92-94 Square Plasky, 1030 Brusseles

Japan (☎ 03-3587 2038, fax 3587 2563) 14th floor, Noa Bldg, 3-5, 2 Chome Azabudai, Minato-Ku, Tokyo 106

Malaysia (☎ 03-2732 3335, fax 2732 7555) Level 2, Menara Chan, 138 Jalan Ampang, 50450, Kuala Lumpur

New Zealand (☎ 04-473 5401, fax 499 1011) 31 Pipitea St, Thorndon, Wellington; PO Box 3940

Papua New Guinea (☎ 211 914, fax 217 220) 4th floor, Defense House, Champion Parade, Port Moresby, NCD; PO Box 6117

UK (☎ 020-7584 3661, fax 7584 2838, e fijirepuk@compuserve.com) 34 Hyde Park Gate, London SW7 5BN

USA (☎ 202-337 8320, fax 337 1996, e fijiemb@earthlink.net) 2233 Wisconsin Ave, NW, Suite 240, Washington, DC 20007

Foreign Embassies & Representatives in Fiji

The following countries have diplomatic representation in Fiji.

Australia (☎ 338 2211, fax 338 2065, e austembassy@connect.com.fj) 37 Princes Rd, Tamavua, Suva

China (☎ 330 0251, fax 330 0950) 147 Queen Elizabeth Drive, Suva

European Union (☎ 331 3633, fax 330 1084, e eudelfiji@eu.org.fj) 4th floor, Fiji Development Bank Centre, Victoria Parade, Suva

Federated States of Micronesia (☎ 330 4566, fax 330 0842) 37 Loftus St, Suva

France (☎ 331 2233, fax 330 1894, e presse@ambafrance.org.fj) 1st floor, Dominion House, Thomson St, Suva

India (☎ 330 1125, fax 330 1032, e hicomindsuva@connect.com.fj) Suite 270, Suva Central, Suva PO Box 471

Japan (☎ 330 2122, fax 330 1452) 2nd floor, Dominion House, Thomson St, Suva

Your Own Embassy

It's important to realise what your own embassy – the embassy of the country of which you are a citizen – can and can't do to help you if you get into trouble. Generally speaking, it won't be much help in emergencies if the trouble you're in is remotely your own fault. Remember that you are bound by the laws of the country you are in.

In genuine emergencies you might get some assistance, but only if other channels have been exhausted. For example, if you need to get home urgently, a free ticket is exceedingly unlikely – the embassy would expect you to have insurance. If you have all your money and documents stolen, it might assist with getting a new passport, but a loan for onward travel is out of the question.

Korea (☎ 330 0977, fax 330 3410) 8th floor, Vanua House, Victoria Parade, Suva
Malaysia (☎ 331 2166, fax 330 3350) 5th floor, Air Pacific House, Butt St, Suva
Marshall Islands (☎ 338 7899, fax 338 7115) 41 Borron Rd, Samabula, Government Buildings, Suva.
Nauru (☎ 331 3566, fax 330 2861) 7th floor, Ratu Sukuna House, Suva
New Zealand (☎ 331 1422, fax 330 0842, e nzhc@connect.com.fj) 10th floor, Reserve Bank Bldg, Pratt St, Suva
Papua New Guinea (☎ 330 2244, fax 330 0178) 3rd floor, Credit Corp Bldg, Gordon St, Suva
Tuvalu (☎ 330 1355, fax 330 1023) 16 Gorrie St, Suva
UK (☎ 331 1033, fax 330 1046, e ukinfo@bhc.org.fj) Victoria House, 47 Gladstone Rd, Suva
USA (☎ 314 466, fax 300 081, e usembsuva@connect.com.fj) 31 Loftus St, Suva

CUSTOMS

If you are travelling with expensive camera or computer equipment, carry a receipt to avoid possible hassles when returning home.

Visitors can leave Fiji without paying value-added tax (VAT) on: up to $400 per person of duty-assessed goods; 2L of liqueur or spirits, or 4L of wine or beer; 500 cigarettes or 500g of cigars or tobacco, or all three under a total of 500g; and personal effects.

Pottery shards, turtle shells, coral and trochus shells and giant clamshells cannot be taken out of the country without a permit. You can bring as much currency as you like into the country but can't take out any more than you brought in.

Quarantine

Importation of vegetable matter, seeds, animals, meat or dairy produce is prohibited without a licence from the Ministry of Agriculture & Fisheries. Domestic pets require a permit to enter Fiji and will be kept in quarantine in Suva for up to a month.

MONEY

It's good to have a few options for accessing money – take a credit card, a debit card, some travellers cheques and a small amount of cash. Banks in larger places like Suva and Nadi can give cash advances on major credit cards and there are a growing number of ATMs around, however, if you're plastic cards get swallowed by a machine, you'll need an alternative like travellers cheques. In an emergency, you can have money wired to you in Suva through Western Union.

Before you head out to remote parts of Fiji, check in the appropriate chapter to make sure you can access money, exchange currency or change travellers cheques.

Currency

The local currency is the Fiji dollar ($); it's fairly stable relative to Australian and New Zealand dollars. All prices quoted herein are in Fiji dollars unless otherwise specified.

The dollar is broken down into 100 cents. Bank notes come in denominations of $50, $20, $10, $5 and $2. There are coins to the value of $1, $0.50, $0.20, $0.10, $0.05, $0.02 and $0.01. Even though Fiji is now a republic, notes and coins still have a picture of England's Queen Elizabeth II on one side.

Exchange Rates

To check current exchange rates see w www.oanda.com. At the time of writing exchange rates were as follows:

country	unit		F$
Australia	A$1	=	1.20
Canada	C$1	=	1.35
euro zone	€1	=	2.20
India	R100	=	4.15
Japan	¥100	=	1.68
Malaysia	MYR1	=	0.55
New Zealand	NZ$1	=	1.15
UK	UK£1	=	3.29
USA	US$1	=	2.05

Exchanging Money

The best currencies to carry are Australian, New Zealand or US dollars, which can be exchanged at all banks.

The most common commercial banks operating in Fiji include Fiji Westpac, ANZ and National Bank (previously the government-owned National Bank of Fiji). Bank hours are 9.30am to 3pm Monday to Thursday, 9.30am to 4pm Friday. The ANZ at Nadi airport provides 24-hour service. While banks in larger towns keep standard business hours, branches in smaller towns may not open every day.

Exchange bureaus include:

American Express (☎ 772 2325, Nadi Airport Concourse, 25 Victoria Parade, Nadi) It has a good reputation for quick replacement of lost or stolen cards or cheques.

Thomas Cook (☎ 330 1603, fax 330 0304, 30 Thomson St, Suva) • (☎ 770 3110, fax 770 3877, cnr Main & Sukuna Sts, Nadi)

Western Union Suva: (☎ 331 4812, cnr Victoria Parade & Gordon St) It does global money transfers – handy in an emergency.

Travellers Cheques You can change travellers cheques in most banks and exchange bureaus, and at larger hotels and duty-free shops. It's a good idea to take travellers cheques in both small and large denominations to avoid being stuck with lots of cash when leaving.

The 24-hour ANZ bank at Nadi International Airport charges $2 on each transaction. Other banks and exchange bureaus don't normally charge a fee.

ATMs Most ATMs accept the main international debit cards including Cirrus, Plus and Maestro. The ANZ has an ATM at Nadi International Airport and you'll find more in town at Nadi and Suva. There's also one in Savusavu, but have a backup plan (like travellers cheques) in case it's out of order. Although more commonplace, you won't find ATMs in remote areas so plan ahead.

Credit Cards Restaurants, shops, mid- to upper-range hotels, car rental agencies, tour and travel agents will usually accept all of the major credit cards. Visa, American Express, Diners Club and MasterCard are widely used. Some resorts charge an additional 5% for payment by credit card. Cash advances are available through credit cards at most banks in larger towns.

Security

While it's unlikely that you'll be robbed, it does happen, so try to keep all valuables out of sight and lock your door while you're out or sleeping. Most resorts have a safe where you can store your moneybelt. You can also avoid becoming utterly destitute by stashing a small amount of cash or a couple of travellers cheques in a separate place to where the bulk is stored.

Costs

Travelling independently in Fiji is good value compared to many Pacific countries. Nevertheless, as tourism is a major industry, entrepreneurs have grown wise to it and – if you're not careful – it can be easy to spend a lot of money. Restaurants, transport and shops can be extremely good value, particularly in more remote areas, however, anything geared for tourists is far more pricey. On average, budget travellers can expect to pay about $50 to $75 per day for food, transport and accommodation. If you stay in dorms and dine on corned beef, you can do it for cheaper. Island hopping is generally fairly pricey; if you're planning to move around a lot, expenses will go up. It's good to plan your route to avoid backtracking. Diving will obviously drive your costs skyward. See also the Accommodation and Food sections later in this chapter.

If you're on a tight budget, self-catering can be a good option; try local markets for fruit and veg. Carry lots of small bills as many vendors and hole-in-the-wall restaurants won't have change and may try to keep yours. When looking for a taxi, try for a 'return taxi', on its way back to base (see the Getting Around chapter). And finally, always ask for walk-in rates at hotels – they can be a fraction of the advertised rate.

Tipping & Bargaining

Tipping is not expected or encouraged in Fiji; however, if you feel that the service is worth it, tips are always appreciated. At many resorts you can drop a tip in the 'Staff Christmas Fund' jar.

Indigenous Fijians generally do not like to bargain, however it's customary in Indo-Fijian stores, especially in Nadi and Suva. Indo-Fijian shop owners and taxi drivers

VAT Tax

VAT is charged on most things in Fiji (including accommodation, food and transport). Between the time of research and the time we went to print, the government announced an increase in the VAT from 10% to 12.5%. Prices listed in this book include the 10% VAT, so you may come across slightly higher prices on items or services subject to VAT.

consider it bad luck to lose their first customer of the day, so you can expect an especially hard sales pitch in the morning.

POST & COMMUNICATIONS

Fiji Post & Telecommunications Ltd (w *www.fijipost.com*) is generally quick with its actual posting (if a little slow at the counter) and has offices throughout the country. Post offices are open from 8am to 4pm weekdays and from 9am to noon Saturdays.

Postal Rates

To mail a letter within Fiji costs $0.17. Postcards sent internationally cost $0.25, while letters (up to 30g) cost $0.48 to Australia, $0.96 to Europe, $0.35 to New Zealand, $0.89 to North America and $0.89 to the UK.

Sending Mail

Sending mail is straightforward; by the time you've gotten to the front of the queue, you'll know the process by heart. Surface mail is cheaper but slow; air mail can usually make it to Australia or New Zealand within the week and Europe or North America within 10 days. If you're really in a hurry, there's an international express mail service available through the main post offices.

Receiving Mail

It's possible to receive mail at poste restante counters in all major post offices. Mail is held for up to two months without a charge. It's also possible to receive faxes at Fintel (Fiji International Telecommunications) in Suva and major post offices (see Fax later in this section).

Telephone

You'll find a phone in most mid-range and top-end hotel rooms. While local calls are often free, hefty surcharges are added onto long distance calls. The cheapest way to phone home is by direct dial with a public phonecard; as they have a limited credit, it's also a good way to stop your relatives from chatting away your savings. Phonecards can be purchased at post offices, newsagents and some pharmacies and come in denominations of $3, $5, $10, $20 and $50. You'll find public phones outside the post office but they're generally just for decor (they're rarely functioning). You'll also find them at resorts and around town. Fintel, in downtown Suva, also provides an international phone service.

Before you leave, check with your phone company at home; many have local numbers in Fiji that'll put you through to an operator in your home country. You can then call collect or charge your call to a calling card.

There are no area codes within Fiji. Be aware that national calls are charged according to time. Rates on public phones are $0.20 per three minutes for a local call; around $0.20 per 45 seconds between neighbouring towns; and $0.20 for each 15 seconds for more distant calls (eg, Nadi to Suva or between islands). Collect calls are more expensive and, when using operator assistance, there's a minimum charge of three minutes plus a surcharge of $1.20 applies.

Most towns have automatic telephone exchanges, however, some remote areas have a manual exchange service. Islands are linked by cable and satellite to worldwide networks.

Vodaphone (☎ *331 2000, fax 331 2007;* w *www.vodafone.com.fj*) is the only mobile phone company in Fiji. It operates a GSM digital service and has roaming agreements with Australia's Telstra, Optus and Vodafone, New Zealand's Bell South and the UK's Vodafone. Ask for rates before you leave home – you may end up paying international rates for local calls. Mobile phones can be rented from some car rental agencies.

Useful numbers include:

Emergency	☎ 911
International collect calls	☎ 031 + number
International directory inquiries	☎ 022
International operator assistance, bookings	☎ 012
Local collect calls	☎ 030 + number
Local directory inquiries	☎ 011
Police (emergency)	☎ 917

The international dial-in code for Fiji is ☎ 679 followed by the local number. To use International Direct Dial (IDD), dial ☎ 00 plus the country code given below. The following rates are per minute:

country	code	rate (F$)
Australia	☎ 61	1.42
Canada	☎ 1	2.40
France	☎ 33	2.40
French Polynesia	☎ 689	1.51
Germany	☎ 49	2.40
Japan	☎ 81	2.40
New Zealand	☎ 64	1.42
Tonga	☎ 676	1.42
USA	☎ 1	2.40
Vanuatu	☎ 678	1.51

ekno Communication Service

Lonely Planet's ekno global communication service provides low-cost international calls – for local calls you're usually better off with a local phonecard. Lonely Planet's ekno also offers free messaging services, email, travel information and an online Travel Vault, where you can securely store all your important documents. You can join online at **w** www.ekno.lonelyplanet.com. The access number in Fiji is ☎ 00 800 7126.

Fax

You can send and receive faxes from major post offices. If you're faxing internationally, try **Fintel** *(☎ 331 2933, fax 330 1025; 158 Victoria Parade; open 8am-8pm Mon-Sat)* in Suva. At post offices, incoming faxes cost $1.20 per page and sending a local/regional/international fax costs $1.65/9.65/12.15 per page. Additional pages are usually a little cheaper. Check out the Fiji Post's website for offices offering fax services *(**w** www.fijipost.com)*.

Email & Internet Access

In Fiji's urban centres, the Internet is the best thing since ready-ground kava; cybercafés are appearing overnight in Suva, Nadi and Lautoka and access is offered in most resorts. Setting up an internet-based email account such as Lonely Planet's ekno is the easiest and most affordable way of keeping in touch while you're on the road. However, be aware that using the Internet isn't particularly cheap anywhere in Fiji and tends to be extortionate in resorts. Expect to pay between $0.10 to $0.25 per minute.

DIGITAL RESOURCES

The Web is a goldmine for travellers. You can research your trip, hunt down bargain air fares, book hotels, check on weather conditions or chat with locals and other travellers about where to go and where to steer clear of.

Lonely Planet *(**w** www.lonelyplanet.com)* has summaries on the ins and outs of travelling to most places on earth as well as postcards from other travellers and the Thorn Tree bulletin board, where you can ask questions before you go or dispense advice when you get back. The website's subwwway section links you to the most useful travel resources elsewhere on the Web.

Try the following websites for useful information on Fiji.

Australian Department of Foreign Affairs & Trade (**w** www.dfat.gov.au/consular/advice) Keeps a close eye on Fijian happenings

Fiji Government (**w** www.fiji.gov.fj) Contains press releases, news and immigration updates

Fiji Post (**w** www.fijipost.com) Fiji's daily newspaper online

Fiji Village (**w** www.fijivillage.com) Geared for overseas Fijians, this site is updated with daily news and has excellent links to local events, including music, movies and sport. The only catch is the US$35 subscription fee.

Fiji Visitors Bureau (**w** www.bulafiji.com) Offers information on accommodation, activities and getting around, with links and an email directory

Fijilive (**w** www.fijilive.com) Live updates on Fijian news

NZ Ministry of Foreign Affairs & Trade (**w** www.mfat.govt.nz) The South Pacific Update is an excellent resource for economic and business news

Pacific Islands Report (**w** pidp.eastwestcenter.org/pireport) An excellent place to get news summaries covering Pacific events

South Pacific Tourism Organisation (**w** www.spto.org) A web travel directory with info on South Pacific countries

BOOKS

Most books are published in different editions by different publishers in different countries. As a result, a book might be a hardcover rarity in one country while it's readily available in paperback in another. Fortunately, bookshops and libraries search by title or author, so your local bookshop or library is best placed to advise you on the availability of the following recommendations. Many of the books listed below can also be ordered online through the **USP Book Centre** (☎ *321 2500, fax 330 3265;* **w** *www.uspbookcentre.com; University of the South Pacific, Suva)* or bought on the campus. Other books can be purchased at the Fiji Museum in Suva.

Lonely Planet

If you're planning on spending much time underwater, Lonely Planet's *Diving & Snorkelling Fiji* is indispensable, with detailed information on over 70 of Fiji's best dive sites as well as the finer points of safety, dive conditions and underwater photography. It's also got lots of colour photos to help you identify those underwater critters. The *Fijian phrasebook* or the *South Pacific phrasebook* will help you chat with locals and the *South Pacific* guidebook is great if you're planning on visiting any of Fiji's South Pacific neighbours. If you've got youngsters in tow, *Travel with Children* is packed with useful information for family travel.

History & Politics

Yalo i Viti (1986), by Fergus Clunie and published by the Fiji Museum, is recommended if artefacts are your thing; it explains the significance of the Fijian object you'll see in the museum.

Exodus of the I Taukei, Lako Yani ni Kawa I Taukei (2002), by Andrew Thornley, is the story of Methodism in Fiji from 1848–78 and considers the impact of missionaries, their collaboration with indigenous Fijians and their modes of evangelism. The book was written as a means of understanding Fiji's contemporary political arena.

For insight into more-recent history, *Broken Waves – A History of the Fiji Islands in the Twentieth Century* (1992) is written by Brij V Lal, a well-informed and respected historian. He also authored *Power and Prejudice – The Making of the Fiji Crisis* (1988), which looks at the coups of the 1980s and their aftermath. *More Letters From Fiji, 1990-1994 – First Years Under a Post-coup Constitution*, by Len Usher, also looks at this period of Fiji's history.

Confronting Fiji's Future (2000) is an academic work that went to print about the same time that Speight initiated the 19 May 2000 coup. It gives a mainly Indo-Fijian perspective of Fijian society over the past couple of decades.

Government by the Gun: the unfinished business of Fiji's 2000 Coup (2001) considers the hows and whys of the 2000 coup by looking more specifically at the development of indigenous Fijian society.

Changing Their Minds: Tradition & Politics in Contemporary Fiji & Tonga (1998) is an intriguing look at how traditions have been created, altered and interwoven into the political scene.

Biography

If you're interested in precolonial history, try to find *Journals of Baron Anatole von Hugel* by Jane Roth & Steven Hooper. Published by the Fiji Museum, it's an interesting account of the baron's experiences of living in Fiji between 1875 and 1879. *The Inheritance of Hope: John Hunt, Apostle of Fiji* (2000), by Andrew Thornley, looks at the life of an English missionary in Fiji from 1839 to 1848.

Life in Feejee, or, Five Years Among the Cannibals (1851), by A Lady (aka Mary Davis Wallis), are the memoirs of the wife of a Yankee trading captain. A reprint can be purchased at the Fiji Museum shop.

My Twenty-One Years in the Fiji Islands, by Totaram Sanadhya, is an interesting first-hand account of the indenture system. Written in the 1910s, a later edition (1991) is available at the Fiji Museum.

Beyond the Black Waters – A Memoir of Sir Sathi Narain (1996), by Satya Colpani, follows Narain's life from when his family migrates from India to Koro to his involvement and politics and position as a prominent Indo-Fijian in industry and business.

Fiction

See Literature in the Arts section of the Facts about Fiji for contemporary fiction by locals. *South Pacific Literature: From Myth to Fabulation* (1992), published by the Institute of Pacific Studies, is a survey of Pacific Islanders and their work and has an extensive bibliography.

Fiji (1988), by Daryl Tarte, is the ultimate trashy Fijian novel, a sprawling saga following over a century of Fijian history through the experiences of a plantation family. Based on the Tarte family of Taveuni, it's an easy read and dips into a wide range of historical subjects.

Veiled Honour, by Satya Colpani, is a novel set in Fiji during the postcolonial era and, with a cast of characters from many backgrounds, is the story of conflict between family duty and the desire for freedom.

Traditional Culture

Myths and Legends of Fiji and Rotuma (1967), by AW Reed & Inez Hames, has lots of short stories with characters such as the powerful shark-god Dakuwaqa and the great snake-god Degei.

Holy Torture (1974), by Muneshwar Sanadeo, is a glimpse into the rituals of Indo-Fijians, starring knives, oil, fire and resistance to pain. *Kato'aga: Rotuman Ceremonies*, by Elizabeth Inia, explores the rituals, spirituality and chants of Rotuman.

For a look at traditional indigenous Fijian healing practices, read *The Straight Path of the Spirit: Ancestral Wisdom and Healing Traditions in Fiji* (1999) by Richard Katz. *Secrets of Fijian Medicine*, by MA Weiner, will give you an insight into the traditional uses of plants while *Traditional Handicrafts of Fiji* (1997), by Tabualevu, Uluinaceva & Raimua, looks at weaving, pottery and *masi*.

For boatspotters, *Traditional Sailing Canoes in Lau* (1993) by Gillett, Ianelli, Waqaratoqu & Qaica, has photos and construction details of the vessels.

Contemporary Society

My Village, My World: Everyday Life in Nadoria (2001), by Solomoni Biturogoiwasa, a villager of the Rewa Delta, describes village life within the context of modern Fiji. Asesela Raviwu's *Development or Dependence: The Pattern of Change in Fijian Villages* considers the unanticipated, negative aspects of modernisation on Fijian villages. *Moving Through the Streets* (1994) looks at the lifestyles of Fijian teenagers in Suva and the challenges they face.

Living on the Fringe (2000), by Winston Halapua, describes the continued displacement of Fijian descendents of Melanesians brought to Fiji as plantation labourers in the 1800s.

Photography

Children of the Sun (1996), photos by Glen Craig and poetry by Bryan McDonald, is Fiji's most popular coffee-table book. The stunning photography of smiling locals in front of spectacular landscapes was taken over an eight-year period on Craig's many visits to Fiji. You should be able to find a copy at the FVB, the museum or USP's bookstore.

Fiji, the Uncharted Sea, by Frederico Busonero, has great underwater photography. *Rotuma, Fiji's Hidden Paradise* (1996), by Ian Osborn, has beautiful photos that will have you packing your bags for this remote island group.

Environment

Fiji – Beneath the Surface (2000), by Professor Patrick Nunn, is an interesting compilation of 52 articles about the Fiji environment and its mysteries. The articles appeared as weekly columns in the *Fiji Times*.

FILMS

Both the original 1948 *Blue Lagoon*, starring Jean Simmons, and the 1979 remake with Brooke Shields, were shot in the Yasawa islands. Milla Jovovich came back to film *Return to the Blue Lagoon* on Taveuni in 1991.

More recently, the 2001 blockbuster *Cast Away*, starring Tom Hanks, was filmed on Monuriki in the Mamanuca Group – not nearly so far from civilisation as the film would have you believe. To follow in Tom's footsteps, see the Activities section in the Mamanuca Group chapter.

If you've seen *Contact* with Jodie Foster and are wondering where 'heaven' really lies, that scene was aptly filmed in Fiji too.

The FVB sells various videos promoting the Fiji islands.

NEWSPAPERS & MAGAZINES

The *Fiji Times*, founded in Levuka in 1869, is the oldest newspaper in the country and also claims to be 'the first newspaper published in the world' each day, due to its proximity to the International Date Line. The *Fiji Times* also publishes the newspapers *Nai Lalaki* in Fijian, and *Shanti Dut* in Fiji-Hindi. The *Daily Post*, established in 1987 is also published as *Nai Volasiga* in Fijian. Magazines include *Pacific Islands Monthly* and *Island Business*, which cover regional issues, and the *Review*, which is Fiji-oriented.

Australian newspapers (at least a few days old) are available at some Suva newsagents for an inflated price. If you're a news fanatic, it's easier (and cheaper) to have a quick look at your home paper's website.

Freedom of the Press

The eight different governments that have passed through Fiji's parliament over the past 18 years have each tried their hand at controlling the country's media. So far, Fiji's journalists have managed to emerge from the political upheaval muzzle-free, with a media touted by the World Press Freedom Review as among the most free and robust in the South Pacific. It's been far from easy – during coups, journalists have been attacked and arrested without charge, television stations have been looted and newspapers have been temporarily shut down. While journalists aren't subject to any specific laws that could bar press freedom, access to information is strictly guarded by the government and many journalists are ruled by a social code of ethics that makes questioning or criticising chiefs a tricky business.

Fiji's media have managed to safeguard their much heralded freedom and fend off the clutches of government through the Fiji Media Council, an independent, united front of journalists from competing companies and all backgrounds. In Fiji's difficult political climate, unity spells good news.

Refer to the Tourist Offices section earlier in this chapter for details of magazines that may contain some useful information for travellers to Fiji.

RADIO & TV

The government-sponsored Fiji Broadcasting Commission has stations in English (Radio Fiji 3 and FM 104), Fijian (Radio Fiji 1) and Fiji-Hindi (Radio Fiji 2 and 98 FM).

The ever-popular Bula 100 plays an eclectic mix of pop, rock, reggae and dance with some unlikely Anne Murray, Phil Collins and Bee Gees thrown in. Tune in for the World Chart Show, Take 40 Australia, Roots Rhythm and UK Top 10. The station also plays 10% local content: listen for Seru Serevi, Danny Costello, Michelle Rounds, Karuana Gopalan, The Freelancers and The Black Roses.

The independent commercial station FM 96 began as Communications Fiji Limited in 1985. It has 24-hour broadcasting with music, sports and community information in English and Fiji-Hindi.

Radio Pacific (FM 88.8), managed by the USP Student Association, began broadcasting in May 1996. Student volunteers host programmes with music and information from different Pacific countries, as well as some academic programmes. The government licence binds them to avoid political and religious topics.

Fiji received its first TV transmission in October 1991, when Television New Zealand played a live telecast of World Cup rugby matches. The Fiji Television Company received its licence in August 1993. There is just one station – appropriately named Fiji One – however it plays 90% foreign sitcoms and serials. Check the *Fiji Times* or the fortnightly *TV Guide* magazine for programming. Cable TV was introduced in 1996.

VIDEO SYSTEMS

The various video systems – PAL, NTSC and Secam – are incompatible. The system used in Fiji is PAL G, as in Australia and New Zealand. Unless you're content to just sit and watch the cover, ensure that any video purchases you make are compatible with the system in your home country.

PHOTOGRAPHY

Film & Equipment

Fiji is extremely photogenic. While film and photography equipment is readily available, it's often best to bring dependable film from home. Always check expiry dates and, if intending to take lots of shots, buy 36-exposure film which will be less bulky to carry. For most conditions, 100 ISO will be good; 400 ISO film is better for darker, forest conditions. There are labs with same-day processing services in Nadi, Lautoka and Suva.

Unless you're a serious photographer, weight and simplicity of operation are the biggest factors. While photos from throwaway cameras aren't likely to lead you into a career in photography, they are surprisingly good quality, have underwater options and release you from any stress about losing expensive equipment.

For more earnest travel photography (portraits, landscapes, architecture, wildlife and macro shots), it's best to have equipment that gives you flexibility. An SLR camera with a combination wide angle and zoom lens is great. Make sure your equipment and flash are working well, take spare batteries and consider bringing a polariser.

Don't leave your camera gear exposed to the sun, heat, humidity or salty sea air; fungal growth on camera lenses isn't uncommon in the tropics. If you plan to stay in Fiji or the tropics for more than a few weeks, it may be a good idea to keep equipment in airtight containers with activated silica gel (available at pharmacies). If travelling around in small boats, definitely store your camera and film in a waterproof bag or container.

Technical Tips

Fiji's midday sun can be bright and harsh, leading to overexposed photos, so you'll need to adjust your camera settings accordingly. The best light conditions are generally in the early morning and late afternoon. People can often turn out as silhouettes on overly bright backgrounds; it's sometimes best to overexpose your photos, or, if your camera has one, to employ the contrast- adjustment setting. A flash can also be used to highlight the foreground. Check out Lonely Planet's *Travel Photography: A Guide to Taking Better Pictures* for more useful tips.

Restrictions At a *yaqona* ceremony you will normally have to wait until after the formal ritual before taking photos; always ask first. Don't wander around villages photographing and filming people's private space, unless invited. Try not to flash expensive gear around.

Underwater Photography Novelty cameras are a fun introduction to underwater photography. Some resorts and dive centres offer underwater cameras for hire, with tuition and sometimes processing facilities. Special underwater cameras are an expensive investment. Alternatively, standard cameras can be used with special waterproof housings and an underwater strobe flash, or, on sunny days, with underwater slide film. As a general rule, close-up shots will be more successful. Give preference to high shutter speeds to avoid camera shake and blurred fish. Water absorbs certain wavelengths, and red filters can be used to reduce the exaggerated blue. If you are bringing your own equipment, make sure your lights can be charged on 240V, or bring a converter.

VIDEO

Make sure you are familiar with your camera and its limitations. For a successful travel video, consider light conditions and avoid glare, panning too quickly and camera shudder. Try to avoid filming in the wind as it can drown out any commentary and sound like a lot of racket. Take precautions to protect your gear from humidity, heat and sea air.

TIME

The concept of time in Fiji is fairly flexible ('Fiji time'), so don't get too stressed if people are not punctual for appointments or if transport is running late (or early); just go with the flow.

Although the 180° meridian passes through the Fiji archipelago, the International Date Line doglegs so that all Fiji islands lie to the west of it. Fiji is 12 hours ahead of GMT/UTC. Daylight is from about 6am to 6pm. Fiji introduced daylight savings (from November to February) relatively recently, in part to be in the running to be the first country to see in the new millennium! There was intense rivalry between competing countries, which include Tonga and Kiribati.

When it's noon in Suva, corresponding times elsewhere are as follows:

same day	time
Sydney	10am
New Caledonia & Vanuatu	11am
Auckland	noon
Tonga	1pm

previous day	time
London	midnight
Samoa	1pm
San Francisco	4pm
New York	7pm

Subtract one hour from these times if the other country does not have daylight savings in place.

ELECTRICITY

Electricity is supplied at 240V, 50 Hz AC. Many remote areas and island resorts rely on solar and generator power. It is best to buy adaptors prior to leaving home. Many of the resorts and hotels have universal outlets for 240V or 110V shavers and hair dryers. Outlets are of the three-pin type and use flat two- or three-pin plugs.

WEIGHTS & MEASURES

Fiji follows the metric system, with distance measured in kilometres, goods bought in kilograms or litres, and temperature registered in degrees Celsius. Refer to the conversion chart on this book's inside back cover.

LAUNDRY

Most resorts and hotels will do your laundry for a small fee. A load is normally about $5, although some places will charge by item, which can become costly. People travelling away from cities, towns and resorts may wish to carry laundry soap and a scrubbing brush, although village stores usually stock these items. In rural areas, women sit down in the creeks or rivers fully clothed to do their washing. Same-day laundry and dry-cleaning services are available in Nadi and Suva. Consult the telephone directory (Fiji's *Yellow Pages*).

TOILETS

Toilets are the sit-down type with public toilets in cities and larger towns, hotels and resorts, and sometimes near small groups of shops on country roads. It's a good idea to carry an emergency supply of toilet paper.

Most remote villages don't have toilets, and the local creek is used for washing. Ask about the local bathing customs, don't just strip off near the village. For a toilet, make do with the bush or the beach, making sure you are a suitable distance from any creeks or rivers, and bury your toilet paper.

HEALTH

Travel health depends on your predeparture preparations, your daily health care while travelling and how you handle any medical problem that may develop. While the potential dangers can seem quite frightening, in reality few travellers experience anything more than upset stomachs.

Those arriving directly from a temperate climate may initially find the tropical heat and humidity a bit overwhelming. Fiji is malaria-free, though some other Pacific countries, such as Vanuatu, have the disease. Obtain a doctor's advice about antimalarials if you also plan to visit such countries. There are occasional outbreaks of dengue fever and filariasis in Fiji (both are mosquito-transmitted diseases). Hepatitis A and B also occur in Fiji.

Predeparture Planning

Immunisations No jabs are required for travel to Fiji, unless you have been travelling in a part of the world where yellow fever may be prevalent. Ensure that your normal childhood vaccinations (polio, tetanus, diptheria) are up-to-date. Plan ahead for getting vaccinations; some of them require more than one injection, while some vaccinations should not be given together, during pregnancy or to people with allergies – discuss with your doctor.

Also consider vaccinations for Hepatitis A and B and tuberculosis (TB).

Health Insurance Make sure that you have adequate health insurance, especially if you plan to go diving. See Travel Insurance under Visas & Documents earlier in this chapter for details.

Travel Health Guides Lonely Planet's *Healthy Travel Australia, New Zealand & the Pacific* is a handy pocket-sized book and is packed with useful information including pretrip planning, emergency first aid, immunisation and disease information and what to do if you get sick on the road. *Travel with Children,* from Lonely Planet, also includes advice on travel health for younger children.

Other Preparations Make sure you're healthy before you start travelling. If you are going on a long trip make sure your teeth are OK. If you wear glasses take a spare pair and your prescription.

If you require a particular medication take an adequate supply, as it may not be available locally. Take part of the packaging showing the generic name rather than the brand, which will make getting replacements easier. It's a good idea to have a legible prescription or letter from your doctor to show that you legally use the medication to avoid any problems.

Basic Rules

Food Vegetables and fruit should be washed with purified water or peeled where possible. Beware of ice cream that is sold in the street or anywhere else it might have been melted and refrozen; if there's any doubt (eg, a power cut in the last day or two), steer well clear. Shellfish such as mussels, oysters and clams should be avoided, as should undercooked meat, particularly in the form of mince. Steaming does not make shellfish safe for eating.

Ciguatera This is a type of food poisoning caused by eating tropical and subtropical fish that have accumulated certain toxins through their diet. The toxins are contained in algae, which is eaten by smaller reef fish, which are in turn the prey of larger fish. It is best to avoid eating big reef predators such as snapper, barracuda and grouper. Ocean fish such as tuna, wahoo and Spanish mackerel are safe to eat, and small reef fish that the locals eat and recommend should be OK.

The symptoms of ciguatera poisoning include nausea, vomiting, diarrhoea and stomach cramps, alternating fevers and chills, and tingling in the skin and mouth. A feeling of weak muscles and joints and aching pain in the fingers and feet may sometimes last weeks or even months. Hot may feel cold and vice versa.

Water The water in Fiji's major towns, hotels and resorts is generally safe to drink, but the same cannot be said of all villages and islands. The water supply in the Rakiraki area in northern Viti Levu has been deemed unsafe. Many of the resort islands of the Mamanucas pipe or barge their water from the mainland.

The number one rule is *be careful of the water* and especially ice. If you don't know for certain that the water is safe, err on the side of caution. Take care with fruit juice, particularly if water may have been added. Milk should be treated with suspicion as it is often unpasteurised, though boiled milk is fine if it is kept hygienically. Tea or coffee should also be OK, as the water should have been boiled.

Water Purification The simplest way of purifying water is to boil it thoroughly.

For a long trip, consider purchasing a water filter, either a 'total filter', which takes out all parasites, bacteria and viruses and makes water safe to drink; or simple filters (which can even be a nylon mesh bag). Simple filters take out dirt and larger foreign bodies from the water so that chemical solutions work much more effectively; if water is dirty, chemical solutions may not work at all. Simple filtering will not remove all dangerous organisms, so if you cannot boil water it should be treated chemically. Chlorine tablets will kill many pathogens, but not some parasites like giardia and amoebic cysts. Iodine is more effective in purifying water and is available in tablet form. Follow the directions carefully and remember that too much iodine can be harmful.

Environmental Hazards

Heat Exhaustion Dehydration and salt deficiency can cause heat exhaustion. Take some time to acclimatise to high temperatures and make sure you drink sufficient liquids – don't rely on feeling thirsty to indicate when you should drink. Not needing to urinate or dark yellow urine is a danger sign. Remember to always carry a water bottle with you on long trips.

Salt deficiency is characterised by fatigue, lethargy, headaches, giddiness and muscle cramps; salt tablets may help, but adding a little extra salt to your food is better.

Heatstroke This serious, occasionally fatal, condition can occur if the body's heat-regulating mechanism breaks down and body temperature rises to dangerous levels. Long, continuous periods of exposure to high temperatures and insufficient fluids can leave you vulnerable to heatstroke.

The symptoms are feeling unwell, not sweating very much (or at all) and a high body temperature (39° to 41°C or 102° to 106°F). Where sweating has ceased, the skin becomes flushed and red.

Severe, throbbing headaches and lack of coordination will also occur, and the sufferer may be confused or aggressive. Eventually the victim will become delirious or convulse. Hospitalisation is essential, but in the interim get victims out of the sun, remove their clothing, cover them with a wet sheet or towel and then fan continually. Give fluids if they are conscious.

Prickly Heat This itchy rash is caused by excessive perspiration trapped under the skin. It usually strikes people who have just arrived in a hot climate. Keeping cool, bathing often, drying the skin and using a mild talcum or prickly heat powder or resorting to air-conditioning may help.

Sunburn You can get sunburnt surprisingly quickly, even through cloud. Use sunscreen, a hat, and barrier cream for your nose and lips. Calamine lotion or Stingose are good for relieving mild sunburn. Protect your eyes with good-quality sunglasses, particularly if you will be near water and sand a lot.

Infectious Diseases

Diarrhoea Simple things like a change of water, food or climate can all cause a mild bout of diarrhoea, but a few rushed toilet trips with no other symptoms is not indicative of a major problem.

Dehydration is the main danger with any diarrhoea, particularly in children or the elderly. Under all circumstances, fluid replacement (at least equal to the volume being lost) is the most important thing to remember. Weak black tea with a little sugar, soda water, or soft drinks allowed to go flat and diluted 50% with clean water are all good. With severe diarrhoea a rehydrating solution is preferable to replace minerals and salts lost. Commercially available oral rehydration salts (ORS) are very useful; add them to boiled or bottled water. In an emergency you can make up a solution of six teaspoons of sugar and a half teaspoon of salt to a litre of boiled or bottled water. Keep drinking small amounts often. And stick to a bland diet as you recover.

Seek medical help urgently if you experience any of the following: diarrhoea with blood or mucus (dysentery), any diarrhoea with fever, profuse watery diarrhoea, or severe or persistent diarrhoea.

Fungal Infections These infections occur more commonly in hot weather and are usually found on the scalp, between the toes (athlete's foot) or fingers, in the groin and on the body (ringworm). You get ringworm (which is a fungal infection, not a worm) from infected animals or other people. Moisture encourages these infections.

To prevent fungal infections, wear loose, comfortable clothes, avoid artificial fibres, wash frequently and dry yourself carefully. If you do get an infection, wash the infected area at least daily with a disinfectant or medicated soap and water, and rinse and dry well. Apply an antifungal cream or powder like tolnaftate (Tinaderm). Try to expose the infected area to air or sunlight as much as possible and wash all towels and underwear in hot water – change them often and let them dry in the sun.

Cuts, Bites & Stings

Bites & Stings Bee and wasp stings are usually painful rather than dangerous. However, for people who are allergic to them, severe breathing difficulties may occur and require urgent medical care. Calamine lotion or Stingose spray will give relief and ice packs will reduce the pain and swelling.

The sting of certain cone shells can be dangerous or even fatal. There are various fish and other sea creatures that have harmful stings or bites or are toxic to eat – seek local advice.

Cuts & Scratches Skin punctures can easily become infected in hot climates and may be difficult to heal. Wash well and treat any cut with an antiseptic such as povidone-iodine. Where possible avoid bandages and Band-Aids, which can keep wounds wet. If the sore is not healing and starts spreading, consult a doctor as antibiotics may be needed. Coral cuts are notoriously slow to heal and if they are not adequately cleaned, small pieces of coral are likely to remain embedded in the wound.

Avoiding Mosquito Bites

While malaria is not a significant risk in Fiji, several other potentially serious mosquito-borne diseases do occur. Travellers are best to avoid mosquito bites at all times (both to avoid diseases such as dengue and for general comfort!). The main messages are:

- Wear light-coloured clothing.
- Wear long trousers and long-sleeved shirts.
- Use mosquito repellents containing the compound DEET on exposed areas of your body (prolonged overuse of DEET may be harmful, especially to children, but its use is considered preferable to being bitten by mosquitoes that transmit diseases).
- Avoid perfumes or aftershave.
- Use a mosquito net impregnated with mosquito repellent (permethrin) – it may be worth taking your own.
- Impregnate clothes with permethrin, which deters mosquitoes and other insects.

Dengue Fever This viral disease is transmitted by mosquitoes. Generally, there is only a small risk to travellers except during epidemics, which are usually seasonal (during and just after the rainy season).

The *Aedes aegypti* mosquito, which transmits the dengue virus, is most active during the day, unlike the malaria mosquito, and is found mainly in urban areas, in and around human dwellings.

Signs and symptoms of dengue fever include a sudden onset of high fever, headache, joint and muscle pains (hence its old name, 'breakbone fever') and nausea and vomiting. A rash of small red spots appears three to four days after the onset of fever. Dengue is commonly mistaken for other infectious diseases, including malaria and influenza.

You should seek prompt medical attention if you think you may be infected. Aspirin should be avoided, as it increases the risk of haemorrhaging. Recovery may be prolonged, with tiredness lasting for several weeks.

There is no vaccine against dengue fever. The best prevention is to avoid mosquito bites at all times.

Filariasis This is a mosquito-transmitted parasitic infection found in many parts of the Pacific. Travellers aren't at risk – infection requires repeated exposure to the parasite over many, many years – but if you're wondering why some Fijians, particularly those who work in waterlogged agricultural areas, have swollen ankles and legs, it's probably filariasis.

Intestinal Worms These parasites are most common in rural, tropical areas. The different worms have different ways of infecting people. Some may be ingested on food such as undercooked meat (eg, tapeworms) and some enter through the skin (eg, hookworms). Infestations may not show up for some time, and although they are generally not serious, if left untreated some can cause severe health problems later. Consider having a stool test when you return home to check for these and determine the appropriate treatment.

Snakes Fiji's most common snake is the *dadakulaci,* or banded sea krait, and you are likely to see it when snorkelling or diving. Although placid, its venom is three times more potent than that of the Indian cobra. The yellow-bellied sea snake can be aggressive, and the burrowing snake is venomous but seldom seen. To minimise your chances of being bitten do not approach any sea snake, and wear boots, socks and long trousers when walking through undergrowth where snakes may be present. Don't put your hands into holes and crevices, and be careful when collecting firewood.

Snake bites do not cause instantaneous death, and antivenenes are usually available. In the event of a bite, keep the victim calm and still, wrap the bitten limb tightly, as you would for a sprained ankle, and then attach a splint to immobilise it. Then seek medical help. First-aid methods, such as tourniquets and sucking out the poison, are comprehensively discredited.

Jellyfish Heeding local advice is the best way to avoid contact with these sea creatures, which have stinging tentacles. Stings from most jellyfish are rather painful. Dousing in vinegar (or urine) will deactivate any stingers that have not 'fired'. Calamine lotion, antihistamines and analgesics may reduce the reaction and relieve the pain.

SOCIAL GRACES

While indigenous Fijians seem very laid back, their complex codes of behaviour are fairly strictly followed. As a foreigner, Fijians will generally forgive your gaffes in social etiquette, however, you'll get more out of your experiences and are far less likely to offend people if you are aware of local customs. If you are unsure of what's expected, just ask.

If you are travelling with children, Fijians will expect them to be quiet when indoors, and to be respectful of elders.

Staying with a Family

Should you be invited to stay with a Fijian family, prepare yourself for a novel and heart-warming experience. Fijians are masters at entertaining and go out of their way to make guests feel as comfortable as possible.

When you visit an indigenous Fijian family, bring some *yaqona* with you. This is for your *sevusevu* – a formal presentation whereby you request permission to visit the village from the chief and, in effect, the ancestral gods. Also bring a small gift for your hosts from each guest.

Indo-Fijians are also very hospitable. If you're invited to someone's house, you'll certainly be offered a cup of tea and usually a delicious meal. In rural areas, men and women often socialise and eat separately. While many Indo-Fijian men enjoy drinking *yaqona* socially as much as indigenous Fijians, it isn't the custom for guests to bring *yaqona* to an Indo-Fijian home. If you want to bring something, sweets for the kids are usually appreciated. Some men also drink alcohol, often following *yaqona* (called 'washdown'). Women tourists who feel like drinking can be considered honorary men for the occasion.

The custom throughout Fiji is to finish drinking *yaqona* and/or alcohol before the dining. This can result in some very late meals.

In the Village

Try not to show up at a village uninvited, or, if you do, ask the first person you meet if it is possible to visit their village. They will probably take you to see the chief. Never wander around unaccompanied: gardens, backyards and *bure* are someone's private realm. Even in remote areas the land, beaches and reefs are usually owned by a *mataqali* (extended family or land-owning group).

Fijian culture demands that visitors be treated as honoured guests. It is common for villagers to invite visitors into their home and offer food, even if they are very poor. It is polite to accept, and also a good chance to chat with locals. Try to reciprocate hospitality by leaving some basic groceries such as sugar, tea or tinned meat, which you can buy at the village shop. If you intend to travel outside the main tourist areas, consider carrying some small gifts with you.

Always take a *sevusevu* when visiting a village. Around 500g of *taga yaqona* (pounded kava, which costs about $14 per kilogram) is good or, even better, take a bundle of *waka* (kava roots). You'll find kava at markets, service stations and some shops. Don't bring alcohol, some villages ban it. In most villages *yaqona* is drunk every day, but some villages abstain completely, so ask the person taking you on the visit. Request to present the yaqona to the *turaga-ni-koro* (hereditary chief), who will welcome you in a small ceremony on behalf of the village. In this ceremony, the *sevusevu* is presented to the spirits of the ancestors, gaining you permission to visit the village and its land. Wandering around without the *sevusevu* ceremony risks the wrath of the spirits. *Sevusevu* ceremonies usually develop into a friendly *talanoa* (gossip session) around the *yaqona* bowl, so be prepared to recount your life story.

When visiting a *bure* leave your shoes outside. Always enter a *bure* through the back door – the front door is reserved for the head of the house. Stoop when entering (doorways are often low anyway), and quietly sit cross-legged on the pandanus mat. If you are in the presence of someone of high social rank, such as the chief and his family, it is polite to keep your head at a lower level than theirs.

Fijians consider the head private, even sacred, so *never* touch a person's head or hair. Carry your bags in your hands, not over your shoulder and remove your hat and sunglasses when in the village; wearing either is considered extremely rude. It's also offensive to question the authority of a *ratu* (male chief), *adi* (female chief) or *tui* (king), to speak badly of anyone or to criticise people personally. Pushing people to talk about contentious topics such as politics is definitely not the done thing. Don't camp outside if you have been offered a place to sleep inside a home; it can embarrass the hosts if they think their *bure* is not good enough. It's also important to dress appropriately in a village; see Dress later.

It is unusual for villagers to use a tourist unreasonably as a source of money, but it can happen. The greater danger is of tourists taking advantage of Fijian hospitality, often unintentionally. If you do stay in a village, contribute food or money (about $10 per day to cover your costs). When taken somewhere by private boat always offer to pay your share to cover fuel costs. As a rule Fijians are exceptionally polite and will not ask you for money, but will let you know if you are behaving in an insensitive manner or if you have overstayed your welcome.

Because of the custom of *kerekere*, or shared property, children or even adults may ask you for your shoes, jewellery or other travelling gear. If you don't want to give the item away, you can usually get out of awkward situations by saying that you can't do without it. Try not to flash around expensive items that are beyond the reach of villagers.

The Trouble with Kava

Kava drinking is as much a part of Fiji as beaches and *bure*. *Burau*, a ceremonial kava-drinking ritual, was originally a daily rite in days of yore. In those days, kava drinking was the prerogative of chiefs, priests and important male elders. The priest knelt on the floor to drink the liquid from a shallow *tanoa* bowl, made of either pottery or sacred *vesi* timber. As it was tabu (taboo) for priests to touch food or drink with their hands, they'd often suck the kava through a straw.

Late in the 18th century, Tongan's passed along new ways of drinking kava to the Fijians. Kava started to be served using coconut-shell cups and deep, wooden *tanoa* bowls, and was consumed in a less formal and more social circle ritual – much how it's dished up today. The long plaited cords on kava bowls, studded with egg-cowry (a symbol of divine fertility), and extending from the kava bowl to the chief, are a relatively recent addition and form a link with the spirits. If the link is broken (ie if you step over the cord), it's believed that the spirits will mete out a deadly sentence.

The original Fijian *burau* ceremony was an essential part of the old religion, and therefore condemned and brought to a halt by the missionaries. The circle rituals were tolerated, however, as these rituals didn't have the *burau's* restrictions on who could and couldn't drink it, everyone and his dog began swigging the murky beverage, and still do today.

After drinking your first cup of kava, you may well wonder why. Rest assured, it's not simply for that furry feeling you develop on your tongue, nor for the numb lips or even for the steadily dulled brainwaves. Kava has properties that combat depression, reduce anxiety, and lower blood pressure – news that spread like wildfire through health-obsessed Western countries in the 1990s. Kava quickly became in high demand and when trade peaked in 1998, Fiji and neighbouring Vanuatu were exporting US$25 million worth of the stuff each year.

But the good times didn't last. A German study done in 2001 indicated that kava potentially caused liver damage and by November of 2002, most of Europe as well as Canada and the USA had either banned or put harsh warnings and restrictions on kava. Trade disappeared and Fijian farmers lost their means of supplementing their subsistence lifestyles with money for school fees and petrol. There was little left to do but drown their sorrows in some good kava-drinking sessions.

Reviews later revealed that the vast majority of individuals examined in the German study were using other drugs that affect the liver, yet the bans remain. Pro-kava activists claim that the positive properties of kava are proving too competitive for the major pharmaceutical companies. Others claim that Western chemists haven't had enough experience working with kava, extracting it or prescribing it.

What *is* the trouble with kava? Its taste, perhaps, but with each cup you down, you're less likely to care.

Around the kava bowl – Alexander Turnbull Library, Te Puna Matauranga o Aotearoa

Many locals think that all tourists are wealthy and that the standard of living is much higher in other countries. Travellers are often asked to become a pen pal or even to sponsor someone to migrate. If you are not keen, a polite refusal should be OK.

Sunday is considered a day of rest when families spend time together and attend church. Visits by travellers may not be appreciated by the chief.

Yaqona Drinking

Yaqona, otherwise known as kava, is an infusion prepared from the root of *Piper methysticum*, a type of pepper plant. It holds a place of prominence in Fijian culture – in the time of the 'old religion' it was used ceremonially by chiefs and priests only. Today *yaqona* is drunk socially as part of daily life, not only in villages but across the different races and in urban areas. 'Having a grog' is used for welcoming and bonding with visitors, for storytelling sessions or merely for passing time. Soon after your arrival in Fiji you will be offered a drink of kava. When visiting a village you will usually be welcomed with a short *sevusevu* ceremony, where you will be initiated into kava-culture.

There are certain protocols to be followed at a kava ceremony and in many villages it is still a spiritual experience. Sit cross-legged, facing the chief and the *tanoa*, or large wooden bowl. Women usually sit behind the men and won't get offered the first drink unless they are the guest of honour. Never walk across the circle of participants, turn your back to the *tanoa* or step over the cord that leads from the *tanoa* to a white cowry (it represents a link with the spirits).

The drink is prepared in the *tanoa*. The dried and powdered root, wrapped in a piece of cloth, is mixed with water and the resulting concoction looks like muddy water. You will then be offered a drink from a *bilo* (half a coconut shell). Clap once, accept the *bilo*, say '*bula*' (meaning 'cheers' or, literally, 'life'), and drink it all in one go (best to get it over with quickly anyway!). Clap three times in gratification. The drink will be shared until the *tanoa* is empty. You are not obligated to drink every *bilo* offered to you, but it is polite to drink at least the first.

Yaqona is a mild narcotic and has been used as a diuretic and stress reliever for pharmaceutical purposes. Despite a huge amount of build-up from other travellers, it's not *that* awful tasting (kind of like a murky medicine) and the most you're likely to feel from one *bilo* is a furry tongue. After a few drinks you may feel a slight numbness of the lips. Long sessions, however, with stronger mixes can make you drowsy and very relaxed and some heavy drinkers develop *kanikani*, or scaly skin.

Dress

Precolonial Fijian adults wore very little and children ran around naked. Girls from about seven to puberty used a skimpy apron, and afterwards the short *liku*, the skirt of womanhood (made out of grass or strips of pandanus leaves). Men wore just the *malo*, a loincloth. The missionaries were aghast at this wardrobe and imposed a puritanical dress code that stuck. Today, indigenous Fijian women generally wear long dresses with sleeves and underskirts, and men wear shirts and *sulu* (skirts to below the knees), or long pants. Similarly, most Indo-Fijian women cover up in long saris. The dress code in the urban centres is not so strict, with a mix of traditional and Western styles.

Men and women are expected to dress modestly. You will rarely see adult Fijians swimming and when they do they cover up with a T-shirt and sulu. Western-style bathers are fine at resorts, but in other areas, avoid offence by using a sulu to below the knee and a T-shirt to cover your shoulders. This applies to both men and women. Don't swim or sunbathe naked or topless, unless at an exclusive or remote resort. See Women Travellers in this chapter.

When you're in a village be careful not to offend the chief by wearing a hat or cap – if you want protection from the sun, use sunblock, look for a shady tree or use an umbrella. It's also rude to wear sunglasses, especially when meeting people.

Socialising

It is rare to see public displays of affection between men and women so curtail your passions in public to avoid embarrassing or offending locals.

Indo-Fijian Temples

Refrain from eating meat on the day you intend to visit a Hindu temple and remove your shoes before you enter.

Photography

Fijians are usually happy to have their photo taken (or are too polite to say no anyway) but always ask first. Consider sending photos as a thank-you present for villagers' hospitality. You will normally have to wait until after the formal ritual of a *sevusevu* ceremony before taking photos in a village; ask first.

WOMEN TRAVELLERS

Attitudes Towards Women

Domestic violence is a serious problem in Fiji with sexual abuse and violence on the rise. Progress made by national and international women's pressure groups has deteriorated since the coup of 2000 with economic hardship seen as a major contributor. Violence against women occurs in both the Indo-Fijian and indigenous Fijian communities. In many indigenous areas, a *bolubolu* ceremony is still legally accepted as a reason not to charge convicted rapists and abusers. *Bolubolu* is the traditional form of apology and reconciliation. The father of the victim often receives the apology.

As a traveller, it is highly unlikely that you will witness or experience this side of society. Be aware, however, that men in this environment may view the influence of Western women as a threat to their own position and therefore might discourage their wives from talking with you.

In general, women travellers will find Fijian men friendly and helpful, especially if you are travelling with a male partner. You'll be treated with more respect by both men and women if you follow the local dress codes (see Social Graces earlier in this chapter).

If you're travelling alone, you may experience whistles and stares but you're unlikely to feel threatened. Nevertheless, some men will assume lone females are fair game and several female readers have complained of being harassed or ripped off, particularly in touristy areas. You may even strike the opposite problem of being totally ignored, especially by Indo-Fijian men. If you get a blank response when trying to get information or buy a ticket, seek help from someone who does acknowledge your existence. Nobody should walk alone on the streets of Suva after dark, particularly women. Even if you're in a group, it's safer to take a taxi.

Try to ask local women for practical advice if you are unsure of how to act; if you can't get a response, attempt to follow their lead. Meeting Fijian women is definitely easier in larger towns than in the villages, where you are unlikely to get much more than a friendly smile.

Safety Precautions

Here are a few tips:

- Follow your instincts; if you feel unsafe or uncomfortable with someone, leave
- Don't hitchhike
- Avoid walking at night, particularly alone and especially in Nadi and Suva
- Don't go drinking with Fijian men, however friendly they are to begin with. It's rare but the friendliness may be false and you could end up losing your wallet.
- Wearing a wedding ring may deter unwelcome comments or advances
- Draw the curtains! There are 'window shoppers' in some rural areas. It's also common for men to appear at a woman's window if he's interested in her.

What to Wear

The Fijian dress code is conservative, especially in the rural areas. Although you can get away with it in a resort, a woman in a short skirt, brief shorts or sleeveless top is unusual anywhere else and will attract lots of attention. Indo-Fijian women generally wear long saris and indigenous Fijian women wear big floral caftans down to the ankles. In Suva the code is slightly more liberal. To avoid hassles, respect the local dress code and cover your knees and shoulders. Refer to Social Graces in this chapter for local attitudes to dress and behaviour.

Organisations

There are several women's organisations where you can meet local women, including the following.

Fiji WIP Project – National Council of Women (☎ 331 1880) Stinson Parade, Suva

Fiji Women's Crisis Centre (☎ 331 3300 88 Gordon St Suva • ☎ 814 609, Labasa • ☎ 665 0500, Lautoka)

Fiji Women's Rights Movement (☎ 331 3156) 88 Narseys Bldg, Renwick Rd, Suva. This prominent community organisation deals with issues such as domestic violence, women in trade unions and women's legal rights. It also assists rape victims

Women's Action for Change (☎ 331 4363) 350 Waimanu Rd, Suva

DAVID WALL

View from Monuriki, the Mamanucas

CASEY & ASTRID WITTE MAHANEY

A formal kava ceremony

DAVID WALL

Suva Market

PHIL WEYMOUTH

Dive school, South Beach, Mana

CASEY & ASTRID WITTE MAHANEY

White-tip reef shark, Savusavu Bay, Vanua Levu

DAVE LEVITT

Blue ribbon eel, Kadavu island

CASEY & ASTRID WITTE MAHANEY

Porcelain crab, Bligh Water, Vanua Levu

CASEY & ASTRID WITTE MAHANEY

Snorkelling offshore

CASEY & ASTRID WITTE MAHANEY

Diving in the Kadavu Group

GAY & LESBIAN TRAVELLERS

Fiji's constitution states that discrimination must not occur on the basis of sexual orientation and, precoup, Chaudhry's government was all for legalising homosexual activity. This has brought about heated arguments from the present conservative and very Christian government. In 2002, a new Family Law bill was put forward, once again sparking the debate of legalising homosexuality and same-sex marriages. Sadly, the publicity surrounding the debate has brought greater hostility towards homosexuals in Fiji, with two prominent gay men (the Red Cross leader John Scott and his partner) murdered in July of 2002.

Public displays of affection are considered offensive in Fiji in general; as a gay or lesbian couple, the risks of receiving unwanted attention for outwardly homosexual behaviour are high. In general, as long as you are relatively private, you should feel safe travelling around Fiji.

Organisations

For pretrip planning advice consult the latest *Spartacus International Gay Guide* and *Outrage* magazines. Both **w** www.travelandtranscendence.com and **w** mygayweb.com list gay-friendly accommodation and nightclubs and have bulletin boards for travellers' questions and advise. Also check out **w** www.qrd.org and **w** www.planetout.com.

DISABLED TRAVELLERS

In Pacific countries disabled people are simply part of the community, looked after by family where necessary. In some cities there are schools for disabled children but access facilities, such as ramps, lifts and braille, are rare. Many resorts are designed with multiple levels, lots of stairs and sandy paths, making them difficult for some people to manoeuvre on. Buses do not have wheelchair access and pavements have high kerbs.

Nevertheless, people will go out of their way to give you assistance when you need it. Airports and some hotels and resorts have reasonable access; before booking a particular resort, check if it suits your needs. Access-friendly resorts include Tokatoka Resort Hotel and Beachside Resort in Nadi and Treasure Island Resort in the Mamanucas. Hideaway Resort on the Coral Coast, Viti Levu will also cater to special needs.

Organisations

For pretrip planning advice try the Internet and disabled people's associations in your home country. The **Fiji Disabled People's Association** *(☎ 331 1203, fax 332 1428; 355 Waimanu Rd, Suva)* may also be able to provide advice.

SENIOR TRAVELLERS

Fiji is a good place for senior travellers. It is relatively disease-free and has many options for transport and accommodation. You can choose to stay at resorts, take tours, travel in groups or roam around independently. It is easy to hire vehicles and explore the larger islands. Some travel agents offer discounts for groups or those with a seniors card. For pretrip planning advice, try senior-traveller associations in your home country.

TRAVEL WITH CHILDREN

Fiji is a major family destination and is very child-friendly. Some resorts cater specifically for children, with babysitting, cots and high chairs, organised activities and children's pools. However, many smaller exclusive resorts do not accept children or relegate them to a specific period during the year. Some resorts have lots of levels and sand paths, which make using prams and strollers difficult. Larger resorts that are well set up for kids include Shangri-La's Fijian Resort on Viti Levu's Coral Coast, Plantation Island Resort in the Mamanucas and Jean-Michel Cousteau Fiji Islands Resort on Vanua Levu. Tokatoka Resort Hotel is near Nadi International Airport and good for those awaiting flights.

Travelling around with kids is fairly easy. Some car-rental companies will provide baby seats. If you intend to take public transport, a backpack for transporting young children is a good idea. Long-life milk is readily available, as is bottled spring water and fruit juice. Nappies, formula and sterilising solution are available in pharmacies and supermarkets in the main cities and towns, but if you are travelling to remote areas or islands, take your own supplies. Consider using cloth nappies wherever you can. Many small boats don't carry enough life jackets and never have child-sized ones; if you're planning to island hop, you might want to consider bringing your own Coast Guard approved inflatable life jackets.

Children are valued in Fiji, and childcare is seen as the responsibility of the extended family and the community. Everyone will want to talk with your kids and invite them to join activities or visit homes. Babies and toddlers are especially popular – they may tire of having their cheeks pinched! Fijian men play a large role in caring for children and babies, so don't be surprised if they pay a lot of attention to your kids. Fijian children are expected to be obedient and spend lots of time playing outdoors. Backtalk and showing off is seen as disruptive to the fabric of the community, so when visiting a village, try to curb any crying, tantrums and noisy behaviour.

Lonely Planet's *Travel with Children* has useful advice on family travel, and has a section on Fiji.

DANGERS & ANNOYANCES

Fiji is still a pretty safe place for travellers. When you're in Nadi or Suva, it's best not to walk around at night, even in a group, as muggings are not uncommon. Don't hitchhike; while it's commonly done by locals, as a foreigner, you're a sitting duck for muggers. As a precaution, use a moneybelt and keep your valuables in a safe place. It's rare but travellers may be asked if they want marijuana (see Legal Matters later in this chapter).

As you exit customs at Nadi airport, you'll likely be swarmed by touts who will do their best to get you into their shuttle van and on the road to their employer's resort. If you're unsure of where you want to stay and want to avoid these mobs while you consider your options, head directly into the FVB in the airport. It's got lots of information on accommodation.

Sword sellers are not as common as they used to be, since the FVB has tried to curtail the practice. If anyone becomes overly friendly, wants to know your life story and begins carving your name on a long piece of wood, just walk away, even if they pursue you claiming that you have to pay for the rubbishy item. If you are travelling for an extended period you may tire of being asked where you are staying. While this is often just innocent conversation, it can also be a way of judging how much you're going to be charged for dinner.

Developing tropical ulcers from something as simple as a mosquito bite or scratch can sometimes be a hazard (see Health earlier in this chapter); do your best to keep it clean. If you are unlucky enough to be caught in a natural disaster such as a cyclone or flood, ask locals for advice on where to seek protection from the elements.

Swimming

Contrary to Fiji's image promoted overseas, many beaches, especially on the large islands, aren't great for swimming. The fringing coral reefs often become too shallow at low tide. Avoid swimming or snorkelling alone and be very careful of currents and tidal changes. Always seek local advice on conditions.

Some of the most beautiful sea creatures such as the scorpion fish and lionfish are also highly venomous. Avoid the temptation and keep your hands to yourself! Sea urchins, crown-of-thorns starfish and stonefish can be poisonous or cause infections. Barracuda eels, which hide in coral crevices, may bite and some sea snakes are venomous. Jellyfish and fire coral can cause nasty stings, and cone shells often have a tiny venomous harpoon; don't pick them up off the beach. Sea lice or stingers can also be a nuisance.

Shark attacks on divers and snorkellers are rare in Fiji. Reef sharks don't normally attack humans for food, but they can be territorial. Avoid swimming near waste-water outlets, areas where fish are being cleaned, and the mouths of rivers or murky waters. If you are lucky enough to see a shark, just move away calmly.

LEGAL MATTERS

The only drug you are likely to come across is marijuana. It's totally illegal; don't seek it out or buy it as the risk is too high. It is not uncommon for drug users in Fiji to be imprisoned in the psychiatric hospital. It's also illegal to drink and drive. Refer also to the Customs and Gay & Lesbian Travellers sections earlier in this chapter for information on legal restrictions.

BUSINESS HOURS

Fijians are not known for their punctuality and usually adhere to 'Fiji time'. Most businesses open from 8am to 5pm weekdays, and from 8am to 1pm on Saturdays. Government offices are open from 8am to 4.30pm Monday to Thursday, 8am to 4pm Fridays. Many places close for lunch from 1pm to 2pm. Although the postcoup Sunday observance's ban on trading has now been lifted, little happens on Sunday. For indigenous Fijians it is a day for church, rest and spending time with family. Activities may be restricted at resorts.

PUBLIC HOLIDAYS & SPECIAL EVENTS

Fijians celebrate a variety of holidays and festivals. New Year's Day is celebrated all over Fiji: in villages, festivities can last a week or even the whole month of January. There is also a day commemorating the man considered Fiji's greatest statesman, Ratu Sir Lala Sukuna. Annual public holidays include:

New Year's Day	1 January
National Youth Day	late March/early April
Easter (Good Friday and Easter Monday)	March/April
Prophet Mohammed's Birthday	May
Ratu Sir Lala Sukuna Day	first Monday in June
Queen's Birthday	mid-June
Constitution Day	July
Birth of Lord Krishna	August/September
Fiji Day (Independence Day)	early October
Diwali	October/November
Christmas Day	25 December
Boxing Day	26 December

Fijian festivals include:

February or March

Hindu Holi (Festival of Colours) People squirt coloured water at each other; mostly in Lautoka.

March or April

Ram Naumi (Birth of Lord Rama) A Hindu religious festival and party on the shores of Suva Bay. Worshippers wade into the water and throw flowers.

August

Hibiscus Festival Held in Suva, with floats and processions.

Hindu Ritual Fire Walking Performed by southern Indians in many temples (try the Maha Devi Temple, Howell Rd, Suva).

September

Lautoka's Sugar Festival Lautoka comes alive with fun fairs, parades and the crowning of the Sugar Queen.

October or November

Diwali Festival (Festival of Lights) Hindus worship Lakshmi (the goddess of wealth and prosperity); houses are decorated and business is settled. Candles and lanterns are set on doorsteps to light the way for the god. This is a great time for shopping as there are lots of sales.

Ram Leela (Play of Rama) Primarily a Hindu festival, theatrical performances celebrate the life of the god-king Rama and his return from exile. It's held at the Bulileka Ram Leela Temple (Bulileka, Labasa) around the first week of October, and has been celebrated here for over 100 years.

ACTIVITIES

On your trip to Fiji you can either pack in lots of different activities or laze around and do very little.

Village Visits

Many tours include a village visit in their activities. Some villages have become affected by busloads of tourists parading through their backyards every other day and the *sevusevu* ceremony and *meke* can seem somewhat put on. Other village tours, especially those run by the villagers, are smaller in scale with perhaps not have so much going on, however, the whole experience can feel much more genuine.

The village tours from Levuka on Ovalau are fantastic and Navala, in Viti Levu's highlands, is one of Fiji's most picturesque villages. Avoid visiting villages on Sunday, as it is considered a day for church and rest. Refer to the Social Graces section earlier in this chapter for village etiquette.

Hiking

It is culturally offensive to simply hike anywhere – you need to ask permission, be invited or take a tour. For more details see Social Graces and Camping in this chapter. You should ask local villagers or hotel staff to organise permission and a guide. Good boots are essential all year round. Carry plenty of water, good maps, a compass, a warm jumper and a waterproof coat. Be sure to tell others where you are heading in case you get lost or have an accident.

Viti Levu and Taveuni are the best islands for hiking. Kadavu is more isolated but equally beautiful. Colo-i-Suva Forest Park on Viti Levu and the Lavena Coastal Walk and Tavoro Falls on Taveuni have marked trails and don't require guides. The Vidawa Forest Walk on Taveuni is a full-day guided tour. Other good places for hiking are Mt Tomanivi on Viti Levu near Nadarivatu, and Koroyanitu National Heritage Park and Mt Koroyanitu near Lautoka. For an easy but scenic walk, follow the Coral Coast Scenic Railway from the Shangri-La's Fijian Resort to the beautiful Natadola beach. For more information on the walks and guided tours, see the Taveuni, Suva and Viti Levu Highlands chapters.

If you will be in Fiji for a while, consider contacting the Rucksack Club in Suva (contact details available from the FVB). It organises regular walks and excursions.

Cycling

Cycling is a good way to explore Viti Levu, Vanua Levu (the Hibiscus Hwy) and parts of Ovalau and Taveuni. With the exception of Kings and Queens Roads, most roads, especially inland, are rough, hilly and unsealed, so mountain bikes are definitely the best option. Consider taking a carrier (a small truck) up to Abaca and riding back down to Lautoka. Be sure to carry lots of water and watch out for mad drivers who aren't used to minding cyclists. The best time to go is the drier season (May to October), and note that the eastern sides of the larger islands receive higher rainfall. Take waterproof gear and a repair kit to be self-sufficient, as it is difficult to get bike parts in Fiji. Maps are available from the government Map Shop in Suva. If you wish to take a bike on a domestic flight, make sure it is a demountable type.

Some resorts have bikes for hire. Expect to pay around $10 to $15 for half a day. See Mountain-Biking under Activities in the Nadi section of the Viti Levu chapter.

Bird-Watching

The best places for bird-watching are Taveuni and Kadavu. Taveuni has a better infrastructure than Kadavu, and is cheaper and easier to travel around. The Tunulao Rainforest on Vanua Levu is home to the rare silktail and rainforests around Savusavu are popular bird hangouts. On Viti Levu, Colo-i-Suva Forest Park near Suva has great bird-watching, as does the area near Waidroka Bay Resort on the Queens Road. See the Flora and Fauna section of the Facts about Fiji chapter and consider picking up a copy of *Birds of the Fiji Bush*, by Fergus Clunie & Pauline Morse, Fiji Museum, 1984.

Horse Riding

There are a few places in Fiji where horse riding is an organised activity. Try Ratuva's, near Sigatoka on Viti Levu's Coral Coast and Vatuwiri Farm in southern Taveuni.

Visiting Archaeological Sites

Fiji has a number of fascinating archaeological sites. However, the Tavuni Hill Fort and the Sigatoka Sand Dunes, both near Sigatoka, are the only sites set up for visitors. Other sites include the many ring-ditch (see the 'Ring-Ditch Fortifications' boxed text in the Viti Levu chapter) sites in the Sigatoka Valley and Rewa Delta; the Wasavula Ceremonial Site in Labasa; and the remains of an extensive village in Nukubolu near Savusavu.

Diving

Fiji's warm, clear waters and abundance of reef life make the islands a magnet for divers. Visibility regularly exceeds 30m, though this is reduced on stormy days or when there is a heavy plankton bloom. The drier months of May to October have more reliable visibility.

The beauty of Fiji is that, with a well-established dive industry, you can have great access to diving regardless of whether your accommodation funds extend to budget or luxury. When choosing a place to stay, decide whether the sole purpose of your trip is diving or whether you also want to pursue other activities. Some resorts specialise in diving, and exclusive resorts often include diving in the daily tariff. Prices for a two-tank dive range from $85 to $180. Check for half-price dive specials from mid-January to the end of March. Most operators rent out equipment (in varying states of maintenance) if you don't want to lug your own gear around but you may prefer to bring your own buoyancy control jacket, regulator, mask, snorkel and fins.

Make sure that your travel insurance covers scuba diving and emergency treatment for the unlikely event that you need an air transfer and stint in a recompression chamber. Attach a small whistle or a marker tube to your equipment for signalling; divers lost in the water are extremely difficult to spot. Refer to individual island chapters for specific information on dive operators and resorts.

Many travellers take the opportunity to learn scuba diving while in Fiji, and most operators offer courses for beginners as well as certification and advanced courses. Open-water certification courses, either by the Professional Association of Diving Instructors (PADI), or less commonly by the National Association of Underwater Instructors

(NAUI), take four to five days to complete and cost between $350 and $600. Equipment rental is about $30 per day. Make sure your instructor is qualified; check with the **Fiji Dive Operators Association** *(FDOA; ☎ 885 0620, fax 885 0344; w www.fijidive.com; Savusavu)* or the FVB. FDOA members are required to abide by international diving standards, a code of practice and a code of ethics, and support the Fiji Recompression Chamber Facility. Other operators may offer cheaper diving, but perhaps less reliable instruction, equipment and safety procedures.

Some dive operators offer courses in languages other than English. Mana Island Resort and Beachcomber Island Resort, in the Mamanuca Group, both have instruction in Japanese, and Ovalau Watersports on Ovalau and Dolphin Bay Divers on Taveuni offer courses in German.

Decompression illnesses, both the bends and arterial gas embolism (AGE), are perhaps the biggest dangers in diving. The bends occurs in divers when not enough time is allowed while rising to the surface to let the body's tissues expel the gases. Instead, the gases form bubbles in the brain, spinal cord or peripheral nerves. Symptoms include numbness, difficulties with muscle coordination, nausea, speech defects, paralysis, convulsions, and personality changes. Other symptoms include excessive coughing and difficulty in breathing, chest pain, a burning sensation while breathing and severe shock. Small nitrogen bubbles trapped under the skin can cause a red rash and an itching sensation known as diver's itch, but these symptoms usually pass in 10 to 20 minutes.

AGE occurs when the air in your lungs expands from ascending too quickly, causing very serious and more immediate effects than the bends. It's important to get a diver suffering from decompression illness to a recompression chamber as quickly as possible to avoid permanent tissue damage – be assertive if you or other divers experience symptoms. There's a **recompression chamber** in Suva *(☎ 330 5154, 24-hour service ☎ 336 2172)* and a medivac system that transfers dive accident victims to the chamber.

Divers Alert Network (DAN) is an international membership association of individuals and organisations. It operates a 24-hour diving emergency hotline for members, with advice on early treatment, evacuation and hyperbaric treatment of diving-related injuries. Membership is reasonably priced and includes DAN TravelAssist, a benefit that covers evacuation, as well as insurance including decompression illness. For more information, check w www.diversalertnetwork.org. The 24-hour emergency line for DAN SEAP (Southeast Asia Pacific) members is ☎ 61 8 8212 9242. DAN America members should call ☎ 919 684 4326.

The FVB publishes an annual glossy *Fiji Islands Dive Guide*. Also try the Internet and diving magazines. Lonely Planet's *Diving and Snorkelling Guide to Fiji* gives full coverage of Fiji's dive sites and safety and you may like to pick up a laminated Fiji fish identification card (available from most dive shops).

Dive Sites Fiji has vast unexplored regions as well as many dive sites of world renown. The soft corals of the Rainbow Reef and the Great White Wall of the Somosomo Strait near Taveuni, the Beqa Lagoon off southern Viti Levu and the Great Astrolabe Reef off Kadavu are all spectacular. There is no such thing as the best diving site, especially in Fiji. Each dive site has something special or unique. Sites range from the safe and easy, to wall dives in fast currents, to dives with reef sharks.

Mamanuca Group Easily accessed from the Nadi/Lautoka area, the Mamanucas have lots of popular dive sites including the Supermarket, patronised by sharks, and the Circus with its colourful array of clown fish. The Malolo Barrier Reef protects the group, and the currents through its passages provide nutrients, promoting soft and hard coral growth. Inside the barrier reef the waters are generally calm with many coral reefs and abundant fish life. There are exciting dive sites outside the barrier reef at the Namotu and Malolo Passages, where you can see batfish, manta rays and turtles. It often gets rough here and should therefore only be attempted by experienced, adventurous divers.

Despite the large number of tourist resorts in the Mamanucas, the coral ecosystems are still good. Most of the resorts have their own dive operations. Day-trippers to resorts such as Beachcomber Island Resort or Musket Cove Resort may be able to

Sink or Swim: Choosing a Dive School or Operation

In general, diving in Fiji is very safe, with a high standard of staff training and good equipment maintenance. However, as with anywhere in the world, some operations are more professional than others, and it is often difficult, especially for inexperienced or beginner divers, to select the best operation for their needs. Here are a few tips to help you select a well set-up and safety-conscious dive shop.

1. Is it a member of the FDOA? The Fiji Dive Operators Association is made up of dive centres that meet certain safety and staff training standards. A list of members is available from the **FDOA** (☎ 885 0620, fax 885 0344, **w** http://fijidive.com).
2. Are its staff fully trained and qualified? Ask to see certificates or certification cards – no reputable shop will be offended by this request. Guides must reach 'full instructor' level (the minimum certification level) to be able to teach *any* diving course. To guide certified divers on a reef dive, guides must hold at least 'rescue diver' or preferably 'dive master' qualifications. Note that a dive master cannot teach – only fully qualified instructors can do that. A school that allows uncertified divers to go out with a dive master is breaking all the safety rules.
3. Does it have safety equipment on the boat? Legally, a dive boat must carry oxygen and a first-aid kit, radio and flares. An easy way to check this is to ask what kind of oxygen equipment they carry, and see if they can show it to you. Do not dive with any operator not carrying oxygen.
4. Is its equipment OK and its air clean? This is often the hardest thing for the new diver to judge. A few guidelines are:

a. Smell the air – open a tank valve a small way and breathe in. Smelling dry or slightly rubbery is OK. Smelling of oil or car exhaust tells you they do not filter the air correctly. Go somewhere else.

b. When the equipment is put together, are there any big air leaks? All dive centres get some small leaks at some time, and usually will explain that a tiny bit of air loss is unimportant. This is true, and not a reason to reject a dive shop. However, if you get a big hiss of air coming out of any piece of equipment, ask to have it replaced. Usually that solves the problem. If you have three or more equipment failures, seek another dive shop.

5. Is it conservation-oriented? Most good dive shops explain that you should not touch corals or take shells from the reef. If any dive guide suggests that they spear fish or collect clams during the dive, please report the guide to the FDOA.

Diving in Fiji is wonderful and varied. Some areas are more suitable for experienced divers, some for beginners. In general terms, if you want to learn to dive, or are relatively inexperienced, the best areas are the Mamanucas, the northwest Coral Coast, and the north of Viti Levu. For more experienced divers, the most spectacular reefs are off the western Coral Coast, Kadavu, Vanua Levu and Taveuni. All divers are recommended to ensure their travel insurance covers them for scuba diving. There is a recompression chamber in Suva, contactable in an emergency on ☎ 336 2172.

Helen Sykes

arrange a dive. Inner Space Adventures, based at Newtown Beach, and Dive Tropex, based at the Sheraton on Denarau Island, both take diving trips from Nadi (see the Viti Levu chapter for details). It is also possible to charter a yacht from Musket Cove Marina for diving in the Mamanucas.

Yasawa Group The Yasawa Group has spectacular reefs with vibrant corals, walls, underwater caves and plenty of unexplored areas. Westside Watersports has a dive operation on Tavewa and there are dive operations at Wayalailai Resort (on Wayasewa) and Octopus Resort (on Waya).

Viti Levu Dive sites off Viti Levu include the Mamanucas (see the earlier Mamanuca Group entry), the Coral Coast, Beqa Lagoon and Nananu-i-Ra.

The main advantage of diving on the Coral Coast is the proximity of sites to the coast, and the wide range of accommodation available. The inside reefs can be reached by small boat, currents are usually moderate and you will see reasonably good coral and small reef fish. To see bigger pelagic fish and more spectacular coral you have to dive the outer reefs and passages. The large barrier reef surrounding the islands of Beqa and Yanuca forms Beqa Lagoon – one of the world's top diving locations. The reef and its various passages have a number of excellent sites, with coral heads, walls, tunnels, undercuts, abundant soft coral and large fish. Dive operators located at Pacific Harbour take trips to the lagoon.

There are many dive sites and unexplored areas around Nananu-i-Ra, which is just off the northernmost point of Viti Levu. Divers can expect to see soft and hard corals, black coral, walls, caves, large fish, dolphins, turtles and the occasional whale cruising through Bligh Water.

Coral Coast Scuba Ventures at Shangri-La's Fijian Resort and SPAD-South Pacific Adventure Divers cater to many of the Coral Coast resorts. There are also dive operations at Waidroka Bay Resort, Pacific Harbour and at Momi Bay.

Lomaiviti Group This is still a relatively unexplored area and has lots of diverse sites, particularly for beginners but also for experienced divers. There's lots of fish, rays and the occasional shark. Ovalau Watersports is based in Levuka and most of the island resorts have their own operations, including the backpacker resort on Leluvia, the mid-range Naigani, the more expensive Moody's Namena on Namenalala, and the exclusive Wakaya.

Kadavu The diving reputation of Kadavu was established on the Astrolabe and Soso Reefs during the 1980s. The reefs north of the island are also beautiful and are sheltered from the southeast trade winds. The most spectacular dives are the passages between the lagoons and the open sea and on the outside face of the barrier reefs. Expect to find abundant soft and hard corals, caves, vertical walls and lots of fish.

Kadavu is a remote and rugged island away from the mainstream tourist destinations, and remains a relatively new frontier for diving in Fiji with lots of scope for exploratory diving. Dive operators include Albert's Sunrise and Dive Kadavu.

Taveuni & Vanua Levu Fiji's northern region has developed a reputation as one the best areas for diving in Fiji. The vast number of reefs offer all that the diver could wish for: lots of soft coral; huge walls, over-hangs and caves; reef; and pelagic fish.

The best sites, including Rainbow Reef and Great White Wall, are on the outer barrier reefs in the Somosomo Strait, between the islands of Vanua Levu and Taveuni. Somosomo Strait dive sites often have strong currents and involve drift diving.

Taveuni dive operations include Aquaventure and Swiss Fiji Divers based in Matei and Dolphin Bay Divers in the south. Taveuni Island Resort, Garden Island Resort and the upmarket offshore island resorts of Matangi and Qamea Beach Club each have their own dive operations.

Vanua Levu operations include Eco Divers-Tours and L'Aventure Jean-Michel Cousteau, both in the Savusavu area. The upmarket Nukubati Island Resort dives the Great Sea Reef off northern Vanua Levu.

Lau Group Due to its distance from the rest of Fiji, the Lau Group is still relatively unexplored in terms of diving. There is reportedly great potential in the area, with dive sites as good as, or better, than the best found in the rest of the country.

Live-Aboard Operators Due to the number of readily accessible dive sites in Fiji, live-aboards are not as popular as in some dive localities. They can, however, be a good option for exploring reefs where the usual operators don't go.

Green Turtle – one of the underwater creatures you may encounter

The Responsible Diver

The popularity of diving is placing immense pressure on many sites and environmentalists say that Fiji's reefs are beginning to show wear and tear. Please consider the following tips when diving to help preserve the ecology and beauty of reefs.

- Do not use anchors on the reef, and take care not to ground boats on coral. Encourage dive operators and regulatory bodies to establish permanent moorings at popular dive sites.
- Avoid touching living marine organisms with your body or dragging equipment across the reef. Polyps can be damaged by even the gentlest contact. Never stand on corals, even if they look solid and robust. If you must hold on to the reef, only touch exposed rock or dead coral.
- Be conscious of your fins. Even without contact, the surge from heavy fin strokes near the reef can damage delicate organisms. When treading water in shallow reef areas, take care not to kick up clouds of sand. Settling sand can easily smother the delicate organisms of the reef.
- Practice and maintain proper buoyancy control. Major damage can be done by divers descending too fast and colliding with the reef. Make sure you are correctly weighted and that your weight-belt is positioned so that you stay horizontal. If you have not dived for a while, have a practice dive in a pool before taking to the reef. Be aware that buoyancy can change over the period of an extended trip: initially you may breathe harder and need more weight; a few days later you may breathe more easily and need less weight.
- Take great care in underwater caves. Spend as little time in them as possible as your air bubbles may be caught within the roof and thereby leave previously submerged organisms high and dry. Taking turns to inspect the interior of a small cave will lessen the chances of damaging contact.
- Don't collect or buy corals or shells. Aside from the ecological implications, taking home marine souvenirs depletes the beauty of a site and spoils the enjoyment for others.
- Ensure that you take home all your rubbish and any litter you may find as well. Plastics in particular are a serious threat to marine life. Turtles can mistake plastic for jellyfish and eat it.
- Resist the temptation to feed fish. You may feed them food that is detrimental to their health; disturb their normal eating habits; or encourage aggressive behaviour. This is especially true of shark feedings that have become popular in Fiji.
- Try not to disturb marine animals. In particular, do not ride on the backs of turtles as this causes them great anxiety.

The luxurious 33m yacht *Nai'a* (☎ *345 0382;* **w** *www.naia.com.fj)*, based at Pacific Harbour, has the reputation of being the best live-aboard in Fiji. It takes up to 18 passengers in nine air-conditioned rooms, all with en suites. A seven-day charter costs $5400 per person (double occupancy) including all meals, tanks, weights and unlimited air refills.

The *Fiji Aggressor* (☎ *504-385 2628 USA;* **w** *www.livedivepacific.com)* is a live-aboard dive operation that is based in Nadi. It is part of the worldwide Aggressor fleet, which consists of a number of luxury live-aboard boats. This boat is 32m-long and has eight cabins to accommodate a maximum of only 16 guests. Facilities include sundecks, air-conditioned rooms, wheelchair access, quality diving gear and photo equipment. Cruises cost $4800 per person, twin share and normally leave on Saturday returning the following Saturday. It includes 5½ days of diving.

Snorkelling

Snorkelling in Fiji's warm waters is a definite highlight. There are beautiful reefs teeming with amazing life. Snorkelling is often fantastic very close to the coast, making it a relatively inexpensive and easy pastime compared to diving. Many snorkellers get a taste for the underwater experience and use it as a stepping stone to diving, while others are content without the fuss of all that heavy equipment. All you need is a mask, snorkel and fins. Ideally wear a T-shirt and waterproof sunscreen as it is easy to become absorbed by the spectacle, lose sense of time and scorch your back and legs.

If you have not snorkelled before or are not a confident swimmer, familiarise yourself with the equipment in a pool or shallow water. Learn how to clear your snorkel, so that you don't panic and tread over the fragile coral. Keep to the surface if you feel more comfortable there and never dive too deep. It is best to swim with a partner, to always use fins and to ask locals about currents. Some operators who take snorkellers on their dive trips may just dump you overboard with a buoy, on a barrier reef, far from land. If you are not confident, ask for a life jacket. It is common to see reef sharks but don't panic, they're probably more scared of you. The most beautiful creatures can be poisonous so avoid touching anything. Also avoid being washed against the reef as coral cuts can turn into nasty infections.

You are likely to see brilliant soft and hard corals, multitudes of colourful fish of various shapes and sizes, sponges, sea cucumbers, urchins, starfish, Christmas-tree worms and molluscs. Crustaceans are more difficult to spot and many only come out at night. Night snorkelling is a fantastic experience if you can overcome your fear of the unknown!

Snorkelling becomes even more enjoyable if you can recognise different species. See the previous Diving introductory section for details of books that can help you make the most of Fiji's underwater world.

Snorkelling Sites Most resorts offer snorkelling and have equipment for hire. However, always check first when going to a remote budget resort – it can be frustrating if you are in a gorgeous location without any equipment. If you are a keen snorkeller it may be worth having your own equipment for greater flexibility. Dive operations usually take snorkellers to outer reefs if there is room on the boat, although some prefer to keep the activities separate and have special snorkelling trips.

In many places you can snorkel off the shore, however, often you can only swim at high tide and channels can be dangerous. The best sites on Viti Levu are at Natadola Beach (watch the current here though), Nananu-i-Ra and Beqa Lagoon. Viti Levu's Coral Coast is not that great for snorkelling as it is usually a fair way to the drop, much of the reef is dead and swimming is mostly tidal.

The best snorkelling sites are on the outer islands. Notable sites include: the Mamanucas and Yasawas (superb reefs with mostly hard coral); Vanua Levu's rocky coastline, especially near Mumu's Resort; Taveuni's Vuna Reef; Kadavu, offshore of the Matava, Astrolabe Hideaway Resort and Jona's Paradise Resort on Ono; and the Lomaiviti Group's Caqelai and Leleuvia.

Surfing

It is believed that surfing has existed in Fiji for hundreds of years. Surfing reefs over warm, crystal-clear, turquoise-blue water is a very special experience. The majority of Fiji's rideable breaks are on offshore reefs that require boat trips. When choosing accommodation, also consider the price of getting to the surf. The best surf spots are in barrier-reef passages where the powerful swells from the open ocean break onto the reefs – along Viti Levu's south coast and along western Viti Levu in the Mamanuca Group. There are also breaks at Kadavu and Taveuni. The dry season (May to October) is the best time to go due to low pressures bringing in big surf.

Riding the dangerous southern Mamanuca reef-breaks should only be attempted by experienced surfers. If you want to stay at the popular surf resorts on Tavarua and Namotu, book well in advance. It is also possible to charter a yacht from Musket Cove Marina on Malololailai (Plantation Island) to access the breaks – it can be an OK deal for a group. Some breaks are likely to be out of bounds unless you are staying at the resorts. See the Mamanuca Group chapter for more information.

There are a few places on mainland Viti Levu where you can paddle out to the surf including the Sigatoka River mouth along the Coral Coast. Natadola Beach sometimes has small surf that can be good for beginners and there's bigger surf offshore (requiring a boat). Suva has a reef-break at the lighthouse – you need a boat to get there. See Momi Bay, Sigatoka, Korolevu, Pacific Harbour and Yanuca in the Viti Levu chapter for more information.

Kadavu's Cape Washington has good surf but no place to stay. There are breaks on Kadavu's passages near Astrolabe Hideaway Resort. Lavena Point on Taveuni also has rideable though inconsistent waves.

You should be aware that Fijian villages usually have fishing rights to, and basically own, adjacent reefs. Some resorts pay the villages for exclusive surfing rights, which has led to disputes between competing surfing and diving operations. If you would like to explore lesser-known areas you will need to respect local traditions and seek permission of the local villagers.

Surfboards can be hired in Nadi at Viti Surf Legend. They can also arrange trips to the beach-breaks at Natadola and Sigatoka. You can also pick up gear at Wai Tui Surf in Suva. If you are a keen surfer, bring your own board and in winter take a light wetsuit or vest; surfing booties and a helmet are also a good idea.

FVB publishes *Fiji Islands Surfs Up*, a brochure with surf resorts throughout the country. You can also check out their website at **w** www.bulafiji.com/web/surf.

Sea & Dive Kayaking

Sea and dive kayaking are becoming increasingly popular in Fiji. It is a great way of exploring the coast at a gentle pace. Dive kayaks, which can carry lunch, snorkelling gear and scuba gear, can be double the fun.

The islands of Taveuni, Vanua Levu, Yasawa and Kadavu are great for kayaking. Some keen kayakers paddle Taveuni's rugged Ravilevu Coast, but generally the western sides of the islands are preferred as they're sheltered from the south-east trade winds.

Many of Fiji's resorts have kayaks for guest use, or for hire at about $20/30 for a half-/full day. There are also special kayaking tours available during the drier months between May and November. Some combine paddling with hiking into rainforests, snorkelling, fishing and village visits, and have support boats that carry camping gear and food. They don't necessarily require that you have previous experience. For more information on kayak tours, see the Yasawa Group, Vanua Levu and Kadavu Group chapters.

Independent travellers planning extended trips should check weather forecasts, watch the tides and currents, and wear a life jacket, hat and plenty of sunscreen. Ideally, take a signalling device or even a mobile phone or radio and always let someone know of your plans.

River Trips

Bilibili (bamboo rafting) and kayaking trips can be made on the Navua River in Namosi Highlands (see Viti Levu Highlands in the Viti Levu chapter). Many village trips also include a ride on a *bilibili* (see Natokalau Village Trips in the Levuka section of the Lomaiviti Group chapter and the Waitabu Marine Park in the Taveuni chapter). The *Shotover Jet* through the mangroves at Denarau Island near Nadi is a quick thrill (see Nadi in the Viti Levu chapter).

Windsurfing

Many resorts have windsurfers for guests. Wave jumpers should consider the surf-break off the Namotu Island Resort on Namotu (Magic Island) in the Mamanucas (refer to the Mamanuca Group chapter). You will have to take your own board out there.

Boat Chartering & Fishing

Villages have rights over the reefs and fishing so you cannot just drop a line anywhere; seek permission first. Many of the more expensive resorts offer game-fishing tours and boat chartering. Matangi Island Resort, in the Taveuni island group, specialises in saltwater fly-fishing. The smaller resorts will also arrange for local boats to take you fishing. Consider the southeast trade winds when choosing the best spot – the leeward sides of the islands are generally calmer. For boat chartering see Activities under the Mamanuca Group and Taveuni chapters.

Sailing

Yachties are often looking for extra crew and people to share costs. Approach the marinas, ask around and look on the notice boards.

Fiji's marinas include the Suva Yacht Club; Vuda Point Marina between Nadi and Lautoka; Levuka Marina on Ovalau; Musket Cove Marina on Malololailai in the Mamanucas; and The Copra Shed Marina and Waitui Marina, both at Savusavu on Vanua Levu. The designated ports of entry are Suva, Levuka, Lautoka and Savusavu. Refer to Visas & Documents earlier in this chapter.

The main yachting season is June, July and August, but there are races and regattas throughout the year. Fiji Regatta Week and the Musket Cove to Port Vila Regatta are held in September. Obviously the Fijian reefs necessitate good charts and crews with sailing experience.

For organised cruises and charters, refer to the individual island chapters. Musket Cove Marina hires a range of vessels for sailing around the Mamanucas and Yasawas, including some that are fully crewed with skipper and cook. There are also private boats for sail and adventure cruises from Savusavu's marinas. By Fijian law, you must have a local guide on all chartered boats.

Contact individual yacht clubs for further information, and pick up a copy of the *Yacht Help Booklet, Fiji* available from FVB. *Landfalls of Paradise – The Guide to Pacific Islands,* by Earl R Hinz, University of Hawaii Press, and Michael Calder's *Yachtsman's Fiji* are also popular references.

COURSES

The USP in Suva *(w www.usp.ac.fj)* runs some informal courses on different subjects. Also check the *Fiji Times* diary page, which sometimes advertises classes. Indian cultural centres have three-month programmes, including *kathak* (classical dance), vocal/harmonium, tabla, sitar, yoga and Hindi language. While classes are mostly for local children, you may be able to negotiate something.

WORK

Those travelling to Fiji for reasons other than a holiday must declare this on their arrival card. They will be given a visa for 14 days and will have to apply for subsequent extensions. Those wishing to live or work in Fiji for more than six months will require a working visa. These can be difficult to get and need to be organised at least two months prior to travelling to Fiji. Application forms can be obtained from any Fijian embassy and must be completed and sent by the applicant to the immigration authorities in Fiji. Your application will normally only be approved if supported by a prospective employer and if your skills cannot be found locally. If you want to conduct business in Fiji, contact the **Fiji Trade and Investment Board** *(☎ 331 5988, fax 330 1783; w www.ftib.org.fj; 6th floor, Civic Tower, Victoria Parade, Government Bldgs, Suva)*.

Volunteer Work

There are two types of volunteer work available to foreigners in Fiji. One is through an overseas aid organisation such as Australian Volunteers Abroad, British Voluntary Service Overseas and GAP Activity Projects. Responsible organisations will only go where invited, pay their staff local wages, and teach volunteers the local language and respect for traditional culture and customs. The other option, usually taken up by ex-pats, is to help a Fijian charitable or community organisation, such as the Fiji Women's Rights Movement (refer to Women Travellers earlier in this chapter). The Fiji Museum in Suva is often looking for volunteers (see the Suva section in the Viti Levu chapter). Greenpeace, the World Wide Fund for Nature (WWF), National Trust for Fiji (w www.nationaltrust.org.uk/main) and South Pacific Action Committee for Human Ecology and Environment *(Spachee)* also have offices in Suva. (See the Ecology & Environment section in the Facts about Fiji chapter for contact details.) Volunteers are required to apply for a work permit.

ACCOMMODATION

Five-star hotels, B&Bs, hostels, motels, treehouses, bungalows on the beach and campgrounds – there's no shortage of accommodation options in Fiji.

With prices ranging from dorm beds as low as $10 per night to exclusive resorts charging well over $1000, there's something for every budget. Accommodation prices are subject to 12.5% VAT and it's worth checking if this tax is included in the price quoted before signing in. It's often possible to get cheaper walk-in rates, particularly during the low season, in February and March.

While Nadi itself is nothing special, it has a lot of places to stay and can be a good base from which to organise tours and meet other travellers with up-to-date advice.

Reservations

If you're after a short stay in one place, consider prebooking hotel or resort accommodation as a package deal. You'll almost always get a cheaper price than the quoted 'rack rate', particularly during low season. You'll need to book well in advance for popular resorts. If you just turn up, you may not get the resort of your choice, however, you may get about 25% off for a 'walk-in' rate.

If you're looking to stay a bit longer and want to move around, avoid paying too much in advance and keep your options open. There are many places to choose from so if you're not happy for some reason, you won't be tied by prepaid reservations and can just move on. Be aware, however, that places do tend to get booked out in the busy months.

Remote islands, such as Kadavu, have few places to stay and the main form of transportation is by small boat. In this case, avoid being left stranded without a vacancy in your price range by prebooking – this will also ensure you'll be met at the airport or ferry.

If you're making reservations at mid- or budget-range places, especially while you're on the road, don't be completely surprised if you show up and nobody's heard of you. Administration can sometimes be a little less than organised and reservations that are made don't always seem to make it into the book.

Camping

Don't just set up camp anywhere without permission. Most of Fiji's land, even in seemingly remote areas, is owned by the indigenous population, by *mataqali* (extended families) or villages. If you are invited to camp in villages, avoid setting up next to someone's *bure*. Doing so can be misinterpreted as implying that you feel the house is not good enough for you to stay in. While camping is not very common in Fiji, there are a couple of camping areas on Viti Levu, Vanua Levu and Taveuni. Expect to pay around $12 per person per night. For details of the location of camping areas refer to the individual island chapters.

Hostels

The Cathay chain has budget accommodation at Lautoka, Saweni Beach, the Coral Coast and Suva. It gives discounts for HI and Nomad card holders. There are many cheap hotels with dormitory accommodation and some hotels and resorts have converted a room or two into dorms – often a great bargain as you'll have access to all of the resort's facilities.

Guesthouses

Guesthouses are normally cheap hotels. In some dodgy neighbourhoods (particularly in Suva and Nadi) certain guesthouses rent their rooms by the hour for pursuits other than sleeping. These places are usually unsafe, scuzzy and best avoided. In remote areas, there are basic government guesthouses that are mostly used by government workers, however, travellers are usually accepted if there is a vacancy.

Hotels

Fiji has many budget hotels, especially in the Nadi/Lautoka area, the Coral Coast and Suva on Viti Levu. Spartan rooms are available for around $40 to $60 for a double. Many budget hotels have dormitories for about $12 a night – a good option for solo travellers who want to meet other like souls. Some have communal cooking facilities and individual lockers.

There are also lots of mid-range hotels with prices from around $70 and $150 for doubles; discounts may apply if the hotel is not busy. Amenities usually include air-con, tea- and coffee-making facilities, and a restaurant, bar and pool.

Resorts

The term 'resort' is used loosely in Fiji and can refer to any accommodation located anywhere near the sea, and ranges from backpacker-style to exclusive luxury, to a farm on Taveuni. If you are prepared to put up with rudimentary facilities and services, you can find an inexpensive piece of paradise. There are some beautiful coral islands where you can stay cheaply in simple thatched-roof *bure* in idyllic settings. Most offer meal plans, which are fixed-price packages that generally include breakfast, lunch and dinner.

Wailoaloa and Newtown beaches near Nadi have a concentration of 'backpacker resorts'. Although the black-sand beaches aren't that great and it's pretty isolated, it is an OK place to get over your jetlag or wait for a flight. There are many backpacker resorts on the offshore islands, including the Yasawas, on Mana in the Mamanucas, Kadavu, Nananu-i-Ra, and Leluvia and Caqelai near Ovalau. The standards of many of these places can slide up and down with popularity; normally they ask for payment up front, so before embarking try to get information from travellers who have just been there. Popular places can become overcrowded and less popular places can feel totally abandoned. Transport is usually by small open boat, which can be risky in rough weather.

For those who are happy to spend up to a few hundred dollars per day for extra comfort, services and activities, there are many popular resorts in the Mamanucas, on Viti Levu's Coral Coast, on Taveuni, as well as on more remote islands. Mainland resorts have the advantage of more options for tours, entertainment and shopping, however, with the exception of beautiful Natadola

Beach, offshore islands usually have better beaches. If you are just looking for water sports or a relaxing time on the beach, choose an offshore island. There is a trend towards small, exclusive resorts on privately owned islands; these are best suited to couples with a very healthy bank balance or on a honeymoon spree.

Rental Accommodation

Most of the long-term rental accommodation is in Suva and Pacific Harbour, and to a lesser extent in Nadi. There are also a number of houses for rent on Taveuni. Renting apartments or rooms with weekly rates may be a cheap option if you are looking for a fixed base from which to take day trips. Normally apartments have cooking facilities, and if you are in a small group, a joint effort to buy groceries, fresh fruit and vegetables from the local market can save a fair bit of money.

FOOD

Local Food

Fiji is the multicultural hub of the Pacific, and its food is a blend of indigenous Fijian, Polynesian, Indian, Chinese and Western influences. Traditional Fijian foods include *tavioka* (cassava) and *dalo* (taro) roots, boiled or baked fish, and seafood in *lolo* (coconut cream). Meat (pork or beef) is fried and accompanied with the *dalo* roots and *rourou* (boiled dalo leaves) in *lolo*. *Kokoda* is a popular traditional dish made of raw fish marinated in coconut cream and lime juice. Seasonal tropical fruits include bananas, guava, pineapple, mango and pawpaw (papaya).

Lovo are traditional indigenous Fijian banquets in which the food is prepared in an underground oven. A hole is dug in the ground and stones are put inside and heated by an open fire. The food is wrapped in banana leaves and cooked slowly on top of the hot stones. You may get a chance to try *lovo* at resorts or on a village visit.

Indo-Fijian dishes tend to be heavily spiced. A typical meal is a meat, fish or vegie curry with rice, lentil soup and roti (a type of flat bread). Chinese food is generally the Western-takeaway affair with stir-fries, fried rice, chop suey, chow mein and Chinese curries. Sometimes you'll find the added delicacy of bêche-de-mer (sea cucumber) on the menu.

If you are invited to share a meal with a Fijian or Indo-Fijian family, you will experience authentic Fijian food. At home, Fijians generally eat with their hands and sit on woven mats. In Indo-Fijian homes there may be a strict protocol for eating, such as using

LIZ THOMPSON

Preparing the lovo (earth oven)

Boiled Bat

Fancy some boiled *beka* (bat) for dinner? Long ago it was a popular indigenous Fijian dish but these days only the older generations dine on it. It's difficult to know if its consumption stems from a scarcity of food, an actual fondness for the meat, or a dare. If you ask younger Fijians what they think of it, they'll turn up their noses in disgust. And if you smell it cooking or taste it, you'll likely join them. Apparently it's ghastly.

only your right hand, so you may want to ask your host for advice. You will be provided with plenty of food, whether your hosts can afford it or not and some hosts will even wait for you to have your fill before they start eating – if that is the case, leave enough for everybody. Try to reciprocate by buying some groceries for the family.

You may get to taste Fijian 'bush food' while hiking in the highlands, such as freshwater prawns and *tavioka* roasted on a small open fire, and dipped in a banana-leaf bowl of water, salt, lime juice and chillies.

Although turtles are an endangered species and there are strict controls on their capture and eating, turtle meat can still be found in markets. If villagers offer you *vonu* (turtle), politely refuse. An adult female is about 20 to 50 years old before she can lay eggs.

Village children catch the crabs that swarm along beaches under a full moon, and then hold a feast. Fishing for flounder is also popular by moonlight. It involves wading into shallow water to spear or net the fish.

Avoid eating large predatory reef fish such as snapper, barracuda and groupers, as these sometimes carry the ciguatera toxin (refer to Health earlier in this chapter).

Fast Food

Fijians are facing nutritional problems as, like much of the world, they forgo traditional foods for Western-style tinned and packaged foods. Corned beef enjoys colossal popularity and the number of fast-food outlets is growing quickly in the main towns. If you've got a craving for pizza, fried chicken or greasy Indian or Chinese takeaway, you shouldn't have any difficulties finding some.

Restaurants

Fiji's main towns, especially Nadi and Suva, have a good variety of restaurants ranging from cheap cafés to fine dining. Most have a combination of adapted Chinese, Indian and Western dishes, and Japanese food is becoming increasingly popular. It's more difficult to find indigenous Fijian food although many resort restaurants do have *lovo* nights, which are often accompanied by a *meke*.

Cheap restaurants charge between $5 and $10 for main meals. Restaurants normally close early – don't expect to find many places open after 9pm.

Vegetarian Food

Being vegetarian in Fiji is pretty easy. Most resorts will cater to vegetarians and tourist restaurants almost always have at least one token vegie meal on the menu. Some places even have a huge variety of tasty meals without meat. If you're partial to Indian food you've got it made – a huge number of Indo-Fijians are strict vegetarians and so it's difficult to find an Indo-Fijian restaurant that doesn't have lots of vegie options. You'll find Govinda's Vegetarian Restaurant and Hare Krishna restaurants in Lautoka, Suva and Lambasa, where you don't have to worry about any meat having found its way into your food.

The only time a person's vegetarian-ness can prove tricky is on visits to indigenous Fijian villages. If you are planning such a tour, be sure to tell the guide or tour operator that you're vegetarian when you book the tour to avoid an embarrassing and uncomfortable situation later when you're dished up a big plate of meat.

Self-Catering

Every large town in Fiji has a fresh fruit-and-vegetable market and at least one supermarket where you can buy basic groceries. Most villages have a small shop, but, as most villagers grow their own fresh produce, the stock is often limited to pre-packaged goods, such as tinned fish and corned beef. Some backpacker places have cooking facilities and also sell basic groceries. If you are a guest in a village it is a good idea to buy some goods at the local shop for your host family. See the Language chapter for useful food-related vocabulary.

DRINKS

Nonalcoholic Drinks

Both local and imported mineral water and soft drinks are available in Fiji. Most of the milk available is long-life. Fresh local fruit juices and smoothies are great, but don't be misled by 'juice' on a menu – it often means sickly sweet cordial. The chilled water from green coconuts is much more refreshing.

Alcoholic Drinks

Most restaurants and bars stock a variety of local and imported spirits and beer. Fiji Bitter and Fiji Gold are locally brewed beers. Most of the wines available are from Australia or New Zealand. You can expect to pay about $3 for a glass of beer, although the upmarket resorts will charge more. A 750ml bottle of Fiji Rum is about $20.

Yaqona

Yaqona, also called kava or grog, is the national drink and is an integral part of Fijian life. It is mildly narcotic, looks like muddy water and makes your tongue go furry. You won't escape trying it! Refer to the Social Graces section earlier in this chapter.

ENTERTAINMENT

On Sundays, it's a good idea to organise activities in advance, or attend a Fijian church service to hear some great singing. Nadi has minimal nightlife, although the larger mainland resort hotels have discos, live bands, *meke*, *lovo* nights and fire-walking performances. Beachcomber Island Resort in the Mamanucas has a reputation as a party island for young backpackers. Suva, with its cosmopolitan and student population, is the nightlife capital; while it does have a few great bars and clubs, don't expect Rio.

Every major town has at least one cinema. Suva and Lautoka have comfortable Village cinema complexes with recent, mainstream Western releases, Indian Bollywood films and great popcorn. Admission costs around $5. Check the entertainment section in the *Fiji Times* for what's showing.

SPECTATOR SPORTS

Rugby Union and soccer are Fiji's major competitive sports. Rugby, especially popular with indigenous Fijians, is the one sport that has continually put Fiji on the world sporting scene. Even if you're not a fan, it's worth going out for a local rugby match on Viti Levu just to watch the crowd. Every village has its rugby field, and interested visitors may be invited to join an informal game. Soccer is especially strong with Indo-Fijians, and Gujeratis have their own competition.

The British brought the golfing habit to Fiji. There are golf courses on Denarau Island and along Viti Levu's Coral Coast and also at Pacific Harbour and Suva. Other popular sports include cricket, basketball, netball, volleyball, squash, badminton, tennis, lawn bowls, surfing, chess, athletics and boxing.

With the Pacific Games held in Suva in 2003, the capital's facilities have increased and improved and more regional sporting events are likely to be held here. Refer to the sports pages of the *Fiji Times* for venues and events.

Women's Turf

Until recently, Fijian women with an interest in rugby could do little other than cheer on the men's teams. However, these days, more and more women are donning shorts and boots and getting muddy on the field. The Fiji Rugby Union is slow to support them and the players suffer verbal abuse from both men and women. Following a women's national competition, female spectators called into a radio show to rage about how disgraceful the players looked in their kit. With some severely twisted logic, some even blamed women's rugby as responsible for the increase in rape and incest in Fiji. Soon after the competition, Colo-i-Suva Village banned its women from playing.

Overall, the insults seem only to motivate the players to prove their ability. And they're doing a great job of it. Players who've done stints with North American teams have come away feeling that Fijian women are a notch above their competitors. Fijian women's teams have played and beaten Australian teams and are hoping to have their new league team ready for the Women's World Cup in 2006. If you're interested in rugby, check the newspapers for game times and go out and cheer on the women's teams – they'll appreciate the support.

SHOPPING

The main tourist centres of Nadi, the Coral Coast and Suva have lots of handicraft shops. Lautoka and Savusavu are quieter and the salespeople are less pushy. You can also buy interesting handicrafts direct from villages, particularly woven goods and carvings.

Traditional artefacts, such as war clubs, spears and chiefly cannibal forks, are popular souvenirs. So too are *yaqona* bowls of various sizes (miniature ones for salt and pepper), woven pandanus mats, baskets from Kioa, sandalwood or coconut soap, and *tapa* cloth in the form of wall hangings, covered books and postcards. Pottery can be a good buy – if you can get it home in one piece. Don't buy any products derived from endangered species such as turtle and avoid the temptation of buying shells.

Clothing shops in Suva and Nadi have *bula* shirts (in colourful tropical prints) and fashion by local designers. There are also vibrant saris and Indian jewellery on sale.

CASEY & ASTRID WITTE MAHANEY

Don't be tempted, shells are important for the ecology of the sea

Fijian ceramic jewellery is sold in the Government Crafts Centre in Suva.

The Fiji Museum shop in Suva has some interesting books, posters and postcards.

Indo-Fijian History & Culture

LIZ THOMPSON

ROBYN JONES

ROBYN JONES

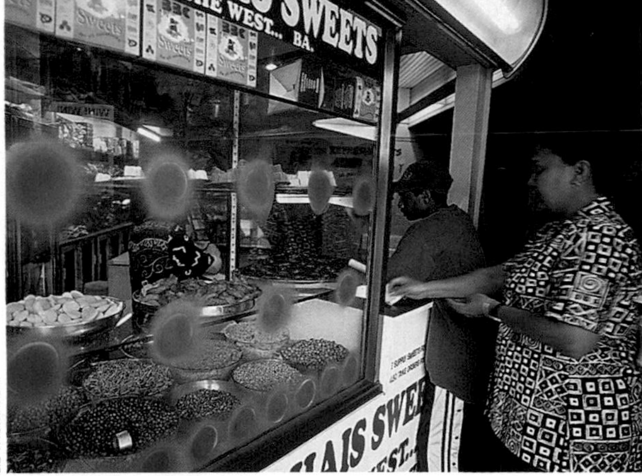

LIZ THOMPSON

Previous Page: Sri Siva Subramaniya Swami Temple, Nadi (Photograph by Robyn Jones)

Top: Indo-Fijian dance group

Middle Left: Statue of a Hindu goddess, Vanua Levu

Middle Right: Statue of Ganesh, Vanua Levu

Bottom: Indian sweet shop, Suva

Indo-Fijian culture means more than Indians living in Fiji. It is a unique blend of beliefs and customs that's developed over centuries out of remarkable historical circumstances. Indo-Fijian culture is heavily intertwined with indigenous Fijian life and culture; without the Indo-Fijian account, you're only getting half the story.

History

Most Indo-Fijians today are the descendents of indentured labourers who began arriving in Fiji from India in the late 1800s to work for the British in cane fields and sugar mills. Many were young illiterate farmers recruited from villages across India, but there was also a mix of castes ranging from Chamars (lower castes) to Brahmins (higher castes).

In the mid-1900s, on completion of their contracts, independent Indian farmers began leasing land to earn a living in sugar cane, cotton, tobacco and rice cultivation. By the time indenture was abolished in 1919, some Indians had diversified further, becoming shopkeepers, clerks, public servants and domestic help. The big move into commerce began in the 1930s, following the arrival of a second wave of mainly business migrants from India.

Over the next few decades, the Indians focused on consolidating their lives and laying the foundations for a future in their adopted country. By the 1940s, Indians outnumbered indigenous Fijians and a campaign for equal citizenship was well underway. In the postwar years Indo-Fijians became more socially and politically organised, and education took on new impetus. During the 1950s and 1960s their numbers in businesses and the professions swelled. Many young Indo-Fijians were sent to study overseas and returned as doctors, lawyers and teachers, brimming with Western influences and ideas about nation building. Among them were future leaders including Mahendra Chaudhry and Jai Ram Reddy.

Fiji became independent from 96 years of colonial administration in 1970. For the next 15 years Indo-Fijians felt fairly secure under Prime Minister Ratu Sir Kamisese Mara, whose Alliance Party promoted multiracialism. But in the mid-1970s race relations took an ugly turn when nationalists, warning of an Indian takeover, demanded the repatriation of all Indians. It was during this period that an unflattering racial stereotype of Indo-Fijians as greedy and self-serving emerged. Political disillusionment with the major parties soon set in.

In the mid-1980s many Indo-Fijians turned to the new Fiji Labour Party (FLP) and its platform of social reform. In 1987 a FLP-NFP (Indo-Fijian National Federation Party) coalition won the elections under the leadership of Dr Timoci Bavadra. Dr Bavadra's cabinet was mainly Fijian but the new government was labelled Indian-dominated by nationalists. In May 1987 the Bavadra government was overthrown in a military coup led by Lieutenant Colonel Sitiveni Rabuka. Indo-Fijian insecurities reached new heights when, in 1990, a new racially biased constitution was introduced to concentrate power in the hands of indigenous Fijians. Two years later Rabuka became prime minister following the first elections since 1987.

During the early 1990s thousands of skilled and professional Indo-Fijians fled the country, and by the mid-1990s Rabuka as prime minister came under local and international pressure to review the 1990 constitution. As a result a new and fairer constitution, including a Bill of Rights, was declared in 1997. Parliamentary seats were still allocated according to ethnicity, but Indo-Fijians were relatively better off under this system.

In the May 1999 elections Rabuka was rejected and Fiji's first Indo-Fijian prime minister, FLP leader Mahendra Chaudhry, came to office. Within a year, Chaudhry's social-reform agenda and his style proved too much for the establishment and nationalists. In 2000 the Chaudhry government was overthrown, following a coup led by George Speight. The 1997 constitution was ditched and an all-indigenous interim government was appointed by the military. Once again deprived of their rights, Indo-Fijians began leaving the country in droves. But many also remained to see the crisis through, including cane-farmer Chandrika Prasad, who took the interim regime to court. He challenged the abrogation of the 1997 constitution and won, paving the way for the 2001 general elections (see the History section in Facts about Fiji for more information).

ROBYN JONES

Left: Sri Siva Subramaniya Swami Temple – the Hindu lord assumes many forms

The Indian in Indo-Fijian

With some five generations having been raised in Fiji, the Indo-Fijian community has forged a strong identity in its adopted homeland. This identity is neither Fijian nor Indian proper, but a unique blend of these cultural traditions. For an Indo-Fijian, being ethnic Indian as opposed to being indigenous Fijian is about a certain type of upbringing and way of life. The outlook and aspirations of Indo-Fijians are very much informed by India's value systems, which have been inherited over the years. Much emphasis is placed on education and hard work to ensure a secure future for oneself. Add thriftiness for good measure and you have the core of the Indo-Fijian package.

India remains an important cultural beacon for Indo-Fijians, influencing ritual practices, culinary traditions, dress and entertainment. Today these aspects of Indo-Fijian life provide some of the more obvious signs of cultural distinction between Indians and non-Indians.

Food and the rituals surrounding preparation and consumption continue to reflect the traditions of India. Most Indo-Fijians enjoy home-made rotis (traditional breads) straight from the kitchen. Steaming curries are served with roti and rice and accompaniments such as chutney and yogurt often complete the meal. Many Indo-Fijians have a weakness for traditional sweets (*mithai*) and on special occasions, such as religious festivals, younger family members are often taught *mithai* making. But home is not the only place you would find Indo-Fijians enjoying and sharing in these popular cultural imports from India. Spot an Indo-Fijian around lunch time at school, the workplace or the outdoors and you can be sure the unashamedly ubiquitous curry combo is not too far away.

Tradition, pride and identity have also ensured that saris, the colourful Indian dress worn by women, remain popular in Fiji. In recent years, taking cue from India's fashion trends and films, the Muslim- and Punjabi-influenced *salwaar-kameez* has also become *de rigeur*, especially among the younger generations. Most Indo-Fijians are practising Hindus, Muslims or Sikhs, and across the country, temples and mosques lend a particularly Indian feel to the landscape. The domes, minarets and red flags atop bamboo poles in backyards also serve as a reminder of the strength of Indo-Fijian adherence to the faiths of India (see Religion in the Facts about Fiji chapter).

Entertainment and recreation continue to have a decidedly subcontinental flavour for many Indo-Fijians, with the local cinemas providing a regular dose of Hindi-language Bollywood film and music. Indo-Fijian home-entertainment systems are often tuned to provide Bollywood on tap, as well as an endless supply of Hindi-pop music videos. Apart from the pure escapism value, Bollywood films also provide many with the only connection they have with India and subcontinental Hindi.

The Fijian in Indo-Fijian

While India may well provide a cultural beacon, most Indo-Fijians today have never been to India, nor feel any particular kinship with that country. Over a century of living together with indigenous Fijians has had a profound effect on the Indo-Fijian identity and lifestyle.

As a result, Indo-Fijians have largely done away with the rigidities of India's caste and social structure, adopting instead the laid-back Melanesian way of life. In Fiji, schools, higher-education institutions, the workplace and places of worship do not discriminate according to caste or class differences. As a result the relative ease with which Indo-Fijians socialise and engage is arguably one of the characteristics which sets them apart from Indians – especially the middle classes in India. For example, in Fiji wedding invitations from economically disadvantaged or rural relatives are seized upon by their well-to-do relatives as an opportunity to catch-up with relatives and indulge in feasting and celebration. Such disregard for social codes would be frowned upon in India. Wedding practices have actually undergone changes in the Melanesian environment. Whereas in India wedding rituals vary widely across the country, in Fiji they have largely been standardised.

One of the more significant cultural departures from India has been the emergence of a Hindi dialect unique to Indo-Fijians. Known as 'Fiji-Hindi', it is an amalgam of regional dialects spoken by earlier indentured labourers from India. Today it is used in all informal family and social settings. In India, it would be regarded as *toota-phoota*, or broken Hindi. But its universal use among Indo-Fijians as well as its distinct grammatical rules and vocabulary, have contributed to its increasing acceptance as a legitimate dialect. The current community debate about whether Fiji-Hindi should be used occasionally on national radio instead of *shud*, or 'Standard Hindi' demonstrates this cultural confidence.

Indian Fijian Tensions

Most aspects of Indo-Fijian lifestyle and culture have comfortably coexisted with the indigenous Fijian way of life for over a century. Occasionally, however, cultural differences between the two communities have proven rich fodder for political agitators, despite the fact that simmering racial tensions can also be attributed to other factors, including a racially based electoral system.

The majority of Indo-Fijians still belong to disadvantaged classes. But the domination of a few in economic activities, and their high visibility in professional and white-collar occupations have often been used by politicians to fan the coals of resentment, especially among the disenfranchised. For a long time, Indo-Fijians have been blamed for the economic plight of indigenous communities. And ever since the early part of last century, the threat of eventual Indian domination has been a recurring theme in Fiji politics, and recycled quite effectively by opportunists and extremists. Such fear-mongering often succeeded in driving a wedge between the two communities. When the democratically elected governments were overthrown in 1987 and 2000, the first thing the coup leaders did was to separate the indigenous Fijian government ministers from their Indo-Fijian colleagues.

The symbols of Indo-Fijian success – new cars, big houses, expensive saris and gold jewellery serve as a constant reminder of what makes Indo-Fijians different as well as threatening. One coup leader has even referred to the way Indians 'look different and smell different' when justifying his actions to the international media. The fact is, the Indo-Fijian threat can and has often served as a perfect smokescreen for other agendas.

Coming Together

Despite the obvious differences between the two main communities, the extent to which they coexist and influence each other demonstrates the goodwill that has grown over the years.

The soccer field is a place of shared experiences. The game first became popular in Fiji among Indians in the postindenture period. Today, indigenous Fijians and others have all joined in. The goodwill that has been generated is reflected in the way the players engage on and off the field. In some of the main soccer districts such as Lautoka and Labasa, it is not uncommon for players to speak each other's languages and hold regular curry, beer and kava nights.

In some areas of Fiji, Indo-Fijian and indigenous Fijian cultures have merged to such an extent that these communities are regarded as oddities in the rest of the country. This is pronounced in the cane belts of Viti Levu – also known as the 'Western side'. After years of working alongside Indo-Fijians, many indigenous cane farmers speak Fiji-Hindi fluently, while their families immerse themselves in Bollywood films like any other Indo-Fijian farming family. The more die-hard Indophiles even sing Hindi film songs. Some Indo-Fijians in these rural areas also speak the local Fijian dialects. Indo-Fijian devotional songs or *bhajans* have even been recorded and released commercially by indigenous Fijian artists.

This comfortable coexistence in the Western side found political expression in the Fiji Labour Party, especially in its early days. Both Labour prime ministers deposed in the coups – the indigenous Fijian Timoci Bavadra and the Indo-Fijian Mahendra Chaudhry – have come from the west. In the mid-1980s the Labour Party emerged as the main opposition to the established parties, with its work and issues-based agenda. Unions and the urban intellectuals championed its causes, but it was the combined support from indigenous Fijians and Indo-Fijians in the Western side that underpinned the Party's multiracial appeal. Indigenous Fijians in the west, disgruntled with the political dominance of their mainly eastern chiefs, threw their support behind the Labour Party, thus cooperating with a large constituency of Indo-Fijian cane growers.

Cultural Immersion

The best way to experience Indo-Fijian culture is to share a meal at the home of an Indo-Fijian. To increase the chances of being invited, you can always meet sociable Indo-Fijians at some of their favourite celebrations, haunts, shops and cultural venues. Annual festivals and events provide some of the best opportunities. *Diwali* (Festival of Lights) takes place around October or November, and a good way to join in the fun is by buying some sweets and candles and sharing them with Indo-Fijians. Religious events include temple fairs where thousands of Indo-Fijians gather to watch rituals and enjoy folksy meals. In Suva the South Indian firewalking festival during July or August begins with a procession and culminates at the **Mariamma Temple** *(Howell Rd, Samabula)*. In the north, the *Ram Leela* festival is held at the Mariamman Temple in Vunivau, Labasa around October. During the rest of the year, visitors are welcome at Hindu and Sikh temples, but temple etiquette must be followed, including wearing conservative dress, removing footwear and abstaining from non-vegetarian meals on the day of your visit.

Fairground activities also accompany the soccer season, which runs from February to October. Club soccer matches are played on weekends throughout the season, culminating in the interdistrict tournament, held in a different location each year (**w** www.fijifootball.com). On the sidelines there is fierce culinary competition under tin sheds, where *pulau* (aromatic fried rice), curry and roti are sold. Be prepared to eat with your fingers and put up with the distorted Bollywood and folk music blaring around you.

If you want to hear and watch the real Bollywood thing, there are cinemas in all major towns and cities with regular sessions of Hindi films (without subtitles); newspapers carry screening details. Bollywood music tapes and CDs are usually available in duty-free centres, as well as at music stores such as Procera Music Stores (☎ 339 4911). In major Indo-Fijian shopping areas, such as Toorak and Cumming Streets in Suva, there is a wide variety of stores selling Indian spices, saris and knick-knacks.

There are plenty of good restaurants around the country serving Indian meals, including the familiar North Indian specialties such as tandoori and naan. For a traditional Indo-Fijian cuisine, inquire about seasonal vegetables such as *duruka, katahar* (jackfruit) and *kerela* (bitter melon). Do not forget to ask for pickles and chutneys made from local fruits such as mangoes, *kumrakh* (star-apple) and tamarind.

Tackling the Tongue

Most Indo-Fijians speak English as well as Fiji-Hindi. English is the main form of communication with other races, but it is not uncommon to find non–Indo-Fijians speaking the lingo at times. In places such as markets, a handful of words can go a long way when bargaining.

Kaise *(KAY-say)*	The common Indo-Fijian hello
Kaise hai *(KAY-say hey)*	How are you?
Tik hai *(TEEK-hey)*	I'm well
Fir Milio *(PHIR Mil-lio)*	A colloquial 'We'll meet again'

Getting There & Away

Centrally situated in the South Pacific, Fiji is one of the main airline hubs of the Pacific region (Hawaii is the other). Many travellers visit Fiji on round-the-world (RTW) tickets or on a stopover between Australia, New Zealand and North America. Those visiting Fiji on a package tour should consider enhancing their trip with some independent travel; get out and explore Fiji for a week or two (perhaps on a budget) and then finish up with a few days in a plush resort. Many agents will allow you to extend your stay on either side of your accommodation package.

> **Warning**
>
> The information in this chapter is particularly vulnerable to change. You should check directly with the airline or a travel agent to make sure you understand how a fare (and the ticket you may buy) works. See the airline websites listed for up-to-date fares and information. In addition, the travel industry is highly competitive and there are many lurks and perks.
>
> The upshot of this is that you should get opinions, quotes and advice from as many airlines and travel agents as possible before you part with your hard-earned cash. The details given in this chapter should be regarded as pointers and are not a substitute for your own careful, up-to-date research.

AIR

Airports & Airlines

Most visitors to Fiji arrive at Nadi International Airport, situated 9km north of central Nadi. A few flights from Sydney and nearby Pacific countries also land at Nausori airport near Suva.

On arrival you will be greeted by a sea of smiling faces and guitar serenading. Most of these people will be representatives of local accommodation or the many travel agencies on the ground floor and first floor concourse of the airport. Usually, representatives of the Fiji Visitors Bureau (FVB) will be there to help you, and it's worth ducking into their office to escape the crowd and get an update on available accommodation and activities. The arrivals and customs area also has a board displaying the names and rates of hotels in the Nadi area that are members of the Fiji Hotels Association.

The airport has a 24-hour ANZ bank with currency exchange ($2 commission fee per transaction) just next to the FVB office. There are many travel agencies, airline offices and car-rental offices in the arrivals area, as well as a post office, cafeteria, restaurant, duty-free shop, newsagency and luggage storage area. Luggage storage costs $3 to $6 per day.

Airlines with direct services to Nadi include Fiji's Air Pacific, Qantas Airways, Air New Zealand, Aircalin, Air Nauru and Solomon Airlines.

Nausori International Airport, 23km northeast of downtown Suva, is Fiji's second airport. Air Fiji has flights to Tuvalu and Tonga, and Royal Tongan Airlines also has flights to Tonga. Air Pacific now has a direct route from Sydney. Otherwise the airport is mostly used for domestic purposes.

The following international airlines have representatives in Fiji. All telephone numbers are for Nadi, unless otherwise stated.

Air Fiji (☎ 672 2521, in Suva ☎ 331 3666, **W** http://airfiji.net) Sales agents for Air India
Air Nauru (☎ 672 2795, in Suva ☎ 331 3731, **W** www.pacificislands.com/airlines/nauru.htm)
Air New Zealand (☎ 672 0070, in Suva ☎ 330 1671, **W** www.airnz.co.nz)
Air Pacific (☎ 672 0888, in Suva ☎ 330 4388, **W** www.airpacific.com) General sales agents for Air Canada, British Airways, Cathay Pacific Airways and Malaysia Airlines
Air Vanuatu (☎ 672 2521, in Suva ☎ 330 0771, **W** www.airvanuatu.com)
Aircalin (☎ 672 2145, **W** www.aircalin.nc) General sales agents for Air France
Polynesian Airlines (☎ 672 2521, *in Suva* ☎ 331 5055, **W** www.polynesianairlines.co.nz)
Qantas Airways (☎ 672 2880, *in Suva* ☎ 331 1833, **W** www.qantas.com.au)
Royal Tongan Airlines (☎ 672 4355, in Suva ☎ 330 9877, **W** www.royaltonganairlines.com)
Solomon Airlines (☎ 672 2831, in Suva ☎ 331 5889, **W** www.solomonairlines.com.au)

Buying Tickets

It is always worth putting aside a few hours to research the current state of the travel market. Start early: some of the cheapest tickets have to be bought months in advance and some popular flights sell out quickly. Talk to other recent travellers – they may be able to stop you making some of the same old mistakes. Look at the advertisements in newspapers and magazines, search the Internet, consult reference books and watch for special offers – then phone travel agents for bargains. (Airlines are useful for supplying information on routes and timetables; however, except at times of airline ticketing wars, they do not supply the cheapest tickets.) Find out the fare, the route, the duration of the journey and any restrictions on the ticket. Then sit back and decide which ticket is best for you.

Use the fares quoted in this book as a guide only. They are approximate and based on the rates advertised by travel agents at the time of research. Most are likely to have changed by the time you read this. Quoted air fares do not necessarily constitute a recommendation for the carrier.

If you are travelling from the UK or the USA, you will probably find that the cheapest flights are being advertised by obscure bucket (discount) shops whose names haven't yet reached the telephone directory. Many such firms are honest and solvent, but there are a few rogues who will take your money and disappear, to reopen elsewhere a month or two later under a new name. If you feel suspicious about a firm, don't give them all the money at once – leave a deposit of 20% or so and pay the balance when you get the ticket. If they insist on cash in advance, go somewhere else. Once you have the ticket, ring the airline to confirm that you are actually booked onto the flight.

You may decide to pay more than the rock-bottom fare and opt for the safety of a better-known travel agent. Firms such as STA Travel, which has offices worldwide, or Travel Cuts in Canada are not going to disappear overnight, leaving you clutching a receipt for a nonexistent ticket, and they offer good prices to most destinations.

It's sensible to buy travel insurance as early as possible. If you buy it the week before you fly, you may find, for example, that you're not covered for delays to your flight caused by industrial action.

Round-the-World Tickets & Circle Pacific Fares RTW tickets are often real bargains. One that takes in the Pacific will be between US$1400 and US$2500, depending on where you want to stop. They are usually put together by a combination of two or more airlines and permit you to fly anywhere you want on their route systems so long as you do not backtrack. Most tickets are valid for up to one year.

The cheaper RTW tickets usually have more restrictions such as fewer choices of where you can stop, large fees to change flight dates and mileage caps. It's also worth checking the minimum and maximum number of stops you can make and how many different airlines you can use. An alternative type of RTW ticket is one put together by a travel agent using a combination of discounted tickets.

Circle Pacific tickets use a combination of airlines to circle the Pacific – combining Australia, New Zealand, the USA and Asia. As with RTW tickets, there are advance purchase restrictions and limits to how many stopovers you can take. These fares are likely to be about 15% cheaper than RTW tickets.

Air Passes Intercountry flights in the Pacific can be expensive. The only really workable way to travel to more than a handful of countries is by using an air pass. Fortunately, there are lots to choose from. New deals are always coming up so it's worth checking with your travel agent or searching the Internet. Conditions apply and seating can be limited, so book early.

Polynesian Airlines' Polypass (which is also called Pacific Explorer Airpass) covers Australia's east coast, New Zealand, and a number of South Pacific countries including Fiji, Samoa, the Cook Islands, and Tonga. Valid for up to 45 days, a ticket including six stops is US$1099; tickets inclusive of Hawaii and/or LA cost US$1699/1349 and stops in Tahiti cost an extra US$175/350 one way/return. The pass is not valid for travel in December or January.

There are also Circle the South West Pacific passes, which include flights with five airlines. Travel must start and finish in Australia, must be completed within 28 days, and there's a minimum stay per destination of five nights. It costs A$780 to A$1200 (depending on which countries you visit) for travel to two of the Solomon Islands, Vanuatu, Fiji or New Caledonia, and around A$180 to A$500 for an extra country.

Air Pacific's Triangle Fare links Fiji, Samoa and Tonga for F$667. The fare is only available from the USA and South America, and travel must be completed within 60 days. You must stop in each of the three countries and can fly on Air Pacific, Polynesian Airlines or Air New Zealand flights. There are also limited offers on other Triangle Fares, such as New Zealand, Fiji and Vanuatu.

The South Pacific pass allows for travel with lots of different airlines (including Air Pacific and Qantas) for a maximum of 6 months, with a minimum of two stops and a maximum of eight. Each flight costs between US$160 and US$320. The ticket covers the South Pacific as well as flights to Australia and New Zealand.

Qantas Boomerang pass is only available in connection with air or sea travel to/from Australia, New Zealand or Fiji from outside the region; it is not available to residents of these countries. It covers Fiji, Vanuatu, Tonga, Western Samoa and the Solomon Islands with a minimum of two stops and a maximum of ten. Tickets range in price, depending on how many 'zones' you cross. Travel within the South Pacific Islands costs US$160 per flight; between Australia or New Zealand and the Pacific Islands costs US$200 per flight.

Travellers with Special Needs

If you have special needs of any sort – you've broken a leg, are vegetarian, in a wheelchair, taking the baby, terrified of flying – let the airline know as soon as possible so that it can make arrangements accordingly. You should remind it when you reconfirm your booking (at least 72 hours before departure) and again when you check in at the airport. It may also be worth ringing airlines before you make your booking to find out how they can handle your particular needs.

Children under two travel for 10% of the standard fare (or free, on some airlines) as long as they don't occupy a seat. They don't get a baggage allowance either. 'Skycots' should be provided by the airline if requested in advance; these will take a child weighing up to about 10kg. Children aged two to 12 can usually occupy a seat for half to two-thirds of the full fare and get a baggage allowance. Push chairs (strollers) can often be taken as hand luggage.

You can take bicycles to pieces and put them in a bike bag or box, but it's much easier to wheel your bike to the check-in desk, where it should be treated as a piece of baggage. You may have to remove the pedals and secure the handlebars sideways so that it takes up less space in the aircraft's hold; it's best to check all this with the airline well in advance, preferably before you pay for your ticket.

Departure Tax

An international departure tax of F$20 applies to all visitors over 12 years old.

The USA

Fiji is a major stopover between west-coast USA and Australia and New Zealand. Fiji is about six hours from Hawaii and 12 hours from west-coast USA. Fares from the USA vary greatly in price depending on season and ticket restrictions. Los Angeles–Nadi with Air New Zealand is about US$1030/1500 for low/high season.

The *New York Times*, the *Los Angeles Times*, the *Chicago Tribune* and the *San Francisco Examiner* all produce weekly travel sections. **ANZA** *(☎ 800-269 2166; **w** www.anza-travel.com)* is an American online travel agent specialising in travel to the South Pacific. **All Travel** *(☎ 800-300 4567, fax 310-312 5053; **e** alltravel@all-travel.com; **w** www.all-travel.com)* also specialises in travel to this region, as does **South Seas Adventures – Sunspots** *(☎ 800-334 5623; **e** info@sunspotsintl.com; **w** www.sunspotsintl.com; 1918 NE 181st St, Portland, Oregon)*, customising holiday packages and dive packages to Fiji.

For student discounts **STA Travel** *(☎ 800-777 0112; **w** www.statravel.com)* has offices in major cities.

Canada

Fiji is a popular stopover between Canada and Australia and New Zealand, and for those on RTW tickets. Air Canada shares with Air Pacific on this route. Fares for Vancouver–Nadi via Honolulu start at about C$1860/2200 for low/high season. Fares from Ottawa or Toronto are C$100 more; these generally fly via Chicago and LA.

Toronto's *Globe & Mail*, the *Montreal Gazette*, the *Toronto Sun* and the *Vancouver Sun* are good places to look for cheap fares.

Flight Centre *(☎ 888-967 5355; w www.cheapflights.ca)* usually offer the best prices; you're likely to get a better price if you go into one of their offices than if you book online. Check the website for the agency nearest you. **Travel Cuts** *(☎ 866-246 9762; w www.travelcuts.com)* is Canada's national student travel agency and has offices in all major cities.

Australia

Air Pacific is the main carrier between Australia and Fiji, and Qantas Airways tickets to Fiji are usually seats on Air Pacific planes. The flight time is about 3¾ hours from Sydney and about 4½ hours from Melbourne.

Excursion fares from Sydney or Brisbane are typically A$750/990 return for low/high season. Add A$50 to fares from Melbourne. Advance purchase fares are cheaper, but less flexible.

Good places to hunt for bargain flights include **Hideaway Holidays** *(☎ 02-9743 0253, fax 9745 3568; w www.hideawayholidays.com.au)* or **Talpacific Holidays** *(☎ 02-9244 1850, fax 9262 6318; e sydney@talpacific.com; w www.talpacific.com)*.

New Zealand

Air Pacific operates services from Nadi–Auckland, Nadi–Wellington and Nadi–Christchurch. Air New Zealand also flies Nadi–Auckland and has shared services on the other routes. From Auckland to Fiji (three hours) costs about NZ$950/1140 for low/high season. Flights from Wellington are about NZ$225 extra and from Christchurch NZ$275 extra. It is possible to get better deals so you should shop around.

Try **Travel Online** *(w www.travelonline.co.nz)* or **Talpacific Holidays** *(w www.travelarrange.co.nz)*, also **Air New Zealand** *(w www.airnewzealand.co.nz)* and **Go Pacific** *(☎ 09-914 4048, fax 09-377 0111; e mike@gogogo.co.uk; 151 Victoria St, Auckland)*. **STA** *(w www.statravel.co.nz)* and **Flight Centre** *(w www.flightcentre.co.nz)* are also popular travel agents in New Zealand.

Other Pacific Countries

Many airlines provide connections between Fiji and other Pacific countries including Air Nauru, Aircalin (New Caledonia), Nadi–Papeete (Tahiti), Solomon Airlines and Royal Tongan Airlines. Air Pacific flies Nadi–Honiara, Nadi–Apia (Western Samoa), Nadi–Port Vila (Vanuatu), and Nadi–Fua'amotu. Air Fiji flies Suva–Funafuti (Tuvalu) and Suva–Tonga service.

Flights within the Pacific can be expensive, so to cover a number of countries, consider an air pass (see the Air Passes section earlier in this chapter).

The UK

London is the travel discount capital of Europe. Airline ticket discounters are known as bucket shops in the UK, and many advertise in the travel pages of the weekend broadsheets, such as the *Independent* on Saturday and the *Sunday Times*. Look out for the free magazines, such as *TNT*, which are widely available in London, often from outside the main railway and underground stations.

Try **Travel Cuts** *(☎ 020-7255 2082; 295a Regent St, London)*, who are agents for STA; **Trailfinders** *(☎ 020-7938 3939; w www.trailfinders.co.uk)*, **Bridge the World** *(☎ 020-7734 7447; w www.b-t-w.co.uk)* and **Flightbookers** *(☎ 020-7757 2000; w www.ebookers.com)*.

A return ticket from London to Nadi costs about £840/980 in the low/high season.

Continental Europe

Generally there is not much variation in air fare prices for departures from the main European cities, but deals can be had, so shop around. Expect to pay around €955/1216 for low/high season.

OTU Voyages *(☎ 0825 817 817; w www.otu.fr)* is a French network of student travel agencies that can supply discount tickets to travellers of all ages. You'll find offices in most French cities. It's also worth trying **Nouvelles Frontières** *(☎ 0825 000 747; w www.nouvelles-frontieres.fr)* as wel as **Voyageurs du Monde** *(w www.vdm.com)*.

In the Netherlands is **Wereldcontact** *(☎ 0343-530530; w www.wereldcontact.nl; Hoofdstraat 166, Driebergen)* specialising in flights to the South Pacific. You can also try **NBBS Reizen** *(☎ 0900-1020300; e info@nbbs.nl; w www.mytravel.nl; Linnaeusstraat 28, Amsterdam)*.

In Germany, **Adventure Travel** *(☎ 0911-979 9555, fax 979 9588; e support@adventure-holidays.com; w www.adventure-holidays.com; Wacholderbergstr. 29 90587 Veitsbronn)* specialises in South Pacific travel.

Asia

Air Pacific has flights from Nadi to Japan, South Korea and Thailand. Most flights to/from Southeast Asia go via Australia or New Zealand.

Hong Kong is the discount plane-ticket capital of the region; flights to Nadi with Air Pacific cost about HK$2470. Hong Kong's bucket shops are at least as unreliable as those of other cities. Ask the advice of other travellers before buying a ticket. STA, which is reliable, has branches in Hong Kong, Tokyo, Singapore, Bangkok and Kuala Lumpur.

SEA

Travelling to Fiji by sea is difficult unless you're on a cruise ship or yacht. Few of the shipping companies will take passengers on cargo ships and those that do will usually charge hefty rates. It is virtually impossible to leave Fiji by cargo ship unless passage has been prearranged. However, you could try asking your local shipping agents, or go to the docks and personally approach the captains.

Cruise Ship

Although few cruise ships have Fiji on their itineraries, it is a possibility. Recently, a cruise or two has stopped in Levuka (on Ovalau), Taveuni, Savusavu (on Vanua Levu), and the Yasawas. These ships have hailed from the east coast of Australia and Hawaii. If you're hoping to visit Fiji by cruise ship, you need to talk to your travel agent well in advance.

Yacht

Fiji's islands are a popular destination and stopover for yachts cruising the Pacific. The best time to sail is in the 'winter' from early November to late April when the southeasterly trade winds are blowing. During the 'summer' months (May to October), winds change direction more often and the chance of finding yourself in a storm or cyclone is greater.

Yachts need to head for the designated ports of entry at Suva, Lautoka, Levuka or Savusavu, to clear customs, immigration and quarantine. Present a certificate of clearance from the previous port of call, a crew list and passports. Before departing, you'll again need to complete clearance formalities (within 24 hours), providing inbound clearance papers, your vessel's details and your next port of call. Customs must be cleared before immigration, and you must have paid all port dues and health fees. For more information see Visas & Documents in Facts for the Visitor.

Other marinas in Fiji include Vuda Point Marina (between Nadi and Lautoka), Port Denarau, and Musket Cove Marina on Malololailai (Plantation Island) in the Mamanucas. Yachties are often looking for extra crew and people to share day-to-day costs. If you are interested, ask around the

Isa Lei, a Fijian Farewell Song

As your boat departs from the shore or you hike off from the village, Fijians are likely to sing you this farewell song written by a student in the early 20th century for his forbidden love, Isa. While her social standing may have separated Isa from her lovesick suitor, it couldn't keep what became Fiji's number-one song from reaching her ears. By the time you leave Fiji, you too may well know it by heart.

Isa Isa Vulagi lasa dina
Isa Isa you are my only treasure
Nomu lako au na rarawa kina
Must you leave me so lonely and forsaken
Cava beka ko a mai cakava
As the roses will miss the sun at dawning
Nomu lako au na sega ni lasa
Every moment my heart for you is yearning

Isa lei, na noqu rarawa
Isa Lei, the purple shadows fall
Ni ko sa na gole e na mataka
Sad the morrow will dawn upon my sorrow
Bau nanuma na nodatou lasa
Oh forget not when you are far away
Mai Viti nanuma tiko ga
Precious moments from Fiji

Vanua rogo na nomuni vanua
Isa Isa my heart was filled with pleasure
Kena ca ni levu tu na ua
From the moment I heard your tender greeting
Lomaqu voli me'u bau butuka
Mid the sunshine we spent the hours together
Tovolea ke balavu na bua
Now so swiftly those happy hours are fleeting

marinas and look on the noticeboards. For more details see the Activities section in the Facts for the Visitor chapter.

ORGANISED TOURS

While travelling independently is easy in Fiji, many visitors prearrange some type of package tour. It may be the ideal option if you have limited time, prefer an upfront, all-inclusive price, wish to stay in a particular resort, or have special interests and activities, such as diving. Most travel agents will be able to organise this type of trip and can often arrange cheap deals. There are many options, and prices depend on the season, type of accommodation and length of the trip.

Although not pushed by travel agents, with most package deals it's possible to extend your stay in Fiji on either side of your tour, giving you a chance to experience Fiji independently as well as time to relax and be pampered in a resort. This is the perfect option for those looking to add a bit of adventure to their beach holiday.

Getting Around

By using local buses, carriers and ferries you can get around Fiji's main islands relatively cheaply and easily. If you'd like more comfort or are short on time you can use air-conditioned express buses, rental vehicles, charter boats and small planes.

AIR

Domestic Air Services

Fiji is well serviced by internal airlines, which have frequent and generally reliable flights. Some may find the light planes scary, especially if it's windy or turbulent, but the views of the islands, coral reefs and lagoons are fantastic.

The international airports on Viti Levu, at Nadi and Nausori (near Suva), are also the main domestic hubs. Other domestic airports include Savusavu and Labasa on Vanua Levu, Matei on Taveuni, Vunisea on Kadavu, Bureta on Ovalau and, in the Mamanucas, Malololailai and Mana. Many other small islands also have airstrips. There are flights to outer islands where there is no accommodation for tourists and an invitation is needed to visit – in some cases it is illegal to turn up uninvited. Rotuma, Gau, Koro, Moala and Vanua Balavu, and Lakeba in Lau have airstrips but receive few visitors, while other islands such as Vatulele, Yasawa and Wakaya have their own airstrips that serve the upmarket resorts.

Air Fiji and Sun Air have regular inter-island flights by light plane. Most of Air Fiji's services operate out of Nausori, while Sun Air is based in Nadi. Prices on shared routes are almost identical.

Air Fiji (e *airfiji@connect.com.fj;* w *www.airfiji.net; in Suva ☎ 331 3666, fax 330 0771; in Nadi ☎ 672 2521, fax 672 0555; at Nausori airport ☎ 347 8077, fax 340 0437; in Labasa ☎ 881 1188, fax 881 3819; in Savusavu ☎ 885 0173; in Levuka ☎ 344 0139, fax 344 0252; in Matei ☎ 888 0062)* operates daily flights from Suva to Labasa,Levuka, Nadi, Savusavu, Taveuni and Kadavu. From Nadi, there are daily flights to Suva, Savusavu, Mana, Labasa, Taveuni and Kadavu via Suva.

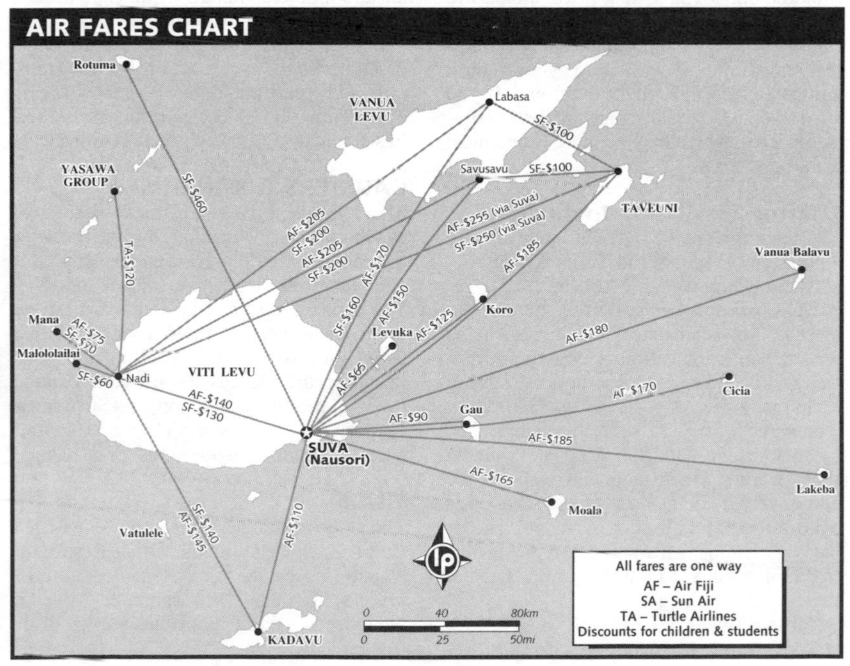

Sun Air *(e sunair@connect.com.fj; w www.fiji.to; at Nadi airport ☎ 672 3016, fax 672 3611; in Suva ☎ 330 8979, fax 330 2089; at Nausori airport ☎ 347 7310, fax 347 7377; in Labasa ☎ 881 1454, fax 881 2989; in Savusavu ☎ 885 0141; in Matei ☎ 888 0461)* has daily services to major tourist destinations (except Ovalau), including Suva, Labasa, Savusavu, Kadavu, Malololailai (Plantation Island Resort and Musket Cove Resort) and Mana. See the Air Fares Chart for prices. For overseas reservations contact: Australia: (☎ 02-9232 5866, fax 02-9223 9358); New Zealand: (☎ 09-913 7583, fax 09-478 1372) and USA/Canada: (☎ 310 376 8956, fax 310 376 9804).

Air Passes

Air Fiji has a 30-day Discover Fiji Pass for $540 (US$270). It is sold only outside Fiji in conjunction with an international air fare. There is a choice of three set itineraries, including: Nadi–Taveuni–Suva–Kadavu–Nadi; Nadi–Taveuni–Suva–Levuka–Suva–Nadi; and Nadi–Savusavu–Suva–Kadavu–Nadi–Malololailai–Nadi. It's best to book your seats, as the small planes often fill up quickly. Children under 12 pay half price, infants are charged 10%. There is a US$60 predeparture cancellation fee, and reimbursement is minimal once in Fiji. If you change your mind it will cost US$70 per flight to reroute. If you are a student, a 25% discount applies to regular air fares, which may be more economical than the air pass.

Charter Services & Joyflights

Charter services and joyflights are available with Island Hoppers and Turtle Airways.

Island Hoppers *(☎ 672 0410, fax 672 0172; w www.helicopters.com.fj)* offers transfers to most of the Mamanucas island resorts, as well as helicopter flights departing from Denarau island and Nadi airport. A flight to Malololailai by helicopter costs $370 return (compared with $224 by seaplane and $120 by small plane with Sun Air). A 20-minute flight over the Sabeto mountain range and the gorges of Mt Evans, east of Lautoka, costs $140 per seat (four to six passengers). The Islands & Highlands trip is $230 per person (for a trip lasting 35 minutes). Children under two fly free of charge.

Turtle Airways *(☎ 672 1888, fax 672 0095; w www.turtleairways.com; New Town Beach, Nadi)* has a fleet of seaplanes departing from Newtown Beach or the resorts on Denarau. As well as flight seeing, it provides transfer services to the Mamanucas, Yasawas, the Fijian Resort (on Queens Rd), Pacific Harbour, Suva, Toberua Island Resort and other islands as required. A flight to Malololailai by seaplane costs $224 return (compared with $120 by Sun Air). The charter service is $790/1050 per flying hour for a five-seater Cessna/seven-seater DeHavilland Canadian Beaver.

BUS

Fiji's larger islands have extensive and inexpensive bus networks. Catching the local buses is a cheap and fun way to get around. While they can be fairly noisy and smoky they are perfect for the tropics, with unglazed windows and pull-down tarpaulins for when it rains. There are bus stops but you can often just hail buses, especially in rural areas. See the respective destination chapters for details.

Reservations

Reservations are not necessary for local buses. If you are on a tight schedule or have an appointment though, it may be a good idea to buy your ticket in advance, especially for coach trips and tours over longer distances (eg, Suva to Nadi). Pacific Transport and Sunbeam issue timetables (available from the FVB), but for most local buses just ask around the bus stations.

CARRIERS & MINIBUSES

Many locals drive small trucks (known as carriers) with a tarpaulin-covered frame on the back. These often have passenger seating and some run trips between Nadi and Suva. You can pick up a ride in Nadi's main street. They leave when full and are quicker than taking the bus. Similarly, Viti Minibuses shuttle along the Queens Rd between Lautoka (pick-up near the bus station) and Suva (pick-up near the market), and charge $10. However, the drivers are notorious for speeding.

TRAIN

The only passenger train is on Viti Levu's Coral Coast between the Fijian Resort and Natadola Beach. It is a scenic jaunt for tourists. For details, see Yanuca & Around in the Queens Rd & Coral Coast section of the Viti Levu chapter.

CAR & MOTORCYCLE

Ninety percent of Fiji's 5100km of roads are on Viti Levu and Vanua Levu, of which about one-fifth are sealed. Both of these islands are fun to explore by car or on motorcycles.

Road Rules

Driving is on the left-hand side of the road. A licence from an English-speaking country will suffice, otherwise, you'll need to obtain an International Driving Permit. The speed limit is 80km/h which drops to 50km/h in towns. Many villages have speed humps to force drivers to respect the village pace. Seat belts are compulsory for front-seat passengers. Should you pick up a parking fine in Suva it's likely to be around $2.

As a rule, local drivers often speed, stop suddenly and overtake on blind corners, so take care, especially on gravel roads. Buses also stop where and when they please. There are lots of potholes, and sometimes the roads are too narrow for two vehicles to pass, so be aware of oncoming traffic. Avoid driving at night as there are many pedestrians and wandering animals – especially along the southeast coast of Viti Levu, on Vanua Levu and Taveuni. Watch for sugar trains in the cane-cutting season, as they have right of way.

Rental

Rental cars are relatively expensive in Fiji. Despite this, it is a good way to explore the larger islands, especially if you can split the cost with others. Rental motorcycles and scooters are also available in Nadi and Suva (see following). The perimeter of Viti Levu is easy to get to know by car: Queens Rd and most of the Kings Road are sealed. Most other roads are unsealed and are better for 4WD vehicles.

Some rental agencies will not allow their cars to be driven on unpaved roads, which limits exploration of the highlands. It is possible to take vehicles on roll-on, roll-off ferries to Vanua Levu or Taveuni, but again, some companies do not allow this. The ferry costs are pretty expensive and vehicles are available to rent on both these islands anyway. If you do take a car on a ferry to Vanua Levu, it's best if it's a 4WD.

The shorter the hire period, the higher the rate. Delivery and collection charges usually apply. Avis Rent a Car rates for four to six days with unlimited travel are $100/170 per day for a small car/4WD with air-con. Thrifty Car Rental has cheaper rates for slightly older cars. Some companies will hire at an hourly rate or per half-day, while some have a minimum hire of three days. It's usual to pay a deposit by credit card, although some companies require a minimum cash payment per day as well as a passport-size photograph. Some will give discounts for advance bookings.

A valid overseas or international driving licence is required. Third party insurance is compulsory and personal accident insurance is highly recommended if you are not already covered by travel insurance. The minimum-age requirement is 21, or in some cases 25.

Ask the FVB about the various companies. Generally, the larger, well-known companies have better cars and support, but are more expensive. Consider what's appropriate for you, including how inconvenienced you might be if the car breaks down, what support services are provided, the likely travel distance, insurance, if value-added tax (VAT) is included and the excess or excess waiver amount (what you pay to waiver paying the excess). Common exclusions, or problems that won't be paid for by the insurance company, include tyre damage, underbody and overhead damage, and theft of the vehicle. Check brakes, water, and tyre pressure and condition before heading off.

The main towns have service stations, but fill up the tank before heading inland. If you do run out of fuel, it might be available in village shops. Expect to pay about $1.20 per litre of petrol in Fiji.

The easiest place to rent vehicles is on Viti Levu. Most rental agencies have offices at Nadi International Airport; the established companies also have offices in other towns and rental desks at larger hotels.

Some of the more reputable car-rental agencies on Viti Levu include:

Avis Rent a Car (e aviscarsfj@connect.com.fj) Avis has branches at Nadi airport (☎ 672 2688, fax 672 0482), Nausori airport (☎ 347 8963) and in Suva (☎ 331 3833)

Budget Rent a Car Budget has branches at Nadi airport (☎ 672 2735, fax 672 2053) and Nausori airport (☎ 347 9299)

Hertz There are Hertz branches in Nadi (☎ 672 3466, fax 672 3650) and Suva (☎ 338 0981)

Thrifty Car Rental (e rosiefiji@connect.com.fj) Thrifty has offices at Nadi airport (☎ 672 2755, fax 672 2607) and in Suva (☎ 331 4436)

Car-rental agencies on Vanua Levu and Taveuni have mostly 4WDs due to the island's rough roads.

Budget Rent a Car (☎ 881 1999, fax 881 3654) Hot Springs Hotel, Labasa; (☎ 888 0291, fax 888 0275) Somosomo, Tavenui – 4WD vehicles only

Although not widely available, motorcycles and scooters are not a bad way to travel in Fiji. Similar traffic rules and rental conditions as mentioned above for car rental, apply to motorcycles and scooters. Rental per day cost around $30/50 scooters/125cc motorcycle.

Beat Rentals (☎ 672 1471) Queens Rd, Martintar, Nadi; (☎ 338 5355, 991 2587) Grantham Rd, Nabua, Suva
Westside Motorcycle Rental (☎ 672 5878, e mihajoltd@connect.com.fj) 27 Gounder St, Nadi

BICYCLE

Fiji's larger islands have good potential for cycling, although some areas are too hilly and rugged. Viti Levu has long, flat stretches of sealed road along the scenic Coral Coast, and it is possible to cycle around the perimeter of the island by the Kings Road and the Queens Road. Take a carrier up to a highland location such as Abaca and ride back down. You could also cycle along Vanua Levu's unsealed roads from Savusavu along Natewa Bay (no accommodation around here) and along the Hibiscus Hwy from Buca Bay, where you can take the ferry over to Taveuni. Ovalau also has a scenic unsealed (mainly flat) coastal road.

The best time to go would be in the 'drier' season (May to October). If you intend to do a lot of cycling bring your own bicycle and repair kit. Mountain bikes are best for exploring the interior. Bicycles can be rented on the Coral Coast, Taveuni and Ovalau. Bicycles can be rented in Nadi, Teveuni and Ovalau Wacking Stick Adventure Tours near Nadi runs mountain-bike tours. Rental bikes can be in pretty poor condition, so test the brakes and gears beforehand.

The biggest hazard is the unpredictable traffic – Fijian drivers can be pretty manic. Avoid riding in the evening when visibility is low. Travel light but carry plenty of water – it can be hot and dusty. You can usually buy coconuts and bananas from villages along the way. Storage at Nadi airport is relatively expensive; the cheapest place to store bikes is at backpacker hostels. For more information see Cycling under Activities in the Facts for the Visitor chapter.

HITCHING

Hitching is never entirely safe in any country, and we don't recommend it. Travellers who decide to hitch should understand that they are taking a small but potentially serious risk.

Hitching in Fiji, however, is common. Locals do it all the time, especially with carriers. It is customary to pay the equivalent of the bus fare to the driver. Hitchhikers will be safer if they travel in pairs and let someone know where they are planning to go. Crime is more prevalent around Suva, although there have been cases of hitchhikers being mugged around Nadi.

BOAT

With the exception of the upmarket resort islands, often the only means of transport to and between the islands is by small local boats, especially for the backpacker resorts. Life jackets are rarely provided and usually the boats have no radio-phones. If the weather looks ominous or the boat is overcrowded, consider postponing the trip.

Interisland trips for sightseeing and catamaran transfers are available in the Mamanucas, and the Yasawas: see these chapters for more details. In other areas, however, it is difficult to explore and hop from island to island unless you have a charter boat or yacht. In Kadavu, for example, transport is mostly by small village or resort boats. Apart from the Suva–Kadavu ferry, there is no organised transport here and most resorts have their own boats.

Ferry

Regular ferry services link Viti Levu to Vanua Levu and Taveuni, and also Viti Levu to Ovalau. See the Fiji colour map at the beginning of this book for ferry routes. The Patterson Brothers, Beachcomber Cruises and Consort Shipping boats are large roll-on, roll-off ferries, carrying passengers, vehicles and cargo. They have canteens where you can buy drinks, snacks and light meals.

Ferry timetables are notorious for changing frequently. Boats sometimes leave at odd hours and there is often a long waiting period at stopovers. The worst thing about the long trips is that the toilets can become disgusting (take your own toilet paper). There are irregular boats that take passengers from Suva to Lau, Rotuma and Kadavu.

Beachcomber Cruises (☎ 330 7889, fax 330 7359) Taina's Travel Service, Suite 8, Epworth Arcade, Suva; (☎ 666 1500, fax 666 4496) Lautoka; (☎ 885 0266, fax 885 0499) Savusavu; (☎ 888 0216, fax 888 0202) Tavenui
Consort Shipping (☎ 330 2877, fax 330 3389) ground floor, Dominion House Arcade, Thomson St, Suva
Grace Ferry Services (☎ 885 0602) Savusavu
Hussein's (☎ 888 0134) Naqara, Tavenui
Kadavu Shipping (☎ 331 2428, fax 331 2987) Office No. 1, Old Millers Wharf, Walu Bay, Suva
Patterson Brothers Shipping (☎ 331 5644, fax 330 1652) Suites 1 & 2, Epworth Arcade, Nina St, Suva; (☎ 881 2444, fax 881 3460) Labasa; (☎ 666 1173, fax 666 7269) Lautoka; (☎ 344 0125) Levuka

Nadi–Mamanucas South Sea Cruises (*☎ 675 0500, e southsea@connect.com.fj*) has the fast catamaran *Tiger IV* shuttling daily between Denarau Marina and the Mamanuca islands. There is also another catamaran, *Malolo Cat,* connection to Musket Cove Marina on Malololailai. Refer to Getting Around in the Mamanuca Group chapter for information on both these services.

Nadi–Yasawas South Sea Cruises' new catamaran, the *Yasawa Flyer*, has daily services between the Viti Levu mainland (Nadi's Denarau Marina) and the Yasawas (Waya/Waya Lailai, Naviti and Tavewa). Refer to the Yasawa Group chapter for details.

Nadi–Beachcomber Island–Lautoka–Northern Viti Levu–Vanua Levu The Beachcomber Cruises catamaran *Lagilagi,* operates between the Viti Levu mainland (Nadi's Denarau Marina and Lautoka) and Vanua Levu (Savusavu). It stops at Beachcomber Island (in the Mamanucas) and on request, Nananu-i-Ra (off Northern Viti Levu). The service runs twice weekly (Tuesday and Saturday). The route is: Denarau Marina (departs 6am)–Beachcomber Island–Lautoka (departs 7am)–Nananu-i-Ra (on request)–Savusavu (departs 12.30pm)–Lautoka–Denarau Marina. The one-way trip between Viti Levu and Vanua Levu will cost you $90.

Suva–Savusavu–Taveuni Consort Shipping's MV *Spirit of Free Enterprise (SOFE)* does voyages twice a week Suva–Koro–Savusavu–Taveuni return. It departs Suva on Wednesday at 10am arriving at Koro 7pm, Savusavu (seat/bunk $40/75) at 11pm, and Taveuni at 6am on Thursday (seat/bunk $45/85). It departs Taveuni around noon on Thursday arriving at Savusavu at 5pm, Koro at 3am and Suva at 9am on Friday. The stop at Koro is about one hour and the Suva–Taveuni trip involves a 13-hour stopover in Savusavu, but the return trip has a much shorter stopover in Savusavu. The second trip departs Suva on Saturday at 6pm arriving at Koro on Sunday at 3am, Savusavu at 8am and Taveuni at 2pm. It then departs Taveuni at noon on Monday arriving at Savusavu at 5pm, Koro at midnight and Suva at 8am on Tuesday.

Beachcomber Cruises' 500-passenger ship the *Adi Savusavu*, previously known as *Dana Star* has better facilities than the *SOFE* and has Suva–Savusavu–Taveuni voyages three times weekly. It departs Suva on Tuesday at 10am, Thursday at noon, and Saturday at 6pm. The Suva–Savusavu trip costs $45/65 for economy/first class per person and takes about 11 hours. The ferry from Savusavu then continues for an extra five hours to Taveuni ($22/45 economy/first class from Savusavu to Taveuni, $50/70 economy/first class from Suva to Taveuni).

Grace Ferry has a Savusavu–Buca Bay–Taveuni bus-ferry service ($15) involving 1½ hours by bus to Natuvu, Buca Bay, and 1¾ hours by ferry to Waiyevo (Taveuni) across the Somosomo Strait. The bus departs Savusavu bus station Monday, Wednesday and Friday at 8.30am to connect with the ferry at 1pm. The return trip starts with the ferry trip from Taveuni to Buca Bay Tuesday, Thursday and Saturday at 8.45am.

Lautoka–Ellington Wharf–Nabouwalu (Viti Levu)–Labasa Patterson Brothers plies this route four times a week ($50). It involves a bus ride (3½ hours) from Lautoka, a trip on the *Ashika* ferry (3¾ hours) and a trip on another bus to Labasa (four hours).

Suva–Natovi–Nabouwalu–Labasa Patterson Brothers travels this route daily ($43), except Sunday and public holidays. It involves a bus ride (1½ hours) from Suva, a ferry trip (4½ hours) and another bus to Labasa (four hours).

Suva–Natovi–Buresala–Levuka This Patterson Brothers service ($24), runs daily except Sunday, involves a bus ride (1½ hours) from Suva (Western Bus Terminal, Rodwell Rd) to Natovi Landing, followed by a ferry to Buresala Landing (one hour) and another bus to Levuka (one hour).

Suva–Bau Landing–Leleuvia–Levuka Daily services except Sunday leave at noon (contact Leleuvia Island Resort for bookings) and include Suva–Leleuvia ($30 one way) and Suva–Levuka ($50 one way).

Suva–Kadavu Kadavu Shipping has irregular passenger services on the MV *Bulou-ni-Ceva* ($42 one way).

Suva–Rotuma Kadavu Shipping has irregular passenger services on the MV *Bulou-ni-Ceva* ($90/130 for deck/saloon).

Suva–Lau Group There are several cargo/passenger boats that visit the Lau Group. Vanua Balavu and Lakeba both have budget accommodation, otherwise you need to be invited to stay by a local.

Ika Corporation (☎ 330 8169, fax 331 2827) Yatulau Arcade, Rodwell Rd, Suva. Ika has fortnightly trips from Suva to Cicia, Vanua Balavu, Lakeba, Nayau, Tuvuca and Mago ($60 one way, excluding meals).

Saliabasaga Shipping (☎ 330 3403) GPO Box 14470, Walu Bay, Suva. Saliabasaga has fortnightly trips aboard the MV *Tunatuki* to Lakeba, Nayau, Cicia, Tuvuca, Vanua Balavu and occasionally Moce and Oneata ($80 one way with meals).

Taikabara Shipping (☎ 330 2258, fax 332 0251) Muaiwalu Complex, Old Millers Wharf, Rona St, Walu Bay, Suva. Taikabara has fortnightly trips aboard the *Taikabara* to the Southern Lau Group. It visits Lakeba, Vanuavatu, Komo, Kabara, Moce, Fulaga, Namuka, Vatoa, Ogea Levu and Ono-i-Lau ($70/80 one way for deck/cabin, including meals). It costs an extra $10 to visit the far south of the group (Vatoa and Ono-i-Lau).

Suva–Moala Group There is no accommodation for visitors to the Moala islands – you would need to be invited to stay by a local. **Khans Shipping** *(☎/fax 330 8786; Mauiwalu Complex, Rona St, Walu Bay, Suva)* has almost weekly trips aboard the two cargo/passenger boats, the *Te Maori* and *Cagidonu*. They make the journey to Moala, Matuku and Totoya in the Moala Group and Gau and Nairai in the Lomaiviti Group. A one-way fare is $50/80 without meals/VIP room including meals.

Yacht

Yachting is a great way to explore the Fiji archipelago. It is possible to charter boats or hitch a ride on cruising vessels. See the Sea section of the Getting There & Away chapter or Activities in the Facts for the Visitor chapter.

LOCAL TRANSPORT

Taxi

You will find taxis on Viti Levu, Vanua Levu, Taveuni and Ovalau. The bus stations in the main towns usually have taxi depots and there is often an oversupply of taxis, with drivers competing for business. There are some good cabs, but most are rickety old dinosaurs bound for or retrieved from the wrecker. Most taxi drivers are Indo-Fijians keen to discuss life and local politics. They invariably have relatives in Australia, New Zealand or Canada.

Unlike in Suva, taxi drivers in Nadi, Lautoka and most rural areas don't use their meters. First ask locals what is the acceptable rate for a particular trip. If there is no meter, confirm an approximate price with the driver before you agree to travel. Cabs can be shared for long trips. For touring around areas with limited public transport such as Taveuni, forming a group and negotiating a taxi fee for a half-day or day may be an option.

Always ask if the cab is a return taxi (returning to its base). If so, you can expect to pay $1 per person or less (remember to confirm the going rate with a local), as long as the taxi doesn't have to go out of its way. To make up for the low fare, the driver will usually pick up extra passengers from bus stops. You can usually recognise a return taxi, as most have the name of their home depot on the bumper bar.

ORGANISED TOURS

Fiji has many companies providing tours within the country, including trekking, cycling, kayaking, diving, bus or 4WD tours. Cruises to the outer islands such as the Mamanucas and Yasawas are popular. There is also a sailing safari called Tui Tai from Savusavu to Taveuni, Kioa and Koro (see Cruises in Vanua Levu). Viti Levu has the most tours, and Ovalau, Taveuni and Vanua Levu also have a few. See the respective destination chapters.

Feejee Experience *(c/o Tourist Transport Fiji ☎ 672 3311; **e** ttf@connect.com.fj)* has a fun four-day loop around Viti Levu ($269), together with a trip and accommodation at Savusavu on Vanua Levu (ferry-bus via Nabouwalu and catamaran return) with/without a trip to Beachcomber Island for $565/425. A side-trip just including Beachcomber Island costs $410.

There are also several live-aboard dive boats (see under Activities in the Facts for the Visitor chapter).

Viti Levu

Highlights

- Trek the mountains of Koroyanitu National Heritage Park and enjoy the spectacular views to the Mamanucas and Yasawas
- Stretch out on Natadola Beach, undoubtedly Viti Levu's best beach
- Take a river trip by kayak or raft through the wilderness and gorges of the Namosi Highlands
- Stroll around central Suva and its colonial buildings, visit the fascinating Fiji Museum
- Circle the island by bus or car via the Queens and Kings Road
- Snorkel, dive, kayak or windsurf over the crystal blue reefs around Nananu-i-Ra
- Glimpse the highland way of life and see the traditional *bure* architecture at the village of Navala
- Visit the Tavuni Hill Fort, the Sigatoka Sand Dunes and the Ka Levu Cultural Centre

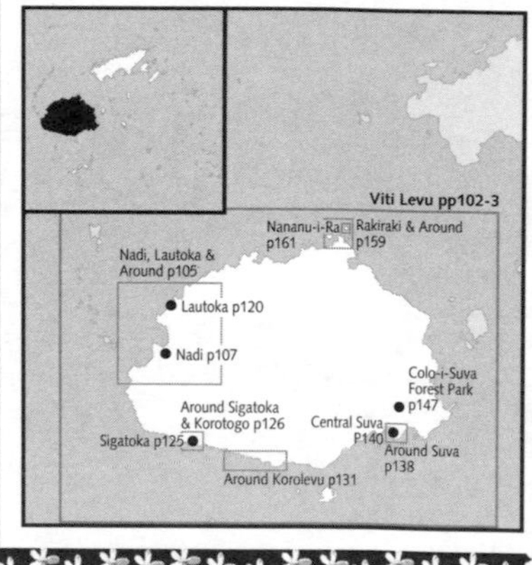

At 10,400 sq km, Viti Levu (Great Fiji) is Fiji's largest island. It's also the political, administrative and industrial centre of the archipelago and home to around 75% of Fiji's population (581,000). The west especially, is home to a high proportion of Indo-Fijians, most of them fourth-generation descendants of indentured labourers brought to Fiji to work in the cane fields. Many still reap a meagre living from growing cane.

The roughly oval-shaped island (146km from east to west and 106km from north to south) has a mountainous interior scattered with remote villages. The highest Fijian peak, Tomanivi (Mt Victoria, 1323m) is at the northern end of a high backbone running north-south. Rugged ranges and hills slope steeply down to the lowlying coast. Viti Levu has four large rivers: the Rewa and the Navua Rivers form fertile delta regions near Suva; the Sigatoka River flows south to the Coral Coast; and the Ba River flows north.

While Viti Levu has much to offer the curious, adventurous traveller, with the exception of Natadola Beach and the OK beaches of the Coral Coast, the mainland may disappoint those after a 'beach' holiday. You will have to pay extra for a boat or plane to the offshore and outer islands to find idyllic, deserted beaches.

Climate

The central highlands lie in the path of the prevailing southeast trade winds, resulting in higher rainfall and lush rainforest on the eastern side of the range. In contrast, the drier western slopes are mostly open grasslands, which turn light yellow to brown in the dry season (May to October).

Orientation

Suva, the country's capital, largest city and main port, is in the southeast, on the rainier side of Viti Levu. Most travellers, however, arrive in the west at Nadi International Airport. Nadi and Suva are linked by the Queens Road (sealed), along the southern perimeter of Viti Levu (221km), and Kings Road (mostly sealed), around the northern side of the island (265km).

Many minor roads lead to isolated coastal areas and into the highlands. Most are unsealed and often too rough for non-4WD vehicles. Between the wetter months of November and April, some roads can become impassable.

Nadi International Airport is 9km north of central Nadi and 24km south of Lautoka, the country's second largest city. Fiji's 'Sleeping Giant' (Sabeto Range) lies between – offering great trekking opportunities and views to the tiny offshore islands of the Mamanucas.

South of Nadi, the Queens Road winds past more cane country. Momi Bay (on the dusty Old Queens Road), the lovely Natadola Beach and the Sigatoka Sand Dunes are interesting detours.

The fertile Sigatoka Valley (known as Fiji's 'salad bowl'), formed by Fiji's second-largest river, extends far into the highlands. Farther east the Queens Road hugs the beautiful Coral Coast. This long stretch of wide fringing reef, broken only by passages adjacent to rivers and streams, is a stunning sight from the air. Past Korolevu, the Queens Road turns away from the shore and climbs up over the southern end of the mountain range that divides eastern and western Viti Levu. Almost immediately the vegetation becomes lusher. Deuba and Pacific Harbour have the last OK mainland beaches before Suva and the offshore islands of Beqa and Yanuca in the Beqa Lagoon beckon divers and surfers.

Heading north from Suva, the Kings Road passes Nausori and then the small town of Korovou. Kings Road then heads northwest over the hills through an unsealed section, and down by the beautiful Viti Levu Bay to Rakiraki. There are spectacular views of the mountains, indented coast and the offshore islands, including Nananu-i-Ra. An alternative rough, unsealed route from Korovou (4WDs only) skirts the northeast coast, passing Natovi Landing and rejoining the Kings Road farther north near Viti Levu Bay.

Just before the small town of Tavua there is a turn-off to Nadarivatu and Tomanivi, Fiji's highest peak. The scenery returns to sugar-cane farming as the Kings Road passes through Tavua, bypasses the agricultural town of Ba and ends up in Lautoka.

There are three roads up from the coast to the Nausori Highland villages of Navala and Bukuya (via Ba, Nadi and Sigatoka).

Accommodation

On arrival at Nadi International Airport you will be bombarded with a huge range of accommodation options. Nadi itself has an oversupply of places to stay. If you haven't already decided where to go, it can be worth staying a night or two in the Nadi-Lautoka area to assess your options and hear other travellers' tales.

At the time of writing there was a free phone within airport arrivals where, if you are organised (and awake enough) you can book accommodation yourself. Alternatively, do some homework at the FVB.

Just outside the airport there are cheap, local buses along the Queens Road and most of the hotels have free transfer vehicles awaiting international flights, so it is best to already have some idea of where to go for the first night.

Nadi is a highway town stretching over 10km between the airport and downtown. It is easy and cheap to get around by local buses, which you can catch just outside the airport entrance. If you want to be close to the shops Nadi has a couple of budget options in busy downtown. While a bit more isolated, it is peaceful at the nearby beach on Nadi Bay. Places along or near the main road are convenient if you are awaiting domestic connections or you want quick access to buses. Most places offer free airport transfers for international flights, so you don't necessarily have to stick close to the airport.

While Nadi town has good restaurants and infrastructure for travellers it can be a bit of a tourist trap. Lautoka is quieter, with a more authentic local atmosphere, and is easy to get around on foot. There is also accommodation between the two towns at Vuda Point and near the Sabeto Range.

Unlike the offshore islands, budget places on the mainland will generally have hot showers and 24-hour power, unless they are in remote villages.

There are also plenty of places to stay along the Queens Road (Coral Coast), and in Fiji's capital, Suva. Kings Road accommodation is relatively sparse, except for the lovely and convenient offshore island of Nananu-i-Ra.

Getting There & Away

Most travellers arrive in Fiji at Nadi International Airport (although some do arrive at Suva's Nausori airport). The Getting There & Away chapter contains fares and contact details of airline offices. Nadi is also Fiji's main domestic transport hub. From here there are flights to many of the other larger islands, reliable boat services and cruises to offshore islands and a regular and cheap local bus network. Refer to the Getting Around chapter and individual island chapters for information on interisland flights and ferry services.

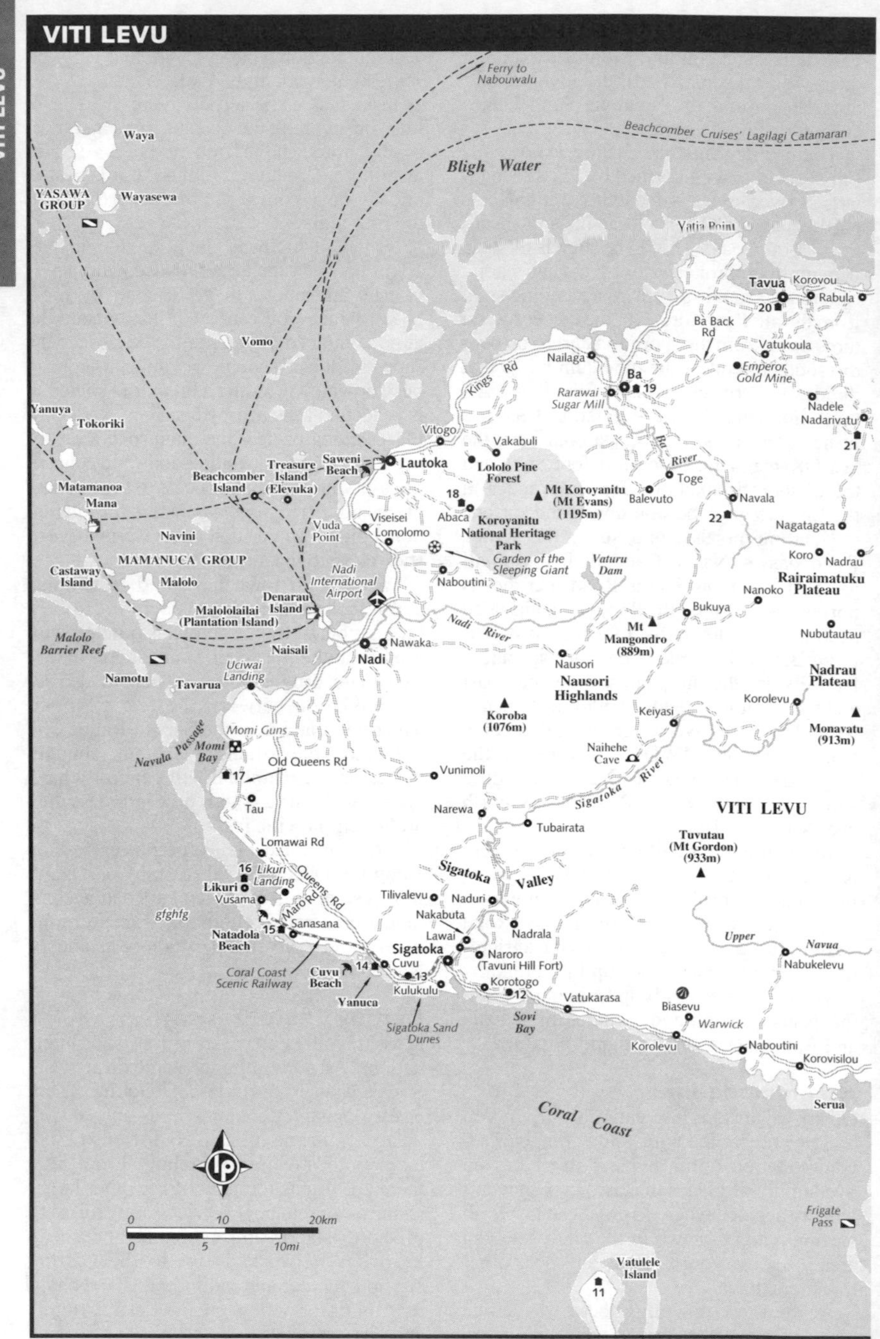
VITI LEVU
Ferry to Nabouwalu
Beachcomber Cruises' Lagilagi Catamaran
Bligh Water
Waya
YASAWA GROUP
Wayasewa
Yatia Point
Tavua
Korovou
Rabula
Ba Back Rd
Vatukoula
Emperor Gold Mine
Nadele
Nadarivatu
Vomo
Nailaga
Kings Rd
Ba
Rarawai Sugar Mill
Yanuya
Tokoriki
Vitogo
Vakabuli
Lautoka
Saweni Beach
Lololo Pine Forest
Treasure Island (Elevuka)
Beachcomber Island
Matamanoa
Mana
Mt Koroyanitu (Mt Evans) (1195m)
Balevuto
Toge
River
Navala
Abaca
Koroyanitu National Heritage Park
Viseisei
Vuda Point
Lomolomo
Navini
MAMANUCA GROUP
Nagatagata
Garden of the Sleeping Giant
Vaturu Dam
Koro
Nadrau
Castaway Island
Malolo
Nadi International Airport
Naboutini
Rairaimatuku Plateau
Nanoko
Denarau Island
Malololailai (Plantation Island)
Bukuya
Nadi River
Mt Mangondro (889m)
Nubutautau
Malolo Barrier Reef
Naisali
Nadi
Nawaka
Nausori
Namotu
Tavarua
Uciwai Landing
Nausori Highlands
Nadrau Plateau
Koroba (1076m)
Korolevu
Keiyasi
Monavatu (913m)
Momi Guns
Navula Passage
Momi Bay
Naihehe Cave
Old Queens Rd
Vunimoli
Sigatoka River
Tau
Narewa
Tubairata
VITI LEVU
Lomawai Rd
Tuvutau (Mt Gordon) (933m)
Likuri Landing
Likuri
Queens Rd
Sigatoka Valley
Vusama
Maro Rd
Tilivalevu
Naduri
gfghfg
Nakabuta
Sanasana
Natadola Beach
Lawai
Nadrala
Upper Navua
Sigatoka
Naroro (Tavuni Hill Fort)
Nabukelevu
Coral Coast Scenic Railway
Cuvu Beach
Cuvu
Korotogo
Kulukulu
Yanuca
Vatukarasa
Biasevu
Sovi Bay
Warwick
Sigatoka Sand Dunes
Korolevu
Naboutini
Korovisilou
Serua
Coral Coast
0
10
20km
5
10mi
Frigate Pass
Vatulele Island
11
12
13
14
15
16
17
18
19
20
21
22

VITI LEVU

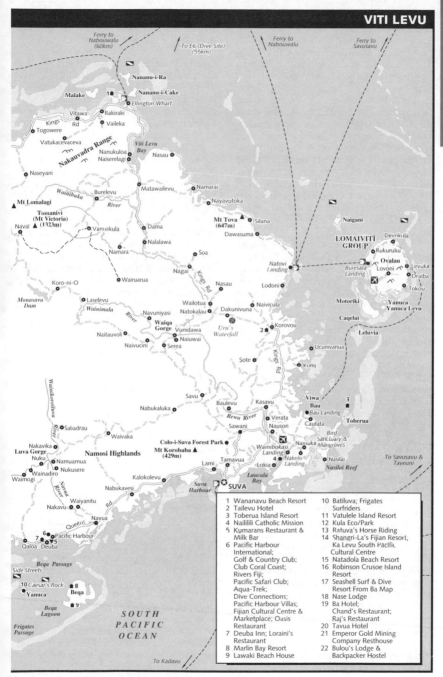

1. Wananavu Beach Resort
2. Tailevu Hotel
3. Toberua Island Resort
4. Naililili Catholic Mission
5. Kumarans Restaurant & Milk Bar
6. Pacific Harbour International; Golf & Country Club; Club Coral Coast; Rivers Fiji; Pacific Safari Club; Aqua-Trek; Dive Connections; Pacific Harbour Villas; Fijian Cultural Centre & Marketplace; Oasis Restaurant
7. Deuba Inn; Loraini's Restaurant
8. Marlin Bay Resort
9. Lawaki Beach House
10. Batiluva; Frigates Surfriders
11. Vatulele Island Resort
12. Kula Eco/Park
13. Ratuva's Horse Riding
14. Shangri-La's Fijian Resort, Ka Levu South Pacific Cultural Centre
15. Natadola Beach Resort
16. Robinson Crusoe Island Resort
17. Seashell Surf & Dive Resort From Ba Map
18. Nase Lodge
19. Ba Hotel; Chand's Restaurant; Raj's Restaurant
20. Tavua Hotel
21. Emperor Gold Mining Company Resthouse
22. Bulou's Lodge & Backpacker Hostel

Getting Around

Local buses are cheap, regular and a great way to travel around the island and mix with the locals. Express buses link the main centres of Lautoka, Nadi and Suva, along both the Queens and Kings Roads. Most will pick up or drop off at the hotels and resorts. Look for timetables from Pacific Transport and Sunbeam Transport offices in Lautoka. There are also many bus companies operating on a local level. Even remote inland villages, such as those in Viti Levu's highlands, have regular (though less frequent) services. These trips might take awhile as they stop in many villages along the way. Before heading to an isolated area, check that there is a return bus so that you don't get stranded without any accommodation – sometimes the last bus of the day stays at the final village.

There are also lots of tourist buses. **Feejee Experience** (run through Tourist Transport Fiji – details following) has recently started up, carting budget travellers around Viti Levu and linking some of the most popular places and sites. It can be a fun and social way to get around, especially if you are short on time and friends. The travel pass is packed full of activities and allows you to stop and start as you like. The four-day 'Hula Loop' of Viti Levu ($269) includes Natadola Beach, Sigatoka Sand Dunes, highland trekking, tubing on the Navua River, Suva nightclubs, *bilibili* rafting on the Wainabuka River, kayaking and longboarding and snorkelling on Nananu-i-Ra. Other passes include trips to Vanua Levu and Beachcomber Island (see Organised Tours in the Getting Around chapter). Contact Sun Vacations (see Travel Agencies later under Nadi) for more information.

Minibuses and carriers (small trucks) also shuttle locals along the Queens Road. Taxis are plentiful, but drivers don't always use meters, just confirm the price in advance. Viti Levu is also easy to explore by car or motorbike, although for the unsealed highland roads you'll generally need a 4WD. See the Getting Around chapter for a list of car-rental and motorbike and scooter hire.

For those in a hurry or after a scenic flight there are cheap, regular light plane flights between Nadi and Suva for about $140.

Viti Levu Bus Services There are a range of companies and services available.

Fiji Holiday Connections *(☎ 672 0977, Suite 8, arrival concourse, Nadi International Airport)* operates a minibus shuttle between Nadi and Suva (about 3½ hours) along the Queens Road, and will pick up and drop off travellers at hotels along the Coral Coast. There is also an express service that takes about three hours. It has early morning departures from Nadi and departs from Suva in the early afternoon; book a day in advance. It also has minibuses for hire within Viti Levu.

Pacific Transport Limited *(Nadi: ☎ 670 0044; Lautoka: ☎ 666 0499; Sigatoka: ☎ 650 0088; Suva: ☎ 330 4366)* has a regular service (about six express buses daily) between Lautoka and Suva ($12, 6/5 hours for regular/express) via the Coral Coast on the Queens Road. The first express bus leaves Lautoka at 6.30am, the last about 6pm. It is generally OK to turn up at the bus station, but you can book in advance for an extra $0.50.

Sunbeam Transport Limited *(Lautoka: ☎ 666 2822; Suva: ☎ 338 2122)* runs the Lautoka–Suva express services via the Queens Road ($12, 5 hours).

Tourist Transport Fiji *(☎ 672 3311, toll free 0800 672 0455;* **e** *ttf@connect.com.fj;* **w** *www.new-zealand.com/fiji/ttf)* offers coach tours and are agents for Feejee Experience.

United Touring Fiji *(Nadi airport: ☎ 672 2811, fax 672 0389; Suva: ☎ 331 2287)* has a daily express air-con coach service between Nadi and Suva (about $30, 4½ hours) along the Queens Road. It has daily departures from Nadi about noon, and from Suva around 7.30am. From Nadi International Airport to Korolevu costs $20.

Nadi

Nadi (pronounced n**an**-di) is Fiji's third-largest city (population 30,900) and is the country's tourism hub. While not the ideal destination in itself, it is a convenient base from which to organise your trip around Viti Levu or to outer islands. Nadi has heaps of places to stay, from budget dorms to luxury resort hotels and there are many organised day trips on offer. The main street is packed with restaurants and souvenir shops, and the produce market and the Swami Temple are well worth a visit. Inland are the Nausori Highlands, and to the north lies the beautiful Sabeto mountain range.

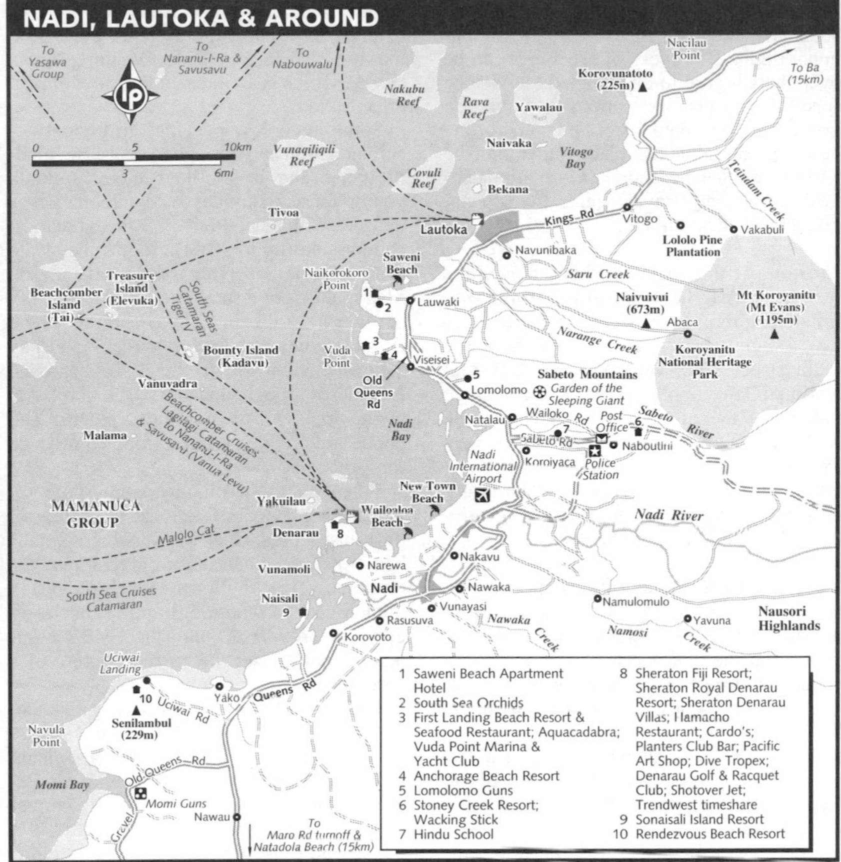

Orientation

From Nadi airport the Queens Road heads north to Lautoka and 9km south to downtown Nadi. Nadi's main street extends from the Nadi River southward for about 800m to the T junction at the large Swami temple. From here the Queens Road continues right to Suva, while the Nadi Back Rd bypasses the busy centre and rejoins the Queens Road back near the airport. The road to the Nausori Highlands leads off into the mountains from the Nadi Back Rd.

The market, bus station and post office are downtown just east of the main street.

Just north of downtown, between the mosque and the Nadi River, Narewa Rd leads west for 6km to Denarau Island. It has Nadi's most upmarket resorts, a manicured golf course and Denarau Marina from where most tours and boat services depart for the offshore islands of the Mamanucas and Yasawas.

Near Martintar, Wailoaloa Rd also turns west off the Queens Road and after 1.75km hits Wailoaloa Beach. To reach New Town Beach, turn right off Wailoaloa Rd after 1.25km and continue for another 1.25km. This quiet spot has several budget places to stay, a golf course and the Turtle Airways seaplane base. You can also get to Wailoaloa Beach along Enamanu Rd.

Information

Tourist Offices The **Fiji Visitors Bureau** *(FVB; ☎ 672 2433, fax 672 0141; e fvbnadi@connect.com.fj; w www.BulaFiji.com)* is a good source of information for travellers.

The office is at the Nadi airport arrivals concourse and is open to meet all international flights. The racks of brochures can be overwhelming, so to obtain useful advice be specific. The visitors' comments book can give some up-to-date insight on some of the budget places. Note that places other than the FVB claiming to be 'tourist information centres' are actually travel agents that do not give independent advice.

Money At the airport arrivals concourse there is an **ANZ bank** (open for all international flights). Elsewhere banks usually give a slightly better rate. Downtown on the main street **ANZ**, **Westpac** and **Colonial National Bank** all have ATMs and exchange money and there is also an ANZ ATM at the McDonald's on the Queens Road. Also try **Thomas Cook** *(Main St, Nadi; open 9am-5pm Mon-Fri, 8.30am-noon Sat)*. The larger hotels also exchange money and usually pay a little less than the banks.

Post & Communications There is a post office in downtown Nadi near the market, and another at Nadi airport, across the car park from the arrivals area near the cargo sheds. Public phones are usually easy to find and private phones can be used with the phone-card system.

These services can be found just about everywhere in Nadi, including many of the budget hotels. Expect to pay 10 to 20 cents per minute.

There are a few options in Martintar, including the **West Coast Cafe** *(open 5pm-11pm)*. At **Onyx Internet** *(☎ 672 0088; Room 201, Capricorn International Hotel, Martintar)* you can also download images from digital cameras onto CD.

Cybercafe *(501 Main St, Nadi)* is in town near the petrol station. At the other end of the main street **Noveix Microsystems** also has lots of terminals.

At the Nadi International Airport arrivals concourse try the travel agencies (Rosie Tours, Sun Vacations on the ground floor and at Ratu Kini's upstairs).

Travel Agencies Most of Nadi's many travel agencies are at the Nadi International Airport arrivals area on the ground and first floors. Domestic plane tickets can be bought directly from the Air Fiji and Sun Air offices at the arrivals concourse. Before committing to any local trips with the agents it is a good idea to have a look at the Fiji Visitors Bureau (FVB), which is an independent government organisation.

Some agencies specialise in budget accommodation and offer good deals. Be mindful though that it is in their interest to book you up for as many days accommodation as they can with places that offer them the most commission (up to 30%!). So, just be aware that you're not receiving independent advice. Many of the good small budget places struggle when the cream is taken off, so where possible contact the resort directly and pay the owner when you get there. This approach is hindered though, due to the lack of reliable phone lines at some remote places, and phonecard credit is quickly gobbled up even for local calls.

When booking offshore budget accommodation get details such as: the safety of the transport (especially if it includes small-boat trips); the cleanliness and facilities; the type and price of food available; and any hidden costs. If possible, quiz other travellers or browse through the FVB's comments book to get the current picture of a particular place.

Argo Travel & Foreign Exchange *(☎ 670 1645, e argotravel@connect.com.fj, 267-269 Main St, Nadi)* is a good spot for organising tickets with Sun Air, Air Fiji and Air Pacific: if the location in town is more convenient than the airport.

Awesome Adventures Fiji *(South Sea Cruises ☎ 675 0499, or toll free 0800 6750 499, e awesomeadventure@connect.com.fj, w www.awesomeadventures.co.nz)* offers island hopping aboard the *Yasawa Flyer* and various budget-accommodation packages for the Mamanucas and Yasawas.

Margaret Travel Service *(☎ 672 1988, fax 672 1992, upstairs Nadi airport concourse)* specialises in budget accommodation.

Rosie, The Travel Service *(Adventure Fiji ☎ 672 2755, fax 672 2607, e info@rosiefiji.com, w www.rosiefiji.com, Nadi airport concourse)* organises road tours, cruises and accommodation, and are agents for Thrifty Car Rental.

Sun Vacations *(☎ 672 4273, fax 672 5829, w www.sunvacationsfiji.com, Nadi airport concourse)* books accommodation, transport and tours.

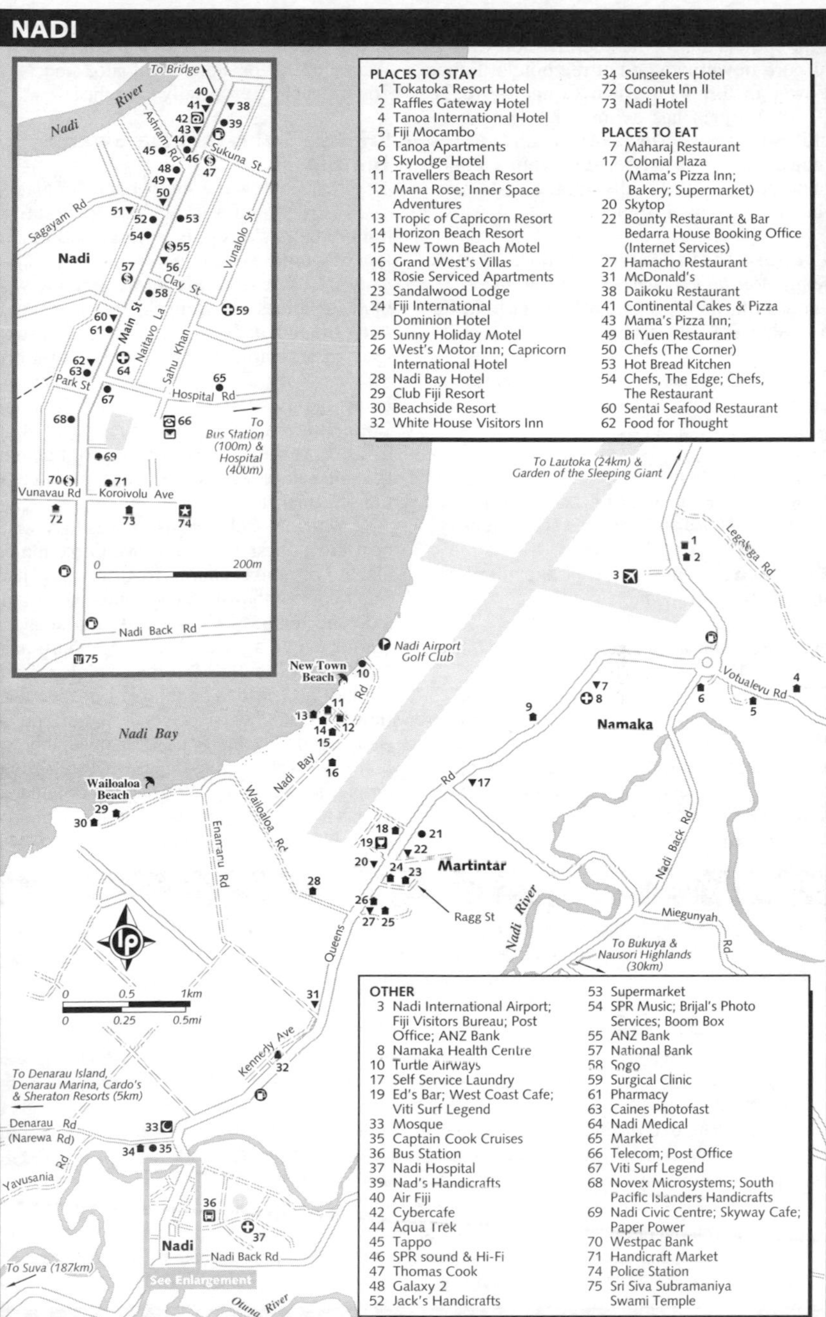
NADI

PLACES TO STAY
1 Tokatoka Resort Hotel
2 Raffles Gateway Hotel
4 Tanoa International Hotel
5 Fiji Mocambo
6 Tanoa Apartments
9 Skylodge Hotel
11 Travellers Beach Resort
12 Mana Rose; Inner Space Adventures
13 Tropic of Capricorn Resort
14 Horizon Beach Resort
15 New Town Beach Motel
16 Grand West's Villas
18 Rosie Serviced Apartments
23 Sandalwood Lodge
24 Fiji International Dominion Hotel
25 Sunny Holiday Motel
26 West's Motor Inn; Capricorn International Hotel
28 Nadi Bay Hotel
29 Club Fiji Resort
30 Beachside Resort
32 White House Visitors Inn
34 Sunseekers Hotel
72 Coconut Inn II
73 Nadi Hotel

PLACES TO EAT
7 Maharaj Restaurant
17 Colonial Plaza (Mama's Pizza Inn; Bakery; Supermarket)
20 Skytop
22 Bounty Restaurant & Bar Bedarra House Booking Office (Internet Services)
27 Hamacho Restaurant
31 McDonald's
38 Daikoku Restaurant
41 Continental Cakes & Pizza
43 Mama's Pizza Inn;
49 Bi Yuen Restaurant
50 Chefs (The Corner)
53 Hot Bread Kitchen
54 Chefs, The Edge; Chefs, The Restaurant
60 Sentai Seafood Restaurant
62 Food for Thought

OTHER
3 Nadi International Airport; Fiji Visitors Bureau; Post Office; ANZ Bank
8 Namaka Health Centre
10 Turtle Airways
17 Self Service Laundry
19 Ed's Bar; West Coast Cafe; Viti Surf Legend
33 Mosque
35 Captain Cook Cruises
36 Bus Station
37 Nadi Hospital
39 Nad's Handicrafts
40 Air Fiji
42 Cybercafe
44 Aqua Trek
45 Tappo
46 SPR sound & Hi-Fi
47 Thomas Cook
48 Galaxy 2
52 Jack's Handicrafts
53 Supermarket
54 SPR Music; Brijal's Photo Services; Boom Box
55 ANZ Bank
57 National Bank
58 Sogo
59 Surgical Clinic
61 Pharmacy
63 Caines Photofast
64 Nadi Medical
65 Market
66 Telecom; Post Office
67 Viti Surf Legend
68 Novex Microsystems; South Pacific Islanders Handicrafts
69 Nadi Civic Centre; Skyway Cafe; Paper Power
70 Westpac Bank
71 Handicraft Market
74 Police Station
75 Sri Siva Subramaniya Swami Temple

To Bridge
Nadi River
Ashram Rd
Sukuna St
Sagayam Rd
Vunalolo St
Nadi
Clay St
Main St
Naitavo La
Sahu Khan
Park St
Hospital Rd
To Bus Station (100m) & Hospital (400m)
Vunavau Rd
Koroivolu Ave
0
200m
Nadi Back Rd
To Lautoka (24km) & Garden of the Sleeping Giant
Legalega Rd
Nadi Airport Golf Club
New Town Beach
Votualevu Rd
Namaka
Nadi Bay
Nadi Bay Rd
Wailoaloa Beach
Wailoaloa Rd
Enarraru Rd
Martintar
Ragg St
Nadi River
Nadi Back Rd
Miegunyah Rd
To Bukuya & Nausori Highlands (30km)
Queens Rd
0 0.5 1km
0 0.25 0.5mi
Kennedy Ave
To Denarau Island, Denarau Marina, Cardo's & Sheraton Resorts (5km)
Denarau Rd (Narewa Rd)
Yavusania Rd
Nadi
Nadi Back Rd
To Suva (187km)
See Enlargement
Ouna River

Bookshops Nadi has few bookshops. Your best options are the handicraft shops at the airport, downtown and at the hotels. Paper Power in the Nadi Town Council Arcade (Civic Centre) has a limited selection of children's books; **Devia** *(Main St, Nadi)* has magazines. Consider donating your second-hand books to the Nadi Library upstairs in the Town Council Arcade.

Laundry The **Self Service Laundry** *(Queens Road, Martintar; open 9am to 5pm Mon-Fri and 9am to 1pm Sat)* charges $3 per load for a wash and $3 for a dryer.

Medical Services For medical treatment, contact any of the following.

Dr Ram Raju Surgical Clinic (☎ 670 0240) 2 Lodhia St, Nadi
Nadi Hospital (☎ 670 1128) Market Rd, Nadi
Namaka Medical Centre (☎ 672 2288) Corner of Queens Road and Namaka Lane, Namaka

Emergency Emergency phone numbers include the following.

Ambulance (☎ 670 1128)
Fiji Visitors Bureau emergency hotline (☎ 0800 6721 721)
Police (☎ 670 0222)

Warning You may be pestered by sword-sellers and overly keen souvenir vendors. While Fiji is a relatively safe place to travel, there are occasional muggings and thefts in the Nadi area, not limited to lone travellers. Avoid wandering with valuables or packs along the beach or quiet roads such as Wailoaloa Rd or along Wailoaloa and New Town Beaches, especially at night.

Sri Siva Subramaniya Swami Temple

The focal point at the southern end of Nadi's main street and set against a beautiful mountain backdrop is a large, colourful Hindu temple *(☎ 670 0016; open 5am-8pm daily)*. Before this elaborate temple was built, devotees worshipped here in a small *bure* (thatched dwelling). Wander around the main temple to see the Hindu Lord Shiva's various forms, all incarnations being manifestations of the One Supreme Lord. This is a Murugan temple and worship of Lord Murugan is equivalent to the worship of nature. He is the guardian deity of the seasonal rains.

Visitors are welcome as long as they wear neat and modest dress, and haven't consumed alcohol or nonvegetarian food that day. It is fine to take photos in the grounds but not inside the temple. Annual festivals such as Karthingai Puja, Panguni Uthiram Thiru-naal (April) and Thai Pusam attract devotees from around the world. The temple has four full-time priests who perform eight pujas (prayers) daily and, for a fee, are available for home and vehicle blessings. Devotees circle around the temple where they offer banana, smash a coconut, burn some camphor and receive blessing from the priest.

Hindu Symbolic Rites

There are lots of tiny Hindu temples and shrines dotted around the countryside. A Hindu temple symbolises the body, the residence of the soul. Union with God can be achieved through prayer and by ridding the body of impurities (meat cannot be eaten on the day of entering the temple, and shoes must be removed).

Water and fire are used for blessings. Water carried in a pot with flowers is symbolic of the Great Mother (the personification of nature), while burning camphor symbolises the light of knowledge and understanding. The trident represents fire the protector and the three flames of purity, light and knowledge.

The breaking of a coconut represents the cracking of three forms of human weakness: egotism (the hard shell), delusion (the fibre) and material attachments (the outermost covering). The white kernel and sweet water represent the pure soul within.

Fire walking is a means to become as one with the Great Mother. Hindus believe that the body should be enslaved to the spirit and denied all comforts. They believe life is like walking on fire and that a disciplined approach, like the one required in the ceremony, helps them to achieve balance, self-acceptance and to see good in everything.

Diving

The good-value **Inner Space Adventures** *(☎/fax 672 3883; New Town Beach)*, near Mana Rose accommodation, offers budget dive trips to the Mamanucas and charges $110 for a two-tank trip, including all gear, lunch and transfer from Nadi hotels. Open-water certification costs $380.

Dive Tropex *(☎ 670 1888)*, based at the Sheraton Fiji Resort on Denarau island, has good, fast boats and covers a wide range of dive sites in the Mamanucas. A two-tank dive trip costs $150, or $620 for open-water certification.

Aqua-Trek *(☎ 670 2413; w www.aquatrek.com; 465 Main St, Nadi)* has a shop with diving and snorkelling gear for sale, but no excursions from Nadi.

River Rafting & Kayaking

Based at Pacific Harbour, **Rivers Fiji** *(☎ 345 0147; w www.riversfiji.com)* picks up from Nadi hotels. It offers exciting river-rafting and kayaking trips to the superb Namosi Highlands.

Mountain Biking

Based at Stoney Creek Resort, **Wacking Stick Adventure Tours** *(☎ 672 4673, 995 3003; w www.wackingstickadventures.com)* rents good mountain bikes for $12/20 for a half/full day and sends you off with a map to explore the cane fields, foothills of the Sabeto Mountains and Valley. For $10 extra you can hire a guide.

The full-day organised tours are also worthwhile. The Sleeping Giant Bike and Hike tour ($125) visits the Garden of the Sleeping Giant, bikes around the Sabeto area, visits a hot spring, heads up the valley by 4WD to Nalesutele for a *sevusevu*, hikes to a cave through jungle and to a waterfall. It is offered daily, except Sundays. On the Natadola Beach Bike Tour ($95) you'll ride through farmland via the village of Malomalo, stop at Natadola for bodysurf and snorkel (equipment provided) and return to Nadi by carrier. Tours collect participants from Nadi hotels and lunch is included.

Another day trip combines biking, some hiking and visiting a village and waterfall for $55. A sunset ride from Stoney Creek Resort to the local hot spring costs $15 (lanterns and headlamps provided). Those who are fit can even follow the Eco Challenge bike route in the Nausori Highlands. This trip (accompanied by a support vehicle) includes a ride from Ba, an overnight stay in Navala, a drive to Bukuya and another ride to the dam near Navalawa. Visit the website for details.

Golf & Tennis

The **Denarau Golf & Racquet Club** *(☎ 675 9710)* caters mainly for guests of the Sheraton hotels. It has an immaculately groomed 18-hole golf course with bunkers in the shape of sea creatures. Green fees are $95 for 18 holes and $55 for nine holes. The all-weather and grass tennis courts cost $20 per hour and racket hire is $10 per person.

Nadi Airport Golf Club *(☎ 672 2148; $15 for 18 holes)*, near Turtle Airways at New Town Beach is a much cheaper option. Clubs and pull-cart are an extra $25.

Jet-Boat Trips

For those in need of an adrenalin rush, the New Zealand company **Shotover Jet Fiji** *(☎ 675 0400; e shotoverjet@connect.com.fj; $59/25 per adult/child, 30mins)* has a roaring, hair-raising tear around the Nadi River mangroves. The mad jet-boat drivers perform 360-degree spins and frighteningly close shaves. It departs from Denarau Marina and there's a courtesy minibus for transfers from hotels.

Horse Riding

The **Sonaisali Island Resort** *(☎ 670 6011; e info@sonaisali.com)* has one-hour horse-riding trips for $13/26 per child/adult.

At Club Fiji Resort horse riding can be arranged for $20 per hour. There are also horses for hire at Natadola Beach, a good day trip from Nadi.

Day Trips & Organised Tours

Offshore Islands For those lovely white-sand beaches and crystal blue waters head for the stunning offshore islands of the Mamanucas and Yasawas. The Mamanucas are close enough for an easy day trip. **South Sea Cruises** *(Awesome Adventures ☎ 675 0499; w www.awesomeadventures.co.nz)* has a regular catamaran shuttle running a loop around the group three times daily. Malololailai, Beachcomber, Mana and Castaway islands also usually take day-trippers; confirm in advance to check if you can have lunch or use a resort's facilities. The last trip goes in the opposite direction, which gives flexibility for visiting a couple of places in the same day or returning to one of the islands to sleep. South Sea Cruises also has a sailing trip to the island where the Tom Hanks film *Cast Away* was filmed.

Beachcomber Cruises (☎ *666 1500;* **w** *www.beachcomberfiji.com)* run their own day trips to Beachcomber Island where there are lots of watersports on offer. **Captain Cook Cruises** (☎ *670 1823;* **w** *www.captaincook.com.au)* has a day trip to Tivua Island by tall ship and a three-day sailing safari to the Mamanucas and Southern Yasawas. **Oceanic Schooner Company** (☎ *672 2455,* **e** *funcruises@connect.com.fj)* also has sailing trips from Denarau and Musket Cove Marina on Malololailai has yachts for charter. Most cruises, sailboats and regular catamaran shuttles leave from Nadi's Denarau Marina, and some from Lautoka's Queens Wharf.

South Sea Cruises also runs a daily shuttle by large catamaran to the Yasawas, which is a good way of sightseeing the group. To avoid being stuck on the boat the whole day, hop off at one of the southern resorts, spend an hour or two, and pick up the boat on its return. It's advisable to confirm arrangements in advance.

Blue Lagoon Cruises (☎ *666 3938;* **w** *www.bluelagooncruises.com)* and Captain Cook Cruises have floating hotel-type cruises to the Yasawas. They are generally pre-booked, although sometimes they offer last-minute deals. See the Yasawa Group and Mamanuca Group chapters for more information.

Organised trips to Robinson Crusoe Island (also called Likuri island) just offshore from Viti Levu and south of Nadi (see later in this chapter) is an easy and fun day excursion.

Scenic Flights Most domestic flights are scenic, especially on a sunny day. It takes only 10 minutes from Nadi to the Mamanucas: Malololailai (Sun Air) and Mana (Air Fiji or Sun Air). Confirm in advance to use a resort's facilities. The islands, coral reefs and depths of blues and greens are gorgeous from above – snorkellers and divers will drool at the sight. Flights over the Nausori Highlands and the patchwork farmland of the Sigatoka Valley are also spectacular. See under

Traditional Bure

Travellers who want to experience a bit of indigenous Fijian culture can stay in a *bure* or traditional thatched dwelling. These days *bure* refers to just about any accommodation with or without a hint of traditional features.

In the past, these homes were dark and smoky inside, with no windows, usually only one low door, and with hearth pits where the women would cook. The packed-earth floor was covered with grass or fern leaves and then finely woven pandanus leaf or coarse coconut-leaf mats. Sleeping compartments were at one end, behind a bark-cloth curtain, where people slept on woven mats and with wooden headrests.

Traditional *bure* are usually rectangular in plan, with timber poles and roof structure lashed together with coconut-fibre string. Thatch, woven coconut leaves or split bamboo is used as wall cladding, and rooves are thatched with grass or coconut leaves. Communities band together to finish a *bure* in a few weeks and re-thatch every couple of years. Most villages still have some traditional-style *bure* and new homes are usually simple and rectangular in plan; however, as the traditional structure of village life breaks down and natural materials become scarcer, most people now find it easier or cheaper to build with materials that require less maintenance: concrete block, corrugated iron and even flattened oil drums.

Bure Kalou

In the days of the old religion, every village had a temple, or *bure kalou*, also used as a meeting house for the men. These buildings had a high-pitched roof and usually stood on terraced foundations. The *bete,* or priest, who was an intermediary between the villagers and the spirits, lived in the temple and performed various rituals, including feasting on slain enemies and burying important people. A strip of white *masi* (bark cloth) was usually hung from the ceiling, serving as a connection to the spirits. The construction of such a temple required that a strong man be buried alive in each of the corner post holes.

Domestic Air Services in the Getting Around chapter for details on Turtle Airways floatplanes and Island Hoppers helicopters.

Visiting the Highlands Organised tours can also be an OK way to have a look at the high country and visit interior villages.

The highland village of Abaca in the Koroyanitu National Heritage Park is an easy day trip from Nadi or Lautoka; **Mount Batilamu Trek** has trips to this region. **Adventures in Paradise** offers Cannibal Cave and Waterfall day tours on the Coral Coast, where it is based, and will collect guests from Nadi hotels. See the Viti Levu Highlands section later in this chapter for contact details, and more on organised tours and visiting the mountains independently. **Rosie, The Travel Service** (see Travel Agencies earlier in this section) has daily (except Sunday) full-day trekking to the Nausori Highlands from Nadi for $58 including lunch. It also offers six-day, five-night tours to the central highlands.

Places to Stay – Budget

Most places have free airport transfers for international flights. Consider whether you prefer downtown (lots of places to eat and shop), at the grey-sand New Town or Wailoaloa Beaches (fairly isolated but peaceful) or along the Queens Road (on the main bus route). Campers will have to head further afield (Saweni Beach south of Lautoka and Seashell Surf & Dive Resort near Momi Bay are the closest places).

Along the Highway The Martintar suburb, halfway between Nadi and the airport along the Queens Road, can be a bit sleazy at night but is becoming a good area to stay. There are a number of services close by and regular buses along the Queens Road.

Nadi Bay Hotel (*☎ 672 3599; e nadibay@connect.com.fj; Wailoaloa Rd; dorms/singles/doubles $18/48/56, singles/doubles/triples with private bathroom $75/90/100, apartment $85/110/130)* is one of Nadi's best budget places. It is just 400m off the Queens Road by the cane fields on Wailoaloa Rd. The hotel is small but it has lots of options, from cheaper fan-cooled 10-bed dorms to new air-con dorms ($22). The air-con rooftop apartment (with cooking facilities) has fantastic views to the bay and the mountains, and can also be a 6-bed dorm costing $25 per person. Unlike dorms, room rates include a continental breakfast. Clean and welcoming, the hotel has a swimming pool to laze around, a pleasant outdoor **dining area** *(breakfast from $6, lunch $7-9, dinner $11-16)* with good food at reasonable prices, as well as Sky TV, lots of local artwork, and laundry service ($7 a bag). Credit cards are accepted.

White House Visitor's Inn *(☎ 670 0022; 40 Kennedy Ave; dorm beds $11, singles/doubles with fan & bathroom $35/45, doubles with air-con $45)* is fairly small and a bit shabby, but it is reasonably clean and has a friendly atmosphere. There are small four- or five-bed fan-cooled dorms. A simple breakfast (toast and coffee) is included in the price and there is a communal kitchen. The adjacent restaurant serves Chinese meals for $6 to $15. It is a 15-minute walk from downtown, or $3 by taxi.

The budget rooms at **West's Motor Inn** and the **Capricorn International Hotel** both along the Queens Road in Martintar, and **Raffles Gateway Hotel** opposite the airport, can be good options (see Places to Stay – Mid-Range later in this section).

Sandalwood Lodge *(☎ 672 2044, fax 672 0103; e sandalwood@connect.com.fj; Ragg St; singles/doubles from $75/80 to $85/90)*, 200m off the Queens Road down Ragg St, is an excellent option for self-caterers and families. It has 33 good-value self-contained serviced rooms in a double-storey building surrounding a grassy courtyard and cute palm-shaded swimming pool. Each room has a small kitchen, TV, phone, private balcony or doors to the garden. The Family Room is spacious (for up to six) and the Orchid Wing has newer furnishings and fittings. Children under 16 are free and extra adults are $7. There are restaurants at nearby hotels.

Rosie Serviced Apartments *(☎ 672 2755, fax 672 2607; Queens Road; $44/66/88 for studio/one-/two-bedroom apartments sleeping four/five/eight)*, while not particularly attractive (by the roadside and up two flights of stairs), are a cheap option for groups or families looking for lots of space and self-catering facilities.

New Town Beach This area has a cluster of new homes for the well-to-do and plenty of options for the budget traveller. At the end of a dusty, unsealed road it is a good alternative for escaping the bustling town, however, just be aware Nadi Bay beaches have dark silty sand, no coral, and shallow waters. Once you've come to terms with this, you should find it is a peaceful spot to catch the breeze, watch the sunset and the changing hues of the Sabeto Mountain Range. It's also a good spot to watch the seaplanes and boats come and go. There is a dive operation (see Diving earlier), fishing trips and horse riding (contact tour desk at Travellers Beach Resort). Travellers Beach Resort and Horizon Beach Resort welcome outsiders to their restaurants, and the beachfront bar at Travellers Beach is the local watering hole. Self-caterers are best to stock up in Nadi town, however there is a small store and a shop at the new mid-range Grand West's Villas, both within a short walk along the road to Nadi.

Travellers Beach Resort *(☎ 672 3322; ⓔ beachvilla@connect.com.fj; dorm beds $11, singles/doubles with fan $33/40, with air-con $40/55, fan/air-con villas $66/77)* has lots of budget accommodation options, friendly staff and the poolside **bar and restaurant** *(dinner mains around $14)* serves good food right on the beach. The best rooms in the front building face the pool and beach, and the rooms upstairs on the corners in the rear building are bright and breezy. The villas, on a separate site, have kitchens with microwave and TV and comfortably sleep four people; some are open plan, others have separate rooms. Longer-term rates are negotiable, as are rental cars. Visa and MasterCard are accepted.

Tropic of Capricorn Resort *(☎ 672 3089; 11 Wasawasa Rd; air-con dorm $15, apartment rooms with fan/air-con $40/60)* is a new place with clean and airy dorms, beach access and a cute pool. The **apartments** are in another building, back from the beach near Mana Rose. Here you can take a whole two-bedroom apartment (price negotiable) or just a double room and share kitchen and living areas. The upstairs units are brighter and have a veranda.

Horizon Beach Resort *(☎ 672 2832; ⓔ horizon@connect.com.fj; 10 Wasawasa Rd; dorm beds $10, singles/doubles/family with fan $35/40/50, with air-con $40/50/60, with air-con & sea view $50/60/66)* has friendly staff and a pool. Dorm rates include breakfast. The sea-view air-con rooms are bigger and better value than the fan-cooled rooms. Meals cost around $7/10 for lunch/dinner.

New Town Beach Motel *(☎ 672 3339, 672 3420; 5 Wasawasa Rd; dorms/doubles/family room $13/40/50)* is quiet, clean and homey with a fan-cooled, five-bed dorm. Meals are $7/9 for lunch/dinner. It has a nice swimming pool and deck in the back garden.

Mana Rose *(☎ 672 3333; dorms/double $15/45)* is a stopover for Ratu Kini Boko's Village Resort on Mana island in the Mamanucas. The double-storey house has six-bed dorms and a fan-cooled double room with en suite. Prices include breakfast. There are comfy communal lounge areas and a kitchen and laundry for guests.

Wailoaloa Beach This area is around 1.5km southwest of New Town Beach. Lack of transport is a disadvantage here.

Beachside Resort *(☎ 670 3488, fax 670 3688; ⓔ beachsideresort@connect.com.fj; Wailoaloa Beach; air-con garden-view/ocean-view doubles $70/90, fan-cooled bure $140 or studio/mountain-view room $45/55)* is a cute place with the comforts of a mid-range place and an excellent restaurant. While it doesn't have its own beach frontage (it's 80m back from the beach) it has a cosy scale and atmosphere. The 15 air-con rooms in the triple-storey building overlook the gardens and swimming pool and there are also fan-cooled *bure* with two rooms each, which can be divided into studios. Up to two children under 12 years are free. The poolside **Coriander Café** *(lunch/dinner $10/16)* is a highlight here – the interesting blackboard menu featuring cassava wedges, fruit smoothies and good coffee.

Club Fiji Resort *(☎ 670 2189; ⓔ reservations@clubfiji-resort.com; Wailoaloa Beach; dorm beds $14, garden/ocean-view/beach bure $55/90/121, hotel doubles $150)* can be a good place for a Nadi stopover. The grounds are pleasant, on a stretch of dark-sand beach. There are 24 fan-cooled *bure*; you pay extra for the sea breeze and view, better maintenance and newer furnishings. One of the rear *bure* is used as a 10-bed dorm. There is a good salt-water pool and a large bar-restaurant *bure* (OK meals $15 to $20) which sometimes has live entertainment. Windsurfing and paddleboards are free and horse riding can be arranged for $20 per hour. There is a daily shuttle bus to downtown Nadi ($2.50) leaving at 10.15am and returning at 1pm. Otherwise a taxi costs $6.

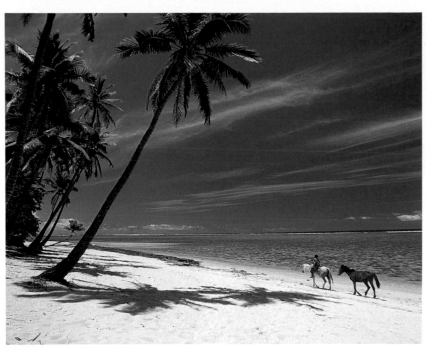

Beach resort, Coral Coast, Viti Levu

Biausevu Waterfall, Coral Coast, Viti Levu

Sunset view from Denarau island

ALL PHOTOGRAPHS BY DAVID WALL

ROBYN JONES

Sigatoka Valley, Viti Levu

ROBYN JONES

Banded Iguana

DAVID WALL

Sugar-cane train near Lautoka, Viti Levu

ROBYN JONES

Navala village, Viti Levu Highlands

Downtown Nadi In town near the post office, market and bus station, **Nadi Hotel** (*☎ 670 0000; Koroivolu Ave; dorm beds $15, doubles/triples with fan $50/70, with air-con in old bldg $60/80, in new bldg $70/90*) is frequented mostly by locals. The male and female dorms (each with 10 beds and en suite) are on opposite sides of the swimming pool and are not bad value. Standard fan-cooled rooms are OK but can be a bit musty and air-con rooms in the old building are pretty dingy. The deluxe versions in the newer building are better, though it can be noisy with the disco next door (Tuesday to Saturday to 1am).

Sunseekers Hotel (*☎ 670 0400; Narewa Rd; dorms/singles/doubles with fan $8.80/35/40*) is a convenient spot, only a few minutes' walk over the bridge to the northern end of downtown. The hotel, with up to 100 beds, is reasonably clean and an OK option for travellers on a tight budget. Dorms have six to 10 beds. Some rooms have a private toilet and shower. There is an outdoor deck and bar and you may, or may not, find water in the swimming pool.

Coconut Inn II (*☎ 670 1169; 37 Vunavau Rd; dorm beds $11, singles/doubles with fan $33/40, with air-con $45/60*) is a small, low-key place just off the main street. Look around as rooms vary in terms of natural ventilation and light, some with no external windows.

Places to Stay – Mid-Range

Most of the mid-range hotels are located along the Queens Road between Nadi town and the airport, an important consideration given the early morning departure times of many international flights. Most are used as airport stopovers only and the restaurants offer typically tourist fare and entertainment. If they don't appear busy, ask about reduced 'walk-in' rates. Day rooms (for those awaiting night-time flights) are usually about half price and for a maximum of six hours between 6am and 6pm. Rooms will generally have air-con, TV, phone and fridge, and the hotel will usually have tour desks, luggage storage and courtesy airport transfers.

Raffles Gateway Hotel (*☎ 672 2444, fax 672 0620; e rafflesresv@connect.com.fj; doubles with air-con $55, deluxe doubles/quad $125/150, suites $170*) is good value and convenient (directly opposite the airport). Families especially will enjoy the pleasant gardens and water slide into the enormous freeform swimming pool. Standard rooms upstairs are generally better than those on the ground floor. Deluxe rooms are more spacious and suites have an indoor and outdoor sitting area. Up to two children under 16 years can share with parents for free. Day rooms cost $90. There is a pool-side bar and **restaurant** (*meals around $18*), which isn't a bad spot to hang out while waiting for a flight.

Tokatoka Resort Hotel (*☎ 672 0222, fax 672 0400; e tokatokaresort@connect.com.fj; Queens Road; studios per double/triple $145/165, one-bedroom villas per double/quad $205/255, two-bedroom villas $325*), is also just opposite the airport. The atmosphere and set up are good for families and it has a great swimming pool with water slide, a pleasant garden, and good wheelchair and pram access. It has 74 villa-style units, most with cooking facilities. The two-bedroom villas sleep up to seven people. Self-caterers will find the small supermarket handy and the restaurant-bar (*lunch around $7-17, dinner $16-25*) serves meals by the pool. Child-minding is available for $3.50 per hour.

Skylodge Hotel (*☎ 672 2200, fax 672 4330; e skylodge@connect.com.fj; Queens Road; rooms with air-con from $121, cottage units $135*) has more spacious grounds and is another good spot for families. It has mini- golf, mini-tennis, a games pavilion and playground, and a good swimming pool. The rooms in the building near reception are for up to three adults, or two adults and two children. Three- to eight-room cottages are dotted around the large open garden. These self-contained units (up to four people) are also available for long-term rental.

Fiji International Dominion Hotel (*☎ 672 2255, fax 672 0187; e dominionint@connect.com.fj; Queens Road; singles/doubles/triples from $125/130/140*) is a large hotel with 85 rooms, about 4.5km south of Nadi airport. All rooms have views to the garden and swimming pool and deluxe rooms (with a bigger bed) cost another $25 per person. Children under 12 years occupying a separate room are half price. Amenities also include tennis courts. Meals are available at the **restaurant** (*dinner $14-20*), and there is a *meke* (dance performance that enacts stories and legends) on Saturday night ($22 including a glass of wine and buffet meal).

The **West's Motor Inn** *(☎ 672 0044, fax 672 0071; e westsmotorin@mail.connect.com.fj; Queens Road; singles or doubles/triples $60/75, deluxe doubles/triples/family $105/125/135)* is good value and has happy staff. Rooms have ceiling fans and air-con, and the more spacious deluxe versions have a TV and overlook the pool and enormous mango tree. There are standard rooms in the main building but those in what was previously the Sandalwood Inn next door, are generally lighter and better ventilated. Some have balconies and adjoin another smaller pool. The pool-side bar and **restaurant** *(dinner $14-19.50)* offers OK meals.

Capricorn International Hotel *(☎ 672 0088, fax 672 0522; e capricorn@connect.com.fj; Queens Road; singles or doubles $85-110, family suite doubles $135)*, just south of West's Motor Inn, offers OK-value typical mid-range accommodation and has nice gardens and a swimming pool. Some of the family suites (with cooking facilities) also open on to the pool area. Each extra bed (for those over 12 years) is $20. Some rooms that have been set up with three single beds are good value for backpackers.

Grand West's Villas *(☎ 672 4833; e hexagongroup@connect.com.fj; Nadi Bay Rd; doubles/family $99/145)* is in an odd place on a dusty road among the cane fields on the edge of the airstrip about 300m from New Town Beach. However it could be a good place for families to stopover, or for longer term if you have your own transport. Within the large fenced compound it has 22 new two-bedroom double-storey air-con villas, a restaurant and a nice swimming pool with water slide.

Places to Stay – Top End

There are two large, upmarket hotels within a few minutes' drive southeast of the airport. Both offer perfectly comfortable but pretty standard business-type rooms (air-con, TV and refrigerator), room service, fitness and convention centres, swimming pools and 24-hour cafés.

Fiji Mocambo *(☎ 672 2000, fax 672 0324; e mocambo@connect.com.fj; w www.shangri-la.com; singles/doubles $190/200)* is managed by Shangri-La Hotels. Most of the 128 rooms here have mountain views and there is a nine-hole golf course and tennis courts. There are live bands Friday and Saturday nights.

Tanoa International Hotel *(☎ 672 0277, fax 672 0191; e tanoahotels@connect.com.fj; doubles $190, executive rooms $200)* has a sleepy islander feel about it. The 135-room hotel began as a Travelodge but is now locally owned. The **restaurant** *(all-day dining $9-16, dinner $19-30)* serves standard fare.

Tanoa Apartments *(☎ 672 3685, fax 672 1193; deluxe rooms $164, penthouse $210, 3-bedroom apartment $220)* is a quiet place with just 23 self-contained and serviced apartments (for up to six people). It is on the hill overlooking the roundabout, just south of the airport. There is a swimming pool, and some of the rooms have great mountain views. Weekly and non-serviced long-term rates are negotiable.

Places to Eat

Nadi is a tourist town catering well for a variety of tastes and budgets. Most places serve a mixture of traditional Fijian, Indian, Chinese and Western dishes, and there are lots of cheap lunch-time eateries downtown. Most restaurants and cafés serve a traditional Fijian dish or two, and some of the resorts have special *lovo* nights, where food is cooked in a pit oven.

Restaurants A medium-priced restaurant, **Chefs, the Edge** *(☎ 670 3131; Sagayam Rd; open 10am-10pm)* has good food has good-value meals in an air-con café-setting. **Chefs, the Restaurant** *(☎ 670 3131; Sagayam Rd; open 10am-2pm & 6pm-10pm Mon-Sat)* is one of Nadi's more expensive restaurants, for those seeking international cuisine and candlelit dinners.

Maharaj *(☎ 672 2962; Queens Road, Namaka; dishes $6-15)* is on the main road near the airport. Though the location is nothing special, is has Nadi's best curry and also does takeaway.

Mama's Pizza Inn *(☎ 670 0221; large pizza $15-23)*, downtown and at the Colonial Plaza in Namaka on the Queens Road, is a good inexpensive option for pizza and pasta. The large pizza is huge, or try the yummy vegetarian bolognaise spaghetti for $6.50. Both Mama's and **Continental Cakes & Pizza** (see later under cafés) will deliver pizza if you pay the taxi fare.

Sentai Seafood Restaurant is the best place for Chinese dishes and, as the name suggests, has good seafood.

Nadi has two good Japanese restaurants, though best avoided by hungry backpackers on a budget. **Daikoku Restaurant** *(☎ 670 3622; à la carte meals $18-29)*, in town near the bridge, has yummy teppanyaki for $22 to $48. It can be reasonable for lunch if you stick to sushi ($5 to $7) or noodles ($12 to $18). **Hamacho** *(☎ 675 0177; Denarau; teppanyaki $63-74, sukiyaki $58)*, near the Sheraton Royal, is a nice spot but more pricey.

Martintar has a couple of restaurants. **Nadi Bay Hotel** (see Places to Stay earlier) has a pleasant outdoor dining area and excellent food. **Bounty Restaurant & Bar** *(☎ 672 0840, Queens Road, Martintar)* is a down-to-earth place with OK-value all-day breakfast, lunch ($4 to $13) and dinner ($12 to $28) and a friendly bar with icy beer. **Skytop** *(Queens Road, Martintar)*, a rooftop bar opposite Fiji International Dominion Hotel, has $5 goulash and beef ribs for $12.

A few of the other small resort restaurants are worth going further afield for. **Beachside Resort** (see Places to Stay) near Wailoaloa Beach has a trendy menu. **Stoney Creek Resort** *(☎ 672 2206; Sunday lovo lunch/buffet dinner $18/15)* is a great spot north of town in the Sabeto foothills, surrounded by cane fields and cradled by the mountains.

Cardo's *(☎ 675 0900; Denarau Marina; mains $11-24, medium pizza $14)* is worth a try if you crave seafood or a good steak, and are prepared to spend a bit more for a taxi. Contemplate the lives of the rich and famous from the veranda overlooking the cruise boats and luxurious yachts.

Visitors are welcome at the fine-dining **restaurants** at the Sheraton resorts on Denarau. See also, the First Landing Seafood Restaurant in Vuda Point later.

Cafés For good coffee and milkshakes, head to **Surf Republic** *(Main Street, downtown Nadi)*. **Continental Cakes & Pizza** *(☎ 670 3595; Main St, Nadi; medium pizza $9-18)*, a few doors up from Mama's, has good coffee and pizza, and supplies many of the hotels with cakes and croissants. Lambshank rolls cost $4.50. **Chefs (the Corner)** *(Sagayam Rd; open 8am-9pm Mon-Sat)* has good-value quality meals, including curries ($7), cakes, coconut pies, coffee ice cream.

West Coast Cafe *(Queens Road, Martintar)* serves snacks, pies and sandwiches ($6 to $10) and has email and Internet services.

The **kiosk** at Domestic departures at the airport has good-quality local food at local prices, while the one at International Departures is priced for tourists. If you have a bit of time to kill before a flight try the poolside bar at the Raffles Hotel, opposite the airport entrance.

Fast Food Try the small cafés, such as **Skyway**, around the Nadi Civic Centre – while not squeaky clean, they often have good, cheap food and are popular with locals. *Tavioka* (cassava), Indian snacks, curries and chop suey are usually under $4.

Hot Bread Kitchen *(downtown Nadi and at Colonial Plaza, Namaka)* has tasty mutton pies for $1.20 and fresh orange juice $1.80 a litre. **Food for Thought** *(8am-6pm Mon-Sat)*, upstairs off the main street, has vegetarian *thali* (plate meal) for $5 and Internet access.

Rik's Café *(Queens Road, Martintar)* has good-value fish and chips for $5. **McDonald's** *(cnr Queens Road & Enamanu Rd)*, about 2km north of town, is very popular with locals.

Self-Catering Nadi has a large produce **market** *(Hospital Rd)*, which sells lots of fresh fruit and vegetables. Good-quality meat, however, is not so easy to come by. There are several large **supermarkets** and **bakeries** downtown as well as along the Queens Road at the Colonial Plaza and at Namaka.

Entertainment

While Nadi has nowhere near the variety of nightlife as Suva, there are a few good bars and the upmarket hotels usually have something happening at weekends. **Ed's Bar** *(Queen's Rd, Martintar)* and **Mama's Pizza** downtown on the main street are good places for a drink. **Fiji Mocambo** hotel has live bands, karaoke and rave music on Friday and Saturday nights. There is a cover charge and a dress code (no flip-flops or shorts). The Sheraton Royal on Denarau has a disco at the **Planters Club bar**, Wednesday night firewalking and Saturday night *meke* ($50/25 per adult/child over 12 including a *lovo* dinner.

There are a few cinemas downtown that show a mix of Hollywood and Indian Bollywood movies (admission is $3). The Hindi movies sometimes have English subtitles. The **Galaxy 2** *(Ashram Rd)* has four screenings daily except Sunday. Check the *Fiji Times* for information on what's showing.

Shopping

Nadi's Main St is largely devoted to souvenir and duty-free shops.

Jack's Handicrafts, Sogo, Tappo and Nad's Handicrafts all sell crafts, clothing and jewellery. There is an outdoor handicraft market near the Civic Centre, where you can bargain. There are also many stores selling colourful Indian saris and intricate gold jewellery. Its always good to get handicrafts from their source, South Pacific Islanders Handicrafts is a co-op.

Popular souvenirs include printed designs on *masi* (bark cloth) and *tanoa* (*kava* bowls). See the Shopping section in the Facts for the Visitor chapter for more information.

Surf Republic has a small art gallery with indigenous and Indo-Fijian craft. The Pacific Art Shop at the Sheraton Fiji Resort on Denarau also has quality arts and handicrafts. There are a few local artists doing interesting work such as Penny Casey (☎ 999 4569); Nadi Bay Hotel has some of her paintings. Also watch out for works by Fred Whippy (☎ 666 1195), Craig and Leibling Marlow (☎ 670 1081) and Robert Kennedy (☎ 652 0227).

SPR Music and the Boom Box are good places to sample music by local bands and Indian Hindi stars. At SPR Sound & HiFi (☎ 6700 478) you can buy Bollywood videos and DVDs.

Viti Surf Legend (Queens Road, Martintar) has boards for sale and hire, and Aqua-Trek has dive and snorkelling gear.

Getting There & Around

Nadi International Airport is 9km north of downtown Nadi and there are frequent local buses from just outside the airport along the Queens Road to town ($0.50); otherwise a taxi is $10. Most of the hotels have free transfer vehicles awaiting international flights. From Nadi bus station (downtown Nadi) there are buses to Lautoka and Suva, non-express buses can be picked up at regular bus stops along the Queens Road.

Buses depart from New Town Beach for downtown Nadi ($0.50, 15 minutes) at 6.30am, 7.30am, 8.30am and 11.15am, 4pm and 5pm daily (except Sunday). A taxi costs $3/5/10 to the Queens Road/downtown/airport. Boat transfers to the budget resorts on Mana island depart from New Town

A Sweet Success Turned Sour

Sugar cane is still the mainstay of the Fijian economy and the origin of multicultural Fiji. Well suited to the hot and relatively dry climate of western Viti Levu, it is mostly grown by small Indo-Fijian tenant farmers. In cutting season (the latter part of the year) the air can be hazy from farmers burning the crops. The cane is cut manually, oxen plough the paddocks, and cute little sugar engines haul their long load along a complicated network of narrow tracks to Lautoka's mill. Watch out for the over-wide trucks that take over the roads.

The colonial capitalist economy relied on sugar for its existence, and the Australian-owned Colonial Sugar Refining Company (CSR) gained phenomenal power and influence in Fiji. In the early 1880s it established mills at Lautoka, Nausori and Ba and at Labasa on Vanua Levu and in 1926 took over the mill at Rakiraki.

The colonial government, keen to attract foreign investment, facilitated the purchase of land and arranged for cheap labour from India through the indenture system. CSR later shifted the burden of heavy production costs by subcontracting the sugar-growing work and leasing land to ex-indentured Indians. A minority of the Indians became rich cane farmers, leading to resentment among white plantation owners. CSR profits hinged on long working hours (a 50-hour week) and heavy workloads, between 1914 and 1924, CSR reaped the best profits in its history. However, after the abolition of indenture and the resulting labour shortage, company land was divided and rented to small tenant farmers.

There was industrial trouble from 1942 to 1960 with disputes over wages, cane prices and conditions and in 1972 CSR cut its losses and pulled out of Fiji. The mills and its freehold land were nationalised and the Fijian government is still a major shareholder in the industry. Suffering from outdated infrastructure, the industry has been experiencing serious financial problems, only exacerbated by the drought in recent years and uncertainty for farmers as 100-year land leases expire.

Beach ($40/70 per person one way/return, 45 minutes to 1½ hours depending on weather conditions and tide).

Most boat trips to the Mamanucas and Yasawas depart from Denarau Marina and most organised tours will pick up guests from the hotels. You can also get to Denarau island independently. West Bus Transport (☎ 675 0777) has six buses daily (less frequently on Sunday) from Nadi bus station to Denarau island. The first is at 8.30am and the last at 5pm ($0.50, 30 minutes).

Taxi drivers are always on the lookout for business. They don't use meters so confirm prices in advance. Remember if they are returning to base, you pay less (see the Getting Around chapter for hints and for car and motorbike rental, as well as interisland air and boat services).

Around Nadi

Foothills of the Sabeto Range

Explore the countryside between Nadi and Lautoka either by local bus, mountain bike, motorbike, hire car, taxi or organised tour.

The **Garden of the Sleeping Giant** *(☎ 672 2701; adult/child/family $9.90/4.90/24.90; open 9am-5pm Mon-Sat, Sunday by appointment)*, at the foothills of the Sabeto mountain range (Sleeping Giant), is a peaceful place for a picnic or to spend a few hours relaxing among the orchids, lily ponds and forested tracks. About 6km north of Nadi airport turn off the Queens Road inland along Wailoko Rd for about 2km. A taxi from Nadi will cost around $12.

Further north along the Queens Road visit **Lomolomo Guns** for a short walk and a great view. The abandoned WWII battery, built to protect Nadi Bay, is on a rise at the foot of the Sabeto Mountains. The turn-off is 400m north of Lomaloma police station and about 8.5km north of the airport. Follow the dirt road for about 300m, turn left and follow the road up and around for about 400m.

Places to Stay & Eat On a rise popping out of the cane fields, **Stoney Creek Resort** *(☎ 672 2206; e stoneycreek@connect.com.fj; dorms/bure $16/40-66)* commands a 360-degree view of the mountains and Nadi Bay. The surrounding area can be explored by mountain bike. Accommodation is simple, cute and airy. The dorm building has a communal area largely open to the elements and view, with 16 beds in more enclosed cubicles. The small fan-cooled *bure* (or shack) faces the Sleeping Giant, and the larger one has a panoramic mountain view from the bed, seen through mosquito screening. The **restaurant** *(breakfast/lunch/dinner $8/10/18, Sunday lovo lunch/buffet dinner $18/15)* overlooks the pool to the Sleeping Giant.

The resort is in a hidden spot inland and northeast of the airport. Head north along the Queens Road for 3km, then 6km east along Sabeto Rd (700m past the police post and post office). It provides a free airport shuttle, otherwise a taxi is $7/12 from the airport/town. There are also regular 'Sabeto' buses from Nadi bus station, which can be picked up at the Sabeto Rd/Queens Road junction (12 buses between 8am and 5.30pm).

Viseisei & Vuda Point

About 12km north of Nadi airport the Queens Road bypasses the village of Viseisei, which receives tourists on organised tours. Viseisei was the home of the late Dr Timoci Bavadra, whose government was deposed by Fiji's first coup in 1987. The *mataqali* (extended family or landowning group) here own and lease several of the Mamanuca islands to resorts. Local buses between Nadi and Lautoka go past the village.

About 1km north of Viseisei there is a turn-off from the Old Queens Rd to Vuda Point peninsula, which juts out towards the Mamanucas between Nadi and Lautoka. According to local legend the first Melanesians arrived in Fiji at this spot. It is a farmland area with a couple of resorts and the **Vuda Point Marina** *(☎ 666 8214; e vudamarina@connect.com.fj)* and Shell, Mobil and BP oil terminals.

The turn-off to Vuda Point is about 11km south of Lautoka and about 12km north of Nadi airport, situated at the top of a steep hill off the Old Queens Road. The marina is about 3.5km further west at the end of the point. A taxi between here and the airport costs about $12.

Places to Stay & Eat At Vuda Point marina, **The Hatch** coffee shop is *the* place for an affordable lunch and dinner (bookings advised). It has sandwiches, burgers and Chinese dishes. The marina also has a good **store**

(open 7.30am-7pm daily), laundry and other services for yachties. Travellers are welcome at the Yacht Club **restaurant and open-air bar** *(dinner around $10)* and also, next door at First Landing Resort **restaurant.** Both are nice spots for a sunset meal on the beach.

Located in a nice spot on the water's edge, **First Landing Resort** *(☎ 666 6171, fax 666 8882; e firstlanding@connect.com.fj; superior/deluxe/ocean-view cottages $121/143/176)* has views to the Mamanuca islands. It is next door to the Vuda Point Marina, which means there is easy access out to the Mamanucas. The air-con cottages (up to four people) have mosquito-screened verandas spaced in a large garden. Rates include breakfast. It has a lovely freeform swimming pool and you can snorkel and swim off the sandy beach at high tide. There is a good dive operation here, **Aquacadabra** *(☎ 666 6171; w www.aquacadabradiving.com)*, which runs dive trips to the Mamanucas and Southern Yasawas reefs ($155 for two-tank dive including equipment hire). The pleasant beachfront **First Landing Seafood Restaurant** *(snacks $10, mains from $20)* specialises in seafood and also has wood-fired pizza, curry and pasta dishes. It's a 15-minute drive from Nadi airport.

Anchorage Beach Resort *(☎ 666 2099, fax 666 5571; e anchorage@connect.com.fj; garden-view/ocean-view/panorama singles or doubles $132/143/154; mains $10-17.50)* is on a great hilltop site with panoramic views south over Nadi Bay and west to the Mamanucas. An extra adult costs $24 and discounts apply during low season. Some units have cooking facilities. It's an OK option if you want to feel away from it all: the beach is a five-minute walk down the hill and there is a small pool but no organised activities. Heading west from the Queens Road, the resort is on the left, about 2km along Vuda Point Rd.

Uciwai Landing

Uciwai Landing, used by surfers to access the Mamanuca breaks and island resorts on Namoto and Tavarua, is 18km southwest of Nadi.

Rendezvous Beach Resort *(☎ 651 0571; e rendezvous@infofiji.com; dorms/singles/doubles $45/60/110)* is a surf and dive camp run by a local surfer and his Japanese dive-instructor wife. You wouldn't come here for the beach; quick access to the Mamanuca surf breaks and dive sites are the attraction. Accommodation is in simple but clean bungalows and meals are included in the price.

Surfing boat fees are $35/50 for half-/full-day trip (full day includes packed lunch). Guided snorkelling boat trip cost $30 per person, two-tank dive trips $120 and open-water course $400.

Rendezvous is about 5km along unsealed Uciwai Rd, and the turn-off from the Queens Road is 13km south of Nadi. The resort organises transfers by car ($20/25 Nadi town/International Airport). There are local buses to Uciwai departing from Nadi bus station at 8am and 1pm Monday to Saturday.

Denarau Island

This island (2.55 sq km) is an upmarket, picture perfect world in itself, a world away but just 6km west of downtown Nadi. The island is a reclaimed mangrove area and the beach has dark-grey sand, however the Sheraton Resorts take day-trippers to a private offshore island with white-sand beaches.

Sheraton Royal Denarau Resort *(☎ 675 0000, fax 675 0818; e sheratondenarau@sheraton.com; garden-view/beachfront rooms $460/680)*, previously the Regent Fiji, was Fiji's first luxury hotel. It has 274 rooms in spacious luxuriant gardens.

Sheraton Fiji Resort *(☎ 675 0777, fax 675 0818; w www.sheraton.com/fiji; singles or doubles $520-803)* has 292 rooms, all with ocean views. While Sheraton Royal has a traditional feel set within the tropical gardens, Sheraton Fiji has more of a modern Mediterranean style. Prices quoted are rack rates (normal prices without discounts): there are seasonal price variations and most patrons arrange some sort of package deal or discount.

Sheraton Denarau Villas *(☎ 675 0777, fax 675 0818; w www.sheraton.com/denarauvillas; deluxe/beachfront rooms $580/700, suites $785/935, villas $1070-1560)*, are an option if you are after the Denarau setting and resort facilities but prefer an apartment with cooking facilities. The 82 stylish new villas have two and three bedrooms, with some rooms separating off as guestrooms.

Young families are well catered for with a daily entertainment programme for children and a baby-sitting service.

Trendwest *(☎ 0800 6750 855)* is a new timeshare resort being built on the island. It has one-, two- and three-bedroom villas and a large pool with a swim-up bar.

There are local bus services to Denarau island (see Getting There & Around); a taxi from Nadi town costs $10 and from the airport $22.

Naisali Island

Like Denarau, Naisali (42 hectares) is on the edge of the mangroves, this long, flat island, is just 300m off the mainland, and about 12km southwest of Nadi. The resort is on a dark-sand beach with quick access and great views to the Mamanucas.

Sonaisali Island Resort *(☎ 670 6011, fax 670 6092; w www.sonaisali.com; doubles $335, ocean-view/beachfront/family bure $410/460/550)* is a 110-room resort with a large freeform swimming pool, sunken bar and poolside, beachfront restaurant. The rooms in the double-storey building have sea views. There are also thatched *bure* with high ceilings and elevated verandas as well as two-bedroom beachfront family *bure*. Rates include a buffet breakfast and the optional meal package, including a two-course lunch and a three-course dinner, costs $60/30 per adult/child.

Naisali is a 25-minute drive and 3-minute boat shuttle from Nadi airport. Turn off the Queens Road at Nacobi Rd and drive for a couple of kilometres by sealed road to the resort landing and taxi stand.

LAUTOKA

pop 43,274

Lautoka, the administrative centre of the Western Division, is Fiji's second port and is the largest city after Suva. This waterfront town has the beautiful Mt Evans Range (Koroyanitu Range) as a backdrop. If you want to avoid the tourist hype of Nadi, Lautoka is a simpler place to get around on foot and can be a good base for shopping and taking trips to the Mamanuca and Yasawa Groups. In cutting season, sugar trains putt along the main street lined with royal palms and there is a small botanical garden nearby. There is a large produce and handicraft market near the bus station, from where buses travel to Suva via the Kings Road to the north and via the Queens Road to the south.

The Lautoka Sugar Mill has been operating here since 1903 and the local economy relies heavily on the sugar industry. You will see lots of little sugar trains shuttling the cane to the mill during cutting and crushing season in the latter half of the year. There is also the smell of wood-chips in the air, exported from the Queens Wharf.

Koroyanitu National Heritage Park is a fantastic place for hiking (see the Viti Levu Highlands section later in this chapter).

Saweni Beach is fairly unappealing but popular with locals for weekend picnics. It is 2km off the Queens Road and the turn-off is 6km south of Lautoka, or 18km north of Nadi airport. Along the way is **South Sea Orchids** *(☎ 666 2206, fax 666 6283)*, which is owned by the Burness family whose great-grandfather was the interpreter at the signing of the deed of Fiji's cession to Great Britain in 1874 (he is the man with the long white beard on the $50 note). Green thumbs will love the landscaped gardens, orchid collection and commercial nursery. South Sea Orchids offers 1½-hour tours of its property. The tours are normally prebooked through **Tourist Transport Fiji** *(☎ 672 3311)* or **UTC** (☎ 672 2811) and cost $47. Expect to pay about $30 for a return taxi ride from Lautoka if you want the cab to wait while you take the tour. See Getting There & Around later for local bus services.

Information

Money There are several banks downtown that will change money and travellers cheques. There are ANZ ATMs on Naviti St, Yasawa St and near the cinema on Namoli Ave. The Cathay Hotel will also change money at bank rates. SITA Travel is also a money exchange.

Post & Communications The **post office** *(cnr Vitogo Parade & Tavewa Ave)* has a few public telephones.

Compuland, upstairs on Vitogo Parade has email and Internet services, as does the Downtown Post Shop on Yasawa St and SITA Travel on Naviti St.

Travel Agencies The following travel agencies can arrange tours.

Beachcomber Cruises/Ferries/Resort office (☎ 666 1500, fax 666 4496, w www.beachcomberfiji.com) 1 Walu St

Blue Lagoon Cruises (☎ 666 3938, fax 666 4098, w www.bluelagooncruises.com) 183 Vitogo Parade

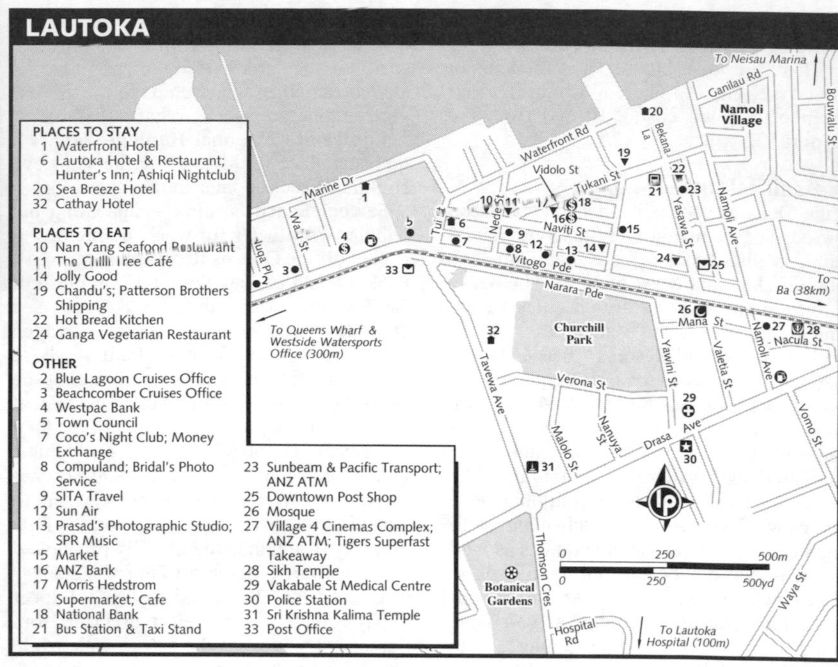

Patterson Brothers Shipping (☎ 666 1173) 15 Tukani St
SITA World Travel (☎ 666 136) 22 Naviti St
Sun Air (☎ 666 4753) Vidolo St

Medical Services For medical treatment, contact either of the following.

Lautoka Hospital (☎ 666 0399) Thomson Crescent
Vakabale St Medical Centre (☎ 665 2955, 995 2369) 47 Drasa Avenue

Emergency In an emergency, contact:

Ambulance (☎ 666 0399)
FVB emergency hotline (☎ 0800 721 721)
Police (☎ 666 0222)

Places to Stay

For village stays and accommodation in the Koroyanitu National Heritage Park see the Viti Levu Highlands section later in this chapter.

Sea Breeze Hotel *(☎ 666 0717, fax 666 6080; Bekana Lane; singles/doubles/triples/family with air-con & sea view $40/49/52/56, singles/doubles with fan $33/37)* is at the end of a quiet cul-de-sac on the waterfront, and close to the market and bus station. Rooms without the sea view are cheaper. Fan-cooled rooms are often booked out; all rooms have en suites. This is a good place for getting over jet lag before heading inland or to the offshore islands. It has a breakfast room upstairs, a quiet bar and TV lounge downstairs, and a swimming pool.

Cathay Hotel *(☎ 666 0566; e cathay@fiji4less.com; Tavewa Ave; dorm beds $12, singles/doubles with fan $33/44, with air-con $46/55)* is a good place to meet other travellers. There is a swimming pool, bar, a TV lounge, and a restaurant that serves OK meals for $4 to $8; the fruit smoothies are good. Check out the various dorms (up to four people in each) as some are less ventilated than others.

Lautoka Hotel *(☎ 666 0388; e ltkhotel@connect.com.fj; 2-12 Naviti St; dorm beds $15, old-wing singles or doubles with shared bathroom $30, singles or doubles with air-con & private bathroom $40, deluxe singles or doubles $65)* is popular with both locals and travellers. The old wing has grungy but spacious rooms with a sink. Dorms hold a maximum of eight people, check for sagging beds. Most rooms don't have external windows. The dorms and rooms at the front with windows facing the street have better ventilation. Some of the dorms have fans and air-con. The new wing has good air-con motel rooms (deluxe) around a small swimming pool.

Saweni Beach Apartment Hotel *(☎ 666 1777; e saweni@fiji4less.com; camp sites per person $7, dorm beds $11, ocean-view/poolside apartment doubles $55/50, 'brownhouse' doubles $40)* is a low-key place for budget self-caterers, about 6km southwest of Lautoka, and 2km off the Queens Road. The 12 fan-cooled one-bedroom apartments are clean and spacious. The 'brown house', recently renovated and painted orange, is closer to the beach and is a good option. The beach isn't great and there are no organised activities so you'll have to create your own fun. There is a small swimming pool and a bar. See Getting There & Around later.

Waterfront Hotel *(☎ 666 4777, fax 666 5870; e waterfront@connect.com.fj; Marine Drive; rooms/suites $115/135)* is the only upmarket hotel in Lautoka, catering mainly to business travellers. Its 47 rooms are in a modern double-storey building. It has a spacious lounge and bar, an outdoor deck, a swimming pool, conference facilities and a good restaurant. 'Superior' rooms are not bad value and the suites are spacious.

Places to Eat

Lautoka has fewer restaurants than Nadi or Suva, however there are lots of inexpensive lunchtime eateries frequented by locals. They usually offer Indian, Chinese and traditional Fijian fare.

Ganga Vegetarian Restaurant *(cnr Naviti & Yasawa Sts)* is one of the town's best options. It is a popular Hare Krishna restaurant with air-con, serving good vegetarian meals. It is near the bus station and market. Prices range from under $2 for simple dishes, soups and lassi, to $5 for a *thali* (food platter) with assorted curries, relish and rice or naan and a fruit juice. It also has lots of brightly coloured ice cream, assorted *buja* (mixed nuts and peas) and sweets (available as gift boxes).

The Chilli Tree Café *(☎ 665 1824; 3 Tukani St)* is recommended for coffee, cake, quiche and sandwiches (around $7).

Jolly Good *(cnr Naviti & Vakabale Sts)* is a popular outdoor venue with inexpensive Indian, Chinese and traditional Fijian fast food for under $4. **Chandu's** *(15 Tukani St; meals around $6)* is a low-key place opposite the bus station, which has quite good meals for both lunch and dinner. The **café** at the Morris Hedstrom supermarket also has good-value fast food. **Tigers Superfast Takeaway** *(Namoli Ave)* near the cinema, is very popular with locals who are seeking a quick bite.

The **Lautoka Hotel** *(mains $8-15)* serves reasonable pizza, Chinese, Indian and European meals.

Nan Yang Seafood Restaurant *(☎ 665 2668; Nede St; soups $9-15, seafood $13-28)* serves up good-quality Chinese food. **Fins Restaurant** at the Waterfront Hotel is the most upmarket restaurant and has nice views out to the harbour.

Self-caterers will be happy with Lautoka's produce **market**.

Entertainment

Lautoka has a **Village 4 cinema complex** *(Namoli Ave)*, just south of Vitogo Parade. There are lots of nightclubs in town. If you are game on Friday and Saturday nights, try **Coco's Night Club** in Naviti St, or the **Ashiqi Nightclub** or the **Hunter's Inn** *(Tui St)*, both at the Lautoka Hotel.

Getting There & Around

Lautoka is 33km north of Nadi and 24km north of Nadi airport. Local buses shuttle between the two towns every 15 minutes during the day and less frequently in the evening. There are also regular express buses along the Kings and Queens Roads, as well as carriers (small trucks) and Viti minibuses to Suva. Both Sunbeam and Pacific Transport have offices in Yasawa St opposite the market.

Lautoka is easy to get around on foot. Taxis are plentiful and short rides are relatively cheap.

Local buses leave from Lautoka bus station to Saweni Beach six times daily, with the first leaving at 6.45am and the last at 5.15pm. Alternatively any local bus to Nadi will drop you at the turn-off, from where it is an easy walk along 2km of unsealed road. A Taxi will cost approximately $7/20 to Lautoka/Nadi airport.

Southern Viti Levu

There are many resorts along this stretch, especially along the Coral Coast east of Sigatoka, as well as a few budget places geared towards backpackers. Highlights are Natadola Beach, the Sigatoka Sand Dunes, the Tavuni Hill Fortification, the Sigatoka Valley and near Pacific Harbour, river trips in the Namosi Highlands and diving in the Beqa Lagoon.

The sealed and scenic Queens Road largely hugs the coast; unsealed roads head inland off the highway and up into the highlands. Both **Sunbeam Transport Limited** (*☎ 650 0168*) and **Pacific Transport Limited** (*☎ 650 0688; Sigatoka*) have regular buses along the Queens Road.

MOMI BAY

South of Nadi the Queens Road winds through cane fields, and the first interesting detour is to Momi Bay and along the coast on the Old Queens Road – recommended only if you are taking a leisurely drive. The turn-off is about 18km from Nadi (27km from the airport, 46.3km from Lautoka). Some local buses take this dusty unsealed route, but if you jump off you will have to wait a while for the next one. The 29km of unsealed road takes you through beautiful farmland, cane fields and pine plantations. There are lots of small temples and mosques in the area.

The **Momi Guns** site is worth a quick stop. It is a WWII battery on a hilltop overlooking the strategic Navula Passage, about 6km from the Queens Road turn-off, coming from Nadi. The camouflaged bunkers have been restored and there is a display with historical photos. During WWII Fiji formed a strategic link between the USA and Australia, and New Zealand and Fijian soldiers were posted here.

Places to Stay & Eat

Seashell Surf & Dive Resort (*☎ 670 6100; e seashell@connect.com.fj; camping per tent $10, dorm beds $55, lodge singles or doubles/triples $60/70, bure doubles or triples $150, family bure $200*) is an isolated place, however it has access to good dive sites and surf offshore in the Mamanucas. While the beach isn't great (snorkelling and windsurfing at high tide only) there's a nice swimming pool and beachfront bar. Accommodation is fan-cooled: six-bed fan-cooled dorm rooms (meals included in the rate); better lodge rooms with shared facilities; and *bure* with cooking facilities and fridge. The family *bure* is for up to six people.

Restaurant meals are about $10/20 for lunch/dinner, otherwise meal plans are $35 per person. Self-caterers (*bure* only) should bring supplies from the Sigatoka or Nadi markets as the local shop sells only basic items as well as cheap takeaway curries.

Diving with Scuba Bula (based at the resort) is $110 for a two-tank dive and $440 for an open-water course. Snorkelling trips are $20. Boat trips to the reef-breaks around Namotu are $30 per head.

Getting There & Away

The resort is about 30km from Nadi. From Nadi, travel about 11km along the Old Queens Road, then turn right and continue for another 1.5km. Airport transfers by resort minibus are $15 each way and taxis are $45 (45 minutes). Local buses (Dominion Company) depart from Nadi bus station ($2, one hour, three times daily). There are also daily local buses from Sigatoka ($3, one hour, 1.30pm daily) and taxis charge $40.

ROBINSON CRUSOE ISLAND

This small coral island, also known as Likuri, is near the passage into Likuri Harbour just offshore north of Natadola Beach.

Robinson Crusoe Island Resort (*☎ 651 0100; e robinsoncrusoe@connect.com.fj; dorm beds $65, double small bure $70, double bure island/beach $75/80*) is a small-scale budget resort and one of Fiji's best party islands. It is pretty basic but has a nice white-sand beachfront with spectacular sunsets. Accommodation is simple and comfortable (small thatched private *bure* or bunk beds in the large dorm) with communal bathrooms. Showers are by bucket and hand-pump. Buffet meals (included in the rate) are served in a large horseshoe-shaped shelter with a sandy central area for performances. The entertainment programme is intense, beginning as your boat is 'attacked by cannibals' on your arrival!

Activities on offer include windsurfing, snorkelling, volleyball and use of paddle boards. Boat trips to lovely Natadola Beach (including snorkelling, often with turtles) cost $30 per person (minimum of seven people) and the nearby mangroves are great to explore by kayak. Aqua-trek Robinson Crusoe dive shop offers two-tank dive excursions for $102, while open-water dive courses cost $450.

There are day trips from Nadi and Coral Coast hotels daily, except Monday and Saturday, leaving at 10am and returning at 4.30pm ($80 per person). There is also a cruise to the island combined with a trip on the Coral Coast Scenic Railway (see Yanuca & Around later in this chapter) and there were plans to introduce a two-day sailing adventure from Musket Cove in the Mamanucas to Likuri ($250 including meals, accommodation and transfers).

A free shuttle bus service from Nadi hotels takes you to the **boat landing** *(Maro Rd)*, at the first bridge, about 6km off the Queens Road on the road to Natadola Beach. The boat ($45 return per person) takes 30 minutes along the river to the island, which is very close to the coast (about a 15-minute boat ride).

NATADOLA BEACH

In between Momi Bay and Sigatoka is the gorgeous white-sand Natadola Beach. It is mainland Viti Levu's best beach; most other beaches in this area and along the Coral Coast have wide, flat fringing reefs that only allow swimming at high tide. Take care when swimming here, however, as conditions vary and there can be strong currents. Sometimes there is good body surfing. If you want to snorkel, surf or windsurf take your own gear. The setting is idyllic, but watch your valuables as there have been reports of theft. The small upmarket resort opposite the beach is the only development so far, however, several large resort chains have their eyes on the site, pending government infrastructure. Hopefully further development won't cut off public access to the beach.

Local villagers offer horse riding along the beach ($10) and sell green coconuts for drinking and necklaces; some can be a bit pushy. Locals are not allowed to enter the resort and travellers cannot have a drink without buying lunch. Consider bringing your own picnic and drinks. There is no public telephone, although the resort should let you use its phone in an emergency.

Places to Stay & Eat

Natadola Beach Resort *(☎ 672 1001, fax 672 1000; w www.natadola.com; doubles $350, 2-bedroom suites $530)* is a cute, small-scale, luxury resort. It has 11 comfortable fan-cooled rooms with private courtyards. There is an attractive swimming pool and landscaped garden. No children under 16 years are accepted. The resort's **restaurant-bar** *(lunch around $15, dinner $20-30)*, with open-plan courtyard and Spanish-style rendered walls, is open to the public.

Villagers from nearby Sanasana, interested in a share of the tourism dollar, may offer **village stays**. Expect to pay about $25 for accommodation and meals in a basic village dwelling. Ask for **Ilami Nabiau** at the police post at the Queens Road-Maro Rd turn-off or contact **Save** *(☎ 650 0800)* or **Baravi** *(☎ 650 0222)* in Sanasana village.

Getting There & Away

Natadola Beach is fairly isolated and makes a good day escape from Nadi. The Maro Rd turn-off heads south to Natadola off the Queens Road, 36km from Nadi (45km from the airport, 66km from Lautoka) just past the police post. There is a temple with a life-sized goddess on the corner. Continue along the gravel road for 9.5km, past a school, a mosque and two bridges, and turn left at a T-junction. You will pass another mosque before reaching the beach.

While there are no direct buses from Nadi, there are regular Paradise buses from Sigatoka bus station to Vusama/Natadola ($2, about one hour). There are six buses daily (fewer on Saturday, none on Sunday), the first leaving Sigatoka at about 6.30am and the last at about 5.45pm. The Coral Coast Scenic Railway runs tours to this beach (see Yanuca & Around later in this chapter). Keen walkers could follow the track between Yanuca and Natadola Beach. It is a pleasant 3½-hour walk. You can catch the train or a bus back.

YANUCA & AROUND

Past the turn-off to Natadola, the Queens Road continues southeast, winding through hills and down to the coast at Cuvu Bay and Yanuca about 50km from Nadi.

The station for the **Coral Coast Scenic Railway** *(☎ 652 8731; Queens Road)* is at the causeway entrance to the Fijian Resort. It offers scenic rides along the coast on an old, diesel sugar train, past villages, forests and sugar plantations, to the beautiful Natadola Beach. The railway was once used for transporting cane and passengers to the Lautoka Mill. The 14km trip takes about 1¼ hours, leaving at 10am and returning at 4pm ($75 including barbecue lunch at the Natadola Resort). It is a popular trip with families and guests of the Fijian Resort suffering hangovers or sunburn. Better value is the Rail-a-Way-Sail-a-Way train-bus-boat day trip for $99, combining a one-way train ride and a trip to Robinson Crusoe. Children under 12 are half-price or free if under six.

Ka Levu South Pacific Cultural Centre *(☎ 552 0200; tour 10.30am-3.30pm Tues-Sun; admission $80)* is on the Queens Road opposite the entrance to the Fijian Resort. The theatrical performance includes a kava ceremony, a tour of a replica of a traditional village, a re-enactment of the Deed of Cession, contemporary Indian dancing, and legends of the Pacific.

Places to Stay & Eat

Adjoining the Cultural Centre is **Trader Jacks** and the **Pig Hunters Bar**. There is budget accommodation here in a 20-bed dorm ($65). Rates include three meals and a daily *lovo* feast and free entry to the cultural centre tour (good value considering the price tag of the tour itself).

Shangri-La's Fijian Resort *(☎ 652 0155, fax 650 0402; **w** www.shangri-la.com; lagoon-view/ocean-view singles or doubles $370/410, family room $510; studios or suites $680, beach bure $950)* is a huge 436-room resort with over 500 staff. The resort, established in the late 1960s, covers the entire 43-hectare island of Yanuca. About 50km from Nadi, Yanuca is just offshore and linked to the mainland by a causeway.

The resort is very family-oriented (85% of their clientele); two children can share with parents for free and there is babysitting ($15 three hours), teenagers' club and 'little chiefs' club'. Room rates include buffet-style breakfast and dinner, expect to spend about $10 for lunch. Most guests are on package deals.

Getting There & Away

The Fijian Resort is about a 45-minute drive from Nadi and 11km west of Sigatoka. There are regular express buses, minibuses and carriers travelling along the Queens Road. A taxi to Nadi airport is about $65 while the Coral Sun coach is $25.

SIGATOKA & AROUND

pop 8000

Sigatoka (pronounced sing-a-toka) is a small town 61km southeast of Nadi and 127km west of Suva. The town is near the mouth of the Sigatoka River, Fiji's second-largest river. It is predominantly a farming community as well as a service town for tourists drawn to the Coral Coast resorts. There is a produce market in the heart of town, a few souvenir shops, a large mosque and a fantasy-style, privately owned mansion on the hill behind the town.

Information

You can seek medical assistance at **Gerona Medical and Surgical Clinic** *(☎ 652 0128, after hrs 652 0327; Sigatoka Valley Rd; open 8.30am-4pm & 7pm-9pm Mon-Fri, 8.30am-1pm & 7pm-9pm Sat, 7pm-9pm Sun)*.

Horse Riding

At **Ratuva's Horse Riding** *(☎ 650 0860)* you can hire horses for riding along the beach. It charges $20 per hour, and $15 per hour for groups of five or more. It's located on a hill about 5.5km from Sigatoka on the left towards Nadi.

Surfing

Sigatoka has Fiji's only beach-break. Most other areas have fringing reefs but here the fresh water has prevented their formation. The break is over a large, submerged rock platform covered in sand. Surfing is at the point-break at the mouth of the Sigatoka River and beach-breaks pound the shore.

Sigatoka Sand Dunes

These large windblown dunes *(admission $5, open daily from 8am to 6pm)* are along a beach near the mouth of the Sigatoka River. The dunes are about 5km long, up to 1km wide and on average about 20m high, rising to about 60m at the western end. Do not expect golden Sahara-like dunes, as the fine sand is a grey-brown colour and largely covered with vines and shrubs. The dunes have been forming over millions of years. The alluvial sediment washed downriver

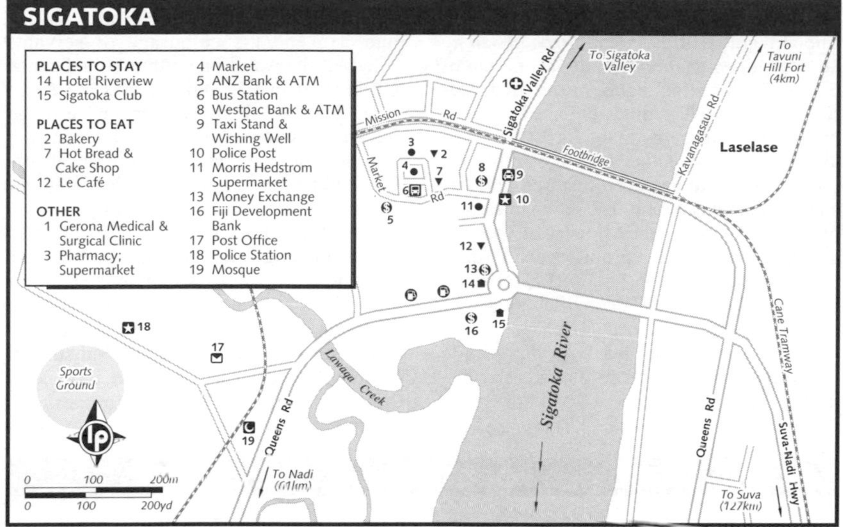

and out to sea is brought ashore by waves and then blown inland by the southeast trade winds.

Human skeletal remains and pottery shards were discovered here suggesting that there was a village near the eastern end of the dunes in prehistoric times. The state-owned part of the area was declared a national park in 1989 in an attempt to help preserve the site.

The dunes are quite spectacular and a great place for a walk. On a hot day visit before 11am or after 3pm. Enter through the Sigatoka Sand Dunes visitor centre at the western end of the dunes, 4.5km west of Sigatoka on the Queens Road. From here there are trails to the dunes; avoid eroding the fragile dunes. Allow about one hour for the round walking tour.

Sigatoka Valley

The Sigatoka River's tributaries originate as far away as Tomanivi (Mt Victoria) and the Monasavu Dam. The river has long provided a line of communication between mountain peoples and coast dwellers, and the fertile river flats are productive agricultural land. Almost 200 archaeological, cultural or historically significant sites have been found in and around the valley; sadly, many of the sites are being taken over by farmland or housing.

This fertile river valley is known as Fiji's 'salad bowl'. Cereals, vegetables, fruits, peanuts and sugar cane are grown here, mostly on small-scale farms. The Sigatoka Valley Rural Development Project (SVRDP) coordinates cropping programmes and provides training for farmers on up-to-date techniques and irrigation systems. Much of the produce ends up at the municipal markets, and vegetables such as eggplant, chilli, okra and root crops like *dalo* (taro), *tavioka* (cassava) and yams are exported to Canada, Australia, New Zealand and the USA. It's a great landscape to fly over, with the mountains, the patchwork valley, the muddy brown river flowing into the blue ocean, and the Coral Coast's vast fringing reef.

Two valley villages are known for their **pottery**: Lawai and Nakabuta. The latter is home to one of Fiji's best potters, Diana Tugea. Visitors are welcome at both villages. If turning up unannounced, you should ask the first person you meet to guide you. They will take you to a pottery *bure* with various works on display. Large, smooth cooking pots are the traditional pots from this area, but small items such as pottery pigs and *bure* are also sold to tourists who visit the area. You can visit these villages by just hopping on a local bus (see Getting There & Around later).

Tavuni Hill Fort

The Tavuni Hill Fort *(adult/child/family $6/3/15; open 8am-5pm Mon-Sat)* is one of the most interesting sights in the area. Defensive sites such as this were used in times of war. While there are many like it scattered all over Fiji, this is the most accessible for visitors. The site has been restored and has an information centre. It was set up in a combined effort between the Ministry of Tourism and the people of Naroro, and received funding from the European Union (EU). It now provides income to the local villagers whose ancestors lived in the fort.

A clan of Tongans led by Chief Maile Latemai established the defensive fort. The mid- to late 18th century was an era of political and social upheaval in Tonga and the chief left his country to escape a family dispute. He and his entourage of servants sailed all the way in a double-hulled canoe and arrived in the Sigatoka area in about 1788. They originally set up in Korotogo but were kept on the move by constant tribal warfare. Eventually the local tribes accepted the newcomers, and the chief was given some land and a local wife.

The steep limestone ridge, about 90m high at the edge of a bend in the Sigatoka River, was an obvious strategic location for a fortification. From this position the surrounding area could easily be surveyed, both upstream and downstream. Substantial earthworks were carried out to form *yavu* (bases for houses) and terraces for barricade fencing. There are also a number of grave

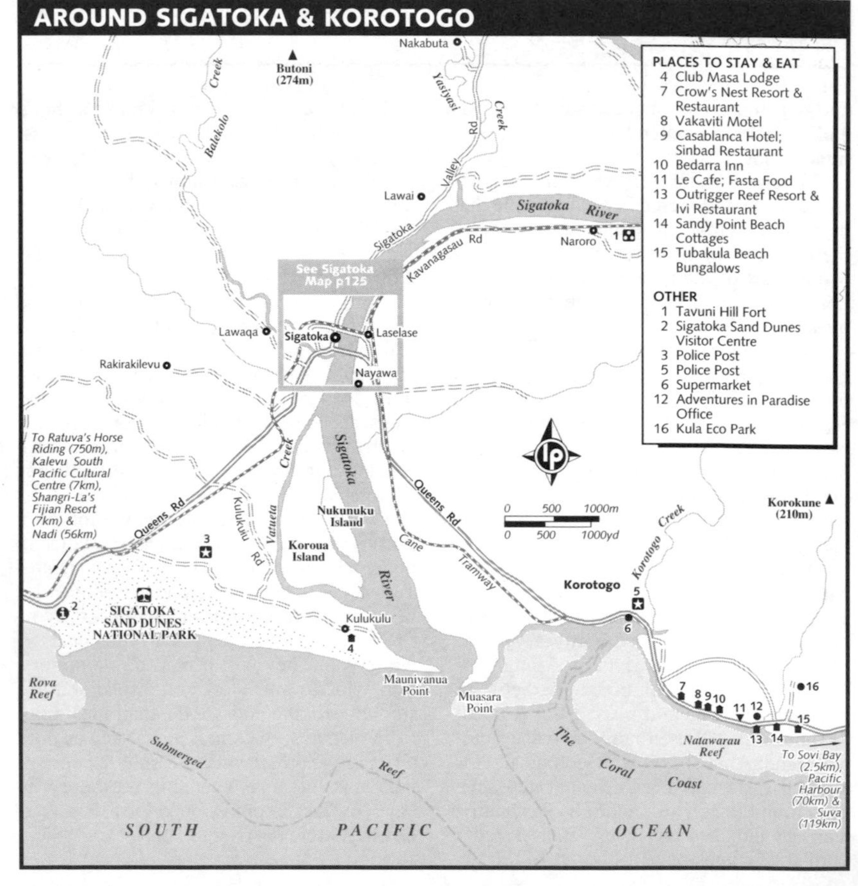

The Kai Colo Uprising

The last significant tribal conflict in Fiji was the Kai Colo Uprising of 1875–6. The Kai Colo (mountain people of inland Viti Levu) opposed the cession of Fiji to Great Britain in 1874 and the imposition of the new politics and religion by the colonial regime.

The measles epidemic of 1875 destroyed about one-third of Fiji's population, totally wiping out some villages. The Kai Colo interpreted this both as a deliberate effort by the European invaders to destroy them and as a punishment from their gods for discarding the traditional ways. Any faith in the new church dissolved and they returned to the old religion and tribal warfare, descending into the Sigatoka Valley and attacking and burning villages of their traditional enemies.

Sir Arthur Gordon saw this as a direct threat to the viability of the fledgling colonial administration, and in order to quash this 'rebellion' and set an example, formed a constabulary of over 1000 Fijian men under the Nadroga Chief Ratu Luki. This force ascended the valley, destroying hill forts and hanging, imprisoning or dispersing the chiefs involved. Sir Gordon's strategy was to pit Fijian against Fijian, on the one hand reinforcing the link with the new laws and, on the other, distancing the colonial government from the bloodshed.

sites, a *rara* (ceremonial ground), a *vatu ni bokola* (head-chopping stone), and some beautiful curtain figs and an *ivi* (Polynesian chestnut tree) on the site.

Souvenirs, snacks and drinks are for sale. Your guide will probably joke about his cannibal past and pinch you to see how tasty you might be! Tavuni is about 4km north of Sigatoka on the eastern side of the river, above Naroro village. There are regular local buses that pass Tavuni Hill (about $0.60). They leave Sigatoka bus station along Kavanagasau Rd heading for Mavua (seven times on weekdays between about 7am and 5.30pm). A taxi to the fort is about $5 one-way.

Places to Stay

Sigatoka town can be a convenient stopover, however there are better budget options nearby in Korotogo. Although not unsafe, prostitutes hang out at night near these two small hotels.

Sigatoka Club *(☎ 650 0026; dorms/singles/doubles $15/25/45)*, by the bridge, is the local watering hole with pool tables and $4 meals. It has basic accommodation in a five-bed dorm or private rooms. **Hotel Riverview** *(☎ 652 0544; dorms/singles/doubles $15/35/45)*, across the roundabout from the Sigatoka Club, has air-con dorm rooms.

Club Masa Lodge *(☎ 651 1347; camping per person $18, dorms/doubles $30/40)* is a surfie hangout south of town near the river's mouth and the Sigatoka Sand Dunes. There is a communal veranda area, and electricity's until 9.30pm. Prices include breakfast and dinner, and lunch can be ordered. It has ocean and river access for surfing, windsurfing and canoeing; bring your own gear.

About 2km southwest of Sigatoka, turn off the Queens Road at Kulukulu Rd and continue a further 2km along the dusty road. Turn left at the T-junction facing the dunes and continue for about 1km to Kulukulu village. Club Masa is another 200m farther south. There are Sunbeam buses that depart from Sigatoka bus station for Kulukulu village six times daily, less often on Sunday. A taxi will cost about $5 from Sigatoka. It's a 50-minute drive from Nadi airport ($40 by van).

Places to Eat

For nice lunches, try **Le Café** *($10)* on the main street near the larger bridge. There are **bakeries** and many cheap eateries near the market and bus station serving inexpensive Chinese, Indian and traditional Fijian meals. Both hotels also serve meals. Self-caterers can stock up at the **market** and the **Morris Hedstrom supermarket**.

Getting There & Around

The cheapest and most fun way to travel along the Coral Coast from Suva or Lautoka is by open-air bus. Express buses running from Suva take about 2¾ hours, while the trip from Lautoka takes about 2¼ hours. Add about an hour for non-express buses.

Alternatively, there are express air-con coaches going from Nadi International Airport to Korolevu. There are also carriers and Viti minibuses as well as taxis.

Paradise Valley *(☎ 994 169)* buses travel up the Sigatoka Valley on the western side. Lawai is about 4km north of Sigatoka. Nakabuta is twice as far ($5 by taxi, $0.60 by bus, or a 10-minute drive). There are regular buses to Naduri, which pass Lawai and Nakabuta (every one to two hours from about 6.30am to 7.30pm). On weekends services are less frequent. Heading inland by local bus offers beautiful scenery. Try a ride to Keiyasi village about 55km upriver ($5, about four hours return). The morning buses generally return (check with the bus driver), while the afternoon buses stay in the village overnight.

KOROTOGO & AROUND

The Coral Coast begins at the Sigatoka River, a 45km stretch of fringing reef dropping off dramatically into deep ocean. In most parts of the coast the beach is tidal and, except for some lagoons, is only suitable for swimming and snorkelling at high tide. Sovi Bay 2.5km east of Korotogo is OK for swimming, however be careful of the strong channel currents.

The Queens Road hits the coast again near the settlement of Korotogo, and about 8km east of Sigatoka, there are a few places to stay and eat, a souvenir shop, and a travel agent across a quiet service road from an ordinary beach. Here the Queens Road was diverted to provide foreshore frontage for the colossal Outrigger Reef Resort, which carefully grooms the sand on its beachfront. East of the creek the beach improves, with a few lagoons with some live coral for snorkelling, and budget accommodation on the foreshore.

Further east, the section of the Queens Road between Korotogo and Korolevu is the most beautiful. The road winds along the shore, with scenic bays, beaches, coral reefs and mountains, an especially spectacular trip at sunrise or sunset.

Kula Eco Park

This well-run wildlife sanctuary *(☎ 650 0505; w www.fijiwild.com; adults/children $15/7.50; open 10am-4.30pm daily)*, just across the road from the Outrigger Reef Resort entrance, is well-worth visiting. An educational centre for local children, it has a captive-breeding programme for the endangered Fiji peregrine falcon and Fiji's crested and banded iguanas. Take your time to wander along the walkways, through the big aviary and up the hilly forest bushwalking trails that ends with a rope-bridge crossing. There are hawksbill sea turtles (hand fed three times daily, 11am, 1pm and 3.30pm), a raptor centre with owls, goshawks and peregrine falcons, Fiji's musk parrots, collared parrots (the Kula bird), honeyeaters, fruit bats eating bananas upside down, and enclosures where banded iguanas hide camouflaged in the shrubbery.

Diving

Coral Coast Scuba Ventures *(☎ 652 8793)* based at Shangri-La's Fijian Resort takes dive trips to some of the Coral Coast reefs and passages around the area. A two-tank dive costs $190 and an open-water course is $600.

Organised Tours

Adventures in Paradise *(☎ 652 0833; e wfall@connect.com.fj)* offers day trips to the Naihehe cave for $100 (see the Viti Levu Highlands section later in this chapter), and tours to Biausevu and the Savu Na Mate Laya waterfall near Korolevu for $90. Tours include a village visit, kava ceremony, lunch and transport from Coral Coast and Nadi hotels. Its office is in a small group of shops just west of Outrigger Reef Resort. **Rivers Fiji** pick up from Coral Coast resorts (see Pacific Harbour later).

Places to Stay – Budget

Tubakula Beach Bungalows *(☎ 650 0097; e tubakula@fiji4less.com; dorm beds $15, up-to-3-person bungalows poolside/ocean-view/beachfront $60/70/80, for renovated bungalows add $20)*, on the beachfront east of Outrigger Reef Resort, is a good budget option. It has 27 A-frame, fan-cooled, bungalows with cooking facilities, in a decent stretch of beach (for Coral Coast standards). The renovated beachfront bungalows are good value and dorm accommodation (three to four beds) is in eight small rooms with communal cooking facilities. There are spacious grounds, a swimming pool, restaurant and bar, mini-market, and there's a communal TV lounge and games area.

Vakaviti Motel *(☎ 650 0526; e bulavakaviti@connect.com.fj; dorm beds $15, motel doubles/triples $65/77, bure $75/87)*, a nice hillside place with a jungle-like garden, is about 500m west of Outrigger Reef Resort. It has four fan-cooled self-contained motel rooms with cooking facilities that open onto a nice swimming pool with views over the treetops to the ocean. There are two other buildings (one for up to six people) at the bottom of the garden. The motel was up for sale at the time of writing.

Crow's Nest Resort *(dorm beds $15)* has a nice little elevated six-bed dorm (no cooking facilities) on top of its restaurant and overlooking the pool. In the low season you may find you have it to yourself! See Places to Stay – Mid-Range later for more details

Casablanca Hotel *(☎ 652 0600; singles/doubles $45/55 plus $8 per extra person, large unit $65)* run by Mostafa, an Egyptian-Australian, is where Mediterranean meets the South Pacific. Prices here are fair and the staff friendly and helpful. The eight units are clean and spacious with good cooking facilities and a fridge. All rooms have nice ocean views and there is a small saltwater swimming pool.

Places to Stay – Mid-Range

Bedarra Inn *(☎ 650 0476, fax 652 0116;* **e** *bedarrahouse@connect.com.fj; doubles $125)* is a small hotel with a swimming pool and pleasant gardens, just west of the Outrigger Resort. It is a good option for those after a more intimate atmosphere than the larger resorts, accompanied by fine food. The main house has a lofty central bar/entertainment area and two family rooms and two double rooms. There is a separate *bure* for those who want to maximise their privacy and a new double-storey hotel wing with 16 air-con rooms. The family rooms are spacious and can easily fit four (children under 16 are free). The daily tariff includes breakfast. Bedarra has the best restaurant in the area – it is open to outsiders and they have a pick up and drop off service for the guests of local hotels. Van transfers are $30 from Nadi airport.

Crow's Nest Resort *(☎ 650 0513, fax 652 0354;* **e** *crowsnest@connect.com.fj; up-to-4-person unit $88)* is 7km east of Sigatoka town in Korotogo. It is on a hillside site across the road from the beach. It has 17 good self-contained split-level units with balconies and sea views that were quite a bargain at the time we passed. Each has a double bed and two single beds, ceiling fans, air-con, and cooking facilities. The resort has a nice swimming pool and a sun-deck adjacent to the restaurant (see Places to Eat later). It also has dorm accommodation (see Places to Stay – Budget earlier).

Sandy Point Beach Cottages *(☎ 650 0125, fax 652 0147;* **e** *cbcom@connect.com.fj; singles/doubles or triples $70/80, family cottage $130)* is a family-oriented place with just five self-contained cottages. It has spacious grounds on a nice stretch of beach. The family cottage sleeps five people. There is a 10% discount if you stay longer than seven days; book ahead for the busy months between June and September. There is a freshwater swimming pool but no restaurant. Cottages are by far outnumbered by big parabolic aerials (satellite dishes), which resort owner Bob Kennedy uses to get the latest weather maps and keep an eye on approaching cyclones.

Places to Stay – Top End

Outrigger Reef Resort *(☎ 650 0044, fax 652 0074;* **w** *www.outrigger.com/fiji; doubles $410, 4-person bure $480)* is a huge beachfront resort on the Korotogo hillside. It has 167 air-con rooms in the four-storey main building, with balconies or verandas and superb views over the resort grounds and coral reef. Down the elevators (yes elevators, the only resort in Fiji with elevators!) are the 47 Fijian-style *bure* with high ceilings lined with hand-painted *tapu* cloth, spread around the resort grounds and gardens to the beachfront. Near the 70m swimming pool are another 40 hotel rooms in the old Reef Resort building revamped beyond recognition. There are three restaurants, bars, shops, a sports club, and a nightclub. The Friday night entertainment programme includes Fijian firewalking ($15 per person), buffet dinner ($35) and *meke* performances (visitors welcome).

Places to Eat

There are a few options for dining out.

Bedarra Inn Restaurant *(☎ 650 0476; mains $14-30)* has excellent food and a friendly bar. It has pick up and drop off service for the guests of local hotels.

Le Cafe *(☎ 652 0877; dishes around $10; open 4pm-10pm daily)* just west of the shops has a Swiss chef Jean Pierre, who offers tasty pizzas and European-style food. The shops next door to Le Café includes a general store and **Fasta Food** – an inexpensive eat-in or takeaway.

The **restaurant** at the Crow's Nest Resort in Korotogo is decked out with nautical memorabilia. It was temporarily closed when we came around, but it normally offers European and local dishes at reasonable prices.

Sinbad Restaurant *(dishes $5-10)* at the front of the Casablanca Hotel offers OK Chinese, curries, pizza and European dishes.

If are prepared to spend a bit more try dining at the colonial-style **Ivi Restaurant** at the Outrigger Reef Resort.

Getting There & Around

There are regular express and local buses along the Queens Road. A taxi from Korotogo to Sigatoka is $4, and around $40 to Nadi. Queens Deluxe Coaches has air-con buses from Nadi to Korotogo ($5, one daily) departing Nadi International Airport at 7.30am and passing the Outrigger Resort at 6.45pm.

Fire Walking

Fijian *Vilavilairevo* (literally 'jumping into the oven') is practised on the island of Beqa, off southern Viti Levu. The ability to walk barefoot on white-hot stones without being burned was, according to local legend, granted to a local chief by the leader of the *veli*, a group of little gods. Now the direct descendants of the chief *(Tui Qalita)* serve as the *bete* (priests) who instruct in the ritual of fire walking. The spirits of the little gods are summoned to watch the performance held in their honour.

Preparations for fire walking used to occupy a whole village for nearly a month. Firewood and appropriate stones had to be selected, costumes made and various ceremonies performed. Fire walkers had to abstain from sex and refrain from eating any coconut for up to a month before the ritual. None of the fire walkers' wives could be pregnant, or it was believed the whole group would receive burns. Pregnant women were also barred from the vicinity of the pit.

Traditionally, only performed on special occasions in the village of Navakaisese, nowadays it is performed for commercial purposes and has little religious meaning. Other villages, on Beqa and neighbouring Yanuca, use fire walking as a source of income. Time and cost considerations in modern resort performances have led to smaller fire pits requiring less firewood. Costumes can now be reused and tabu periods have been reduced to a few days. There are regular performances at the Pacific Harbour Cultural Centre, at the larger resort hotels, and at Suva's annual Hibiscus Festival.

Hindu The Hindu fire walking is part of an annual religious festival coinciding with a full moon in July or August and lasting 10 days. It takes place at many temples in Fiji, including the Mariamma Temple in Suva.

Preparations for the ceremony are overseen by a priest and take three to 10 days, with the fire walking the climax of the ritual. During this period participants isolate themselves, abstain from sex and eating meat, and meditate to worship the goddess Maha Devi.

They rise early, pray until late at night, survive on little food or sleep and dress in red and yellow, which symbolises the cleansing of physical and spiritual impurity. Yellow turmeric is smeared on the face as a symbol of prosperity and power over diseases.

On the final day the participants at the Mariamma Temple bathe in the sea. The priests pierce the tongues, cheeks and bodies of the fire walkers with three-pronged skewers. The fire walkers then dance in an ecstatic trance for about 2km back to the temple for the fire walking.

Devotees' bodies are whipped before and during the ceremony. If fire walkers are focused on the divine Mother they should not feel pain.

A decorated statue of the goddess is placed facing the pit for her to watch and bless the ceremony. It only takes about five seconds to walk along the pit, which is filled with charred wood raked over glowing coals, and the walk is repeated about five times to chanting and drumming.

Hindu fire walking is a religious sacrament performed mostly by descendants of southern Indians. It is a means by which a devotee aspires to become one with the Mother. Their body should be enslaved to the spirit and denied all comforts. They believe life is like walking on fire; discipline helps them to achieve a balanced life, self-acceptance and to see good in everything.

KOROLEVU & AROUND

The village of Korolevu is 90km from Nadi airport, (31km east of Sigatoka and 24km east of Korotogo) and 71km west of Pacific Harbour. There are many resorts spread along this stretch of the coast, from budget to top-end places.

There is a souvenir shop west of Korolevu in the small village of Vatukarasa: **Baravi Handicrafts** *(☎ 652 0364)* sells local crafts, clothes and jewellery and is open daily.

East of Korolevu, the Queens Road turns away from the shore and climbs over the southern end of Viti Levu's dividing mountain range. To the east of this range the road improves and the scenery changes to lush rainforest and the road winds its way past wider bays.

Activities

Take care while swimming, currents can be dangerous and there have been drownings near here. At Hideaway Resort there is a right-hand break at the passage about 100m from the shore for experienced surfers – the best chances of good **surf** are between January and May. It is also possible to surf offshore from Waidroka Bay Resort and at Frigates in the Beqa Lagoon.

Mike's Divers *(☎ 653 0222; e info@divefiji.com)* a local dive operation based at Votua village, takes dive trips to some of the nearby reef passages. Rates are $125 for a two-tank dive trip or $450 for an open-water course.

SPAD-South Pacific Adventure Divers *(☎ 672 4246; e spaddivefiji@connect.com.fj)* is a dive operation used by guests at upmarket resorts in Korolevu (Warwick, Naviti and Hideaway Resorts). It runs dives to the main reef off Korolevu, as well as dive sites at Beqa Lagoon and the offshore island of Vatulele. Rates are $130 for a two-tank dive trip ($240 for two-tank dive excursions to Beqa or Vatulele including lunch) and $550 for open-water courses. Both dive operations will pick up divers from most places around Korolevu. Waidroka Bay Resort has its own dive set up (see Places to Stay later in this section).

Adventures in Paradise (see Organised Tours under Korotogo & Around earlier in this chapter) has trips to the village of Biausevu, inland from Korolevu, and a local waterfall where you can **swim**. The turn-off to Biausevu is about a 15-minute drive east of Hideaway Resort. The village is 2.5km inland, and the waterfall is an easy 15- to 30-minute walk from the village.

Places to Stay – Budget

The Beachhouse *(☎ 653 0500, toll free 0800 6530 0530; e info@fijibeachouse.com; camping per person $12, five-/three-/two-bed dorm $19/22/24, doubles $55)* offers budget-chic accommodation, excellent service and a friendly atmosphere in a lovely beach setting. It is 7km east of Korolevu and 89km from Suva, just off a bend in the Queens Road. It has a couple of double-storey timber buildings with double rooms upstairs, dorm rooms downstairs, and cute private garden rooms among an established tropical garden. The beachfront is quite pleasant, with a grassy area under coconut trees where people lay around, a small deck close to the water to sit and drink at sunset or night, and a nice little stretch of white-sand beach. Bathrooms and toilets are in an adjacent building. Meals are at **Coconut Café** *(breakfast/lunch/dinner $4/7/9)* in the restored original copra plantation cottage. As well as good meals and plunger coffee, the milkshakes and smoothies

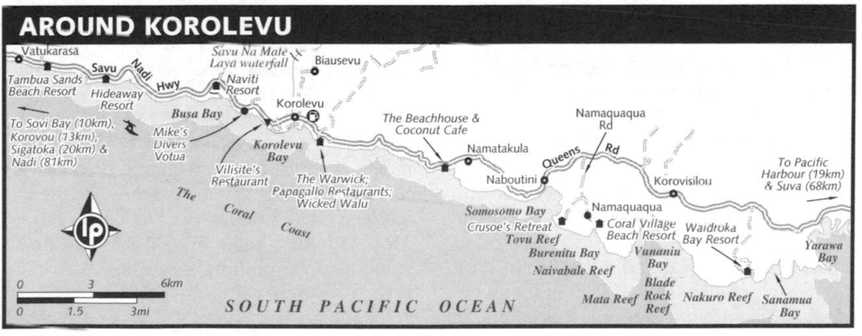

($4) are yummy and afternoon tea is free. There is also a simple communal kitchen. This place is very popular, so you might need to book ahead.

Use of canoes is free, there is snorkelling equipment for hire ($3 per day) and guided hikes are $5 per person. Diving the reef passages nearby is with Mike's Divers (See earlier under activities).

Waidroka Bay Resort *(☎ 330 4605; dorm beds $18, lodge rooms per person $55, bure doubles/triples $100/140)* is on a beautifully secluded section of the coast 69km west of Suva. Run by an American family, the resort is well-equipped for adventurous divers and surfers. Accommodation in the lodge is simple (maximum of three people in a room with shared facilities) there is also a big, eight-bed dorm *bure*. The four fan-cooled oceanfront *bure* are comfortable and have verandas facing the water. The communal building has a **restaurant** *(open 8am-8pm)*, a TV lounge and shop. Meal packages are $40 per day, otherwise lunch is under $10 and dinner is $12 to $18. It is a fairly remote place and there are no self-catering facilities.

Diving is $110 for a two-tank dive, plus $15 for equipment rental. Snorkel trips are $20 per person but you can also snorkel along the shore. There are six surf beaks near Waidroka ($15 per person for a boat) and it's a half-hour boat trip to surf Frigate Passage ($45 per person). The resort can hire out some reasonably good surfboards ($25 per day), but it is best to bring your own. Fishing, kayaking, trekking, village visits and trips to Pacific Harbour are also offered.

The 4km of unsealed road through steep hills and forest into the resort is a bit rough and very steep in parts. Transfers from Nadi airport or from the Queens Road turn-off to meet the bus can be organised if you call ahead. Expect to pay $80 to $100 for a taxi from Nadi.

Coral Village Beach Resort *(☎ 650 0807; e corvill@connect.com.fj; dorm beds without/with meal package $17/40, bure single or double/triple $60/80, bure with meal package $80 per person)* is a small low-key place in a nice and isolated coastal valley next to Namaquaqua village and near Crusoe's Retreat. The Queens Road turn-off to the resort is 50km from Sigatoka and 77km from Suva. There is a good beach and lagoon for swimming, and an offshore reef for snorkelling. It has an eight-bed dorm (no cooking facilities), spacious double or twin fan-cooled *bure*, and very large family *bure*, which can sleep five people comfortably. The daily meal includes breakfast and dinner only, but you can order extra snacks/meals ($7 to $10) at the restaurant-bar.

There are nature walks, fishing, and snorkelling trips, diving and other activities can be arranged with Crusoe's Retreat next door. There is dance and kava drinking at the local village on Tuesdays ($8 per person). The road into the resort is about 5km off the Queens Road, so call ahead to be picked up at the turn-off.

Places to Stay – Mid-Range

Waidroka Bay Resort *(bure doubles/triples $100/140)* has comfortable, fan-cooled, oceanfront *bure* (see Places to Stay – Budget earlier in this section).

Crusoe's Retreat *(☎ 650 0185, fax 652 0666; w www.crusoesretreat.com; bure up-to-3-adults or 2-adults & 2-children sea-view/seaside $150/180)* is a beautiful, hilly beachfront setting, well off the beaten track. The 28 spacious fan-cooled *bure* are comfortable and good value. Three meals a day will cost around $100 per adult. There is a tennis court and a foot-shaped saltwater swimming pool and use of the glass-bottomed boat and snorkelling equipment are free. The resort dive shop charges $150 for a two-tank dive trip or $15 per person for snorkelling trips to outer reefs. Crusoe's Retreat is 90km from Nadi, 80km from Suva and 5km from the Queens Road. Return transfers from Nadi International Airport cost $100 per person, half price for children under 12 years.

Tambua Sands Beach Resort *(☎ 650 0399, fax 652 0265; e tambuasands@connect.com.fj; beachfront/ocean-view bure doubles $120/100 plus $20 per extra adult)* is a quiet place along a reasonably good beach and best suited for those wanting to relax at a small-scale resort. It offers fairly simple and comfortable fan-cooled *bure*, but no cooking facilities. *Bure* rates include breakfast, and meals at the resort's restaurant cost around $10/25 lunch/three-course dinner. The resort has a small swimming pool and nice setting. Most activities, including village tours, horse riding and snorkelling gear, cost extra. The resort is approximately halfway between Nadi and Suva.

Places to Stay – Top End

Hideaway Resort *(☎ 650 0177, fax 652 0025; w www.hideawayfiji.com; up-to-3-person bure fan cooled/air-con $240/260, beachfront bure doubles with air-con $310, up-to-4-person 2-bedroom bure $410)* is a popular resort on a good stretch of beach. The frangipani *bure*, set back in the garden, are smart and have an outside bath/shower and spa. The two-bedroom *bure* are well-ventilated and good value for families, while the spacious air-con *bure* couples. Rates include a buffet breakfast and the meal plan ($40 per person per day) includes lunch and two-course dinner.

The resort has a fun atmosphere, with lots of amenities, entertainment and a surf break just offshore (see Activities earlier). It has *lovo* nights on Sunday, a nightly house band, weekly fire walking, *meke* and kava ceremonies. The resort has an excellent swimming pool and non-motorised activities are included in the tariff. Diving is with SPAD-South Pacific Adventure Divers (see Activities earlier in this section).

There are two other upmarket resorts further east, both members of the Warwick International Hotel chain.

The **Naviti Resort** *(☎ 653 0444, fax 653 0099; w http://navitiresort.com.fj; doubles and up to two children mountain-view/ocean-view $190/220)* is popular with families, with good wheelchair and pram access. A hilly backdrop protects the beach and it has a small, private island. All of its 140 air-con rooms either have balconies (nicer) or outdoor patios. Meal packages are $60 per adult.

The **Warwick Fiji Resort** *(☎ 653 0555, fax 653 0010; w www.warwickfiji.com; up-to-3-person or 2-adults plus 2-children mountain-view/ocean-view rooms $300/340, Warwick Club rooms/suites $470/630)*, about 5km east of the Naviti, has 250 rooms and is one of Fiji's largest resorts.

Both resorts can offer good-value all-inclusive package deals and facilities are interchangeable. The Naviti is a few kilometres west of Korolevu and the Warwick about 2km east of the village. Lots of activities and non-motorised sports (including golf, tennis, horse riding and windsurfing) are included in the price and there is *meke* and fire walking twice weekly. Diving is with SPAD-South Pacific Adventure Divers (See Activities earlier).

Places to Eat

Coconut Cafe *(☎ 653 0500, breakfast $3-5.50, light lunch $7, dinner around $9)*, at The Beachhouse colonial cottage near Korolevu, is a popular spot with backpackers (see Places to Stay earlier) and a nice place for a break if you are travelling along the Coral Coast. It has good coffee and fresh-fruit smoothies. For dinner place an order before 4pm.

Vilisite's Restaurant *(☎ 653 0054)*, between the Naviti and Warwick resorts, has a veranda overlooking the water. It has á la carte and set-menu dishes for lunch and dinner. Octopus, fish fillets and fruits cost $19.50, while a meal of 16 king prawns, fried rice and a fruit platter is $32.

Visitors are welcome at the larger resorts restaurants. At the Warwick Resort, the **Papagallo Restaurant** *(mains $17-28)* serves good pizza and pasta dishes for $10 to $20 and the **Wicked Walu** *(dinner only; seafood $20-34)*, is on a tiny island linked to the resort by a causeway. The **restaurant** *(mains $10-20)* at the Hideaway Resort is also open for visitors.

Getting There & Around

There are plenty of buses shuttling along the Queens Road (to Suva or Nadi costs approximately $7 one way) and drivers will pick up and drop off at the resort gates. The Warwick and the Naviti have a free shuttle bus for guests running between the resorts and to/from Nadi International Airport. Taxis to the airport cost about $85/95 one-way/return for the 1½-hour ride, or $20 for the 20-minute drive to Sigatoka (28km).

PACIFIC HARBOUR & NAVUA

The vegetation east of Korolevu is greener and denser as you approach rainy Suva. In the Deuba and Pacific Harbour area, the Queens Road hugs the coast, with the offshore island of Beqa in sight.

Pacific Harbour is 78km east of Sigatoka (139km from Nadi) and 49km west of Suva. It is an unusual town for Fiji, a planned upmarket housing and tourism development (which has never taken off) with meandering drives, canals and a golf course, and many, *many* vacant blocks. It rains a lot here and the town itself is fairly unexciting, however the Beqa Lagoon offshore has world-class diving and an awesome surf-break and inland are the spectacular Namosi Highlands (see the Viti Levu Highlands section later). The beach at Deuba is the closest OK beach to Suva. Just 45 minutes by car from Suva, Pacific Harbour is a convenient weekend beach escape from the capital, and some residents commute daily to work in Suva.

The small town of Navua, on the banks of the wide Navua River, is 39km west (a 20-minute drive) from Suva and 143km from Nadi. Early in the 20th century, sugar cane was planted here and a sugar mill built, but this activity ceased as the drier western region proved more productive. Farmers of the delta region then turned to dairy farming, cattle grazing, rice and other crops. Many of the old buildings in the town date from the beginning of the 20th century.

Things to See

Take a sunset or sunrise walk up to the hilltop for a superb view of Beqa Lagoon.

The **Fijian Cultural Centre & Marketplace** *(☎ 345 0177)*, about 1km east of the Pacific Harbour International Resort, has seen better days, and is geared towards tour groups by the busload. It has a few gift shops and the cultural centre is OK for a quick caricature of Fijian history. Children may enjoy taking the **Lake Tour** in a *drua* (double-hulled canoe) around the small islands that have an artificial village with a 'warrior' as skipper and guide. There is a temple, chief's *bure*, cooking area with utensils and a weaving hut. Fijian actors dressed in traditional costumes carry out a mock battle. The boat stops along the way to show traditional techniques for canoe-making, weaving, pottery and *tapa* (also known as *masi,* or bark cloth). There are three fire-walking and *meke* performances weekly (Tuesday, Thursday and Saturday).

Activities

Pacific Harbour International Resort allows visitors to use the facilities and join tours. Dinghy sailing, windsurfing, or coral viewing in a glass-bottomed boat costs $15 and a one-hour horse ride is $10/15 per child/adult. Cruises to offshore Yanuca are $60 per person. The **Pacific Harbour Golf & Country Club** *(☎ 345 0048)* designed around lakes and canals, is about 2km inland from the Queens Road. Green fees are $20/25 for nine/18 holes.

Diving At Pacific Safari Club, **Aqua-Trek** *(☎ 345 0324, in Nadi 670 2413;* **e** *aquatrekbeqa@connect.com.fj)* is one the best diving operations in the area. Rates are $160 for a two-tank dive, but a dive package in excess of 12 dives works out to about $50 per dive. Open-water courses are $600.

Dive Connections *(☎ 345 0541;* **e** *diveconn@connect.com.fj; 16 River Drive)* takes dive trips on either the 12m *Scuba Queen* or 7m aluminium *Dive Master*. A two-tank dive, including all equipment and picnic lunch, costs $130, or $100 for just tanks and weights. An open-water course is $395. For snorkellers, trips are $45 including lunch. It has a comfortable self-contained one-bedroom unit for divers. Ask about package deals.

Surfing There is first-class surfing at Frigate Passage and surf camps on Yanuca (see Yanuca later in this chapter).

River Tours Based at Pacific Harbour, **Rivers Fiji** *(☎ 345 0147, mobile 999 2349;* **w** *www.riversfiji.com)* offers excellent kayaking and rafting trips to the Namosi Highlands north of Pacific Harbour.

Discover Fiji Tours *(☎ 345 0180, fax 345 0549;* **w** *www.discoverfijitours.com)* based in Navua, has several tours to the Navua River area. The 'Magic Waterfall' trip costs $80 per person and includes lunch and *bilibili* (bamboo rafting) down the Navua River to Nakavu village. You can be picked up and dropped off at Pacific Harbour and Suva hotels. A five-hour trip with a cruise up the Navua River in a 25-horsepower punt (1½ hours upriver, one hour downriver) to Namuamua village for lunch costs $55. It also offers one- to four-day guided treks across Namosi Highlands, with camping overnight in villages, and a three-day, two-night camp on the banks of the Navua River.

Wilderness Ethnic Adventure Fiji *(☎ 331 5730;* **w** *www.wilderness.com.fj)* offers tours to the Navua River, picking up passengers from Pacific Harbour as well as from Suva hotels (see under Organised Tours in the Suva section later in this chapter).

There are also market boats and local buses to/from Namuamua and Nukusere villages about 20km upriver. The trip can take up to two hours, depending on the river's water level and general conditions.

Places to Stay – Budget

Pacific Safari Club *(☎ 345 0498, toll free 0800 3450 498; dorms/singles/doubles $18/40/45)* has spacious and comfortable rooms with fully equipped cooking facilities. It is in a convenient spot on the canal and has friendly and helpful management. Turn inland on River Drive, opposite the Pacific Harbour International Resort, and before the canal take the first street on the left.

Accommodation at the **self-contained flat** *(singles/doubles $30/40)* next to the Dive Connections office in Pacific Harbour is good value. Contact **Dive Connections** *(☎ 345 0541; e diveconn@connect.com.fj)* for bookings.

Club Coral Coast *(☎ 345 0421; e clubcoralcoast@connect.com.fj; singles or doubles/triples $70/100, budget singles or doubles $25)* has a nice swimming pool and a tennis court. Family rooms with a double bed and a mezzanine with twin single beds can be good-value. Budget rooms are a squeeze and have shared facilities. Turn inland on River Drive, opposite the Pacific Harbour International Resort, cross the canal and take the first left at Belo Circle.

Deuba Inn *(☎ 345 0544; e theislander@connect.com.fj; Queens Road, Deuba; dorms/singles/doubles $10/17/27, up-to-five-person units $50-60)* is an old pineapple-canning factory and homestead with a nice garden and a good restaurant. It is just a kilometre west of the Pacific Harbour International resort and a few minutes' walk from the local beach. The cheaper rooms and dorm (five people) are basic prefab boxes with a shared bathroom. The units with cooking facilities are a better deal for groups.

Places to Stay – Mid-Range & Top End

Pacific Harbour International *(☎ 345 0022, fax 345 0262; e centrapacharb@connect.com.fj; singles or doubles $143 plus $25 per extra adult, suites $275)*, previously the Centra Resort, was built in the early 1970s. The resort has spacious grounds, standard air-con rooms, a swimming pool, tennis, windsurfing, snorkelling, diving, horse riding, tennis, a kids' club and a reasonable dark-sand beach for swimming. Canoeing and tennis are included in the rates but most other activities and tours cost extra. Diving is with Aqua-Trek (see Activities earlier).

Pacific Harbour Villas *(☎/fax 345 0959; e hps@fijirealty.com; villas nightly/fortnightly $100/600)*, spacious modern houses on the quiet streets around the golf course, can be a good option for families or groups. Check the location first if you don't have your own transport.

Places to Eat

Kumaran's Restaurant and Milk Bar *(☎ 345 0294; mains $5-12)*, across the Queens Road from the Pacific Harbour International entrance, is a good place for cheap simple food. It has Indian, Chinese and European food to eat-in or takeaway (try the take way roti parcels). There are a couple of cheap **takeaways** in the Fijian Cultural Centre & Marketplace as well as the **Oasis Restaurant** *(☎ 450 617; mains from $15; open lunch & dinner)*, which has burgers and sandwiches from $4.50 to $7.

Loraini's Restaurant at Deuba Inn has good-value meals (mains under $10), including curries, Chinese and European dishes, and very friendly service. It also has a bar with happy hour from 6pm to 7pm.

Nautilis Restaurant *(mains $12.50-22.50)* at Pacific Harbour International resort welcomes visitors.

There is a supermarket in the Cultural Centre, a good produce market in Navua, and roadside stalls sell fruit and vegetables.

Getting There & Around

Pacific Harbour is about an hour's express bus ride from Suva and around three hours from Nadi. There are frequent Pacific Transport and Sunbeam Transport Lautoka–Suva buses travelling the Queens Road as well as vans and carriers. The first bus from Pacific Harbour to Lautoka leaves at about 7.50am and the last at around 7pm. The first bus to Suva leaves at 8.45am and the last is at 9.40pm. A taxi to Suva costs $35 and to Nadi about $100.

The regular express buses along the Queens Road stop at Navua, 10km east of Pacific Harbour. They take about 50 minutes from Suva and about 3¼ hours from Nadi.

OFFSHORE ISLANDS

Offshore from Pacific Harbour, a 64km-long reef encloses the 360-sq-km **Beqa Lagoon** and the islands of Beqa and Yanuca. The lagoon has many famous dive sites: Side

Streets (soft corals, coral heads and gorgonian fans); Frigate Pass (a 48m wall with large pelagic fish, including white-tip reef sharks); and Caesar's Rocks (coral heads and swim-throughs). Surfing is first-class at **Frigate Passage**, southwest of Yanuca. It has left-hand waves, which can get really big. The break has three sections, which join up under the right conditions: the outside take-off, a long, walled speed section with a possibility of stand up tubes; and an inside section breaking over the shallow reef and finishing in deep water.

Beqa

The high island of Beqa (area 36 sq km), about 7.5km south of Pacific Harbour, is visible from the Queens Road and even from Suva. The island is about 7km in diameter with a deeply indented coastline and a rugged interior with ridges averaging 250m and sloping steeply down to the coast. The surrounding coral reef is famous for its dive sites. Beqa has two upmarket resorts, one budget resort and eight villages. The villagers of Rukua, Naceva and Dakuibeqa are known for the tradition of fire walking.

Lawaki Beach House *(☎ 992 1621; e info@lawakibeachhouse.com; dorm beds $70, bure doubles $80 per person)* is a new budget place on the southwestern side of the island at Lawaki. There is good snorkelling off the secluded pristine white-sand beach and visits to the nearby village. Catering for a maximum of 10 guests, it has just two double *bure* with en suites and verandas and a six-bed dorm. The Swiss-Fijian hosts have a spacious beach house with kitchen and communal area for guests. Three meals are included in the daily rate, and payments are by cash only.

Transfers to Lawaki Beach House are by small open local boats which can be hired at Navua for about $100. Otherwise try to join a local village boat to Beqa for $15 a head (no timetable). Be aware that the boat trip can be rough, and depending on the weather, it may be unsafe as they normally do not carry life vests or a radio.

Marlin Bay Resort *(☎ 330 4042, fax 330 4028; w www.marlinbay.com; double bure $400)* caters mostly for divers on prebooked packages. It has 25 luxury air-con *bure*, a large restaurant-lounge *bure* and a pool on a nice coconut-tree fringed beach on the western side of the island. Meal plans are $110 per person per day. Rates include snorkelling, kayaking, unlimited shore diving, hiking to waterfalls and village visits. Two-tank dive trips cost $160. Boat transfers from Pacific Harbour are $100 per person return.

Yanuca

Not to be confused with Yanuca (Shangri-La's Fijian Resort) near Sigatoka, or Yanuca near Ovalau, this small island with beautiful beaches is within the Beqa Lagoon, 9km west of Beqa. **Frigates Passage** surf-break is south of the island. Visited mainly by day-trippers, divers and surfers, it has two surf camps and one small village.

Batiluva *(☎ 343 1019, 992 0019; e batiluva@pacific-harbour.com; dorms/bure doubles $100/220)* is a surf camp offering fairly comfortable accommodation in a large 12-bed dorm *bure* or in the 'love shack' (a *bure* for couples or a small family of three – minimum stay two nights). The beach here is quite pretty, but for a good snorkel you need to go on a short boat trip (free of charge). 'Gourmet jungle meals' and daily boat trips to the surf break are included in the price.

Frigates Surfriders *(☎ 345 0801, 925 3097; surfers/nonsurfers camping or dorm beds $75/35)* run by Penaia, a local surfer, is also a basic surf camp on a small white-sand beach. There is a beach-hut dorm and a camping area where you can pitch your own tent for the same price. Rates include three meals and daily surf trips. Snorkelling, diving, canoeing and trekking can also be arranged.

Boat transfers from Pacific Harbour to Frigate Surfriders or Batiluva are $40 return by small open boat.

Vatulele

pop 950 • area 31 sq km

The beautiful island of Vatulele is 32km south of Korolevu, off Viti Levu's southern coast and west of Beqa Lagoon. It is 13km long and mostly flat, the highest point just 33m above sea level, with scrub and palm vegetation. The western coast is a long escarpment broken by vertical cliffs formed by fracturing and uplifts. A barrier reef up to 3km offshore forms a lagoon on the eastern and northern ends with two navigable passages at the northern end.

Vatulele has four villages and one exclusive resort. The villagers live mostly off subsistence farming and fishing and are one of

Fiji's two main producers of *masi*. Vatulele has **archaeological sites**, including ancient rock paintings of faces and stencilled hands, and unusual geological formations, including limestone caves and pools inhabited by red prawns that are considered sacred.

Vatulele Island Resort (☎ *655 0300, fax 655 0262;* w *www.vatulele.com; villa $2200 per couple per night, minimum four nights)*, an exclusive intimate-scale place, is definitely one of Fiji's best top-end resorts and with a price to match. The location is idyllic and the architecture stunning – a mix of thick, Santa Fe–style rendered walls with the lofty thatched roofs of traditional Fijian *bure*. The 18 open-plan, split-level villa are well spaced for privacy, each with an outdoor terrace and its own stretch of white-sand beach and turquoise lagoon. There are no excuses if you can't relax here! Gourmet meals, alcohol and most activities are included in the rate; dive packages and game fishing are available.

Getting There & Away Unless you are a resort guest or charter a boat, you are unlikely to visit this beautiful island. There is an airstrip and return transfers are by resort charter plane to Nadi ($616 per adult, 25 minutes). SPAD-South Pacific Adventure Divers organises excursions to dive sites around Vatulele Island (See Activities under Korolevu & Around).

Suva

Nestled on the harbour with views to the surrounding mountains, Suva (pronounced **soo**-va) is one of the most laid-back capitals you're likely to come across. With wooden, colonial buildings, a friendly population (358,495) and something close to a cosmopolitan air, this small city has a certain charm about it; it's worth spending a day or two taking in the museum, lounging in the cafés or checking out the nightlife. You can also catch up on some of your shopping in Suva's myriad of stores or head out to the nearby Colo-i-Suva Park for a quiet escape into the lush rainforest.

Suva is Fiji's political and administrative capital and home to about half of the country's population. As the largest city in the South Pacific, Suva has become an important regional centre with the University of the South Pacific, the Forum Secretariat and many embassies to prove it. Students from throughout the Pacific reside here, as do many public servants and a growing expat community. As with most cities, urbanisation has also brought new difficulties; crime and poverty have increased in recent years (see Dangers & Annoyances later in this section) and around half of Suva's inhabitants are crowded into settlements on land that has no title.

On a less serious but equally grey note, clouds tend to hover over Suva and frequently dump rain on the city (around 300mm each year). You may, however, find the rain a welcome relief to the heat and humidity that often cloak the city.

HISTORY

The Fijians who originally lived on Suva Peninsula had a small settlement on the site of the present day Government House. Like the infamous Chief Cakobau of Bau, they were the traditional rivals of the Rewans of the Rewa Delta to the east. In the 1850s, with the help of King George of Tonga, Chief Cakobau defeated the Rewans and, soon after, proclaimed himself Tui Viti, or King of Fiji.

As King, Cakobau took it upon himself to give away bits and pieces of Fiji to foreign settlers who began arriving in the country in the mid 1800s. Cakobau also managed to acquire giant debts with the American immigrants and, by 1862, his inability to pay them off became apparent when he attempted to cede Fiji to Britain in exchange for debt clearance.

Up until this time, the only Europeans in the Suva area had come from Melbourne, seeking new sources of fortune after the decline of the gold rushes and subsequent downturn in the Australian economy. In Cakobau's debts the Aussies saw their chance; in 1868, the newly formed Australian Polynesia Company agreed to clear Cakobau's debts with the Americans in return for the right to trade in Fiji and a large chunk of land, 90 sq km of which covered the Suva Peninsula.

While it was not his land to trade, the powerful Chief Cakobau had the Suva villagers relocated and welcomed a new group of Australians to the area in 1870. The new settlers cleared dense reed from what is now downtown Suva and tried growing cotton and sugar cane. Their attempts at farming on the peninsula's thin topsoil and the soapstone base failed and most of the settlers' efforts ended in bankruptcy. In an effort to increase land values, two Melbourne merchants, WK Thomson and S Renwick, encouraged the government to relocate the capital from Levuka to Suva with incentives in the form of land grants. As Levuka had insufficient room for expansion and the government was looking for a fresh start for white settlement, the government officially moved to Suva from Levuka in 1882.

In the 1880s Suva was a township of about a dozen buildings. Later, sections of the seashore were reclaimed and trading houses constructed, and by the 1920s it was a flourishing colonial centre. Large-scale land reclamation was carried out in the 1950s for the Walu Bay industrial zone.

Suva most recently hit the international headlines in May 2000 when George Speight and his military entourage held the government hostage in Suva's Parliament Buildings (see History in Facts About Fiji chapter).

ORIENTATION

Suva is on a peninsula about 3km wide by 5km long, with Laucala Bay to the east and Suva Harbour to the west. Most of the peninsula is hilly apart from the narrow strip of land on the eastern edge of the city where you'll find Suva's main drag, Victoria Parade, as well as the market and wharf. The

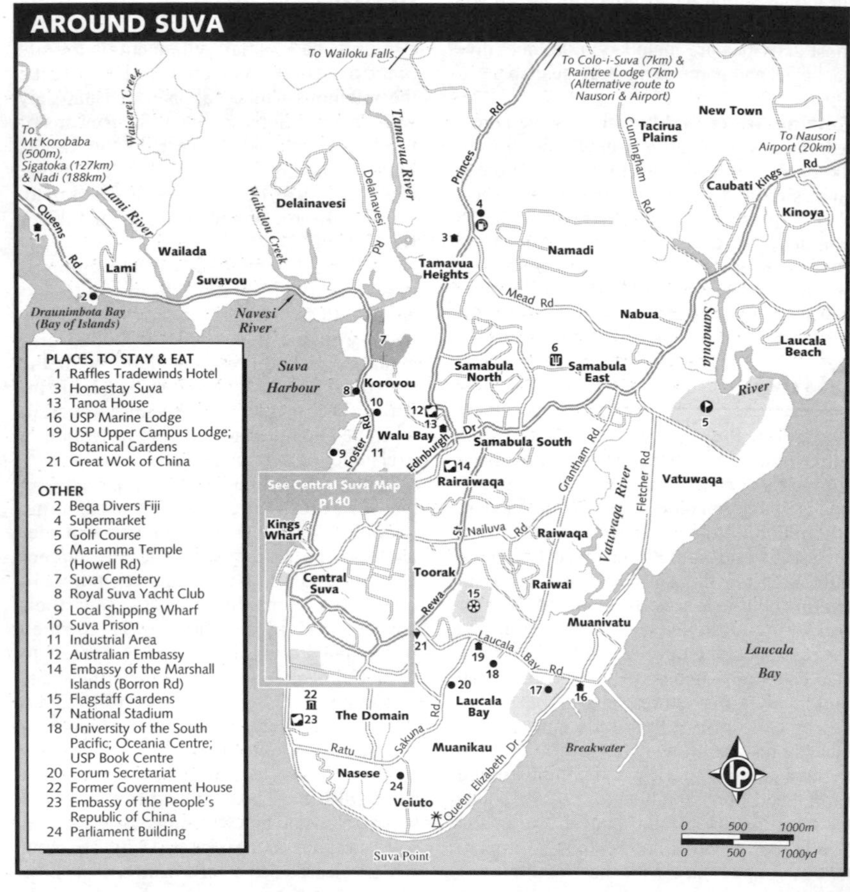

The Headstrong Reverend Baker

Thomas Baker, a Wesleyan Methodist missionary, was killed on 21 July 1867 by the Vatusila people of Nabutautau village, deep in the isolated Nausori Highlands. A few years earlier Baker had been given the task of converting the people of the interior of Viti Levu to Christianity. Out of impatience, martyrdom, foolhardiness or the urge for success, he had ignored advice to keep to areas under the influence of already converted groups. Many felt it was almost inevitable that he would offend the highlanders in some way.

The highlanders associated conversion to Christianity with subservience to the chiefdom of Bau. As they were opposed to any kind of extended authority, knocking off the Reverend may well have been a political manoeuvre. However, a second theory maintains that it was Baker's own behaviour that brought about his nasty end. Apparently, the local chief had borrowed Baker's comb to festoon his voluptuous hairdo. Insensitive or forgetful of the fact that the chief's head was considered sacred, Baker snatched the comb from the chief's hair. Villagers were furious at the missionary for committing this sacrilege and killed and ate him in disgust. According to one local, his ancestors ate everything, 'even tried to eat his shoes'.

Twenty years after Baker's death, a mission teacher, guided by a repentant eater, recovered the Reverend's humerus from within the overgrown fork of a large shaddock tree. The bone had been placed there as a trophy. Baker's uneaten shoe is exhibited in the Fiji Museum.

random layout of downtown Suva is attributed to Colonel FE Pratt, surveyor general in 1875. The many people who wanted the plans modified stumbled over a lack of funds and Suva unfolded to Pratt's creative design.

The suburb of Toorak tumbles up onto the hill east of Suva Market. Originally Suva's posh neighbourhood (named after Melbourne's exclusive suburb), it has fallen from grandeur. In this area, Waimanu Rd passes the hospital in the northeast and then rolls down into town, becoming Renwick Rd at Nubukalou Creek and then Victoria Parade.

Victoria Parade is Suva's main business strip where many of the city's restaurants, shops and clubs congregate. Heading south, it will take you past the Government Buildings, Albert Park and to Thurston Gardens and the museum. Beyond the museum, it's renamed Queen Elizabeth Drive and heads out past Suva Point and round to the University and National Stadium on the eastern side of the peninsula.

Drivers may find central Suva's one-way streets, angled intersections and contorted loops a bit challenging at first. There are three major roads in and out of the city: the Queens Road from Nadi; Princes Rd to the northeast (the scenic route to Nausori); and the Kings Road from Nausori and the International Airport. Kings Road meets Princes Road closer to Suva, where it turns into Edinburgh Drive. Edinburgh Drive and Queens Road converge at Walu Bay roundabout; if you're heading downtown, head south at this roundabout onto Rodwell Rd which you can follow past the bus station and market, across Nubukalou Creek and into central Suva.

Maps

You can pick up photocopies of a basic map of Suva at the Fiji Tourist Bureau and at many larger hotels. If you're looking for something more detailed, head around the back of the Government Buildings to **The Map Shop** *(☎ 321 1395; Room 10, Department of Lands and Surveys; open 8am-1pm & 2pm-3.30pm Mon-Fri, closes 3pm Fri)*. It stocks a good map of Suva and the surrounding areas, as well as large survey maps of the rest of Fiji.

INFORMATION

Tourist Offices

Fiji Visitors Bureau *(FVB; e infodesk@fijifvb.gov.fj; w www.bulafiji.com)*, has its head office *(☎ 330 2433, fax 330 0970; cnr Thomson & Scott Sts; open 8am-4.30pm Mon-Fri, 8am-4pm Fri, 8am-noon Sat)* in Suva where friendly staff will go out of their way to help you find what you're looking for. It stocks countless brochures and schedules for Suva and the surrounding area. It also has a 24-hour, toll-free visitors' **helpline** *(☎ 0800 721 721)* to handle complaints and emergencies.

The **South Pacific Tourism Organisation** *(☎ 330 4177, fax 330 1995; e info@spto.org;*

CENTRAL SUVA

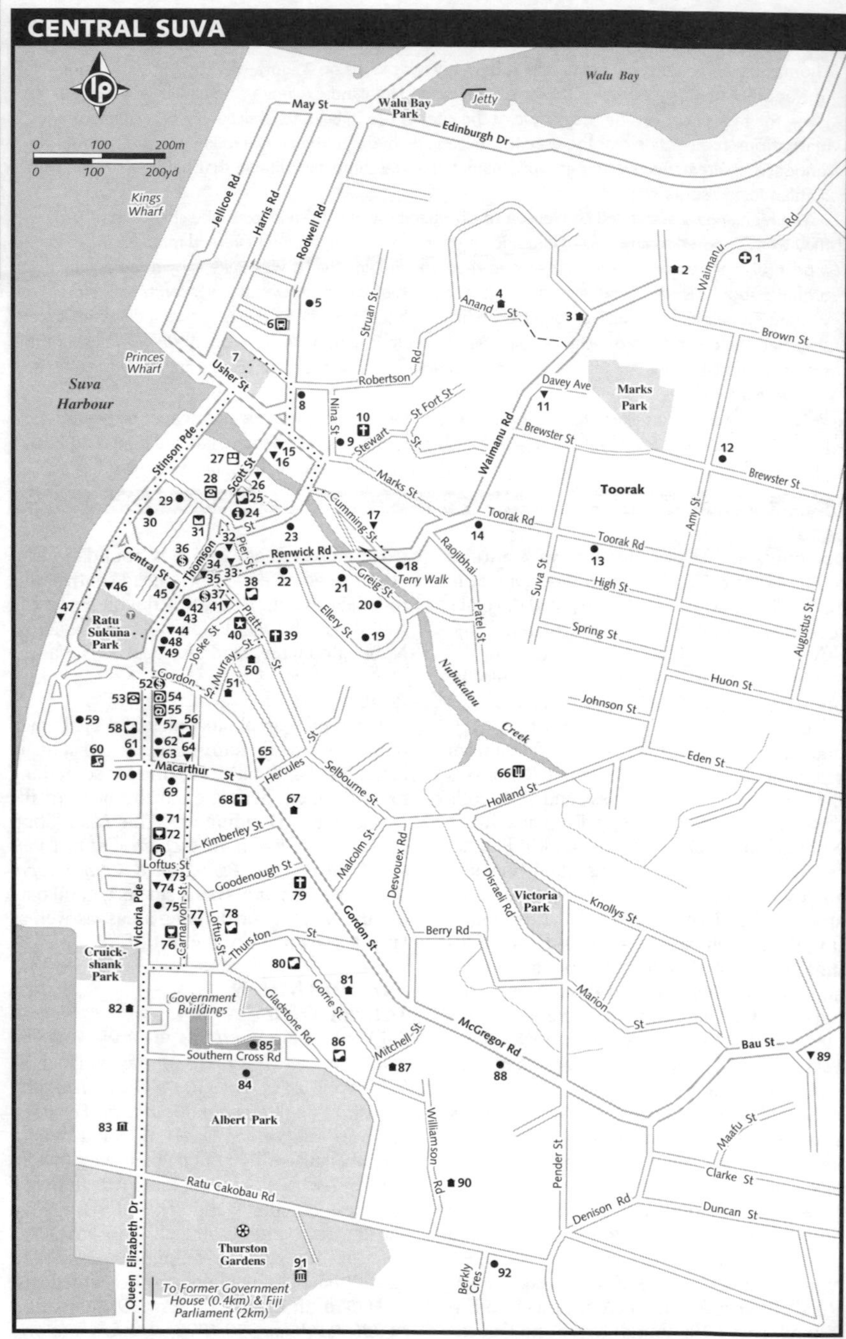

w http://spto.org; 3rd floor, Dolphin Plaza, Victoria Parade) has an office in Suva; for more information see Tourist Offices in the Facts for the Visitor chapter.

Money

Westpac Bank *(☎ 330 0666, fax 330 0275; 1 Thomson St; open 9.30am-3pm Mon-Thur, 9.30am-4pm Fri)* and the **ANZ bank** *(☎ 330 1755, fax 330 0267; 25 Victoria Parade; open 9.30am-3pm Mon-Thur, 9.30am-4pm Fri)* both change money and travellers cheques. Westpac has an ATM outside Village 6 Cinema Complex and ANZ has a number of ATMs outside the bank and will also do credit card advances. **Thomas Cook** *(☎ 330 1603; 21 Thomson St; open 9am-4pm Mon-Fri, 9.30am-noon Sat)* also changes travellers cheques and foreign currency. If you need money in a hurry, **Western Union** *(☎ 331 4812; cnr Victoria Parade & Gordon St; open 8am-4.45pm Mon-Fri, 8am-1.45pm Sat)* does worldwide money transfers.

Some hotels, including the budget South Seas Private Hotel and Travel Inn, will also change travellers cheques for guests at bank rates without added commission.

Post & Telephone

There are a number of card phones around the city, including outside the **GPO**. From **Fintel** *(☎ 331 2933, fax 330 1025; 158 Victoria*

CENTRAL SUVA

PLACES TO STAY

2 Motel 6
3 Annandale Apartments
4 Colonial Lodge
50 Town House Apartment Hotel
51 Sunset Apartment Motel
67 Southern Cross Hotel
81 Travel Inn
82 Holiday Inn
87 Suva Motor Inn
90 South Seas Private Hotel

PLACES TO EAT

11 Korea House
15 Hot Bread Kitchen
16 Ultra Roast Station
17 Govinda's Vegetarian Restaurant
26 Harbour Centre; Pizza King; Bob's Hook; Line & Sinker
32 Chef's Restaurant & Ice Cream Parlour
33 Republic of Cappuccino
35 Headworks
41 Lantern Palace; Hare Krishna Restaurant
44 Rivendell; Gathera; Wai Tui Surf
46 JJ's Bar & Grill
47 Tiko's Floating Restaurant
49 Fusion; Korean Embassy; Vanua Arcade
57 New Peking
62 Bad Dog Cafe; Victoria Wines & Spirits; Pizza Hut; O'Reilly's
64 Zen Restaurant
65 Da Kyung Garden
73 Dolphin Plaza Food Court; Republic of Cappuccino; Representative of the Federated States of Micronesia; South Pacific Tourism Organisation
74 Daikoku Restaurant
77 Old Mill Cottage
89 Aberdeen Grill

OTHER

1 Hospital
5 Supermarket
6 Bus Station; Taxi Stand
7 Suva Municipal Market
8 Morris Hedstrom Supermarket
9 Beachcomber Cruises; Patterson Brothers Shipping
10 Centenary Methodist Church
12 Fiji Recompression Chamber Facility
13 Gangaram's Laundry & Drycleaners
14 Indian Cultural Centre
18 Pharmacy Plus
19 Boulevard Medical Centre; Central Boulevard Pharmacy; Downtown Boulevard Shopping Centre; Kahawa; The Boom Box
20 Suva Bookstore
21 Procera Music Shop
22 Ransam
23 Former Garrick Hotel Building
24 Fiji Visitors Bureau (FVB)
25 French Embassy; Japanese Embassy; Consort Shipping Line; Hunts Travel; Dominion House Arcade
27 Village 6 Cinema Complex
28 Telecom Fiji
29 Fiji Philatelic Bureau
30 Curio & Handicraft Centre
31 GPO
34 Jack's Handicrafts; Thomas Cook
36 Westpac Bank
37 ANZ Bank
38 New Zealand Embassy
39 Roman Catholic Cathedral
40 Police Station
42 Office Works
43 Air New Zealand
45 Air Pacific; Qantas
48 Fuji Film
52 Western Union
53 Fiji International Telecommunications (Fintel)
54 Bav's Internet Services
55 Alpha Net Café; Sun Air
56 Malaysian Embassy
58 European Union Representative
59 Town Hall & Suva City Council
60 Suva Olympic Pool
61 Old Town Hall; Ashiyana; Ming Palace; Jackson Takeaway; Greenpeace
62 Air Fiji
66 Shree Laxmi Narayan Temple
68 Holy Trinity Cathedral
69 Government Crafts Centre; Embassy of Nauru
70 Suva City Library
71 Enjoy Cafe
72 Traps Bar
75 Historic Cogwheel
76 The Barn
78 US Embassy
79 St Andrew's Church
80 Embassy of Tuvalu
83 Grand Pacific Hotel Building
84 Kingsford Smith Pavilion
85 The Map Shop
86 British Consulate
88 Alliance Française
91 Fiji Museum; Botanic Gardens Clock Tower
92 Spachee

Parade; open 8am-8pm Mon-Sat) you can make international phone calls and send faxes and telegrams. You can also call home from **Telecom Fiji** *(☎ 311 2233; Victoria Parade; open 8.30am-4.30pm Mon-Thur, 8.30am-4pm Fri)*, across the street from the GPO.

Email & Internet Access

Springing up left and right, Internet cafés will soon be as common as curries in Suva. **Bav's Internet Services** *(Victoria Parade; per min/hr $0.10/5; open 8am-10pm Mon-Thur, 8am-1am Fri & Sat, 9am-8pm Sun)* has a fairly speedy connection and is one of the cheapest in town. **Alpha Net Café** *(☎ 330 0211; Victoria Parade; per min $0.10; open 8am-8pm Mon-Thur, 8am-5pm Fri & Sat, 10am-4pm Sun)* offers Internet access and also repairs laptops. **Fintel** *(see Post & Communications earlier; per min $0.15)* has a number of well-connected computers; you purchase your time online via debit cards in denominations of 15/30/60/120 minutes.

There are also a number of laid-back coffee houses around Suva that offer Internet access. There are two computers at the **Republic of Cappuccino** *(per min $0.15, $1 minimum charge)* and one at **Kahawa** *(per min $0.20)*. At the back of **Enjoy** *(min/hr $0.10/5)* there are eight brand-spankin' new computers; the atmosphere isn't exactly cosy but you can take your pearl jelly tea in with you. For opening times and contact details of these cafés, see Places to Eat later in this chapter.

Travel Agencies

Travel agencies in Suva include:

Air Fiji (☎ 331 3666, fax 330 0771) 185 Victoria Parade. Open 8am to 5pm Monday to Friday and 8am to noon Saturday.

Air New Zealand (☎ 331 3100, fax 330 2294) Queensland Insurance Bldg, Victoria Parade. Open 9am to 5pm Monday to Friday, 9am to noon Saturday.

Air Pacific (☎ 330 4388, fax 330 2860) CML Bldg, Victoria Parade.

Hunts Travel (☎ 331 5288, fax 330 2212) 1st floor, Dominion House arcade. Open 8am to 5pm Monday to Friday, 8am to noon Saturday. Hunts can book domestic and international flights along with hotels and cars.

Qantas (☎ 331 1833, fax 330 4795) CML Bldg, Victoria Parade.

Sun Air (☎ 330 8979) Victoria Parade. Open 8am to 4.30pm Monday to Friday and 8am to noon Saturday.

See the Getting There & Away chapter for contact details of interisland-ferry agencies.

Bookshops

The **USP Book Centre** *(☎ 321 2500, fax 330 3265; University of the South Pacific; w www.uspbookcentre.com)* is stocked with a fantastic selection of local and international novels, Lonely Planet guides for destinations around the globe and books covering everything from land rights to legends of the Pacific region (many published by USP's very own Institute of Pacific Studies). Other than a sale table of random novels, it's all a bit pricey but the pickings are superb. You can order books online from their website; they'll courier them to your doorstep overseas.

The gift shop at the **Fiji Museum** *(☎ 331 5944; e fijimuseum@connect.com.fj; open 9.30am-4pm Mon-Thur, 9.30am-3.30pm Fri, 9.30am-4pm Sat)* also has a fairly good selection of Fijian history books (many no longer in print outside of Fiji) as well as cookbooks and bird books from the area.

Suva Bookstore *(☎ 331 1355; Greig St; open 7.30am-5pm Mon-Fri, 7.30am-1pm Sat)* has a small selection of children's books as well as Fijian and Indo-Fijian cookbooks. **Office Works** *(☎ 331 4200; Victoria Parade)* has a small selection of novels from the likes of Jeffrey Archer, Judith Krantz and Tom Clancy. **Republic of Cappuccino** on Renwick Road and **Kahawa** (see Places to Eat in this section) both have book exchanges.

Libraries

The **Fiji Museum** *(☎ 331 5944, fax 330 5143; e fijimuseum@connect.com.fj; Thurston Gdns)* has a good reference library but you must call in advance to request a visit. The **Suva City Library** *(Victoria Parade; 9.30am-6pm Mon-Fri except Wed noon-6pm, 9am-1pm Sat)*, next to the old town hall, has a small library on the ground floor.

The best Pacific collection is at the **university library** *(open 8am-10pm Mon-Thur, 8am-6pm Fri, 9am-6pm Sat, 1.30pm-6pm Sun)*, a large resource centre for the whole of the region. If you're happy to hand over a $50 deposit, you can borrow books from the general library. Books from the Pacific collection, however, cannot be borrowed and visitors can only use this part of the library for one day. Reduced hours apply during university holidays.

South Pacific Action Committee for Human Ecology & Environment *(Spachee; ☎ 331 2371, fax 330 3053; cnr Ratu Cakobau Rd & Berkley Crescent)* aims to create awareness of issues that affect environment, sustainability and growth in the South Pacific region and has a small reference library on these topics. **Greenpeace** *(☎ 331 2861)*, on the first floor above the old town hall building on Victoria Parade, also has a reference library.

Cultural Centres

The Fiji Museum promotes indigenous Fijian culture (see Fiji Museum later in this section). Other cultural centres include:

Alliance Française (☎ 331 3802, fax 331 3803; **W** http://alliancefrancaisefj.tripod.com) 14 McGregor Rd. Open 9am to 6.30pm Monday to Thursday, 9am to 6pm Friday. Watch French videos or check out the French-language library.

Indian Cultural Centre (☎ 330 0050) Corner of Toorak & Waimanu Rds. This centre promotes Indian culture and offers classical music lessons, dance and yoga classes.

Laundry

Most resorts and hotels will do your laundry for about $5 a load. Same-day laundry and dry-cleaning services are also available at **Gangaram's Laundry & Drycleaners** *(☎ 330 2369; 126 Toorak Rd)*.

Medical Services

Boulevard Medical Centre has a good reputation and is conveniently located in downtown Suva with a pharmacy nearby. Visits to the GP are usually $10 to $20.

Boulevard Medical Centre (☎ 331 3355, fax 330 2423) 33 Ellery St. Opening hours are from 8.30am to 5pm Monday to Friday and 8.30am to 11.30am Saturday.

Central Boulevard Pharmacy (☎ 330 3770) Shop 13, Downtown Boulevard Shopping Centre. Opening hours are 8.30am to 5.30pm Monday to Thursday, 8.30am to 6pm Friday and 8.30am to 1pm Saturday.

Colonial War Memorial Hospital (☎ 331 3444) Waimanu Rd.

Fiji Recompression Chamber Facility (☎ 885 0630, fax 885 0344) Corner of Amy & Brewster Sts.

Pharmacy Plus (☎ 330 5300) 190 Renwick Road. Open 8.30am to 5.30pm Monday to Thursday, 8.30am to 6pm Friday and 8.30am to 2pm Saturday. You can get your prescriptions filled here and stock up on such things as vitamins, baby needs and sunscreen.

Emergency

Some useful emergency numbers are:

Ambulance	☎ 330 1439
Emergency	☎ 000
Fiji Recompression Chamber Facility emergency	☎ 3362 172
FVB Emergency Hotline	☎ 0800 721 721
Police	☎ 331 1222
Tourist Police	☎ 330 2433 + 215

Warning

Despite its small size, Suva suffers many of the same dangers as most urbanised centres. Pickpockets roam; keep your valuables out of sight, particularly in crowded areas like the market or dance floors. As night descends, be sure to follow the locals' lead and take taxis everywhere; cab fares are cheap and muggings are common.

WALKING TOUR

While Suva isn't brimming with sights, its downtown area has a number of colonial buildings and places of interest, making it a pleasant place to wander around. Allow a few hours for this tour, giving you a chance to check out shops and duck into a cafés away from the midday heat. Most places are closed on Sundays, and Saturday mornings are the busiest, especially around the market.

Using the Central Suva map as a guide, begin at the **FVB** building (1912). Opposite it, to the east, is the **Garrick Hotel** (1914). Grand in its day, it's now home to the Sichuan Pavilion Restaurant. Head south to the tiny park just past Thomas Cook where you'll find a historical marker commemorating the arrival of the first missionaries in 1835, the annexation of Fiji by Britain in 1874, public land sales in 1880 and the proclamation of Suva as the capital of Fiji in 1882. Continue south down Suva's main street, **Victoria Parade**, which is lined with shops, nightclubs and restaurants. You'll find **Ratu Sukuna Park** on your right; this is a favourite hangout for locals and the sight of many demonstrations, rallies and concerts. Cross the park to the waterfront for a view across Suva Harbour to the mountain ranges and the distinctive **Joske's Thumb**. With the water on your left, head north for a browse through the **Curio & Handicraft Centre** *(open 8am-5pm Mon-Sat)* where you can hone your bargaining skills. There are endless souvenir stalls packed with woven and wooden goods and, with so much of competition, prices are generally reasonable.

Return to your waterside promenade, crossing Nubukalou Creek to the bustling **Suva Municipal Market** *(Rodwell Rd; mornings, Mon-Sat)*. This is a great place to buy kava for village visits (the unpounded roots are better) and to sample some local delicacies. Vendors sell exotic fruit and vegetables, *nama* (seaweed), multicoloured fish, bound crabs, pungent spices, neon Indian sweets, and fresh fruit drinks from glass tanks. There are vendors from all backgrounds selling their goods at the market – Fijian, Indo-Fijian and Indo-Chinese. The top floor has mostly tobacco and kava, the seafood is downstairs closest to the water, and the produce is impossible to miss.

Following the map, head southeast to busy **Cumming St**, which in the 1920s was known for its *yaqona* saloons and 'dens of iniquity'. Today it's lined with curry houses and sari shops. At the end of Cumming St turn right into Renwick Rd. If you walk on the left side of the street, you'll get a good view of the facades of the old wooden buildings on the right. You may want to stop in at **Republic of Cappuccino** for a pick-me-up before taking a left onto Pratt St. About a block down on the left is the **Roman Catholic Cathedral** (1902), built of sandstone imported from Sydney and one of Suva's most prominent landmarks. Head right at Murray St, right again at Gordon St, and then left back onto Victoria Parade. Continue along past the **Fintel building** (1926) and the **old town hall** (1904). Now home to several restaurants, the old town hall building was once used for dances, bazaars and performances. The **Suva Olympic Pool** is set back between this building and the **Suva City Library** (1909).

Turn left onto Macarthur St for a browse in the **Government Crafts Centre**. Take the first right onto Carnarvon St where you'll find the Old Mill Cottage and, opposite it, a **rusting cogwheel** uncovered during excavations for the Native Lands Trust Board (NLTB) building. It is thought to be a remainder of Fiji's first sugar mill opened by Brewer & Joske on this site in 1873. Growing sugar cane in this wet area, however, proved unsuccessful.

The impressive **Government Buildings** (1939 and 1967) at the end of Carnarvon St are set on heavy foundations atop reclaimed land over a creek bed. As you circle around it to Victoria Parade, you'll spot statues of two influential Fijians (Ratu Cakobau and Ratu Sukuna) in the gardens. The Department of Lands & Survey is of interest, as it was the scene of the 1987 coup. While Parliament has now moved to new (and apparently equally coup-able) premises, government departments and the courts remain here.

Farther along Victoria Parade is **Albert Park**, named after Queen Victoria's husband. The Polynesia Company gave this land to the Fijian Government as an incentive for moving the capital to Suva. Outfitted with a cricket ground, tennis courts and football pitch, it's often the scene of weekend games. The **Kingsford Smith Pavilion** is at the back of the park, named after the famous aviator who landed here. On the seaside opposite the park is the imposing and somewhat haunted-looking **Grand Pacific Hotel** (1914). Built by the Union Steamship Company, its ship-style architecture is reminiscent of the luxury liners that once plied the seas. The now dilapidated building was recently bought by a Japanese company; apparently if they don't begin renovations within two years, the government has the right to reclaim it – although it's questionable as to what end.

Winging It

Charles Kingsford Smith was the first aviator to cross the Pacific, flying in his little Fokker trimotor, *The Southern Cross*, from California to Australia. The longest leg of the flight was the 34-hour trip from Hawaii to Fiji. Suva's Albert Park, with its hill at one end and the Grand Pacific Hotel at the other, was made into a makeshift landing strip for his arrival. Trees were still being cleared after Smith had already left Hawaii. Kingsford Smith and his crew arrived on 6 June 1928, and were welcomed by a crowd of thousands, including colonial dignitaries who had gathered at the Grand Pacific Hotel to witness and celebrate this major event. Because the park was too short to take-off with a heavy load of fuel, Smith had to unload, fly to Nasilai Beach and reload for take-off to Brisbane and Sydney. Kingsford Smith and his crew were presented with a ceremonial *tabua* (whale's tooth) as a token of great respect.

ROBYN JONES
Thurston Gardens, Suva

ROBYN JONES
Guard outside the Government Buildings, Suva

LIZ THOMPSON
Vendor at Suva Market

SCOTT DARSNEY
Fiji Museum, Suva

ROBYN JONES
Painted temple doors, Viti Levu

ROBYN JONES

Seaplane, Mamanuca Group

ROBYN JONES

Beachcomber Island

PHILIP GAME

Beach on Turtle Island, Yasawa Group

JOHN BORTHWICK

Boys from a village in the Yasawas

At the corner of Ratu Cakobau Rd, Victoria Parade becomes Queen Elizabeth Drive. On the left is **Thurston Gardens**, closed at the time of writing for renovations but due to reopen in the near future. Originally opened in 1913, these botanical gardens are named after Sir John Bates Thurston, an amateur botanist who introduced many ornamental plant species to Fiji. You can wander through this peaceful park to the **Botanic Gardens Clock Tower** (1918) and the **Fiji Museum** (see later in this chapter).

If you continue south along the waterfront, you'll pass the **former Government House**. The original government house (1882), built on this site for Governor Des Voeux, was struck by lightning and burnt down in 1921; the present structure dates back to 1928. With Fiji now a republic, the house and grounds have become the president's residence and are not open to the public. The entrance is guarded by a soldier in the standard white handkerchief *sulu*.

It's worth continuing along the seawall a ways for views of the mountains. The walk is lined with dramatic, old jungle-like trees and, if the tide is out, an abundance of crabs and fish in tidal pools. A lookout point is about 1.5km along from where there are views of Nukulau, a small offshore island to the east. If you've had enough leg stretching, you can hop on one of the green and white striped buses back into the city centre.

FIJI MUSEUM

Chock-full of excellent exhibits and well-maintained artefacts, the Fiji Museum *(☎ 331 5944; e fijimuseum@connect.com.fj; Ratu Cakobau Rd; adult/child $3.30/free; open 9.30am-4pm Mon-Fri, 9.30am-4pm Sat)* is well worth a few hours of your time. With excellent descriptions, the museum takes you through the history of Fiji's peoples, cultures, languages, animal life, pottery and more recent migration, as well as the more gory accounts of warfare and cannibalism. There is a beautiful, traditional *drua* on display (1913), the last of these large ancient catamarans to be built. At first glance, the museum doesn't look very big, but on the other side of the shop is a larger, two-storey wing that looks at early traders and settlers, blackbirding and Indian indenture. Upstairs is the small **Indo-Fijian Gallery** with local, contemporary artwork.

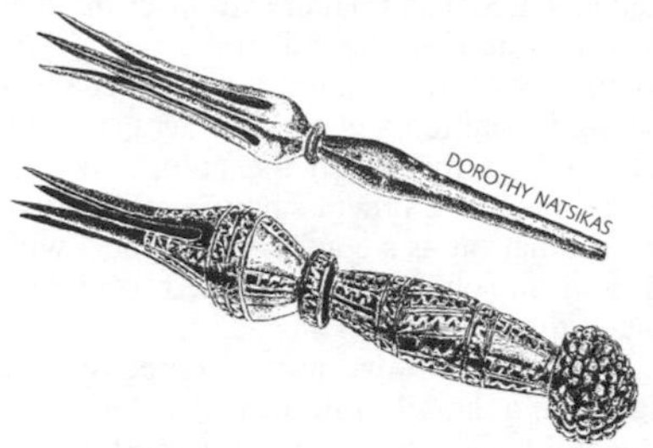

Cannibal Forks – On display at the excellent Fiji Museum

The museum continues to undertake archaeological research and collects and preserves oral traditions. Many of these are published in *Domodomo*, a quarterly journal on history, language, culture, art and natural history that is available in the museum's gift shop. It also organises craft demonstrations with one of Fiji's best-known potters, Taraivini Wati. Contact the museum for times.

PARLIAMENT OF FIJI

Opened in June 1992, the parliament complex *(☎ 330 5811; Battery Rd)* was designed in post-1987-coup climate, and the aim of maintaining indigenous-Fijian values is apparent. Traditional arts and structures are mingled with a contemporary feel. The main building, *vale ne bose lawa* (parliament house), takes its form from the traditional *vale* or family house and has a ceremonial access from Ratu Sukuna Rd. The complex is 5km from the city centre. It's easiest to reach by taxi; however, you can hop on a bus along Queen Elizabeth Drive and walk along Ratu Sukuna Road for 1km.

As the site of the 2000 coup, the parliament buildings are no longer very accessible to the public. If you would like to visit, you must arrange it beforehand by calling the parliament buildings; unexpected guests will be turned away.

UNIVERSITY OF THE SOUTH PACIFIC

With beautiful lawns and excellent facilities, the USP's main **Laucala Campus** *(☎ 331 3900, fax 330 1305)* is a pleasant place to visit. Once the site of a New Zealand seaplane base, the campus has over 11,000 students. USP has smaller campuses in other Pacific countries, the university has a total population of over 1.5 million. USP is a fee-paying institution and most students rely on scholarships for which the competition is fierce. The government's policy of 'positive discrimination' is a controversial one – with 50% of all scholarships awarded to indigenous Fijians.

Inside the northwestern entrance, on the right, is a small **botanical garden** with peaceful trails winding around Pacific trees and plants. You can also visit **USP Oceania Centre** where you can see temporary exhibits of paintings and carvings and sometimes even catch an artist at work. The university's main entrance is off Laucala Bay Rd and is a 10 to 15-minute drive from downtown Suva. There are frequent buses to the USP: the Vatuwaqa bus departs opposite the Dominion arcade in Thomson St, near the FVB or you can hop on a Raiwaga bus from Victoria Parade. The taxi fare from the city is about $3.

PLACES OF WORSHIP

Despite their cosmopolitan lifestyle, the majority of Suva's Indo-Fijians and indigenous Fijians are still very religious and dash off to temple or church on a regular basis. While few of these buildings are interesting in themselves, a couple are worth a gander if you're in the neighbourhood.

Just east of downtown, the bright orange and blue **Shree Laxmi Narayan Temple** *(Holland St)* generally has a caretaker around to let you in for a look. (See Special Events later in this chapter for Mariamma Temple details.)

Holy Trinity Cathedral *(cnr Macarthur & Gordon Sts)*, with its unique boat-shaped interior, interesting Fijian tapestries and wood-beamed ceiling is a peaceful retreat. The gigantic tree in front of the church is a showcase of Pacific plants with cacti and ferns making themselves at home in its branches. The **Catholic Cathedral** is, unfortunately, most often locked (see Walking Tour earlier). For a rousing chorus of song on a Sunday morning, head to the **Centenary Methodist Church** *(Stewart Street)*.

If you entered town via Queen's Road, you likely passed Suva's **cemetery**. Graves are dug by the inmates from the prison next door (1913), and then decorated with bright cloth.

COLO-I-SUVA FOREST PARK

As you wander deep into the wilds of this lush rainforest, complete with clear natural pools, singing birds and gorgeous vistas, you will find utter tranquillity away from the hustle and heat of the city. In total, Colo-i-Suva Forest Park (pronounced tholo-ee-**soo**-va) *(☎ 332 0211; admission adults/children $5/0.50; open 8am-4pm Mon-Sun)* covers about 2.45 sq km. With just a touch of Indiana Jones in the rope swings over water and stone steps across streams, the 6.5km of walking trails are superb maintained. There are three natural swimming holes, as well as picnic tables, shelters and change rooms. Home to 14 different species, the park is a hotspot for bird watching; keep your eyes open for the scarlet robin, spotted fantail, Fiji goshawk, sulphur-breasted musk parrots, Fiji warblers, golden dove and the barking pigeon.

The park was established in 1953. Like the surrounding area, the forest here was logged in the late 1940s and early 1950s, and while the surrounding area remains extensively cleared, the park area was replanted with introduced mahogany. The Waisila Creek flows through the park, down to Waimanu River and is the water catchment for the Nausori/Nasinu areas.

The park is located 11km north of Suva on Princes Road. The Visitor Information Centre is on the left side of the road as you approach from Suva; buy your ticket here and then head to the entrance booth on the other side of the road. There have been reports of tourists sneaking in through the park exit in order to avoid the admission fee; please think twice before attempting this as the minimal fee is vital to maintaining the trails.

The park receives an annual rainfall of 424cm, with showers approximately four days each week. The trails can be extremely slippery so be sure to wear good footwear. If you drive out to the park, leave any valuables at the Visitor Information Centre, not in your car, as robberies are not unheard of. Camping is not allowed in the park. (See Raintree Lodge in Places to Stay later.)

The Sawani bus leaves Suva bus station every half-hour ($0.65, 20 mins). The forest station is on the left on top of the hill, just before Raintree Lodge. If driving, take Princes Rd out of Suva, past Tamavua and Tacirua villages.

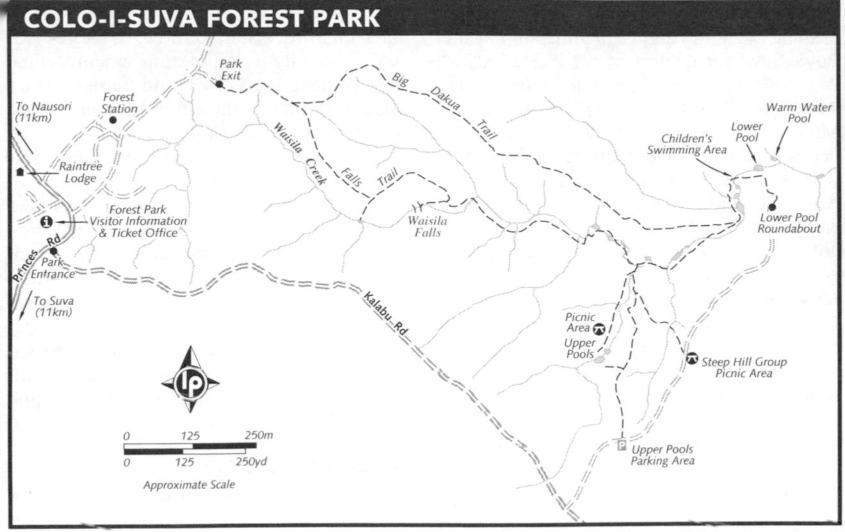

ACTIVITIES

Not much happens in Suva on Sunday so try to organise activities in advance or attend a Fijian church service to hear some uplifting, boisterous singing.

Bushwalking

Colo-i-Suva Forest Park is an easy place for bushwalking close to Suva (see earlier in this section for details). You can also hike to Mt Korobaba, about a one- to two-hour walk from the cement factory near Lami. Joske's Thumb is an enticing spectacle for serious climbers; check with FVB about getting permission. A climb to this peak was featured in the film *Journey to the Dawning of the Day*.

Keen trekkers should contact the Rucksack Club for weekly walking adventures either inland or to other islands. The membership changes regularly, as most of the 80 to 100 members are expats on contract in Fiji. Ask the FVB for the latest contact number. The club hosts fortnightly meetings in appreciation of Fiji's beauty and culture, with guest speakers and performers.

Swimming

Seldom crowded, the giant, outdoor **Suva Olympic Swimming Pool** *(224 Victoria Parade; open 10am-6pm Mon-Fri & 8am-6pm Sat Apr-Sept, 9am-7pm Mon-Fri & 7am-7pm Sat Oct-Mar)* is an oasis on a hot day. Entry is fantastically cheap – adults pay $1.65 and children (13 years and under) $0.80. There is a kiddies play area, lap-lanes and change cubicles for a $2 deposit. Keen lap swimmers can also attend the **university's 25m pool** *(admission $2; open 7am-6pm daily)*.

Between Suva and Colo-i-Suva, **Wailoku Falls** is not a good place for a dip as muggings are a *very* common occurrence.

The nearest decent beach is at Deuba, Pacific Harbour. It is a 50-minute drive from Suva, although by local bus it can take much longer. Alternatively, there are the freshwater pools at Colo-i-Suva Forest Park.

Diving

Beqa Divers Fiji *(☎ 336 1088, fax 336 1047; 75 Marine Drive, Lami)* is about a 10-minute drive from Suva. It offers daily, two-tank dive trips to Beqa Lagoon, gear rental and diving courses including Open Water PADI ($495), Rescue Diver ($420), PADI Dive Master ($880) and instructor courses.

The Holiday Inn can organise dive trips to Beqa Lagoon with **Aqua-Trek**, based at Pacific Harbour (see that section earlier).

Surfing

There is a surf-break near Suva lighthouse, accessible by boat; the **Fiji Surf Association** *(☎ 336 1358)* may be able to give some advice on how to get out there and local conditions.

Sailing

Visiting yachties can get membership at the **Royal Suva Yacht Club** *(☎ 331 2921, fax 330 4433; e rsyc@connect.com.fj; office open 9am-1pm & 2pm-4pm Mon-Fri, 9am-1pm Sat)*. Mooring fees are $50 for the first day and $15 per day thereafter. For room in the boatshed with/without cradle it's $50/20 daily and hardstand is $50 for the first day and $10 per day thereafter. The club has bathrooms with hot water, and a laundry, which are open 24 hours a day. There's also a restaurant, an ATM and a kid's playground. The bar here *(open 8am-10pm Mon-Thur, 8am-midnight Fri & Sat)* is a popular watering hole for yachties and locals and has great views of the Bay of Islands and the mountains, including Joske's Thumb. Even without a yacht, overseas visitors are welcome and can be signed in. The notice board in the clubhouse is a good place to find boats looking for crew.

ORGANISED TOURS

Wilderness Ethnic Adventure Fiji *(☎ 331 5730, fax 331 5450)* offers several tours that pick up from Suva hotels. There are rafting and canoeing tours ($99/60 adult/child) on Navua River, half-day tours to Nasilai village ($49/33 adult/child) and city tours of Suva ($79/44 adult/child).

Discover Fiji Tours *(☎ 345 0180, fax 345 0549; e discoverfiji@connect.com.fj)*, based in Navua, also offers canoe trips 20km inland along the Navua River to a giant waterfall. (See under Navua in the Queens Road section earlier in this chapter for more about Navua River).

Adventure Fiji can organise four- to six-day 50km highland treks through the province of Ra. By bus, boat train and foot, you'll follow a route used by missionaries since 1849. Accommodation and meals are in villages along the route. The trek is run from May to October with a maximum of 15 people aged 12-60 years. Visit the tour desk at the Holiday Inn for current prices, more information and to book.

SPECIAL EVENTS

Check with the FVB to see if there are any special events coinciding with your stay. In August, Suva has a week-long **Hibiscus Festival** with food stalls, parades, Fijian fire-walking demonstrations, fair rides and the crowning of Miss Hibiscus. Much of the money raised from the event goes to local charities. Started in 1956, the festival was originally a day of amusement, when government workers could replace their starched white shirts with bright *bula* shirts – a colourful tradition that stuck.

There are several Hindu religious festivals observed in Suva and around the country. Fire walking and body piercing is held at the **Mariamma Temple** *(Howell Rd, Samabula)*, also in August. In March or April each year, there is a party on the shores of Laucala Bay to celebrate the birth of Lord Rama, with offerings, flowers and swimming in the bay. Dawali, the Hindu festival of lights, falls in late October or early November and is celebrated with fireworks and huge sales in the shops.

PLACES TO STAY

Suva has some excellent budget accommodation, some good mid-range motels for those looking to self-cater, and a couple of plusher alternatives. There are also several dodgy places along the northern stretch of Robertson Road that are the haunts of prostitutes and their clients; if you notice no other travellers and a lot of traffic, you may want to move on.

Places to Stay – Budget

Raintree Lodge *(☎ 332 0562, fax 332 0113; e raintreelodge@connect.com.fj; Princes Rd, Colo-i-Suva; camping/dorms/doubles $10/18-20/50, all with shared bathroom and kitchen)* offers Suva's best budget accommodation on the edge of the rainforest. The wooden, 20-bed dorms are surprisingly cosy and the lush surroundings are gorgeous. Camping is in a field next to one of the lakes but can be a rather muddy ordeal in the rain. The lodge is on 3 acres with an extremely impressive layout; privacy and views for each building were achieved with only one tree being cut down. Facilities at the lodge include fishing, volleyball, canoeing, swimming, and mountain bikes (free with deposit). There's a lakeside *lovo* on Sundays, kava sessions many evenings and a bar with a great cocktails and a pool table. Staff are fantastically friendly, the atmosphere relaxed and the restaurant is superb (see Places to Eat later in this section). The lodge also offers upmarket *bure* (see Places to Stay – Top-End later in this section). Raintree Lodge is about 10km

Home Away From Home

On the outskirts of Suva, away from the flashy shops and colonial homes, thousands of people are living in tiny, corrugated iron huts. In April of 2002, more than 60,000 Fijians were landless and squatting, a number that is continuously climbing with the country's unsolved land issues.

Indigenous Fijians have traditional ownership rights to almost 80% of the country's landmass, large tracts of which they've leased to Indo-Fijian farmers for the past century. However, with these leases coming to an end and ethnic friction heightened by recent political events, many indigenous landowners are turfing Indo-Fijian farmers off property where their families have lived for generations. Most Indo-Fijians are fleeing to the cities for safety. Unfortunately, with their livelihood gone, many families are ending up in suburban squatter settlements.

These impromptu, crowded towns are not strictly Indo-Fijian. The substantial pay-cuts and rise in unemployment that have followed the country's numerous coups have left many urban indigenous Fijians unable to pay the rent. Their only means of survival is also to head for the squatter settlements. These dilapidated settlements have little sanitation and often no water supply.

In 1994, the government of the day approved a policy to upgrade squatter settlements. Since then, many landless families have been promised resettlement, particularly evicted Indo-Fijians. However, the constant juggling of politics and politicians in Fiji has left many families squatting for more than a decade. Some have turned to begging and others attempt to sell crafts to tourists, but for the majority of these families, the future does not look bright.

from Suva, next door to Colo-i-Suva Park. It's a cool retreat from the city but don't forget your bug repellent. Catch the Sawani bus from Suva's bus terminal (20 mins; $0.65).

Colonial Lodge *(☎/fax 330 0655; 19 Anand St; dorms/singles/doubles with shared bathroom $17/38/48, single/double with en suite $50/60, all include breakfast)* is your best option if you're wanting to stay closer to the city centre. A restored colonial home, the lodge is run by a friendly family. There's a veranda where you can lounge in a hammock and dinner is sometimes available; ask ahead. Private rooms upstairs are much brighter than those downstairs with the exception of the one room with en suite; it's downstairs, huge and lovely. The lodge is only a 20-minute walk from town however the area is notorious for muggings; make sure you get a taxi after dark. The lodge has two dogs to keep you safe; unfortunately they may also wake you up at night.

Sunset Apartment Motel *(☎ 330 1799, fax 330 3446; cnr Gordon and Murray Sts; dorms/singles/doubles $9/42/48)* is minutes from downtown. Dorms are clean and an excellent deal with shared bathroom, a kitchen, 24hr reception and individual lockers. Private rooms are basic but pleasant with a balcony, en suite, fridge and TV.

Tanoa House *(☎ 338 1575; 5 Princes Rd; singles/doubles $20/30, dorm rates for group booking)* is a bit rundown but still has lots of character. Rooms are basic, clean and fan-cooled, each with a sink and shared bathroom. There's a pleasant lounge, garden and small bar. Meals are available if booked in advance.

South Seas Private Hotel *(☎ 331 2296, fax 330 8646; e southseas@fiji4less.com; 6 Williamson Rd; dorms/singles/doubles $12/19/28)* is somewhat reminiscent of a 1940s asylum building; however, with a big garden and comfy lounge, it's an old standby in Suva. Dorms are basic but clean; private rooms are bare and a little rundown. An international student card will get you a dollar discount. You must pay in full on arrival, cash only, although the hotel exchanges travellers cheques at bank rates.

Travel Inn *(☎ 330 5254, fax 330 8646; e travelinn@fiji4less.com; Gorrie St; singles/doubles/triples $22/30/39, self-contained flat $60)* is conveniently located on a quiet street near the Government Buildings, within an easy walk to the city centre. The quaint, old u-shaped building looks like a 1950s motel. Rooms are fan-cooled and paired to share a bathroom and a small stoveless kitchen area. There is a small but reasonably good communal kitchen and dining area, which is open from 7am to 7.30pm. As with South Seas (they're both part of the Cathay chain), payment is cash only on arrival.

Places to Stay – Mid-Range

USP Upper Campus Lodge *(☎ 321 2614, 321 2639, fax 331 4827; e usplodges@usp.ac.fj; singles/doubles with shared facilities $39/45, self-contained singles/doubles $54/64)* has fantastic, bungalow-style units with balconies overlooking the botanical gardens. Comfortable and self-contained with kettles, toasters and microwaves (but no stoves), this is an excellent deal. As a guest, you also gain access to the university's sport facilities. Rooms inside the lodge are clean and spacious but somewhat older and lacking character. Shared bathrooms are spotless and there's a lounge, balcony and fully equipped kitchen. The lodge is on the right as you enter through the uni's northwest entrance. The **USP Marine Lodge** *(same contact as above; singles/doubles $44/59)* is further down the road. Rooms are bright and clean with views of the sea. Doubles have kitchens and all rooms have bathrooms. Reception is at the Upper Campus Lodge.

Town House Apartment Hotel *(☎ 330 0055, fax 330 3446; 3 Forster St; standard singles/doubles $48/60, one-bedroom apartment singles/doubles $60/70, extra adult $12)* has clean apartments with kitchen facilities, a balcony with good views and cheery decor from the 1950s. Standard rooms aren't quite as nice, with a wee balcony but no view.

Motel 6 *(☎ 330 7477, fax 330 7133; 1 Walu St, off Waimanu Rd; standard/deluxe/family room $44/55/77-88)* has new, clean rooms. What they're lacking in character, they make up for with balconies and views of the harbour. All rooms have en suites, deluxe rooms have satellite TVs and fridges and one-bedroom family rooms sleep four. Staff are helpful and, while it's a bit out of town, it's quiet here. Reception is through an unmarked orange door.

Suva Motor Inn *(☎ 331 3973, fax 330 0381; e suvamotorinn@connect.com.fj; cnr Mitchell & Gorrie Sts; standard/2-bedroom flat $90/155)* has spacious rooms with lots of light. They may be without frills but they're tidy, have kitchen facilities and they're built around a courtyard with a pool and water slide. It's good value if you're travelling in a group as standard rooms sleep three and two bedroom flats sleep six.

Annandale Apartments *(☎ 331 1054, 330 2171; 265 Waimanu Rd; nightly/weekly $45/280)* is a great deal, especially if you're planning to stay awhile. All flats are spacious with two bedrooms, a balcony, a fully equipped kitchen, lounge, bathroom and shower. The woman running the place is friendly and it's a 20-minute walk to town. This is a dodgy area at night though; take a taxi.

Places to Stay – Top End

Homestay Suva *(☎ 337 0395, fax 337 0947; e homestaysuva@connect.com.fj; 265 Princes Rd, Tamavua; doubles in house downstairs/upstairs $150/160, singles/doubles in annex $160/180)* is a fabulous place to rest travel-weary bones. This gorgeous colonial house is in large grounds on the Tamavua ridge, with spectacular views over Suva Harbour. Rooms are beautiful, plush and extremely comfortable with air-con, fans and en suites. An excellent breakfast (included in the price) is served on the terrace overlooking the pool and bay. Home-cooked dinners are available on request. Book in advance (no young children).

Raintree Lodge *(☎ 332 0562, fax 332 0113; e raintreelodge@connect.com.fj; Princes Rd, Colo-i-Suva; single & double bure/family bure $110/165, extra person $28)* has beautiful *bure* set in the rainforest. Each one has a balcony with its own private view of the lake and the beds are as comfortable as clouds. The family *bure* sleeps a maximum of 10 people with a loft for children, a lounge and a dining area. Service is excellent. For a description of facilities see Places to Stay – Budget earlier in this section.

Southern Cross Hotel *(☎ 331 4233, fax 330 2901; 63 Gordon St; singles & doubles without/with breakfast $120/135)* is being completely remodelled by its new owners into one of Suva's finest hotels. Polished mahogany floors and panelled walls give rooms a warm, posh country club feel. Each room has a balcony and en suite and there's a pool in the central courtyard. At the time of writing, Korean and Japanese restaurants were also planned for the hotel.

Holiday Inn *(☎ 330 1600, fax 330 0251; e reservations@holidayinnsuva.com.fj; Victoria Parade; standard/superior $175/275)* has a great location on the southern edge of town, across from the Government Buildings and near the museum. Rooms are cool, spacious and clean but somewhat worn. The lobby has had a recent renovation but the bar and garden are still showing a bit of wear and tear. Nevertheless, the pool and garden have an excellent view of the sea.

Raffles Tradewinds Hotel *(☎ 336 2450, fax 336 1464; Queens Road, Lami; standard/deluxe $80/120, 1 child under 16 free in standard, 2 in deluxe)* has outlived its heyday; its glamour shows a bit of wear and its decor definitely tilts towards the 1960s. Nevertheless, it's comfortable, staff are friendly and it has beautiful views out to the sailboats in the harbour. There's a small pool with wooden loungers on the deck, and a bar next to the water. Standard rooms have a small deck with a view, fridge and kettle and deluxe rooms are bigger and brighter with a tub and private deck next to the water. The hotel operates a water taxi to Suva ($44 per person) as well as bay cruises, fishing trips and inner tube rides.

PLACES TO EAT

Restaurants

While not known for its restaurant scene, dining option in Suva are definitely looking up these days.

Raintree Lodge *(☎ 332 0562, fax 332 0113; Princes Rd, Colo-i-Suva; breakfast/lunch or dinner $10/15)* has an excellent restaurant with a covered veranda where you can dine amid the trees over the quarry-cum-lake. The beautiful setting is very peaceful and the service is stellar. The menu has traditional Fijian dishes as well as mixed grills, curries and fresh fish with tasty marinates like citron-vodka. There are good vegie options and the pancakes at breakfast are a must. There is also a kids' menu, unique (if pricey) cocktails and cheesecake for dessert. To get there, see Places to Stay earlier in this section.

JJ's Bar & Grill *(☎ 330 5005; Stinson Parade; light meals outside $9, lunch/dinner inside $18)* has moved to a new location, next to Ratu Sukuna Park. Very popular with Suva's upwardly mobile crowd and expats, it has that American casual-dining feel. The food is excellent, particularly the fresh seafood. Outside on the patio you can enjoy sea views and salads, sandwiches and fish and chips.

Tiko's Floating Restaurant *(☎ 331 3626; open noon-2pm & 5pm-10pm Mon-Sat; mains $25)* is one of Suva's most atmospheric dining options. The cruising vessel is anchored at the seawall across from Ratu Sukuna Park and, if there's a swell, rocks in time to the live local music. Not surprisingly, the speciality is seafood including lobster, prawns, and curried or grilled fish. You can also get a teriyaki steak, chicken or veggie options. Value isn't fantastic but the bar is well stocked and the sea breezes are worth the splurge.

Chef's *(☎ 330 8556; Thomson St; lunch/dinner $16/32; open 11am-2pm & 6pm-9.30pm Mon-Sat)* may be lacking atmosphere, but it's regarded as Suva's top restaurant by many Suvanese. The menu is certainly more exciting than the décor, with Tex-Mex, Indian and pasta dishes for lunch, and Fijian and seafood dishes such as slow roasted snapper for dinner. Cool off downstairs in Chef's **Ice-Cream Parlour** with a scoop of vanilla ice.

Aberdeen Grill *(☎ 330 4322; 16 Bau St, Flagstaff; three-course set meal $19; open 12.30pm-3pm & 6.30pm-10pm Mon-Sat, 6.30pm-10pm Sun)* has an aristocratic, slightly stuffy feel about it. However, you can sit in overstuffed chairs in front of big windows, and dine on fantastic three-course meal deals. If you opt for the menu, you can choose from fish, steak, Cajun chicken, lobster or a rack of lamb. Not the place to go if you're a vegetarian.

Yacht Club *(☎ 331 2921; mains about $14; open 11am-2.30pm & 5pm-9pm daily)* serves a mixture of dishes from around the globe like black peppercorn steak, soy ginger chicken and fish in *lolo*. It also has all-day breakfast ($8.50) and fish and chips ($7.50) for homesick Brits. You can eat outside at picnic tables for a view of the docked boats.

Indo-Fijian There are enough hole-in-the-wall curry houses in Suva to set your head spinning and your mouth watering. This is where those on tight budgets can eat like kings.

Ashiyana *(☎ 331 3000; Old Town Hall Bldg, Victoria Parade; mains $9; open 11.30am-2.30pm & 6pm-10pm Tues-Sat, 6pm-9.30pm Sun)* feels like an Indian diner – if such a thing exists. From your booth you can appreciate the Indian decor while you feast on tandoori, vegie *thali* or the $6 lunch special. Wash it all down with an excellent cup of *chai* (tea).

Hare Krishna Restaurant *(☎ 331 4154; cnr Pratt and Joske Sts; mains $2; open 9am-7.30pm Mon-Thur, 9am-9pm Fri, 9am-3.30pm*

Sat) is popular with local Indo-Fijians for its vegetarian curries and samosas, and even more so for its home-made ice cream ($1.25/2.60 small/large). Service is canteen-style.

Govinda's Vegetarian Restaurant *(☎ 330 9587; 93 Cumming St; Thali Combo $6.50; open 9am-7pm Mon-Fri, 9am-3pm Sat)* is a friendly canteen serving up *dosas* (crepe), curries and Indian sweets.

Old Mill Cottage *(☎ 331 2134; 49 Carnavon St; dishes around $6; open 7am-6pm Mon-Fri, 7am-5pm Sat)*, just around the corner from the Dolphin Plaza Food Court, serves Indo-Fijian fare, canteen style. The balcony is a great place to relax for awhile.

Chinese Suva's most stylish Chinese restaurant, the **Great Wok of China** *(☎ 330 1285; cnr Bau St & Laucala Bay Rd, Flagstaff; dishes around $25; open noon-2pm & 6.30pm-10pm Mon-Fri, 6.30pm-10pm Sat & Sun)*, serves a huge range of spicy Sichuanese dishes. Relax among the bamboo screens and, if you're brave, fill up on delicacies like bêche-de-mer.

Lantern Palace *(☎ 331 4795; 10 Pratt St; mains $10; open 11.30am-2.30pm & 5pm-10pm Mon-Sat, 5pm-10pm Sun)* serves reliable, good-value dishes. It's a bit dark but extremely popular with customers who crowd around big, round tables to feast on seafood, chop suey and Mongolian sizzling grills. Set menus for four to eight people are around $16 per person.

Ming Palace *(☎ 331 5111; dishes $10; open 11.30am-2.30pm & 6pm-10pm Mon-Fri, dim sum 9am-3pm Sun, dinner 6pm-10 Sun)* is inside the grandiose old town hall building and decorated in elaborate Chinese banquet-style. Unfortunately, it's beginning to smell a bit musty. It specialises in Cantonese food and can fulfil your dim sum cravings on Sunday mornings.

New Peking *(☎ 331 2939; 195 Victoria Parade)*, a downtown standby for cheap Chinese dishes, has – sadly – burnt to a crisp. The owners are still serving up a few dishes canteen-style next door while they rebuild the restaurant.

Japanese For excellent Japanese food, it's definitely worth splashing out at **Daikoku Restaurant** *(☎ 330 8968; Victoria Parade; mains $15; open lunch & dinner daily)*. Relax to peaceful music with your Japanese beer ($6.50) or sake ($5.50) as professional teppanyaki chefs whip up a gourmet, sizzling feast before your eyes. Sushi, tempura and sashimi are all delicious and served on beautiful pottery dishes. Bring your own wine for an $8 corkage fee.

Zen Restaurant *(330 6314; level 1, Pacific House, Butt St; mains around $15, lunch special $7; open 11.30am-2.30pm & 6pm-9pm Mon-Fri, 11.30am-2.30pm Sat)* offers casual dining on its covered deck. Specialities include smoked sashimi and Japanese curry. The lunch special is a serious bargain.

Korean Enter through the giant wooden doors of the **Korea House** *(☎ 331 1711; 178 Waimanu Rd; mains $12; open noon-3pm & 5pm-10pm daily)* for *kim chi* (fermented vegetables) and barbequed sweet fish. The walls are simply decorated with masks and the staff are friendly.

Da Kyung Garden *(☎ 359 1224; 43 Gordon St; mains $15; open 10am-10pm Mon-Sat, 12.30pm-10pm Sun)* is lacking in atmosphere but you'll hardly notice as you indulge in Korean barbeque, dumplings, fried eel, *bulgogi* (beef stir-fry) and noodles. Service is with a smile.

Pizzerias

Having 'borrowed' its name from the American chain, **Pizza Hut** *(☎ 331 1825; Victoria Parade; regular/large/giant pizza $8/12/22; open 10am-10pm daily, closes 10.30pm Fri & Sat)* serves OK, inexpensive pizzas with Mediterranean, chicken, seafood and vegetarian toppings. It also serves a few pasta dishes. Takeaway can be ordered up until 9.45pm.

Pizza King *(☎ 331 5762; Harbour Centre, Scott St; pizzas $10; open 11am-2pm & 7pm-10pm daily)* is another place to head to for cheap, thick pizzas.

Cafés & Snack Bars

With some of the best coffees in town, **Republic of Cappuccino** *(☎ 330 0333; Renwick Rd; coffees $3; open 7am-11pm Mon-Sat, 10am-7pm Sun)* is a popular hang-out. Enjoy a latte, fresh juice or cake on a comfy couch while you read the café's newspapers and magazines. It also serves a few so-so sandwiches. There is a smaller outlet in Dolphin Plaza on Victoria Parade.

Kahawa *(☎ 330 9671; Plaza One, Downtown Blvd Shopping Centre, Ellery St; drinks $3;*

open 7am-6pm Mon-Thur, 7am-4pm Fri & Sat, 7am-1pm Sun) is another place to sink into a comfy couch or relax on the patio. It has less of a chain feel about it and there's a notice board to check out, a book exchange and lots of magazines to read as you enjoy coffees, *chai*, smoothies, cakes and cinnamon buns.

Fusion *(☎ 330 9117; Vanua Arcade, Victoria Parade; sandwiches $4; open 8am-5pm Mon-Sat)* has fantastic giant sandwiches, wraps, coffees and the best smoothies in town. There are lots of options for vegetarians. Eat at the barstools, tables in the mall or take it away.

Headworks *(☎ 330 9449; upstairs, cnr of Renwick and Thomson Sts; dishes $4; open 8am-7pm Mon-Sat)* serves smoothies, filled croissants, cakes, lasagne and sandwiches along with coffees and teas. Comfy chairs are on the balcony overlooking downtown Suva. When you tire of the view, you can get your hair done next door in the café's salon.

Bad Dog Cafe *(☎ 330 4662; cnr Macarthur St & Victoria Parade; mains $10; open 11am-11pm Mon-Wed, 11am-1am Thur-Sat)* has tasty soups, pasta, gourmet pizza and pasta and huge coffees. It has an extensive list of foreign beers and cocktails or you can buy wine from Victoria Wines next door and pay a $6 corkage fee. If you're more of a spectator than a reveller, it's also a good place to watch nightclubbers go by on Friday and Saturday nights.

Rivendell *(☎ 330 4662; Queensland Insurance Bldg, Victoria Parade; lunch or breakfast $4; open 7am-4.30pm Mon-Fri, 7am-2.30pm Sat)* serves sandwiches, quiche, burgers, smoothies and cake in an indoor courtyard. It's a good option if you're looking for a quick lunch or for an early breakfast of muesli or French toast.

Ultra Roast Station *(☎ 330 8998; Scott St; coffees $3; open 8am-7pm Mon-Sat)* is a nice place to relax on a sunny day. On the terrace you can enjoy river and mountain views with your coffee, croissant, salad or shake.

Enjoy *(☎ 331 6888; 281 Victoria Parade; snacks & drinks $4, mains $16; open 9am-9pm Mon-Thur, 9am-11pm Fri & Sat, 10am-9pm Sun & holidays)* might well have been beamed over directly from Beijing. Spacious and smoky, with energetic dance music but little atmosphere, you can practice your Chinese while you eat waffles, dip into a hotpot or slurp a pearl jelly tea.

The university has a couple of cheap places to eat. **Southern Cross** *(main entrance; open 9am-10pm Mon-Thur, 9am-5pm Fri-Sun)* is the most pleasant, with coffee and cinnamon buns served outdoors under the shade of an enormous tree. **Mango Tree Kona** *(open 7am-5pm daily)* is a small canteen with a deck and sandwiches for $1.50. Nearby, the main **canteen** *(open 7am-10am, 11.30am-1.45pm & 5.30pm-7.30pm Mon-Fri)* and **Tree Corner** *(open 9am-4pm Mon-Fri)* serve cheap Indo-Fijian and traditional Fijian meals for under $5.

Fast Food

Suva has a few **food courts**: one at Downtown Boulevard Shopping Centre *(Ellery St)*, another upstairs in Harbour Centre *(Scott St)* and one at Dolphin Plaza *(cnr Loftus St & Victoria Parade)*. All have a variety of takeaway-food outlets, including pizza, pasta, Chinese, curries and Fijian dishes for around $5. **Jackson Takeaway** *(open 7am-6pm Mon-Sat, 9am-5pm Sun)* in the old town hall has good-value Chinese food for under $3.50.

Self-Catering

Suva Municipal Market is the best place for fish, fruit and vegetables. There are a couple of supermarkets downtown on Rodwell Rd, facing the market and bus station. At the **Hot Bread Kitchen** *(☎ 331 3919; Scott St; open 5.30am-7pm Mon-Fri, 5.30am-1pm Sat)* you can pick up fresh cheese and onion loaves and coconut rolls. For something to wash it all down with, try **Victoria Wines & Spirits** *(☎ 331 2884; Victoria Parade; open 11am-9pm Mon-Fri, 11am-2pm Sat)*.

ENTERTAINMENT

Pubs, Bars & Discos

While little ole' Suva doesn't rival London or Bangkok with its nightlife, Friday and Saturday nights see Victoria Parade swarming with clubbers and barhoppers. Among the dodgy bars and pubs are a couple of great clubs where you can shake your booty. You don't need to get completely dolled up but if you're wearing shorts or flip-flops you'll be turned away. Watch out for pickpockets on the dance floor and always take a taxi after dark, even if you're in a group – walking home is considered dangerous.

Traps Bar *(☎ 331 2922; Victoria Parade; happy hr 6pm-8pm; open 6pm-1am daily)* is justifiably popular and gets crowded on weekends. The pub-like front room and snooker room are good places to grab a beer and socialise, while the trendy back room has a vibrant dance floor, laser lights and a busy well-stocked bar. The music is a good mixture of current and older dance and pop.

O'Reillys *(☎ 331 2968; cnr of Macarthur St & Victoria Parade; open 6pm-1am daily)* has nothing Irish about it. Despite being more of a bar than a club, it gets packed out on weekends with people dancing with poles and on tables. Music is an odd but fairly good mixture of dance and pop, and the crowd is an equally unusual mixture of students, expats and business people letting down their hair.

The Barn *(☎ 330 7845; Carnavon St; open 6pm-1am daily)* is a rugged, country and western bar with live music nightly except Sunday and Monday. Music is country with a bit of pop and reggae thrown in for good measure. The cowboy crowd is a little older.

JJ's Bar & Grill *(☎ 3305 005; Stinson Parade)* has a comfortable, casual bar where you can relax, sip cocktails and eat bar snacks in the evening.

Check out the *Fiji Times* entertainment section for upcoming events and what's on at nightclubs or ask staff at Republic of Cappuccino for the currently popular hang-outs.

Cinemas

Village 6 Cinema Complex *(☎ 331 1109; Scott St; admission $5)* shows recently released Hollywood and Bollywood films. See the cinema section of the *Fiji Times* for what's screening.

SPECTATOR SPORTS

Fijians are fanatical about their rugby and, even if you aren't that keen on the game, it's worth going to a match. The season lasts from April to September; ask at the FVB if there will be a match during your stay. With the 2003 Pacific Games hosted at Suva's National Stadium, improved facilities may equal an increase in events. Again, check with the FVB or in the local paper for what's on.

SHOPPING

Suva is bursting at the seams with shops; whether you're looking for souvenirs, a new swimsuit or some new music, you've come to the right place.

Souvenirs & Handicrafts

For a good selection of souvenirs, crafts and Fiji-made clothes at reasonable prices, head to **Jack's Handicrafts** *(☎ 330 8893; cnr Renwick Rd & Pier St; open 9am-5.30pm Mon-Fri, 9am-2pm Sat)*.

Moving to a Different Beat

Dancers pay homage to the steady beat of the drums, seemingly oblivious to the spectators. The poorly lit room is crowded with both tourists and locals yelling '*bula*' to one another over the din. As a big, indigenous Fijian man – who should be playing the chief in this scene – approaches with a flower behind his ear and a pitcher of beer on his tray, you don't need any reminding that this is no *meke*. This is Saturday night in Suva, when the country's urban youth let down their hair and pole dance to pop music.

Fiji's urban youth face many of the same difficulties as young people around the globe: teenage parenting, crime, drugs and skyrocketing unemployment (only one in eight school leavers finds a job). However, these youths also find themselves straddling two opposing worlds – the traditional, conservative society of the villages many have left behind, where life was filled with cultural protocols, and the liberal, individualistic lifestyle of the modern and increasingly Westernised city. With 90% of its airtime devoted to Western sitcoms and serials, young people watch television filled with an irrelevant and often unattainable world. The rising club and café culture is bringing together youths from indigenous and Indo-Fijian backgrounds, in the midst of a city filled with ethnic strife. Many face the near impossibility of surviving unemployment in the city; returning 'home' to a village sporting dreadlocks and skin-tight jeans isn't much easier. Youth have little room to voice their own opinions and it's not entirely surprising that many look for routes out of the country.

This is not the Fiji of postcards, of grass skirts and beachside *lovos*, however, it's well worth grabbing a cappuccino or putting on your dancing shoes to check out Fiji's rising urban youth culture. It's an unexpected eye-opener.

Ransam *(☎ 330 8696; upstairs, 6 Ellery St; open 8.30am-5pm Mon-Thur, 8.30am-5.30pm Fri, 9am-noon Sat)* sells local crafts such as wooden trays and bowls and woven baskets. They can also package and ship goods overseas. The **Government Crafts Centre** *(☎ 331 5869; Macarthur St; open 8am-4.30pm Mon-Thur, 8am-4pm Fri, 8am-12.30pm Sat)* sells similar wares of consistently high quality and assists rural artisans in the process; however, it's generally more expensive than elsewhere.

The **Suva Curio & Handicraft Centre** *(Stinson Parade)* has endless stalls and is an interesting place to wander through. It can offer up some fantastic buys but be prepared to bargain! Not all artefacts are as genuine as the vendor would like you to believe; if you aren't an antique expert, only pay what the object is worth to you. In-your-face sword-sellers (renowned for befriending tourists, carving their name in a wooden sword and then demanding to be paid for it) have all but disappeared. Nevertheless, if you are cornered by one, just walk away (unless of course you have a hankering for a new, wooden mini-sword).

Gathera *(☎ 330 5565; Queensland Insurance Bldg, Victoria Parade; open 9am-5pm Mon-Fri, 9am-1pm Sat)* has beautiful goods from throughout the South Pacific. Pick up handmade hammocks, soaps, candles, bedspreads, cards and carvings. It's not cheap but its excellent quality.

The **Fiji Philatelic Bureau** *(☎ 331 2928, fax 330 6088; GPO bldg; open 8am-4pm Mon-Thur, 8am-3.30pm Fri, 8am-noon Sat)* has stamps and first covers from Fiji and other Pacific Islands.

Music

Try **Procera Music Shop** *(☎ 331 4911; Greig St; open 9am-2pm & 2.30pm-5.30pm Mon-Fri, 9am-1pm Sat)* for top Fijian and Hindi releases. **The Boom Box** *(☎ 330 8265; Downtown Blvd Shopping Centre)* has new-ish releases of Euro and US dance, country and reggae music. It's imported and fairly pricey.

Film

For one-hour film processing, **Fuji Film** *(☎ 331 3911; Shop 11, Vanua House, Victoria Parade; open 9am-5pm Mon-Fri, 9am-1pm Sat)* has a reputation for high quality photos. It also sells camera batteries and an array of print and slide film.

Water Sports

If you're looking for beachwear, daypacks, snorkel gear or surf boards, **Wai Tui Surf** *(☎ 330 0287; Queensland Insurance Bldg, Victoria Parade; open 8.30am-5pm Mon-Fri, 8.30am-2pm Sat)* has lots of name brand goods to keep you afloat. **Bob's Hook, Line & Sinker** *(☎ 330 1013; Harbour Centre, Thomson St; open 8am-5.30pm Mon-Fri, 8am-1.30pm Sat)* also sells snorkelling, diving and fishing gear.

GETTING THERE & AWAY

Suva is well connected to the rest of the country by air and interisland ferries, and to western Viti Levu by buses and carriers. Most international flights, however, arrive at Nadi International Airport.

Air

Nausori International Airport is 23km northeast of central Suva. There are no direct local buses between Suva and the airport, but **Nausori Taxi & Bus Service** *(☎ 331 2185, 330 4178)* has regular buses to/from the Holiday Inn hotel in Suva ($2.50). Otherwise, a taxi from the airport to/from Suva costs about $17. Alternatively, cover the 3km to Nausori's bus stations by taxi (about $3), and catch one of the frequent local buses to Suva bus station for about $1.50. Allow plenty of time, as some buses speed while others crawl. Expect to pay about $12 for a taxi ride from Nausori Airport to the Raintree Lodge next to Colo-i-Suva Forest Park.

See the Getting Around chapter for flight routes.

Bus & Carrier

There are frequent local buses operating along the Queens Road and Kings Road from Suva's main bus terminal. If you can cope with busy bus stations and sometimes crowded buses, they are more fun and better value than tourist buses and will stop at resorts along the way upon request.

Small trucks or carriers, with tarpaulin-covered frames on the back, also take passengers along Queens Road. If you're travelling in a group, you can usually get a taxi for little more than the price of a bus.

Boat

From Suva there are regular ferry services to Vanua Levu and Taveuni with **Beachcomber**

Cruises *(☎ 330 7889, fax 330 7359; Suite 8, Epworth Arcade)* and **Consort Shipping** *(☎ 330 2877, fax 330 3389; Grnd floor Dominion House Arcade, Thomson St)* and to Ovalau with **Patterson Brothers Shipping** *(☎ 331 5644, fax 330 1652 Suites 1 & 2, Epworth Arcade, Nina St)*. See the Getting Around Chapter. There are also irregular boats that take passengers from Suva to Kadavu, Lau and Rotuma (see the respective destination chapters).

GETTING AROUND

It is easy to get around central Suva on foot. Local buses are cheap and plentiful and depart from the main bus terminal. There are relatively few buses in the evening and barely any on Sundays.

Taxis are cheap for short trips ($3), and in Suva they actually use the meter! Suva's one-way looping streets may make you think the taxi driver is taking you on a goose chase; drivers along Victoria Parade may get caught on a long run around the market and wharf area. Suva is *not* considered a safe place to wander around at night and it's well worth hopping in a taxi. To order one call **Carnarvon Taxi** *(☎ 331 5315, 331 1393)* or **Sanyo Cabs** *(☎ 331 1221, 330 4541, 331 1038)*.

See the Getting Around chapter for car rental companies.

Kings Road

The Kings Road links Suva to Lautoka via eastern and northern Viti Levu, 265km and about four hours by express bus . This route is just as beautiful as the Queens Road, through remote highland villages and small agricultural towns, and a great trip either by bus or car (best if you hire a 4WD, especially during the wet season, if the road is still unsealed between Korovou and Dama).

Korovou, Rakiraki, Tavua and Ba each have a simple hotel, there is an upmarket resort near Rakiraki and several budget resorts offshore on Nananu-i-Ra.

NAUSORI & THE REWA DELTA

pop 22,000

The township of Nausori is on the eastern bank of the Rewa River, 19km northeast of downtown Suva. It has the country's second-largest airport and is a bustling service centre and transport hub for the largely agricultural and industry workers. If you're passing through there are a few banks and inexpensive eateries near the market and bus stations.

Now a major rice-producing region, the town developed around the CSR sugar mill, which operated here for eight decades until 1959. Growing sugar cane proved more successful on the drier western side of Viti Levu.

Ring-Ditch Fortifications

Defensive fortifications in lowland areas took the form of ring-ditches *(korowaiwai)*. There are many of these eroded circular mounds remaining in the Rewa Delta and you may be able to spot some if you fly over the area. In times of war they were necessary for the survival of a village, forming protection against a surprise attack. A ring ditch was usually about 10m wide with steep, battered sides and a strong fence on the inner bank, which encircled the living areas. Entry was through narrow causeways or drawbridges and gates. The ditch sometimes had dangerous bamboo spikes hidden in the muddy water. Important villages could be surrounded by up to four concentric ditches with offset causeways to divide and expose attackers. Fences were made of coconut posts and bamboo or bundles of reeds. According to AJ Webb, writing in 1885, 'Before the introduction of firearms, these places were simply impregnable to assault, and could only be taken through treachery or by starving the beleaguered.'

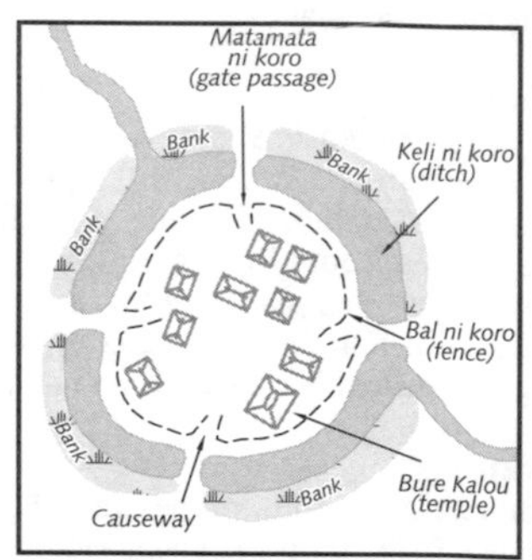

Getting There & Around

The Kings Road from Suva to Nausori is the country's busiest and most congested stretch of highway. The Nausori bus station is in the main street. **Sunbeam Transport** *(☎ 347 9353)* has regular buses to Lautoka via the Kings Road and there are six express services on weekdays (the first at 6am and the last at 5.15pm; on weekends the last bus is at 3pm).

Nausori International Airport The airport is about 3km southeast of Nausori, 22km from Suva. Air Fiji, Air Pacific and Royal Tongan Airlines have international flights through here. Air Fiji and Sun Air have domestic flights (see the Getting Around chapter for details). The airport premises are small, with a newspaper stand (selling a few magazines, books and phonecards) and a snack counter. An ANZ bank opens for international flights only.

There are regular buses from Nausori airport to nearby boat landings: Bau Landing, Wainibokasi Landing (in Naisali village) and Nakelo Landing (in Toberua). From Nakelo Landing there are local village boats, which you may be able to join or hire to explore the area. Chat with locals who may invite you to visit their villages.

Nakelo Landing is on the Wainibokasi River, southeast of the airport. If driving from Nausori, turn left before the airport and then take the first right. Follow the road for about 5km and turn right before Namuka.

Nasilai Village & Naililili Catholic Mission

Nasilai village is home to the well-known potter Taraivini Wati (see Arts in the Facts about Fiji chapter). Pottery is a major source of income for the village, and when large orders are placed, everyone participates in the process, helping to collect and prepare the clay and make the pots. When a baby girl is born in the village, a lump of clay is placed on her forehead. It's believed she will then automatically know how to carry on the pottery-making tradition.

Catholic missionaries built the Naililili Catholic Mission at the turn of the century from France. The stained-glass windows, imported from Europe, incorporate Fijian writing. The delta area on which the mission is built is a flood plain and so the priests no longer live here.

Wilderness Ethnic Adventure Fiji *(☎ 331 5730; w www.wilderness.com.fj)* runs tours of the Rewa Delta and Nasilai village, departing from Suva hotels (see organised tours in the Suva section).

There are regular buses to Wainibokasi Landing from the Nausori bus station. If driving from Nausori, head southeast for about 6km on the road that runs parallel to the Rewa River. Pass the airport entrance and turn right at the T-junction. The landing is a further 1km before the bridge across the Wainibokasi River. There you can catch a boat to the Naililili Catholic Mission, which is almost opposite the landing, or take a short trip downriver to Nasilai village. Ask a local for permission to visit the village and take along some kava for a *sevusevu*.

Bau

If you fly over Bau today it is bizarre to think that in the 19th century such a tiny speck of an island was the power base of Cakobau and his father Tanoa (see History in the Facts about Fiji chapter). In the 1780s there were 30 *bure kalou* on the small chiefly island, including the famous Na Vata ni Tawake, which stood on a huge *yavu* faced with large panels of flat rock. Also of interest are its **chiefly cemetery**, **old church** and a **sacrificial killing stone** on which enemies were slaughtered prior to being cooked and consumed.

To visit the island you must be invited by someone who lives there or have permission from the Ministry of Fijian Affairs (☎ 321 1458). Dress conservatively, take a large *waka* (bunch of kava roots) for presentation to the *turaga-ni-koro* (chief).

There are regular buses from Nausori bus station to Bau Landing, which is northeast of Nausori airport. If you are driving from Nausori, turn left before the airport and after about 4km turn left at the intersection and follow the road to its end. Boats cross to Bau, which is just offshore from the mainland. Boats also leave from Bau Landing for Viwa.

Toberua

This small island (2 hectares) is just off Kaba Point, the easternmost point of Viti Levu, about 30km from Suva.

Toberua Island Resort *(☎ 330 2356, fax 330 2215; w www.toberua.com; deluxe bure singles/doubles $390/455)*, originally built in 1968 as an American millionaire's hideaway, was one of Fiji's earliest luxury resorts. Don't be put off by its proximity to Suva, Toberua only receives about a third of Suva's annual rainfall. It has pleasant communal areas and 14 fine fan-cooled *bure* where up to two children under 16 years can share free of charge. Meal plans for adults are $80/100 for two/three meals per day. At low tide the beach is used for golf and there is snorkelling (you will probably see sea snakes), paddle boating, and tours to the nearby island bird sanctuary and mangroves. A two-tank dive, including equipment costs $170. Transfers involve a taxi from Nausori airport/Suva to Nakelo Landing ($16/30) followed by a boat ($18/35 per child/adult, 40 minutes).

KOROVOU & AROUND

The Kings Road between Suva and Rakiraki is mostly sealed, except for the 56km section between Korovou and Dama, which was undergoing road works at the time of writing. Korovou (one of many towns known literally as 'new village') is not much more than a transport intersection, about 50km north of Suva and 31km from Nausori airport. There are a few shops near the bus stop, and a post office across the river near the roundabout. The Kings Road continues to the northwest and over the hills. Another unsealed road follows the coast to Natovi Landing (a 20-minute drive), from where there are bus/ferry services to Labasa (Vanua Levu) and Levuka (Ovalau). See the Getting Around chapter for details. It is possible to meet the Kings Road again farther on, but only if you have a 4WD, as the road deteriorates as you approach Mt Tova.

Tailevu Hotel *(☎ 343 0028; camp sites $5, dorm beds $8, singles/doubles with private bathroom $20/35, family room $50, cottages $50)*, on the hill overlooking the roundabout has budget accommodation. A family room sleeps five people and self-contained cottages sleep four. The restaurant *(mains $5-10)* becomes the local nightclub on Friday and Saturday nights. **Wailotua Snake God Cave** is about 23km west of Korovou on the Kings Road. Hop on one of the Suva–Lautoka buses and ask the driver to let you off at Wailotua village, where you can request to visit the cave. It is about 1½ to two hours' walk from the village.

Between Korovou and Rakiraki the Kings Road crosses dairy-farming country (soldier settlement farmland given to returned soldiers after WWII), winds through hills and along the Wainibuka River, and passes many small villages where you'll receive a friendly wave. This apparently peaceful area was the subject of much local unrest and targeting of Indo-Fijian families during the 2000 coup. The unsealed section is usually passable although somehow *we* managed to get bogged! It's a slow trip – watch out for mad drivers and the odd timber truck, which hurtle along the gravel, and expect delays at milking time when cows plod along the road. The ones we saw all seemed to have sore feet! You may see the occasional *bilibili* on the river. About 14km from Korovou the Kings Road crosses the beautiful **Uru's Waterfall**.

Natovi Landing

There is a general store at Natovi Landing but little else. Patterson Brothers has a bus/ferry service (daily except Sunday) between Suva–Natovi and Nabouwalu on Vanua Levu. It also has a Suva–Natovi–Ovalau bus/ferry service (daily except Sunday) to Buresala Landing, with a bus connection to Levuka. Ferries also depart for Nabouwalu, Vanua Levu from Ellington Wharf near Rakiraki. See the Getting Around chapter for more information.

RAKIRAKI & AROUND

The scenery is stunning along the Kings Road winding down from the mountains from Dama past Viti Levu Bay and to the beautiful region of Rakiraki, Viti Levu's northernmost tip. The climate on the northern side of the **Nakauvadra Range** is similar to that of western Viti Levu, drier and suited for growing sugar-cane. According to local legend, the imposing mountains are the home of the great snake-god Degei, creator of all the islands. The opening and closing of his eyes is the cause of night and day, and thunder is said to be Degei turning in his sleep.

The turn-off to **Ellington Wharf** is about 5km east of Rakiraki off the Kings Road (at the 112.4km post from Lautoka), and then a further 1.5km by sealed road to the wharf. Nananu-i-Ra (see that section later) is just a short boat ride offshore. Ferries also leave here for Nabouwalu on Vanua Levu and Beachcomber Cruises has a weekly boat to Savusavu and Denarau via Beachcomber Island (see the Getting Around chapter).

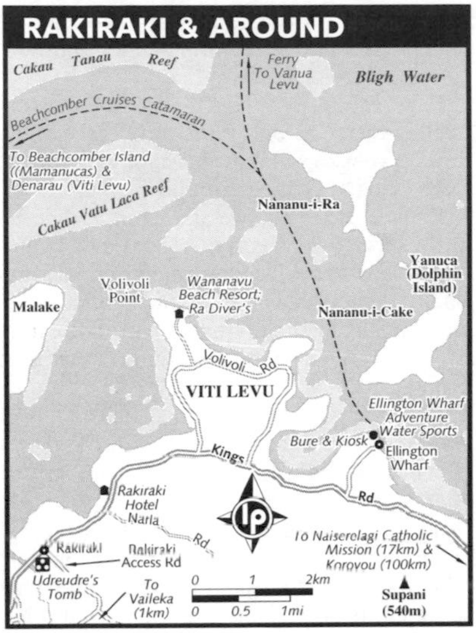

RAKIRAKI & AROUND

There is a turn-off that leads past the sugar mill to the small service town of **Vaileka** (about 2km inland from Rakiraki). Here there is a bus station, taxi stands, market, supermarket and a few cafés (one with Internet access). You can change travellers cheques at the Westpac bank (only open Tuesdays and Thursdays) or at the Colonial Bank.

When heading west out of Rakiraki towards Nadi, keep your eyes peeled for **Udreudre's Tomb**, the resting place of Fiji's most notorious cannibal (see the 'Ratu Udreudre' boxed text later). While it may be overgrown it is just by the roadside on the left, about 100m west of the Vaileka turn-off.

About 10km west of Rakiraki near Vitawa is a large outcrop known as **Navatu Rock**. There was once a fortified village on top of the rock and it was believed that from here spirits would depart for the afterlife.

Naiserelagi Catholics Mission

About 25km southeast of Rakiraki is an old mission (1917) overlooking Viti Levu Bay. The church is famous for its mural depicting a black Christ painted in 1962 by Jean Charlot. The three panels of biblical scenes depict Christ on the cross in a *masi sulu* and a *tanoa* at his feet. Indigenous Fijians are shown offering mats and *tabua*, and Indo-Fijians presenting flowers and oxen. Visitors are welcome and a small donation is appreciated.

From Vaileka or the Kings Road intersection, take the Flying Prince local bus for $1.50, ideally before 9am when buses are more regular. Otherwise it will cost $30 return by taxi. Naiserelagi is just south of Nanukuloa village, on the right past the school. The mission is on the hill, about 500m up a winding track.

Organised Tours

Ellington Wharf Adventure Water Sports *(☎ 669 3366, 942 765, W www.sailboardingsafaris.com)* offers lots of water-based activities including: two-hour snorkelling trips (from $25 per person plus $20 gear hire), windsurfing (from $30 per hour); catamaran sailing lessons and hire, as well as diving. Especially interesting are the sea kayaking trips around the islands and bays (short trips as well as one-, three- and seven-day trips). They also have organised windsurfing tours from Australia and New Zealand.

Eagles Waterfall Tour *(☎ 669 4864, 994 5260)* take trips to Nasesenibua village including a stop at Naiserelagi Mission, kava ceremony and a trek to a waterfall.

Places to Stay & Eat

Vaileka has a few cheap **cafés** near the bus station, and a **cake shop** at the Community Centre building. Ellington Wharf has a small **kiosk** that sells soft drinks, tinned food and snacks.

Budget travellers usually head straight out to Nananu-i Ra, however Ellington Wharf now has a 10-bed dorm **bure** *(☎ 693 333; $20)* with an outside toilet and cold shower; OK as a stopover.

Rakiraki Hotel *(☎ 669 4101; Kings Road; singles/doubles with fan $38/46, with air-con*

Ratu Udreudre

In 1849, some time after Ratu Udreudre's death, Reverend Richard Lyth asked Udreudre's son Ravatu, about the significance of a long line of stones. Each stone, he was told, represented one of the chief's victims, and amounted to a personal tally of at least 872 corpses. Ratavu went on to explain that his father consumed every piece of his victims of war, sharing none. He ate little else, and had an enormous appetite.

from $50/66), 1.8km east of the Vaileka turn-off, offers reasonably good-value rooms. Though musty, the rooms are acceptable and the hotel has a pool, half-size tennis court, lawn bowling and nine-hole golf course nearby. Air-con rooms in the newer building are $88/99 singles/doubles. You can get about a 30% discount for air-con rooms between November and early April. The **restaurant-bar** *(lunch $10; dinner $13-17)*, open to visitors, has standard fare including curries, roasts, fried fish, grilled steak and vegetables.

Wananavu Beach Resort *(☎ 669 4433, fax 669 4499; e wananavuresort@connect.com.fj; garden-view/ocean-view/beachfront bure doubles $185/215/245 plus $25 per extra person, villas $300)*, east of Rakiraki at the northernmost point of Viti Levu, is a good-value mid-range resort run by a New Zealand family. The hillside position has beautiful views of Nananu-i-Ra island and the mainland's mountainous coastline. The 15 comfortable air-con *bure* have balconies, and at a pinch can accommodate up to four people. There are also three self-contained two-bed villas down near the water. Ask about walk-in deals. Meal plans are an extra $88 per person. Visitors are welcome at the **restaurant/bar** *(dinner around $25)*, a great spot with good food. There is a beach nearby, a marina, nice swimming pool, tennis and volleyball courts, diving and snorkelling. Diving is available with Crystal Divers (based at Nananu-i-Ra) or Ra Divers, based at the resort.

The turn-off from the Kings Road is about 3.5km east of the Vaileka turn-off. Follow the unsealed (sometimes muddy) road to the north for about 3km to the resort. Airport transfers from Nadi are $100 by taxi or $15 per person by minivan. A taxi to Vaileka will be $10.

Getting There & Around

Sunbeam has regular express buses along the Kings Road from Suva and Nadi, which stop at Vaileka and the turn-off to Ellington Wharf. To avoid lugging groceries and gear the 1.3km to the wharf however, get off at Vaileka and catch a taxi for around $8. Sharing a taxi from Nadi is another option (about $80).

Nananu-i-Ra is just a 15-minute boat ride from Ellington Wharf. All the resorts on Nananu-i-Ra have their own boat transfers. Arrange your pick-up in advance (there is also a phone at Ellington Wharf). Boat transfers for the budget resorts are around $18 per person return.

From Ellington Wharf there is a Patterson Brothers ferry (a bit of a rusting hulk) three times a week to Nabouwalu, southwest Vanua Levu (see the Getting Around chapter).

Beachcomber's new catamaran, *Lagilagi*, has a service between the Viti Levu mainland (Nadi's Port Denarau and Lautoka) and Vanua Levu (Savusavu). It can call/drop off en-route at Wananavu, Nananu-i-Ra and Ellington Wharf (see the Getting Around chapter).

NANANU-I-RA

Nananu-i-Ra is a beautiful hilly 3.5-sq-km island, roughly triangular in shape with many scalloped bays, white-sand beaches and mangroves. Only 3km north of Ellington Wharf, it is an excellent option for those who want an offshore island experience but minimal boating and associated cost. It is handy to the Nadi area and is especially popular with self-caterers, divers and windsurfers.

The island has no roads and no village – most of the residents are of European descent so there's not much contact with traditional culture here. Great for **trekking**, it has views to the Nakauvadra mountain range on the mainland and birdseye views of turquoise reefs from the grassy hilltops. If you time it right with the tides you can walk around the island in about four to five hours and pass the mangroves at low tide. Part of the island is rocky so shoes are recommended. Weather permitting, **kayaking** around the island would take a similar time.

Diving & Snorkelling

Snorkelling offshore you can expect to see some coral, abundant fish, and, on the north side of the island, many sea snakes. You can also go on snorkelling trips to the outer reefs. with McDonald's Cottages (see Places to Stay later) and Ellington Wharf Adventures Water Sports (see Organised Tours earlier). The surrounding reefs and especially **Bligh Water** to the north have some amazing dive sites. The weather however can be tricky, while rainfall is relatively low it can be very windy.

Ra Divers *(☎ 669 4511; w www.radivers.com)*, based at Nananu-i-Ra will pick up from Wananavu Beach Resort which is on the

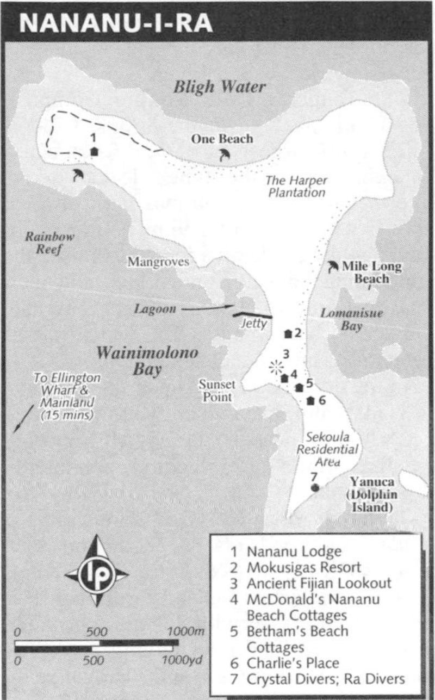

mainland, and from the budget resorts on the Nananu-i-Ra island. It charges $140 for a two-tank dive, plus $25 equipment rental, and $475 for an open-water course.

Crystal Divers *(6694 747; w www.crystaldivers.com)* also based at Nananu-i-Ra island has a good reputation and better boats. They take divers to excellent advanced dive sites further out in the Bligh Water. Diving with them costs $220 for a two-tank dive (including weight belts only).

Windsurfing

The climate here is relatively dry (water supply is sometimes a problem on the island) and its exposure to the trade winds make it especially suited for windsurfing. A lot of visitors come here particularly for this activity, especially from June to August when winds are generally 10 knots or more almost every day. Book ahead over this period. There is some basic windsurf gear for hire from Ellington Wharf Adventures Water Sports.

Organised Tours

For kayaking tours see Rakiraki earlier.

Places to Stay – Budget

There are four inexpensive places to stay on the island and one upmarket resort. It's a good idea to book accommodation in advance, especially if you want a cottage, as the island can get busy. Take cash and plenty of change, as not all of the budget places accept credit cards. All the budget places are well set up for self-caterers (linen and cutlery provided).

Self-caterers could get by with buying supplies from the shop at Betham's Beach Cottages – a small but reasonably well stocked shop – but it is a good idea to pick up some supplementary supplies (especially fruit and vegetables). Both Betham's and McDonald's Nananu Beach Cottages have an outdoor café. The bar and restaurant at Mokusigas Resort, a 10-minute walk from Betham's, is open to outsiders if it is not busy; book first. It is dry here and water supply is sometimes a problem.

Three of the budget places are close together facing the same bay – it's a narrow isthmus and there is another beach east that is generally more exposed to the wind (thus good for windsurfing or kite surfing). Prices are comparable so if you are not happy you have the chance to swap. Power is supplied by generator, which stops after about 10pm.

McDonald's Nananu Beach Cottages *(☎ 669 4633; dorm beds $17, cottage doubles $70 plus $9 per extra person, private house $100)* has the liveliest atmosphere. Dorm accommodation with kitchen and fan (maximum of five people) is in a new building set back in the garden. Of the self-contained cottages (two double and three sleeping up to five) the beachfront *bure* number five is the best. The private house further up the beach (up to five people; no kids) has 24-hour electricity. Meal packages (three meals) are $25 otherwise the outdoor **restaurant/bar** *(breakfast/lunch/dinner from $8/10/20)* has a nice atmosphere. Snorkelling gear/kayaks are $6/8 per half-day. You can snorkel off the jetty (lots of colourful fish) or day trips to the reefs at Bligh Water are $25 per person (minimum four people). Visa and MasterCard accepted.

Betham's Beach Cottages *(☎ 669 4132; e bethams@connect.com.fj; dorm beds $17, cottages $85 plus $10 per extra person)*, between Charlie's and McDonald's, has two spacious dorms with cooking facilities, but no fan, sleeping six to 10 people. The five self-contained beachfront cottages are clean and spacious. Discounts of 20% apply from October to mid December. Betham's beachfront café offers sandwiches for lunch (under $5) and dinner for $11 to $16.

Charlie's Place *(☎ 669 4676; dorm beds $17, cottage doubles $70 plus $9 per extra person)*, run by Charlie and Louise, offers the most privacy. There are two self-contained cottages on the hill, each with well-equipped kitchens and laundry. The more spacious one is used as a dorm and has views to both bays. The other also has a lovely view and is good for families. There is also a cottage in the garden next door. Charlie and Louise give guests mangoes when they are in season.

Nananu Lodge *(☎ 669 4290; camping per person $10, dorm beds $20, cottage doubles $40)* formerly known as Kon Tiki Lodge, is on the northwest point of the island and has a really nice beach. This place was under renovation at the time of writing and prices may go up. Accommodation is set up for self-caterers and campers also have access to basic cooking facilities. There is a small shop selling basics but bring your own food. There's a bar and deck and a wood fire stove for pizza. You can snorkel in front of the resort ($10 equipment hire). There are excellent walks from here over the hill to secluded One Beach (about 45minutes one-way). Try to make it there for mid to high tide if you want to swim or snorkel. The views along the way are spectacular.

Places to Stay – Top End

Mokusigas Resort *(☎ 669 4444, fax 669 4404; suites $286-386)*, is on a narrow, steep ridge with beautiful trees and views to the water on both sides. It was under receivership at the time of writing and part of the jetty had collapsed! It has 20 suites with ceiling fans and balcony and rates based on the quality of the views. Prices include breakfast and transfers. The hilltop restaurant/bar *(mains $19)* has great views to Mile Long Beach. Activities include snorkelling, windsurfing, canoeing, fishing, tennis, working out in the gym and diving.

TAVUA & AROUND

Tavua is a small, quiet agricultural town with lots of temples, churches and mosques. It is on the Kings Road, 67km northeast of Lautoka and 100km from Nadi. Fiji's largest cattle station, Yaqara – with over 4000 head roaming the 70-sq-km property – is midway between Rakiraki and Tavua.

The Emperor Gold Mining Company began mining here in the 1930s. Gold is Fiji's third-largest earner of foreign exchange. Most of the mine's 1500 workers live in **Vatukoula**, a purpose-built town of about 5000 residents, 9km southeast of Tavua. Take a ride on a local bus to see the contrasting housing for workers and their bosses. From Vatukoula, drivers may take the scenic back road to Ba, which passes cane farms and Indian settlements.

In the dry season head up to the hill town of Nadarivatu, from where you can hike to Fiji's highest peak Tomanivi (Mt Victoria). See the Viti Levu Highlands section later in this chapter.

Tavua Hotel *(☎ 668 0522; dorms/singles/doubles/triples $11/44/66/77, air-con room $66)*, is OK if you need to stop on the Kings Road or are heading inland for hiking. It is a classic old hotel with colonial character, sleepy service and a swimming pool. The musty six-bed dorm is near the bar where locals can also crash after a drinking binge. The self-contained rooms are clean and have air-con. The **dining room** *(meals $8-12)* is pleasant.

Regular buses ply the Kings Road, passing through Tavua

BA

pop 12,500

The Kings Road bypasses the township of Ba, and while there is not much reason for the average traveller to stay here, the bustling town is worth a look. It is 38km northeast of Lautoka and 71km from Nadi, on the banks of the Ba River. The bridge over the expansive river was wiped out by Cyclone Kina in 1993 and replaced with the aid of EU finance.

Sugar cane growing is the lifeblood of the region, home to a predominantly Indo-Fijian population. The Rarawai Sugar Mill is on the town's southern outskirts. The industrious locals also mill pine and local hardwood and produce clothing, steel, confectionery, poultry and chalk commercially.

People here are soccer mad. The local team often wins national tournaments – try to catch a match. Ba also boasts Fiji's best racecourse, and the town's horse-racing and bougainvillea festivals are in September.

Places to Stay & Eat

Ba Hotel *(☎ 667 4000; Bank St; singles with fan $30, singles/doubles with air-con $44/55, suite $66)*, the only place to stay in town, has gaudy but clean and comfortable rooms. Catering mainly for local business people it has a reasonable swimming pool and a restaurant-bar *(mains around $7)*. The local watering hole is the **Farmer's Club** next door.

Stop for refreshments at the giant soccer ball – **Raj's Restaurant** *(meals $3)*, across the Elevuka Creek from the mosque. A good option here further east of the river, is **Chand's Restaurant** *(☎ 667 0822; meals $4-7; open daily)* where takeaway curries cost $3. It's closed Sunday nights.

Local buses run regularly along the Kings Road; pick up a timetable from the FVB.

Viti Levu Highlands

The interior of Viti Levu is one of the best places to experience traditional Fijian culture. There are small, largely self-sufficient villages and settlements scattered through the hills. Koroyanitu National Heritage Park and the Nausori Highlands have some fantastic landscapes and are good for trekking. Take a jumper with you, as the mountainous inland areas can get chilly. Refer to the main Viti Levu map on pages 102 and 103.

KOROYANITU NATIONAL HERITAGE PARK

If you are a keen walker or nature lover, the Koroyanitu National Heritage Park up the mountains about 10km southeast of Lautoka is definitely worth a visit. Contact the **Abaca Visitor Centre** *(☎ 666 6644, after the beep dial 1234, fax 666 6590; admission $5)* for more information. There are six villages within the park that receive income from the ecotourism project.

Abaca (pronounced am-barth-a) village is at the base of **Mt Koroyanitu** (Mt Evans). The area has beautiful walks through native Dakua forests and grasslands, bird-watching, archaeological sites and waterfalls.

Trekking

Those who make the one-hour climb to the summit of **Castle Rock**, from Nase Lodge, will be rewarded with panoramic views of the Mamanucas and Yasawas. Local guides will take you hiking for $5 to $10. There is also a two-hour hike to the terraced gardens at Tunutunu and to the Navuratu village site. A full-day hike to Mt Koroyanitu visits the remains of a fortified village.

Mount Batilamu Trek *(☎ 0800 6720 455, 672 3311; e batilamutrek@compuserve.com)* organises 2½-day tours up the Sabeto Valley. The tour starts with a 4WD up to the village of Navilawa for a *sevusevu*. After a night in the village community hall you will be taken on the walk up to Fiji's sleeping giant (Mt Batilamu, five to eight hours). There you'll be rewarded with gorgeous views of Nadi Bay and a bed in Fiji's highest *bure* at about 1150m. On the following day you head down to Abaca and are then transported back to Nadi or Lautoka. Everything will be organised for you, including meals, drinks, transport to and from Nadi/Lautoka hotels for $355. Trips depart Tuesdays and Thursdays from mid-April to mid November.

Places to Stay

You can experience highland village culture by staying with a family in Abaca. **Village stays** are $30 per night, including all meals, for a minimum stay of three nights. Village stays are organised through the Abaca Visitor Centre (see details earlier).

Nase Lodge *(camp sites per person $10, dorm beds $20)* is about 400m uphill from the village and has 12 bunk beds, a living area, cooking facilities, a cold-water shower and toilet. Meals at the village will cost $5/7/10-15 for breakfast/lunch/dinner, but you should also take some groceries as there is only a small village shop. There are barbeque facilities and a *lovo* and entertainment on Thursday nights ($20 per person).

Getting There & Away

Abaca village transport *(☎ 666 6590)* has a carrier, which departs from Lautoka daily, except Sunday. It costs $8 per person each way. Alternatively, there are carriers for hire on Yasawa St next to the Lautoka bus station.

If driving from Nadi, turn right off the Queens Road at Tavakubu Rd, past the first roundabout after entering Lautoka. Continue for about 6.5km, past the police post and the cemetery, then turn right at Abaca Rd. It is a further 10km of gravel road up to the village, suitable for 4WDs only, and about one hour's drive from Lautoka.

NAUSORI HIGHLANDS

The rolling golden grasslands of the Nausori Highlands, in contrast to the lush rainforests of the eastern highlands, are relatively dry with patchy areas of forest. Small villages are scattered in the hills, the more remote the more traditional the villagers in their ways. Sunday is a day of rest, for church and spending time with the family, so visits to villages may be disruptive and unappreciated by the chief. The villagers in Navala are Catholic, while in Bukuya they are Methodist.

If you have your own transport the loop from Nadi to Ba, to Bukuya and back down to Nadi, or down via the Sigatoka Valley is a fun and usually easy day trip. Check road conditions before heading off, especially during the wet season, as bridges occasionally wash out. Fill up on petrol before heading for the hills as there is nowhere to fill up.

Navala

pop 800

Nestled in the rugged grassy mountains is Navala, by far Fiji's most picturesque village. Navala's chief enforces strict town-planning rules: the dozens of traditional thatched *bure* laid out neatly in avenues, with a central promenade sloping down banks of the Ba River. All of the houses here are built with local materials; the only concrete block and corrugated iron in sight is for the school and radio shed (housing the village's emergency radio telephone). The rectangular-plan houses have a timber-pole structure, sloping stone plinths, woven split bamboo walls and thatched roofs. Kitchens are in separate *bure*, and toilets in *bure lailai* (little house).

It is a photographer's delight but you need to get permission to take shots, even from across the bridge. The *turaga-ni-koro* (chief), Karoalo Vaisewa, allows tourists to visit and take photos but they must present a *sevusevu* (a gift such as *yaqona*) and donation of $15. If you arrive independently, ask the first person you meet to escort you to the chief.

Places to Stay & Eat Coming from Ba, **Bulou's Lodge & Backpacker Hostel** *(☎ 666 6644, after the beeps dial 2116; dorms/bure per person $45/55)* is 1km past Navala village and on the right about 50m before a river crossing. The lodge is run by a retired Fijian couple, Seresio and Bulou N Talili, and their son Tui. Activities include visiting the village, horse riding ($20 for a few hours), swimming, and trips up to the Talili's farm (a two-hour walk uphill), from where you can see the offshore islands in the distance. The home is on the river's edge from where you can take *bilibili* trips in the dry season.

There is a traditional *bure* in the garden or you can stay in the 10-bed dorm attached to their house; they have cold-water showers and flush toilets but no electricity. All meals and kava are included in the nightly fee. Bulou's home cooking is good, with plenty of home-grown fruit and vegetables including local dishes such as *palusami* (corned beef, onion and *lolo*, or coconut cream, wrapped in dalo leaves and baked in a *lovo*). It is best to ring in advance in case they have to stock up on food in town. Take some food as a present for the hostel owners. Bulou sells her handicrafts (pandanus mats and printed *masi* cloth) for reasonable prices.

Getting There & Away There are local buses from Ba to Navala (1½ hours) daily, except Sunday. There is one at 5.30pm, but the midday one is better to avoid arriving at the village on dark. Buses return to Ba at 6am and 7.30am and 1.30pm. Ring Bulou's Lodge in advance and they will pick you up from Navala. Carriers cost about $25 for the vehicle. The rough, gravel road has a few patches of bitumen on the really steep bits. While only about 26km away, Navala is about an hour's drive from Ba, past the Rarawai Sugar Mill, through beautiful rugged scenery.

If driving from Ba, there are a couple of turns to watch out for – at the police post take the left turn passing a shop on your right and at the next fork in the road, keep left. The road is rough and rocky, but usually passable as long as the car has high clearance – seek local advice on conditions before heading out. The Ba River floods occasionally and the concrete bridge just before the village becomes impassable.

Bukuya

pop 700

The village of Bukuya is at the intersection of the gravel roads from Sigatoka, Nadi and Ba. The drive from Sigatoka up the Sigatoka Valley is about 1½ hours, as is the journey from Ba via Navala. From Nadi along the

Nausori Highlands Rd it takes about 1½ to two hours. The chief here is an ex-boxing champion. Villagers are more or less self-sufficient for food, except for salt and meat.

Budget travellers have been coming to the village for many years, to Peni's *bure* on the edge of town, however when we past it had pretty much closed and had become very unreliable. At the time of writing new thatched *bure* were being built on a high hilltop nearby overlooking the village. The new *bure* were a few kilometres walk west of the town on the road to Nadi. It looked promising – we'd love to hear how it goes.

Getting There & Away All roads to Bukuya are rough and unsealed, and are best suited to a 4WD or if the weather is fine, at least a vehicle with high clearance. It's a bone-crunching ride in the back of a carrier ($30 to $35 to Navala; $45 to Ba).

There are several operators that take day trips into the highlands (see Activities in the Nadi, Lautoka & Around section earlier in this chapter).

SIGATOKA VALLEY

Local buses are an easy and cheap way of sightseeing. The **Naihehe cave**, about an hour's drive upriver from Sigatoka, was once used as a fortress by hill tribes and has the remains of a ritual platform and cannibal oven. **Adventures in Paradise** *(☎ 652 0833; e wfall@connect.com.fj)* offer guided tours departing Nadi/Coral Coast for $120/100, including lunch and *bilibili* rafting.

NAMOSI HIGHLANDS

The steamy Namosi Highlands north of Pacific Harbour have Fiji's most spectacular mountain scenery (dense lush rainforests, steep ranges, deep river canyons and tall

Cannibalism

Archaeological evidence from food-waste middens shows that cannibalism was practised in Viti from 2500 years ago until the mid- to late-19th century, by which time it had become an ordinary, ritualised part of life. In a society founded on ancestor worship and belief in the afterlife, cannibalising an enemy was considered the ultimate revenge. A disrespectful death was a lasting insult to the enemy's family.

Bodies were either consumed on the battlefield or brought back to the village spirit house, offered to the local war god, then butchered, baked and eaten on the god's behalf. The triumph was celebrated with music and dance. Men performed the *cibi*, or death dance, and women the *dele* or *wate* an obscene dance in which they sexually humiliated corpses and captives. Torture included being thrown alive into ovens, being bled or dismembered, being forced to watch their own body parts being consumed or to have to eat some themselves!

Women and children joined in the eating, but were banned from the formal sacrificial rites and feasting in the spirit house and men's house, known at that time as *bure*. Raw and cooked human flesh was handled like any other meat and eaten with the fingers. Priests and chiefs, as living representatives of the gods, could not touch any kind of food as their hands and lips were considered tabu (sacred). They were normally fed by a female attendant who carefully avoided touching the lips, but for cannibalistic feasts the men fed themselves with special long-pronged wooden forks. Considered sacred relics, these forks were kept in the spirit house and were not to be touched by women or children.

Mementos were kept of the kill to prolong the victor's sense of vengeance. Necklaces, hairpins or ear-lobe ornaments were made from human bones, and the skull of a hated enemy was sometimes made into a *tanoa* or kava drinking bowl. Meat was smoked and preserved for snacks, and war clubs were inlaid with teeth or marked with tally notches. To record a triumph in war, the highlanders of Viti Levu placed the bones of victims in branches of trees outside their spirit houses and men's houses, as trophies. The coastal dwellers had a practical use for the bones: leg bones were used to make sail needles and thatching knives. Sexual organs and foetuses were suspended in trees. Rows of stones were also used to tally the number of bodies eaten by the chief.

Early European visitors and settlers were understandably obsessed with cannibalism, recording gruesome but nevertheless fascinating stories. The traders and beachcombers introduced firearms and had a significant and disruptive influence on the balance of power. At this time Viti was in a state of upheaval, and warring was intense.

waterfalls). If you have your own wheels (preferably 4WD) take a detour as far inland as you can from Nabukavesi, east of Navua. If you intend to visit a village take along some kava. Sunday is observed as a day of rest.

Tour company **Rivers Fiji** (☎ *345 0147*, **w** *www.riversfiji.com)*, based in Pacific Harbour, offers trips to this beautiful area that travellers otherwise rarely see. It is well organised and has excellent equipment.

The day trip to Wainikoroiluva (Luva Gorge) is highly recommended – fine for novices and those of average fitness. The scenery is well worth the two-hours bumpy trip by carrier up the hills to the Namosi Valley. At Nakavika village the chief and his family welcome you to their home for a chat, kava and a *sevusevu*. From here you paddle downstream (four hours) by inflatable kayak over stretches of gentle rapids and past waterfalls. At Namuamua village, where the river joins the Upper Navua to become the Navua River, you take a motorised longboat (1½ hours) to Nakavu or Navua. Food, drinks and equipment are included in the price ($175/160 from Nadi/Suva or the Coral Coast).

For gorgeous gorges and more advanced rapids try the day trip to the Upper Navua River ($180, with food and equipment included). It is more physically demanding and spends seven hours on the water. The one-hour road trip to Nabukelevu village is as rough as it is scenic, then all aboard an inflatable raft down to Wainadiro or Waimogi.

Discover Fiji Tours (☎ *345 0180;* **e** *discoverfij@connect.com.fj)*, based at Navua, has two-day guided treks across Namosi Province, camping overnight in villages, as well as trips with village visits and *bilibili* expeditions on the Navua River (see Pacific Harbour and Navua in the Southern Viti Levu section).

NADARIVATU, NAVAI & KORO-NI-O

The forestry settlement of Nadarivatu (30km southeast of Tavua) is a beautiful highland area. Hike up to Mt Lomalagi (meaning 'sky' or 'heaven' in Fijian) for great views (3-hour return). The **Forestry Office** (☎ *668 9001)* can arrange for **camping**, dorm accommodation or a **homestay** with a local family (bring provisions and give money or groceries to cover costs). Alternatively, seek permission from the manager at Vatukoula's **Emperor Gold Mining Company** (☎ *668 0630)* to stay at the gold-mine **resthouse**. It is spacious and has an open fire.

Navai, about 8km south of Nadarivatu is at the foot of Fiji's highest peak, **Tomanivi** (Adam and Eve's place; 1323m), also known as Mt Victoria. Allow at least five hours return to hike from the village. Guides can be hired for $10. The last half of the climb is practically rock climbing and can be extremely slippery.

The Wainibuka and Wainimala Rivers (eventually merging to form the Rewa) originate around here, as does the Sigatoka River. Past Navai the road deteriorates, and is recommended for 4WD vehicles only. Koro-ni-O ('village of the clouds') and the **Monasavu Dam** are about 25km to the southeast. The Wailoa/Monasavu Hydroelectric Scheme here provides about 93% of Viti Levu's power needs.

Getting There & Away

The turn-off to the hills, crossing Fiji's highest mountain range and eventually ending up in Suva, is about 3km east of Tavua. The windy, rough gravel road climbs sharply, affording spectacular vistas of the coast and takes about 1½ hours by 4WD. Local bus services from Tavua ceased operating due to poor road conditions. The road from Navai to Suva is barely passable; avoid it unless you have a 4WD or are hitching with a carrier.

Mamanuca Group

The Mamanuca Group of about 20 small islands is in a lagoon formed by the Great Sea Reef and mainland Viti Levu. Just west of Nadi and Lautoka, it is popular for day trips.

Like the Yasawa Group to the north, the Mamanucas are very scenic, from larger islands of volcanic formation to tiny coral islands with beautiful white sand, coconut palms and reef-fringed beaches. Most of the habitable islands support a tourist resort (on land leased from nearby villages) and/or a Fijian village community. Most of the islands have grassland and some have dry forest areas and only a few of the smaller islands, such as Monu and Monuriki (made famous in the movie *Cast Away* starring Tom Hanks), retain significant areas of forest with native birds and reptiles. Fire and goats and other introduced animals have degraded the original vegetation.

The Mamanuca islands are usually sunnier and drier than Viti Levu. You often see heavy rain clouds hanging over Nadi and Lautoka while these offshore islands remain unaffected. The resorts usually bring in their water from the mainland by barge, and rely on generator power.

Highlights

- Snorkel or dive in azure waters exploring the beautiful coral reefs
- Surf the fantastic breaks of the southern Mamanucas
- Cruise around the island group or sail to *Cast Away* island (Monuriki) as featured in the Hollywood film
- Take a scenic flight over tiny islets with reef-fringed white-sand beaches
- Party at Beachcomber Island and parasail over the tiny coral islet

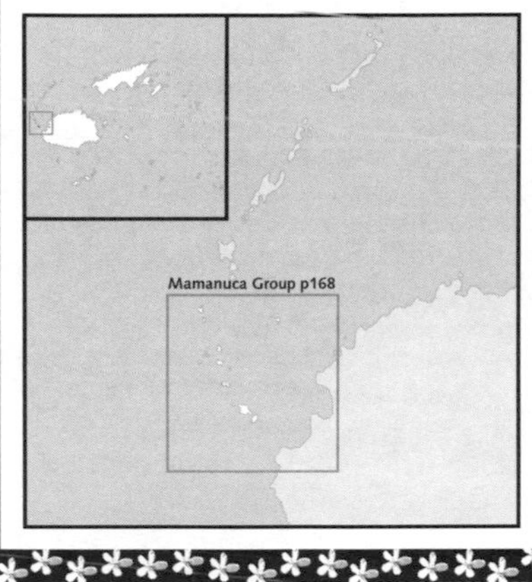

Activities

The Mamanucas are the perfect playground for water sports enthusiasts and most of the upmarket resorts have excellent facilities. Activities such as snorkelling, paddleboating and windsurfing are usually included in the price while motorised water sports such as parasailing, water-skiing, jet-skiing, fishing and island hopping cost extra.

Diving Mamanuca dive sites have an abundance of fish and corals. Gotham City is three pinnacles in a passage in the Malolo Barrier Reef; it has soft coral and is named after the batfish. You are likely to see big fish at The W dive site, which is outside the reef on the edge of an abyss.

Inside the Malolo Barrier Reef is the famous Supermarket, at a depth of 5m to 30m, where several currents converge. Here you can see grey, white and black-tip reef sharks and the occasional bronze whaler.

North Reef, also known as the Circus, has lots of clown fish, schools of pelagics, plate corals, nudibranches, feather stars and a series of pinnacles. Other sites include the Fish Store, Driwas Dream, Yadua Island, Barrel Head, Camel Humps, a cruise-ship wreck and the remains of a WWII B26 bomber. See Diving in the Facts for the Visitor chapter for more information.

Many resorts have their own dive operations. Subsurface, located on Beachcomber Island and Malololailai, is a well-respected operation. Aqua-Trek, based at Mana, is another good dive operation in the area. From Nadi you can dive the Mamanucas with Inner Space Adventures (a no-frills, small diving operation based at Travellers Beach), or Dive Tropex based at the Sheraton on Denarau. The Fiji Recompression Chamber Facility in Suva is 45 minutes away from the Mamanucas by helicopter.

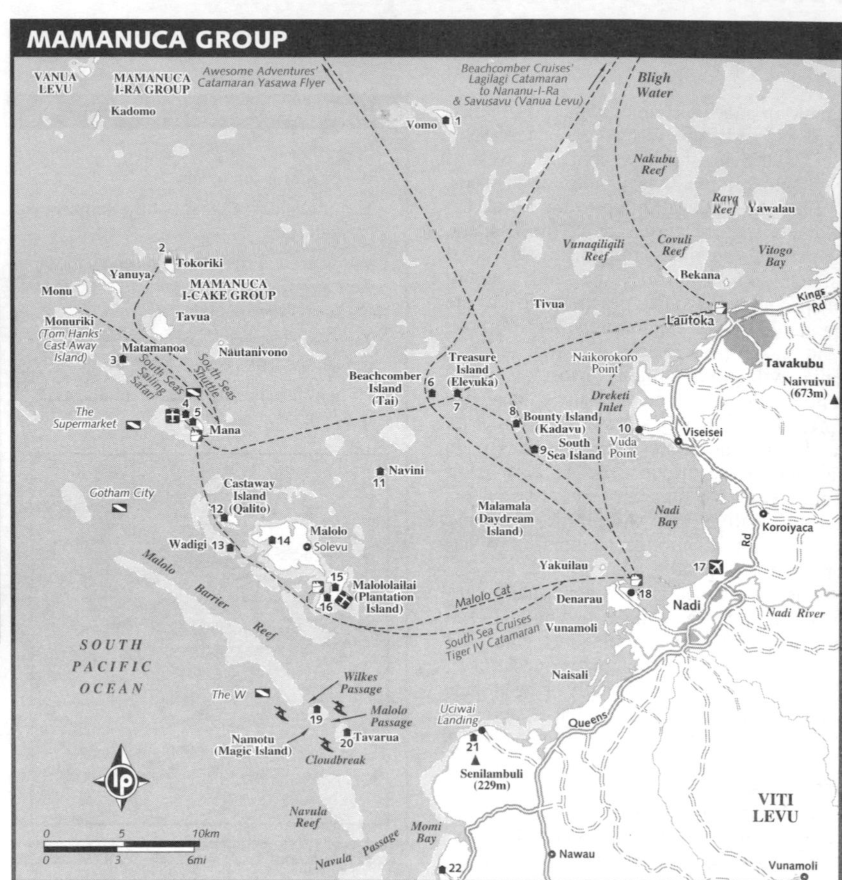

Surfing There are excellent surf-breaks at Malolo and Wilkes Passages. Surfers will have to weigh up the cost and convenience of staying at resorts close to the breaks against staying at cheaper resorts on the mainland, but with extra transport costs for each surf trip. Seashell Cove Resort and Rendezvous Beach Resort, near Momi Bay on Viti Levu, arrange trips to some of the Mamanuca breaks.

Organised Tours

Captain Cook Cruises *(☎ 670 1823; w www.captaincook.com.au; 15 Narewa Rd, Nadi)* offers a day cruise to Tivua, a tiny coral island, on board the sailing ship *Ra Marama,* a 33m former governor's brigantine. It departs Denarau Marina at 10am and returns at 5pm ($79/39.50 per adult/child). The cost includes transfers from Nadi hotels, guided snorkelling, coral viewing in glass-bottom boats, paddle boats and a BBQ lunch. The starlight dinner cruise aboard MV *City of Nadi* ($85/40 per adult/child, three hours) includes an à la carte three-course meal (wine and spirits extra); it departs Denarau Marina daily at 5.30pm. Captain Cook Cruises also has the popular three-day, two-night cruise/camping trip to the Mamanucas and the southern Yasawas (see Organised Tours in the Yasawa Group chapter for more information).

Apart from the Island Express *(Tiger IV)* catamaran transfers (see Getting There & Around later in this chapter), **South Sea Cruises** *(☎ 675 0500, fax 675 0501; e southsea@connect.com.fj)* has an interesting and

MAMANUCA GROUP

1 Vomo Island Resort
2 Tokoriki Island Resort
3 Matamanoa Island Resort
4 Mana Island Resort
5 Ratu Kini Boko's Village Resort; Mereani Vata Backpacker's Inn
6 Beachcomber Island Resort
7 Treasure Island Resort
8 Bounty Island Sanctuary Resort
9 South Sea Island
10 Vuda Point Marina & Yacht Club
11 Navini Island Resort
12 Castaway Island Resort
13 Wadigi Island Lodge
14 Malolo Island Resort
15 Musket Cove Resort; Musket Cove Marina; Dick's Place
16 Plantation Island Resort; Ananda's Restaurant
17 Nadi International Airport
18 Denarau Marina
19 Namotu Island Resort
20 Tavarua Island Resort
21 Rendezvous Beach Resort
22 Seashell Cove Resort

worthwhile full-day combination of *Tiger IV* and sailing cruise aboard the famous *Seaspray*, a two-masted schooner that featured in the *Adventures of the Seaspray* television series. The cruise starts on board the *Tiger IV* to Mana, where you transfer to the sailing ship. Then you cruise through three inhabited islands (including the island where the Hollywood movie *Cast Away* was shot, Monuriki), stop for snorkelling, lunch and village visit ($165 per person). South Sea Cruises also offers day cruises to Mana ($100), Castaway Island ($100), Malolo ($95) and South Sea Island ($90). Cruises include lunch, nonmotorised water sports, use of the resort facilities and pick-up from Nadi hotels.

Oceanic Schooner Company (☎ *672 2455;* e *funcruises@connect.com.fj*) offers a five island champagne day cruise aboard the 30m schooner *Whale's Tale* including champagne, continental breakfast, buffet lunch, an open bar and snorkelling gear. What else could you possibly need? Well, $160.

Fun Cruises Fiji (☎ *670 0243*) offers day trips to uninhabited Malamala ($79 per person). Children under 16 years pay half-price (under 12s are free). Included are a BBQ lunch and open bar for drinks (wine, beer and soft drinks), snorkelling, coral viewing and transfers from Nadi hotels.

Blue Lagoon Cruises (☎ *666 3938;* w *www.bluelagooncruises.com*) has combined cruises of the Mamanuca and Yasawa islands from Lautoka using three different luxury boats. For more information see Organised Tours in the Yasawa Group chapter.

Accommodation

In general, the majority of resorts in the Mamanucas cater for those willing to pay mid-range to top-end prices, and usually guests are on package-deal pre-arranged trips. Some have excellent facilities and services for families, while others don't accept young children. The resorts on Tavarua and Namotu, near the surf-breaks in the southern Mamanucas, cater mostly for surfers.

Along with the great increase in the number of backpackers resorts in the Yasawas, there are now more budget places in the Mamanucas. There is a dive lodge at Plantation Island Resort, Bounty Island and South Sea Island are both good and convenient options, and there are the long-established places on beautiful Mana and dormitory accommodation at the popular Beachcomber Island Resort.

Getting There & Around

Awesome Adventures' (☎ *675 0500, fax 675 0501;* e *southsea@connect.com.fj*) *Tiger IV* (also known as the *Island Express*) is a 27m fast catamaran that runs a loop from Denarau Marina to most of the Mamanuca islands, including: Castaway, Malolo, Mana ($60 one way), Treasure Island ($50), Bounty Island ($40) and South Sea Island ($30). Hopping between islands costs $40. Matamanoa and Tokoriki are linked by smaller launch to Mana ($100). Coaches pick up and deliver guests to Denarau Marina from hotels and resorts in Nadi (free) and on the Coral Coast ($20).

South Sea Cruises' *Yasawa Flyer* (also known as the 'Yellow Boat') also connects with South Sea Island and, on request, Bounty and Beachcomber Islands.

Malolo Cat (☎ *666 6215*), a fast and comfortable 17m catamaran, shuttles between Malololailai (Musket Cove and Plantation Island Resorts) and Denarau Marina three times daily ($40/20 for an adult/child one way, 50 minutes one way).

The price of a light-plane ticket is comparable with catamaran prices, and the flight is much quicker and more scenic. Sun Air and Air Fiji have daily flights (although sometimes the flights are cancelled if there aren't enough passengers) from Nadi to Mana (about $70 one way) and Malololailai (about $60). Turtle Airways offers more expensive seaplane flights to the Mamanuca resorts, as does Island Hoppers (by helicopter). For more information, see Charter Services & Joyflights in the Getting Around chapter. Note that weight limits apply to all flights.

Yachts are a fun way to explore the group and can be hired at Musket Cove Marina on Malololailai.

Warning Travelling by small boat in rough weather can be a problem. This mostly applies to backpackers travelling between Nadi and Mana; you and your gear are likely to get wet. If the weather conditions look suspect, the boat is overcrowded or there are no life jackets on board, consider taking the South Sea catamaran.

BOUNTY ISLAND

Bounty Island, also known as Kadavu, is a 20-hectare coral island just 15km offshore from the mainland. The interior is mostly covered by natural vegetation, home to some endangered bird species and some rare Fiji crested iguana. The island is rimmed by a nice white-sand beach where endangered hawksbill turtles nest and the marine reserve has some pristine coral.

Bounty Island Sanctuary Resort *(☎ 672 2852; e bounty@treasure.com.fj; w www.fiji-bounty.com; dorm bed $55, rooms or tents per person $70)* is a new budget resort, built after plans for a five-star resort were thwarted by the year 2000 coup. True to its name, it is a beautiful place with good snorkelling, excellent food and friendly staff. It works well as a quick destination in itself, or as a stopover between the mainland and the Yasawas' budget resorts.

The dorms and rooms (twin bunk beds) are spacious, clean and have comfortable beds, while the tents have two rooms for up to four people. Toilet and shower are shared, but there are enough facilities to keep everyone happy. Three meals are included in the daily rates. Activities include snorkelling ($5 per day), canoes, kayaks and sailboards ($5 per hour) and trail bikes ($10 per day). Diving and other motorised activities can be arranged with Subsurface – a dive operation on Beachcomber Island.

Transfers are by the South Sea Cruises' *Tiger IV* or Awesome Adventures' *Yasawa Flyer* (see Getting There & Around earlier in this chapter).

SOUTH SEA ISLAND

South Sea Island is a tiny sandy island southeast of Bounty and Treasure Islands. Previously know as Aqualand and set up by South Sea Cruises for day trips, it now also operates as a small budget resort.

South Sea Island *(☎ 675 0499; e awesomeadventure@connect.com.fj; dorm beds $65, double rooms per person $80)* has one double-storey *bure* with a restaurant and bar downstairs and 30 beds (mostly bunks) upstairs. The beach is good for swimming and OK for snorkelling and there is a swimming pool and lots of water-play equipment including free snorkelling gear, paddleboards, sailboards and a sailing catamaran. This island is a good stopover for trips to the Yasawas' budget resorts or for the one-day sailing adventure aboard the *Seaspray*. Prices include three good meals a day. Tranfers are by the *Yasawa Flyer* (see Getting There & Around earlier in this chapter).

BEACHCOMBER ISLAND

Beachcomber Island (Tai) is about 20km offshore from Nadi airport. The tiny island is only 2 hectares at low tide, has a great garden and is circled by a beautiful beach.

Beachcomber Island Resort *(☎ 666 1500, fax 666 4496; e beachcomber@connect.com.fj; w www.beachcomberfiji.com; bunk beds $75, singles/doubles lodge $180/240, beachfront bure $270/320)* has been operating for more than 28 years. It takes only 10 minutes to walk around the island, which is completely covered by the resort. It caters for up to 250 guests, plus day-trippers. While it is not a secluded oasis, it has the reputation of having the best party atmosphere in the Mamanucas, attracting a young singles crowd. Entertainment includes live music and grooving on the sand dance floor.

There are bunk beds in the 84-bed huge dorm *bure*. Lockers are provided. Alternatively, fan-cooled lodge rooms with fridge are good value. There are also 22 comfortable beachfront *bure*. All prices include good buffet-style meals.

Most activities cost extra, but snorkelling equipment is free for house guests. Also on offer are water-skiing ($30 per hour), parasailing ($50), catamaran sailing ($25 per hour), windsurfing ($10 per hour), jet-skiing ($80 per half-hour), canoeing ($14 per day) and fishing trips ($200 for a maximum of four people for two to three hours).

Subsurface *(☎ 666 6738; w www.fijidiving.com)* is an excellent diving operation based on the island. It has Japanese- and English-speaking dive instructors and a wide range of dive courses and speciality programmes. A two-tank dive is $180 and six dives $350, but if you are staying there for a week or so and keen to dive it is best to take an unlimited diving package for $550. Open-water courses are $615. Diving is half-price during February and March for those staying at least five nights.

Transfer is by the resort's fast catamaran and includes courtesy bus pick-ups from the airport, Nadi and Lautoka hotels ($70 return per person). Beachcomber also offers speedboat transfers for late-flight arrivals, with a $30 surcharge.

TREASURE ISLAND

Treasure Island (Elevuka) is a small 6-hectare coral island near Beachcomber Island.

Treasure Island Resort *(☎ 666 6999, fax 666 6955; w www.fiji-treasure.com; bure $395)* caters well for families and honeymooners. The landscaped tropical gardens cover the entire island which is encircled by a nice white-sand beach. It has 67 comfortable air-con beachfront *bure*, each taking up to three adults, or two adults and two children under 16 years. Optional meal packages cost $55/62 for two/three meals daily; otherwise expect to spend $13/17/36 per person for breakfast/lunch/dinner.

There is nightly entertainment in the large, open dining room/bar, a games room and a freshwater pool. The resort has an excellent kids club and baby-sitting is provided. Windsurfing, canoeing, snorkelling, volleyball, minigolf, use of catamarans, paddle boats and sail boats, coral viewing and fishing are all included. Diving trips are organised with Subsurface ($180 for two tanks or $615 for open-water certification).

Treasure Island Resort is serviced by the South Sea Cruise *Tiger IV* catamaran ($50 per person one way).

NAVINI

Navini, a tiny coral island centrally located in the Mamanuca Group, is surrounded by a white-sand beach and offshore reef.

Navini Island Resort *(☎ 666 2188, fax 666 5566; w www.navinifiji.com.fj; 1-bedroom/premier/duplex/honeymoon bure $450/480/520/590)* is a small, family-run resort for a maximum of 22 guests. It is a good place for families or couples who want a friendly intimate atmosphere away from crowds of tourists. The 30 staff outnumber the guests – one of the reasons why there are lots of return customers.

Its nine *bure* are all within 10m of the beach. Duplex *bure* have sitting rooms (maximum five people) and the more spacious 'premier' *bure* (with a maximum of three people) have a veranda on two sides. Honeymoon *bure* have a private courtyard and spa. All guests usually eat at the same table. A meal plan is $85 per adult, $49 for children six to 12 years old, and $36 per child two to five. The food is good, especially the fresh fish.

Snorkelling is excellent just off the beach along the edge of the surrounding reef. Kayaking, windsurfing, volleyball, use of coral viewing boards and morning trips, including fishing and visiting other resorts or villages, are included in the price. Diving can be arranged with Subsurface at Beachcomber Island.

Navini guests are picked up from Nadi or Lautoka hotels, taken by van to Vuda Point Marina and then spend 30 minutes in a speedboat. Return transfers cost $180/90 for an adult/child aged five to 12; children under five are free.

MANA

The beautiful island of Mana is about 30km northwest of Denarau. With its grassy hills, lovely beaches and wide coral reef, it is spectacular to fly over. There is a large luxury resort and two budget resorts next to the village on the southeastern end. The upmarket Mana Island Resort stretches between the north and south beaches over 80 hectares of leased land. The northern beach and the western beach (known as Sunset Beach) are quite good for snorkelling with lots of tiny colourful fish. Also check out the south beach pier, where the fish go into a frenzy under the night lights. Hike up to the tallest hill for a stunning view over the surrounding reefs.

Places to Stay

In the past there was a fair bit of animosity between Mana Island Resort and the neighbouring budget resorts. The resort has erected a fence and placed its water tanks along the division, to make it clear that its facilities, beach shelters and deck chairs are for its own guests only. Things between the resorts are more settled these days now that the budget resorts are getting better organised and are obviously here to stay.

While the two budget resorts appear to be part of the same complex, they are run by brothers who are very competitive. Politics aside, the staff of both places are usually friendly and the party atmosphere can be fun, but it's not a quiet escape. Year after year, we've been receiving mixed reports about both places; avoid paying too much upfront so that you have an option to change if you are not happy. You can use credit cards here but you will need to bring some cash. Beware of theft on the beaches and in the dorms. There is a shop next to Ratu Kini's reception desk selling quite a few basic things for travellers, but it is best to bring your personal items. Soap, a towel, snacks, a torch, kava and mosquito repellent are some handy items to bring to the island.

Ratu Kini Boko's Village Resort *(☎ 672 1959 Nadi; e rtkinihostel@connect.com.fj; camping per person $30, dorm beds $45, single/double bure shared bathrooms $60/80, bure with bathroom $75/95)* has accommodation of various sizes and types, from a concrete house to traditional *bure*. Most of it is set back from the beach in gardens amongst breadfruit trees almost indistinguishable from the village dwellings. One of the dorms is a double-storey large house with lots of different room compartments, while the other is smaller and closer to the beach. Prices include meals. Food quality is variable and is served buffet-style. Activities include snorkelling trips ($10 per person), kayaking ($5 per hour), visits to the island where the movie *Cast Away* was shot ($50 per person including snorkel and lunch) and island hopping $35 per person. There's also diving trips for $150 (two tanks).

Mereani Vata Backpacker's Inn *(☎ 666 3099, 670 2763 Nadi; dorms/doubles $45/80)* has a 10-bed girls dorm with ensuite, another 24-bed dorm and four double rooms. A beachfront shack further into the village is $200. Rates include three meals. Activities include reef-fishing trips ($5), four-island sightseeing ($35), a Tom Hanks picnic ($50), snorkelling, as well as a weekly kava ceremony.

Mana Island Resort *(☎ 665 0423, fax 665 0788; w www.manafiji.com; double garden bure $300, double ocean-view bure or hotel room $400, honeymoon bure $900)*, with 128 *bure* and 32 hotel rooms, is one of Fiji's largest island resorts. It was established in the early 1970s and is now Japanese-owned. Garden *bure* have room for up to four people, and deluxe ocean-view air-con *bure* are spacious, elevated and have a porch. The new honeymoon *bure* are large with open-air spas and decks just a few metres from the water. Resort facilities include a circular pool, tennis courts and a play centre for children. Up to two children under 16 years are free and rates include all nonmotorised water sports. Meal plans are available and the south beach restaurant (mains from $25) is a pleasant spot right on the beach.

There are good dive sites at the main reef off the island. **Aqua-Trek** *(☎ 670 2413; w www.aquatrek.com)* caters for resort divers. A one-tank boat dive costs $80 including equipment and open-water courses cost $600.

Getting There & Away

Mana is serviced by South Sea Cruises' *Tiger IV* catamaran ($60 per person one way). Flying is the quickest and most scenic way to get to Mana, but it may not be an option for backpacker resort guests, as the airstrip is part of Mana Island Resort (for the use of its guests only). Sun Air and Air Fiji have a 15-minute shuttle from Nadi airport to the Mana airstrip several times daily ($70 one way).

In the past, transfers to the budget resorts were in small and unsafe boats. However, lately there's a safer and more reliable boat service. Ideally, get informed about weather conditions, and definitely avoid any overcrowded boats with no life jackets or radio on board. These boat transfers depart from New Town Beach (in front of Travellers Beach Resort) taking 45 minutes to 1½ hours, depending on weather conditions and the tide. The trip costs $40/70 per person one way/return.

MATAMANOA

Matamanoa is a small, high island just north of Mana.

Matamanoa Island Resort *(☎ 666 0511, fax 666 1069; w www.matamanoa.com; bure double $450; unit double $270; min stay three days)* has 20 *bure* on a high point overlooking a lovely beach. All *bure* have a veranda and beach views (half facing sunrise, half sunset). The 13 air-con units have either beach or garden views. The resort does not cater for children under 12 and is best suited to couples who want a relaxing holiday. Rates include breakfast (meal plans cost $56/28 per adult/child) and nonmotorised water sports. Other activities include a 'honeymoon island' picnic and trips to the nearby pottery village of Tavua (on the island of Tavua). Diving is with Aqua-Trek, based on Mana.

Most guests fly or take the South Sea Cruises' *Tiger IV* catamaran to Mana and then the shuttle catamaran to Matamanoa ($100 one way per person catamaran plus shuttle). Seaplane is another option (see Getting There & Around earlier in this chapter).

TOKORIKI

The small, hilly island of Tokoriki has a beautiful, long fine-white-sand beach facing west to the sunset. Near the northern end of the Mamanucas, it has a special remote feel.

Tokoriki Island Resort *(☎ 666 1999, fax 666 5295; w www.tokoriki.com; deluxe bure $570)* caters mainly for couples but also for families. The comfortable air-con *bure* are just a few steps from the beach and rates can include up to four people.

Lunch (around $15) is served on the pleasant terrace and pool area while gourmet candle-lit dinner (mains from $2[illegible]) is in the à la carte restaurant. Breakfast and sports such as tennis, canoeing, sailing and snorkelling are included in the rate. The dive shop here is equipped with excellent boats and gear. It has an interesting clam farming dive site nearby and visits some pristine local sites. A two-tank dive trip costs $150.

Most guests fly or take the South Sea Cruises' *Tiger IV* catamaran to Mana and then the shuttle catamaran to Tokoriki ($100 per person catamaran one way plus shuttle). Seaplane or helicopter ($185 per person each way) is another option: the island has a helipad (see Getting There & Around earlier in this chapter).

VOMO

This wedge-shaped, 90-hectare island rises to a magnificent high ridge and has lovely beaches, good snorkelling and diving.

Vomo Island Resort *(☎ 666 8133, fax 668 500; w www.vomofiji.com; villas per night adult/child $900/320; min stay three nights)* is a luxury resort with a pool, a golf course and 'honeymoon island', Vomolailai, just offshore. The 28 very comfortable, air-con villas each have a spa and a mosquito-proof deck. Rates include gourmet meals and nonmotorised activities.

Guests can arrive by helicopter ($370 return, 15 minutes from Nadi airport or Denarau), seaplane ($220 return, 20 minutes from Wailoaloa Beach) or launch ($440 per couple one-way, one hour from Denarau).

CASTAWAY ISLAND

Reef-fringed, 70-hectare Castaway Island, also known as Qalito, is 27km west of Denarau.

Castaway Island Resort *(☎ 666 1233, fax 666 5753; w www.castawayfiji.com; garden/ocean-view/beachfront bure $510/550/610)* covers about one-eighth of the island. The 65 simple fan-cooled *bure* are quite spacious, sleeping four adults or a family of five, and have intricate *masi* (bark cloth)-lined ceilings. There is a nice centrally-located swimming pool/bar, an open-air pizza bar with sea views, and a great dining terrace *(all-day casual meals $10-14; the à la carte dinner is $14-22)* perched on the point overlooking the water. Alternatively pay $50 per day for unrestricted selection from lunch and dinner menus.

The resort has a clinic with a nurse, a creche and a first-rate kids' club. There are lots of activities on offer and all nonmotorised sports are free. Castaway Dive Centre is excellent and charges $90 for a one-tank dive and $450 for unlimited dives. Open-water courses are $550 per person in a group, or $695 for individual lessons. Several speciality diving courses are also offered.

Castaway Island Resort is serviced by *Tiger IV* catamaran/seaplane/helicopter ($100/240/370). Visitors staying for the day are also often accepted.

MALOLO

Malolo is the largest of the Mamanuca islands with two villages, a resort and a timeshare facility (called Lako Mai), mangroves and coastal forest. The island's highest point is Uluisolo (218m), which was used by locals as a hill fortification and by the US forces in 1942 as an observation point. From here there are panoramic views of the Mamanuca islands and the southern Yasawas.

Malolo Island Resort *(☎ 666 9192, fax 666 9197; W www.maloloisland.com; oceanview/beachfront $440/500)* is on the western side of the island. Formerly Club Naitasi, this place has been renamed and thoroughly upgraded. As well as the white-sand beach and the usual resort amenities guests can go hiking. On the beachfront there are 50 simple but comfortable air-con *bure* with verandas. There is a nice pool and a kids' club and rates, including all nonmotorised water activities, are for two adults and up to two children. There is a hillside restaurant (mains $25) as well as a beachfront bar/restaurant. Optional meal packages are $60/30 per adult/child per day. Diving is with Subsurface at Musket Cove.

Malolo Island Resort is serviced by South Sea Cruises' *Tiger IV* Island Express catamaran from Denarau ($100 return). By seaplane it takes 10 minutes to Malolo ($200 return trip per person).

Americans on Malolo

A US expedition led by Commandant Charles Wilkes visited Fiji in 1840 as part of its exploratory journey of the Pacific. His team, including scientists, artists and a language expert, produced the first reasonably complete chart of the Fiji islands. They ran into strife in the Mamanucas, however, when a disagreement with the people of Malolo got out of hand. Wilkes and his sailors tried to take a local person as hostage and the Fijians retaliated by killing some of the Americans, including Wilkes' nephew. In response, the Americans set alight two villages and killed more than 50 people.

American troops again 'invaded' Malolo in 1942, while training for combat against the Japanese. They set up an observation and signals station on Uluisolo.

WADIGI

This cute, tiny privately-owned island (1.2 hectares) is just west of Malolo.

Wadigi Island Lodge *(☎/fax 672 0901; W www.wadigi.com; island charter per day doubles $2200, extra person per day $800; min stay three nights)*, run by Ross and Jenny Allen, is a unique place catering for a maximum of six people (no children under 12). The luxury three-bedroom suite is perched atop the single hill with gorgeous sea views from the living areas and decks. It is the perfect special place for honeymooners who are on an extravagant splurge. Included are all meals (prepared by two gourmet chefs) as well as the use of snorkelling gear, kayaks, windsurfers and a 4m aluminium boat. Transfers (round trip from Nadi area) can be via helicopter/seaplane/catamaran at $370/240/90 per person.

MALOLOLAILAI

Malololailai is approximately 20km west of Denarau Island and, at 2.4 sq km, the second largest of the Mamanuca Group. Apart from two resorts, there is a time-share resort, a marina with bar, grocery and cafe, dive shop, a restaurant near the airstrip and a gift shop on the hill above Musket Cove.

Musket Cove Marina

In September each year, the **Musket Cove Yacht Club** *(☎ 666 2215, fax 666 2633; W www.musketcovefiji.com)* hosts Fiji Regatta Week and the Musket Cove to Port Vila yacht race. Yachts can anchor at the marina (year round) from $46 a week, as well as stock up on fuel, water and provisions on sale at the general store. The marina also offers a choice of charter yachts ranging in size from 6m to 32m; charter rates vary depending on duration and extent of services required.

Diving

Subsurface at Musket Cove *(☎ 662 2215; W www.fijidiving.com)* is a well-equipped dive shop, with fast dive boats and quick access to great dive sites on the Malolo Barrier Reef. A two-tank dive costs $180, a six-tank package $350, and an open-water course is $615. Plantation Island Resort has its own diving concern, Plantation Divers. It offers two-tank dives ($130), ten-tank packages ($495) and open water courses ($570).

Surfing

There is no official transport from Malololailai to the surf-breaks, but Big Johnnie, a local villager, can get you there. His boat, however, has no life jackets, radio, flares or insurance. He can be contacted at Plantation Island Resort's boatshed, and if one/two-three/four-five people go, rates are $40/30/25 per person. *Emotional Rescue* (☎/*fax 666 6710;* ⓔ *sailfiji@connect.com.fj*), a fast, 17m yacht available for charter for $1200 per day for a maximum of eight people, also offers access to the main surf-breaks.

Places to Stay & Eat

Plantation Island Resort (☎ *666 9333, fax 666 9123;* ⓦ *www.plantationisland.com; hotel rooms $190, beachfront/garden bure per single or double $385/470, per 6 adults $490/570, studio bure doubles $280)* was one of Fiji's first resorts, established in the late 1970s on the good white-sand beach.

The resort is family oriented and the atmosphere is often fun and lively, especially for children. If you are after a quiet, secluded holiday however, this is not the place for you. The 23 two-bedroom *bure* are popular and often booked out, and the 66 one-room studio *bure* are in the garden. Aircon hotel rooms cater for up to two adults and two children under 16. Those on the ground floor have direct access to the beach, while upstairs there is more privacy. The **Dive Lodge** *(per person $44)* a new addition at the back of the resort, is a budget option for those after some diving or surfing from Malololailai. It has six bedrooms with twin beds shared bathrooms and a lounge, no cooking facilities.

Meal packages are $36/55 for two/three meals a day. Otherwise expect to spend around $12 to $20 per person for lunch and $17 to $24 for dinner.

The many activities include snorkelling trips, canoeing, windsurfing, golf, tennis and even lawn bowls.

Musket Cove Resort (☎ *666 2215, fax 666 2633;* ⓦ *www.musketcovefiji.com; beachfront/lagoon/sea-view bure doubles $440/410/375, villa/Armstrong Island villa doubles from $530, hotel rooms $240)* is adjacent to Musket Cove Yacht Club and marina. It has spacious gardens, a large pool and poolside restaurant and a cute island bar by the marina. It caters best for couples and families after a quiet holiday. There are seven types of accommodation, from hotel rooms to self-catering thatched *bure*. Its newer Armstrong Island villas have over-water verandas and a private pool. The air-con rooms located on the first floor of the administration building are good value.

Dick's Place *(mains $12-30, 3-course set menu $30)* serves international cuisine with some Indian and Fijian dishes, weekly BBQs and pig-on-the-spit. Activities such as windsurfing, canoeing, hand-line fishing and snorkelling are included. Game fishing, diving and use of catamarans cost extra.

Ananda's Restaurant *(mains around $20; kids' meals $9)* is next to the general store and a change from the resort restaurants. The food is good and there is live music.

Getting There & Away

The *Malolo Cat* catamaran runs three times daily. Return fares from Denarau Marina near Nadi cost $80/40 per adult/child and take 50 minutes one way. Sun Air has a shuttle service from Nadi to Malololailai ($45 one way). It is a lovely 10-minute scenic flight.

NAMOTU

Namotu, a tiny (1.5 hectares) and pretty island next to Tavarua, has been transformed from not much more than a sand bar to a nicely landscaped resort.

Namotu Island Resort (☎ *670 6439, fax 670 6039;* ⓦ *www.mauigateway.com/~namotu/; shared bure per person $240, bure doubles $630)* is an intimate resort catering for a maximum of 24 people. Idyllic for surfers, windsurfers and divers, it is also a great spot for honeymooners. The restaurant/bar and swimming pool area is surrounded by a veranda with great views to the surf-break and open ocean. Accommodation prices include three meals a day (varied cuisine) and unlimited surfing. Drinks are extra. Children under 12 years are not accepted at the resort.

Surf-breaks include Namotu Lefts, Swimming Pool and Wilkes Passage. Use of kayaks and snorkelling gear is included in the price. Diving is arranged with Subsurface on Malololailai.

Check in and check out is on a Saturday to Saturday basis only. Generally, guests book and pay in advance, but Namotu does occasionally take 'walk-ins'. The resort will arrange for a driver to pick up its guests from Nadi International Airport or from Nadi hotels.

TAVARUA

This small coral island is at the southern edge of the Malolo Barrier Reef which encloses the southern Mamanucas. It is 12 hectares, rimmed by beautiful white-sand beaches and has great surf nearby at Cloudbreak and Restaurants breaks.

Tavarua Island Resort (*☎ 672 3513, fax 670 6395;* **e** *tavarua@connect.com.fj; bure singles/twins $300/450)* is American-run and most of the guests are American surfers on package deals. Accommodation is in simple elevated *bure* spaced along the beach. Rates include all meals, transfers from the mainland and boat trips to the surf-breaks. Drinks are extra.

The minimum stay is one week and bookings need to be made well in advance, although in the low season (December to February) they may accept 'walk-ins'.

The resort organises pick-ups from the Nadi area. Guests are driven to Uciwai Landing and there's a half-hour boat ride to the island.

Yasawa Group

This 90km-long chain of 20 ancient volcanic islands, famous for lovely white-sand beaches, crystal-blue lagoons and rugged volcanic landscapes, is (understandably) a magnet for travellers. Extending north from the Mamanucas (from about 40km northwest of Viti Levu), the group forms a roughly straight line within the Great Sea Reef. The land is mostly hilly; four of the larger islands have summits around 600m above sea level. While the relatively dry climate is a plus for visitors, the land is prone to drought, and Hurricane Gavin wrought havoc in early 1997.

The Yasawas are sparsely populated (5000), with most people living in small isolated villages. There are no shops, banks, postal or medical services and phone and radio-phones are not always reliable.

The locals have their own distinct dialect, which is known as *Vuda*. Travellers may notice that *cola* (pronounced thola) is sometimes used instead of *bula* (cheers), or *vina du riki* instead of *vinaka vakalevu* (thank you very much).

After the famous mutiny on the *Bounty* in 1789, Captain William Bligh paddled through the island group on his way to Timor. His longboat was chased along by Fijian canoes.

With improvements in transportation and the proliferation of budget resorts the Yasawa Group has become a major backpacker destination in recent years.

Highlights

- Cruise, kayak or take a sailing safari through the beautiful waters and high islands
- Hike on the high islands of Waya and Wayasewa
- Swim through the dark chambers of the Sawa-i-Lau caves
- Fly by seaplane over the spectacular island chain

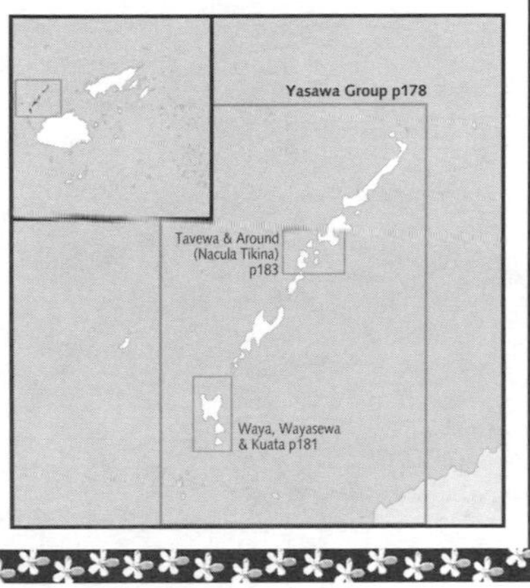

Diving

The spectacular reefs of the Yasawas have brilliant corals, walls, underwater caves, and many areas yet to be explored. Westside WaterSports is an excellent dive operation based on Tavewa (see Tavewa section). It caters for the backpacker resorts, Blue Lagoon Cruises passengers as well as the upmarket Turtle Island Resort. There are also dive operations at Wayalailai Eco Haven Resort (on Wayasewa) and Octopus Resort (on Waya).

Hiking

Bring good boots or sandals, as the hilly islands such as Wayasewa and Waya are great for trekking.

Kayaking

Australian-operated **Southern Sea Ventures** (*☎ 02-9999 0541, in Australia;* **W** *www.southernseaventures.com*) offers 9-day seasonal kayaking trips along the Yasawa chain. The trips (May to October) cost A$1890 per person, for a maximum of 10 people per group. The price includes all meals, two-person fibreglass kayaks, safety and camping gear. The pace of the tour is dictated by the weather and the fitness of the group. Expect to paddle for three to four hours daily, stopping along the way for snorkelling and village visits, and relate to Bligh's experience.

Sailing Safari

Organised sailing safaris are a popular and fun way to experience the Yasawas and a good option for the budget traveller.

Captain Cook Cruises (*☎ 670 1823;* **W** *www.captaincook.com.au; 15 Narewa Rd,*

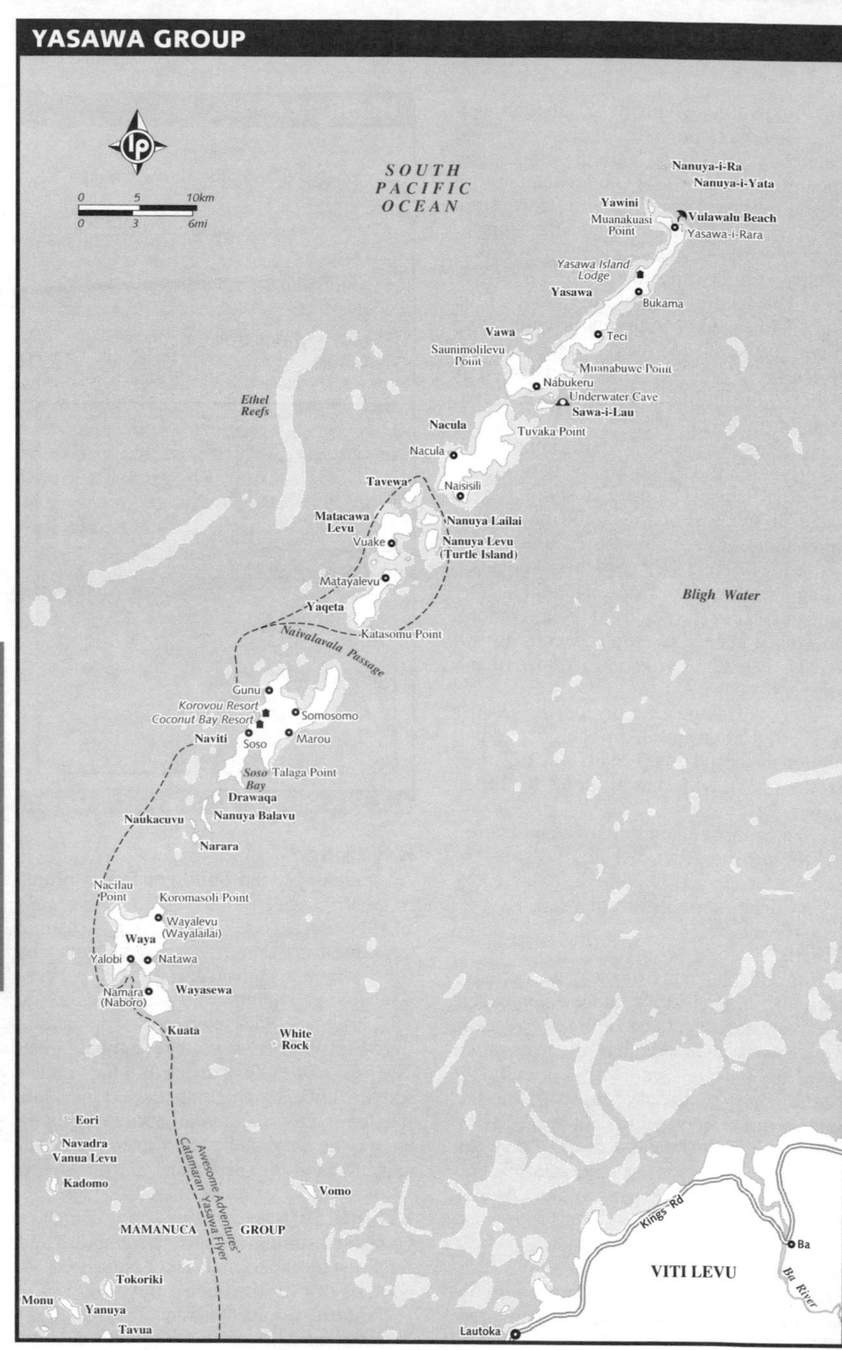
YASAWA GROUP
0 5 10km
0 3 6mi
SOUTH PACIFIC OCEAN
Nanuya-i-Ra
Nanuya-i-Yata
Yawini
Vulawalu Beach
Muanakuasi Point
Yasawa-i-Rara
Yasawa Island Lodge
Yasawa
Bukama
Vawa
Teci
Saunimolilevu Point
Muanabuwe Point
Nabukeru
Underwater Cave
Sawa-i-Lau
Ethel Reefs
Nacula
Tuvaka Point
Nacula
Naisisili
Tavewa
Matacawa Levu
Nanuya Lailai
Vuake
Nanuya Levu (Turtle Island)
Matayalevu
Bligh Water
Yaqeta
Katasomu Point
Naivalavala Passage
Gunu
Korovou Resort
Somosomo
Coconut Bay Resort
Naviti
Soso
Marou
Soso Bay
Talaga Point
Drawaqa
Naukacuvu
Nanuya Balavu
Narara
Nacilau Point
Koromasoli Point
Wayalevu (Wayalailai)
Waya
Yalobi
Natawa
Namara (Naboro)
Wayasewa
Kuata
White Rock
Eori
Navadra
Vanua Levu
Kadomo
Awesome Adventures' Catamaran Yasawa Flyer
Vomo
MAMANUCA GROUP
Kings Rd
Ba
VITI LEVU
Ba River
Tokoriki
Monu
Yanuya
Tavua
Lautoka

Nadi) has sailing trips to the southern Yasawas aboard the tall-ship SV *Spirit of the Pacific*. Swimming, snorkelling, fishing, island treks, village visits, campfire barbeques and *lovo* (food cooked in a pit oven) feasts are all part of the deal. Accommodation is in simple thatched *bure* ashore, or aboard in fold-up canvas beds below the deck cabins. Prices per person, twin share, are $540/648 for a three/four day trip.

Yachts can also be chartered from Musket Cove Marina, which is located on Malolo in the Mamanucas.

Cruises

The floating hotel/cruise ships are an excellent mid- to top-range option for visiting the Yasawas. With good food and comfortable accommodation laid on, take it easy aboard your luxury vessel, pop overboard for excellent snorkelling and diving, drop in on beautiful white-sand beaches and stop to visit local villagers. The main tour operators are Blue Lagoon Cruises and Captain Cook Cruises.

Captain Cook Cruises *(☎ 670 1823; w www.captaincook.com.au; 15 Narewa Rd, Nadi)* offers a three-night Mamanuca and southern Yasawa cruise, a four-night Yasawa cruise, and a seven-night combination cruise onboard the MV *Reef Escape*. The 68m cruise boat has a swimming pool, bars, lounges and air-con accommodation spread over three decks. Accommodation options include cabins with bunk beds, staterooms and deluxe staterooms. Prices per person, twin share, including all meals and activities (except diving) are $1270/1531 (three-night cruise) or $2668/3214 (seven-night cruise) for cabin/stateroom. Children under two years travel free of charge; those up to 15 years pay $300 to $700 per night. Cruises depart from Denarau Marina on Denarau Island, west of Nadi.

Blue Lagoon Cruises *(☎ 666 1662; w www.bluelagooncruises.com; 183 Vitogo Parade, Lautoka)* offers three-, four-, or seven-day Club Cruises to the Yasawas aboard motor-yachts. Club Cruises cost from $671/1006/1809 for two/three/six nights per person in twin-share cabins. Seven-day Gold Club Cruises aboard the luxury MV *Mystique Princess* start at $2354 for twin deluxe staterooms. Children under two pay 11% and those under 12 years sharing with an adult are charged from $165 to $522, depending on the type of cruise. Transfers, cruise activities and food are included but drinks, snorkelling, diving and equipment hire is extra. Diving is with Westside WaterSports (see Tavewa section later in this chapter). Cruises depart from Lautoka's Queens Wharf on Viti Levu.

Blue Lagoon Cruises also has a seven-day Dive Cruise aboard the MV *Nanuya Princess* or MV *Lycianda* departing Lautoka on the first Saturday of each month. It includes all the activities (village visits, kava ceremonies, shore excursions, walks etc) and comforts of a luxury cruise in addition to 15 dives at 15 different dive sites, from south to the northernmost tip and most pristine area of the island group. Prices start at $3000/2000 diver/non-diver.

Accommodation

In the Yasawas budget travellers can have the same access to superb beaches and sites as those staying at the upmarket resorts. Due to the great improvement in transportation to the islands (see this chapter's Getting There & Around text later in this section), new budget places are popping up all over the Yasawas. The long-established places, which used to get overcrowded, are facing tight competition. A dozen or so resorts in the Nacula Tikina (on Nacula, Tavewa, Nanuya Lailai and Matacawalevu Islands) have banded together and, with the help of Turtle Island Resort management, have formed the **NTTA** *(Nacula Tikina Tourist Association; w www.fijibudget.com)* to promote their area.

Budget accommodation ranges from rustic *bure* to simple cottages at the more 'upmarket budget resorts' financed by Turtle Island. Local families usually run the budget places. On some of the islands you will have more contact with traditional culture, though generally the resorts are quite separate from the village. Camping is also available at many of the budget resorts, however self-catering is not usually offered. Expect cold-water showers at these offshore budget places. There are no shops, so it might be an idea to take along your own snacks in case the fare provided doesn't live up to your expectations. Some places require visitors to stay a minimum number of nights and ask for payment upfront.

Coral's True Colour

Coral is usually stationary and looks decidedly flowery, but it's an animal, and a hungry carnivorous animal at that. Although a 3rd-century AD Greek philosopher surmised that coral was really an animal, it was still generally considered to be a plant until only 250 years ago.

Corals belong to the same class of animals as sea anemones and jellyfish. The true reef-building corals or Scleractinia are distinguished by their lime skeletons. It is this relatively indestructible skeleton that forms the reef, as new coral continually builds on old, dead coral and the reef gradually builds up.

All coral formations are made up of polyps, the tiny tube-like fleshy cylinders that look very like their close relation, the anemone. The top of the cylinder is open and ringed by waving tentacles, which sting and draw any passing prey into the polyp's stomach (the open space within the cylinder).

Each polyp is an individual creature, but each can reproduce by splitting to form a coral colony of separate but closely related polyps. Although each polyp catches and digests its own food, the nutrition passes between the polyps to the whole colony. Most coral polyps only feed at night: During the daytime they withdraw into their hard limestone skeleton, so it is only at night that a coral reef can be seen in its full colourful glory.

Hard corals may take many forms. One of the most common and easiest to recognise is the staghorn coral, which grows by budding off new branches from the tips. Brain corals are huge and round with a surface looking very much like a human brain. They grow by adding new base levels of skeletal matter and expanding outwards. Flat or sheet corals, like plate coral, expand at their outer edges. Many corals can take different shapes depending on their environment. Staghorn coral can branch out in all directions in deeper water or form flat tables when they grow in shallow water.

Like their reef-building relatives, soft coral is made up of individual polyps, but does not form a hard limestone skeleton. Without the skeleton that protects hard coral, it would seem likely that soft coral would fall prey to fish, but it seems to remain relatively immune either due to toxic substances in its tissues or to the presence of sharp limestone needles, which protect the polyps. Soft corals can move around and will sometimes engulf and kill hard coral.

Corals catch their prey by means of stinging nematocysts (a specialised type of cell). Some corals can give humans a painful sting. The fern-like stinging hydroid is one that should be given a wide berth.

Getting There & Around

If the idea of a three-hour trip on a small boat doesn't appeal, you will be delighted to hear that there are other options by sea and by air to get to the Yasawas.

Most people travelling to the Yasawas choose to go by the *Yasawa Flyer* (also called the 'Yellow Boat') operated by **Awesome Adventures Fiji** *(☎ 675 0500, fax 675 0501; w www.awesomeadventures.co.nz)*. The comfortable 25m high-speed catamaran has toilets, air-con and snack bar and departs daily from Denarau Marina at 9.15am. It takes about 1½ hours to Kuata or Wayalalai ($65), two hours to Waya ($65), 2¾ hours to Naviti ($75) and 3¾ hours to Tavewa ($85). Inter-island fares are $40 to $50.

The 'Bula Pass' ($240) is a good deal if you want flexibility, allowing unlimited island hopping for 21 days but only one return to Denarau. Awesome Adventures also offer package deals which can be worthwhile if you are short on time. Three/seven night stays (from $200/495 per person) on up to four different islands including transport, meals, accommodation and activities.

Turtle Airways *(☎ 672 1888; e turtleairways@connect.com.fj)* has seaplanes flying daily from Nadi (from Turtle Airways Base in Newtown, 20 minutes from Nadi International Airport) to Tavewa Island. It takes about 30 minutes and costs $100 one-way (a fraction of what the upmarket resort guests pay). It is a spectacular scenic flight and well worth it for at least one leg. The flight, on the small vintage planes (Cessnas or the less noisy De Havilland Beaver), is a great experience itself.

Warning Some of the budget resorts offer their own, cheaper boat transfers to the Yasawas, however be aware that the trip is quite long, across an exposed stretch of water, and weather conditions can change quickly. Depending on the weather and your state of mind, these trips by small boat can be a fun

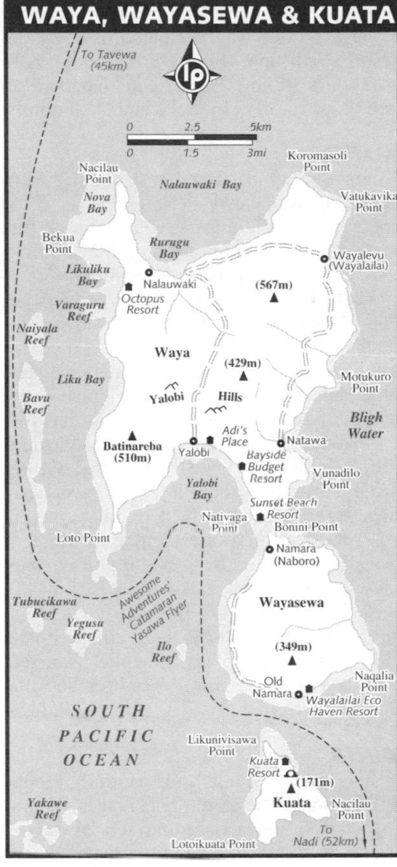

adventure or uncomfortable, vomit-inducing and frightening! Exposure to rain or too much sun may also be a problem if the boat does not have a roof. In the past, passengers have been stranded for hours due to engine failure and in 1999 an overcrowded boat sank! Fortunately no one died but, as one survivor told us, it's worth checking beforehand if boats have sufficient life jackets, a marine radio and are licensed by the Fijian government. Transfers from the *Yasawa Flyer* to the resorts, while usually only a short distance, involve the use of local boats.

Petrol is a limited resource here and travelling around by local boat can expose you to the risk of running out of petrol. So when hopping around advise the budget resorts and the *Yasawa Flyer* of your intended movements to help them plan for food and boat transfers.

WAYASEWA

Also known as Wayalailai (Little Waya), Wayasewa is in the southern Yasawas, about 40km northwest of Lautoka. It has good beaches and coral reefs. The Fijian Government declared Namara village unsafe and had it moved to its present location in 1975 after a rockslide from the cliff damaged some of the buildings. The new **Namara**, also known as Naboro village, also has a spectacular setting. The high grassy hills to the south form a theatrical backdrop for *meke* in the late afternoon light. Villagers welcome tourist groups and present *meke* and host kava ceremonies (see Social Graces in the Facts for the Visitor chapter for information on *yaqona* drinking). Many of the photos in Glen Craig's beautiful photography book *Children of the Sun* were taken on Wayasewa and Waya.

Wayalailai Eco Haven Resort *(☎ 666 9715; camping per person $30, dorm beds $40, singles $45, bure doubles without/with private bathroom $85/105)* is owned and operated by the villagers of Wayasewa and together with Kuata are the closest Yasawa resorts to the mainland. The resort is at the base of a spectacular cliff where the old Namara village used to be. Snorkelling off the beach is OK, but the best place is off Kuata, a short boat ride away. The beachfront *bure* have en suites and are the best option for accommodation. Beds in a 19-bed *bure* or a smaller eight-bed dorm are available. There is also accommodation in the old schoolhouse, which is partitioned into 13 basic single rooms. The minimum stay is three days. All rates include three meals a day. There are shared cold-water showers and flush toilets; water supply can be restricted at times. Drinks and snacks can be bought at reasonable prices, and the restaurant-bar has a lovely raised deck overlooking the beach.

Two-tank diving trips with Dive Trek Wayasewa (based at the resort) cost $140. Guided hikes around the island cost $3 per person. The hike to the top of the cliff passes through high grass, trees and sharp rocks. From the hilltop you have excellent views of the whole Yasawa Group. Other activities include fishing ($10), volleyball, village visits ($14) and the inescapable kava ceremony.

Transfers to Wayalailai can be by *Yasawa Flyer* ($60 one way per person), or by the resort small boat ($80 return, about 1½ to two hours, 40km). Guests can be picked up and dropped off at Lautoka and Nadi hotels.

KUATA

Kuata is a small island just about 1.5km south of Wayasewa. The island is quite spectacular with unusual volcanic rock formations, caves, coral cliffs on the southern end, and great snorkelling just offshore.

Kuata Resort (*☎ 666 9715, island number 666 6644 wait for two beeps then dial 3233; dorms $40, bure doubles $110*) has a coarse sandy beach frontage facing Wayasewa. The other side of the island also has a nice beach and the best snorkelling. The resort has two 15-bed dorms and many traditional style double *bure* with private bathrooms, tightly arranged around the gardens. Three basic meals are included in the daily rate. Overall, the standards here are similar to those at Wayalailai. When they get organised they take you on guided walks of the island ($8), though you can do this on your own, snorkelling trips ($10) and village visits ($14), which are both worthwhile. Transfers to Kuata are by *Yasawa Flyer* for $60 one way per person.

WAYA

Waya has rugged hills and beautiful beaches and lagoons. There are four villages, a nursing station and a boarding school on the island. It is easy to hike to the top of Yalobi Hills, from where you can see the entire Yasawa islands chain. However, hiking across the island requires more preparation as it is 10km each way over the hills.

Places to Stay & Eat

Octopus Resort (*☎ 666 6337, fax 666 6210; camping per person $40, bure garden/ocean/beach $130/150/180, shared bure per person $55*) is one of the most 'upmarket' budget resorts in the Yasawas. It has one of the best beaches in the area, good snorkelling, and a secluded atmosphere. Accommodation is in traditional Fiji-style *bure* with en suites and mosquito nets. The beach *bure* are better value as they have better views and catch the breeze. The food is excellent here and rates include breakfast and dinner (lunch from $6.50). There is solar electricity for lighting, and facilities are simple but comfortable. Activities include village visits with kava ceremony ($18), reef snorkelling trips ($20 per person), a hiking tour up the hill for nice views and lunch ($15) and volleyball. The use of snorkelling gear is free but a $50 deposit is required. They also have a reasonably good dive shop charging $150 for a two-tank dive trip, but you should be able to negotiate better rates for multiple dive trips.

On the southern side of Waya, tucked in the majestic Yalobi Bay, there are more budget places to stay. For a good snorkel you will have to take a boat to a nearby reef or walk to the eastern side of Nativaga Point. There is no power at these three budget resorts.

Adi's Place (*☎ 665 0573, Lautoka; camping per person $20, dorm beds $35, doubles $80*), at Yalobi, is on a nice, protected white-sand beach. The owner, Adi Sayaba, offers basic accommodation in a 12-bed Fijian *bure* dorm, or in double rooms in a house. Three meals are included. While the place is pretty basic, it can serve as an inexpensive base for hiking or you can just chill out and get into the slow pace of a Fijian village lifestyle.

Bayside Budget Resort (*☎ 665 1460; camping per person $30, dorm beds $40, bure doubles $100*), just a 10-minute walk southeast of Adi's Place, is run by Manasa, Adi's bother. It has a 14-bed Fijian *bure* dorm and double rooms in another *bure*. The facilities are all shared and also pretty basic, but the place has a friendly atmosphere and secluded feel. Meals are included in the price.

Sunset Beach Resort (*☎ 672 2832; **e** sunsetbeach@connect.com.fj; camping per person $30, dorm beds $45, bure doubles $140*) is at the southern end of Yalobi Bay, on Nativaga Point where a tidal sandbar connects the big Waya to its smaller neighbour Wayasewa. You can walk across at low tide, and the snorkelling on the eastern side of the point is good. It is an exposed but beautiful site. Accommodation is in simple Fijian-style *bure* along the beach. Prices include three meals.

Getting There & Away

The *Yasawa Flyer* catamaran comes past Yalobi Bay daily ($60 per person each way). Octopus Resort also has its own new boat and picks up guests from Nadi and Lautoka hotels departing from Vuda Marina on Viti Levu ($120 return).

NAVITI

Roughly midway along the Yasawas, and one of the largest (33 sq km) and highest of the group, Naviti has a rugged volcanic profile, up to 380m high. Deep inside Soso Bay, on the southern part of island, is Soso, a politically influential village and home to one the high chiefs of the Yasawas. About halfway up the west coast of Naviti, on a protected bay fringed by a long white-sand beach, there are a couple of budget resorts. The main attraction here is an amazing snorkelling site nearby where you can swim with manta rays.

Korovou Resort *(☎ 666 6644 wait for two beeps then dial 2244; e korovoultk@connect.com.fj; camping per person $24, dorm beds $40, double bure $100)* is a good budget option, well run by friendly staff. Accommodation is in a 12-bed dorm or in double *bure* with toilets and cold showers and meals are included in the rate. All *bure* are spaced along the beachfront with bay views. Snorkelling is OK off the beach. Gear hire is $5 per day and a snorkelling trip costs $15 per person. There are also village visits ($20 per person), guided hikes up the hills ($15) and fish-trolling ($35 for two hours).

Coconut Bay Resort *(☎ 994 2429; dorm beds $40, double bure shared facilities $100, double bure with shower $110-150)* is just five minutes' walk south of Korovou, on the same beach and with similar activities to its neighbour. Accommodation is fine with a 12-bed and a 20-bed dorm, and double bure all on the beachfront. The staff here are also friendly and meals, though simple, are OK and included in the price.

Boat transfers to both resorts are with the *Yasawa Flyer* ($75 each way).

TAVEWA

Tavewa is a small (3 sq km), low island right in the middle of the Yasawa Group, with nice beaches and good swimming and snorkelling. The island is freehold land with no village or chief. There are three long-established budget resorts and a new cottage among the coconut trees of the old copra plantation. The best beach is at the lovely Savutu Point at the southern end of the island, which has excellent snorkelling just offshore.

Sea-kayaks are available for hire ($5 per hour) from Kingfisher Lodge. Diving is with **Westside WaterSports** *(☎ 666 1462, 998 862;*

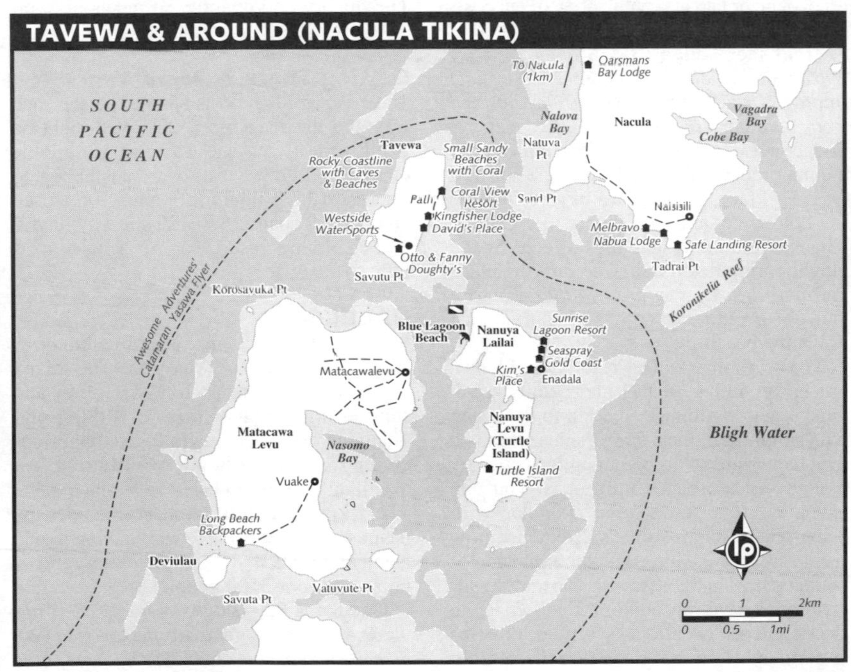

w *www.fiji-dive.com)* which also caters for the budget resorts on nearby islands, Blue Lagoon Cruises passengers, and the upmarket Turtle Island Resort (a two-tank dive costs $145, while an open-water course is $550). The dive shop is on the beach in front of Otto & Fanny Doughty's (see following).

Places to Stay & Eat

Otto & Fanny Doughty's *(☎/fax Lautoka 666 1462, island 665 2820; dorm beds $70, bure doubles $150)* has the prime spot, just inland from the lovely Savutu Point. *Bure* are dotted around the pleasant garden. The large six-bed dorm *bure* is good, though set back from the beach. *Bure* nearest the beach catch more of the sea breeze. Two of the *bure* can fit three to four people, with one more secluded in the jungle and near the beach. Harry is a great cook and prices include three excellent meals; you don't have to take the meal package (less $35 from rates per person per day) and pay for individual meals, breakfast/lunch/dinner $7/15/20. Lunch and dinner can be provided for non-guests given advance warning and everyone is welcome for afternoon tea (3pm to 5pm). A piece of cake (chocolate or banana) with coffee or tea costs $2, and ice cream is $1 per scoop.

Kingfisher Lodge *(☎ 666 6644 wait for two beeps then dial 2288 or 665 2820 contact through David's Place;* e *nacula@hotmail.com; bure single/double $90/160)*, the newer budget place, is best suited for couples after a quiet time. On the beachfront just north of David's Place, it has just one comfortable fan-cooled cottage in a jungle-like garden. You can join in the activities offered by the neighbouring resorts. Jo, who runs the place and lives nearby, can provide meals or you can go to Otto & Fanny's restaurant just down the beach.

The two other budget resorts on Tavewa are fairly similar in feel and quality. Both have spacious grounds adjacent to the beach with simple traditional *bure*. Standards can be a bit haphazard so keep your options open by not paying too much upfront so you can check out the competition. Popular with backpackers for many years, they are now facing stiff competition with the explosion of budget places in the Yasawas. The traditional-style *bure* have mosquito nets and concrete floors and are occasionally visited by crabs and mice. Both offer volleyball, nightly music and kava sessions, fishing ($10 per person), a beach trip to nearby islands ($5-10 per person), village visits ($25 per person) and trips to Sawa-i-Lau caves (about $25 per person, depending on numbers).

Coral View Resort *(☎ 666 2648, Nadi 672 4199;* e *coral@connect.com.fj; camping per person $30, dorm beds $40, standard/superior bure doubles $85/95)* has a fairly ordinary beach with some OK coral about 30m offshore. Savutu Point is a 20-minute walk away. All prices include three basic meals and one free activity per day. The three- to eight-bed dorm *bure* have concrete floors and mosquito nets. There is a basic shared facilities block with flush toilets, and a very large dining and entertainment hut where the hoards used to party.

David's Place *(☎ 665 2820, Nadi airport 672 1820;* e *davidsplaceresort@yahoo.com; camping per person $27, dorm beds $40-45, bure doubles without/with private shower $95/105)* also has cute traditional-style *bure* among the coconut trees. There are two Fijian-style dorm *bure*, one with 12 beds, another with four. Rates include three simple meals a day with *lovo* and BBQ nights. The quality and quantity of meals, as well as the services, are variable.

Getting There & Away

The *Yasawa Flyer* costs $85 per person each way and the seaplane $100, so it might be worthwhile flying one way and boating the other. Coral View has its own transfer boat to Lautoka (three hours minimum, organised on demand) costing $70/120 one way/return. Guests of other resorts can be included for a little extra.

NACULA

Nacula, a hilly volcanic island is the third-largest island in the Yasawas. The island has beautiful beaches for swimming and snorkelling, rugged hills for hiking and villages to visit. There are four villages, including Nacula, home of Ratu Epeli Vuetibau, the high chief of Nacula Tikina. The Tikina (group of villages) includes the islands of Nacula, Tavewa, Nanuya Levu, Nanuya Lailai and Matacawalevu, and is home to about 3500 people.

Oarsmans Bay Lodge *(☎ 672 2921;* e *nacula@hotmail.com; camping per person $20, dorm beds $35, bure doubles $110, family bure*

$270) is near Nacula village, on an excellent white-sand beach facing west and the lovely Nalova Bay which has good swimming and snorkelling at all tides. There is a great view to the lagoon from the 20-bed dorm in the attic above the beachfront sand floor dining-bar. The double *bure* are clean timber-clad units with en suites, louvre windows and ceiling fans. Larger family units have a double bedroom and another room with four bunk beds. Meal packages cost $35 per person. Paddleboats and snorkelling gear are free. There are boat trips to the underwater cave ($30 per person including a small lunch) or snorkelling trips to the Blue Lagoon ($12 per person). Diving can be arranged with Westside WaterSports based at Tavewa.

Safe Landing Resort *(☎ 672 2780; e nacula@hotmail.com; dorm beds $55, bure double without/with bathroom $100/160, double unit sharing bathroom $140)* is near Naisisili at the southern end of the island on a beautiful point with its own bay. It has easy access to good snorkelling, although the beach is tidal. The communal facilities have a beautiful outlook, the atmosphere is great and the staff helpful. There is a choice of standard Fijian-style traditional *bure* or clean-lined units like those at Oarsmans Bay Lodge. Three meals are included in the rate. Boat transfers from the *Yassawa Flyer* or the seaplane 'airport' in Tavewa cost $10 per person. It has free village visits, a couple of small paddleboats, snorkelling gear ($5 per day, snorkel trips $10 per person), island hopping ($10 per person each way) and underwater cave trips ($25 per person).

Nabua Lodge *(☎ 666 9173; e nacula@hotmail.com; dorm beds $45, bure doubles without/with shower $90/120)* is just west of Safe Landing on a flat grassy site with a tidal white-sand beach fringed by reefs. It is managed by an amiable local family from Naisisili, which is only five minutes' walk away. It is a great place to switch to Fiji time and absorb the local Fijian lifestyle. Accommodation is in simple traditional Fijian *bure*. One of the double *bure* has solar-powered dim lights, otherwise there is no electricity (kerosene lamps are provided). Meals are basic, but normally sufficient, and included in the prices. It has some snorkelling gear for hire ($2 per day), and boat trips for fishing or to Blue Lagoon ($10 per head), or to the underwater cave ($25 per person).

Melbravo *(☎ 666 9173; e nacula@hotmail.com; dorm bed $45, bure doubles without/with shower $90/120)* right next door to Nabua Lodge, has a similar set-up, standards and prices to its neighbour.

NANUYA LAILAI

The lovely island of Nanuya Lailai consists of gently sloping hills, mangroves and – on its western side – the famous Blue Lagoon beach, where luxury cruise boats and yachts anchor. A narrow channel separates it from the larger Nanuya Levu (Turtle Island) to the south. Travellers are advised (by signs and enforced at times by security staff) to stay clear of Nanuya Levu Island as well as the section of Blue Lagoon beach which is used by Blue Lagoon Cruises. The settlement of Enadala is located on the lovely eastern beach and has a few family-operated budget resorts.

Sunrise Lagoon Resort *(☎ 651 1195, mobile ☎ 995 1341; e nacula@hotmail.com; dorm beds $40; bure doubles without/with shower $90/150)*, is located at the northern end of the beach, and is the most organised of the Enadala budget places. It has simple traditional-style *bure* and an indoor dining/entertainment area. Three basic meals are included in the rates.

Seaspray *(☎ 666 8962 Lutoka; e nacula@hotmail.com; dorm beds $40, bure with shared facilities $90)* is right next door to Sunrise. Smaller in scale, it offers a similar standard of accommodation and has a lovely outdoor space under the trees.

Both of these resorts can take guests on snorkelling and/or fishing trips ($10 per person), as well as an underwater cave trip ($25 per person).

At the southern end of the beach there are a couple of quieter places to stay that are a little more basic.

Kim's Place *(☎ 672 3225; bure singles/doubles $35/70)*, around the point, has a couple of *bure* with shared facilities and serves afternoon tea.

Gold Coast *(☎ 665 1580; dorm beds $40, bure doubles without/with shower $77/120)* also has a few *bure*, though it was running haphazardly when we came past. At both of these places meals are included and snorkelling, fishing, cave and village trips can be organised for around the same prices as the neighbouring budget resorts.

MATACAWALEVU

Matacawalevu is a 4km-long hilly volcanic island protected by the large Nasomo Bay on its eastern side. Nanuya Levu (Turtle Island) is to the east and to the south, across a protected lagoon which is used for seaweed farming, is Yaqeta. The island has two villages, Matacawalevu on its northeast end and Vuake in Nasomo Bay.

Long Beach Backpackers *(☎ 666 6644 after beep dial 3032); dorm beds $35, bure doubles $77)* is on a lovely long curved beach with a protected lagoon. The site is stunningly beautiful and there is good snorkelling nearby, including an excellent reef drop off on the western side of the island. It has easy access to the small rocky island of Deviulau, home to local seabirds. Accommodation and facilities are pretty basic in Fijian style *bure*. It charges $5 per person for pick ups from the *Yasawa Flyer* or $20 per person to meet the seaplane at Tavewa.

TURTLE ISLAND

Turtle Island (Nanuya Levu) is a privately owned island (2 sq km) with protected sandy beaches and rugged volcanic cliffs. The 1980 film *The Blue Lagoon*, starring Brooke Shields, was partly filmed here, as was the original 1949 version starring Jean Simmons.

Turtle Island Resort *(☎ 672 2921, fax 720 007; w www.turtlefiji.com; deluxe/grand bure doubles from $2200/2700; six-night minimum stay)* is an exclusive resort owned by American Richard Evanson, who after making his fortune in cable television bought the island in 1972 for his own personal hideaway. The 14 two-room *bure* are spaced along the beach. Rates include all food, drinks and most activities. Children are allowed only during July and Christmas holidays. Transfers are by Turtle Airways seaplane charter ($1600 return per couple), a 30-minute flight from Nadi.

SAWA-I-LAU

Sawa-i-Lau is the odd limestone island amid high volcanic islands. The underwater limestone rocks are thought to have formed a few hundred metres below the surface and then uplifted over time. Shafts of daylight enter the great dome-shaped cave (15m tall above the water surface) where you can swim in the natural pool. With a guide, a torch and a bit of courage, you can also swim through an underwater passage into an adjoining chamber. The limestone walls have carvings, paintings and inscriptions of unknown meaning. Similar inscriptions also occur on Vanua Levu in the hills near Vuinadi, Natewa Bay and near Dakuniba on the Cakaudrove Peninsula.

Most Yasawa budget resorts offer trips to the caves and the cruise ships call here.

YASAWA

Yasawa, the northernmost island of the group, has six small villages.

Yasawa Island Lodge *(☎ 672 2266, fax 672 4456; w www.yasawa.com; deluxe bure doubles per night from $1500)* is a remote luxury resort on a gorgeous beach. The 16 air-con bure are spacious with separate living and bedroom areas. Rates include lobster omelettes for breakfast and all à la carte meals (drinks extra) and activities (except for diving, game fishing and massage). The resort has its own dive shop and activities include 4WD safaris and picnics to deserted beaches. Transfers are by Sun Air charter from Nadi (30 minutes, $300 per person each way).

Lomaiviti Group

Although, just off the east coast of Viti Levu, the islands of the Lomaiviti Group feel more like worlds away. Rustic and peaceful, the laidback pace is infectious and travellers tend to stay here far longer than they intended. It helps that the climate of these islands is sunnier and drier than the east coast of Viti Levu.

Steeped in history, Ovalau is one of the largest islands of the group and is the closest to Viti Levu. Picturesque Levuka, Ovalau's main town, was Fiji's earliest European settlement and the country's first capital. The sea south of Ovalau is sprinkled with the tiny coral islands of Leleuvia and Caqelai. Both islands have sandy beaches, good snorkelling and simple, budget resorts. Hawksbill turtles frequent these beaches to lay their eggs.

Gau is the southernmost and largest island of the group. With infrequent air and boat services and nowhere to stay, it's more than well off any tourist track. Wedge-shaped Koro rises abruptly from deep water. It has lush rainforest and great diving nearby, visited by adventure cruises (see Savusavu).

Lying in the east of the group are Nairai and Batiki, both lower than their neighbouring islands and surrounded by large coral reefs. Like many of the islands in the Lomaiviti (or Central) Group, they are difficult to reach and have no facilities for tourists. Makogai, northeast of Levuka, was formerly a leper colony for the southwest Pacific; these days you'll find a Department of Agriculture research station there.

Highlights

- Soak up the relaxed atmosphere and fascinating history of picturesque Levuka – the wild, lawless capital of 19th-century Fiji
- Dive among the rays, sharks and turtles of the area's relatively unexplored reefs
- Trek to the village of Lovoni, set in a lush extinct volcano crater
- Join a tour to the friendly village of Natokalau for a glimpse of indigenous Fijian life and a *bilibili* ride
- Snorkel off the peaceful, sandy island of Caqelai where you'll spot bright coral and other fantastic sea life

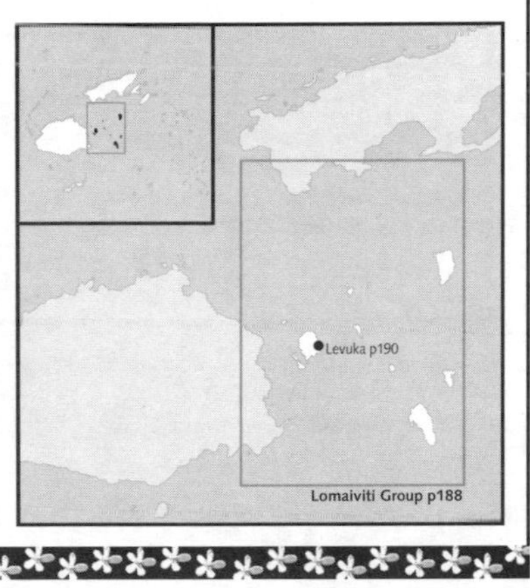

Ovalau

Ovalau's rugged volcanic landscape, sharp peaks and central crater are beautiful. The historic town of Levuka is definitely worth a visit, as is Lovoni village, deep in the extinct caldera. With lots of activities – including hiking, diving, snorkelling and island-hopping – you can easily spend a few days here. If you're looking for beautiful white-sand beaches, head for the offshore coral islands of Leleuvia and Caqelai. The annual migration of a pod of Humpback whales brings them along the east coast of Ovalau; approximately ten swim past in June, July and August. In 2002, two stopped for a rest in Levuka's harbour.

The Bureta airstrip and Buresala ferry landing are on the western side of the island, while Levuka is on the eastern coast. A gravel road winds around the perimeter of Ovalau and another follows the Bureta River inland to Lovoni village.

LEVUKA

pop 3750

Once the lawless centre of the blackbirding trade and a popular port for sailors, whalers and traders, Levuka is one of Fiji's most picturesque towns. Sandwiched between the sea and lush, green mountains, its colourful

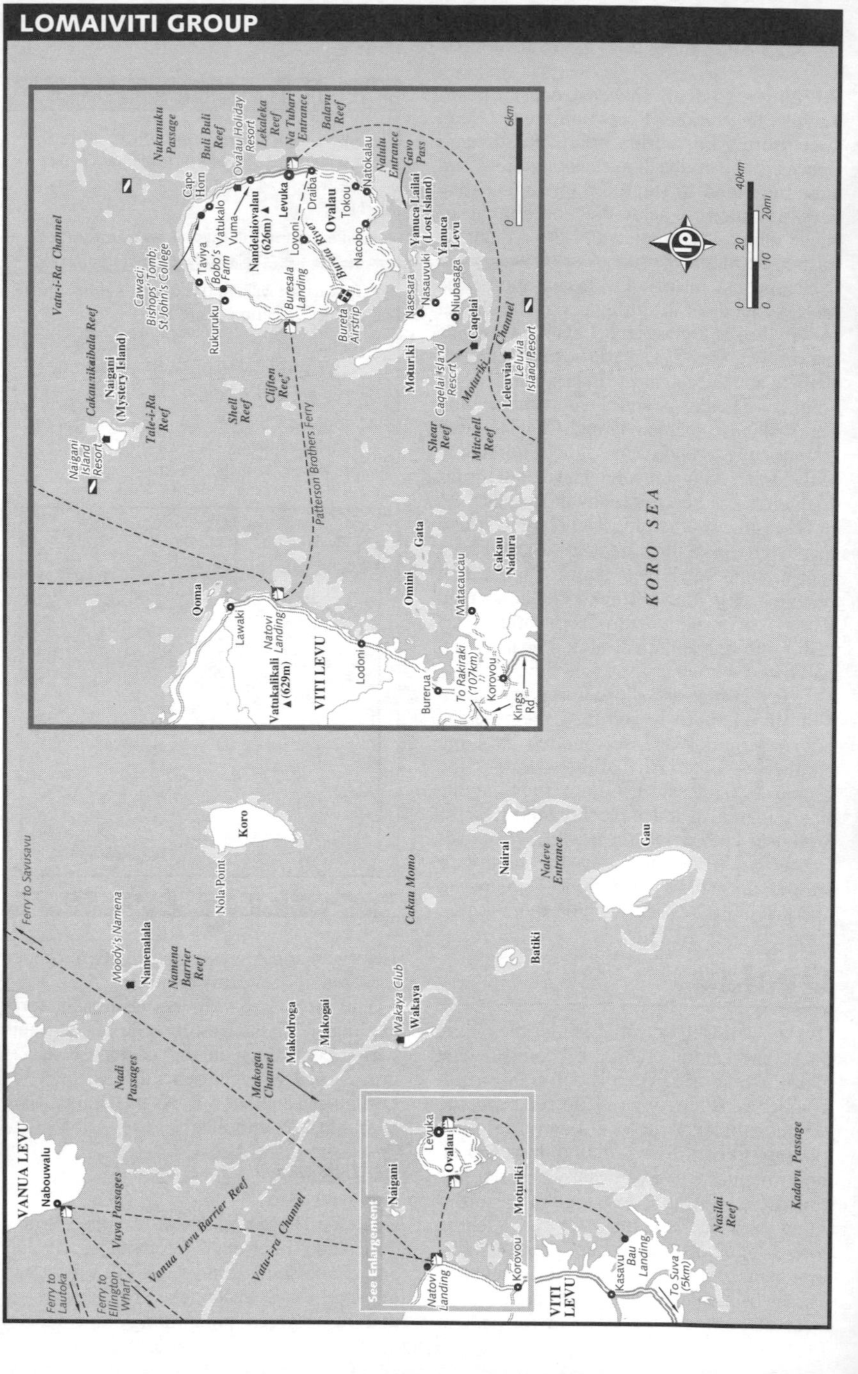

LOMAIVITI GROUP

VANUA LEVU
Nabouwalu
Ferry to Lautoka
Ferry to Ellington Wharf
Ferry to Savusavu
Vuya Passages
Nadi Passages
Moody's Namena
Namenalala
Namena Barrier Reef
Vanua Levu Barrier Reef
Vatu-i-ra Channel
Makogai Channel
Makodroga
Makogai
Nola Point
Koro
Wakaya Club
Wakaya
Cakau Momo
See Enlargement
Naigani
Natovi Landing
Levuka
Ovalau
Korovou
Moturiki
VITI LEVU
Kasavu
Bau Landing
To Suva (5km)
Nasilai Reef
Batiki
Nairai
Naleve Entrance
Gau
Kadavu Passage
KORO SEA
0 20 40km
0 10 20mi

Vatu-i-Ra Channel
Naigani Island Resort
Cakaunikaibala Reef
Naigani (Mystery Island)
Tale-i-Ra Reef
Cawaci; Bishops' Tomb; St John's College
Nukunuku Passage
Cape Horn
Buli Buli Reef
Qoma
Lawaki
Rukuruku
Taviya
Bobo's Farm
Vatukalo
Vuma
Ovalau Holiday Resort
Shell Reef
Nandelaiovalau (626m)
Lekaleka Reef
Vatukalikali (629m)
Natovi Landing
Clifton Reef
Buresala Landing
Lovoni
Levuka
Na Tubari Entrance
VITI LEVU
Patterson Brothers Ferry
Draiba
Bureta River
Ovalau
Balavu Reef
Bureta Airstrip
Tokou
Lodoni
Nacobo
Natokalau
Nalulu Entrance
Moturiki
Nasesara
Yanuca Lailai (Lost Island)
Gavo Pass
Omini
Gata
Nasauvuki
Burerua
Shear Reef
Caqelai Island Resort
Yanuca Levu
Niubasaga
To Rakiraki (107km)
Matacaucau
Mitchell Reef
Moturiki Channel
Caqelai
Korovou
Cakau Nadura
Leleuvia
Leleuvia Island Resort
Kings Rd
0 6km

downtown looks like it's been lifted straight out of a Wild West film. Its tiny population is surprisingly diverse and extremely welcoming to visitors. You'll also find good food, excellent accommodation and lots to do.

As early as 1806, sandalwood traders were stopping at Levuka in search of supplies. Traders began settling here in the 1830s. They built schooners, traded throughout Fiji for bêche-de-mer, turtle shells and coconut oil and eventually began intermarrying with the Fijian population. Other than occasional raids by the Lovoni villagers from the centre of Ovalau, the community was well protected both by the chief of Levuka and the harbour's Lekaleka Reef.

Levuka's heyday was in the mid- to late 19th century; by the 1850s it had become increasingly rowdy, with a reputation for wild drunkenness and violence. In the 1870s a flood of planters and other settlers came to Fiji, and the booming town had a population of about 3000 Europeans and 52 hotels. While the northern end of town was swept away in hurricanes of 1888 and 1905, many of the boom-time buildings remain.

In 1825 the coastal villagers ended their alliance with the chief of Verata (a village on Viti Levu's Rewa Delta), and gave allegiance to Ratu Seru Cakobau, the powerful chief of Bau (an island off the southeast coast of Viti Levu). Cakobau attempted unsuccessfully to form a national government in 1871, and in 1874 ceded Fiji to Great Britain. Fiji thus became a British colony and Levuka was proclaimed its capital. (For more information see the History section in the Facts about Fiji chapter.) It soon became apparent that Levuka was unable to develop as a capital due to the constraints of terrain, and the government was officially moved to Suva in 1882. By the end of the 19th century, trade was also shifting to Suva, and with copra markets plummeting in the 1930s, Levuka declined further.

Today, much of the population remains of mixed Fijian and European descent, with a scattering of Indo- and Chinese-Fijians and a small expat community. You'll soon catch wind of the island's main employer, the Pacific Fishing Company (Pafco), which is located on the edge of Levuka. The rest of the town seems to have been frozen in time; slow-paced and charming, tourism is becoming increasingly important.

Orientation & Information

Beach Street is Levuka's main drag and is lined with historic shopfronts; it's worth strolling along the waterfront walkway. Beach Street continues as a ring road around the island's perimeter. The north of town is marked by Gun Rock and you can follow your nose to the Pafco tuna cannery at the southern end, whose modern buildings contrast starkly with the rest of town.

Ovalau Tourist Information Centre *(Community Centre, Morris Hedstrom Bldg; open 8am-1pm & 2pm-4.30pm Mon-Fri)* features friendly staff who will do their best to help you hunt down any information you're after. You may also want to ask at the Whale's Tale restaurant or Ovalau Watersports. Both have lots of tour notices, accommodation advertisements and friendly owners.

Westpac *(Beach St; open 9.30am-12.30pm & 1.30pm-3pm Mon-Thur, 9.30am-4.30pm Fri)* exchanges travellers cheques and foreign currency and gives cash advances on Visa or MasterCard. **National Bank** *(Beach St; open 9am-4pm Mon, 9.30am-4pm Tue-Fri)* also exchanges travellers cheques and currency.

The **post office** *(Beach St; open 8am-1pm & 2pm-4pm Mon-Fri, 8am-10.30am Sat)* is near Queen's Wharf at the southern end of Beach St; there's a card-phone outside. **The Royal Hotel** has a computer in its office where you can get online for $0.20 per minute.

Air Fiji Travel Centre *(☎ 344 0139, fax 344 0252)* is opposite the community centre. From Ovalau, it only flies to Suva but will book onward flights throughout the rest of Fiji; credit-card payments are accepted. **Patterson Brothers Shipping** *(☎ 344 0125; Beach St; open 8.30am-4.30pm Mon-Fri)* is near the market; see Getting There & Away later in this chapter.

In an emergency, dial ☎ 000 for the ambulance or police. Otherwise, contact the **Levuka Hospital** *(☎ 344 0152; Beach St; outpatient treatment 8.30am-1pm & 2pm-4pm Mon-Fri, 8am-noon Sat, emergencies only after hrs)* at the northern end of town or the **police station** *(☎ 344 0222; Totogo Lane)*.

Walking Tour

A good start is Nasova, about 10 minutes' walk south of the Pafco cannery, where the Deed of Cession was signed in 1874. Surrounded by a white picket fence, **Cession Site** has a memorial commemorating the event.

Across the road is the **Provincial Bure**. In 1970, Prince Charles used it as his headquarters, something locals are sure to tell you. From Fiji's independence until 1994, it was used by the local Provincial Government for meetings and ceremonies. The interior is decorated with woven mats and the walls are still hung with pictures of leaders and Cabinets through the ages. The door to the *bure* is usually open but it's best to ask permission in the building around the back. Next door is **Nasora House**, once the Governor's House and now government headquarters for Fiji's Eastern District. The small building furthest south is where Prince Charles stayed when he visited in 1970 (something else locals will definitely point out). Today it's home to Town Council.

The tuna cannery (Pafco), at the southern end of Levuka, employs about 1000 people, roughly 30% of Ovalau's working population. The factory was established in 1964 as a joint venture between two Japanese companies and the Fijian government to boost the town's dying economy. The Japanese contingency was bought out by the Fijian government in 1987 but the plant floundered and, recently, a new joint-venture was established with an American company. The site has since seen refurbishment, expansion and an increase in employees. The facility processes about 15,000 metric tonnes of tuna (skipjack, yellow fin and albacore) per year from waters around Fiji and other Pacific nations, including the Solomon Islands and Kiribati. It is packed under about 30 different brand names.

Head north along **Beach Street** where the streetscape dates from the late 19th and early 20th centuries. Just in front of the post office is the site of the original **Pigeon Post**, marked by a drinking fountain in the centre of the road. From the timber loft that stood here, pigeons provided the first postal link between Levuka and Suva. The birds flew the distance in under 30 minutes.

A few doors down stands the former **Morris Hedstrom** trading store (1868), the original and first MH store in Fiji. Behind its restored facade is the Levuka Community Centre, library and a branch of the Fiji Museum. A handicraft centre for local artisans is also scheduled to open here soon. The **Fiji Museum** *(admission $2; open 8am-1pm & 2pm-4.30pm Mon-Fri)* appears small but has an amazing number of artefacts and amount

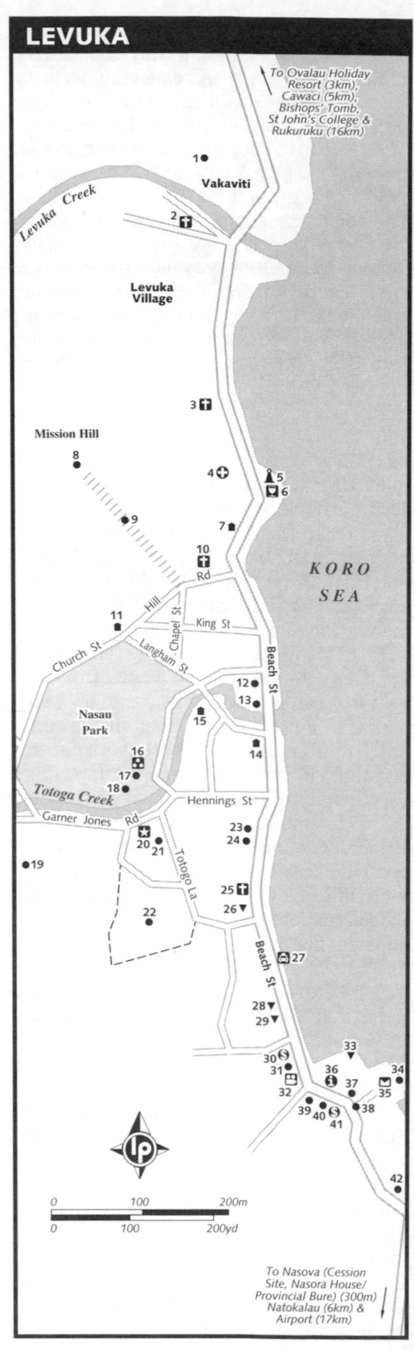

LEVUKA

PLACES TO STAY
7 Mavida Guest House
11 Levuka Homestay
14 Mary's Holiday Inn
15 The Royal Hotel

PLACES TO EAT
26 Emily Cafe
28 Whale's Tale
29 Kim's Paak Kum Lounge; Inn's Boutique Fashion Wear
33 Coffee in the Garden

OTHER
1 Gun Rock
2 Methodist Church & Cemetery
3 Church of the Holy Redeemer
4 Hospital
5 Niukaube Hill War Memorial
6 Levuka Club
8 Methodist School
9 199 Steps of Mission Hill
10 Navoka Methodist Church
12 Patterson Brothers Shipping
13 Market
16 Ruins of Masonic Lodge
17 Former Town Hall
18 Ovalau Club
19 Levuka Public School
20 Police Station
21 Old Police Station
22 Marist Convent School
23 Katudrau Trading Mini-Market
24 Bakery
25 Sacred Heart Church
27 Taxi & Carrier Stand
30 National Bank
31 Levuka Amusement Centre
32 Levuka Cinema; Cinema Café
34 Queen's Wharf
35 Post Office; Customs Office
36 Former Morris Hedstrom Building; Ovalau Tourist Information Centre; Library; Museum
37 Ovalau Watersports
38 Site of Pigeon Post
39 Air Fiji Travel Centre
40 General Store
41 Westpac Bank
42 Pafco Cannery

of information packed into it. It offers a quick lesson in the more interesting stories from local history with old photos of Levuka, intricately carved clubs, a beautiful sitar and hundreds of labelled seashells.

Many of Levuka's original religious and community buildings are still intact. Have a nose-in at the timber interior of the **Sacred Heart Church** *(Beach Street)*, which dates from 1858. The clock in the tower has sounded the time since 1898. From there, head west along Totogo Lane to explore the backstreets. The **Marist Convent School** (1891) is now a busy co-ed primary school. The school was built largely of coral-stone in an attempt to protect it from hurricanes and it remains an impressive monument against the mountain backdrop. It was originally a girls' school opened by Catholic missionaries and run by Australian and French nuns. In 1919, it was converted into a temporary hospital during an influenza epidemic that claimed about five lives a day.

The little weatherboard building on Totogo Lane was Levuka's original **police station** (1874), and across Totoga Creek in Nasau Park you'll find Fiji's first private club – the colonial-style timber **Ovalau Club** (1904). Ask the bartender to show you a letter written by Count Felix von Luckner during WWI, just before his capture on nearby Wakaya. At the time, German enemy ships cruised these waters to sink Allied vessels. His own ship having sunk, the Count attempted to avoid arrest by disguising himself as an English writer on a sporting cruise and signed the letter from Max Pemberton. Next door to the Ovalau Club is the **old town hall** (1898), built in typical British colonial style in honour of Queen Victoria's silver jubilee.

Alongside this, you'll find the stone shell of the South Pacific's first **Masonic Lodge** (1875), burnt to the ground in the heat of the 19 May 2000 coup. So the story goes, a riotous group of people came down from Lovoni in rampant support of George Speight. They headed for the Queen's Wharf but were turned away by armed soldiers, and instead fell upon the Masonic Lodge. Local Methodist leaders had long alleged that the secret Masonic society was in league with the devil and that tunnels led from beneath the lodge to Nasora House, the Royal Hotel, and through the centre of the world to Masonic HQ in Scotland. Some say that church leaders egged the Lovoni mob on and watched in delight as the building went up in smoke.

Return across the creek and follow Garner Jones Rd west to the **Levuka Public School** (1881). This was Fiji's first formal school and many of Fiji's prominent citizens were educated here including Percy Morris and Maynard Hedstrom. If you continue up the steps behind the school you can join some of the locals for a chat at a popular resting spot. Walk back down to Garner Jones Rd, turn left into Church St and pass Nasau Park. There are many old colonial homes on the hillsides and the **199 Steps of Mission Hill** are worth climbing for the fantastic view. The very simple coral and stone Gothic-style **Navoka Methodist Church** (1860s) near the foot of the steps is one of the oldest churches in Fiji.

Head south along Chapel St then east along Langham St and across the creek. **The Royal Hotel** (1860s) is Fiji's oldest hotel, rebuilt in 1903. It is the lone survivor of the once-numerous pubs of the era. Originally it had an open veranda with lace balustrading, but this was built in to increase the size of the rooms.

Back on Beach St, continue north to **Niukaube Hill**, on a point near the water. This was once the site of Ratu Cakobau's Supreme Court and Parliament House. This is also where the first indentured Indian labourers landed in Fiji after being forced to anchor offshore for several weeks in an attempt to control an outbreak of cholera. The site now has a memorial to locals who fought and died in WWI and WWII.

North of here is the Anglican **Church of the Holy Redeemer** (1904). This church was the third attempt; the first two churches were whipped away by hurricanes. Inside, the colourful stained glass was brought from Europe and depicts early residents of Levuka.

Levuka village, once the home of Tui Cakobau, is 200 metres further north. In the **cemetery** next to the village's Methodist Church, you'll find the grave of American consul JB Williams who died in 1860. It was his claims for financial compensation that led Cakobao to hand over Fiji to Britain.

With the chief's permission you can climb the prominent **Gun Rock** for a great view of Levuka. In 1849 Commodore Wilkes, of the US Exploring Expedition, pounded this peak from his ship with cannon fire in an attempt to impress the chief of Levuka. (See the 'Americans on Malolo' boxed text in the Mamanuca chapter for more on Wilkes.) Commodore Goodenough repeated the 'entertainment' in 1874. You can still find cannon ball scars on the rock.

Walk, cycle or take a taxi the 5km north to Cawaci, where you'll find Gothic-style **Bishops' Tomb** (1922) where Fiji's first and second Roman Catholic bishops are entombed on a point overlooking the sea. From here you can see the limestone and coral **St John's College** (1894), where the sons of Fijian chiefs were educated in English.

Cycling

Cycling is a good way to explore Levuka and its surrounding area. The road to the south is fairly flat, and the north is OK until about Vatukalo, after which it gets very hilly. Mountain bikes are available from **Inn's Boutique Fashion Wear** (*☎ 344 0374; 1/4/8 hrs $3/10/15; open 9am-5pm Mon-Fri, 9am-1pm Sat*) and from **Ovalau Watersports** (*☎ 344 0166; 1hr $5, half/full day $10/15; open 8.30am-4pm or 5pm*). The closing times of both rental shops is 'flexible' – check before you set off for the day.

Diving & Snorkelling

The Lomoviti waters offer some great dive sites where you can encounter manta rays, hammerheads, turtles, white-tip reef sharks and lion fish. Colourful hard and soft coral also makes for good reef snorkelling. **Ovalau Watersports** (*☎ 344 0166, fax 344 0633; W www.owlfiji.com; open 8.30am-4pm Mon-Sat*) offers two-tank dives with good gear for $130 per person (minimum of two divers, maximum eight). You can also take your PADI open-water course here for $460 with instruction in English or German. Reef snorkelling trips cost $30 per person.

Organised Tours

Epi's Tour (*10am, Mon-Sat*) takes you uphill through the rainforest and into the crater of an extinct volcano. This is the centre of Ovalau and the site of Lovoni village. Run by the charismatic Epi, a local of Lovoni, this tour is extremely popular. As mist drifts through this colourful village and you sit surrounded by the lush peaks of the volcano, Epi brings history to life through his fantastic storytelling. From the first foot set upon the island to present day, the epic is rife with love, trickery, war and slavery. Epi is also extremely knowledgeable about local herbal remedies and will point out lots of examples during your trek. The tour is a combination of trekking and transport on local carrier. Once you've reached the village and presented your *sevusevu*, you can take a dip in the river. A delicious lunch is provided in one of the village homes. The full day costs $30/40/50 per person for 4/3/2 people. Book the tour through Ovalau Watersports.

Natokalau Village Tour (*9.45am-3pm Mon-Sat*) is an excellent way to experience genuine village life. Kali, your friendly guide, will take you home to Natokalau, about 6km south of Levuka. The tour is completely unpretentious – as you are guided around the village you'll encounter locals going about

Bishop's tomb, Ovalau

Colonial buildings in the former capital of Levuka

Main street, Levuka

ALL PHOTOGRAPHS BY ROBYN JONES

LIZ THOMPSON

Kayaking at Taveuni Island

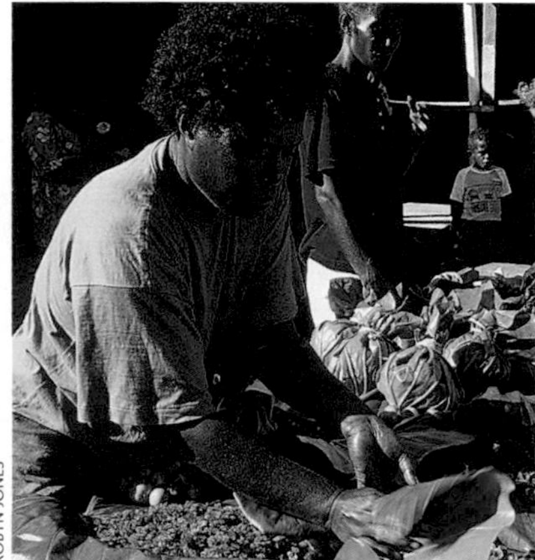
ROBYN JONES

Open-air market, Savusavu, Vanua Levu

ROBYN JONES

Toilets at Nukubolu village, Vanua Levu

ROBYN JONES

Jungle outside Waiyevo, Taveuni

their daily tasks of weaving mats, farming and preparing meals. Kali will take you on a trek up the hillside to Natokalau's original site and on to the burial grounds of his ancestors. Both of these areas are tabu and require you to present a *sevusevu* to the chief first. Kali is extremely good-natured and will teach you about the plants you pass en route, fetch fresh coconuts for you, tell you local legends, and take you on a *bilibili* ride at sea. The tour includes lunch in the village and costs $27.50 per person. Book in advance at Ovalau Watersports.

Henry Sahai *(☎ 344 0096; Mon-Sat)*, a senior citizen of Levuka, will take you on a walking tour of the town, sharing his knowledge of local history and his experiences of living here for around 90 years. The cost is $8 per person; you can book through The Royal Hotel but it's more reliable to book through Henry himself or Ovalau Watersports.

Tea & Talanao Tours are run through Ovalau Watersports. *Talanoa* means 'have a chat', which is exactly what you'll do. Visit the homes of local residents for an insider's perspective on life in Levuka. The cost is $15 per person.

Places to Stay

Levuka Homestay *(☎/fax 344 0777; Church Street; ⓔ levukahomestay@connect.com.fj; ⓦ www.levukahomestay.com; singles/doubles $115/130 including breakfast, extra person $40)* is pure comfort. Newly built and gorgeous, it has a gob-smacking view over the sea and a huge deck with hammocks to enjoy it from. Rooms are beautiful, each unique and tastefully decorated. The atmosphere is relaxed, the lounge has lots of books and videos that you can borrow, and the laid-back owners will go out of their way to ensure that you enjoy your stay in Levuka. Breakfast is straight from your homesick fantasies of banana pancakes, muesli, bacon and eggs and will keep you full for the day. Room rates are extremely reasonable for what's on offer.

The Royal Hotel *(☎ 344 0024, fax 344 0174; ⓔ Royal@connect.com.fj; dorms/singles/doubles/triples $10/18/28/35, cottages $80, all with en suite except dorms, payment by cash only)*, next to Totoga Creek, is the town's most unique option. The weatherboard building is Fiji's oldest hotel and oozes colonial atmosphere, even if it is getting a bit worn at the edges. Each room is a little different from the next, including the tilt of its floor and how lumpy the mattress is. Try to get a room at the front as they have lovely views of the sea. Dorms are in a separate colonial-style house with kitchen facilities. There are more recently built air-con cottages in the front garden (max three people) and a small variety of self-contained cottages in the back garden. The hotel has a gorgeous pool, a bar, a billiard room and shows videos each night at 8pm (sharp!). All facilities are for guests only. Staff range from friendly to…shall we assume hard of hearing?

Mavida Guest House *(☎ 344 0477; dorms/doubles with shared bathroom $10-15/20-30, including breakfast & mosquito nets)* is a rambling house that dates back to the 1860s. With lots of sitting areas, verandas and wooden floors, it's an excellent budget choice. Staff are extremely friendly and shared facilities are clean. Four-bed dorm rooms are spread throughout the house; to reach some private rooms you have to go through a dorm or two.

Mary's Holiday Inn *(☎ 344 0013; Beach St; dorms/singles/doubles with shared bathroom $8/14/27)*, round the corner from The Royal Hotel, has the cheapest beds in town, hot showers, hardwood floors and friendly proprietors. There are no locks on the bedroom doors and, if you're a stickler for clean bedding, you may want to use your own sleeping bag.

Ovalau Holiday Resort *(☎/fax 344 0329; camping per person $10, dorm beds with breakfast $9.50, singles/doubles $35/70, extra person $20)* is about 3km north of Levuka, facing a small bay. Unfortunately, it's getting a bit rundown with nocturnal visits by nibbling rodents. The six-bedroom dorm is fan-cooled and has kitchen facilities, while private rooms are in self-contained weatherboard cottages (maximum six people). There's an OK beach across the road where you can snorkel and kayaks can be hired for $5 per hour. The menu at the pleasant **restaurant** *(breakfast/lunch/dinner $6.50/9.50/15.50; open 7am-9am, noon-2pm and 6.30pm-9pm daily)* changes daily but usually includes fresh seafood. Transport can be arranged by the resort; a taxi from Levuka will cost about $5.

Places to Eat

Restaurants The cosy **Whale's Tale** *(☎ 344 0235; 3-course special $14, mains $9; open 11am-3pm & 5pm-9pm Mon-Sat)* has fantastic soups, salads, seafood and pasta dishes, all made from fresh ingredients. The vegetarian dishes are tasty, the three-course special is a steal and desserts are divine. This place is very popular; it's a good idea to get there early or book a table.

Kim's Paak Kum Lounge *(☎ 344 0059; mains $8; open 7am-2pm & 6pm-9pm Mon-Sat, noon-2pm & 6pm-9pm Sun)* is a great place to dine, especially on the balcony overlooking the water. With an epic menu of Asian and Fijian dishes, it'll keep vegetarians and carnivores happy. Stumped for choice? Try the Thai curry – it's superb. There are also prawns in *lolo*, chicken in oyster sauce and huge bowls of soup. For breakfast there's pancakes and fresh, giant-sized scones. Staff are ultra-friendly.

Emily Café *(☎ 344 0382; pizza $7; open 7am-2pm & 6pm-9pm Mon-Sat)* is a good place to stop for an egg-bun in the morning. It's very basic but friendly and, in the evening, serves great pizza.

Coffee in the Garden *(☎ 344 0471; drinks/snacks/Sunday breakfast $2.50/2/3.50; open 8am-6pm Mon-Sat, 9am-11.30am Sun)* is quite literally that – a secluded garden on the seafront where you can sip iced coffees and nibble on muffins, quiche or calamari. To find it, enter through the large gate to the left of the Community Centre. Tables are set under palm trees and Sunday sees them fill up quickly for a fry-up breakfast.

Cinema Café *(☎ 344 0666; drinks $2; open 8am-4pm Mon-Sat)* is a funky, bright place to have a coffee or a milkshake to the upbeat tunes of old MTV on video. Across from the Community Centre, it's also a great spot for people-watching along Levuka's main drag.

Self-Catering On Saturdays, there's a **produce market** on the north side of Totoga Creek. You can get fresh bread at the **bakery** and most everything else at **Katudrau Trading Mini Market** and the **General Store**, all on Beach St.

Entertainment

Levuka's wild days are long gone and the sleepy town doesn't offer a great deal of evening entertainment. For a drink, try **Ovalau Club** *(4pm-10.30pm Mon-Thur, 2pm-midnight Fri, 10am-midnight Sat, 10am-10.30pm Sun)* or **Levuka Club**; both have 'Members Only' signs posted but welcome guests nonetheless.

There are a number of pool halls where locals shoot to pop music; try the **Levuka Amusement Centre** *(open 10am-10pm Mon-Sat; $0.50 per game)*. Otherwise, head to **Levuka Cinema** *(adult/child $3/1.50)* on Thursday to Sunday for popcorn and slightly out-of-date releases.

Getting There & Away

Air Air Fiji has twice-daily Levuka–Suva flights between Nausori airport and Bureta airstrip on Ovalau (one way/week-return $55/88; 12 minutes). The Bureta airstrip is on the southwestern side of Ovalau, about 40 minutes drive to/from Levuka (minibus/taxi $3.60/$20). Minibuses to the airport depart from outside the Air Fiji Travel Centre at 6.30am and 4pm. Better yet, if you let them know where you're staying, Air Fiji will arrange for the minibus to pick you up at your hotel.

Boat Near the market, **Patterson Brothers Shipping** *(☎ 344 0125; Beach St; Suva/Labasa $22/55; open 8.30am-4.30pm Mon-Fri)* has a bus/ferry service from Levuka to Suva via Natovi ($22; 4 hours; 4am daily). You can also opt to stay on the boat at Natovi to Bau (on Vanua Levu) and then continue by bus to Labasa. Patterson Brothers also run a boat to Leleuvia from where you can continue on to Suva via Bau Landing ($35; Monday to Saturday). You must book at least a day in advance and on Friday for weekend sailings.

Getting Around

Levuka is tiny and easy to get around on foot. There is a taxi stand opposite the Whale's Tale restaurant where carriers depart for Lovoni and Rukuruku. Mountain bikes can be hired in town (see the Activities section earlier).

LOVONI

Lovoni village is nestled within a spectacular extinct volcano crater, in the centre of Ovalau. The village has no accommodation for travellers however there are guided walks from Levuka. (See Organised Tours earlier in this chapter.) The hike can be muddy and slippery so good boots are essential. Bring a *sevusevu* for the chief. Of interest is the **chief's burial site** opposite the church and **Korolevu hill fortification**, high on the crater rim, where villagers took refuge in times of war.

The villagers of Lovoni are extremely proud people. They believe that since Chief Cakobau was only able to defeat them with trickery, not by war, they are the strongest tribe in Fiji (see 'The Enslavement of the People of Lovoni' boxed text following). On 7 July each year, the enslavement of the Lovoni people is commemorated. People of all religions gather in the same church and the history is read out.

Getting There & Away

You can hike in from Levuka with a guide (see Organised Tours earlier in this chapter). There is also a Levuka–Lovoni truck leaving Levuka at 7am and 11am daily, except Sunday, and returning at about 3pm.

RUKURUKU

The village of Rukuruku is a 17km drive north of Levuka. The drive there affords fantastic views across the sea. Near the village is a **black-sand beach** with a view of Naigani island, and a small **waterfall** about 20 minutes' walk up the valley. It's best to arrange a day out there with Bobo (see next) to avoid trespassing on village property.

Places to Stay & Eat

Bobo's Farm (*☎ 993 3632; Rukuruku;* **w** *www.owlfiji.com; $22 per person, breakfast/lunch/dinner $5/7/10)* is a tranquil retreat that is surrounded by a gorgeous garden and lush rainforest. Hand built by Bobo, the two-bedroom cabin includes a small kitchen for use by guests. If you intend to cook for yourself, you'll need to bring your ingredients with you. You can use the fridge in the main house as well as the TV; everything is either solar or wind powered. The main house (also Bobo-built) has a large deck where local villagers often gather for singing and kava drinking. There are lots of fruit trees in the yard and there's a freshwater stream where you can catch prawns or bathe in small, natural pools. Ten minutes upstream is a waterfall and 10 minutes downstream is the black-sand beach. You want more? Well, Bobo can also organise village tours, arrange island hopping, snorkelling and fishing trips. Book ahead through the Whale's Tale or Ovalau Watersports in Levuka; the mobile only works from 10am to noon on Saturdays! Bobo can pick you up by boat from Levuka, Buresala Landing, Leleuvia ($70), Caqelai ($45) or Natovi ($70).

Getting There & Away

A carrier travels to Rukuruku every day (except Sunday) from Beach St in Levuka ($1.50, one hour). A taxi will cost about $20 each way.

The Enslavement of the Lovoni Villagers

In 1870–71 Tui Cakobau's warriors fought against the Lovoni highlanders, who had been raiding the settlement of Levuka and were a threat to Cakobau's authority. After repeated attempts to penetrate the Lovoni fort failed, Cakobau sent a Methodist missionary to subdue the people. At the time, Lovoni had a dwarf priest who had the ability to foresee the future. The priest was the first to notice the approaching missionary and, seeing a brightness emanating from him, believed he came in peace. The missionary read from the *Bible* in Bauan, referring to the Lovoni villagers as the lost sheep of Fiji. He then invited them to a reconciliation feast with Cakobau; whether the missionary was a pawn or party to Cakobau's plans for the feast is unknown.

On 29 June 1871, the Lovoni people came down from the safety of their village to Levuka, and in good faith put aside their weapons. However, as they started their meal, Cakobau's warriors caught them off guard, quickly surrounding and capturing them.

Tui Cakobau sold the Lovoni prisoners as slaves, his takings helping him form government. Families were separated as the villagers were dispersed as far as Kavala (in the Kadavu Group), Yavusania (near Nadi on Viti Levu), Lovoni-Ono (in the Lau Group) and Wailevu (on Vanua Levu). The dwarf priest and two Lovoni warriors were sold to an American circus.

Other Lomaiviti Islands

YANUCA LAILAI

Yanuca Lailai (Lost Island) is an uninhabited island close to Levuka and adjacent to Moturiki. It has a hill with a short, **golden-sand beach** (about 200m long), and the rest of the island is rocky. It is too shallow to swim at low tide but it is possible to snorkel.

The island has rudimentary accommodation, but it was not operational at the time of writing. Ask at **Ovalau Watersports** in Levuka to see if it's open or to arrange for a daytrip.

MOTURIKI

The hilly, lush island of Moturiki is just southwest of Ovalau and home to 10 villages. Although it has no accommodation for travellers, both Leleuvia and Caqelai resorts will take guests to the village of Niubasaga for Sunday church services.

CAQELAI

Just south of Moturiki lies Caqelai – a gorgeous coral island. It's only a 15-minute walk around the island's beautiful **white-sand beaches**, which are fringed with palms and other large trees. If you're lucky you may see **dolphins** and **baby turtles**.

What Lies Beneath

If you head out to the islands south from Ovalau, your boat will likely travel through Gavo Pass, a break in the reef. Many indigenous Fijians believe that beneath these waters lies a sunken village where ancestral spirits continue to reside. Stories of fishermen hooking newly woven mats are whispered around Levuka. When passing over the tabu site, Fijians remove their hats and sunglasses and talk in hushed, reverent tones. It is believed that the spirits are capable of doling out nasty punishments to those who upset them. Whether or not you choose to believe the story, avoid offending and upsetting your hosts by respecting their beliefs and following suit. One tourist who refused to take off his baseball cap sent a Fijian woman into terrified hysterics.

Caqelai Resort (*☎ 343 0366; camping with/without meals $24/12, dorms/bure $28/60, all per person, mosquito nets and meals included, shared bucket toilets & showers*) is a small, immaculately kept place run by the Methodist Church of Moturiki. Those seeking a secluded spot who don't mind roughing it a little will love it here. The facilities are basic but the small *bure* on the water's edge are lovely, the food is superb and the staff are extremely friendly. Dorm accommodation is in weatherboard buildings. There is no alcohol for sale on the island but you can bring your own.

Lionfish and octopuses make snorkelling off the shore fantastic; gear is available for $6 per day. At low tide it's possible to walk out to Snake Island (named after the many black-and-white banded sea snakes found here), for even better snorkelling. Diving can be arranged with Leleuvia's dive shop (see the following Leleuvia section) as well as village trips to Niubasaga on Moturiki for the Sunday church service or boat trips to tiny Honeymoon Island. Other activities include volleyball as well as singing, dancing and kava drinking beside a bonfire on the beach.

Getting There & Away

If you're coming from Levuka, you can book transport and accommodation from The Royal Hotel. One-way transfers cost $15 per person in a group, $30 for one person or $40 for a return day trip (including meals).

From Suva, catch a bus heading down Kings Road from the main bus terminal and get off at Waidalice. You need to call ahead for a boat from Caqelai to pick you up here ($25 each or $40 for one person).

LELEUVIA

Just south of Caqelai sits Leleuvia, another palm-fringed coral island with golden-sand beaches. At low tide a vast area of sand and rock is exposed, a good time to walk around the island to explore the tidal pools. It's also possible to swim off the western side or to do some OK snorkelling and great diving.

Leleuvia Island Resort (*☎ 330 1584; dorms/bure/cabin $30/35/45 per person, including meals*) has, sadly, seen better days. Despite its beautiful setting, management wars have taken their toll. Meals are just OK, however, you can bring your own food and cook for yourself. The dorm is reminiscent of a bunker and the cement cabins are gloomy. *Bure* are definitely the best option but bring your own padlock. The shared facilities (for all but the cabins) include rain/seawater showers and flush toilets. There is a safe for valuables and the office sells snacks and cold beer. Staff are friendly and we're hoping that the new management gets this beautiful oasis back on its feet.

Nautilus Dive Fiji is run separately from the resort and has a good reputation for safe gear and great dives. Single/double dives cost $75/120; if you're planning on staying for a while there are also five- and 10-dive packages. The PADI course costs $390. You can rent snorkelling gear for $10 per day and, for another $10, you can be taken by boat to brighter coral off-shore. The Dive Shop also has one of the best book exchanges we saw in Fiji.

Getting There & Away

Patterson Brothers Shipping *(in Suva ☎ 331 5644, in Levuka 344 0125)* oversees a boat and bus combination journey from Suva to Leleuvia, via Bau Landing; see the Getting Around Chapter. Transfers to the island from Bau Landing take about one hour on a 12-person boat. Conditions can become very choppy, and passengers and their gear can arrive drenched. Don't go if there aren't enough life jackets or if the boat is overcrowded.

WAKAYA

About 20km east of Ovalau, Wakaya is a privately owned island visible from Levuka. It has forests, cliffs, beautiful white-sand beaches, and archaeological sites, including a **stone fish trap**. In some areas you'll find feral horses, pigs and deer roaming freely; in others there are millionaires' houses.

Wakaya Club *(☎ 344 8128, e wakaya@connect.com.fj; garden/ocean-view doubles $2600-12,100, 5-night minimum)* is one of Fiji's most exclusive resorts. If you're looking to be seriously pampered, start saving your pennies.

Getting There & Away

The island is a 20-minute speedboat ride from Levuka; however, as it's private, you'll need an invite to visit.

KORO

Koro has many villages nestled in its lush tropical forests. Roads over the mountainous interior provide for plenty of thrills and wonderful views. A portion of the island is freehold, so foreigners can own a small vine-covered haven; the TV reality series 'Under One Roof' was filmed here. At Dere Bay, a wharf allows you to walk out to good swimming and snorkelling; inland is a waterfall and natural pool. For a traditional Fijian experience, walk from the resorts into the nearby village to meet the chief, celebrate the kava, or listen to the school children sing.

Koro Beach Resort *(☎ 331 1075, fax 330 3160, e fijimiller@connect.com.fj; bure doubles $160, including all meals)* offers budget accommodation close to many great dive sites. The ten bure are set around a white-sand bay, some self-contained, others with shared facilities. The resort has its own restaurant and store, serves great food, and there's good swimming at the door-step.

Dere Bay Resort *(☎ 331 1075, fax 330 3160, e fijimiller@connect.com.fj; bure doubles $400, including all meals)* offers luxury, while keeping the local traditional character. The well-designed bure have soaring ceilings, delightful furnishings, 360-degree outlooks, and spacious verandas. Sit and watch the sand crabs while you wait to be called for another gourmet meal. There's a swimming pool, kayaks, scuba diving equipment, full game-fishing facilities and a resident diving instructor. Friday night is lovo night.

Getting There & Away

Air Fiji flies into Koro from Suva on Saturday ($95), and Turtle Islands or Pacific Island's sea planes regularly fly in from Nadi ($300 one-way) Consort ferries leave Suva twice weekly (deck/air-con cabin $35/65, 8 hours). It's worth the trip just to watch the activities on the wharf when you arrive, but you really need to take a cabin. From Savusavu, the Dere Bay boat costs $100 one-way. Enquire about transport when you book your accommodation; the resorts pick you up from the airport or wharf ($20).

NAIGANI

Naigani, also known as Mystery Island, is a mountainous island about 10km offshore from Ovalau. The island has white-sand beaches, lagoons, a fringing coral reef, the remains of a **precolonial hillside fortification** and 'cannibal caves'. According to locals, 1800 villagers were slaughtered here by marauding tribes. The place is tabu and locals keep away; out of respect, you should do the same.

Naigani Island Resort *(☎ 330 0539, fax 330 0925; W www.fijifvb.gov.fj/resorts/naigani.htm; studios/villas $120/150)*, on the grounds of an old copra plantation, caters to couples, families and small groups. The 17 spacious garden and beachfront villas are great value with two-bedroom villas holding a maximum of five guests. The bar and restaurant are in the restored plantation homestead and daily meal packages cost $45/60 for two/three meals.

The resort has a kids' programme, a golf course, a pool with swim-up bar and a water slide. Snorkelling is excellent immediately offshore and there are good dive sites nearby (via the resort's dive operation). Other activities include nature-trail walks, kayaking, windsurfing, fishing and day excursions to Levuka.

Getting There & Away

Return transfers to/from Suva, via Natovi Landing, are $60/30 per adult/child. Return launch transfers to/from Taviya village, near Rukuruku on Ovalau, are $45.

NAMENALALA

The volcanic island of Namenalala rests on the Namena Barrier Reef, 25km off the southeastern coast of Vanua Levu and about 40km from Savusavu. Namenalala has lovely **beaches** and the island is a natural sailors' refuge. There is an old **ring fortification,** but the villages disappeared long ago. Today there's just one small, upmarket resort.

Moody's Namena *(☎ 881 3764, fax 881 2366; W www.moodysnamenafiji.com; bure per person with meals $378, 5-night minimum, no children under 16yrs; closed Nov-Mar)* has six timber-and-bamboo *bure* on a forested ridge. Diving here is excellent and costs $85 per tank. (Divers must be certified.) Other activities, which include windsurfing, fishing, snorkelling, reef excursions, barbeques, volleyball, use of canoes and paddle boards are included in the rate. The island has a nature reserve for bird-watching and trekking and is home to seabirds, and red-footed boobies and a giant clam farm. The resort closes between November and March to give a little privacy to the hawksbill and green turtles who lay their eggs on these beaches.

Getting There & Away

Guests arrive by charter yacht from Savusavu ($190 per person each way) or by charter seaplane from Nadi ($270 per person, minimum of two people).

Vanua Levu

Dubbed Fiji's best-kept secret, Vanua Levu is making it onto more and more travellers' itineraries. While easily accessible from Viti Levu, it retains a feeling of remoteness and offers a window into the traditional Fijian way of life. Volcanic in origin, Vanua Levu may have few sandy beaches, but its nearby reefs, including the world famous Rainbow Reef, offer some of Fiji's best snorkelling and diving. The island's many deep bays are fantastic for kayaking and the lush, rugged interior rainforest provides for good bird-watching opportunities.

At just over half the size of Viti Levu, Vanua Levu (Big Land) is Fiji's second-largest island. With an area of 5587 sq km, it's home to 18% of the country's total population (139,514). The Fijian administration divides the island into the provinces of Cakaudrove (the southeast), Bua (the southwest) and Macuata (the northwest). Vanua Levu, together with Kioa, Rabi, Taveuni and a number of smaller offshore islands, is known as Fiji's North.

The population on Vanua Levu's southeast coast is predominantly indigenous Fijian and the gorgeous landscape here is brimming with stunning vistas, rainforests and coconut plantations. The small, southern town of Savusavu is the main tourist destination and where you'll find the majority of activities. The central north of the island has a higher population of Indo-Fijians, concentrated around Labasa, Vanua Levu's largest town and administrative and business centre. As well as native forest, there are lots of sugar-cane and commercial pine plantations in this area. Much of the western coast is remote and accessible only by boat.

As on Viti Levu, a mountain range runs along much of Vanua Levu's length, dividing the island into a wetter eastern side and a drier western side.

The coastline of Vanua Levu is irregular and deeply indented; the large Tunulao Peninsula to the east forms the huge Natewa Bay, the longest bay in the South Pacific. Edged by steep, green mountains and frequented by spinner dolphins, the remote village of Korolevu lies here (population 30), reputedly the oldest village on the island and accessible only by invitation and boat.

Highlights

- Rent a jeep and explore the island's lush terrain, passing through remote villages and enjoying breathtaking vistas
- In Savusavu, join an adventure cruise with the Tui Tai for a chance to visit Kiao and Koro and to kayak, snorkel and swim to your heart's content
- Take in the island's plethora of dive sites, including some of Fiji's best
- Kayak around the stunning Savusavu Bay

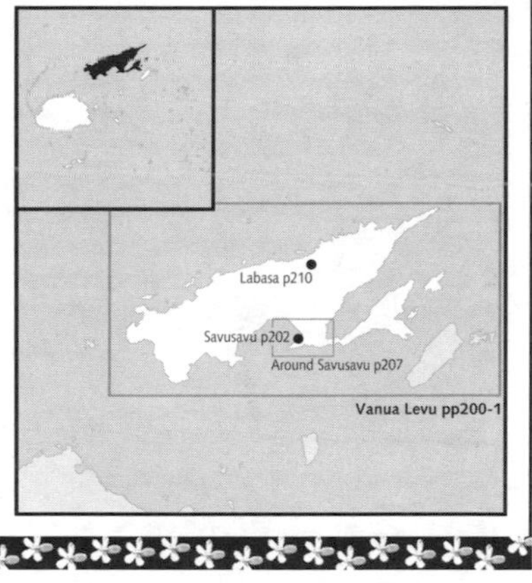

The tourism infrastructure on Vanua Levu remains frail, making it an independent traveller's paradise. Hire a jeep and head off exploring down those wild, tropical roads. Just remember, villagers here are less familiar with tourists and you cannot wander on foot through the countryside without permission from the landowners.

Getting There & Away

Air Vanua Levu is easily reached by frequent flights from Viti Levu. The flight over the reefs and down to Savusavu through the coconut plantations is superb. Both **Sun Air** and **Air Fiji** run twice daily services between Nadi (one hour) and Savusavu. **Sun Air** has regular flights from Suva to Labasa (75 minutes) while **Air Fiji** has twice daily services between Suva and Savusavu (45minutes). Both companies also operate twice daily

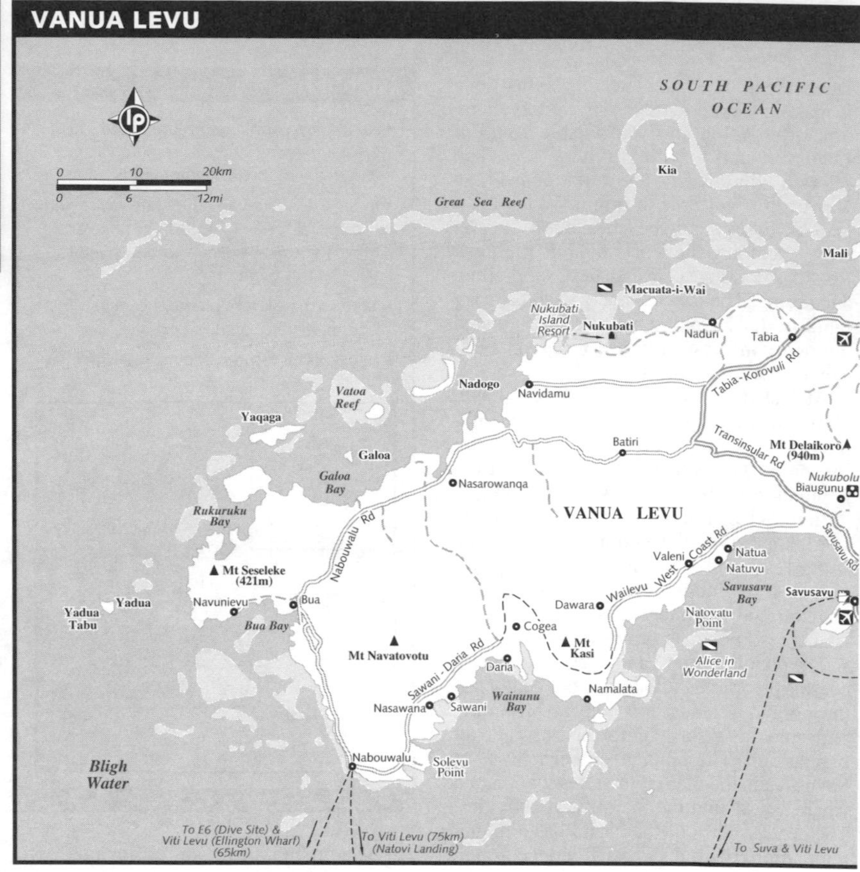

flights between Savusavu and Taveuni (30 minutes). It's often possible to book your seats the day before a flight; however, the planes are small so it's usually safest to book ahead. See the Getting Around chapter for more information.

Boat Travelling to Vanua Levu by boat takes a great deal longer and often it's not much cheaper. However, if you've got the time and a love of the sea, it can be well worth it.

Consort Shipping, **Beachcomber Cruises**, **Lagilagi** and **Patterson Brothers Shipping** all service Vanua Levu, destined for Suva, Ovalau, Ellington Wharf, Lautoka and Taveuni. See the Getting Around chapter for schedules and ticket prices. For **Grace Ferry**, via Buca Bay to Taveuni, buy your ticket at least a day in advance from Hussein's in Savusavu *(☎ 885 0622; open 7.30am-5pm Mon-Sat)*.

Getting Around

There are unsealed roads around most of the island's perimeter. The road from Labasa to Savusavu over the central mountain range is sealed but not well maintained. The coastal road from the airport to the turnoff for the Hibiscus Highway is newly paved and a breeze to drive. The island's main routes are serviced by buses but if you're looking to go off the beaten track at all, it's easier to explore by 4WD. **Budget Rent a Car** in Labasa *(☎ 881 1999)* has 4WD jeeps for hire. Given the bumpy terrain, they're not always in top condition so give them a thorough check before

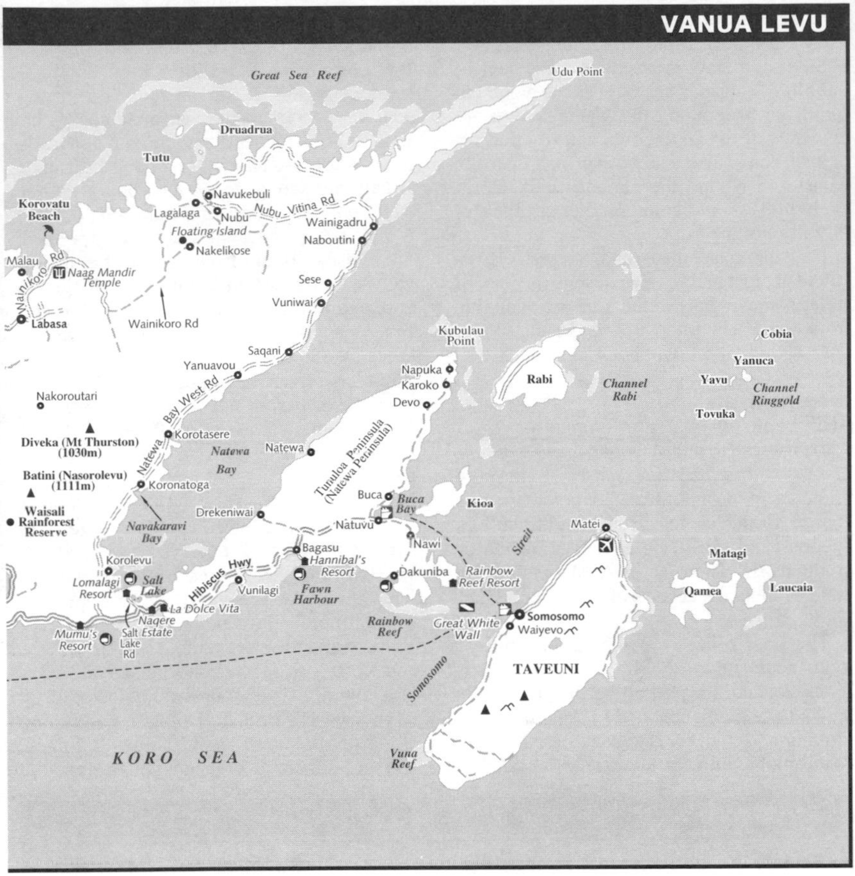

VANUA LEVU

you set out. Budget will also deliver/pickup the jeeps in Savusavu (free if you rent for more than three days). Avoid driving at night as there are lots of wandering animals and pedestrians and service stations are scarce. It's also a good idea to take some food with you on the road as restaurants and shops are nonexistent, except in larger towns (which are rare themselves).

SAVUSAVU

pop 4970

Dusty little Savusavu sits on a peninsula, looking out across Savusavu Bay to the islet of Nawi and the western mountain range. While the town itself may not be so picturesque, the views certainly are and the sunsets can be spectacular.

Savusavu is Vanua Levu's second largest town and home to a mixed population of indigenous Fijians, Indo-Fijians and expats. The economy depended heavily on copra production during the second half of the 19th century but profitability began declining early last century. The majority of the copra was sent to Suva for processing until the mid-1980s when a processing plant was built in Savusavu. This considerably reduced the freight costs; however, most farmers are still struggling to remain viable.

These days, the economy is leaning more and more towards tourism and the town has nicknamed itself 'the hidden paradise'. With more and more visitors arriving, the town is now well serviced by airlines and ferries and its sheltered bay and two marinas make it a popular stop for cruising yachties who can carry out immigration formalities here.

Savusavu Bay once saw a great deal of bubbling volcanic activity; those vents of steam you see along the water's edge are evidence of the geothermal activity that remains. You'll also find **hot springs** near the wharf and behind the playing field. Don't even think about bathing in them as they're literally boiling hot.

Built along one main road, it's pretty difficult to get lost in Savusavu despite the lack of street names. Maps of the area are available from the **Yacht Shop** *(Copra Shed Marina; open 8am-1pm & 2pm-5pm Mon-Fri)*.

Information

ANZ bank *(open 9.30am-3pm Mon-Thur, 9.30am-4pm Fri)* and **Westpac** *(open 9.30am-3pm Mon-Thur, 9.30am-4pm Fri)* both have branches in the main street, opposite the bus station. Both change currency and travellers cheques and give cash advances on major credit cards. There is an **ATM** outside the ANZ branch that accepts all major debit and credit cards.

The **post office** is at the eastern end of town near Buca Bay Rd. There are cardphones outside the post office, near the banks and outside the Copra Shed Marina. If you're looking to get online, **Savusavu Real Estate & Internet Centre** *(☎ 885 0929; Copra Shed Marina; per minute off/online $0.25/0.35; open 8am-5pm Mon-Fri, 8am-noon Sat)* has a few computers. **Plantation Real Estate & Internet** *(☎ 885 0801; per min $0.35; open 9am-4pm Mon-Fri)* has two new computers with quick connections and is generally quiet. They also have a good book exchange.

Laundry service *(open 8am-5pm Mon-Fri, 8am-1pm Sat; $4 wash or dry only, $7/10 wash & dry 6/10kg)* is available at the Copra Shed.

Savusavu is an official point of entry for yachts, with customs, immigration, health and quarantine services all located here. Emergency numbers are **hospital or ambulance** *(☎ 885 0444)*, or **police** *(☎ 885 0222)*. There's a private health centre *(☎ 885 0721; open 8.30am-4pm Mon-Thur, 8.30am-2pm Fri)* in town, near the post office.

Cruises

Perfect for tourists who aren't all that fond of tours, a voyage with **Tui Tai Adventure Cruises** *(☎ 885 3032, 666 1500, fax 666 4496; W www.tuitai.com; Copra Shed Marina)* is a fantastic way to see and do a great deal in a short time. Sailing between Vanua Levu, Taveuni and the more remote islands of Kioa and Koro, you'll get to snorkel, kayak, bike, trek, swim, fish, dive or just lounge on deck to your heart's content. Dolphins swimming alongside the boat, star-lit dinners on deck, and the welcoming villagers you meet on the

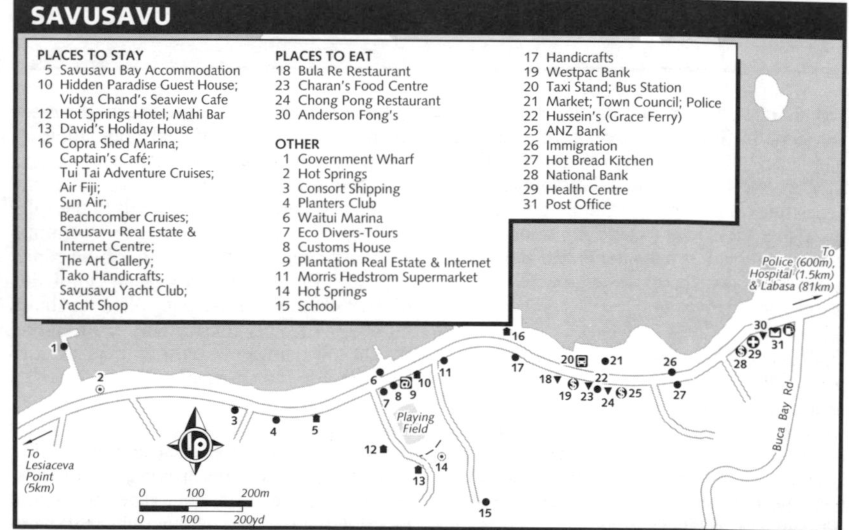

out-of-the-way islands all make it a blissful experience. The crew is brilliant, providing absolutely stellar service and fantastic local food, the equipment is tops, the snorkelling and diving sites are some of the world's best, and the sailboat itself is gorgeous. A four-day cruise costs $920/1700/2650 for dorm bunk/cabin/luxury cabin accommodation, including all meals and activities except bar bills and diving. (There is also a three-day option.) The boat takes a maximum of 24 passengers. Cruises are geared to independent travellers but guides are also available for all activities.

For those looking to charter their own boat, **SeaHawk Yacht Charters** *(☎/fax 885 0787; e seahawk@connect.com.fj)* rents out a beautiful 53ft yacht with captain and a cook/crew for around $400 per person per day, including meals. You can go practically anywhere in Fiji and the crew can help you arrange activities like diving. SeaHawk also offers full-day picnic cruises ($80 per person), half-day sail & snorkel trips ($50 per person), sunset cruises ($45 per person) and overnight cruises ($600 per couple).

Diving

With excellent dive sites in and around Savusavu Bay as well as along the coast towards Taveuni, Savusavu is a diver's mecca. **L'Aventure Jean-Michel Cousteau** *(☎ 885 0188, fax 885 0340; e laventurefiji@connect.com.fj; w www.fijiresort.com; Jean-Michel Cousteau Resort)*, run by the son of Jacques, runs excellent daily dives. Two tank dives cost $160 including gear and you can do the PADI course for $450.

Eco Divers-Tours *(☎ 885 0122; e ecodivers@connect.com.fj; w www.ecodivers-tours.com)* also offers dives in the area. A two-tank dive costs $130, night dives are $90 and the PADI course is $460. They also offer special rates for multi-day diving but it's best to book ahead.

Marinas

Dating back to 1880 and originally one of Fiji's first copra mills, the **Copra Shed Marina** *(☎ 885 0457, fax 885 0989; e coprashed@connect.com.fj)* has been rebuilt into Savusavu's service hub for tourists and expats. In one visit you can book a flight or a boat, check your email, buy postcards, pick up your laundry, swig a beer and devour a pizza. Toilets and hot showers are available for yachties. Moorings in the pretty harbour between Savusavu and Nawi Islet cost $10/150 for a day/month.

A few doors down, the newly opened **Waitui Marina** *(☎ 885 012, fax 885 0344)* is based in a beautiful, restored boatshed with showers, laundry and a private club. Moorings cost $7/42/150 for a day/week/month. Use channel 16 for assistance in locating moorings on arrival.

Other Activities

You can ask at one of the marinas for a lift over to the little **beach** on Nawi Islet or rent a kayak from **Eco Divers-Tours** (see Diving earlier) and paddle the 250m. Eco Divers-Tours also advertises a variety of **village and hiking tours** in the area; ask which ones are available. They can organise guided **kayaking tours** around Savusavu Bay, ranging from three to 14 nights and staying in indigenous Fijian villages. Activities along the way include snorkelling, fishing and swimming. Prices vary according to the trip length and the amount of services required (you can have a boat travel with you) but are generally pretty steep. For a 3-night tour including meals and an extra two nights in a Savusavu hotel, it's around $1580 per person. Plus, you have to rent your own snorkelling gear.

Places to Stay – Budget

In Town For some of the best views on the peninsula, check out **Beachcomber's Driftwood Village** *(☎ 885 0046; e driftwood@connect.com.fj; dorm bed $39)*. The immaculately clean dorm cabin is up on the hill with private lockers, hot showers, and a veranda with a fantastic sea view. The quiet resort has a beautiful pool, good restaurant and bar and a jetty across the street that you can swim or snorkel from. Breakfast is included. They also have equipment for biking, fishing, kayaking and volleyball. Staff are welcoming and helpful. A taxi from town will cost about $3.

Copra Shed Marina *(☎ 885 0457; e coprashed@connect.com.fj; 2-bedroom flat for up to 4 adults $90, studio flat for 2 adults $45)* has a comfortable two-bedroom flat and a studio flat for rent upstairs. Both are self-contained, clean and spacious with sunny sea views and good facilities. The staff here are very friendly. It's best to call ahead as the flats are often booked out on long-term leases, however, you can also get excellent walk-in rates.

David's Holiday House *(☎ 885 0149; camping $7, dorms/singles/doubles $11/20/25, family room $30)* is set in a large garden back from the waterfront. Popular with out-of-town businessmen, this place is simple but friendly. The freestanding dorm (no fan) is clean and camping is across the road, next to the river. Private rooms in the house are basic and sunny. All rooms include breakfast and shared facilities. No top sheet, blanket or mosquito net is provided with any of the beds. There's a 10% discount for weekly rates.

Savusavu Bay Accommodation *(☎ 885 0100; twin with fan/air-con $32/40, family room $60)*, upstairs on the main street, has scrubbed, comfortable rooms but little atmosphere. Each room has a small porch and en suite but many look onto a concrete wall next door.

Hidden Paradise Guest House *(☎ 885 0106; singles/doubles/triples $15/30/45)* has, perhaps, hidden it a little too well. Prices include breakfast and all rooms share facilities, including kitchen. Rooms at the back of the general store and restaurant are basic and getting a little drab. However, if you're looking for somewhere quiet and safe, it's an OK option. Showers are cold.

Around Town **Mumu's Resort** *(☎ 885 0416; camping $5, dorms/singles/doubles $17/35/75, 5-person Pool House $150; 4-person Dream House $80)* sits on ruggedly beautiful Maravu Point, about 17km east of Savusavu. While the place is somewhat run-down, it's full of character with each cabin unique. Ask to see a few before you choose; there's a Fijian *bure*, an American beach house (the Pool House), a cute studio-hut (Garden House) and a concrete cabin (Tank House). Most have cooking facilities and all are clean and comfortable with en suites. For the best views, ask for the Dream House. Camping is up on top of a hill, with views of the sea under the pine, pandanus and coconut trees. The dorm building is clean and basic with cooking facilities (available to campers), a cold shower and toilet; the noisy generator next door may still be a problem. The main house has a comfortable sitting area with views and pet parrots. Simple meals cost $10/15 for breakfast or lunch/dinner and the bar serves beer. There's a small volcanic rock beach beneath the point and a natural swimming hole where you can dip with the colourful fish. At low tide you can walk out to the lagoon between the nearby islands and snorkel with beautiful soft coral and lots more fish. To the east of the resort is another channel where it's possible to swim through caves and see large parrot fish – take extra care with the currents. Local buses ($1 to Savusavu) pass Mumu's five times a day (once only on Sunday) and a taxi to/from Savusavu is $12.

Vatukaluvi Holiday House *(☎ 885 0561; rooms $55)* is a fantastic deal if you're looking for a secluded and self-contained place. A 15-minute drive from town, it's on a rocky point overlooking the Koro Sea and a few desert islands. You can snorkel from the small beach, windsurf or visit nearby hot springs. The house is fully furnished and sleeps a maximum of seven people. The owner can arrange for a cook and cleaner. It's best to book ahead; enquiries can be made through the Copra Shed Marina.

Places to Stay – Mid-Range

Beachcomber's Driftwood Village *(☎ 885 0046; fax 885 0334; ⓔ driftwood@connect.com.fj; double/family bure $125/255)* is a quiet resort with sweeping views of the sea, offering top-end rooms for mid-range prices. The thatched *bure* are private and extremely comfortable and the family cabin sleeps a maximum of six guests. Prices include breakfast. For a full list of facilities, see the previous Budget section. The resort is a $3 taxi ride from town.

Hot Springs Hotel *(☎ 885 0195, fax 885 0430; ⓔ hotspring@connect.com.fj; singles or doubles with fan/air-con $80/125, including breakfast, $22 per extra person, up to 2 children under 12 free)* was built as part of the Travelodge chain and has that typical hotel feel. An old standby, it's smack in the middle of town. Rooms are cool and comfortable with tiled floors and water-view balconies. All have a private en suite and a small fridge. The hotel has a nice pool on a large, sunny deck with more great views. The hotel can arrange tours through Eco Divers-Tours and has a pleasant restaurant and bar.

Places to Stay – Top End

All of Savusavu's top end accommodation is a taxi ride from the town centre.

Koro Sun Resort *(☎/fax 885 0150; e res@korosunresort.com; bure singles/doubles $225/275, triples/quads/quins in 2-bedroom bure $430/480/530)* has beautiful, plush *bure* with four-poster bamboo beds and rock showers. Those on the hillside feel like tree houses, with sea views and birds singing outside. This new, luxurious resort has a gorgeous pool, tennis courts, a nine-hole golf course, kayaks, bikes and snorkelling gear, all free to guests, plus all meals are included. The resort has an excellent children's programme and you can have a massage next to a waterfall, on the edge of the 90-acre rainforest. Diving is available through a branch of L'Aventure Jean-Michel Cousteau Diving that operates from a jetty across the road. The resort is 13km east of Savusavu. A taxi to/from Savusavu costs about $12.

Jean-Michel Cousteau Fiji Islands Resort *(☎ 885 0188, fax 885 0340; w www.fijiresort.com; garden-view/ocean-view bure doubles $850/970, 2-bedroom bure $1140, including all meals and activities except diving, extra person under/over 16 yrs $140/190)* is a resort-lover's resort. Meals are gourmet and *bure* are lavish with large decks and private screened gardens. All meals and activities (except diving) are included in the rate. There are lots of planned activities available, from kayaking to palm weaving to bird-watching, as well as a pool, gym, and a children's programme, although staff seem somewhat disinterested. The resort is 15km southwest of Savusavu on Lesiaceva Point, where Savusavu Bay meets the Koro Sea.

Namale Resort *(☎ 885 0435, fax 885 0400; w www.namale-fiji.com; garden bure singles/doubles $1250/1480, ocean-view bure $1870)* is an exclusive, amazingly expensive resort on the water, 9km east of Savusavu. The price includes all meals and activities except diving. Owned by Anthony Robbins, the American self-help guru, the resort is often booked out with workshop attendees.

About 24km offshore, southwest of Savusavu, is Moody's Namena, on the island of Namenalala (see the Lomaiviti Group chapter for more information).

Places to Eat

Bula Re *(☎ 885 0307; mains about $8; open 8am-9pm Mon-Sat)* serves fantastic food. Meals are Fijian with touches of Chinese, European and Indian cuisines. Dine on fresh seafood, pastas, crepes, salads or tasty vegie dishes like tempeh and curry. You can also indulge in good coffee and cake amid comfortable Fijian décor and music. The staff are very friendly and can let you in on lots of info about Savusavu.

Captain's Café *(☎ 885 0511; Copra Shed Marina; small/medium/large pizza $10/15/20, breakfast $8; open 8.30am-8.30pm Mon-Fri, 9am-9pm Sat, 11am-8.30pm Sun)* is well known for its pizzas but also has fish and chips, sandwiches and full breakfast. The views of the yacht-dotted harbour from the deck make up for its okay food.

Beachcomber's Driftwood Village *(☎ 885 0334; lunch/dinner $7/15)* serves set meals in its open, pool-side *bure*. The food is an imaginative mix of Fijian and Western. In the evening you can dine to the tune of local musicians.

Hot Springs Hotel *☎ 885 0195; breakfast buffet $6.50, Sunday lunch $12.50; breakfast 7am-9am daily, dinner 7pm-9pm daily)* is a great place for breakfast with a view and the buffet will keep you going all day. The daily dinner menu has both Fijian and Western dishes, usually fresh fish and chicken. The Sunday lunch special includes house wine or draught beer and is accompanied by a live string band.

Anderson Fong's *(☎ 885 0066; mains $4; open 7am-5pm Mon-Fri, 7am-1pm Sat)* is a friendly, popular hole-in-the-wall serving Chinese dishes like chicken in oyster sauce or beef in black bean sauce.

Charan's Food Centre *(☎ 885 0448; mains $3; open 7am-6pm Mon-Sat)* is a good place to fill up on cheap, deep-fried fish or chicken with chips, curry or rice.

Chong Pong Restaurant *(☎ 885 0588; mains $5; open Mon-Sat 8am-9pm)* serves your standard Chinese food like chow mein, sweet & sour pork and noodle soup. Up a long flight of stairs, it's simple but has nice views across the main road to the market and sea beyond.

Vidya Chand's Seaview Cafe *(Hidden Paradise Guest House; open 9am-6pm Mon-Fri, 9am-1pm Sat; meals $5)* is bright and cheerful, serving good Indian curries, rice and roti.

Savusavu has a few grocery stores including **Morris Hedstrom Supermarket**. The **market** *(7am-5pm Mon-Fri, 7am-3pm Sat)* has fruit and vegies in season as well as lots and lots of *yaqona* root. The **Hot Bread Kitchen** *(open 6am-8pm Mon-Sat, 6am-1pm Sun)* has fresh loaves daily.

Entertainment

Savusavu Yacht Club *(Copra Shed Marina; open 11am-10pm Mon-Thur & Sun, 11am-1am Fri, 11am-midnight Sat)* has a friendly pub feel about it. With picnic tables on the water's edge, it's a good place for a beer and to meet local expats.

The new **Waitui Marina** *(spirits/wine $3/20)* features a pleasant bar with a deck over the water, a comfy TV/reading lounge and friendly staff. The bar is well stocked and they'll even whip you up some microwave popcorn to enjoy with the view. Ask at Eco Divers-Tours for a free visitor's membership.

Planters Club *(☎ 885 0233; beer/spirits $1.30/2.90; open 9am-10pm Mon-Thur, 9am-11pm Fri & Sat, 10am-8pm Sun)* is in a big, ranch-style house on the western edge of town. With country music, pool tables and darts, it's a popular hangout for local copra farmers.

The **Mahi Bar** *(open 10am-11pm Mon-Sun)* at the Hot Springs Hotel has a large deck with great views and often has live music. Drink prices here are a little steeper.

You might catch a local game of rugby or football on the town's playing field.

Shopping

The Art Gallery *(☎ 885 3054; Copra Shed Marina)* has paintings, cards, sculptures and other work by local artists. **Tako Handicrafts** *(Copra Shed Marina)* also has local handicrafts and postcards. Across the street from the Copra Shed is a shed where a local man sells his wooden carvings. Around the back of the **market** is a room devoted to local woven and wooden handicrafts.

Getting There & Away

Air Fiji *(☎ 885 0173; open 8.30am-4.30pm Mon-Fri, 8.30am-12.30pm Sat)*, **Sun Air** *(☎ 885 0141; open 8am-5pm Mon-Fri, 8am-noon Sat)*, and **Beachcomber Cruises** *(☎ 885 0266, fax 885 0499)* have their offices at the Copra Shed Marina.

See the Getting There & Away chapter for more information about getting to and from Vanua Levu via boat or plane.

Bus The Savusavu bus station and taxi stand are both located in the centre of town, near the market. Buses travelling the sealed highway leaving from Savusavu over the mountains to Labasa ($5.50; three hours; four times daily) depart from 7.30am to 3.30pm Monday to Saturday and from 9.30am to 3.30pm on Sunday. Some buses also take the longer, scenic route from Savusavu to Labasa along Natewa Bay, and depart at 9am ($10, six hours). At 9am and 1pm a bus goes as far as Wainigadru ($5.50, 3 hours) and, at 4.30pm, to Yanuavou ($3.85, 2½ hours).

Buses from Savusavu to Napuca ($5.40, 4½ hours), located at the tip of the Tunuloa Peninsula, depart at 10.30am and 2.30pm daily. The afternoon bus stays there overnight and returns at 7am. A 4pm bus goes to Drekeniwai and on to Buca Bay ($3.85), where it stays overnight. There is no bus from Savusavu to Nabouwalu; you have to catch a morning bus to Labasa and change buses there.

For confirmation of bus timetables, ring **Vishnu Holdings** *(☎ 885 0276)*.

Getting Around

There is an abundance of taxis. They can be hailed on the street or booked. To book a taxi, try **Hot Spring Taxis** *(☎ 885 0226)*. Rates are about $20 per hour. You can also hire small carriers from the bus station – they're really reasonable if you're travelling in a group.

There are buses from Savusavu to Lesiaceva Point for Beachcomber's Driftwood Village and Jean-Michel Cousteau Fiji Islands Resort ($0.50, 15 minutes). The bus leaves Savusavu between 6am and 5pm five times daily, except on Sunday.

Savusavu airstrip is 3km south of town. Local buses do pass the airport every so often; however, a taxi to/from Savusavu only costs $2.

Budget Rent a Car *(☎ 881 1999)* in Labasa will deliver and pick up 4WD jeeps in Savusavu. If you rent for three days, this service is free. The Hot Springs Hotel also has a small car that they rent out for $125 per day.

AROUND SAVUSAVU

Waisali Rainforest Reserve

In the verdant mountains north of Savusavu, lies the protected Waisali Rainforest. While it doesn't offer much of a trek (it's about 20 minutes each way), the foliage is beautiful and the waterfall at the bottom is popular with locals. Take care if it's been raining – the rocks at the foot of the waterfall can be treacherously slippery. There seems to be some dispute over the management of the area and the trails, although new, are unfinished and rough. You can enter the park 20km north of Savusavu, directly off the road to Labasa. It's not properly marked, however there is a large cement block on the right as you head north. Bus drivers should know where to drop you (ask before you board) as should most carrier and taxi drivers. A carrier will cost around $40 return from Savusavu – not bad if you're in a group.

Nukubolu

The remains of the village of Nukubolu are also in the mountains north of Savusavu. The Nukubolu people lived here before Fiji's cession to Britain but met their end following a blunder in etiquette made by their chief, Tui Koroalau. The chief of Cakaudrove, Tui Cakau, sent Chief Koroalau *tabua* (the teeth of sperm whales) along with a request for pigs. Chief Koroalau refused and sent the *tabua* back. *Tabua* have huge ceremonial value for Fijians and returning them is a grave insult. Whether or not Chief Koroalau intended to offend Chief Cakau or just didn't have enough pigs, we shall never know. War broke out and, although the Nukubolu people retreated inland, they could not escape utter defeat by the forces of Cakaudrove.

The remains of the extensive village are on the banks of a creek, in a fertile volcanic crater with hot springs steaming nearby. There are well-preserved stone building foundations, terraces and carefully constructed thermal pools. Locals dry *kava* on corrugated-iron sheets laid over the pools and bathe in the hot springs when sick.

If you've got a 4WD, you can visit the remains of the village. They are on the property of the village of Biaugunu, so take a *sevusevu* for the chief and ask permission first. The turnoff is about 20km northwest of Savusavu. Continue about 8km inland and over a couple of river crossings. You can also rent a carrier from town to take you there and combine it with a trip to Waisali Rainforest Reserve.

TUNULOA PENINSULA

Tunuloa Peninsula, also known as Natewa or Cakaudrove Peninsula, makes up the southeastern section of Vanua Levu. Lush and scenic, it's an excellent area for exploring by 4WD. If you can arrange a guide in Savusavu

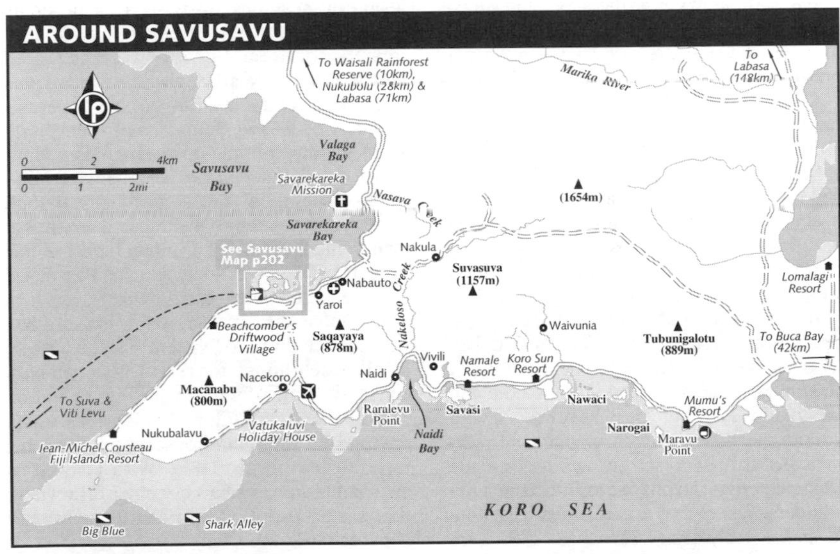

Bêche-de-Mer

European traders flocked to Fiji in the early 19th century to hunt the lucrative bêche-de-mer (sea cucumber). It fetched huge profits in Asia, where it's still considered a delicacy and aphrodisiac.

You are likely to see some of these ugly slug-like creatures while snorkelling or diving. They feed on organic matter in the sand and serve an important role as cleaners in the lagoon ecosystem. There are various types: some are smooth and sticky, some prickly, some black and some multicoloured. After being cut open and cleaned, they are boiled to remove the salt, then sun-dried or smoked. Many find the taste revolting, but it is highly nutritious, with 50% to 60% protein.

Bêche-de-mer is still a lucrative commodity, both for local use and for export, and unscrupulous traders are delivering dive equipment to remote areas and promising high rewards. Villagers of the Bua region are renowned for harvesting the creature. Usually untrained and unaware of the risks, they are encouraged by the traders to dive in deep waters, risking their lives by using faulty scuba equipment. Many end up with the bends and a stint in the Fiji Recompression Chamber and several have died.

or from your resort, it can also offer some great bird-watching and hiking. The bumpy, dirt Hibiscus Hwy runs from Savusavu to the road's end at Napuka, passing copra plantations, old homesteads, waving villagers and thriving forests. The road becomes extremely slippery with the rain; if you've rented a vehicle, double-check to make sure the tyres are good before you set out. There are no restaurants or shops along this route; pack a lunch and bring some water.

About 20km east of Savusavu, the Hibiscus Hwy veers right (south); the turnoff to the left (north) follows the western side of Natewa Bay, an alternative 4WD route to Labasa. About 35km further along the Hibiscus Hwy from this intersection is the turnoff into the village of **Drekeniwai**, where former prime minister Sitiveni Rabuka was born.

Once you hit Buca Bay, the highway turns left (north), becoming more potholed as it heads through the habitat of the rare **silktail bird**. Found only on this peninsula and on Taveuni, the silktail has sadly made it onto the world's endangered-species list with logging being its major opponent. The bird is about 8cm high and is black with a white patch on its tail.

If you turn right (south) at Buca Bay, you'll head through Natuva Village and then up over the mountain to the next village of **Dakuniba**. The road is one big pothole and the going is slow but you'll be rewarded with dazzling views over the forest and out to sea. In a beautiful forest setting, just outside Dakuniba, **petroglyphs** are inscribed on large boulders. Where they are from and what they mean has sadly been lost to history; they are thought to be of ceremonial or mystical significance. Dakuniba means 'behind the fence', and there is a theory that the rocks may have been part of a single structure. Be sure to bring a *sevusevu* for the village chief; the people of Dakuniba are very friendly and may offer to take you to a nearby beach to swim, fish or snorkel. The famous Rainbow Reef is offshore from Dakuniba, but is more easily accessible from the island of Taveuni (see the Taveuni chapter for information).

Places to Stay

Naqere Estate *(☎ 888 0022; e naqere@connect.com.fj; singles/doubles $110/150)* is a beautiful, spacious B&B set in a peaceful garden about 25km from Savusavu. Extremely comfortable with sweeping water views, this is a perfect place to get off the beaten track and relax. Rooms have king-size bamboo beds and your friendly host will whip up three home-cooked meals a day, which are included in the rate. There is a minimum three-night stay, a maximum of four people, and the bathroom is shared. There's a swimming hole nearby, snorkelling off the property and you can kayak a short distance out to a picturesque beach.

La Dolce Vita *(☎ 888 0022)*, is a private home next door to Naqere Estate with a small beach house for rent. Under renovation at the time of writing, the one-bedroom house is self-catering and looks out to sea. Judging by the main house, it will also be tasteful and comfortable. With kayaks, a swimming hole and a very cheerful owner, this is a great option for a family, with reasonable rates expected.

Lomalagi Resort *(☎ 881 6098, fax 881 6099; w www.lomalagi.com; villa doubles $375)*, meaning 'heaven', is hidden high on a hill overlooking beautiful Natewa Bay. About 24km east of Savusavu, the resort is spread out over a hundred-year old working coconut plantation. Each villa is spacious and has a full kitchen and large deck. With a rubber ducky in the tub and not a lot on the walls, the décor of the villas may not be for everyone, however the views are spectacular and you can count on utter privacy. The seawater pool is gorgeous and activities include kayaking, swimming, village trips, snorkelling and biking. Meals are included and are customised for guests. The owner goes out of her way to ensure you have a fantastic stay. No children under 12 are permitted. Someone from the resort will meet you at the airport; if you're driving, turn off at the Salt Lake Rd sign, not far from where the Hibiscus Hwy turns south.

Hannibal's Eco Adventure Resort *(☎ 992 3123; w www.hannibalsresort.com; Nakobo Rd, Bagasu Village)* is very new, set snugly in Fawn Harbour. A true labour of love, its five bright cabins are set in a beautiful garden and have sea views and breezes (no fans). Eco elements include composting toilets (all en suites), an organic garden and solar power. Most staff are from the local village, whom the friendly owners have involved from the start of the project. Activity orientated, you will be able to fish, hike, snorkel and dive here; a white-sand beach is 2km away. All meals and non-motor activities are included, but still the proposed rates seemed high.

The **Rainbow Reef Resort** is southeast of Buca Bay. Accessible only by boat, it's most easily reached from Taveuni. See the Places to Stay text in the Taveuni chapter for more information.

LABASA

pop 24,095

Labasa, Vanua Levu's largest town, is on the northwestern side of the island's mountain range, about 5km inland on the banks of the meandering Labasa River. The fertile riverbanks and reclaimed mangrove swamps have made this area a centre for the sugar industry since colonial days. The Labasa sugar mill was opened on the eastern edge of Labasa in 1894, when huge cane plantations were established. Sadly, in early 2003, Cyclone Ami left Labasa under 1.2 metres of water and all but obliterated the surrounding cane fields. As farmers struggle to restore their livelihoods, you're still likely to see trucks loaded with cane rolling through town and parked in an endless queue outside the mill. Raw sugar, molasses and timber are still exported from Malau, a port north of the mill. Labasa's population is predominantly Indo-Fijian, many of whom are descendants of indentured labourers brought to work on the plantations.

While Labasa is a bustling trade, service and administrative centre for western Vanua Levu, the town itself doesn't have a lot to offer tourists. If you hire a 4WD, however, the surrounding area is great for exploring.

Information

Labasa's main drag is Nasekula Rd; this is where you'll find the majority of shops and services. There are three banks in town, the **National**, **ANZ** and **Westpac**. All change currency and travellers cheques. ANZ also has a 24-hour ATM that accepts foreign debit and credit cards. The **post office** *(Nasekula Rd)* has a row of card-phones outside. At the time of writing, email had not yet hit Labasa.

Northern Travel Service *(☎ 881 1454; cnr Nasekula Rd & Damanu St; open 8am-5pm Mon-Fri, 8am-noon Sat)* is the booking office for **Sun Air** and **Consort Shipping**. Nearby, you'll find **Air Fiji** *(☎ 881 1188; Nasekula Rd; open 8am-4.30 Mon-Fri, 8am-noon Sat)*, **Beachcomber Cruises** *(☎ 881 7788, fax 881 1160; Nasekula Rd; open 8am-5pm Mon-Fri, 8am-1pm Sat)* as well as **Patterson Brothers Shipping** *(☎ 881 2444, fax 881 3460; Nasekula Rd; open 8.30am-1.30pm & 2.30pm-4.30pm Mon-Fri, 8.30am-noon Sat)*.

The **public library** *(open 9am-1pm & 2pm-5pm Mon-Fri, 9am-noon Sat)* at the Civic Centre has a limited collection of books that you can peruse.

East of the river is the hospital and the provincial council's multi-storey office building. Note the stone monolith in front of the building. In the old Fijian religion, such stones were worshipped, as it was believed they embodied the spirit of ancestral gods.

In an emergency, contact the **police** *(☎ 881 1222; Nadawa St)* or the **hospital/ambulance** *(☎ 881 1444; Butinikama-Siberia Rd)*. **My Chemist** *(☎ 881 4611; Nasekula Rd; open 8am-6pm Mon-Thur, 8am-7pm Fri, 8am-3pm Sat)* is fairly well stocked with medicines and vitamins.

Things to See & Do

Just south of town is the **Wasavula Ceremonial Site** on Vunimoli Rd (see the boxed text Monolithic Gods). At the entrance to the site is a sacred monolith that villagers believe grew from the ground. The stone broke about four years ago but the villagers have resurrected it with a bit of plaster. Behind the standing stone is the village cemetery, surrounded by a small, beautiful garden. You will see lots of small stones built into low walls, apparently built as a border to keep unwanted guests at bay. Beyond is the area used during cannibalistic ceremonies – a flat *vatu ni bokola* or head-chopping stone, another rock where the severed head was placed, and a bowl-like stone in which the brain was placed for the chief. It all sounds fairly gruesome but, unless you are given a guided tour, you could probably walk right past most of these stones without noticing. The site is on the left, about 2km south off Nasekula Rd. You can reach it by bus or taxi. Be sure to ask for permission in the village and present a *sevusevu* before you go traipsing about.

Labasa Sugar Mill *(☎ 881 1511)* is about 1.5km east of town. The crushing season is from June to December when a queue of cane-loaded trucks snakes its way out of the mill and down the road. **Waiqele hot springs** is 3km beyond the airport. Take the Waiqele bus ($0.75).

Places to Stay

Labasa Riverview Private Hotel *(☎ 881 1367; Nadawa St; dorm beds $15, singles/doubles with shared facilities $20/30, with en suite $30/40, with air-con and en suite $45/55)* is an excellent option. Rooms are cosy and comfortable and the five-bed dorm has a clean, well-equipped kitchen. The hotel's bar and veranda overlooks the river. A five-minute walk north of town, this place is peaceful, relaxed and has a very friendly proprietor.

Labasa Guest House *(☎ 881 2155; Nanuku St; singles/doubles/triples with shared facilities $22/25/30, singles & doubles/triples with en suite $28/35)* is a friendly place conveniently located near the town centre. Rooms are brightly painted (and we mean *bright*) and have views over the garden. The price of the room depends on its size but all are clean. The kitchen and lounge are available for

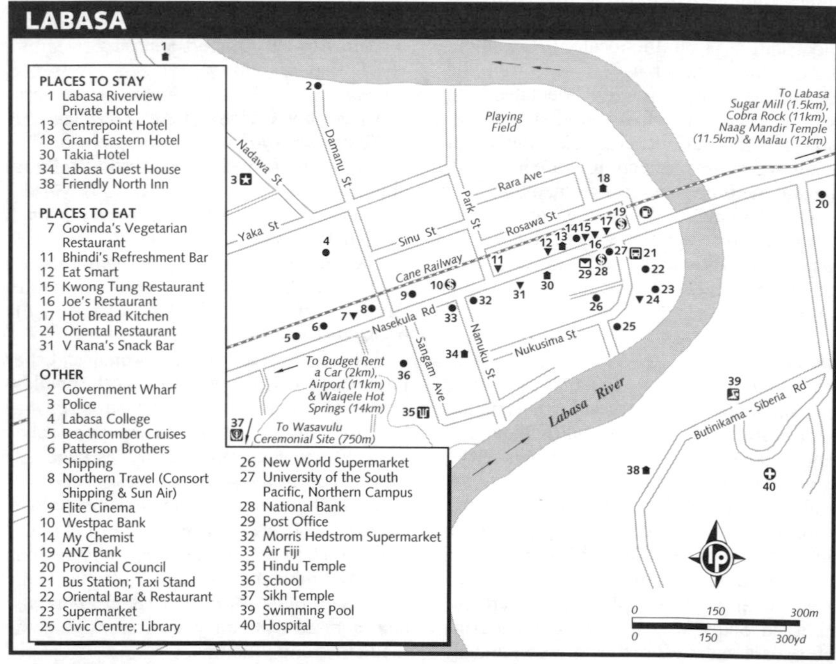

Monolithic Gods

Although the Wasavula Ceremonial Site remains shrouded in mystery, it is thought to be related to similar sites of the *naga* cult found in Viti Levu's Sigatoka Valley. In the old religion, those who betrayed ceremonial secrets would face insanity and death by the ancestral spirits and gods, so what is known about such places is mostly based on hearsay and vague memories.

Before the arrival of Christianity, ceremonial sites were venues for communicating with ancestral gods. Rituals performed at the sites provided a spiritual link between the people and the earth, time, crops and fertility. It is believed that this was where chiefs and priests were installed, where male initiation rites took place and where a *bokola*, the dead body of an enemy, was offered to the gods.

Stone monoliths at the sites were seen as actual gods or as the shrines of gods. These stones were often used for refuge; if someone who had committed a crime made it to the monolith before being caught, their life would be spared.

While the rituals of long ago are no longer practiced at Wasavula Ceremonial Site, the ancestral gods haven't been evicted so easily. It is still revered as a sacred place by the village people and is now where they bury their dead. Some people continue to see the monolith as supernatural; it is said that in photos of villagers with the monolith, the villagers have often vanished from the developed pictures.

guests to use but are somewhat cramped and dingy. You may be able to get cheaper walk-in rates; look for the large pink house on the west side of the street.

Grand Eastern Hotel *(☎ 881 1022, fax 881 4011; W www.tokatoka.com.fj; Rosawa St; standard/deluxe rooms $95/115)* is Labasa's most upmarket hotel, with a beautiful pool and decent restaurant. Rooms don't have much character but do have views of the river, small porches, air-con and private facilities. It's worth paying the extra for the newer deluxe rooms for their river-facing porches.

Friendly North Inn *(☎ 881 1555, fax 881 6429; Butinikama-Siberia Rd; singles/doubles with fan $35/45, with air-con $45/55, apartment with air-con $65, extra mattress/bed $10/15)* is opposite the hospital, east of the river. A 15-minute walk from town, it's utterly quiet. Motel-like rooms all come with en suite and are clean but are lacking in atmosphere. The hotel's large, open *bure* has a TV and beer on tap; meals are available if ordered in advance. A taxi into town will cost $2.

Takia Hotel *(☎ 881 1655, fax 881 3527; Nasekula Rd; singles/doubles with fan $35/45, with air-con & vinyl $55/65, with air-con & carpet $60/70, suite singles/doubles $70/80, $10 per extra person)*, near the bus station, is a three-storey relic from the '70s. Rooms are spacious and clean, each with a TV, fridge and kettle. The vinyl and carpet may come back into style any day now. Try not to get a room next to the noisy road.

Centrepoint Hotel *(☎ 881 1057, fax 881 5057; Nasekula Rd; singles/doubles with fan $38/48, with air-con $48/58, $10 per extra person)* is right in the middle of town but nothing special. Rooms are big and clean and staff seem friendly enough.

Places to Eat

Labasa is teeming with hole-in-the-wall places dishing up Indian or Chinese food.

V. Rana's Snack Bar *(☎ 881 4351; Nasekula Rd; snacks $0.40; open 7am-6pm Mon-Fri, 7am-4pm Sat)* is friendly and has comfortable booths where you can snack on bhajis, samosas and Indian sweets.

Bhindi's Refreshment Bar *(☎ 881 3007; Nasekula Rd; snacks $1.40; open 6.30am-6pm Mon-Thur, 6.30am-7pm Fri, 6.30am-4pm Sat)* serves good home-made snacks including samosas, egg and cheese sandwiches, mutton pies and cakes.

Govinda's Vegetarian Restaurant *(☎ 881 2912; Nasekula Rd; snacks $0.30, thali $7; open 7.30am-7.30pm Mon-Sat, 8am-5pm Sun)* does a fantastic thali, samosas and sweets.

Eat Smart *(☎ 811 6611; Nasekula Rd; mains $3; open 6am-6pm Mon-Thur, 6am-8pm Fri & Sat)* is a fast-food diner serving fish & chips, curries, chop suey and sweet & sour prawns. A beer costs $3.

Kwong Tung Restaurant *(☎ 881 1980; Nasekula Rd; mains $5; open 7am-7pm Mon-Fri, 10.30am-3pm Sat)* is a huge dining hall with dishes of fish in black bean sauce, chicken in chilli sauce and wonton soup.

Joe's Restaurant *(☎ 881 1766; Nasekula Rd; meals $8; open 7am-9pm Mon-Sat, 11am-3pm & 6pm-9pm Sun)* has more creative Chinese dishes like sesame chicken in sweet & sour sauce, Mongolian lamb and sate king prawns. There's a basic bar and a TV blaring in the corner. If you're super hungry, you can order a whole roasted chicken from the appetizer menu.

Oriental Bar & Restaurant *(☎ 881 7321; Nukusima St; meals $5-10; open 10am-3pm & 6.30pm-10pm Mon-Sat, 6.30pm-10pm Sun)* is definitely Labasa's most atmospheric restaurant, with a strong Chinese twist to its Fijian décor. Although it feels slightly upmarket, the prices are extremely reasonable. The bar is fairly well stocked and the menu has a good variety of Chinese dishes, including lots of vegie and a few Fijian options. No caps or vests allowed.

Grand Eastern Hotel *(breakfast/lunch/dinner $10/12/15; 7am-9.30am, 11.30am-2pm & 6.30pm-9pm daily)* serves Western-style food. Decorated with historical photos of Labasa and spilling out onto the deck, it's a pleasant place to dine.

The **Hot Bread Kitchen** *(Nasekula Rd; open 5am-8pm Mon-Thur & Sun, 5am-8.30pm Fri & Sat)* has fresh bread. If you're heading out exploring and need some snacks, head to the **New World Supermarket** *(7.45am-6pm Mon-Thur, 7.45am-6pm Fri, 7.45am-4pm Sat)* near the bus station or the **Morris Hedstrom Supermarket** *(open 7.45am-6pm Mon-Wed, 7.45am-6.30 Thur, 7.45am-7.30 Fri, 7.45-4.30 Sat)* further up the road.

Entertainment

The **Elite Cinema** *(☎ 881 1260; Nasekula Rd; adult/child $3/1)* shows older films, the majority of which are in Hindi. Other than that, there's not much going on in town. You might try the **bar** at the Grand Eastern Hotel for a poolside drink.

Getting There & Away

It is possible to buy tickets in Labasa for bus/boat combinations to Suva and Lautoka. See the Getting There & Away chapter for information on reaching Vanua Levu via boat or plane.

Bus There are regular buses between Labasa and Savusavu ($5.50, five times daily, four on Sunday) departing between 7am and 4.15pm. There is also a 9am bus that takes the long route (about six hours) to Savusavu around the northeast, following Natewa Bay. Buses to Nabouwalu depart at 10.30am and 2pm ($8, Monday to Saturday).

Getting Around

The majority of shops, businesses and hotels are within easy walking distance of the town centre. If you are going further afield, there is no shortage of taxis in Labasa. You'll find the majority of them at the main stand near the bus station. **Budget Rent a Car** *(☎ 881 1999; Vakamasisuasua; 9am-4pm Mon-Fri, 8am-1pm Sat)* has an office a little way out of town where you can rent 4WD vehicles.

The airport is about 11km southwest of Labasa. The turnoff is 4km west of Labasa, just past the Wailevu River. To reach the airport, catch the Waiqele bus from Labasa bus station; it departs between 6am and 4.15pm ($0.55, four times daily Monday to Saturday, as per flight schedule Sunday). A taxi from Labasa costs $8.

AROUND LABASA

The area around Labasa is a great place to explore by 4WD. There are a few points of interest; however, it's definitely the adventure of finding them rather than the sights themselves that make it worthwhile. For all of these sights, you'll need to turn left onto Wainikoro Rd, just past the sugar mill and across from a secondary school. This is the main road out of town to the east.

Cobra Rock

Brightly painted with red, yellow and blue, **Naag Mandir Temple** is built around the sacred Cobra Rock. About 3m in height, the rock's natural curved formation resembles a cobra poised to strike. Covered in colourful flower and tinsel garlands, the rock is beseeched with offerings of fruit, fire and coconut milk. Devotees swear that the rock grows in size and that the roof has had to be raised several times over the years. Remove your shoes before entering the beautifully tiled temple; then circle the rock clockwise three or five times. Several buses pass the temple, including those to Natewa Bay. A taxi costs around $10. If you're driving, the temple is 10km from the turning for Wainikoro Road; you'll pass two smaller temples before you reach Naag Mandir.

Korovatu Beach

Down through dense coconut trees and past the lounging cows lies Korovatu Beach *(admission per car $5)*. The sand is a little coarse but it's a good spot for swimming at high tide. You can also see Malau Wharf from here, with freight ships full of sugar and timber. The beach is popular and can be crowded on holidays. As a note of respect, it's a good idea to wear a T-shirt if you go swimming. You'll find covered areas, picnic tables and toilets here but no water or snacks; bring your own. It's difficult to reach the beach unless you have a car as it's about 3km from the main road. Take the first turn left after Cobra Rock, over the tracks. The road passes strange rock formations and runs through farmed land that used to be a tidal swamp. The beach is on private land; you'll come to a gate where you'll be asked to pay for the upkeep.

Floating Island

This is definitely to be done for the journey rather than the final spectacle. You'll pass rugged scenery, meet some farmers and maybe get lost in a cane field. About 50km northeast of Labasa, the Floating Island is just that – land with trees that bobs on a pond and gets blown around with the wind. As the pond is only about three times the size of the island, it's easy for the island to reach an edge and disguise itself as attached land. You may be able to hop on the island and ride across the small pond, but prepare to get muddy.

To reach the island by 4WD, follow the directions to Cobra Rock and continue following Wainikoro Rd. At the roundabout, this road turns left; follow it through the village. Continue on for 19km and take the turning on the right for Nekelikoso. After 6km, take a left onto Lagalaga Rd. Ask permission at the first house on your right and then follow the track up behind it. When you reach a creek, park and trek right through the long grass to the pond. By this point, you will hopefully have been accosted by the children from the village who will gladly show you the way. Be sure to head out on a full tank of fuel and some food and water; there's nothing in these parts but sugarcane. The dirt road can be rather treacherous; probably not the best trip to make in the rain.

There is a bus to Lagalaga which departs Labasa at 1.30pm for the 2½ hour journey. This bus returns, often almost immediately, leaving you little hope of finding the island and much hope of getting stranded.

NABOUWALU & AROUND

Nabouwalu is a small settlement on the island's southwestern point. Early in the 19th century, European traders flocked to nearby **Bua Bay** to exploit *yasi dina* (sandalwood), which grew in the hills. Today, the ferry landing is about the only draw for travellers.

Nabouwalu has administrative offices, a post office, a small market and a store. Offshore to the northwest, the island of Yadua

The Goods, the Bad & the Ugly

In 1800 the American schooner *Argo* was on its way to the English penal colony on Norfolk Island, 100km north of Auckland, when it was shipwrecked near Oneata, east of Lakeba in the Lau Group. Many of the sailors were killed and eaten by the locals, but Oliver Slater survived by befriending powerful chiefs and helping in their wars with his knowledge of muskets and gunpowder.

The sailors brought with them a disease, thought to be Asian cholera, and a plague broke out in the Fijian islands. Known as *na lila balavu* (wasting sickness), it took a terrible toll and destroyed whole communities. Sick people were walled up in caves, strangled, or even buried alive in an attempt to avoid the spread of the disease.

Slater moved to a village on Bua Bay in Vanua Levu, where his eyes fell upon forests of precious sandalwood. When he was eventually picked up by a passing Spanish vessel, he spilled the beans about the sought after trees growing on nearby hills and later returned to Fiji to facilitate its trade. Ships flocked to the area, which became known as Sandalwood Bay. Cargoes of the fragrant timber fetched high prices in Asia and the Fijians traded it for trinkets, muskets, alcohol and assistance in local wars. As a result the chiefs of Bua gained relative prosperity and prestige.

The sandalwood trade was short-lived as supply was soon exhausted. Slater's luck eventually ran out too – the influential beachcomber was killed on Moturiki in the Lomaiviti Group.

Tabu is home to the last sizeable population of rare and spectacular crested iguana. It became Fiji's first wildlife reserve in 1980.

Places to Stay & Eat

Boats that arrive here are met by buses heading for Labasa but if you do wish to stay overnight in Nabouwalu, there is a **government guesthouse** (*☎ 883 6027; beds $20*). It's often booked out with government workers so be sure to call ahead. There are basic cooking facilities and it's a good idea to bring along some of your own supplies.

Getting There & Away

For ferries, see the Getting There & Away chapter. Nabouwalu can only be reached by bus from Labasa, not from Savusavu. The bus leaves Labasa at 10.30am and 2pm, takes five hours and returns each morning. If you're heading to Savusavu and are not interested in visiting Labasa, ask the driver to drop you off at the junction with the road to Savusavu. You may have to wait at the intersection for about an hour for a connecting bus to Savusavu.

The road from Nabouwalu around the southern coast to Savusavu (127km) is barely passable by 4WD or carrier.

OFFSHORE ISLANDS

Kioa

The island of Kioa (25 sq km) is inhabited by Polynesians originally from the tiny coral reef island of Vaitupu in Tuvalu (formerly Ellice Islands). As their home island suffered from poor soils and overcrowding, the community decided to purchase another more fertile island and relocate some families to reduce the population pressure. Kioa was purchased in 1947 for $15,000; the people of Vaitupu had earned the money working for the Americans who had occupied their islands during WWII. About 600 people now live here, in a colourful and immaculately kept village. The people are very warm and friendly; one of the first things you can see from the sea is a giant sign saying 'Talofa' (the equivalent of Fijian *Bula*). The women are known for their woven crafts and fishing is done from small, traditional *drua*. The people of Kioa have a traditional drink called *toddy*. Made of fermented coconut sap, it's got something more of a kick than kava.

As Kioa is privately owned, you cannot show up without an invitation. There is no accommodation or facilities for tourists, however, Tui Tai Adventure Cruises does make a stop here (see Activities in Savusavu).

Rabi

Rabi (66 sq km), east of the northern tip of the Tunuloa peninsula, is popu lated by Micronesians originally from Banaba (Ocean Island), in Kiribati. At the turn of the 20th century the naive islanders sold the phosphate mining rights of Banaba in return for an annual payment, and sadly their tiny island was slowly ruined. WWII brought these people another blow when the Japanese invaded Banaba and massacred many villagers. Following the war, Rabi was purchased for the Banabans by the British Government and 2000 survivors were resettled here. Today the island has two villages, Uma and Buakonikai, with a total population of 4500.

If you're interested in visiting Rabi, you must first ask permission from the **Island Council** (*☎ 881 2913*). If you're extended an invitation, catch a bus from Savusavu to Karoko where small boats wait for passengers to Rabi ($50 one way). The **Rabi Island Council Guesthouse** (*☎ 881 2913 ext 30; operates Mon, Wed & Fri; dorm beds $50*) has beds in basic, four-bed rooms. The guesthouse is located between the two villages, behind the post office and general store.

Nukubati

This privately owned island is just off the northern coast of Vanua Levu, about 40km west of Labasa. Actually two small islands linked by mangroves, it takes about 30 minutes to walk around at low tide. Once occupied by Fijian villagers, in the 19th century a local chief gave the island to a German gunsmith who settled here with his Fijian wife.

Nukubati Island Resort (*☎ 881 3901, fax 881 3914; Ⓦ www.nukubati.com; bungalow/honeymoon bure doubles $1260/1560*) is a secluded place far from the usual tourist destinations. Suites face a white-sand beach. The steep prices include gourmet meals and boat transfers from Labasa. There is a maximum of 14 guests, only adult couples are accepted, except for whole island bookings at a mere $7000 per night. Activities include tennis, sailing, windsurfing, and fishing. The dive shop caters for experienced divers only.

Taveuni

Taveuni's stunning natural beauty, both under and above the sea, make it a haven for divers, bushwalkers and nature lovers. Nicknamed 'The Garden Island', it's a profusion of tropical plants and flowers, with world-class dive sites on its doorstep. Taveuni is easily accessible and relatively compact, and yet, without a particular town or area singled out as *the* tourist destination, it is far from feeling overrun. Bring an umbrella – this is rainforest territory, and January or February brings the heat and humidity.

The small population (12,000) is spread thinly across the island; there are villages and small towns but no urban centres. The population is mainly indigenous Fijian with a smaller crowd of Indo-Fijians and expats. Taveuni, along with Eastern Vanua Levu and the islands of Qamea, Matagi and Laucala, form the Vanua region of Cakaudrove. Somosomo, Taveuni's largest village, is the seat of the region's chiefly Fijian administration. The island's main source of income is agriculture, mostly copra and to a lesser extent *dalo* and kava crops. These days, tourism is also contributing an increasing amount to the economy.

At 42km in length and about 10km wide, Taveuni is the third-largest Fijian island. It's just 9km from the southeastern end of Vanua Levu, across the indigo waters of the Somosomo Strait. Much of Taveuni's coastline is rugged, set against some of Fiji's highest peaks. Des Voeux Peak reaches up 1195m and the cloud-shrouded Mt Uluigalau, at 1241m, is the country's second-highest summit. The volcanic soil and the abundant rainfall dumped on the island by the prevailing southeasterly winds make Taveuni one of Fiji's most fertile areas.

The island's volcanic past is evident in its black-sand beaches. The beaches at Lavena and Matei have some white sand and are good for swimming and snorkelling. The smaller offshore islands of Qamea, Matagi and Laucala have stunning beaches but are mainly the domain of exclusive resorts. While the northeast of Taveuni is fringed by reefs, the southwest has deep water close to shore. The eastern side of the island has the dramatic waterfalls while the southern coast has dramatic caves and blowholes.

Highlights

- Dive beneath the indigo waters of the Somosomo Strait to visit the incredible Rainbow Reef
- Attend mass at Wairiki Catholic Mission for melodious singing with a sea view
- Trek the lush Lavena Coastal Walk and be rewarded with a swim in a deep waterfall pool
- Kayak along the rugged coast, watching for dolphins and turtles
- Take a guided day hike along the Vidawa Rainforest Trail; to fortified village sites, through verdant vegetation filled with rare birds and past Tavoro Waterfalls
- Snorkel at Vuna Reef and see dazzling coral and improbable creatures

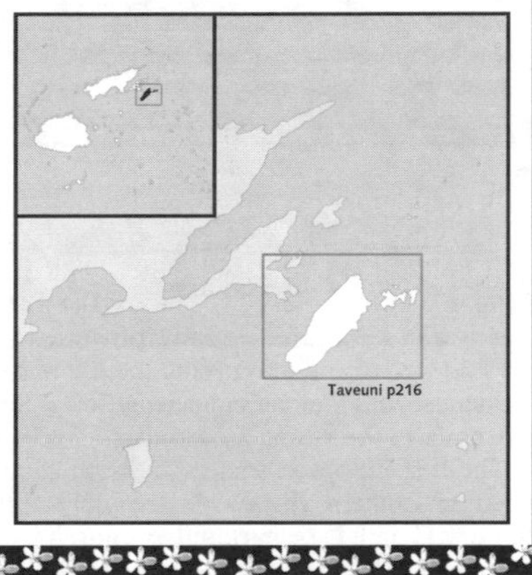

History

According to local lore, the Paramount Chief Tui Vuna who was originally from Moturiki near Ovalau, once presided over the south of Taveuni. His vast army was long undefeated, partly due to the strategic location of the hilltop fort which allowed them to survey the reef for incoming canoes. His opponent, the Tui Cakau of Somosomo, eventually overcame him by bribing the Tui Vuna's relatives to abduct his son. The hilltop fortification still exists in the south, near Vanu Point, however it is now completely overgrown.

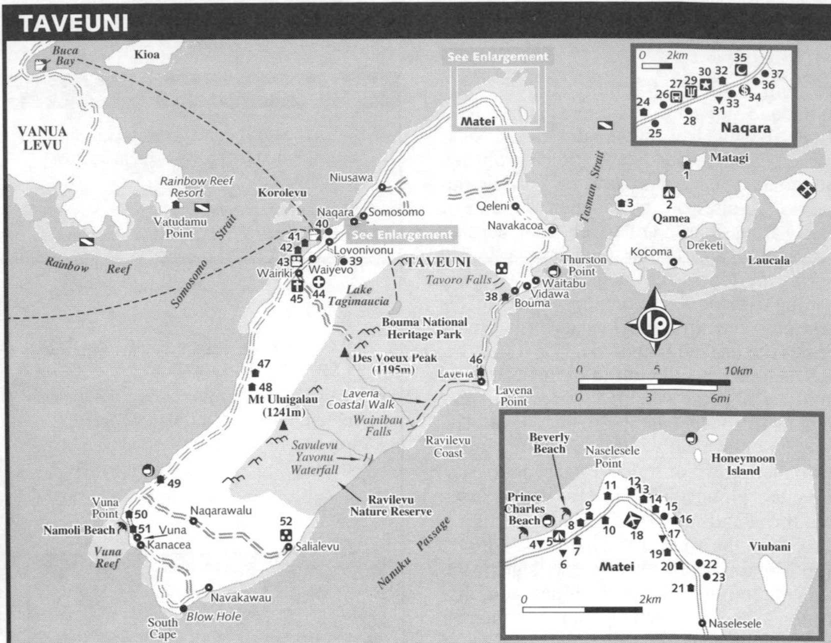

Before Europeans arrived on Taveuni, the Fijian villagers had long been trading, and occasionally warring with the seafaring Tongans. In the mid-19th century the Tongan warlord Ma'afu, already powerful in the Lau Group and attempting to extend his influence, was defeated in a battle at Somosomo, in the island's northeast.

The first European traders and settlers arrived in southern Taveuni in the early 19th century. Land was bartered or purchased from the Tui Vuna and the traders and settlers established plantations and homesteads. Taveuni developed good shipping services and roads for the time. The island's deep fertile soil grew high-quality cotton. When cotton prices collapsed, sugar cane was planted but failed in Taveuni's wet climate. The ruins of the 100-year-old Billyard sugar mill still stand in Salialevu, southern Taveuni. Cattle and sheep grazing also had a short-lived success, as did coffee and tropical fruit plantations, before copra plantations took over.

Flora & Fauna

Taveuni is covered in dense, verdant rainforest and exotic flora and fauna. Its rugged geography has hindered farming, leaving forests and wildlife relatively untouched. You don't have to venture far to encounter ferns, orchids, rare palms and native trees such as *evuevu*, *sinu*, *vutu*, *ivi* and *dilo*. Fiji's national flower, the *tagimaucia,* or *Medinilla waterhousei,* grows only at high altitudes; it's found in Taveuni's Lake Tagimaucia and on one mountain on Vanua Levu. Its petals are white and its branches are bright red.

Taveuni has many copra plantations. Metal bands are placed around the trunks of the coconut trees to stop rats and crabs from climbing up and piercing the coconuts.

Dangers & Annoyances

In recent years, theft has become an increasing problem on Taveuni. While the improving economy may reduce this threat, it's worth taking extra precautions. Always lock your door when sleeping and keep valuables out of sight. Don't wander around alone at night.

All of Taveuni's electricity is supplied by generator. Upmarket resorts have 24-hour power; however, budget and some midrange places only run their generators in the

TAVEUNI

PLACES TO STAY & EAT

1 Matangi Island Resort
2 Campground
3 Qamea Beach Club
4 Island Pizza
5 Beverly Beach Camping; Aquaventure; Swiss Fiji Divers
6 Mrs Harry's
7 Maravu Plantation Resort
8 Taveuni Island Resort
9 Karin's Garden
10 Bibi's Hideaway
11 Garden of Eden
12 Marau Vale
13 Coconut Grove Beachfront Cottages & Cafe
14 Lomalagi
16 Sere-ni-ika
17 Lal's Curry Place
19 Audrey's By the Sea & Sweet Somethings
20 Little Dolphin Treehouse
21 Tovutovu Resort
24 Kool's Accommodation
31 Kumars Restaurant
32 Kaba's Motel
38 Tavoro Waterfalls Visitor Centre
41 Garden Island Resort & Restaurant; Aqua-Trek
42 First Light Inn; Wathi-po-ee Restaurant; Post Office; Ross Handicrafts; Makuluva Restaurant
46 Lavena Lodge
47 The Palms
48 Taveuni Estates
49 Dolphin Bay Divers' Retreat
50 Vatuwiri Farm Resort
51 Vuna Lagoon Lodge

OTHER

15 Raikivi Game Fishing
18 Matei Airport
22 Bhula Bhai Supermarket
23 Taveuni Estate Divers
25 Kaba's Supermarket
26 Grace Ferry Booking Office
27 Bus Terminal
28 Central Indian School
29 Shiri Laxmi Narayan Mandir
30 Police Station
33 Vegetable Stall
34 Colonial Bank; Garden State General Merchants (Budget Rent a Car); Milk Bar
35 Mosque
36 Hot Bread Bakers
37 Krishna Brothers General Merchants (Air Fiji)
39 Waitavala Water Slide
40 Government Wharf; Korean Wharf; Sunset Accommodation
43 Meridian Cinema
44 Hospital; Police
45 Wairiki Catholic Mission
52 Billyard Sugar Mill

evening, usually between 6pm and 10pm. It's a good idea to keep a torch handy to get about in the evenings.

Diving

Taveuni is world-renowned among divers for its spectacular sites. Somosomo Strait (meaning 'good water' in Fijian) has strong tidal currents, which provide a constant flow of nutrients, ideal for soft coral growth and diverse fish life. You can expect to see a gazillion fish, the occasional shark or turtle, fantastic coral and, in November, you may even see pilot whales. The patch reefs of the Somosomo Strait are fairly shallow (10m to 22m) while the strait's fringing reef has wall diving (15m to 30m), larger fish, and is more exposed to weather and surge. Novice divers may find the currents in the Somosomo Strait challenging, however a descent line is generally used; the area is not just for experienced divers as there are many different sites.

Colourful soft-coral sites include the infamous 32km long Rainbow Reef, which fringes the southwest corner of Vanua Levu but is most easily accessed from Taveuni. There are also well-known drift dives along the Great White Wall as well as a plethora of other sites like Cabbage Patch, Blue Ribbon Eel Reef, The Ledge, The Pinnacle, Yellow Grotto, Annie's Bommie and The Zoo and Vuna Reef off southern Taveuni. The island is especially hot and humid in January and February when the water clarity is reduced due to plankton blooms and northerly winds from the equator.

There are a number of dive operations in Matei as well as one in Waiyevo and another in the south at Dolphin Bay Divers' Retreat. The upmarket resorts on the offshore islands of Matagi, Qamea and Laucala have diving for their guests.

Hiking

Taveuni's Lavena Coastal Walk and Tavoro Falls in Bouma National Heritage Park are a must-see for nature lovers. They each have marked trails and don't require the aid of a guide. Avid walkers could also consider the guided Vidawa Forest Walk, also in Bouma, or Des Voeux Peak. If you're super keen and don't mind mud, you can also seek out a guide in Somosomo and trek up to Lake Tagimaucia.

Bird-Watching

Taveuni is one of Fiji's best locations for bird-watching. Over 100 species of birds can be found, partly because the mongoose was never introduced here. Try Des Voeux Peak at dawn for a chance to see the rare orange dove (the male is bright orange with a green head, while the female is mostly green) and the silktail. Another good site is near Qeleni village between Matei and Thurston Point. On the Matei side of the village, follow a 4WD track for 3.5km up the mountain. Here you might see parrots and fantails, particularly between August and September when they're nesting. The deep red feathers of the *kula* parrot were once an important trade item with the Tongans. The forested Lavena coast is also a good spot to see orange or flame doves, Fiji goshawk, wattled honeyeater, and grey and white heron. Vatuwiri Farm Resort at Vuna Point in the south is a great place for viewing fruit bats. You can also see and hear magpies down south, introduced to control insects in the copra plantations.

Getting There & Away

Air The flights between Taveuni and Suva or Nadi are stunning, giving you a chance to peer down at the gorgeous reefs. Both **Sun Air** *(☎ 888 0461)* and **Air Fiji** *(☎ 888 0062)* have two flights daily to/from Nadi (1½ hours) and Savusavu. Sun Air flies to Labasa on Mondays and Fridays while Air Fiji flies two times a day to Nausori near Suva (55 minutes). See the Getting Around chapter for more details.

Matei airport is on the southern tip of Taveuni and is usually open from 8am to 4pm. You'll find both the Sun Air and Air Fiji offices there. There's also an Air Fiji agent in Naqara at **Krishna Brothers General Merchants** *(☎ 888 0051; open 8am-5pm Mon-Fri, 8am-1pm Sat)*.

Boat The Government Wharf for large vessels, including *Spirit of Free Enterprise (SOFE)* and *Adi Savusavu*, is about 1km from Waiyevo, towards Naqara. Smaller boats depart from the Korean Wharf, a bit farther north. Consort Shipping and Beachcomber Cruises both have regular Suva–Savusavu–Taveuni ferries with competitive rates. **Grace Ferry** *(☎ 888 0134; Naqara)* runs a bus/boat trip to Savusavu ($15). The boat departs from the Korean Wharf at 8.45am, landing in Buca Bay from where a bus connects you to Savusavu. In Naqara, the booking office is on the second floor of a large purple building. In Savusavu, it's in Hussein's. Grace Ferry also does occasional transfers to Rabi but you will need to book in advance.

For more information on ferries see the Getting Around chapter.

Getting Around

Taveuni's main road hugs its scenic coast from Lavena in the east, up north and around to Navakawau in the south. At the time of writing it was sealed from Matei to Waiyevo. There are also a couple of inland 4WD tracks. Getting around Taveuni involves a bit of planning, the main disadvantage being the length of time between buses. To get around cheaply and quickly you need to combine buses with walking, or share taxis with a group. You can rent 4WDs in Naqara; however, it's far cheaper to rent a taxi for the day.

To/From the Airport From Matei airport expect to pay about $15 to Waiyevo and $30 to Vuna (Dolphin Bay Divers' Retreat) in a taxi. Matei has many places to stay that are within an easy walk from the airport and most upmarket resorts provide transfers for guests.

Bus Local buses are the best way to meet locals. **Pacific Buses** *(☎ 888 0278)* has a depot in Naqara, opposite the Taveuni Central Indian School. Monday to Saturday, buses run from Wairiki to Bouma at 8.30am, 11.30am and 5pm. The last bus continues to Lavena where the first bus of each morning starts out at 5.45am. On Tuesday and Thursday, all buses go as far as Lavena. On Sunday there is one bus at 3.30pm from Wairiki to Lavena and one from Lavena to Wairiki at 7.30am.

From Naqara, buses run to Navakawau Monday to Saturday at 8.30am, 11.30am and 4.30pm, returning at 5.30am and 11am. On Sunday a bus departs Navakawau at 7.30am and returns from Naqara at 3.30pm. From Matei, buses run to Wairiki at 7am, 11.30am and 3pm Monday to Saturday.

The bus schedule is very lax; buses may show up early or an hour late. Be sure to double check the time of the return bus when you board, just to make sure there is one.

Car In Naqara, **Budget Rent a Car** *(☎ 888 0291; Garden State General Merchants; open 8am-5pm Mon-Fri)* has 4WDs for around $145 per day.

Taxi It's easy to find taxis in the Matei and Waiyevo areas. It may be wise to book ahead on Sunday. Hiring a taxi for a negotiated fee and touring most of the island's highlights in a day will work out cheaper than hiring a car. You may be able to get one for under $100; ask a local to negotiate it for you. For destinations such as Lavena you can go one way by bus and have a taxi pick you up at the end at a designated time (you need to arrange this before you go).

WAIYEVO, SOMOSOMO & AROUND

While not the most picturesque part of the island, this area has the majority of services and can be a good base. Somosomo is the largest village on the island and headquarters for its chiefly leadership. The Great Council of Chiefs' meeting hall was built here in 1986 for the gathering of chiefs from all over Fiji. You'll also find the grave of the missionary William Cross here. Somosomo runs directly into Naqara, the village with the largest shopping area. You'll find supermarkets, the island's one bank, transport links and a few budget hotels. A short taxi ride or a long, dusty walk away is Waiyevo, the administrative capital of the island with the hospital, police station, a budget hotel and resort, and more ferry links. About 2km further south of Waiyevo is Wairiki village, which has a general store, cinema and a beautiful old hilltop Catholic Mission.

Information

Money The only bank on the island is the **Colonial National Bank** *(Naqara; open 9.30am-4pm Mon, 9am-4pm Tues-Fri)*. The bank will exchange currency and travellers cheques but won't do cash advances and doesn't have an ATM. The larger supermarkets and top-end resorts accept credit cards, but you may be charged extra. Some resorts will also change travellers cheques.

Post & Communications The **post office** *(open 8am-1pm & 2pm-4pm Mon-Fri)* is among the shops beneath the First Light Inn in Waiyevo. You can send parcels as well as faxes from here. You'll find a card-phone here as well as outside the supermarkets in Naqara. **Garden State General Merchants** *(☎ 888 0291; Naqara; open 8am-5pm Mon-Fri)* has one computer where you can use the Internet for a pricey $0.50 per minute. **Ross Handicrafts** *(☎ 330 9872; Weiyevo)* also has an Internet connection for $0.40 per minute.

Emergency Taveuni's health facilities are being upgraded thanks to funding from the Australian and Fijian governments. On hand for emergencies are the **hospital** *(☎ 888 0444; Waiyevo)* and **police** *(☎ 888 0222; Waiyevo)*.

International Dateline

For workability, the International Date Line doglegs around Fiji so that everyone is operating on the same time; however, in actuality, the 180° meridian cuts straight through Taveuni, about a 10-minute walk south of Waiyevo. Along the waterside of the road to Wairiki, you'll find a small, red survey beacon marking the spot. If you take the road uphill from Waiyevo (towards the hospital) and cross the field on the right, you'll find a larger board in honour of the meridian, with a bit of local information and a map. It's not all that exciting but worth the 'half in one day half in the other' photo.

Wairiki Catholic Mission

In the mid-17th century, Tongan chief Enele Ma'afu gained control over much of Fiji. His attempt to extend control over Taveuni failed when the Taveuni warriors managed to turn back thousands of Tongan invaders in a canoe battle off Wairiki. The triumphant Taveuni warriors cooked their captured enemies in *lovo* and dined on them with breadfruit – or so the story goes. The mission was built in 1907, thanks to the French missionary who helped the local warriors with their fighting strategy (but, one can assume, not with their dinner plans).

The grand mission looks out over the Somosomo Strait, to the scene of the battle. Its beautiful interior has an impressive beam ceiling and colourful stained glass that reportedly hails from France. In the presbytery, there's a painting of the famous battle. It's worth attending Mass on Sunday at 7am, 9am or 11am; the congregation sits on the floor and belts out in tremendous song.

To find the mission, head south along the coast from Waiyevo; it's about a 20 minute walk. You can't miss the mission on the hill to the left. Behind the mission, a dirt track leads up to a huge white cross. The views from here are superb.

Waitavala Water Slide

This natural water slide is not for the faint of heart. A bruise or two is unavoidable as you fly down these rock chutes. If there's been much rain it can be extremely dangerous; it's definitely best to ask about the conditions first and to watch a local go down the slide before your attempt.

The water slide is about 25 minutes' walk from Waiyevo. With the Garden Island Resort on your left, head north and take the first right at the bus stand. Take another right at the branch in the road, pass a shed and then go left down a hill. You'll see a 'waterfall' sign pointing to the right. Follow this path along the creek (or gushing river, depending on the weather) to the water slide. The river is on the Waitavala estate, which is private land, so if you pass anyone on your way there ask if you can visit.

Des Voeux Peak

At 1195m, Des Voeux Peak is Taveuni's second-highest mountain. On a clear day, the views are fantastic. It's possible to see Lake Tagimaucia and, if you're really lucky, the Lau Group. Try to make it up there by dawn if you are a keen bird-watcher. Allow three to four hours to walk the 6km up, and at least two to return. It's a steep, arduous climb in the heat, so it's best to start out early. To get here, take the inland track just before you reach Wairiki Catholic Mission (if coming from Waiyevo). Alternatively, arrange for a trip up and then walk back at your leisure. On weekdays it's sometimes possible to hitch a ride with Telecom or Public Works Department (PWD) workers who go up to service their equipment. (The First Light Inn can sometimes arrange this for guests.) Taxis can be fairly pricey.

Lake Tagimaucia

Lake Tagimaucia is in an old volcanic crater, in the mountains above Somosomo. At 823m above sea level, masses of vegetation float on the lake, and the national flower, the rare *tagimaucia* (an epiphytic plant) grows on the lake's shores. This red and white flower blooms only at high altitude from late September to late December.

It is a difficult trek around the lake as it is overgrown and often very muddy; you'll need a stick to find firm ground. The track starts from Somosomo where you need to present the Chief with a *sevusevu* and ask permission. Take lunch and allow eight hours for the round trip. Mudu, an elderly man in the village with much knowledge of the lake, may be able to find you a guide.

The Legend of the Tagimaucia

There once lived a young girl with a wild spirit and a tendency to be disobedient. On one fateful day, the mother lost her patience with the girl and beat her with a bundle of coconut leaves, saying she never wanted to see her face again. The distraught girl ran away until she was deep in the forest. She came upon a large vine-covered *ivi* (Polynesian chestnut) tree and decided to climb it. The higher she climbed, the more entangled she became in the vine and, unable to break free, she began to weep. As giant tears rolled down her face they turned to blood and, where they fell onto the vine, they became beautiful white and red *tagimaucia* flowers. Calmed by the sight of the flowers, the girl managed to escape the forest and, upon returning home, was relieved to find an equally calm mother.

Activities

Aqua-Trek Taveuni, based at Garden Island Resort, is a well-equipped dive shop with good boats, Nitrox facilities and a photo centre. It organises dives at Rainbow Reef. Two dives cost $165 and six dives (three days) cost $470 (tanks and belts only). Equipment rental costs $35/25 per day for one/three days or more. Open-water courses cost $660 and one-day dive introductions are $148. The small island of Korolevu, off the resort, has beaches with good snorkelling – trips cost $11 per person plus $6 for fins and booties.

Swimming at Waiyevo in front of the Garden Island Resort is possible two hours either side of high tide. Watch the current though and don't swim near Korean Wharf as sharks are sometimes attracted here by fish cleaning.

Places to Stay

Kool's Accommodation *(☎ 888 0395; Naqara; dorms/singles/doubles $15/20/30)* is a friendly place with basic, clean rooms in a well-maintained building. Private rooms have en suites and there's a kitchen but no fridge. Electricity comes on in the evening. Rooms are fanless. The reception doubles as S&J's Video Club, a pink and purple building across from Kaba's Supermarket.

Kaba's Motel *(☎ 888 0233; Naqara; singles/doubles/triples budget $25/35/55, deluxe 45/55/60)* has big homey rooms with full kitchens, TVs and hot showers. They're a bit dark and some are better than others. The budget rooms are very basic but much brighter with shared bathroom and a kitchen.

Sunset Accommodation *(☎ 888 0229; singles/doubles/triples $15/25/40)* is basic but very cheerful. The cottage-like building has a double and single room, a kitchen and an en suite. Rooms have mosquito nets but no fans, and there's electricity in the evenings. The building is very near the Korean Wharf at Lovonivonu. Look for a sign for Bucalevu School at the bend in the road between Naqara and Waiyevo.

First Light Inn *(☎ 888 0339, fax 888 0387; e firstlight@connect.com.fj; Waiyevo; doubles/ triples with fan $50/60, with air con $60/70, all with en suite)* is a great mid-range option; nothing flashy but clean and very good value. The deck has views over the strait and is a good place to catch the sunset if you can ignore the noise of the neighbouring resort's generator. There is a kitchen for guest use and the friendly owner can help to arrange taxis. The reception doubles as the office for Consort Shipping; rooms are upstairs.

Garden Island Resort *(☎ 888 0286, fax 888 0288; e garden@connect.com.fj; dorms/ singles/doubles $35/150/185, children under 12 free, optional meal plan $80 per person)* is the only top-end place to stay here. It is unremarkable; however, rooms are clean and comfortable with air-con and sea views. There is no beach, but you can swim here at high tide. The lovely pool and restaurant-bar area looks out to the Somosomo Strait and Vanua Levu beyond, and the grounds are dotted with beautiful old flame trees. Two of the hotel rooms have been converted into 4-bed dorms and are good value. The hotel arranges tours of the area for guests only.

Rainbow Reef Resort *(☎ 888 1000, fax 888 1001; w www.rainbowreefresort.com; double bure with/without spa $770/860, family bure $860, including meals, 3-night minimum)* is actually located on Vanua Levu, across the Somosomo Strait from Taveuni. Accessible by boat, it's most easily reached from Taveuni. The closest resort to the famous Rainbow Reef, this small-scale, family-friendly place is on a lovely white-sand beach and has plush beachfront cottages among gardens. Activities include hiking and snorkelling. Diving and tours to Taveuni cost extra. Transfers are $110 return, by boat from Taveuni.

Places to Eat

Garden Island Resort Restaurant *(Waiyevo; breakfast under $10, lunch $10, dinner $20)* is a pleasant place. Tables have a view of the pool and garden and in the evening there's live local music. Meals are mainly Western and not overly inspired, with soups, salads, sandwiches, and grilled fish. The bar is well stocked but, unless you're a guest, you'll only be served alcohol if you've ordered food.

Wathi-po-ee Restaurant and Cannibal Cafe *(☎ 888 0382; Waiyevo; breakfast/lunch or dinner $4/5; open 8am-7pm Mon-Fri, 8am-2pm Sat)* below the First Light Inn, is a basic but friendly place and its thatched outdoor area overlooking the Somosomo Strait is a pleasant place for a beer. For breakfast there's omelettes and sausages while lunch and dinner is mainly Chinese with some *dalo* thrown in for good measure.

Makuluva Restaurant *(☎ 994 5394; Waiyevo; breakfast/lunch $3/4; open 8am-4pm Mon-Fri & Sun)* is in the old market building across from the Garden Island Resort. It's very basic but the cheerful owner whips up great pancakes and hot chocolate for breakfast and Fijian, Indian and Chinese dishes for lunch. Vegetarians will find lots of options here.

Kumars Restaurant *(☎ 888 0435; Naqara; meals $4; open 7am-5.30pm Mon-Sat)*, aka the green curry hut, has Indian dishes as well as a few basic Fijian dishes and the prerequisite chop suey. It's basic and popular with locals.

Milk Bar *(Naqara; snacks $3; open 7am-5pm Mon-Sat)*, disguised behind the Hot Bread Kitchen sign, has a few tables and serves fresh chop suey, pizza and sandwiches.

For self-caterers, **Kaba's Supermarket** *(Naqara; open 8am-5pm Mon-Fri, 8am-1pm Sat)* is fully stocked. Also **MH Supermarket** in Somosomo or the **supermarket** in Wairiki which is open on Sundays. It can be difficult to buy fresh fruit and vegetables as the villagers usually grow their own; try the stalls along the main street of Naqara. **Hot Bread Bakers** *(☎ 888 0504; Naqara; open 6am-8pm Mon-Sat, 6am-noon Sun)* sells fresh breads, buns, cupcakes and tasty pizza.

Entertainment

Meridian Cinema in Wairiki screens mostly Bollywood-style movies on Fridays, Saturdays and Sundays.

Shopping

Ross Handicrafts *(☎ 330 9872; Weiyevo; open 8am-5.30pm Mon-Sat)* is lined with shelves of local wooden and woven crafts. You'll find it next to the Post Office. **Garden Island Resort** also has a small giftshop with local crafts.

SOUTHERN TAVEUNI

The main villages on southern Taveuni are Naqarawalu, in the hills, and, on the southern coast near Vuna Reef, Kanacea, Vuna and Navakawau. The people of Kanacea are descendants of peoples whose island was sold by Tui Cakobau to Europeans. Their ancestors were displaced as punishment for siding with the Tongans in a war.

Things to See

The road south from Waiyevo winds along the rugged coast, through beautiful rainforest, *dalo* and coconut plantations to Vuna and Kanacea villages. Somewhere along this coast, near Taveuni Estates, is an ancient **Warrior Burial Cave**. This cave was once used as a hidden cemetery for warriors, so that their death would be kept secret from enemies. For the same reason some chiefs were buried inside their own *bure*. The lava tube cave runs for about 360m down to the ocean, but, as it is tabu, the entrance has been sealed.

Vatuwiri Farm, at Vuna Point, is another place of interest. In its heyday it was one of the main copra estates on Taveuni and today the 8-sq-km farm is still one of the largest on Taveuni. James Tarte established the estate in 1871 and introduced the magpie into Taveuni to control stick insects. There are some interesting old stone buildings, including rows of workers' cottages built for labourers brought from the Solomon Islands three generations ago. More recently, the Tarte family has diversified into cocoa, vanilla, sugar, cattle, Fijian asparagus, *voy voy* (tree for mats) and tourism. The remains of the old **Vuna village hill fortification**, above the present villages of Vuna and Kanacea, are partly on Vatuwiri land. The Tarte family used to maintain them but a lack of interest from tourists made it unaffordable and today the site is overgrown.

If you continue on to the dramatic, windswept South Cape, you can check out the **Blow Hole**. As the water jumps up through the volcanic rock, it creates many rainbows in the air. It's best at low tide when it can reach up to the top of the palm trees on shore. As testimony to this, the grass on land is dry from the salt water. At high tide it's much less dramatic and you may need to bring a local along to point it out. The water here can be very changeable and, if conditions turn bad, the waves can quite suddenly pound the shore; be wary of climbing down on the rocks.

Activities

Diving and snorkelling on the Vuna Reef is excellent; go through **Dolphin Bay Divers** *(☎/fax 888 0125; W www.dolphinbaydivers.com)* at Dolphin Bay Divers' Retreat where you can do a two-tank/night/shore dive for $130/75/50. It also has multi-day dive packages and offers a number of courses including the PADI ($550), Rescue ($360) and Dive Master ($660). As well as Vuna Reef, it also does dive trips to Rainbow Reef and other sites in the area. Divers taking a course get free accommodation in the dorm and airport transfers from Matei.

Dolphin Bay Diver's Retreat has beautiful coral, moray eels and lion fish right off shore; a guided snorkel costs $15. It also offers trips to Namoli Beach (north of Vuna and Kanacea villages) and the blow hole as well as horse riding trips.

Vatuwiri Farm Resort *(☎ 888 0316)* offers reef fishing, game fishing, horse riding, trips, cattle mustering, trekking, and fruit bat- and bird-watching. *Lady Vuna*, a 12m catamaran, can be chartered for $1000 per night or $750 for a day trip with food and drinks included.

Places to Stay & Eat

Dolphin Bay Divers' Retreat *(☎/fax 888 0125; dorms $10, main-house doubles with private/shared bathroom $50/35, doubles/triples/quads bure with en suite $75/80/85)*, formerly known as Susie's Plantation, has undergone a change of ownership with dramatic improvements. Originally established as a copra plantation in the 1850s, it's set in a very peaceful location with gorgeous sea and sunset views. The atmosphere is laid back and there's excellent diving and snorkelling on site (see Activities earlier in this section). There's a lounge with a book exchange, Internet access and lots of tour options. The double with en suite in the main house is spacious and comfortable and the garden *bure* are pleasant, surrounded by fruit and coconut trees. Dorms are basic but clean and slated for renovation. There's kava drinking in the evenings and on Friday nights there's a *meke*. Breakfast and a three-course dinner are available for $25 and free airport transfers are given to guests staying in a *bure* for three or more nights. Major credit cards accepted.

Vatuwiri Farm Resort *(☎ 888 0316, fax 888 0314; double cottage $110, single homestead room $110, all with en suite; closed from mid-October to early January)* is unlike any other resort you'll set foot in. With horses, cattle and honking geese, a visit here will give you a chance to experience life on a plantation. You can stay with the friendly family in the homestead or opt for one of the two small cottages, far from the geese. Perched on a lawn on the water's edge, these simple cottages have gorgeous views with high tide bringing colourful fish to the doorstep. There are loads of activities available (see Activities earlier in this section), you can swim and snorkel or you can just enjoy the peace and quiet. Three meals a day are available at the house for $70.

Vuna Lagoon Lodge *(☎/fax 888 0627; 627 Salote; dorms/singles/doubles $15/30/50)* has a beautiful setting and should be tried by those wanting contact with Fijian village life. It has simple, clean rooms, two minutes' walk from Vuna village on the edge of Vuna Lagoon. The house has a kitchen, laundry with washing machine, sitting area and electricity from 6pm to 11pm. You can cook for yourself with free fruit and vegetables from the garden; however, you'll need to bring all other supplies with you. Otherwise, home-cooked meals are available for reasonable prices. There is a sandy beach nearby; bring your own snorkelling gear. To find the lodge, turn down the dirt lane towards the coast at Vuna Village; it's the last, blue house on the left. It's best to call ahead to make sure someone is going to be around. Present a *sevusevu* to the chief upon arrival.

The Palms *(☎/fax 888 0241; $65 per person, under 12 half price)* is a 120-year-old Soqulu Plantation home available for rent. With five bedrooms, a big kitchen, a grass tennis court and a beautiful view, it's great value and an excellent place to relax. There are mangos, avocados, pineapples and pears in the garden, a barbecue and *lovo* outside and a cook available on request. The affable owner prefers a week's notice but it's worth calling anyway. The house is on the left just before you reach Taveuni Estates – not surprisingly, it's the one with all the palm trees.

Taveuni Estates *(☎ 888 0044, fax 888 0844; ⓔ taveuniestates@connect.com.fj)* is a luxury home development project about 8km south of Waiyevo. With many of the lots standing empty, the new owners have decided to diversify and are building upmarket villas for rent as well as dorms. If all goes to plan, the dorms will be fantastic, built next to a black-sand beach with a clubhouse and tree-house bar. Rates will probably be around $20 per night. Facilities at the estates include a pool, golf and tennis. The rainforest in this area is also excellent for bird-watching.

Getting There & Away

It's about one hour by car or about two hours by local bus from Matei airport to the Vuna village area. By taxi, expect to pay $35 from the airport, or $25 from the ferry wharf by taxi to Dolphin Bay Divers' Retreat. See Getting Around earlier in this chapter for more information.

TAVEUNI

MATEI & AROUND

Matei is a residential area on Taveuni's northern point. Much of the freehold land has been bought by foreigners searching for a piece of tropical paradise. Within easy vicinity to the airport, there are a number of places to stay here, some of the island's best dining options, dive shops, a couple of OK beaches and nearby snorkelling.

Information

Matei doesn't have much in the way of services. There's a card-phone at the airport and another outside Bhula Bhai Supermarket. Swiss Fiji Divers offers Internet services from 9am-5pm daily.

Diving

Reliable **Aquaventure** *(☎/fax 888 0381; ⓔ aquaventure@connect.com.fj; ⓦ www.aquaventure.org)* is based at Beverly Beach, about 1km west of the Matei airport. A two-tank dive with/without equipment costs $130/150. It also offers single-tank night dives for $90, multi-dive packages and a number of courses including the PADI certificate for $550. Dive sites include Rainbow Reef and the Great White Wall.

Swiss Fiji Divers *(☎/fax 888 0586; e sfd@connect.com.fj; w www.swissfijidivers.com)*, also near Beverly Beach, provides high-quality gear, including computer consoles, masks with underwater communication, and scooters. Two-tank dives cost $190 for tanks and weights only ($40 a day extra for basic equipment rental). An open-water course including all gear costs $760.

Taveuni Estates Dive *(☎ 888 0653; e info@taveunidive.com; w www.taveunidive.com)* is new on the scene. An outpost of Taveuni Estates on Taveuni's southwest coast, it has an enthusiastic manager and the staff are experienced divers. A two-tank dive costs $130 plus an extra $20 for gear, and the PADI course is $530. You'll find it next to the Bhula Bhai Supermarket.

Snorkelling

The three small islands immediately offshore from Naselesele Point have good snorkelling (the third is known as the local 'Honeymoon Island'). You can also snorkel happily at Prince Charles Beach or Beverly Beach. **Aquaventure** will take snorkellers out to reefs if space is available on the dive boat (maximum six) or will take a group of snorkellers (minimum 4) to Qamea ($40 per person). You can also rent gear from them ($20). **Island Pizza** will also take you out to nearby snorkelling sites ($30) and **Taveuni Estates Dive** rents snorkelling gear ($15).

Drua

As a token of appreciation for assisting him in a war against the people of Rewa, Ratu Cakobau presented King George of Tonga with a *drua*, a traditional catamaran. Named *Ra Marama*, the *drua* was built in Taveuni in the 1850s. It took seven years to complete, was over 30m long and could carry 150 people. Hewn from giant trees, it could outsail the European ships of the era.

Drua could involve entire communities in their building and some could carry up to 300 people. Construction often involved ceremonial human sacrifices, and the completed vessel was launched over the bodies of slaves, which were used as rollers under the hulls. The last large *drua* was built in 1913 and is on display at the museum in Suva. If you visit the island of Kioa, north of Taveuni, you can still see fishermen out in small, one-man *drua*.

Other Activities

If you're interested in casting a line, try **Raikivi Game Fishing** *(☎ 888 0371)* who will take you around Qamea in search of sailfish, wahu, maimai and skipjack tuna. A half-/full day costs $420/840 for up to six people.

Island Pizza will take you out trolling for fish ($100 first hour, $50 each additional hour, 4-person maximum) or will take a group of you to Qamea for fishing and a picnic ($40 per person, 6 person minimum). It also rents single kayaks for $10/30/40 for an hour/half-day/day and two-person kayaks for $14/40/60 for an hour/half-day/day.

Places to Stay – Budget

Beverly Beach Camping *(☎ 888 0684; camping with/without own tent $8/10, maximum 12 people)* is about 15 minutes' walk from the airport. The small site is set between the road and a white-sand beach, beneath fantastic, huge, poison-fish trees. It's well maintained and a good place to lay back and relax. The camp has very basic facilities including flush toilets, shower and a sheltered area for cooking and dining. The owner sometimes brings around fresh fruit and vegetables in the morning. He can also provide equipment for snorkelling and fishing.

Bibi's Hideaway *(☎ 888 0443; camping $12, 2-bedroom cottage one/both rooms $50/90, single/double cottage $60/80; bure $80, all with mosquito nets, all self-contained)* has homey, little cottages set in a huge, beautiful garden. A 10-minute walk from the airport, it's very convenient and extremely peaceful. The welcoming family will invite you to help yourself to the luscious produce from the garden; you'll have more bananas, pawpaws, mangoes and guava than you know what to do with. If you're planning to sit outside in the evenings, bring mosquito coils. There's electricity in the evenings but no fans.

Karin's Garden *(☎/fax 888 0511; doubles $95, 2-night minimum)*, with a bird's-eye view of the reef, has a double *bure* with shared kitchen, sitting room and veranda. The wooden rooms are spacious, comfortable and

ROBYN JONES

Beach on Kadavu

SIMON CHARLES

Playing rugby on Kadavu

ROBYN JONES

Local girls, Vunisea

CASEY & ASTRID WITTE MAHANEY

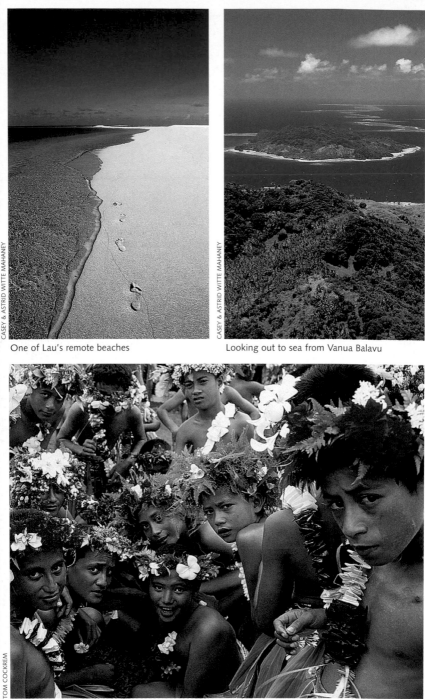

One of Lau's remote beaches

CASEY & ASTRID WITTE MAHANEY

Looking out to sea from Vanua Balavu

TOM COCKREM

Independence Day celebrations, Rotuma

very cozy. There's beach access at the end of the property where, on a clear day, you can see large fish and dolphins swimming past. The owners are relaxed and affable. Rooms have fans and electricity in the evenings.

Little Dolphin Treehouse *(☎ 888 0130; double cottage $90, no children)* is a fantastic place to stay. With a well-equipped kitchen downstairs and comfortable double room upstairs, it has fabulous sea views, lots of books, papaya trees in the yard and is very private. The owners are friendly and may invite you for a snorkelling trip in their boat.

Tovutovu Resort *(☎ 888 0560, fax 888 0722; dorms $15, double/triple bure with kitchen $75/85, double bure without kitchen $65, all private rooms with en suite)* is built on a copra plantation. *Bure* are comfortable and pleasant with hot water, fans and electricity in the evening. The eight-bed dorm at the back of the resort is very simple with a wonky floor, but is nevertheless a good option for backpackers. It has a communal kitchen and deck with views. Bikes can be hired for $15 per day, and snorkelling trips cost $10. It also has a restaurant and family chapel on the hill. Farther up past the end of the airport runway is an old village lookout site. The resort is a 20-minute walk southeast of Matei airport, past the Bhula Bhai Supermarket.

Places to Stay – Mid-Range

Coconut Grove Beachfront Cottages *(☎/fax 888 0328; W www.coconutgrovefiji.com; doubles with en suite in main house $110 per person, double cottages $150-190 per person, all including breakfast & dinner)* is small, well-maintained and very popular. All rooms are spacious and comfortable, and the cottages each have an outdoor rock shower. Through the garden, there's access to a small, white-sand beach from where you can explore in a two-man kayak (hour/half-/full day $15/35/55). The owner goes out of her way to ensure your stay is pleasant and privacy is guaranteed.

Audrey's by the Sea *(☎ 888 0039; cottage $175, no children)* is a quaint, self-contained cottage in a peaceful garden with views through the coconut trees to the sea. The lacy decor may not be everyone's cup of tea but it's comfortable and spacious with a small beach across the road. Audrey is very warm and welcoming.

Places to Stay – Top End

Taveuni Island Resort *(☎ 888 0441, fax 888 0466; W www.taveuniislandresort.com; standard/luxury bungalows $1044/1240 including meals, maximum 14 guests)* is opulent. With the air of a millionaire's clifftop beach house, it's all polished wood and wicker and has a stunning pool, gorgeous views, and a nearby beach. Bungalows are rock and wood and so private, they've got no windows. Not surprisingly, they're popular with honeymooners. Meals are a gourmet's delight.

Maravu Plantation Resort *(☎ 888 0555, fax 888 0600; W www.maravu.net; singles/doubles/triples bure $420/640/780, deluxe bure $460/720/900, family duplex $960, all including meals; children's accommodation free, kids' meal plan $60 per day)* has spacious, plush cottages with a tropical feel to them, dotted among the coconut groves. With big decks, they're private. Meals are sumptuous, there's a lovely pool, pleasant dining area, lots of activities and a small, white-sand beach across the road.

Garden of Eden *(☎ 888 0252; $1250 per week, maximum 4 adults plus children, including all meals)* is a huge, beautiful house with sea views, beach access, a giant garden and lovely pool. There's a loft for the kids and the cook will cater meals to your taste. One month's notice is preferred.

Marau Vale, **Lomalagi** and **Sere-ni-ika** *(W www.fiji-rental-accommodations.com/index.html; from $280-440 per night, including housekeeper)* are three beautiful, beachfront homes for rent with weekly and monthly rates. Ideal for families, houses are spacious and fully equipped. Some have beach access, kayaks and outdoor rock showers. Check out the website for more details and bookings.

Places to Eat

Restaurants & Cafés Surrounded by a pretty patch of golden sand and leafy trees, **Island Pizza** *(☎ 888 8083; regular/large pizza $15/18; open 10am-9.30pm daily)* serves delicious, thin-crusted pizzas on a wooden deck over the water. There's a pleasant sea breeze and views of the planes coming in to land. There's also a swing for you to hop on and sail over the waves as you wait for your food. Prices are very reasonable; a regular pizza is big enough for two. They'll also deliver if you pay the transport. You'll find it next to Aquaventure.

Coconut Grove Cafe *(☎ 888 0328; breakfast $6, lunch $10, dinner $15; open breakfast & lunch 7.30am-3pm, snacks 3pm-5pm, dinner 7pm-9.30pm Mar-Dec)* has great food made from fresh ingredients. The menu includes fresh vegetables, home-made pasta, soups, salads, fish and delicious desserts. Meals are served on the verandah, overlooking the water and nearby islets. Try the best fresh-fruit shakes on Taveuni for $4. Place your dinner order before 4pm. There is an Island Tunes and buffet night twice-weekly.

Karin's Garden *(☎ 888 0511; set dinner-menu $15)* serves excellent European-style dinners from a cliff-top house. The menu is generally meat or fish with home-made bread and the vegetables from the garden. The property has spectacular views at sunset. Book for dinner before 3pm.

Tovutovu Resort *(☎ 888 0560; mains $10; open 8am-10am, noon-2pm & 6pm-8pm daily)* has a comfortable restaurant with an outdoor deck overlooking the offshore island of Viubani. The food is tasty and good value and, on Fridays, there's a well-attended buffet and music night ($15).

Lal's Curry Place *(☎ 888 0705; meals $8; open 11am-9pm Mon-Sat)* serves heaps of great Indian food for a steal. A meal includes soup, curry, roti, rice and chutney.

Mrs Harry's *(☎ 888 0404; meals $6)* takeaway curries are good value and popular among guests at Beverly Beach Camping. Prepared at her house on the hill almost opposite, she'll wow you with her meat, fish and vegie curries, roti and daal. Try to order dinner before 4pm.

Audrey's Sweet Somethings has teas, brewed coffees and excellent cakes, served on the deck with views of the sea. Indulge in some fudge cake or home-made kahlua.

Maravu Plantation Resort *(set lunch/dinner $40/60)* serves gourmet three-course meals with delicacies like stuffed crab. It's pricey but good. Reserve lunch by 10.30am and dinner by noon.

At the time of writing, a new restaurant was about to open on dead man's curve (just past Island Pizza). Promises of fish-and-chip disco were in the air.

Self-Catering **Bhula Bhai Supermarket** *(☎ 888 0462; open 7.30am-6pm Mon-Sat, 8am-11am Sun)*, in Matei, sells a range of groceries, film, stationery, clothing and phonecards and accepts Visa and MasterCard (charge 10%, $90 limit).

Shopping

Coconut Grove Cottages has a giftshop with hand-made cards, local crafts, T-shirts and colourful *sulu*. Maravu Plantation Resort also has a small giftshop with local crafts.

Getting There & Away

Matei is about 45 minutes by bus from Waiyevo and home to the island's airport. (see the introductory Getting Around section earlier in this chapter for more information).

EASTERN TAVEUNI

Eastern Taveuni's wild coast and lush rainforest is a magnet for nature lovers. Having rejected logging in favour of ecotourism, landowners joined with a New Zealand environmental group to form the Bouma Environmental Tourism Project. The aim is to preserve resources while creating an income from visitors and, so far, it's working fabulously. The people of Bouma built fantastic trails that are well-maintained and a must-do for anyone looking to get out into nature.

Scenes for the 1991 movie, *Return to the Blue Lagoon,* were filmed at Bouma National Heritage Park's Tavoro Falls, and at Lavena beach.

Bouma National Heritage Park

This national park *(admission $5)* protects over 80% of Taveuni's total area, covering about 150 sq km of rainforest and coastal forest. The park has several kilometres of bush walks and the three beautiful **Tavoro Waterfalls**, with natural swimming pools. The walking track begins opposite the reception *bure*, south of the river in Bouma.

The first waterfall is about 24m high and only 10 minutes' walk along a flat cultivated path. With a change area, picnic tables and barbecue plates, it's a great place for a dip. The second waterfall, a further 30 or 40 minutes along, is a bit smaller than the first but also has a good swimming pool. The track is quite steep in places, but has steps, handrails and lookout spots to rest. The view through the coconut trees to the zigzagging reef and the island of Qamea beyond is spectacular. As you near the second waterfall, deep in the rainforest, you'll have to cross a river; a rope is suspended across the water to balance you as you leap from stone to boulder. Reaching the third fall involves a hike along a less maintained, often muddy path through the forest for another 30 minutes. Smaller than the other two (about 10m high), it has a great swimming pool and rocks for jumping off (check for obstructions first!). If you bring your snorkelling gear, you'll be able to see the hundreds of prawns in the water.

If you are a keen walker, try the **Vidawa Rainforest Hike**, a full-day guided trek. Beginning at Vidawa village, it passes through the historic fortified village sites of Navuga and follows trails into the rainforest where you'll see lots of birdlife. The trek then takes you down to the **Tavoro Waterfalls**. You can only do this walk with a guide and need to book in advance. The trip runs Monday to Saturday and can take a maximum of eight people ($60/40 for adult/child). It includes pick-up and drop-off at your hotel, guides, lunch, afternoon tea and park fee. Book through Tavoro Waterfalls Visitor Centre.

Places to Stay & Eat **Tavoro Waterfalls Visitor Centre** *(☎ 888 0390; camping $10 per person, meals $5-10; open 9am-4pm daily)* offers simple meals. With picnic tables along the river, it's a lovely spot to picnic or camp. There's a kitchen, toilets and an open shower for campers, as well as a covered eating area. The generator kicks in for the evening. Staff are friendly and will let you store your bags here while you hike up to the falls.

Getting There & Away By local bus, Bouma park is 45 minutes from Matei, and 1½ hours from Naqara. See the introductory Getting Around section earlier in this chapter for bus times. A taxi (up to five people) will cost $20 to $25.

If you are in the mood for a marathon, it is possible to catch the early morning bus to Bouma, make a flying visit to all three waterfalls, and catch the early afternoon bus at about 1.40pm on to Lavena. In a rush you can do the coastal walk before dark and either stay overnight at Lavena or be picked up by a pre-arranged taxi. But this is Fiji – who wants to rush?

Waitabu Marine Park

Opened in 1998, this area is excellent for snorkelling or lounging on the white-sand beach. Only recently opened to tourists, it is only possible to visit the park with a guide. The village of Waitabu has set up a half-day tour that includes a local guide, guided snorkelling, a *bilibili* ride, morning and afternoon tea in the village and transport to and from Matei ($50/25 for adult/12-17 year olds (children under 12 not accepted). There's approximately one trip per week; book with Aquaventure (☎ 888 0381) in Matei.

Lavena Coastal Walk

The 5km Lavena Coastal Walk is well worth the effort to get to. The trail follows the forest edge along a white-sand then volcanic-black beach, passes peaceful villages, and climbs up through the tropical rainforest to a gushing waterfall. It's bliss for those who like the great outdoors. There's some good snorkelling and kayaking here and Lavena Point is good for swimming.

The path is clearly marked and well-maintained. About halfway along the trek, watch for the *vatuni'epa*, bizarre rock pedestals formed by the erosion of the coral base along the coast. Past these, the path seems to disappear at Naba settlement: follow the path onto the beach, then follow the shore past the *bure* and cross the stream to where the path reappears. Further ahead is a suspension bridge at Wainisairi Creek, the only stream to flow out of Lake Tagimaucia. Eventually the trail takes you up the valley of Wainibau Creek. This creek forms the boundary of the Bouma (Wainikeli) and Vuna lands and is also the boundary of the Ravilevu Nature Reserve to the south.

To see and reach the falls at the end of the trail, you have to walk over rocks and swim a short distance through two deep pools. Two cascades fall at different angles into a deep pool with sheer walls. If you're visiting in the rainy season, the rocks near the falls can become slippery, if not flooded; it can be difficult and dangerous, to reach the falls at this time of year. Ask at Lavena Lodge for current conditions. At any time of year (even if it hasn't been raining), violent flash floods can occur and readers have advised staying to the left of the pool, where you can make an easier getaway.

The park is managed through **Lavena Lodge**. Entrance to the park is $5, or $15 including a guide. You can also take a guided sea kayak journey and coastal walk for $40 (including lunch). You can usually order a meal for when you return to the lodge ($10) but it's a good idea to bring along some food and definitely bring water. Kayaks can be hired for $40 per day.

Places to Stay & Eat Lavena Lodge (☎ *888 0116; twins per person $15, maximum 8 people)* is run by friendly, informative staff and has basic rooms, a shared kitchen and bathroom. Rooms are clean and there's electricity in the evening. Next to a beach, this is a great place to relax under the trees after a hard day's hike. Outside the lodge is a *vutu* tree whose flowers only bloom at night; the beautiful white and pink blossoms drop to the ground at sunrise and are used as fish poison.

Meals are available from the lodge ($7/10 breakfast/lunch or dinner). There's a tiny shop in the village with tinned fish and not much else; if you're planning to cook, bring your own supplies.

Getting There & Away Lavena village is about 15 minutes' drive past Bouma, 35 minutes from Matei. However, by local bus it takes about one hour from Matei or just under two from Waiyevo. Expect to pay around $30 for a taxi to/from Matei. See the introductory Getting Around section earlier in this chapter for information on taxi services and the local bus services from Naqara via Matei.

Savulevu Yavonu Falls

The Ravilevu coast is the section from Lavena Point down to Salialevu on the rough, exposed eastern side of Taveuni. It is a straight, beachless stretch of coast with sheer cliffs and open ocean. About halfway along, the 20m-high Savulevu Yavonu water fall plunges off a cliff into the sea. During WWII, ships used the falls as a fresh water depot, going directly under the flow to refill their water reservoir. Access to the falls is by boat only, and is dependent on the weather as the ocean can get very rough on this side of the island. Inquire at one of the dive shops in Metai or at Lavena Lodge.

OFFSHORE ISLANDS

Qamea, Laucala and Matagi are a group of islands just east of Thurston Point, across the Tasman Strait from northeastern Taveuni. Qamea and Laucala are located inside a lagoon formed by a single barrier reef, which wraps around the southeast side, broken only by a passage east of Laucala. All three of the islands have lovely white-sand beaches. The original inhabitants of Qamea and Laucala were displaced by local chiefs in the mid-19th century for siding with Tongan chief Enele Ma'afu during a war. Today, Laucala and Matagi are privately owned and each island has an upmarket resort, catering mainly to diving and game-fishing enthusiasts. Generally the only travellers who see these beautiful islands are resort visitors, although Qamea does have a struggling campground. If you are lucky enough to fly over the islands, the view is superb.

Matagi

area 1 sq km

Stunning horseshoe-shaped Matagi, formed by a submerged volcanic crater, is 10km off Taveuni's coast. Its steep rainforest sides rise to 130m. The bay faces north to open sea and there is a fringing reef on the southwest side of the island.

Matangi Island Resort (☎ *888 0260, fax 888 0274;* W *www.MatangiIsland.com; singles/doubles/triples bure $280/610/720, deluxe bure $360/850/970, treehouses $1070, all including meals and most activities)* is built along a white-sand beach. Spacious deluxe *bure* have umbrella-esque rooftops, while the fantastic 'treehouses' are perched 5m up in the tree canopy with views to the beach, Qamea, Taveuni and beyond. Children are accepted in all but the treehouses. Activities include windsurfing, kayaking, water-skiing and saltwater fly-fishing. Matagi boasts 30 dive spots within 10 to 30 minutes of the island; a two-tank dive is $180 at the resort's dive shop. Transfers to the island cost $120 per adult.

Qamea

area 34 sq km

Qamea is the closest of the three islands to Taveuni, only 2.5km east of Thurston Point. Its six villages came under harsh attack by Cyclone Ami in early 2003. The island's coast has a number of bays with white-sand beaches and a narrow mangrove inlet on the west side. The interior, especially on the north side, is covered with steep green hills and sloping valleys. Qamea is rich in birdlife and is notable for the *lairo*, the annual migration of land crabs. For a few days from late November to early December, at the start of their breeding season, masses of crabs move together from the mud flats towards the sea.

There is a **camping ground** on Qamea, in a small bay with views of Matagi. There are basic facilities and meals available. You can snorkel and hike, and the owner, Robert Mitchell, can arrange village visits. You need to contact him before arriving to make sure someone will be around; as they have no phone, the easiest way is to ask Robert's brother, Cyril, who manages the Air Fiji desk at the airport. To get to the camping ground, ask about chartering a boat at **Island Pizza** or ask Cyril; it's about $60 one way.

Qamea Beach Club *(☎ 888 0220, fax 888 0092; W www.qamea.com; bure singles/doubles/triples $820/1100/1240, double villa $1400, including meals and transfer, children under 13 not accepted)*, located along a lovely white-sand beach, has a fresh spring-water swimming pool and luxury *bure* with hammocks and views. There is excellent snorkelling just offshore as well as windsurfing, sailing, outrigger canoeing, nature walks, village visits and fishing trips. There is also a dive shop here with reasonable rates.

Laucala

area 30 sq km

Just 500m east across the strait from Qamea, Laucala is privately owned by the estate of the late US millionaire Malcolm Forbes. At the time of writing the island's upmarket resort was closed indefinitely to visitors.

Kadavu Group

The rugged Kadavu (ka**nd**-a-vu) Group, comprised of Kadavu (Fiji's fourth-largest island), oval-shaped Ono, Galoa and a number of smaller islands, is about 100km south of Viti Levu. The main island is irregular in shape and so deeply indented that it is almost cut in three by deep bays. The impressive Nabukelevu (Mt Washington) is the highest peak at 838m. The lush rainforests, especially on the eastern side, are home to a wide variety of birdlife, including the indigenous Kadavu honeyeater, Kadavu fantail, velvet fruit dove and the colourful Kadavu musk parrot.

The explorer Dumont d'Urville sailed past the island in 1834 and named the long fringing reef after his ship, the *Astrolabe*. When space at Levuka (on the island of Ovalau) proved limited, Kadavu's Galoa Harbour was considered as a potential site for the new colonial capital. Otherwise, the group has remained removed from Fiji's major historical events. Tourism development here has been slow due to its isolation and lack of infrastructure.

Kadavu's 72 villages or settlements (population 12,000) rely largely on subsistence agriculture and the export of local produce to the mainland. Each village has its own fishing grounds, and resorts negotiate to use the areas for diving, surfing or fishing. There are few roads on Kadavu and most transportation is by boat.

The prevailing southeasterly winds can batter the exposed southeastern side of the island. Expect some rough weather from April to August.

Highlights

- Surf, dive or hike at the dramatic Cape Washington
- Experience the rugged and remote feeling of the island group
- Snorkel or dive the spectacular coral reefs
- Take a seasonal kayaking tour
- Stay in a traditional *bure* on the beach at one of the budget resorts

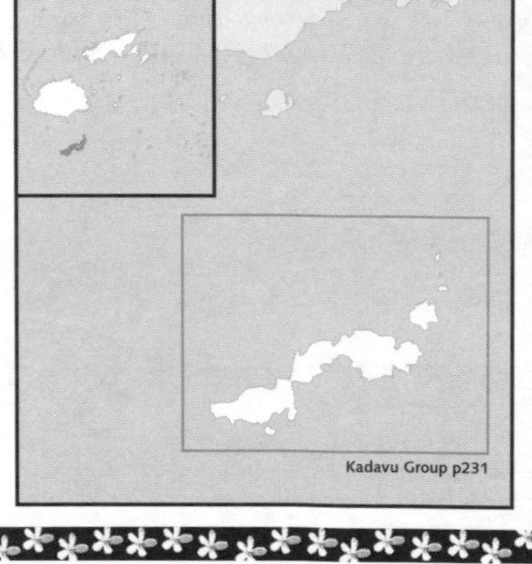

Orientation

The small town of Vunisea is Kadavu's administrative centre, with the island's police station, post office, hospital (all on the top of the hill) and airstrip. It is on a narrow isthmus with Namalata Bay to the west and North Bay to the east. Vunisea is easy to get around on foot, but of little interest to the traveller.

Information

Money Most of the resorts in Kadavu are distant from Vunisea. Some resorts do accept credit cards but bring cash with you especially if you are staying at the budget resorts.

Post & Communications The Vunisea post and telephone offices are on top of the hill, a short walk from the airstrip. This **shop** *(open 8am-3pm Mon-Fri)* sells some groceries, clothes and stationery. Kavala Bay, at the northeastern end of the island, also has a post office.

Medical Services Vunisea's relatively new hospital was opened in 1996, with the help of Australian aid, as part of a $7 million project to improve Kadavu's health services. Services are fairly limited though, so if you really feel unwell escape Kadavu. Divers suffering from the bends can be transferred to the Fiji Recompression Chamber Facility in Suva by Medivac helicopter service.

Emergency In the event of an emergency, dial the **police** *(☎ 333 6007)* or the **hospital** *(☎ 333 6008)*.

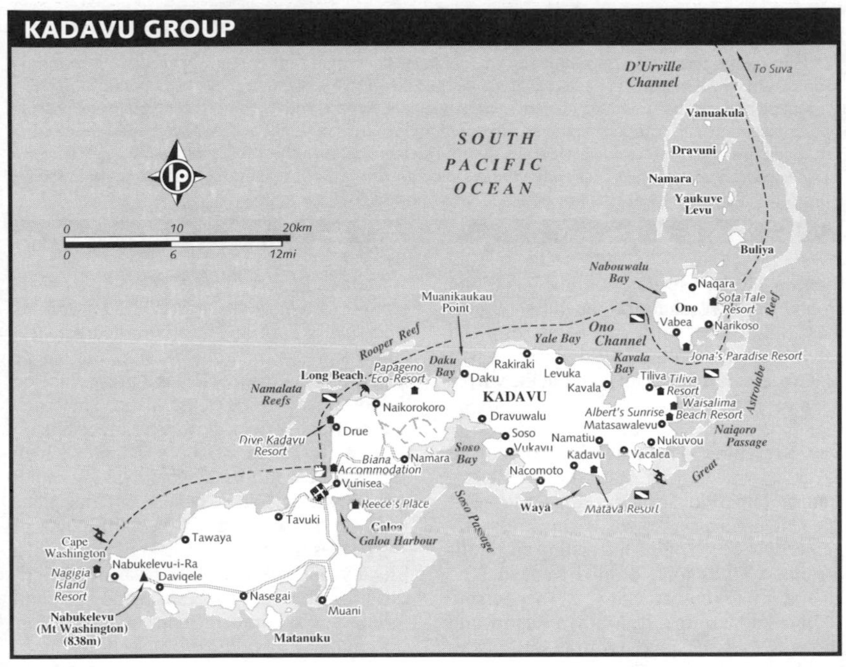

Dangers & Annoyances

The ferry trip to Kadavu from Suva can be rough and the timetable is erratic; fly instead. The small boats used for transfers to/from the airstrip often don't have life jackets or radios.

Activities

Remote and rugged Kadavu is a great place for nature lovers, hikers and bird-watchers. The mountains have rainforests, numerous waterfalls and hiking trails used mainly by school children. Ask locals if a track is clear before heading off. The isolated villagers are very traditional so when visiting a village, ask to speak to the *turaga-ni-koro* first, remove your hat and don't carry things on your shoulders (see Social Graces in the Facts for the Visitor chapter).

There are a few nice beaches and most places to stay have some equipment for snorkelling and other water sports.

Diving Most travellers are attracted to Kadavu for its reefs, which offer some excellent diving. The famous **Great Astrolabe Reef** skirts the eastern side of the Kadavu Group. Expect brilliantly coloured soft and hard corals, vertical drop-offs and a wonderful array of marine life, including lots of reef sharks. However, diving on the reef is variable, ranging from disappointing to terrific. The weather quite often dictates which sites are suitable to dive, and visibility can range from 15m to 70m.

Matava Resort *(☎ 330 5222)* offers dives from the **Soso Passage** to **Naiqoro Passage**, featuring excellent manta ray, cave and shark dives. Albert's Sunrise *(☎ 333 6086)* runs dives to the Naiqoro Passage and, during rough weather, sites on the sheltered side of Ono. Dive Kadavu *(☎ 331 1780)* has an excellent set-up with good equipment and fast boats with up to four dives per day. Dive Kadavu can take divers just about anywhere in Kadavu, but go more frequently to the **Namalata reefs**, which are about 5km from the northwest coast of the island and which are more sheltered from the prevailing winds than the Astrolabe Reef. Two-tank morning dive trips cost $180 (weights and tanks) plus $30 for gear. Open-water courses are $660. Snorkelling trips with the divers are $30 per person and underwater cameras are available for hire.

The Battle of the Shark & Octopus Gods

Dakuwaqa the Shark God once cruised the Fiji islands challenging other reef guardians. On hearing rumours of a rival monster in Kadavu waters, he sped down to the island to prove his superior strength. Adopting his usual battle strategy he charged at the giant octopus with his mouth wide open and sharp teeth prepared. The octopus, however, anchored itself to the coral reef and swiftly clasped the shark in a death lock. In return for mercy the octopus demanded that the people of Kadavu be forever protected from shark attack. In Kadavu the people now fish without fear and regard the shark as their protector. Most won't eat shark or octopus out of respect for their gods.

Surfing The best surfing in Kadavu is found around **Cape Washington**, at the southernmost end of Kadavu. It gets plenty of swell activity all year round. **Vesi Passage**, off Matava, also has powerful surf, but the waves often get blown out.

Sea Kayaking The season for organised kayaking trips is from May to September – contact **Tamarillo Sea Kayaking** *(☎ 04-801 7549 in New Zealand; w www.tamarillo.co.nz/index.html)* which offers interesting and well-organised kayak tours around Kadavu. The eight-day tours cost around $2200 per person.

Dive Kadavu Resort, **Matava Resort** and **Jonas Paradise** have two-person ocean kayaks for hire.

Places to Stay

In Kadavu most of the places to stay are distant from the airport, and the only way to get there is by boat. Consider transportation time and cost when choosing accommodation. Most of the budget places allow camping.

Places to Stay – Budget

Jona's Paradise Resort *(☎ 330 7058, 339 6538; e jonasparadise@connect.com.fj; camping per person $50, dorm beds $60, bure per person with/without shower $100/80)* has one of the best beaches in Kadavu, with good snorkelling directly in front of the resort. It's ideal for those who want a quiet time in rustic accommodation. The eight simple thatched *bure* are spaced along the beachfront and the dorm *bure* has four beds. There are flush toilets and hot-water showers, and four of the *bure* have en suites. Meals are included in the price, but bring extra snacks. There is a minimum three-night stay. The diving operation (charging $145 for a two-tank dive trip) did not yet have proper instructors. Jona has a good boat and return transfers from Vunisea airstrip are $110 per person.

Matava Resort *(☎ 330 5222; e matava@connect.com.fj; dorm beds $18, bure doubles with shared bath $55, waterfront/oceanview bure doubles with bath $100/120, panoramic view house per night $220)* is a great place on the southeastern side of the island. The beach out the front is tidal; however, a reef links it to a picturesque offshore island, which makes a great snorkelling or kayaking trip. It can be windy and exposed, but the place feels remote and ruggedly beautiful.

The resort has been taken over by a friendly and enthusiastic English and American trio. The nine *bure* are rustic but comfortable, with timber floors and verandas. Oceanview *bure* or the private self-contained houses with great views are the best options, and the *bure* with shared facilities are good value. The small dorm has four beds. The resort has solar electricity and hot water showers. A meal package is $50, served on the veranda of the big restaurant-bar *bure*.

A nearby dive site has manta rays year round. The dive gear is new and a two-tank dive is $115 (tanks and weight belts) plus $25 daily for full gear hire; it is $500 to do the open-water course. There is also bushwalking, village and waterfall visits, kayaking, windsurfing and surfing. The boat trip from Vunisea airstrip to Matava ($30 per person one way, 50 minutes) can be a bit rough.

Albert's Sunrise *(☎ 333 6086; camping per tent $10, dorm beds $12, bure singles/doubles $16/30)* is on a beach on the northeastern corner of Kadavu, close to Naiqoro Passage. It is run by Ruth, the wife of the late Albert O'Connor, a Fijian descendent of an Irish beachcomber who came to Kadavu in 1804 and married the daughter of a local chief. There are six thatched *bure*, with mosquito nets (bring mosquito repellent) and woven floor mats but no electricity. The toilet blocks have flush toilets and cold showers. The food is simple and costs $25 per day or $6/10/13 for breakfast/lunch/dinner. Self-caterers can pay $3 to use the kitchen. Snorkelling is OK in front of the resort at high tide and gear hire costs $5 per day. Diving is usually good ($110 for two-tank dives, including all gear), but equipment and boats are pretty basic. The Astrolabe Reef is just a 10-minute boat ride away. Other activities include volleyball, hikes to a village, and waterfall/reef trips for $15/10 per person with a minimum of four. Day hikes to villages can also be arranged.

Transfers from Vunisea airstrip cost $60/50 for one/two or more persons. The trip takes about 1½ to two hours, depending on the weather, and the boat travels on whichever side is calmest.

Waisalima Beach Resort *(☎ 331 6281; e info@waisalimafiji.com; camping per site $8, dorm beds $60, bure doubles without/with shower $160/230)* is at the northeastern end of Kadavu island, within walking distance of Albert's Sunrise, and with views across the channel to Ono. It has a long stretch of sandy, tidal beach, which is OK for swimming at high tide. For a good snorkel here the best option is to join a boat trip ($25 per person). Accommodation is in traditional-style *bure* with hot showers and rates include three meals a day. Diving costs $60 per tank plus $25 per day for diving gear. Also on offer are boat trips to a 40m waterfall or a village visit ($25 per person). Return boat transfers from Vunisea airstrip cost $80 per person.

Reece's Place *(☎ 333 6097; camping per person $6, dorm beds $10, bungalow doubles $20)* is on a nice spot on the northern point of Galoa island, just southeast of Vunisea. Overall the place is pretty basic and service can be erratic. However, it is cheap and relatively close to Vunisea. Bill Reece loves to tell stories about the history of the island, expound on medicinal plants and show you the point where people once went to die so that their spirits could leave them for the afterlife. Snorkelling off the island is poor, but good if you manage to get them to take you by boat to the nearby reef ($10 per person). Meals are simple, but good value at $6/8/10 for breakfast/lunch/dinner. Transfers from Vunisea are $6 each way in a small open boat.

Travellers may get stranded in Vunisea. **Biana Accommodation** *(☎ 333 6010; singles/doubles $40/60)* has basic rooms with mosquito nets. Rates include breakfast, and lunch or dinner is $5. Biana, about 2km north of the airport near the wharf, has nice views over Namalata Bay. The proprietors have purchased a new boat to use for beach day tours, so if needed you could negotiate transfer to the resorts around the island.

Thema *(☎ 333 6156; accommodation per person $10)*, allows people to stay in her home near the airport. She can arrange visits to a nearby waterfall.

Places to Stay – Top End

Dive Kadavu Resort *(☎ 331 1780 fax 330 3860; w www.divekadavu.com; oceanview bure singles/doubles $320/560, quads per person $220)* caters mainly to divers. It is on the western side of Kadavu, sheltered from the prevailing southeasterly winds, and conveniently located for travellers arriving by plane. The lovely beach is good for swimming and snorkelling at all tides.

The resort has 10 comfortable fan-cooled *bure*, all with verandas, insect screening, hot water and good ventilation. The food is good and the hillside restaurant-bar is a nice spot to relax between dives. Rates include meals and airport transfers. Children under 10 are not accepted. There are standby rates and discounts for long stays.

As well as diving (see Diving earlier in this chapter), there are also day trips to the sheltered Ono side of the Astrolabe Reef and to King Kong Reef on the southwestern end of the island, with a stop for a picnic lunch at a village or beach. Use of windsurfers, paddle boards and sea kayaks is free and there are forest walks in the hills, village visits and a weekly *lovo*. Airport transfers take 15 minutes by resort boat.

Papageno Eco-Resort *(☎ 330 3355, fax 330 3533; w www.papagenoecoresort.com; bungalow singles/doubles $260/440)*, previously known as Malawai, is 14.5km northeast of Vunisea. It is a quiet, upmarket, family-friendly retreat for up to 16 guests. The five comfortable fan-cooled cottages

Canoe Rollers

The beachcomber William Diaper visited Kadavu in 1843 with Ratu Qaraniqio of Rewa. He witnessed live captives from Nabukelevu being used as canoe rollers, to help the dragging of the chief's enormous *drua* (double-hulled canoe) across the Kadavu isthmus.

facing a nice sandy beach are spacious and can comfortably accommodate three people, or four in the larger cottage. Rates include meals and return boat transfers from the airstrip (30 minutes one way). Activities include snorkelling boat trips, village and school visits and diving can be arranged with Dive Kadavu Resort, a short boat ride away. There is a nice walk up to a small waterfall in the hills with beautiful views down to the coast. The quality meals, incorporating plenty of home-grown fruit and vegetables, are served in the plantation house and a local band plays for guests. There is a minimum stay of three nights. Anneliese, the Californian owner, organises cultural exchanges for school children.

Nagigia Island Resort *(☎ 331 5774, satellite phone 872 761 960578; e sales@fijisurf.com; double cottages per person less/more than 7 nights $200/150, dorm cottage per person less/more than 7 nights $90/110)* opened in 2000. This surf-resort is on an absolutely stunning site near Cape Washington, at the southwestern end of Kadavu. There are fantastic views over the clear water and reefs to the surf-break and across to the imposing Nabukelevu. At the time of writing it had seven cottages perched over the water. Surfing here is good with a choice of five breaks including King Kong lefts just offshore. The surf-breaks produce rideable waves all year round with bigger swells during mid-year. Apart from surfing, there are nice walks nearby, including to Cape Washington lighthouse for a swim in the Nasoso Beach caves. A visit to the village of Nabukelevu-i-ra, just across the water on Kadavu, is also a must. This is also a great spot for snorkelling and there is a night snorkelling trip. Diving, which can be arranged with Dive Kadavu, is also pretty good down here, with great cave formations to explore and pristine coral.

Good food is served in the restaurant-bar overlooking the surf-break. Meal plans are $50 per person. The boat service is $24 for unlimited access to all surf-breaks close to the island, but you can also paddle out to the main break. Return boat transfers from Vunisea airstrip are $120 per person.

At the time of writing there were two upmarket places under construction. **Sota Tale Resort** *(☎ 330 3567; e spenkar@worldnet.att.net)* on a beautiful site on Ono Island and very close to the Astrolabe Reef; and **Tiliva Resort** *(☎ 331 5127; www.tilivaresortfiji.com)* at the northern end of Kadavu island.

Places to Eat

The airport has a kiosk selling a few snacks, and there are small stores in Vunisea, Kavala Bay, Albert's Sunrise and near Matava Resort. Most of the resorts are very remote, so even if all your meals are provided it may be an idea to take along snacks, especially to the budget resorts.

Getting There & Away

Air Air Fiji has daily return flights from Nadi to Kadavu, via Nausori airport near Suva (1½ hours). Sun Air has daily flights to Kadavu from Nadi (45 minutes). It is advisable to check timetables and always confirm flights the day before departure. See the air fares chart in the Getting Around chapter.

It is a beautiful flight (sometimes turbulent) over stunning reefs to Kadavu from either Nadi or Suva. The approach to Vunisea's **Namalata airstrip** *(☎ 333 6042)* over Namalata Bay has a spectacular view of Nabukelevu, which rises steeply at the southwestern point of Kadavu. Ideally, have your accommodation and transfers booked in advance, otherwise you could be stranded in Vunisea.

Ferry Suva to Kadavu on the ferry MV *Bulou-ni-ceva* is $42 per person one way. This service is mostly for cargo and local use, and it is irregular and unreliable, taking anything from four hours to two days! It visits Vunisea, Kavala Bay and Nabukelevu-i-Ra. The trip can be bearable or terrible, depending on the weather you strike. Contact **Kadavu Shipping** *(☎ 331 2428)* in Suva.

Getting Around

Kadavu's few roads are restricted to the Vunisea area, except for one rough, unsealed road to Nabukelevu-i-ra around the southern end of Kadavu. It's easy to walk around Vunisea or to hitch a ride. Small boats are the group's principal mode of transport. Each resort has its own boat and will pick up guests from Vunisea airstrip; make sure you make arrangements in advance. Boat trips are expensive due to fuel costs and mark-ups. Most boats don't have life jackets or radios. In rough weather it can be a wet and bone-crunching trip to the more remote resorts.

Lau & Moala Groups

The Lau Group is about halfway between the main islands of Fiji, to the west, and the Kingdom of Tonga, to the east. The group has about 57 small islands, scattered over 400km from north to south. Geographically, Lau is subdivided into northern and southern Lau, and the Moala Group lies to the west of southern Lau. Together the island groups are under the administration of the Eastern Division. The climate in this region is drier than in most parts of Fiji.

Most islands of the Lau Group are made of composite materials; some are pure limestone and a few are volcanic. Interrupted periods of uplift permitted coral to grow over the limestone, creating great masses of reefs. Relatively recent volcanic activity is evident by the lava domes on top of the limestone bases of some of the smaller islands.

The islanders of southern Lau are well known for their crafts: Moce, Vatoa, Ono-i-Lau and Namuka produce *masi* (bark cloth) and the artisans of Fulaga are excellent woodcarvers.

Highlights

- Snorkel or dive the fantastic coral reefs of this pristine region
- Visit Lakeba's Oso Nabukete cave
- Experience the interesting blend of Fijian and Tongan cultures
- Sail to the stunning Bay of Islands on Vanua Balavu

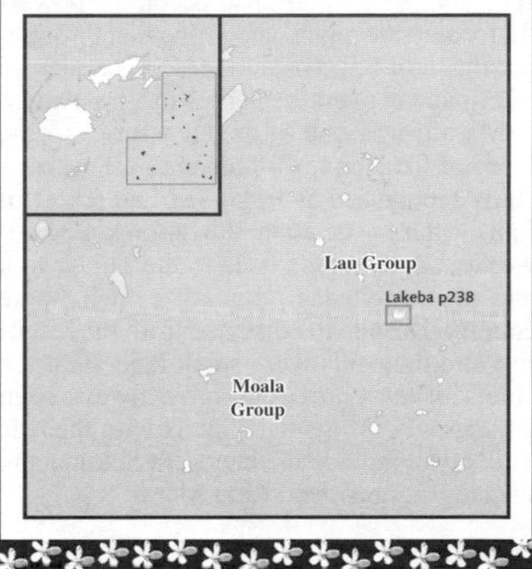

History

Because of Lau's proximity to Tonga, the islanders have been greatly influenced by Polynesian people and culture. The southeast trade winds made it easy to sail from Tonga to Fiji, but more difficult to return. A revolution in canoe design facilitated traffic and trade between the island groups. Tongan and Samoan canoe-builders began settling in Fiji in the late 1700s, bringing with them their innovative canoe designs as well as other decorative skills and crafts. They intermarried with Fijians, and the Tongan influence is expressed in names, language, food, decoration, architecture and physical features.

Both Captain Cook and Captain Bligh sighted the Lau Group on their explorations in the late 18th century. The first real contact with Europeans was in 1800 when the American schooner *Argo* was wrecked on Bukatatanoa Reef east of Lakeba. The ship was on its way to deliver supplies to the penal colony of Norfolk Island. Fijians of Oneata looted the wreck for muskets and gunpowder and the sailors lived with the islanders until being killed in disputes. Oliver Slater survived to become influential in Bua, Vanua Levu (see the boxed text 'The Goods, the Bad & the Ugly' in the Vanua Levu chapter).

The first Christian missionaries entered Fiji via Lau. Two Tahitians from the London Missionary Society (LMS) tried unsuccessfully to set up in Lakeba, then moved on to establish themselves in Oneata in 1830, where they managed to convert a small number of people. Wesleyan missionaries William Cross and David Cargill settled in Lakeba in 1835. They arrived with an emissary of King George of Tonga and, out of respect for the king, the Tui Nayau (king or prominent chief of Lau) made them welcome. He and his people, however, were not interested in being converted. Cross and Cargill developed a system for written Fijian and produced the first book in that language. The Tui Nayau eventually accepted Christianity in 1849.

Northern Lau was traditionally allied with the Cakaudrove province (eastern Vanua Levu and Taveuni), but by the mid-19th century the region became dominated by Tonga. In 1847 Tongan nobleman Enele Ma'afu, cousin of King Taufa'ahau of Tonga, led an armada of war canoes to Vanua Balavu to investigate the killing of a preacher. Six years later the king appointed Ma'afu governor of the Tongans in Fiji. After the murder of 17 Wesleyans, Ma'afu took Vanua Balavu by force and subjugated its inhabitants. He then established Sawana village near Lomaloma as his base. The Tongans assisted in local Fijian wars in return for protection by Chief Cakobau of Bau. By 1855 Ma'afu had become a powerful force in the region and influential throughout much of Fiji. His aim was to conquer all of Fiji and convert the people to Christianity.

Ma'afu was one of the signatories to the Deed of Cession to Britain and became officially recognised as Roko Tui Lau (chief of Lau). After his death in 1881, Tongan power weakened, the title passed to the Tui Nayau, and many Tongans returned to their home country. Despite the distance from the rest of Fiji and their relatively small land area, the chiefs of the Lau Group have always been surprisingly influential. Chiefs with the title Tui Nayau include the late Ratu Sukuna and the current president, Ratu Mara.

Diving

The remote Lau Group is still relatively unexplored in terms of diving. The Lau waters are officially protected by the Fijian government and commercial fishing is prohibited in the area. The upmarket resorts near Vanua Balavu have their own dive operations.

Nai'a Cruises, an excellent live-aboard operator, offers special charters to Lau. *Fiji Aggressor*, another live-aboard, also visits Lau. See Live-Aboard Operators in the Facts for the Visitor chapter.

A Local Delicacy

One week after the full moon in November, the people of Vanua Balavu witness the annual rising of the *balolo* (tiny green and brown sea worms). At sunrise the Susui villagers collect worms by the thousands. The catch is first soaked in fresh water, then packed into baskets and cooked overnight in a *lovo* (underground oven). The fishy-tasting baked worms are considered a delicacy.

Accommodation

Lakeba and Vanua Balavu have budget accommodation. You can also visit other parts of Lau on a live-aboard dive boat (see Diving earlier in this chapter).

There is little other infrastructure for travellers and there are no banks.

Getting There & Away

Moala, Vanua Balavu, Cicia, Lakeba and Kaibu have airstrips. Air Fiji flies Suva–Vanua Balavu and Suva–Lakeba.

There are regular cargo and passenger boats to the Lau group (see Getting There & Away later in this chapter and the Getting Around chapter for details).

Yachties require permission to visit the islands. Details are given under Travel Permits in the Facts for the Visitor chapter. Contact the Lau provincial headquarters in Lakeba (see the Lakeba section later in this chapter).

Northern Lau

Northern Lau's largest island is Vanua Balavu. It has an airstrip, as does Kaibu. The islands of Naitauba, Kanacea, Mago and Cicia are important for copra production.

VANUA BALAVU

Vanua Balavu and the eight other smaller islands within the same enclosing barrier reef, were named the 'Exploring Isles' by Commodore Wilkes of the US Exploring Expedition, who charted the northern Lau Group in 1840. This beautiful island, roughly a reversed S-shape and averaging about 2km wide, has lots of sandy beaches and rugged limestone hills. The **Bay of Islands** at the northwestern end of the island is used as a hurricane shelter by yachts. Along the eastern coast there is a road that has occasional passing carriers (small trucks). Taveuni is visible in the distance, 115km to the northwest.

The largest village on the island is **Lomaloma** on the southeast coast. In the mid-19th century Tonga conquered the island and the village of Sawana was built next to Lomaloma. Fifth-generation Tongan descendants still live in Sawana, and the houses with rounded ends show the influence of Tongan architecture. The first of Fiji's ports, Lomaloma was regularly visited by ships trading in the Pacific. In its heyday Lomaloma had

Fatal Attraction

There is a freshwater lake near the village of Mavana, on the northeast corner of Vanua Balavu, which is considered sacred. The people of Mavana gather here annually for a fun ceremony authorised by their traditional priest. Naked except for a leaf skirt, they jump around in the lake to stir up the muddy waters. This provokes the large fish known as *yawa* (a type of mullet usually only found in the sea) to spring into the air. It is believed that the male fish are attracted to the female villagers and thus easily trapped in the nets. Legend has it that the fish were dropped into the lake by a Tongan princess while flying over the island on her way to visit her lover on Taveuni.

many hotels and shops as well as Fiji's first botanical gardens, though little remains of its past grandeur. The Fijian inhabitants of Vanua Balavu trace their ancestry to Tailevu (southeastern Viti Levu) and Cakaudrove (eastern Vanua Levu and Taveuni). Today the people of Vanua Balavu rely largely on copra and bêche-de-mer (sea cucumber) for their income.

Places to Stay

Moana's Guesthouse (☎ *895 006; rooms per person $50),* at Sawana, is a perfect place for those after peace and solitude. There is not much to do but snorkelling, fishing, visiting some villages and experiencing a bit of pristine Fiji. The guesthouse is built in traditional Tongan style, has two bedrooms and a living area. Guests also have the option to stay in one of the two beach *bure*. Rates include three meals.

Getting There & Away

Vanua Balavu is 355km east of Nadi, about halfway to Tonga. Air Fiji has one flight a week (Tuesdays) from Suva to Vanua Balavu. See the air fares chart in the Getting Around chapter.

If you have plenty of time you can also reach the island by cargo/passenger boat. Saliabasaga Shipping and Ika Corporation both have fortnightly trips from Suva to the Lau Group, including Vanua Balavu. See Boat in the Getting Around chapter for details. A one-way fare with Saliabasaga Shipping is $80, including meals. Expect to spend about a week on board.

KAIBU

Kaibu (3.5 sq km) is a privately owned island in the northern Lau Group, 55km west of Vanua Balavu. It shares a fringing reef with the larger island of Yacata.

Kaimbu Island Resort *(w www.fiji-islands.com/kaimbu.html)* has been closed for renovation but is due to reopen mid-2003. It is a very exclusive resort with only three *bure* for a maximum of six guests. Generally, only couples are accepted unless the whole island is reserved.

Activities offered include diving on the barrier reef, lagoon snorkelling, sports fishing, sailing, water-skiing, wind surfing, catamaran sailing, trekking, cave visits and picnics on an uninhabited island. The island has its own airstrip and guests reach the resort by charter plane.

Southern Lau

Lakeba, being the hereditary seat of the Tui Nayau (chief of Lau), is the most important island in southern Lau. There are 16 other islands, mostly within 100km southeast of Lakeba. Vatoa and Ono-i-Lau are more isolated and farther south.

LAKEBA

Lakeba is a roughly circular-shaped volcanic island, approximately 9km in diameter, with a small peninsula at its southern end. Its 54 sq km big is home to 2000 people. There is a road around its perimeter and several roads across the interior. To the east is a wide **lagoon** enclosed by a barrier reef.

The island has nine villages. Yams, coconuts and *kumala* (sweet potatoes) grow well on the fertile coast and the interior is covered with grasslands, pandanus and pine plantations.

Lakeba was historically a meeting place for Fijians and Tongans; it was also the place where Christian missionaries first entered Fiji via Tonga and Tahiti. Lakeba was frequently visited by Europeans before

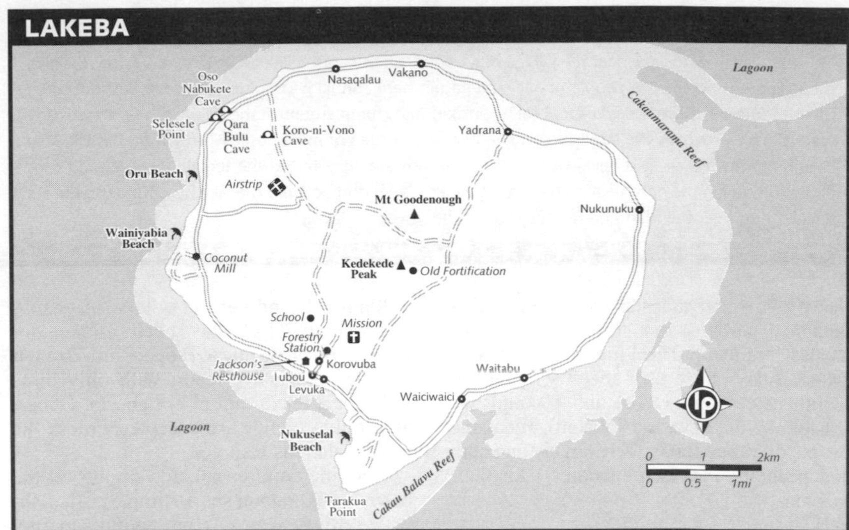

the trading settlement had been established at Levuka.

The island has several caves worth visiting, especially **Oso Nabukete**, which translates as 'too narrow for pregnant women'. Take some kava as a *sevusevu* (gift) to Nasaqalau, where you can arrange a guide (bring your own torch). The island also has an **old fortification** in the middle of the island at Kekekede Peak where the people retreated in times of war.

The **provincial office** *(☎ 882 3164)* for the Lau Group is in **Tubou** at the southern end of Lakeba. There is also a **police station** *(☎ 882 3043)*, **post office**, **telephone exchange**, **hospital** *(☎ 882 3153)* and **guesthouse** here, and some of the nearby **beaches** are good for snorkelling and swimming. Enele Ma'afu, the once-powerful Tongan chief, is buried here, as is Ratu Sir Lala Sukuna, formerly an influential Tui Lau who established the Native Lands Trust Board in 1940.

Shark Calling

The villagers of Nasaqalau perform a shark-calling ritual in October or November each year. About a month prior to the ceremony, the spot is marked by a post and a flag of *masi* (bark cloth) and a traditional priest ensures no-one goes near the post or fishes in the area. On the designated day the caller, standing neck-high in the water, chants for up to an hour. A school of sharks, led by a white shark, will be drawn to the place. Traditionally, all of the sharks except the white shark are killed and eaten by the villagers.

Places to Stay

Call the **Lau provincial office** *(☎ 882 3164)* to check if you can visit the island and to book accommodation.

Jackson's Resthouse *(☎ 823 188; accommodation per person $35)*, run by Kesosoni Qica, can accommodate up to 10 people. Price includes three meals.

Getting There & Away

Air Fiji has one flight a week (Thursdays) from Suva to Lakeba that take 75 minutes one way (see the air fares chart in the Getting Around chapter). There is a bus from the airstrip to Tubou and carriers and buses circle the island.

If you have plenty of time (and the inclination) you can also reach the island by boat. Ika Corporation, Saliabasaga Shipping and Taikabara Shipping each have fortnightly trips from Suva to the Lau Group, including Lakeba. See Boat in the Getting Around chapter for details. A one-way fare including meals is $66.

Moala Group

The three islands of this Group – Moala, Totoya and Matuku – are geographically removed from Lau but administered as part of the Eastern Division. They are about halfway between Kadavu and the southern Lau Group, southeast of the Lomaiviti Group. The islands are the eroded tops of previously submerged volcanic cones that have lifted more than 3km to the sea surface. Totoya's horseshoe shape is the result of a sunken volcano crater forming a land-locked lagoon. The volcano was active 4.9 million years ago. Matuku has rich volcanic soil, steep wooded peaks and a submerged crater on its western side. However, this beautiful island is generally inaccessible to visitors. Each of the islands has villages.

MOALA

Moala (65 sq km) is the largest and most northerly of the group. It is about 160km from Suva and 110km from Lakeba. The island is roughly triangular in shape, with a deeply indented coast. The highest peak reaches 460m and has two small **crater lakes**. It has extremely fertile soil and supports nine villages. The villagers produce copra and bananas, which they send to Suva, a night's sail away. The ancestors of Moala's inhabitants came from Viti Levu.

Travellers can visit Moala if they've been invited to stay with a local family; however, there is no formal accommodation on the island.

Getting There & Away

Air Fiji has flights from Suva to Moala once a week (Thursdays). See the air fares chart in the Getting Around chapter.

Khans Shipping has cargo/passenger boats that make the trip most weeks. Khans visits Moala, Matuku and Totoya in the Moala Group as well as Gau and Nairai in the Lomaiviti Group. See under Boat in the Getting Around chapter for details.

Rotuma

Rotuma (population 3000) is an isolated, 30-sq-km volcanic island, 450km northwest of Suva. Its shape resembles a whale, with the larger body of land linked to the small tail end to the west by the Motusa isthmus. It is about 13km long by 5km at its widest point, with extinct volcanic craters rising up to 250m. The smaller offshore islands of Uea, Hatana and Hofliua, 3km to 6km west of Rotuma, are important seabird rookeries. Uea is a high, rocky island and the spectacular Hofliua is also known as 'split island' because of its unusual rock formation. Endemic wildlife includes the Rotuman gecko and the red-and-black Rotuman honeyeater.

Rotuma is a province of Fiji, but – unlike predominantly Melanesian Fiji – its indigenous population is Polynesian with a distinct culture that has developed over hundreds of years. Tongans invaded Rotuma during the 17th century and the Tongan influence is evident in the language and dance.

In 1791, Europeans on the HMS *Pandora* stopped here to search for mutineers from the *Bounty*. Rotuma became an important port, and the local people were exposed to traders, runaway sailors and convicts. During the mid-19th century, Tongan Wesleyan and Marist Roman Catholic missionaries introduced their versions of Christianity. By the 1870s the religious groups were warring and, in response to the unrest, the Rotuman chiefs decided to cede their home to Britain. Rotuma became joined politically to the Fijian colony in 1881.

Most young people leave their remote island home to find work, and about 6500 ethnic Rotumans live on other Fijian islands, mostly in Suva on Viti Levu. Villagers fish and grow fruit (including oranges and bananas), root crops and coconuts in the fertile soil. There is no bank or shopping centre, just a cooperative. Rotuma produces copra, which is processed at the mill near Savusavu on Vanua Levu. In 1988 Rotumans demonstrated their wish to become independent from Fiji, but the movement was quashed by the Fijian government. In the early 1990s the island hit the news over bad debts and bank-loan scandals.

Highlights

- Be among the few to travel to this remote island group
- Stay in a village and experience the vibrant Polynesian culture
- See the islands' beautiful and unusual landscapes, and visit ancient archaeological sites

ROTUMA GROUP

Things to See & Do

Experience staying with villagers on this beautiful remote island. The best **beaches** are at Oinafa and at Vovoe, west of **Sororoa Bluff**. There are good views from this bluff and from **Mt Suelhof** (256m). There are **archaeological sites** at Sisilo (Graveyard of the Kings), Ki ne he'e and Tafea Point (stone walls). (See Books in the Facts about Fiji chapter for reference to an excellent photography book.)

Places to Stay

For many years travellers were decidedly unwelcome and cruise ships have been stopped from visiting the island. However, the Rotuman chiefs now allow small numbers of visitors. Bring cash and don't turn up unannounced. First call the island's **district officer** *(☎ 889 1011, 889 1089)* to organise a village stay.

Rotuma Island Backpackers *(☎ 889 1290; camping per double $15)* in Motusa has village stays. It is extra for meals and you'll need to bring your own tent.

Getting There & Away

Air Sun Air has a weekly flight on Saturdays from Nadi via Suva (Nausori Airport) to Rotuma (3¼ hours). See the air fares chart in the Getting Around chapter.

Boat Contact **Kadavu Shipping** *(☎ 331 2428, Suva)* for information on the passenger service on the MV *Bulou-ni-Ceva* ($90/130 for deck/cabin). The trip takes two days.

The Origin of Rotuma

Rotumans believe their ancestors came from Samoa. The spot where the island presently lies was nothing but open sea until the arrival of Samoan chief Raho and his favourite grandchild. The little girl was unhappy in her homeland as her cousin was always annoying her. To escape his torment, she convinced her grandfather to take her away to live on another island. For days and nights their entourage sailed westward in an outrigger canoe, but failed to find land. Eventually the chief threw some Samoan soil overboard. The soil grew to form a beautiful, fertile island, which he named Rotuma. Some of the soil scattered, forming the other small islands. Rotumans commemorate this legend in their dance and song.

Yachts occasionally visit the island, and must obtain permission to anchor from the Ahau government station in Maka Bay, on the northern side of the island.

Language

One of the reasons many visitors from the English-speaking world find Fiji such a congenial place to visit is that they don't have to learn another language – the majority of the local people they come in contact with can speak English, and all signs and official forms are also in English. At the same time, for almost all local people, English is not their mother tongue – indigenous Fijians speak Fijian at home and Indo-Fijians speak Fiji-Hindi (also known as Fijian Hindi and Fiji Hindustani). If you really wish to have a better knowledge of the Fijian people and their culture, it's important that you know something of the Fijian languages – and, no matter how poor your first attempts at communicating, you'll receive much encouragement from Fijians.

FIJIAN

The many regional dialects found in Fiji today all descend, at least partly, from the language spoken by the original inhabitants. They would have come from one of the island groups to the west, either the Solomons or Vanuatu, having left their Southeast Asian homeland at least 1000 years previously and spread eastwards by way of Indonesia, the Philippines and Papua New Guinea. From Fiji, groups left to settle the nearby islands of Rotuma, Tonga and Samoa, and from there they spread out to inhabit the rest of Polynesia, including Hawaii in the north, Rapa Nui (Easter Island) in the east, and Aotearoa (New Zealand) in the south. All the people in this vast area speak related languages belonging to the Austronesian language family.

There are some 300 regional varieties (dialects) of Fijian, all belonging to one of two major groupings. All varieties spoken to the west of a line extending north-south, with a couple of kinks, across the centre of Viti Levu belong to the Western Fijian group, while all others are Eastern Fijian.

Fortunately for the language learner there is one variety, based on the eastern varieties of the Bau-Rewa area, which is understood by Fijians throughout the islands. This standard form of Fijian is popularly known as *vosa vakabau* (Bauan), though linguists prefer to call it standard Fijian. It's used in conversation among Fijians from different areas, on the radio and in schools, and is the variety used in this chapter.

In Fijian, there are two ways of saying 'you', 'your', and 'yours'. If you are speaking to someone who is your superior, or an adult stranger, you should use a longer 'polite' form. This form is easy to remember because it always ends in *-nī*. In all other situations, a shorter 'informal' address is used.

Pronunciation

Fijian pronunciation isn't especially difficult for the English speaker, since most of the sounds found in Fijian have similar counterparts in English. The standard Fijian alphabet uses all the English letters, except 'x'. The letters 'h' and 'z' are used for borrowed words only and occur rarely.

Since the Fijian alphabet was devised relatively recently (in the 1830s), and by a missionary who was also a very competent linguist, it is phonetically consistent, ie each letter represents only one sound, and each sound is represented by only one letter.

As with all Pacific languages, the five Fijian vowels are pronounced much as they are in languages such as Spanish, German and Italian:

a as in 'father'
e as in 'bet'
i as in 'machine'
o as in 'more'
u as in 'flute'

Vowels have both short or long variants, with the long vowel having a significantly longer sound. In this guide a long sound is indicated by a macron (stroke) above the vowel, eg, **ā**. An approximate English equivalent is the difference between the final vowel sound in 'icy' and 'I see'. To convey the correct meaning of a word it's important that vowel length is taken into account in your pronunciation. For example, *mama* means 'a ring', *mamā* means 'chew it', and *māmā* means 'light' (in weight).

Note that *māmā* takes about twice as long to pronounce as *mama*.

Most consonants are pronounced as they are in English, but there are a few differences you need to be aware of:

- **b** pronounced with a preceding nasal consonant as 'mb'
- **c** as the 'th' in 'this' (not as in 'thick')
- **d** pronounced with a preceding nasal consonant as 'nd'
- **g** as the 'ng' in 'sing' (not as in 'angry')
- **j** as the 'ch' in 'charm' but without a following puff of breath
- **k** as in 'kick' but without a following puff of breath
- **p** as in 'pip' but without a following puff of breath
- **q** as the 'ng' in 'angry' (not as in 'sing')
- **r** trilled as in Scottish English
- **t** as in 'tap' but without a following puff of breath, often pronounced 'ch' before 'i'
- **v** pronounced with the lower lip against the upper lip (not against the upper teeth as in English) – somewhere between a 'v' and a 'b'

Occasionally on maps and in tourist publications you'll find a variation on the spelling system used in this guide – it's intended to be easier for English speakers to negotiate. In this alternative system, Yanuca is spelt 'Yanutha', Beqa 'Mbengga', and so on.

Further Reading

A good introduction to the language is Lonely Planet's *Fijian phrasebook*, written by Paul Geraghty, which provides all the essential words and phrases travellers need, along with grammar and cultural points. Lonely Planet's *South Pacific phrasebook* covers the languages of many South Pacific islands – ideal if you are visiting a few countries in one trip. Those interested in further studies of Fijian will find George Milner's *Fijian Grammar* (Government Press, Suva, 1956) an excellent introduction to the language. Likewise, Albert Schūtz's *Spoken Fijian* (University Press of Hawaii, Honolulu, 1979) is a good primer for more advanced studies.

Greetings & Civilities

Hello.	*Bula!*
Hello. (reply)	*Io, bula/Ia, bula.* (more respectful)

'Fijinglish'

Here are a few English words and phrases used in Fijian but with slightly different meanings:

Fijian English	English
grog	kava
bluff	lie, deceive
chow	food, eat
set	OK, ready
step	cut school, wag
Good luck to ...!	It serves ... right!
Not even!	No way!

Good morning.	*Yadra.*
Goodbye.	*Moce.* (if you don't expect to see them again)
See you later.	*Au sā liu mada.*

You may also hear the following:

Where are you going?
O(nì) lai vei? (used as we ask 'How are you?')

Nowhere special, just wandering around.
Sega, gādē gā. (as with the response to 'How are you' – no need to be specific)

Let's shake hands.
Daru lùlulu mada.

Yes.	*Io.*
No.	*Sega.*
Thank you (very much).	*Vinaka (vakalevu).*
Sorry. (general)	*(Nì) Vosota sara.*
What's your name?	*O cei na yacamu(nì)?*
My name is ...	*O yau o ...*
Pleased to meet you.	*Ia, (nì) bula.*
Where are you from?	*O iko/kemunì mai vei?*
I'm from ...	*O yau mai ...*
How old are you?	*O yabaki vica?*
I'm ... years old.	*Au yabaki ...*
Are you married?	*O(nì) vakawati?*
How many children do you have?	*Lē vica na luvemu(nì)?*
I don't have any children.	*E sega na luvequ.*
I have a daughter/son.	*E dua na luvequ yalewa/tagane.*

Language Difficulties

I don't speak Fijian/English.	*Au sega ni kilā na vosa vakaviti/vakavālagi.*

Do you speak English? — *O(nì) kilā na vosa vakavālagi?*
I understand. — *Sā macala.*
I don't understand. — *E sega ni macala.*

Getting Around

Where is the ...? — *I vei na ...?*
  airport — *rārā ni waqavuka*
  (main) bus station — *basten*
  bus stop — *ikelekele ni basi*

When does the ... leave/arrive? — *Vica na kaloko e lako/kele kina na ...?*
  bus — *basi*
  plane — *waqavuka*
  boat — *waqa*

I want to go to ... — *Au via lako i ...*
How do I get to ...? — *I vei na sala i ...?*
Is it far? — *E yawa?*
Can I walk there? — *E rawa niu taubale kina?*
Can you show me (on the map)? — *Vakaraitaka mada (ena mape)?*
Go straight ahead. — *Vakadodonu.*
Turn left. — *Gole i na imawì.*
Turn right. — *Gole i na imatau.*

Compass bearings (north, south etc) are never used. Instead you'll hear:

on the sea side of ... — *mai ... i wai*
on the land side of ... — *mai ... i vanua*
the far side of ... — *mai ... i liu*
this side of ... — *mai ... i muri*

Around Town

I'm looking for ... — *Au vāqarā ...*
  a church — *na valenilotu*
  the ... embassy — *na ebasì/valenivolavola ni ...*
  the market — *na mākete*
  the museum — *na vale ni yau māroroi*
  the police — *na ovisa*
  the post office — *na posi(tōvesi)*
  a public toilet — *na valelailai*
  the tourist office — *na valenivolavola ni saravanua*

What time does it open/close? — *E dola/sogo ina vica?*
May I take your photo? — *Au tabaki iko mada?*

Useful Fijian Food Words

bele – green leafy vegetable, served boiled
bu – green coconut
bulumakau – beef
dalo – taro, a starchy root, usually boiled
luve ni toa – chicken
ika – fish
ivi – a type of chestnut from the ivi tree
kokoda – raw fish marinated in lime juice, served with chilli and onions
lolo- coconut milk
lovo – food cooked in an underground oven on hot stones
nama – seaweed that looks like miniature green grapes
niu – brown coconut
palusami – corned beef, onions and lolo wrapped in dalo leaves and baked in a lovo
rourou – boiled dalo leaves (similar taste to spinach)
tavioka – cassava
ura – freshwater prawns
uto – breadfruit – boiled, or baked in a lovo
vakalolo – a pudding of mashed starchy roots like cassava and dalo, and fruit such as breadfruit. The pudding is made with a sweet sauce of caramelised sugar-cane juice, mixed and boiled with lolo, kneaded and rolled into balls, coated with more sweet sauce and wrapped in leaves. In the old days vast quantities of this delicacy were made for traditional feasts.

I'll send you the photo. — *Au na vākauta yani na itaba.*

Accommodation

Where is a ...? — *I vei ...?*
  hotel — *dua na ōtela*
  cheap hotel — *ōtela saurawarawa*

A note of caution. The term 'guesthouse' and its Fijian equivalent, *dua na bure ni vulagi*, often refer to establishments offering rooms for hire by the hour.

I'm going to stay for... — *Au na ...*
  one day — *siga dua*
  one week — *mācawa dua*

I'm not sure how long I'm staying.
Sega ni macala na dedē ni noqu tiko.

Emergencies – Fijian

Help!	*Oilei!*
Go away!	*Lako tani!*
Call a doctor!	*Qiria na vuniwai!*
Call an ambulance!	*Qiria na lori ni valenibula!*
I've been robbed!	*Butako!*
Call the police!	*Qiria na ovisa!*
I've been raped.	*Au sā kucuvi.*
I'm lost.	*Au sā sese.*
Where are the toilets?	*I vei na valelailai?*

Where is the bathroom?
I vei na valenisili?
Where is the toilet?
I vei na valelailai?

Food

restaurant	*valenikana*
Chinese/Indian restaurant	*valenikana ni kai Jaina/Idia*
food vendor	*volitaki kākana*
breakfast	*katalau*
lunch	*vakasigalevu*
dinner	*vakayakavi*

Shopping

How much is it?	*E vica?*
That's too expensive for me.	*Au sega ni rawata.*
I'm just looking.	*Sarasara gā.*
bookshop	*sitoa ni vola*
clothing shop	*sitoa ni sulu*
laundry	*valenisavasava*
market	*mākete*
pharmacy	*kēmesi*

Health

I need a doctor.	*Au via raici vuniwai.*
Where is the hospital?	*I vei na valenibula?*
I'm constipated.	*Au sega ni valelailai rawa.*
I have a stomachache.	*E mosi na ketequ.*
I'm diabetic.	*Au tauvi matenisuka.*
I'm epileptic.	*Au manumanusoni.*
I'm allergic to penicillin.	*E dau lako vakacā vei au na penisilini.*
I have my own syringe.	*E tiko na noqu icula.*
I'm on the pill.	*Au gunu vuanikau ni yalani.*
condoms	*rapa, kodom*
contraceptive	*wai ni yalani*
diarrhoea	*coka*
medicine	*wainimate*
nausea	*lomalomacā*
sanitary napkin	*qamuqamu*

Time & Dates

What time is it?	*Sā vica na kaloko?*
today	*nikua*
tonight	*na bogi nikua*
tomorrow	*nimataka*
yesterday	*nanoa*
Monday	*Mōniti*
Tuesday	*Tùsiti*
Wednesday	*Vukelulu*
Thursday	*Lotulevu*
Friday	*Vakaraubuka*
Saturday	*Vakarauwai*
Sunday	*Sigatabu*

Numbers

0	*saiva*
1	*dua*
2	*rua*
3	*tolu*
4	*vā*
5	*lima*
6	*ono*
7	*vitu*
8	*walu*
9	*ciwa*
10	*tini*
11	*tínikadua*
12	*tínikarua*
20	*rúasagavulu*
21	*rúasagavulukadua*
30	*tólusagavulu*
100	*dua na drau*
1000	*dua na udolu*

FIJI-HINDI

Fiji-Hindi (sometimes called Fiji Hindustani) is the language of all Indo-Fijians. It has features of the many regional dialects of Hindi spoken by the Indian indentured labourers who were brought to Fiji from 1879 to 1916. (Some people call Fiji-Hindi 'Bhojpuri', but this is the name of just one of the many dialects that contributed to the language.)

Many words from English are found in Fiji-Hindi (such as room, towel, book and reef), but some of these have slightly different meanings. For example, the word 'book' in Fiji-Hindi includes magazines and pamphlets, and if you refer to a person of the opposite sex as a 'friend', it implies that he/she is your sexual partner.

Fiji-Hindi is used in all informal settings, such as in the family and among friends. But the 'Standard Hindi' of India is considered appropriate for formal contexts, such as in public speaking, radio broadcasting and writing. The Hindu majority write in Standard Hindi using the Devanagari script with a large number of words taken from the ancient Sanskrit language. The Muslims use the PersoArabic script and words taken from Persian and Arabic. (This literary style is often considered a separate language, called Urdu.) Indo-Fijians have to learn Standard Hindi or Urdu in school along with English, so while they all speak Fiji-Hindi informally, not everyone knows the formal varieties.

Some people say that Fiji-Hindi is just a 'broken' or 'corrupted' version of standard Hindi. In fact, it is a legitimate dialect with its own grammatical rules and vocabulary unique to Fiji.

Pronunciation

Fiji-Hindi is normally written only in guides for foreigners, such as this, and transcribed using the English alphabet. Since there are at least 42 different sounds in Fiji-Hindi and only 26 letters in the English alphabet, some adjustments have to be made. The vowels are as follows:

a	as in 'about' or 'sofa'
ā	as in 'father'
e	as in 'bet'
i	as in 'police'
o	as in 'obey'
u	as in 'rule'
ai	as in 'hail'
āi	as in 'aisle'
au	as the 'o' in 'own'
oi	as in 'boil'

Fiji-Hindi also has nasalised vowels, as in French words such as *bon* and *sans*. This is shown with a tilde over the vowel (eg, **ã**) or with the letter 'n' if there's a following consonant.

The consonants **b**, **f**, **g** (as in 'go'), **h**, **j**, **k**, **l**, **m**, **n**, **p**, **s**, **v**, **y**, **w**, and **z** are similar to those of English. The symbol **č** is used for the 'ch' sound (as in 'chip') and **š** is used for the 'sh' sound (as in 'ship').

Pronunciation of other consonants is a little tricky. Fiji-Hindi has two 't' sounds and two 'd' sounds – all different from English. In 't' and 'd' in English, the tip of the tongue touches the ridge behind the upper teeth, but in Fiji-Hindi it either touches the back of the front teeth (dental) or is curled back to touch the roof of the mouth (retroflex). The dental consonants are shown as 't̪' and 'd̪' and the retroflex ones as 'ṭ' and 'ḍ', and they're important in distinguishing meaning. For example:

āt̪ā/āṭā	coming/flour
t̪ab/ṭab	then/tub
d̪āl/ḍāl	dhal (lentils)/branch

You can substitute the English 't' and 'd' for the retroflex ones and still be understood. There are also two 'r' sounds different from English. In the first, written as **r**, the tongue touches the ridge above the upper teeth and is flapped quickly forward, similar to the way we say the 't' sound in 'butter' when speaking quickly. In the second, written as **ṛ**, the tongue is curled back, touching the roof of the mouth (as in the retroflex sounds) and then flapped forward. You can sometimes substitute English 'rd' for this sound.

Finally, there are 'aspirated' consonants. If you hold your hand in front of your mouth and say 'Peter Piper picked a peck of pickled peppers', you'll feel a puff of air each time you say the 'p' sound – this is called aspiration. When you say 'spade, spill, spit, speak', you don't feel the puff of air, because in these words the 'p' sound is not aspirated. In Fiji-Hindi, aspiration is important in distinguishing meaning. Aspiration is indicated by the use of an 'h' after the consonants – for example:

pul/phul	bridge/flower
kālā/khālā	black/valley
t̪āli/t̪hāli	clapping/brass plate

Other aspirated consonants are:

bh	as in 'grab him' said quickly
čh	as in 'church hat' said quickly

ḍh	as in 'mad house'
gh	as in 'slug him'
jh	as in 'bridge house'
ṭh	as in 'out house'

Note that some books use a different system of transcription. For example, 'aa' may be used for **ā** and 'T', 'D', 'R' for **ṭ**, **ḍ** and **ṛ**.

Greetings & Civilities

There are no exact equivalents for 'hello' and 'goodbye' in Fiji-Hindi. The most common greeting is *kaise* (How are you?). The usual reply is *ṭik* (fine). In parting, it's common to say *fir milegā* (We'll meet again).

More formal greetings are: *namasṯe* (for Hindus), *salām alaikum* (for Muslims) – the reply to the latter is *alaikum salām*.

There are no equivalents for 'please' and 'thank you'. To be polite in making requests, people use the word *ṯhoṛā* (a little) and a special form of the verb ending in *nā*, eg, *ṯhoṛā nimak denā* (Please pass the salt).

They also use the polite form of the word 'you', *ā̃p*, instead of the informal *tum*. Polite and informal modes of address are indicated in this guide by the abbreviations 'pol' and 'inf' respectively.

For 'thanks', people often just say *ačhā* (good). The English 'please' and 'thank you' are also commonly used. The word *ḏhanyavāḏ* is used to thank someone who has done something special for you. It means something like 'blessings be bestowed upon you'.

Yes.	*hā̃*
No.	*nahī̃*
Maybe.	*sāyiṯ*
I'm sorry. (for something serious)	*māf karnā*
What's your name?	*āpke/ṯumār nām kā hai?* (pol/inf)
My name is ...	*hamār nām ...*
Where are you from?	*āp/ṯum kahā̃ ke hai?* (pol/inf)
I'm from ...	*ham ... ke hai*
Are you married?	*šāḏi ho gayā?*
How many children do you have?	*kiṯnā laṛkā hai?*
I don't have any children.	*laṛkā nahī̃ hai*

Emergencies – Fiji-Hindi

Help me!	*hame maḏaḏ karo!*
Go away!	*jāo!*
Call the doctor/police.	*ḍokṭā ke/pulis ke bulāo*
Where is the hospital?	*āspaṯāl kahā̃ hai?*
I've been robbed.	*čori ho gayā*
I've been raped.	*koi hame reip karis*

Two boys and three girls.	*ḏui laṛkā aur ṯin laṛki*

Language Difficulties

Do you speak English?	*āp/ṯum English bolṯā?* (pol/inf)
Does anyone here speak English?	*koi English bole?*
I don't understand.	*ham nahī̃ samajhṯā*

Getting Around

Where is the ...?	*... kahā̃ hai?*
shop	*ḏukān*
airport	*eyapoṭ*
(main) bus station	*basṭen*
market	*mākeṭ*
temple	*manḏir*
mosque	*masjiḏ*
church	*čeč*

You can also use the English words hotel, guesthouse, camping ground, toilet, post office, embassy, tourist information office, museum, cafe, restaurant and telephone.

I want to go to ...	*ham ... jāe mangṯā*
Is it near/far?	*nagič/ḏur hai?*
Can I go by foot?	*paiḏar jāe sakṯā?*
Go straight ahead.	*sidhā jāo*
Please write down the address.	*ṯhoṛā eḍres likh denā*

By the ...	*... ke pas*
coconut tree	*nariyal ke peṛ*
mango tree	*ām ke peṛ*
breadfruit tree	*belfuṭ ke peṛ*
sugar-cane field	*gannā kheṯ*

When does the ... leave/arrive?	*kiṯnā baje ... čale/ pahunče?*
ship	*jahāj*
car	*moṭṭar*

You can also use the English words bus, plane, boat.

Food & Drink

to eat, food	*khāna*
to drink	*pinā*
tea	*čā*
yaqona (kava)	*nengonā, grog*
liquor	*d̪āru*
beer	*bia*
water	*pāni*
I don't drink alcohol.	*ham d̪āru nahĩ pit̪ā*
I don't eat hot (spicy) food.	*ham t̪it̪ā nahĩ khāt̪ā*
I don't eat meat.	*ham gos nahĩ khāt̪ā*
I eat vegetables.	*ham t̪arkāri khāt̪ā*
Just a little.	*t̪oṛā t̪hoṛā*
Enough!	*bas!*
very good	*bahut̪ačhā*

Health

I'm ...	*hame ...*
diabetic	*čini ke bimāri hai*
epileptic	*mirgi awe*
asthmatic	*sā̃s fule ke bimāri hai*
I'm allergic to penicillin.	*penesilin se ham bimār ho jāi*
I have a stomach-ache.	*hamār peṭ pirāwe*
I feel nauseous.	*hame čhānṭ lage*
I'm constipated.	*peṭ kaṛā ho gayā*
condom	*konḍom/raba*
contraceptive	*pariwār niyojan ke dawāi*
medicine	*dawāi*
sanitary napkin	*peḍ, nepkin*
tampon	*ṭampon*

Time & Dates

What time is it?	*kit̪nā baje?*
It's ... o'clock.	*... baje*
When?	*kab?*
today	*āj*
tonight	*āj rāt̪ke*
tomorrow	*bihān*
yesterday	*kal*

English days of the week are generally used.

Numbers

1	*ek*
2	*d̪ui*
3	*t̪in*
4	*čār*
5	*pānč*
6	*čhe*
7	*sāt̪*
8	*āṭh*
9	*nau*
10	*das*
100	*sau*
1000	*hazār*

Note: English numbers are generally used for 20–99.

Glossary

achar – Indian pickles
adi – female chief
arkatis – agents under commission collecting indentured labourers

baigan – eggplant
balabala – tree ferns
bêche-de-mer – sea cucumber, with an elongated body, leathery skin and a cluster of tentacles at the mouth; they were gathered by early traders and are sold in China and Southeast Asia as a delicacy and aphrodisiac
beka – flying fox
bele – leafy green vegetable
bete – priests of the old Fijian religion
bhaji – spinach, or any leafy green vegetable
bhindi – okra
bilibili – bamboo raft
bilo – drinking vessel made from half a coconut shell
bolubolu – traditional custom of apology and reconciliation
breadfruit – a tree of the Pacific Islands, the trunk of which is used for lumber and canoe building; the fruit, which has a texture like bread, is cooked and eaten
bua – frangipani
bula – cheers (literally, 'life')
bula shirt – tapa or floral design shirt
burau – ceremonial *yaqona*-drinking ritual
bure – thatched dwelling
bure bose – meeting house
bure kalou – ancient temple

cibi – death dance
copra – dried coconut kernel, used for making coconut oil

dadakulaci – banded sea krait, Fiji's most common snake
dakua – a tree of the kauri family
dalo – the taro plant, cultivated for its edible root stock
dele – (or *wate*) a dance where women sexually humiliated enemy corpses and captives
dhaniya – coriander
drua – double-hulled canoe; traditional catamaran

girmitiya – indentured labourer; the word comes from the *girmit*, the Indian labourers pronunciation of 'agreement'

ibe – a mat
ibuburau – drinking vessels used in *yaqona* rites
ika – fish
ivi – Polynesian chestnut tree

jalebi – an Indian sweet
jira – cumin

kai colo – hill people
kaihidi – Indo-Fijian
kaivalagi – literally, 'people from far away', Europeans
kaiviti – indigenous Fijian
kanikani – scaly skin from excessive kava use
kasou – very drunk
kava – the Polynesian pepper shrub *(Piper methysticum)*, or a drink prepared from its aromatic roots
kerekere – custom of shared property
kokoda – fish salad
koro – village headed by a hereditary chief
kumala – sweet potato

liku – the traditional skirt of womanhood, made out of grasses or strips of *pandanus* leaves – this tradition was phased out by the missionaries
lolo – coconut cream
lovo – feast in which food is cooked in a pit oven

malo – see *masi*
mangrove – a tropical tree that grows in tidal mud flats and extends looping prop roots along the shore
masala – curry powder
masi – (also known as *malo* or *tapa*) bark cloth with designs printed in black and rust; different styles are also made in other regions of the South Pacific
mataqali – extended family or landowning group
meke – a dance performance that enacts stories and legends

nama – an edible seaweed that looks like miniature green grapes
narak – hell
NAUI – National Association of Underwater Instructors

open-water course – a certification diving course run by PADI or NAUI

PADI – Professional Association of Diving Instructors, the world's largest diving association
paidar – on foot
paisa – money
pandanus – a plant common to the tropics whose sword-shaped leaves are used to make mats and baskets
piala – small metal enamelled bowl
puri – deep-fried, flat Indian bread

rara – ceremonial ground
ratu – male chief
roti – Indian flat bread
rourou – taro leaves

saqa – trevally fish
seo – an Indian savoury snack
sevusevu – the presentation of a gift to a village chief and, by extension, to the ancestral gods and spirits; the gift is most commonly *yaqona* however *tabua* is the most powerful *sevusevu*; acceptance of the gift means the giver will be granted certain privileges or favours
sulu – skirt or wrapped cloth worn to below the knees

tabu – forbidden or sacred, implying a religious sanction
tabua – the teeth of sperm whales, which carry a special ceremonial value for Fijians; they are still used as negotiating tokens to symbolise esteem or atonement
taga yaqona – pounded kava
takia – Fijian canoe
talanoa – to chat, to tell stories
tanoa – *yaqona* drinking bowl
tapa – see *masi*
tavioka – cassava, a type of root crop
tevoro – a god of the old Fijian religion
tikina – a group of Fijian villages linked together
trade winds – the near-constant winds that dominate most of the tropics
tui – king
turaga – chief
turaga-ni-koro – hereditary chief

vale – a family house
vale lailai – toilet
vanua – land, region, place
vasu – a system in which a chiefly woman's sons could claim support and ownership over the property of her brothers from other villages
vatu ni bokola – head-chopping stone used during cannibalistic rituals
veli – a group of little gods
vesi – ironwood, considered a sacred timber
vilavilairevo – fire walking (literally, 'jumping into the oven')
vinaka – thank you
Viti – the name indigenous-Fijians used for Fiji before the arrival of Europeans

waka – bunch of kava roots
wakalou – climbing fern species
wate – see *dele*

yaqona – (also known as kava) a mildly narcotic beverage drunk socially
yasana – a province formed by several *tikina*
yavu – bases for housing

LONELY PLANET

You already know that Lonely Planet produces more than this one guidebook, but you might not be aware of the other products we have on this region. Here is a selection of titles that you may want to check out as well:

Diving & Snorkeling Fiji
ISBN 0 86442 771 9
US$16.99 • UK£10.99

South Pacific
ISBN 1 86450 302 5
US$25.99 • UK£16.99

Fijian Phrasebook
ISBN 0 86442 219 9
US$5.95 • UK£3.50

Diving & Snorkeling Tahiti & French Polynesia
ISBN 1 86450 071 9
US$16.99 • UK£10.99

Tahiti & French Polynesia
ISBN 1 74059 229 8
US$21.99 • UK£13.99

South Pacific Phrasebook
ISBN 0 86442 595 3
US$6.95 • UK£4.99

Australia
ISBN 1 74059 065 1
US$25.99 • UK£15.99

New Zealand
ISBN 1 74059 196 8
US$24.99 • UK£14.99

Rarotonga & the Cook Islands
ISBN 1 74059 083 X
US$16.99 • UK£10.99

Vanuatu
ISBN 1 74059 239 5
US$19.99 • UK£12.99

Hawaii
ISBN 1 74059 142 9
US$21.99 • UK£14.99

Oahu
ISBN 1 74059 201 8
US$16.99 • UK£11.99

Available wherever books are sold

Index

Text

Bold indicates maps.

Bold indicates maps.

Boxed Text

MAP LEGEND

CITY ROUTES

Freeway .... Freeway
Highway .... Primary Road
Road .... Secondary Road
Street .... Street
Lane .... Lane
.... On/Off Ramp
.... Unsealed Road
.... One Way Street
.... Pedestrian Street
.... Stepped Street
.... Tunnel
.... Footbridge

REGIONAL ROUTES

.... Tollway, Freeway
.... Primary Road
.... Secondary Road
.... Minor Road

BOUNDARIES

.... International
.... State
.... Disputed
.... Fortified Wall

HYDROGRAPHY

.... River, Creek
.... Canal
.... Lake
.... Dry Lake; Salt Lake
.... Spring; Rapids
.... Waterfalls

TRANSPORT ROUTES & STATIONS

.... Train
.... Underground Train
.... Metro
.... Tramway
.... Cable Car, Chairlift
.... Ferry
.... Walking Trail
.... Walking Tour
.... Path
.... Pier or Jetty

AREA FEATURES

.... Building
.... Park, Gardens
.... Market
.... Sports Ground
.... Beach
.... Cemetery
.... Campus
.... Plaza

POPULATION SYMBOLS

CAPITAL .... National Capital
CAPITAL .... State Capital
CITY .... City
Town .... Town
Village .... Village
.... Urban Area

MAP SYMBOLS

.... Place to Stay
.... Place to Eat
.... Point of Interest

.... Airfield, Airport
.... Anchorage
.... Bank
.... Bus Terminal
.... Caravan Park
.... Cave
.... Church
.... Dive Site, Snorkelling
.... Golf Course
.... Hindu
.... Hospital
.... Lookout
.... Monument
.... Mosque
.... Museum
.... National Park
.... Parking
.... Police Station
.... Post Office
.... Pub or Bar
.... Shopping Centre
.... Swimming Pool
.... Synagogue
.... Telephone
.... Temple
.... Tourist Information
.... Toilet
.... Zoo

Note: not all symbols displayed above appear in this book

LONELY PLANET OFFICES

Australia
Locked Bag 1, Footscray, Victoria 3011
☎ 03 8379 8000 fax 03 8379 8111
email: talk2us@lonelyplanet.com.au

UK
10a Spring Place, London NW5 3BH
☎ 020 7428 4800 fax 020 7428 4828
email: go@lonelyplanet.co.uk

USA
150 Linden St, Oakland, CA 94607
☎ 510 893 8555 TOLL FREE: 800 275 8555
fax 510 893 8572
email: info@lonelyplanet.com

France
1 rue du Dahomey, 75011 Paris
☎ 01 55 25 33 00 fax 01 55 25 33 01
email: bip@lonelyplanet.fr
www.lonelyplanet.fr

World Wide Web: www.lonelyplanet.com *or* AOL keyword: lp
Lonely Planet Images: www.lonelyplanetimages.com